THE AMERICAN PARTY SYSTEM

REPRINTS IN GOVERNMENT
AND POLITICAL SCIENCE

Editor-in-Chief: Richard H. Leach
DUKE UNIVERSITY

The
American Party System

by
CHARLES E. MERRIAM
and
HAROLD FOOTE GOSNELL

Fourth Edition

With a New Introduction by
ROBERT E. MERRIAM

Johnson Reprint Corporation

New York and London

1969

INTRODUCTION

Charles E. Merriam was the restless inquiring son of an Iowa merchant-politician, with the insatiable intellectual curiosity of a well-trained (Iowa, Columbia, Berlin) nineteenth-century scholar. Charles Merriam was strongly influenced during his formative years not only by his father and his older brother but also by three outstanding scholar-observers: Lord Bryce, Professor W. H. Dunning of Columbia, and Dr. Hugo Preuss of Berlin. It was Bryce who told young Merriam to get at least 10 years of practical political activity. Dunning, his mentor for many years, advised Merriam not to attempt to develop a "Systematic Politics" until he had more experience behind him. And the example of the scholar-politician Preuss, a member of the University of Berlin faculty as well as of the Berlin City Council, unquestionably pointed the direction Merriam was to take.

For Charles Merriam, the life of scholar-teacher was not enough. City Councilman in Chicago, almost-Mayor of the city, leading member of Teddy Roosevelt's Progressive Party, propagandist in Italy in World War I, adviser to Presidents, founder of inter-disciplinary mechanisms for the study of politics and social development, Charles Merriam constantly was experimenting, finding ways to apply the techniques of political theory to the practice of politics and government. His singular contribution was the building of a bridge between the world of ideas and the world of politics in the very best and broadest sense of that word.

In 1922, Charles Merriam recorded his observations in *The American Party System* (subsequently revised in conjunction with Professor Harold Gosnell). This tour through the intricacies of party mechanisms, voting patterns and procedures, and apparent *vs.* shadow influences in partisan activities, clearly reflected the experience of an activist in politics. But the scholar was ever dissatisfied with the available material and pointed to the many voids in empirical data. Indeed, it was this volume which launched Professor Gosnell on some of his useful studies of voting patterns.

The mysteries of the American political party system have for some time baffled the general public. Chicago has long been a case study. Today I live in a block on which the only house was once occupied by "Big Bill" Thompson, last Republican Mayor of Chicago. This same block now houses the Democratic National Committeeman from Illinois and last head of the pre-Daley Democratic Machine, Jacob Arvey, as well as the top Democratic precinct captain in the city, former market-master of Maxwell Street, and the recent Republican minority leader in the Illinois House of Representatives. This illustrates that the American political system is still evolving from its frontier days. Charles Merriam introduced many people, his son included, to this most mysterious mechanism. We are still discovering it.

Robert E. Merriam

THE AMERICAN PARTY SYSTEM

THE AMERICAN PARTY
SYSTEM AN INTRODUCTION TO
THE STUDY OF POLITICAL PARTIES
IN THE UNITED STATES · *Fourth Edition*

CHARLES EDWARD MERRIAM, *Professor Emeritus of Political Science, University of Chicago*

HAROLD FOOTE GOSNELL, *Research Consultant, Washington, D. C. Formerly of the Department of Political Science in the University of Chicago*

THE MACMILLAN COMPANY · *New York* · *1949*

PREFACE

I N THE YEARS SINCE 1940 WHEN THE THIRD EDITION OF THIS BOOK appeared, we have seen the passing of Franklin D. Roosevelt, the rise of Harry Truman, the third party candidacy of Henry Wallace, the Republican capture of Congress in 1946, the turbulent affairs of the Eightieth Congress, the surprising Democratic victory in 1948, the collapse of Axis fascism abroad, and the growing rivalry between the system of free enterprise as exemplified by civilization in the United States and the communist way of life as exemplified in the Soviet Union. These events have left their imprint upon our party system. A revision of the book is, therefore, appropriate.

The book has been thoroughly revised and completely reset. Two new chapters have been added, one on suffrage and one on public opinion surveys. Reference has been made to an increasingly important body of literature, much of which has been contributed by psychologists, sociologists, market research analysts, government public opinion analysts, public relations specialists and statisticians.

Another feature of this edition is the elaborate form in the appendix on the characteristics of successful and unsuccessful candidates for elective office. It is designed to be a guide to test certain hypotheses regarding the personal attributes of political leaders, the effectiveness of different campaign techniques, and the relationship between economic, social and political changes. It is hoped that this form may aid in the gathering of comparable material regarding different campaigns which can later be used as a basis for generalizations regarding the patterns of American political behavior. It includes items on cultural background, personal developmental history embodying culturally conditioning factors, characteristics of interpersonal relations at different age periods, attributes at time of election, techniques employed and social situation and party organization.

Charles E. Merriam
Harold F Gosnell

TABLE OF CONTENTS

THE AMERICAN PARTY SYSTEM

CHAPTER I

THE PLACE OF THE PARTY SYSTEM IN THE MODERN WORLD [1]

"The proverbial wisdom of the populace in the streets, on the roads, and in the markets, instructs the ear of him who studies man more fully than a thousand rules ostentatiously arranged."—Anonymous, 1804.

POLITICAL PARTIES OF THE AMERICAN TYPE ARE PART AND PARCEL OF the democratic system of government.[2] In a dictatorship, where the single party in power tolerates no rivals or opposition groups, there is no party system in the American sense. In a book on American political parties it is therefore necessary to consider the relationship of democracy to the party system.

Peculiar national conditions have produced the American party type. Viewed from the perspective of world history, it is a comparatively new form of organization. Its origin cannot be pushed much further back than 1828 when manhood suffrage was first tried in fourteen of the twenty-four American states. It is true that some time before this the Swiss had experimented with direct democracy in their town meetings, but they had not as yet developed political parties which could function in a representative democratic government. The authors separately have discussed elsewhere the meaning of democracy, representation, and representative government.[3]

[1] This chapter was written by Dr. Gosnell.

[2] A democratic party system has been defined as a system under which the bulk of the adult male population has the right to vote, under which there is freedom of association and freedom of expression, under which decisions are reached by a majority, and under which there exists a constitutional consensus. The meaning of constitutional consensus was made very clear by the events in Germany under the Weimar Republic. After 1929 the rapid growth of the intolerant parties, the National Socialist party at one extreme and the Communist party at another extreme, made it impossible to operate the parliamentary system, and President Hindenburg resorted to the device of government by decree. The Weimar parties were unable to integrate the German people so as to produce a parliamentary majority.

[3] Charles E. Merriam, *Systematic Politics* (Chicago, 1945); H. F. Gosnell, *Democracy: Threshold of Freedom* (New York, The Ronald Press, 1948).

Democratic representation is a form of group action made possible by the invention of the device of majority rule. The American colonists brought with them from Great Britain experience with the use of this device and with various schemes for choosing representatives. Such success as the democratic party system early attained in the United States derived from a respect for tradition, simple tastes, common interests, and the willingness of the average citizen (who was usually a small, independent farmer) to accept the leadership of the educated and the wealthy.

While the political parties first grew up under a rural economy and a handicraft type of industry, they were soon tested by the far-reaching changes brought about by the industrial revolution. As the United States became increasingly urban, industrialized, and capitalistic, the freedom to choose one's party came to be regarded as the concomitant of an economic system of free competition. Political theorists such as Thomas Jefferson, who prophesied dire consequences to our democratic institutions if the people were piled up in cities, would have been confounded to see how adaptable the political forms proved to be to the new economic molds. The industrial revolution brought with it mechanical and social inventions which made it possible for the parties to operate upon a vast scale. The new abundance created by the improved methods of exploiting the country's rich resources allowed a system of universal free education which permitted the masses to enjoy the products of the printing presses. If the United States had been as large in 1800 as it is now, it is doubtful whether national election campaigns could have been conducted. As the country expanded, the political parties learned to use such inventions as the steam railroad, the telegraph, the telephone, the modern printing press, the automobile, the sound truck, the motion picture, the radio, and television to carry their messages to the voters over vast expanses of territory. Our relative security and our economic prosperity permitted political experimentation.

PARTIES AND MAJORITY RULE

One of the outstanding characteristics of the American party system is that it is a two-party system, in contrast to the multiple-party systems which are found in the democratic countries of Continental Europe.

In one sense all democratic party systems are two-party systems. The doctrine of government by consent has proved to be workable only when some convention such as the principle of majority rule has been adopted. Those nations which did not adopt the majority rule principle either ceased to be self-governing or opened the way to dismemberment or stagnation. In Spain, Switzerland, Hungary, and Poland, bitter experience demonstrated the necessity of adopting a device for arriving at a decision without obtaining the consent of all.[4] For instance, in the Poland of the sixteenth century unanimous consent was required for elections, the levying of taxes, and communal self-government. The veto of any individual deputy or squire kept the Poles from forming a strong government which could resist foreign pressure.

Once the principle of majority rule is adopted, the next question becomes: How will this majority be obtained? In the United States and Great Britain the majority is formed by the leaders of one of the major parties who have been able for over a hundred years to marshal sufficient numbers of the voters to form governments. The two-party system implies that no party will have such overwhelming power that it is hopeless for the opposition to strive to obtain a majority. On the other hand, the multiple-party system requires the leaders of different parties to come together to form a coalition government since no one party comes near to a majority. In either case it is necessary for the party leaders to make many compromises. Under the two-party system, the bargains between diverse elements are made before the election, and under the multiple-party system they are made after the election.

The Two-Party System

The two-party system based upon electoral divisions has been characteristic of English-speaking peoples. It has been regarded by some commentators as a superior form of party development.[5] In

---

[4] Ladislas Konopczynski, "Majority Rule," *Encyclopaedia of the Social Sciences*, X (June, 1933), 55–60; and A. M. Holden, "Imperative Mandate in the Spanish Cortes of the Middle Ages," *American Political Science Review*, XXIV (1930), 886–912.

[5] A. L. Lowell, *The Government of England* (new ed., New York, 1912); James C. Charlesworth, "Is Our Two-Party System 'Natural'" *Annals of the American Academy of Political and Social Science*, Vol. 259 (September, 1948), 1–9.

the United States and Great Britain there has never been a time when there were only two parties, but in these countries the minor parties have been relatively insignificant, and the central tendency has always been toward a twofold division of the voters. Under this system, the important fact is that the preponderant party has the power to operate the machinery of the government by itself.

In Great Britain and America the two-party system has been the result of a high degree of homogeneity, the general use of a common language, the presence of long-standing traditions, the absence of intolerant minorities, the general acceptance of the economic system of free enterprise, and the belief in democratic devices. In addition to these general conditions, there are peculiar political institutions in England and America which have conditioned party growth. In both countries the single-member district system of representation has been employed for selection of national legislators. This plan has discouraged minority parties and prevented their getting any firm foothold in the national lawmaking body. In England, however, it did not block the rise of the Labor party. After 1918, when universal adult suffrage was adopted in Britain, the Labor party became a major party and the Liberal party was squeezed between it and the Conservative party.

The position of the executive in English-speaking countries has also contributed to the formation of the two-party system. In England the Prime Minister has the power to dissolve Parliament, which means that he has a firm whip hand over his party followers in the House of Commons. If any members of the party in power entertain thoughts of breaking off and forming a new party group, they are brought to their senses by the party whip who warns them of the trouble and expense of a new election and of the danger of their being defeated if the party leaders should choose to concentrate their efforts to that end. In the United States the election of the President by a majority in the electoral college has had a similar effect upon party development. Any party which cannot approach a majority in the electoral college must give up hope of controlling the most important political office. Consequently, even in times of great crisis, as in the Civil War period, the voters have clung to the old biparty tradition. In this period the Republican party sprang into life full grown. The Whig party disappeared and the Republican party became a major party in 1856.

The American two-party system has been severely criticized by some foreign observers. While James Bryce was on the whole sympathetic, M. Ostrogorski repudiated the system altogether. The two-party plan came, said he, from the Middle Ages when men were divided into hostile camps and must be either orthodox or heterodox. But now many new questions divide men's minds, and the party rests "on political conditions which have ceased to exist." Rigid parties are no longer needed, and party domination is no longer necessary. "Party as a wholesale contractor for the numerous and varied problems present and to come should give place to special organizations, limited to particular objects, and forming and reforming spontaneously, so to speak, according to the changing problems of life and the play of opinion brought about thereby. Citizens who part company on one question would join forces on another."

Ostrogorski suggests, therefore, the "substitution of special and more elastic organizations for the permanent and stereotyped parties." Here he seems to look toward the group or multiparty system in place of the biparty plan; and in this connection he suggests the utility of the preferential vote as a means of securing freer grouping of citizens.[6]

Criticisms against the two-party system have not changed the liking of Americans for it. The system has provided strong governments in times of crisis and it has avoided ministerial crises such as have been common in France. In a country as large as the United States the system has been useful as a means of integrating diverse elements that must be brought together to form a government.

The Multiple-Party System

The electorates of the Continental democratic countries of Europe have lacked the cohesiveness of the British and American electorates and consequently they have been divided into many small parties, no one of which can command a parliamentary majority by itself.[7] Religious, nationalistic, economic, and political differences have split

[6] M. Ostrogorski, *Democracy and the Organization of Political Parties* (New York, 1902).

[7] For a brief discussion of the French, Belgian, German (Weimar), and Swiss multiple-party systems, see H. F Gosnell, *Why Europe Votes* (Chicago, 1930). For a more extended analysis, consult Herman Finer, *Theory and Practice of Modern Government* (London, 1932); C. Friedrich, *Constitutional Government and Politics* (New York, 1937); H. F. Mallory, *Political Handbook of the World* (New York, published annually by Harper and Bros.).

the voters into many different groups and prevented their forming into two main armies. Thus in France there are seven or eight main parties, in Switzerland five or six, and in Belgium four.

In a very illuminating analysis of the French party system, André Siegfried pointed out that there were parties born of the French Revolution, the clerical and the anticlerical parties, and there were parties born of the industrial revolution, the conservative and the working class parties.[8] While there is some overlapping in these two divisions, *i.e.*, a clerical party may have conservative tendencies and a Marxist party may be anticlerical, yet they reveal two fundamental cleavages which are not so prominent in the United States.

Religious tolerance in America has discouraged formation of ecclesiastical political parties. In France, Belgium, Italy, Switzerland, and other democratic countries of Continental Europe, however, there are strongly organized Catholic parties which are interested in securing government support and protection for the church and its activities.[9]

Nationalistic and linguistic differences may also furnish the basis of party separatism. This is shown in Belgium, where there is a Flemish nationalist party, and in the Union of South Africa, where there is a Nationalist party based upon the cleavage between the Boers and the English. On the other hand, neither Switzerland's nor Canada's linguistic differences have proved a basis for formation of separate parties.

Perhaps the most important reason why Continental European democracies have had multiple-party systems is to be found in the economic composition of the population. As compared with the United States, class stratification there has been more marked, and the labor groups have been more diligent in building up their own organizations. The result has been the formation of labor, socialist, and communist parties which are bitterly hostile to the capitalistic or conservative parties.

The multiple-party system is also the product of certain political institutions. In France under the Third Republic the lack of the power of dissolution made it impossible for the Premier to discipline

---

[8] *France: A Study in Nationality* (New Haven, 1930).

[9] Ludwig Bergsträsser, "Catholic Parties," *Encyclopaedia of the Social Sciences*, III (December, 1930), 271–75.

the party members, as the Prime Minister can in Great Britain, with the threat of new elections. Consequently, the seven or eight main parties in the French Chamber of Deputies continued operations during the entire legislative period. Under its new Constitution this feature of the French government was modified so as to strengthen the Premier somewhat. In Switzerland the lack of a responsible parliamentary system leaves room for a multiple-party system. The plural executive does not have to resign when its measures are voted down in the National Council; therefore various combinations of party groups are possible. The system of representation may also encourage the multiplication of parties. Switzerland, France, Holland, and Belgium have forms of proportional representation.

The One-Party System

At the other extreme from the multiple-party system stands the one-party system or the totalitarian regime.[10]

In recent times there developed one-party dictatorships, which, whether fascist or communist, possessed the following in common:

(1) The party is restricted to a small fraction of the community. In Russia less than one per cent of the total population are Communists of party standing; in Fascist Italy and Nazi Germany only 5 per cent of the total population were members of the legal party.

(2) The official party has a "monopoly of legality," i.e., no other party has any legal standing. No other party may organize, agitate, discuss, or carry on any activities coming under the head of party or political functions. All such forms of behavior are illegal and are liable to severe punishment There are of course social groups in a given community, but they must be careful to avoid anything like partisan association or activity.

(3) The so-called party is closely organized from top to bottom and plays an important role in the conduct of public affairs. The party assemblies are more significant than the meetings of the remaining parliamentary bodies, and the party leaders also have an important position in administration. While the power of final decision rests in the hands of the ruling head of the state, the advice of the party leaders and party organization is important and influential.

[10] M. Ascoli and A. Feiler, *Fascism for Whom?* (New York, 1938); G. S. Ford (ed.), *Dictatorship in the Modern World*, 2nd ed. (Minneapolis, 1939); E. Heimann, *Communism, Fascism or Democracy¹* (New York, 1938); I. Silone, *The School for Dictators* (New York, 1938).

(4) Policies depend in large measure for their administration upon the party leaders, either directly or indirectly. In military administration this is difficult to deal with, but in other branches of the state activity much can be done in the way of party supervision and control.

All this constitutes a form of organization of political power but in no sense a party as the term is generally employed. The elements of free association, free organization, free candidacy, free discussion, free criticism of policies and presentation of counter policies, free voting on issues or personnel are all absent. The outcome is a closed corporation of political activists who choose their own membership [11] and compel the community to accept the lines of action they determine—by persuasion and example if possible, but if not, by intimidation and force. There may be some latitude in discussion, but not in organization or opposition. The terror and the purge are never far away in theory or in practice.

It is of course possible to call such an arrangement a one-party system, but in fact it is precisely the opposite of a party system, and can be correctly characterized as a pseudo-party system. It is a very limited aristocracy maintained by violence, if necessary.

The one-party system is the product of the disturbed social and economic conditions following World War I. It is true that despotism is an old form of government, but the modern authoritarian regimes differ from those of former periods in that they are mass movements, which have at their disposal all of the implements of modern technology and psychology.

The democratic party system has taken little root in those countries where the peasants were isolated, where there was a large amount of illiteracy, where the means of communication were not fully developed, and where there were relatively few large cities.[12] In such countries the businessmen were timid and were dominated by the landed aristocracy. The voters could not read the ballots, to say nothing of the newspapers, and they were usually controlled by organized bands of armed men. It is interesting to note that the modern one-party system was first established in Soviet Russia where all of the conditions described above prevailed.

[11] See Merriam, *The New Democracy and the New Despotism* (New York, 1939), on qualifications for membership.

[12] Francis Delaisi, *Les Deux Europes* (Paris, 1929).

Even an industrialized country may turn to an authoritarian regime when national humiliation and economic and political insecurity make desperate remedies attractive. Immediately following 1918, Italy and Germany were among the states that were dissatisfied and insecure. The Italians lacked the resources of a great power, and they felt they were deprived of colonial outlets for their expanding population. Mussolini, in his famous march on Rome in 1922 and in his subsequent extensions of his power, exploited the national disillusionment of the Italians regarding the peace settlement. The Italians were told that they had won the war but lost the peace because they failed to attain their territorial ambitions in Europe and in Africa. Similarly, Germany, humiliated and disarmed by the terms of the Versailles Treaty, felt insecure. The failure of the League of Nations to correct the inequities of the treaty and the attitude of the Allies toward Germany's demands with reference to reparations and arms equality increased the Germans' sense of injury. Adolf Hitler had the organizing genius and the oratorical skill to exploit these feelings at a critical time. Fascism, with its emphasis upon nationalism, has proved to be more brittle than Communist dictatorships which have had an international program.

It appears that the one-party system also flourishes when economic conditions become unbearable and the people have lost hope in their economic and political institutions. One of the principal reasons for the rise of dictatorship in Europe following World War I was the economic chaos which the war left in its wake. The revolutionary process started in Russia which was left exhausted and disorganized by the war. The Bolsheviks, a resolute band of Marxist revolutionaries, took advantage of the chaos found in their vast country to impose a new dictatorship in the name of the proletariat. Lenin and his followers took over the secret police from the Czarists and adapted the device for their own purposes. Liberties were suppressed in the name of the state and a new authoritarianism was born. Following World War II the Russian Communists again took advantage of the want, disorder, and hopelessness found in the devasted and disordered Europe. Their fifth columns, the Communist parties and secret societies, sought control of the key governmental and trade union posts. At appropriate times they staged coup d'etats in neighboring states by means of inside and outside pressures. Democracy survived in those countries which enjoyed a relatively high standard of living even at the lowest points of the business cycle and where the people still had some faith in economic liberalism. In spite of a permanent depression in certain industries, Great Britain survived two devastating wars. While the French did not feel the depression of the thirties until much later than other European peoples, their morale was weakened and they succumbed to the divisive military and psychological tactics of the Nazis in 1940. Democracy in France survived the defeat of its armies and the disgrace of German occupation. The Swiss and the Scandinavians were particularly successful in weathering the economic and war crises. Democratic symbols might have survived in Germany in the thirties if some way had appeared to save the economic structure of the Republic. During the time that Germany could borrow funds to keep her industries going, the antidemocratic sentiment made comparatively little headway.[13] The National Socialist party did not begin to expand its electoral support until unemployment had reached alarming proportions in the German Republic.

In particular countries the rise of the one-party system may be traced to lack of a tradition of self-government and free institutions. While the German people had a brief experience with the democratic system of government under the Weimar Constitution from 1919 to 1933, this experience was not calculated to recommend democratic institutions since it was associated in the popular mind with economic adversity at home and political frustration in international relations. During the Weimar epoch, Germany was ruled by a political bureaucracy which was deeply rooted in the traditional power of the aristocracy, the plutocracy, and the army. The transition from the benevolent paternalism of semiabsolutist government to the liberalism of democratic institutions was too abrupt. It may also be said that in Italy the parliamentary system from 1870 to 1922 had always been in the hands of a small ruling class which exploited the ignorance and the indifference of the masses.

A people that wishes to try popular government must agree to allow disagreement. Without a general consensus of opinion favorable to democratic methods, the system is impossible. Where a considerable minority is found which is hostile to the democratic tech-

[13] R. L. Buell and others, *New Governments of Europe* (New York, 1935).

niques, then it is impossible to make a multiple- or a two-party system work. A fascist dictatorship was established in Germany when a majority of the German voters indicated that they were opposed to democratic methods. What the German people lacked in 1933 was a faith in their own ability to solve their difficulties by parliamentary methods. They were unable to practice self-integration.

The constitutional consensus which was lacking in Germany during the twenties and thirties has been present so far in the United States. The American two-party system has not intensified class strife. It has softened it. Throughout American history the major parties have cut across class lines. They have included members from every sectional, racial, religious, class, and occupational grouping in the country.[14] The major parties have been national parties. Parties which have been based on narrow class interests have not thrived in the American atmosphere.

The end of the war has not brought peace to the world. It is idle to deny the growing antagonism between the United States and the Soviet Union. Many Americans believe that the Communist party dictatorship presents a threat to world peace. On the other hand, it is clear that the Communist leaders regard the American way of life, the Marshall Plan, our interest in free discussion and in free flow of goods, our continued prosperity, the continued success of our political institutions, and the present nonpartisan foreign policy being pursued by our Government as threats to their aspirations. A striking contrast between the American and Communist ways of life is to be found in the ethical foundations of the two systems. Whereas the American way of life is founded upon the religious conviction of the soundness of the Golden Rule, the Soviet system is based upon a materialistic philosophy which has no place for brotherly love. American democracy can meet the challenge of the Communist attacks in so far as we can convince the rest of the world that we can live up to our ideals. There are many aspects of American party life which give indications that we are not living up to our highest ethical principles.

[14] See Chapters V and VI, below.

CHAPTER II

WHAT SUFFRAGE MEANS

"Your every voter, as surely as your chief magistrate, exercises a public trust."
—Grover Cleveland, Inaugural Address, March 4, 1885.

SUFFRAGE, IN A NARROW SENSE OF THE TERM, IS THE RIGHT OR privilege of the individual to take part in the selection of public officials and to vote on propositions presented to the electorate. Opinions on its legal nature have differed widely, but three general theories of suffrage may be postulated.[1]

The first, or individualistic, interpretation views the right of suffrage as an innate natural right of man.[2] This theory demands universal and equal right of suffrage, i.e., every adult citizen has the right to vote, and the ballot of every voter has the same value. The demand for universal and equal suffrage has been enormously useful for propaganda purposes on the part of groups that have been excluded from the franchise. Fantastic meanings have been read into this concept, but nevertheless they produced powerful emotional drives. Another individualistic position states that the vote is an individual positive right similar to a property right. This theory dates back to the feudal regime since it conceives of the vote in terms of status, usually connected with the possession of real property or some other form of wealth. A vestige of it remains in modern England in the form of the business premises vote and in the United States in the seven states having the poll tax requirement for voting.

A second conception of suffrage views the franchise not as a right of the individual but as a function to be performed in the interest of the community. This idea has been criticized because it is enormously difficult to define what is the "common interest" to the satisfaction

[1] H. F. Gosnell, *Democracy: Threshold of Freedom* (New York, The Ronald Press, 1948). The Ronald Press has permitted the authors to draw upon materials in this book for the present chapter.

[2] John Locke, *Complete Works* (London, 1823), Vol. IV, *Two Treatises of Government*; J. J. Rousseau, *Contract Social*.

of all groups. If the definition of common interest is left to a group like a political party, grave abuses may arise. Fascist countries held to the totalitarian view of suffrage and they swept away the guarantees of individual rights and liberties which have been associated with democracy.

The third, or dualistic, theory of suffrage combines the individualistic and totalitarian views. According to this theory the individual voter must consider his obligations to the state, and the collective body must protect the rights of the individual. Marking a ballot is an official function performed for the state; suffrage is both an individual right and a social function. A voter has duties as well as rights. Certain qualifications such as age, residence, and citizenship can easily be justified under this theory.

PROPERTY QUALIFICATIONS FOR VOTING

The property qualification for voting prevalent in the American colonies was borrowed from England where it originally came from the feudal theory, according to which voting was patrimonial in character, a privilege attached to the status of the taxpayer or freeman or burgess or freeholder. Chief Justice Holt, in the case of *Ashby v. White* (1703), said that the election of knights belonged to the freeholders of the counties, and was an original right vested in and inseparable from the freehold, and that it could no more be severed from the freehold than the freehold itself can be taken away.

In Great Britain the rise of the industrial system and the expansion of trade brought more emphasis upon a pecuniary system of values. Demands for extension of the suffrage were first made by the new plutocracy of manufacturers and merchants who were anxious to remove the restrictions placed upon trade by the feudalistic regime.

In England and the United States, the struggle of the propertyless classes to secure the suffrage was upon occasions accompanied by violence. But usually the development of economic power by groups seeking the suffrage was sufficient. In the 1840's the British Chartist agitators employed the method of the strike and the riot. In America the abortive rebellion of Dorr and his followers in Rhode Island indicated that the struggle might possibly have reached a violent stage if concessions had not been made.

Theories of suffrage may be tested by considering what difference the enfranchisement or disfranchisement of certain economic groups makes. Have any of the prophecies regarding the dangers of giving the poor man the vote been realized in practice? Has there been a tendency for the propertyless classes to use the ballot as a means for redistributing wealth? Has the character of the public officeholder declined since adoption of universal adult suffrage?

The abolition of the property qualifications for voting in the United States started with the westward movement. The existence of free land in the western territories of the United States made the definition of suffrage in terms of property owning meaningless. On the frontier land was practically free to those who had the initiative and drive to settle it. When new western states were admitted to the Union most of them omitted the property qualifications for voting, a situation which had its repercussions in the East. Gradually the older states abandoned the landowning and taxpaying qualifications. Whereas at the time of the Revolution seven of the thirteen colonies had land property qualifications and the six remaining colonies allowed substitution of personal property for real estate on the payment of taxes, in the early state constitutions only five retained the real estate qualifications. By 1830, fourteen of the twenty-four states had adult male suffrage.[3]

The far-reaching consequences of the broadening of the suffrage in the United States can be analyzed by studying some of the older states. In New York State, for instance, in the period before democratization of suffrage, the political leaders were for the most part recruited from the wealthy landowners, the merchants, and the lawyers, who at this time were very closely associated with the landed proprietors and merchants. An estimated 60 per cent or more of the political officeholders were from wealthy families.[4] After the suffrage changes, the proportion of persons from the upper income groups that entered politics was much lower. Political activity among the lower income groups greatly increased. Among the possible results of the broader franchise may be listed: the development of party organization and election campaign techniques the rise of organ-

[3] K. H. Porter, *History of Suffrage in the United States* (Chicago, 1918).
[4] Gabriel Almond, "Plutocracy and Politics in New York City" (University of Chicago, Ph.D. thesis, 1938).

ized economic groups representing interests respectively of business, labor, and agriculture; the passage of social and labor legislation covering such questions as the right to organize and the regulation of conditions of work; the adoption of the goal of universal free education; the withdrawal of many of the plutocrats from political life; and the establishment of exclusive social sets.

Especially in local politics the effects of universal adult suffrage have been far-reaching. Whereas one hundred and fifty years ago prominent merchants and social leaders took an active part in municipal affairs, the actual control of party organization in many American cities is now in the hands of political bosses. There have been comparatively few prominent municipal bosses who were members of a socially recognized family. No parents of any of the prominent bosses were found on the social register of their particular cities.[5]

DISFRANCHISEMENT OF RACIAL GROUPS

In so-called democratic countries where there are two widely divergent racial groups, both numerous, it is improbable that democratic principles will be completely applied. Those states which have large colored populations have found it extremely difficult to realize in practice the dogma of political equality. Conflict has arisen between the ideologies of democracy and white supremacy not only in the United States but also in the English-speaking dominions of South Africa and Australia. It might also be stated as a sociological principle that when one racial or nationalistic group lives side by side with another of different social status, the dominant group tries to institutionalize its alleged superiority by political means. If the racial group which is held to be culturally inferior is easily distinguishable by color of skin or some other physical difference, it is difficult to solve questions involving race relations by the ritual of voting. Two such groups, which usually frown upon miscegenation, tend at times to set up a biracial organization. One of the essential conditions of democracy is the existence of constitutional consensus. This does not exist when the stigmatized or submerged racial group is believed to be an actual threat to the supremacy of the dominant cultural group. In Brazil, Mexico, and other Latin American coun-

[5] H. Zink, *City Bosses in the United States* (Durham, 1930).

tries, the dogma of white supremacy has less vogue than in English-speaking countries. North Americans have many lessons in democratic equality to learn from the neighbors to the south of them.

The former Confederate States in the United States, the Union of South Africa, Australia, Barbados and many other jurisdictions where two or more racial groups are set apart by caste lines do not put into operation the democratic system of free elections.[6] The submerged racial group is usually inferior in its economic position. Large numbers of Negroes in the southern states of the American Union are tenant farmers or sharecroppers who are attached to the land and have low standards of living. As a result of their limited educational opportunities, general social ostracism, and lack of economic resources, they have not developed a militant nationalistic movement.

The democratic system may be used in places where the submerged racial group is in a decided minority. This is the situation found in the northern part of the United States where Negroes vote freely. Here the colored group is relatively insignificant in size. In 1944, for instance, Negroes were only 9.3 per cent of the total population in Chicago and 6 per cent in New York City. On the other hand, they were almost 50 per cent of the total population in the state of Mississippi. As the Negro vote has increased in size and influence in the northern states with continued migration from the South, the friction between the races in political and other matters has become more pronounced.

Negroes did not vote in the North before the Civil War except for a scattered number of free Negroes in the New England states who were permitted to vote.[7] All of the other northern states disfranchised free Negroes by putting the word "white" in the qualifications for

[6] On conditions in the United States, see Gunnar Myrdal, *American Dilemma: The Negro and Democracy* (New York, Harper & Brothers, 1944); H. F. Gosnell, *Democracy: The Threshold of Freedom* (New York, The Ronald Press, 1948); Paul Lewinson, *Race, Class and Party* (London and New York, 1932); on the Union of South Africa, L. Buell, *The Native Problem in Africa* (New York, 1928). In Brazil, Mexico, and the Latin American countries in general there is a greater tolerance of racial differences, and in so far as these countries are democratic the above generalizations should be modified.

[7] E. Olbrich, *The Development of Sentiment on Negro Suffrage to 1860* (Madison, 1912); C. P. Patterson, *The Negro in Tennessee* (Austin, Texas, 1922); G. T. Stephenson, *Race Distinctions in American Law* (New York, 1910); K. H. Porter, *History of Suffrage in the United States* (Chicago, 1918). Free Negroes could vote in North Carolina until 1835.

most part educated in the North. The corruption was largely the fault of the northern white carpetbaggers and southern white scalawags who used the Negro voters for their own selfish ends. Graft and inefficiency in government were not confined to the South during the seventies of the nineteenth century. The Tweed scandals in New York and the scandals of the Grant administration were in no way connected with the voting of colored persons. The reaction of the southern whites toward the reconstruction governments was bound to be highly unfavorable for psychological as well as for political and economic reasons. Negro voting was looked upon as an event which turned the social order upside down, and as a means which the northerners used to punish the southern aristocrats for starting the rebellion.[13]

The disfranchisement of Negroes in the southern states furnishes interesting and valuable material regarding the effects of nonparticipation in the political process, even though it is difficult to say whether disfranchisement is the result of the Negroes' inferior social and economic position or whether they lack economic strength because of their political disabilities, or both. It is clear, however, that the Negroes in the South do not receive the full benefits from the state services to which they are entitled by reason of the amount of taxes they pay and their needs. They fail to receive their fair share of the public funds, whether for schools or for such improvements as sewerage, streets, lights, and paving, and they also suffer discrimination in public carriers and in places to live. Their weak political position has also meant that they could do little to protect themselves against lynchings and race riots.

The use which Negroes make of the suffrage in the jurisdictions where they vote is a matter of theoretical interest as they constitute a kind of control group for those disfranchised.[14] A number of ques-

[13] F. B. Simkins and R. H. Woody, *South Carolina During Reconstruction* (Chapel Hill, 1932), gives a very objective account of the reconstruction period on the character of Negro officeholders. See A. A. Taylor, "Negro Congressmen a Generation After," *Journal of History*, VII (April, 1932); J. R. Lynch, *The Facts of Reconstruction* (New York, 1913); and M. Langston, *From a Virginia Plantation to the National Capitol* (Hartford, 1894).

[14] This subject is more fully discussed in Gosnell, *Democracy: Threshold of Freedom* (New York, The Ronald Press, 1948) and *Negro Politicians* (Chicago, 1935); Myrdal, *op. cit.*; Henry Lee Moon, *Balance of Power: The Negro Vote* (Garden City, N. Y., 1948).

tions might be raised. What have the Negroes done in the way of building party organizations of their own? Have they been mere tools of the white bosses?

The new Negro voters in the northern centers have not had the money or the training with which to build powerful political machines, yet they have gradually worked up into party councils until they hold a considerable number of ward and district captaincies.

As Negro voters became more and more numerous in the northern cities they began to demand representatives of their own in the various lawmaking bodies. They have been successful in electing representatives to the state legislature in at least nine states. As long ago as 1876 a colored man was sent to the Illinois General Assembly. Other northern states followed suit and some of the border states likewise.[15]

No Negroes were in Congress during the first quarter of the twentieth century, but in 1928 a Republican Negro candidate in Chicago was successful in securing a seat in the House of Representatives, which since 1943 has been held by a Negro Democrat. In New York City a Negro congressman was elected in 1944. Colored men have also been elected as judges in both New York and Chicago. Although the advances of the group have been seemingly blocked when they acquired enough power and influence to attract considerable attention, the group generally consolidated and preserved the gains which had already been made. No Negroes have been chosen recently to important administrative posts which had control over considerable political patronage, but the Negro voter has enabled some of the colored leaders to bargain for lesser positions. Colored persons are now found on the police force, the teaching staffs, and the general clerical staffs of the northern cities where they constitute a considerable proportion of the population.

Negro politicians have displayed considerable political acumen and have been able to rally their forces by clever manipulation of political symbols. From time to time these ward bosses have come up from the slums. Nevertheless they have been very vigorous characters, sometimes with higher principles than the corresponding white bosses. The Negro political bosses possess considerable race pride and generally use their political and economic power to im-

[15] M. N. Work, *Negro Year Book* (Tuskegee. Alabama, 1914–1915).

prove the status of their group. When some question which they regard as vital to the interest of the race is raised they cannot be bulldozed or bribed.[16]

Have political methods won for the Negro voters occupational openings or other advantages? Even during the dark days following the disfranchisement in the South, the Negroes, because they had potentialities as voters, were given some recognition in the federal government. Various Republican and even Democratic Presidents appointed Negroes to such positions as register of the Treasury, minister to Haiti and consular agent. In the South it became more and more difficult to appoint Negroes to local federal positions with power and prestige, but in the North and in Washington, D. C., Negroes gradually forged ahead. There are now large numbers of Negroes in the postal service and the revenue service.[17]

As voters Negroes have become a pressure group. The civil rights and fair employment practices acts found in northern and border states are in part the product of Negro agitation.[18] White politicians have made these concessions in order to win supporters from the group. As legislators the Negroes have usually been on the side of the party machine. These lawmakers have held that their primary obligations are to secure certain benefits for their group and to protect their group against discriminatory legislation. They feel that this can best be done by going along with the dominant political organization. One of the essentials of the democratic system is that various groups must be made the judge of their own best interests. While efficiency experts would criticize the voting behavior of Negro legislators, the Negro weeklies and the rank and file of the "black belt" have different views. Negro politicians have not secured as much in the war of governmental services as they might have secured under different political conditions. But it is clear that they have secured more in the North in the way of educational facilities and protection of persons and property than their disfranchised brothers have attained in the South.

[16] H. F. Gosnell, *Negro Politicians*; Myrdal, *op. cit.*
[17] Gosnell, *op. cit.*, Chap. XIV.
[18] *Ibid.*, p. 14.

CITIZENSHIP AS A REQUIREMENT FOR VOTING

Citizenship is a concept which has been associated with the individualistic theory of suffrage. The modern idea of citizenship is derived from the ancient and medieval municipality, but it is based upon a territory and a nationality. The triumph of nationalism and industrialism over feudalism was closely associated with the rise of democratic ideologies. At present all so-called democratic countries specify citizenship as one of the qualifications for voting.

Citizenship may be acquired in modern states in one of three ways: by birth within the territory of a state; by birth of parents who are citizens of a state; and by naturalization. In connection with standards for suffrage, the first two methods do not concern us. The requirements for naturalization, however, are also in effect requirements for the exercise of the suffrage. Immigration and naturalization are important topics in the American democracy. What are the qualities that aliens need to fit them to act as voters?

Citizenship is a matter to be determined by the law of a particular state, since it concerns the status of an individual with reference to that state. Naturalization laws vary widely in details, but contain certain common essentials. An immigrant must reside for a given period of years, usually five, in the country in which he seeks citizenship. He must produce witnesses as to his good moral character and he must swear loyalty to his new fatherland.[19]

Five years and three months is the minimum residence period for naturalization in the United States. Prior to the Naturalization Act of 1906, which centralized administration in the Federal Bureau of Naturalization, the acquiring of citizenship was left for the most part to the states, and many grave abuses arose. Many persons naturalized before 1906 did not fulfill even the minimum residence qualification. Gavit has presented figures which indicate great increases in naturalization around elections during this period.[20] During the past forty years, however, naturalization has been carefully regulated, and on the average it takes a person about ten years to

[19] R. W. Flournoy and M. O. Hudson, *A Collection of Nationality Laws of Various Countries as Contained in Constitutions, Statutes and Treaties* (New York, 1929), p. 31.

[20] J. P. Gavit, *Americans by Choice* (New York, 1922).

complete the process. Naturalized citizens thus have time to learn something of the English language and something about American government.

In the United States over one-third of both the foreign-born males and females were aliens in 1940, but of these aliens many more males had their first papers than females.[21] Following the Cable Act of 1922, the percentage of foreign-born women naturalized has been lower than that of the men. A majority of the aliens who have not applied for citizenship are women, who must now take out their own papers even though they marry American citizens.

Nonnaturalization is most prevalent among immigrants from certain European countries. Two-thirds or more of the Irish, Swedish, Norwegian, and German immigrants were naturalized in 1940 as compared with one-half of the Polish, Italian, and Hungarian. This does not mean that a causal relationship exists between birth in southeastern Europe and nonnaturalization. These data show that the variations are related to length of residence in this country. A smaller proportion of Polish and Italian immigrants were naturalized in 1940 because these groups have been in the country for a shorter time than most other immigrants.

A large number of adult persons, particularly women of Polish, Russian, and Italian birth, have been disfranchised by the requirement of citizenship for voting. Several years ago one of the authors made a study of naturalization and nonnaturalization in the city of Chicago.[22] Since adult foreign-born persons in Chicago in 1940 constituted nearly 6 per cent of all adult foreign-born persons in the United States, the findings in the Chicago study are significant. Comparisons between naturalized and nonnaturalized adults showed that newness to the country, extreme youth, bachelorhood, lack of family cares and responsibilities, lack of schooling, and lack of knowledge regarding American political situations were all related to non-

---

[21] Of the adult male aliens approximately 38 per cent are declarants. Of the adult female aliens only 18 per cent are declarants. For original figures, see *Seventeenth Census of United States,* 1940, Vol. III, Part 1.

[22] H. F. Gosnell, "Non-naturalization: A Study in Political Assimiliation," *American Journal of Sociology,* XXXIII (May, 1928), 930–939; "Characteristics of Nonnaturalized," *ibid.,* XXXIV (March, 1929), 847–855; unpublished materials in the possession of the writers. See also Gosnell, *Democracy: The Threshold of Freedom* (New York, The Ronald Press, 1948).

naturalization. These influences, particularly ignorance of the English language and ignorance of American political methods, may be regarded as important in elections.

Ignorance was the greatest single cause of nonnaturalization. Most of the nondeclarants were ignorant of American political affairs, the English language, or the provisions of the naturalization laws. This ignorance is understandable, when associated with short residence in this country. In other cases it was due to apathy. Some aliens feel the requirements for naturalization are too difficult, and others do not want to renounce allegiance to their old country. With the lapse of time nondeclarants are gradually diminishing.

Application of the rules laid down in the naturalization law is of importance because it indicates what kind of persons are kept from becoming voters. In the United States naturalization is regarded as a judicial matter, although in some European countries it is treated as an administrative matter. The American courts apply the rules to the individual aliens coming before them. The Bureau of Naturalization investigates the cases before the courts act, searching out those who seek to avoid the law, and aiding those who are anxious to comply with the law.

Naturalization records show that ignorance of the English language, timidity, and inertia are the chief reasons for failing to complete the naturalization process. They also indicate that misconduct, including false statements, offenses involving moral turpitude, defective witnesses, and unwillingness to accept naturalization in the army are also grounds for refusing applications for citizenship. The courts have cancelled the naturalization certificates of persons shown to be hostile to the principles of the Constitution.[23]

In view of the characteristics of the nonnaturalized, fairly valid grounds exist for excluding this element from the electorate. At one time there were as many as seventeen states in the American Union which permitted persons who had taken out first papers to vote. This was done to attract immigrants to sparsely settled states in the Middlewest. It greatly retarded the naturalization process in these states.[24] As the western states became more populous and as the character of the immigrants began to change in the United States,

[23] L. Gettys, *The Law of Citizenship in the United States* (Chicago, 1934).
[24] Gavit, *op. cit.*, p. 217.

the liberal provisions regarding alien voting were abandoned. Every American state now insists upon citizenship as a requirement for voting.

OPERATION OF WOMAN SUFFRAGE

Women did not get the vote until comparatively recent times because of the legal, religious, social, and economic disabilities they have suffered throughout the ages. Before they could win the ballot, women had to secure greater independence in the home, in the church, in the courts of law, in the schools, in the professions, and in the workshops. One hundred and fifty years ago, women had few property rights, little control over marital status, no freedom of association, and highly limited professional opportunities.

Under the feudal system, the patriarchal organization of the family and the burden of their home duties, which included spinning and weaving, left the women practically no time or opportunity for politics. With the coming of the industrial revolution, wealthy bourgeois women acquired property to protect and leisure time to use for that protection. At the same time, working-class women were often forced to seek employment in the factories. Women industrial workers became potential trade unionists, and labor organizers became defenders of equal rights for women.

The countries which first adopted woman suffrage were predominantly Protestant and bourgeois. Coeducation, attacks on the double standard of sex morals, a liberal economic tradition, defense of women by the great literary leaders, employment of women in gainful occupations, and gradual removal of the legal disabilities suffered by women became closely associated with the demand for equal political rights to women. As their economic independence increased, women demanded political and legal independence. Women were employed more and more in schools, offices, and factories. Women secured the right to vote in states where they had secured emancipation along economic, social, and other lines.

Equal suffrage for men and women has not been achieved without organization and hard work. In 1848 a convention in Seneca Falls was called by Elizabeth Cady Stanton, Lucretia Mott and a number of other women, most of them Quakers, as a beginning of a long period of agitation. The convention was the result of the refusal of abolitionists meeting in London to admit women delegates to their convention. Ridiculed in many quarters, women suffragists secured the support of William Lloyd Garrison, Wendell Phillips, Channing, Whittier, and Emerson. Later in the century, the American sociologist, Lester F. Ward, maintained that the female sex was originally and is naturally superior to the male.[25]

While most of the woman suffrage crusaders lived in the eastern part of the United States, the first victories were in the West. The eastern suffragists, however, in an indirect way paved the way for the unexpected adoption of woman suffrage by the territory of Wyoming in 1869. Various interpretations have been given regarding the action of the territorial legislature. It was thought that the concession might attract women settlers, who were much needed, as the men outnumbered the women four to one. A bit of partisan byplay was involved according to another account. It was also thought that the action would serve to advertise Wyoming.[26] In fact, it did attract national attention, partly because of the pressure activities of the suffragists.

Women's part in national politics in the United States began with the admission of Wyoming as a state in 1890. Gradually the adjoining states followed suit. The Populist movement aided the suffragists to win victories in Colorado (1893), Idaho (1896), and Utah (1896). The next fifteen to twenty years were lean ones for the American suffragists, but they kept up their courage and intensified their pressure activities. Their efforts were rewarded when the Progressive revolt of 1912 broke the hold of the old line party machines in some of the western states. By 1915 the population of the suffrage states was 17 per cent of the total.

In 1890 the National American Women's Suffrage Association was founded on two earlier societies, the National Woman Suffrage Association and the American Woman Suffrage Society. The new organization published a weekly magazine and claimed a membership of 200,000 by 1914. The slow and steady pressure tactics which it used were repudiated in 1912 by Alice Paul, one of the organizers, and

---

[25] *Dynamic Sociology* (New York, 1883), p. 648; *Pure Sociology* (New York, 1903), Chap. XIV.

[26] James Bryce, *The American Commonwealth* (New York, 1920), II, 605–605.

Mrs. August Belmont, who founded the Congressional Union, later known as the National Woman's Party, which used the more dramatic strategy of mass meetings, picketing, and hunger strikes for woman suffragists put in prison.

Following World War I, women were granted the vote by a constitutional amendment passed in 1920.

The newly enfranchised women voters had to be organized and educated in political matters before they could make effective use of the ballot. They had to learn how to perform the routine tasks of democracy.

Some women had been used as political canvassers even before they could vote.[27] Women labor organizers were used for political work. Conservative women, particularly those having social prestige, made excellent political workers. The winning of the vote greatly intensified the political activity of women in the party organizations as canvassers, speakers, delegates to party conventions, members of party committees, and candidates. Special political conventions were held for women, and women's publications were issued.

As soon as they could vote themselves, women took a very active part in the canvassing of votes. Fifteen years after the adoption of equal suffrage in Colorado it was reported that "Where the size of the community justifies canvassing in any systematic way, women are employed in somewhat larger numbers than men." [28] After 1920, the number of woman party canvassers increased several thousand-fold. Women took up party work slowly in the South, but in the urban communities of the North many became precinct captains. One ward leader in Chicago boasted that one-fourth of his precinct captains were women. A study of local party leaders in Philadelphia discovered one Rosie Popovits, regarding whom her ward leader said, "She is the best man on the ward committee." [29] On the other hand, women have secured no recognition in the political clubs of New York City, where strong prejudices against women politicians still exist.[30] The success of women as canvassers has been outstand-

[27] Gosnell, *Democracy: Threshold of Freedom* (New York, The Ronald Press, 1948).

[28] Helen Sumner, *Equal Suffrage* (New York, 1909), p. 64.

[29] J. T. Salter, *Boss Rule* (New York, 1935), p. 193.

[30] R. V. Peel, *The Political Clubs of New York City* (New York, 1935), pp. 127, 248.

ing in Cincinnati, where they furnished the backbone of the volunteer organization which inaugurated and supported the city-manager form of government.[31]

Except where legislation or party regulations require the same number of men and women on the party committees, women have made slow headway in securing positions as higher party executives such as ward, city, county, and state committeemen. State central committees composed of an equal number of men and women were provided by party rule in Colorado as early as 1906. A few of the county central committees followed the example of the state committees. This same plan of representation was adopted by the Democratic National Committee in 1920 and the Republican Committee in 1924. In practice some of the women on these committees have found their position disappointing.[32]

Overriding all obstacles, American women have risen to positions of power and leadership in their parties. One five occasions nearly one-fifth of the delegates to the Democratic national convention have been women. At the Republican national conventions since 1920, from 7 to 12 per cent of the delegates have been women.[33]

TABLE 1

Year	REPUBLICAN		DEMOCRATIC	
	Delegate	Alternate	Delegate	Alternate
1912	2	–	2	1
1916		9	11	11
1920	27	129	93	206
1924	120	277	199	310
1928	70	264	152	263
1932	88	305	208	270
1936	61	222	252	333
1940	78	231	208	347
1944	99	264	174	332
1948	112	254	193	322

M. J. Fisher and B. Whitehead, "Women and National Party Organization," *American Political Science Review*, XXXVIII (Oct., 1944), p. 896.

[31] C. P. Taft, *City Management: The Cincinnati Experiment* (New York, 1933), pp. 235–236.

[32] Emily Newell Blair, "Women in the Political Parties," *Annals of the American Academy of Political and Social Science*, CXLIII (May, 1929), 222–223.

[33] S. Breckinridge, "Activities of Women Outside the Home," in President's Committee on *Recent Social Trends*, p. 741 (New York, 1933), compiled the following figures from the National Democratic and Republican Convention *Proceedings* for the various years:

Since 1916 women have served on the important convention committees in both parties.

WOMEN AS ELECTIVE OFFICEHOLDERS

The right to vote is not complete without the right to run for elective office. What avails the suffrage to a given group if it cannot send its own representatives to the lawmaking bodies to defend its interests? Once that eligibility to run for elective office is established, the question then becomes: How soon can the group capture a sufficient number of elective positions to protect itself? How soon can women leaders acquire the political experience necessary to compete successfully with the men?

American women were elected to school offices even before they could vote. In places where they later obtained the school suffrage, many more were selected as school officers. After obtaining full suffrage in the state of Colorado, a woman won the office of state superintendent of public instruction in 1894 and women have held it continuously since that date.[34] Colorado women also ran successfully for elective local offices.

Women, like other newly enfranchised groups, found it easier to capture legislative positions than to win important executive posts. Many women were elected as state legislators before a woman governor was chosen. Beginning in Colorado in the nineties, a number of women served as state representatives.[35] After 1920 women began to run for legislative positions all over the United States. Schoolteachers, widows of legislators, lawyers, doctors, and homemakers were among the women candidates. Thirty-four sat in the state legislative sessions in 1921.[36] Twenty-five years later there were 230 women serving as state legislators.[37] The highest proportions were secured in Arizona, New Jersey, New Mexico, and Utah (all over 6 per cent), but in absolute numbers more were elected in Connecticut and New Hampshire.

[34] Sumner, *op. cit.*, p. 131; Secretary of State of Colorado, *Abstract of Votes Cast.*

[35] Sumner, *op. cit.*, p. 130.

[36] Breckinridge, *op. cit.*, p. 323. Figures compiled by the League of Women Voters and by American Legislators' Association differ slightly from these.

[37] *Washington Post*, September 12, 1946.

American women state legislators have on the whole been well qualified. The early Colorado women legislators were said to have "averaged above the men members as a whole in intelligence, but one of them could be classed with the most able of the men." [38] Over four-fifths of the early women legislators had had college or university training.[39] In 1932 Dr. Breckinridge found that "nearly two-thirds of the women elected since 1920 have been identified with women's organizations in their communities and states" and "over three-fourths of them showed a special interest in that which is generally called women's legislation." [40] A good fraction of the women lawmakers had had previous experience in public affairs.

Miss Sumner stated in categorical fashion some years ago that "a man of very doubtful honesty may be nominated and elected, but not a woman." [41] This pious hope has not been borne out by subsequent events.[42]

State-wide elective positions have also been won by women in a number of commonwealths. Only in Oklahoma are women still fighting for the constitutional right to run for governor, lieutenant governor, secretary of state, state auditor, attorney general, state treasurer, superintendent of public instruction, and state examiner.[43] In one state or another women have been elected to all of these positions excepting that of attorney general. Two women have been elected to gubernatorial office, Mrs. Nellie Tayloe Ross of Wyoming (1924) and Mrs. Miriam Ferguson of Texas (1924 and 1932), both of whom may be said to have "inherited" their places. Mrs. Ross was nominated by a Democratic convention to fill out the unexpired term of her husband, who died in office, and Mrs. Ferguson was selected to fill the place of her husband, a former antisuffragist, who

[38] Sumner, *op. cit.*, p. 130.

[39] Dorothy A. Moncure, "Women in Political Life," *Current History*, XXIX (January, 1929), 641.

[40] *Op. cit.*, 330–331.

[41] *Op. cit.*, 92.

[42] Gosnell, *Democracy: Threshold of Freedom* (New York, The Ronald Press, 1948), p. 72.

[43] State Election Board, *Directory of the State of Oklahoma*, 1935, p. 135. State Question No. 211 as shown by the records of the Secretary of State: "To amend Section 3, Article 6, of the Constitution of Oklahoma so that women, as well as men, shall be eligible to the office of Governor, Lieutenant Governor, Secretary of State, State Auditor, Attorney General, State Treasurer, Superintendent of Public Instruction, and State Examiner and Inspector." Vote—Yes, 114,968; No, 154,669.

was disqualified because he had been convicted of misappropriation of state funds during his administration as governor. Mrs. Ferguson's re-election was bitterly contested and she won by a very narrow margin. The women elected to executive posts have in general rendered acceptable service. In New York State a woman secretary of state, however, was convicted of misappropriation of funds.

Twenty-nine years after the passage of the woman suffrage amendment there were 7 women members of the House of Representatives and one woman member of the United States Senate. The Seventy-ninth Congress (1945–1947) marked the high point of women's membership in the House when ten women, or 2 per cent of the total, served. A woman senator was elected from the state of Arkansas, in 1932, to fill the vacancy caused by the death of her husband. She owed her re-election to the full term partly to the efforts of the late Senator Huey P. Long. In 1948 Mrs. Margaret Chase Smith was nominated and elected senator from the state of Maine largely on the basis of her own efforts. Of the women members of the House, two have served ten consecutive terms and are now reaping some of the benefits of the seniority rules. A close observer of Washington affairs has said regarding the congresswomen:

Even though the women don't talk much, they have an excellent record of attendance and miss few roll calls . . . No members work harder than they do on their committee assignments, and more and more of them are being placed on important committees. They are conscientious and willing to work, facts which their masculine colleagues appreciate and make use of.[44]

APPOINTIVE POSITIONS

Women's success in winning elections for their own candidates has extended their opportunities for appointive positions in the public service. This has involved overcoming their lack of experience, lack of confidence, and a hostile attitude on the part of the men. In governmental employment as in private employment women have had to battle for equal pay for equal work and for chances to advance to higher posts.

[44] Alice Roosevelt Longworth, "What Are Women Up To?" *Ladies' Home Journal*, LI (March, 1934), 9.

The number of women in public service has increased remarkably since women gained the suffrage. In Colorado equal suffrage in the nineties brought "women employment in somewhat greater numbers as clerks and stenographers in public offices, and the equalizing in most public positions of their salaries with those of men doing the same work." [45] Elsewhere women were appointed as factory inspectors, as members of state boards of education, as charity commissioners, as health commissioners, as librarians, and as other state officers or employees long before 1920. Since then women strengthened their hold upon clerical, social service, and library positions, and they won in addition the headships of some important state departments. North Carolina had a woman commissioner of public welfare in 1921; Pennsylvania had a woman in a similar post in 1923; and New York had a woman chairman of the State Industrial Board in 1926.

Nearly ninety years ago women obtained a few federal clerical positions. The Civil Service Act of 1883 opened a number of opportunities to them in spite of the fact that many of the examinations were given to male applicants only. Just prior to 1920, the newly established Women's Bureau made a report which led to the liberalizing of the civil service examination rules as far as women were concerned. Since 1920 women have continued to struggle against discrimination in the federal service. The Federal Reclassification Act of 1923 marked some distinct steps forward in the direction of equal pay for equal service. In 1947, 46 per cent of the federal civilian employees in the District of Columbia and 24 per cent of those in continental United States were women.

Women have also been placed in positions of responsibility by presidential appointment. In the years immediately preceding their enfranchisement, they held such positions as chief of the Children's Bureau, member of the Industrial Commission, member of the United States Employees' Compensation, Assistant Attorney General, Chief of the Women's Bureau, judge of the Juvenile Court, Commissioner of the District of Columbia, and Civil Service Commissioner. After securing the vote, women have won such offices as Assistant District Attorney, Municipal Judge for the District of Columbia, Consular Agent, Collector of Customs, Collector of In-

[45] Sumner, *op. cit.*, p. 178.

ternal Revenue, Trade Commissioner, division chief in the State De-
partment, judge of the Customs Court, member of the Board of Tax
Appeals, Ambassador, member of the Social Security Board, United
States Delegate to the United Nations Assembly, and Secretary of
Labor.

GENERAL VIEW OF SUFFRAGE

Suffrage is a precious right which has been vigorously sought by
those to whom it has been denied. To get a government based on a
limited suffrage to extend the franchise is not an easy task. No
group which has a monopoly of political power wishes to dilute the
control of that monopoly.

In the United States, as in other democratic countries, suffrage has
been extended when certain conditions have been fulfilled. These conditions have been economic independence on the part of the group
seeking the vote, mobility on its part, disturbed political conditions
caused by war, carefully planned organization and propaganda, and
favorable modes of thought.[46]

Once the suffrage has been obtained, the newly enfranchised group
must learn how to use the ballot. It must be organized to come to the
polls and then to exercise choices which will promote its own interests and the general interest. Suffrage does not automatically bring a
group to the seat of political power.

Imperfect as the right to vote may be, without it a group is at
considerable disadvantage. Suffrage does make a difference in the
services rendered by the government, in the opportunities for public
employment, in the chances for rising to a position of power and
prestige, and in the self respect of the group.

[46] Gosnell, *Democracy: The Threshold of Freedom* (New York, The Ronald
Press, 1948).

CHAPTER III

EVOLUTION OF MAJOR PARTY ISSUES [1]

"Considered nationally political parties in the United States may be described as loose alliances to win the stakes of power embodied in the presidency. The centripetalism generated by this office more than any other factor discourages the development of the multiplicity of parties anticipated by the founders of the constitution."
—Arthur W. Macmahon, "Political Parties in the United States," *Encyclopaedia of the Social Sciences* (New York, The Macmillan Company, 1933), XI, 596.

DETERMINATION OF PARTY POLICIES

ONE OF THE FUNCTIONS OF THE POLITICAL PARTY IS TO AID IN THE formulation of public policies, in the shaping of issues on which various groups in the community divide. To what extent, upon what subjects, in what way, it may be asked, do political parties act in the process by which the community states and settles broad questions of social, economic, and political policy? It will be found that at this point more than at any other there is widespread misunderstanding of the actual work of the parties. The unsophisticated may assume that common action on common policies is the only function of the party, while the oversophisticated may conclude that the party has nothing to do with these questions. An objective analysis will reveal the true part played by the political organizations in the

[1] This chapter does not purport to give a well-rounded discussion of the evolution of party issues. That would require another book. See W. E. Binkley, *American Political Parties: Their Natural History* (New York, 1943); C. A. M. Ewing, *Presidential Elections* (Norman, Okla., 1940); Edgar E. Robinson, *The Evolution of American Political Parties* (New York, 1924); F. R. Kent, *History of the Democratic Party* (New York, 1928); W. S. Myers, *The Republican Party: A History* (New York, 1928); A. N. Holcombe, *Political Parties of Today* (New York, 1924); J. A. Woodburn, *Political Parties* (New York, 1924); K. H. Porter, *National Party Platforms* (New York, 1924); *American Year Book*, 1910 to date, and the *World Almanac*. The standard histories of the United States give a detailed discussion of many of these questions, notably A. M. Schlesinger, *The Political and Social Growth of the United States* (New York, 1941), and S. E. Morison, *The Oxford History of the United States* (London, 1927).

shaping of issues and help to clear away some of the frequent misunderstandings about the real work of the party.

In every community there are broad differences upon questions of public interest. Persons holding similar views tend to come together in groups for conference, for statement of principles, and for effective organization to carry them through into practical action. This is ostensibly the primary purpose of political parties. This task involves a wide variety of functions, some governmental and others partly governmental, including formulation of political platforms, nomination and election of candidates, control over legislative, administrative, and even judicial activities, and continuous attention to public opinion. To carry out these principles or policies is the ideal purpose of the political party, to rally to them widespread support, interest, activity, and enthusiasm. Whatever other influences may actually be at work, campaigns of the party are always conducted in the name of certain high principles or general policies for which the party stands. These policies are always nominally designed for the common good as that good is interpreted by the particular party.

In practice these programs may be closely connected with the benefit of various social and economic interests, following the lines of class or section or both, interpreting the needs and desires of these elements of the population. Each interest will inevitably endeavor to translate its demand or desire into the most logical formula, the most attractive shape, the highest moral appeal. East and West, North and South, Capital and Labor and Agriculture intellectualize and moralize their claims if possible. Each struggles for the possession of the precious support of science, morality, tradition, deftly or clumsily weaving its propaganda in party form. A large taxpayer of New York may find the income tax an invasion of states' rights, or undesirable, or immoral; and the cotton manufacturer may find prohibition of child labor contrary to the principles of state's rights and economically unsound. The brewer and distiller may denounce the invasion of personal liberty by "dry" laws, and the utility owner may find regulation of rates unconstitutional or unwise. The shipper and the railroad may develop different theories of justice, and the railway employees may find still another canon of social equity. Incidentally by their very appeals all parties pay tribute to the prevailing ideas of science, morality and democracy.

It is not necessary or correct to assume that these groups are insincere or hypocritical in their protestation that their program or policy is conducive to the general interest of the whole community. On the contrary the enthusiasm and fervor of their effort arise from its wholehearted sincerity. Without conscious intent they identify the interest of their group with that of the larger group, and thus are able to speak in the interest of the greater group. This gives heartiness and genuineness to the movement instead of artificiality and insincerity. Agriculture, Labor and Manufacturing are equally convinced of the justice of their cause and its desirability from the national point of view. There are many cynical exceptions to this, but as a rule the statement is correct.

Party programs and policies, then, serve to unite individuals and groups, to bring them into the party ranks and to hold them there, as long as the issues hold, or unless more significant ones arise. In the strongest partisan the party belief is nearer to custom or tradition; in the next circle of party adherence, a general tendency or predisposition to follow the party may be observed; but in the outer circle of those more open to argument, the party belief takes the form of a lively conviction that the party program, legislative or administrative, is superior for reasons immediately ahead. The Republican whose grandfather voted for Lincoln, the Republican who believes that "on the whole" the party is most "efficient," the Republican who disapproves the New Deal are different types. To these may be added the independent who comes in for the campaign on some specific issue. In the same way the Democrat whose grandfather fought with Lee, the Democrat who believes that "on the whole" the party is most favorable to the plain people, and the Democrat who believes in the New Deal are three different types, and to these may also be added the independent who comes in for the campaign on some specific issue.

The platform and the program, notwithstanding their very obvious limitations, are recognitions (1) of the existence of a common interest in the group which is placed in the position of a paramount interest prior to that of all subsidiary groups, and (2) of the necessity of an appeal to reason rather than mere force in the adjudication of the question at issue. In very many instances these nominal recognitions are mere lip service without the ring of sincerity and straightforwardness, but if this were always true or were believed to be true the party platform would be given no consideration by the voters. In point of fact, party currency has been very seriously depreciated by the frequent counterfeits and useless paper in circulation, but a certain value still remains.

BRIEF HISTORICAL VIEW OF MAJOR PARTY ISSUES

Historically, there have been five broad divisions between parties. The first was that between Federalists and Democrats; the second between Whigs and Democrats; the third between Republicans and Democrats before the Civil War; the fourth between Republicans and Democrats in the post-bellum period until 1929; and the fifth between the "New Dealers" and their opponents. With certain variations, the two-party tradition has persisted.

Federalists and Republican Democrats

At the time of the first clearly defined electoral division between the major parties in the United States (1800), there were only about five million people in the country, nearly one-fifth of whom were slaves. Two-thirds of the people lived along the Atlantic seaboard, within fifty miles of tidewater. The roads were few and bad, even in the older communities, and the United States was still overwhelmingly rural and agricultural. The total population in towns with more than 10,000 inhabitants was only about 200,000. The largest city of the day was Philadelphia which could boast of only 70,000 people. New York was second with a mere 60,000, and Boston trailed with its 25,000. There was very little manufacturing, and American capital was invested mostly in agriculture and shipping. The social institutions of this period presented a sharp contrast to those of the twentieth century. The newspapers were small in size and circulation. Editorials were more important than news items. The schools were largely aristocratic and religious, and the great bulk of the population was illiterate. Religious intolerance had not yet been completely eliminated from the state constitutions and statute books.

The principal figures in the first political division were Alexander

Hamilton, President Washington's brilliant Secretary of the Treasury, and Thomas Jefferson, the first President's equally brilliant Secretary of State.[2] Hamilton apparently won the ear of the father of his country since his so-called Federalist measures were put through, including the funding of the national debt, assumption of the revolutionary debts of the states, adoption of a protective tariff for the infant American industries, establishment of the United States Bank, adoption of a sound national currency, the granting of special favors to American shipping, provision of adequate national defense, and a foreign policy which was more favorable to England than to revolutionary France. These policies were so distasteful to Jefferson that he resigned from the cabinet.

Thomas Jefferson narrowly missed being elected President of the United States in 1796 when John Adams, a Federalist, beat him by a margin of four electoral votes, but he came back in 1800 to crush his opponents. His cohorts were first called Republicans and later Democrats. These anti-Federalists had complained in Congress that "This plan of a National Bank is calculated to benefit a small part of the United States, the mercantile interest only; the farmers, the yeomanry, will derive no advantage from it," that the protective tariff would operate "as an oppressive indirect tax upon agriculture" and that the funding system was aimed to help the very wealthy.[3] Writing to Madison in 1799, Jefferson proposed that all possible emphasis in the campaign be put upon the Alien and Sedition Laws, the direct tax, the army and navy, the "usurious loan to set these follies on foot," and the pictures of "recruiting officers lounging at every court-house and decoying the laborer from his plough."[4] On a program calling for freedom of the press, repeal of heavy taxation on the farmers, protection of the constitutional rights of the states, and curtailment of the rising power of capitalism and finance, the Jeffersonians were swept into power, and it was many years before elements of the Hamiltonian system were again found in the program of a successful major party. Jefferson, the sage of Monticello, exer-

[2] C. G. Bowers, *Jefferson and Hamilton, the Struggle for Democracy* (Boston, 1925); C. A. Beard, *Economic Origins of Jeffersonian Democracy* (New York, 1915); Henry J. Ford, *Alexander Hamilton* (New York, 1925); C. E. Merriam, *American Political Theories* (New York, 1916).

[3] Cited by C. A. Beard, *American Party Battle* (New York, 1928), p. 35.

[4] Bowers, *op. cit.*, p. 444.

cised great influence over his successors, Madison and Monroe, and in the face of the rising democratic tide the Federalist leaders soon found themselves without followers.

Democrats and Whigs

The second broad division between the major parties was between the Democrats and the Whigs, covering the campaigns of 1832 and 1836, and, less sharply outlined, the campaigns of 1840, 1844, 1848 and 1852.[5] During the period from Washington's administration to that of Andrew Jackson, vast changes had taken place in the social and economic characteristics of the country. Since the Revolution the territory of the country had more than doubled, the number of states had increased from 13 to 22, the amount of capital invested in manufacturing had been greatly augmented, the means of transportation had been improved, and the frontier had moved considerably farther westward. However, the country was still only 7 per cent urban, and the apparently inexhaustible supply of land determined to a large extent the economic and political system. Farming was the leading occupation, and in a country where land was free, property qualifications for voting were largely meaningless.

Andrew Jackson's election to the Presidency in 1828 marked an end of exclusive aristocratic leadership in American political parties, and with it the blossoming of the spoils system and the development of executive party leadership. In contrast to the highly educated and cultivated Jefferson, Jackson had attended school for only a few terms, had never learned to write or spell English correctly, and had little knowledge of literature and science.

The issues raised during this period were the continuance of the United States Bank, which the Whigs favored and the Jacksonian Democrats opposed, and the maintenance of a strong national executive, which the Whigs opposed and the Jacksonians upheld.[6] The tariff, strict and loose construction of the Constitution, and slavery

[5] A. M. Schlesinger, Jr., *The Age of Jackson* (Boston, 1945); C. G. Bowers, *The Party Battles of the Jackson Period* (Boston, 1922); G. W. Johnson, *Andrew Jackson* (New York, 1927); D. T. Lynch, *An Epoch and a Man: Martin Van Buren and His Times* (New York, 1929); Allan Nevins, *Polk: The Diary of a President* (New York, 1929); Merriam, *op. cit.* It should be noted that the term "Whig" was not used urtil 1834.

[6] W. A. McDonald, *Jacksonian Democracy* (New York, 1906); W. E. Dodd, *Expansion and Conflict, 1825–65* (Boston, 1915).

were in the background, emerging from time to time, yet not making definite lines of demarcation. Jackson himself was a good deal of a nationalist, as he showed in his stand on nullification, and the Whig party was unwilling or unable to take a stand on the slavery question. The campaign of 1840 was a personal battle in which the Whigs adopted no platform at all, preferring to rally around the personality of General Harrison. In the struggle of 1844 the Democratic party committed itself to territorial expansion, but the Whigs under Clay did their best to evade the issue. The contest of 1848 was again characteristic in its lack of clear-cut issues of general significance.

The class alignment again arrayed the commercial and trading interests, especially those controlled by the United States Bank, on the side of the Whigs, while the Democrats appealed more successfully to the agrarian group and the smaller shopkeeper.[7] Sectionalism also entered into this contest, with the southern and western territory inclining toward the Democrats and the eastern group of states favoring the Whigs, although by no means was an unbroken front presented.

Republicans and Democrats: War Issues

The third alignment was that between Republicans and Democrats in the memorable campaigns of 1856 and 1860.[8] During the period from 1840 to 1860 the population of the country had nearly doubled; methods of transportation and communication had been vastly improved by the development of the railroad, the steamboat, the telegraph, and postal reform; and the inauguration of a system of free public education had laid the foundation for huge newspaper circulations. The North, with its system of free labor (large parts of it immigrant labor), small farms, industries, banks, and philosophy of enterprise, was outstripping the South with its slave labor, leisure and gentleman class, large plantations, and aristocratic ideology. The North, which was exploiting the industrial and mineral

[7] R. C. H. Catterall, *The Second Bank of the United States* (Chicago, 1903).

[8] A. Craven, *The Repressible Conflict, 1830–1861* (Baton Rouge, 1939); Theodore C. Smith, *Parties and Slavery, 1850–1859* (New York, 1906); A. B. Hart, *Slavery and Abolition* (New York, 1906); C. G. Bowers, *The Tragic Era: The Revolution after Lincoln* (Boston, 1929); G. F. Milton, *The Eve of Conflict: Stephen A. Douglas and the Needless War* (Boston, 1934).

resources of the country, was growing more rapidly in population and wealth than the South, whose chief asset, the soil, was declining in fertility. The storm broke when it appeared that the slave power, the elite of the "Cotton Kingdom," had tightened its grip on the national government. The breaking of the Missouri Compromise of 1820 by the Kansas-Nebraska bill in 1854 led to the creation of a new party, called the Republican party. The dictum of the Dred Scott decision of 1857 that Congress could not prohibit slavery in the territories contributed to its rapid growth. This drew together such diverse elements as the Northern Whigs who opposed the Kansas-Nebraska bill, the Democratic "Barnburners" who resisted the opening of new territory to slavery, and the Free Soilers who held that national power should bar slavery from the territories.

The new Republican party turned to Abraham Lincoln as its standard bearer in 1860 because this backwoodsman lawyer was not so violent as Seward and others.[9] His "house divided" speech did not go so far as Seward's "irrepressible conflict" statement, and he was regarded as being closer to the farmers than his eastern rival. The grain growing farmers of the north central part of the United States were determined to keep the slavocracy out of the territories, and at the same time they wanted to preserve the southern markets for their products. Even the diplomatic Stephen A. Douglas, with his ingenious doctrine of squatter sovereignty, could not keep the Democratic party together during the crisis. The southern delegates bolted the Democratic convention and nominated a candidate of their own, John C. Breckinridge. The relatively peaceful processes of party competition did not function in this critical moment of the national life, although party organizations held together longer than did the ecclesiastical. The Democratic party was split by the issues of the day, but it survived the ordeal of the Civil War fought over slavery and the maintenance of the Union.

During the reconstruction period the Republican party kept the war issues well to the front and side-stepped other questions. Negroes were freed in order to help win the war, and during Reconstruction they were given the vote in order to build up the southern constituency of the Republican party.[10] General Grant's popular

[9] P. M. Angle (ed.), *The Lincoln Reader* (New Brunswick, N. J., 1947).
[10] W. E. B. DuBois, *Black Reconstruction* (New York, 1935).

plurality in 1868 over Seymour was based partly on the southern Negroes. In 1872 Grant found Greeley, the candidate of the Liberal Republicans and Democrats, a weak opponent in spite of the fact that the Republican party was becoming more and more vulnerable to attacks. Strenuous efforts were made to obtain a verdict of public opinion upon the honesty and efficiency of the Republican administration, but the war issue was still too strong to make this possible.

The loss of southern support due to the activities of the Ku Klux Klan and the loss of northern support due to the scandals of the Grant administration resulted in a popular defeat of the Republican party in the famous disputed election of 1876 between Hayes and Tilden. Hayes, the Republican candidate, however, was given the electoral majority by a partisan decision of an electoral commission.[11] This election marked the end of the reconstruction period in politics, since President Hayes withdrew the federal troops from the southern states, thereby abandoning that territory for his party.

The principal issue that divided the two major parties in the next four elections was the tariff issue.[12] The 1880 campaign between Garfield and Hancock saw the beginning of this line of cleavage between the parties, but it was not until 1888 that it was clearly drawn. In his electoral battle with Blaine in 1884, Grover Cleveland, the first successful Democratic candidate since Buchanan, urged the fulfillment of his party's platform calling for a revision of the tariff. Again in 1888 and 1892, when he was running against Harrison, Cleveland risked his political future by advocating tariff revision.

From 1876 to 1896 the margin between the two major parties was a close one and there were conservative and liberal elements in both. Much of the material of which the party platforms were made was practically identical in both parties. In 1888 there were nineteen planks in the Republican platform and twelve in the Democratic.[13] Of these nine were the same in both platforms and in only one was there a significant difference. The parties agreed on the maintenance

[11] P. L. Haworth, *The Hayes-Tilden Disputed Presidential Election of 1876* (Cleveland, 1906).

[12] R. G. Caldwell, *James A Garfield: Party Chieftain* (New York, 1931); H. C. Thomas, *The Return of the Democratic Party to Power in 1884* (New York, 1919); D. S. Muzzey, *James G. Blaine* (New York, 1934); Allan Nevins, *Grover Cleveland: A Study in Courage* (New York, 1932); Pearl Robertson, "Grover Cleveland as a Political Leader" (Ph.D. thesis, University of Chicago, 1937).

[13] The numbering of the planks is somewhat arbitrary and may be variously calculated.

of the Union, on a homestead policy, on early admission of the territories, on civil service reform, on pensions, on banning trusts, on sympathy with Ireland, and on exclusion of foreign contract labor. Republicans declared in favor of personal rights and the free ballot, while Democrats declared for a written constitution with specific powers. In addition to these items the Republican platform declared against Mormonism, in favor of bimetallism, for reduction of letter postage, in favor of free schools, adequate fortifications, the Monroe Doctrine, protection of fisheries, and included carefully safeguarded statements regarding prohibition.[14] They disagreed upon the tariff alone.

In 1892 there were twenty planks in the Republican platform and twenty-two in the Democratic. Among these there was only one point of divergence, namely, the tariff. Many other planks were identical, as, for example, opposition to the trusts, maintenance of the gold and silver standard, civil service reform, opposition to the Czar, friendliness for Ireland, a liberal pension system, deep waterways, the Nicaragua Canal, the World's Fair, admission of territories, and protection of railroad employees. The Republicans again declared in favor of freedom of the ballot, while the Democrats denounced the federal election law. The Republicans declared for an irrigation policy and the Democrats for homesteads. The Republicans favored extension of foreign commerce, free thought, postal free delivery, temperance (again carefully safeguarded), selection of federal officers for the territories from among territorial residents; while the Democratic party demanded stricter immigration laws and free schools, denounced the sweating system, and opposed sumptuary laws.[15]

Republicans and Democrats: Industrial Issues

The election of 1896 marked the beginning of a new era in American politics.[16] Repudiating the policies of its only successful candi-

---

[14] "The first concern of all good government is the sobriety of the people and the purity of their homes. The Republican Party cordially sympathizes with all wise and well-directed efforts for the promotion of temperance and morality."

[15] Sec. 21: "We are opposed to all sumptuary laws as an interference with the individual rights of the citizen."

[16] W. J. Bryan, *The First Battle: A Story of the Campaign of 1896* (Chicago, 1896); H. Croly, *Marcus Alonzo Hanna* (New York, 1912); P. Hibben, *The Peerless Leader: William Jennings Bryan* (New York, 1929).

date since the Civil War, the Democratic party embraced the inflationary theories of the Populists and presented as its candidate William Jennings Bryan, the "silver-tongued orator from the Platte."
Although Bryan was never destined to win the Presidency, he was a
strong individual force behind the income tax amendment, direct
election of senators, the woman suffrage amendment, and the prohibition era. His attempt to lead the western farmers to victory was
blocked by the wealth of the East and the skill of Mark Hanna in
winning votes for his candidate, William McKinley. As a matter of
fact, the Bryan campaign placed the Republican party firmly in the
saddle, to be dislodged only by internal dissension in 1912 and by
the depression in 1932.

Curiously enough, at the time that the Republican party had become the spokesman for big business, a young man was rising in the
councils of the party who was later to challenge this orientation.[17]
Theodore Roosevelt, candidate for vice president on the Republican
ticket in 1900, tried to emulate the example of Bryan by barnstorm-
ing the country in a special train, while his more sedate running
mate, President McKinley, remained in the White House. An as-
sassin's bullet, which struck down President McKinley a few
months after his second inauguration, elevated the young "Teddy"
to the Presidency far sooner than he himself could have hoped in
his wildest dreams. At first the new President insisted that he would
carry out McKinley's policies. As one commentator put it later: "He
did. He carried them out and buried them."

For a while Roosevelt did what he could to reassure the business
interests. It also appears that his eye was fixed on the 1904 campaign
and he did not want to make any serious mistakes which might
jeopardize his nomination. When the 1904 Convention met, his
friend Senator Lodge, a conservative, was instrumental in drawing
up the platform. In this year there was no clear-cut issue presented
by the major parties, since Judge Parker, the Democratic candidate,
had repudiated the Bryan policies. But in 1908 it was Roosevelt who
wrote the party platform. When his candidate, Judge Taft, a few
years later as President appeared to go back on some of these poli-

[17] H. F. Pringle, *Theodore Roosevelt* (New York, 1931); Theodore Roosevelt,
Autobiography (New York, 1913); Mark Sullivan, *Our Times, 1900–1925* (New
York, 1926–1935).

cies, Roosevelt lined up with the insurgent Republicans who disliked the high Republican tariffs, the coolness of Republican leaders toward organized labor, and the close identification of these leaders with the financial and industrial barons. The outcome of this Rooseveltian shift was the Progressive campaign of 1912.[18] Deprived of the Republican nomination by the "steam-roller" methods of the reactionary elements in the party which controlled the Convention, Roosevelt started a new and militant progressive movement.

In 1912 there were distinct issues between the Republican and the Progressive parties regarding the courts, constitutional amendments, direct legislation, and primaries, as well as problems of taxation, currency, social and industrial justice. While these were largely ignored during the campaign by the Democratic candidate, Woodrow Wilson, this was not the case after the election.[19] Wilson won by a plurality, and as President he pushed through a far-reaching legislative program which included the Federal Reserve Act, the Income Tax Amendment, the revision of the tariff, rural credits legislation and the Federal Trade Commission Act. In the 1916 campaign the Democratic party stood on its record, which attracted a sufficient number of the former Progressives to win the Presidency again. Justice Hughes failed to convince some of the westerners of his progressive tendencies, and Woodrow Wilson won a great personal victory.

That the Republican party still enjoyed the confidence of a large majority of the American people was clearly shown by the Harding landslide election in 1920. The main issue at this election was the verdict to be rendered on the Democratic administration, the conduct of World War I, and the nature of the peace. The Democratic candidate, James M. Cox, campaigned on the program that the League of Nations was the only practical means of maintaining permanent peace.[20] Prominent Republicans such as Hughes tried to distinguish between "the" and "a" League of Nations, and their many qualifications left the voters in a fog. The selection of Harding as a candidate by a Senate coterie was an indication of a reaction

[18] C. G. Bowers, *Beveridge and the Progressive Era* (New York, 1932); Victor Rosewater, *Back Stage in 1912* (Philadelphia, 1932).

[19] R. S. Baker. *Woodrow Wilson: Life and Letters*, 4 vols. (Garden City, 1927–1931); W. E. Dodd. *Woodrow Wilson and His Work* (Garden City, 1932).

[20] James M. Cox, *Journey Through My Years* (New York. 1946).

against strong executive leadership.[21] A singular complex of racial, nationalistic, and class conditions led to the overwhelming triumph of the Republican party.

The split in the ranks of the Democratic party in 1924 over the issues of prohibition and religious and racial tolerance reduced that party to its lowest state in its entire history. Only 28.8 per cent of the total vote and 35 per cent of the major party vote was Democratic in this year. John W. Davis, a compromise candidate, could not heal the breach in time for the election. In the meantime Senator La Follette of Wisconsin, who felt that Roosevelt had deprived him of the Progressive leadership in 1912, attempted a campaign upon the issues of economic and social justice, stressing the demands of the discontented agrarians. Calvin Coolidge, who became heir to the Republican nomination upon Harding's death, refused to take up the challenge and fell back upon the claim that his party had brought prosperity.[22] Neither Davis nor La Follette could make the scandals of the Harding administration an issue.

Again in 1928 the Republicans reverted to the prosperity appeal, asserting that business was more secure under Republican than under Democratic rule. The urban, wet, and Catholic background of Al Smith, the Democratic candidate, was also used as a basis of the Republican attack. Even the South was divided on this issue. As it was put, "If Al Smith is elected it will be due to three things, the solid South, liquor, and the foreign and Negro vote. If he is elected he is shrewd enough to bring foreigners here to increase the foreign vote. His plan would bring half a million a year. In ten years Tammany would as completely dominate the United States as it now dominates New York." [23] Smith tried in vain to make water power control, party corruption, and efficient public-spirited administration the main issues, but Hoover talked in generalities and allowed his supporters to build up the myth that he was a superman. Hoover won by a comfortable margin.

[21] H. M. Daugherty and T. Dixon, *The Inside Story of the Harding Tragedy* (New York, 1932).

[22] William Allen White, *A Puritan in Babylon* (New York, 1938).

[23] Quoted by the *Chicago Tribune*, September 30, 1928. See also R. V. Peel and T. C. Donnelly, *The 1928 Campaign* (New York, 1931).

New Deal Democrats and Republicans

The fifth broad division between the major parties began to take form after the onslaught of the depression which began in 1929.[24] Hoover had been elected under what appeared to be most favorable auspices, but there were rumblings of disorder which had not escaped his notice.[25] While he had been an efficient Secretary of Commerce, the burdens and responsibilities of the trying days of the business crash wore down his nerves. The depression was a situation made to order for the Democratic candidate, Franklin D. Roosevelt, who had not been carried away by the false prosperity of the twenties.[26] However, the lines of the New Deal program were not drawn during the campaign. Both candidates pledged themselves to economy and a balanced budget; both were agreed on desirability of drastic farm relief and unemployment relief; both opposed cancellation of the war debts; and both came out for tightening railroad and public utility regulation. There were the usual charges and countercharges about the efforts made by each of the parties to meet the problems of the day, and there were some differences of opinion regarding prohibition, the tariff, unemployment insurance, public utility holding companies, and the operation of government power plants. But one looks in vain in the platforms of the parties or the speeches of the candidates for the battle lines of the "New Deal."

A reading of the platforms of the major parties for 1936 shows that both parties had changed considerably during the interval. Both accepted in 1936 certain policies which were either not mentioned or rejected in previous campaigns. There was now no disagreement regarding a system of managed currency, federal regulation of security exchanges, and use of federal funds for the relief of unemployment and destitution.

The chief differences between the two major parties in 1936 concerned such questions as the relation of the national government to business, maintenance of national credit, efficient and honest administration of relief, the type of policy best suited to relieve the eco-

[24] C. A. Beard and M. A. Beard, *America in Midpassage* (New York, 1939); R. V. Peel and T. C. Donnelly. *The 1932 Campaign* (New York, 1935).

[25] Theodore Joslin, *Hoover Off the Record* (Garden City, 1934).

[26] Ernest Lindley, *Franklin D. Roosevelt* (New York, 1931); Frances Perkins, *The Roosevelt I Knew* (New York, 1947).

nomic distress of the farmers, the best method of administering
social security, the relative merits of a Roosevelt "New Deal" administration and a Republican administration under a "Kansas
Coolidge" such as Alfred M. Landon. A brief consideration of these
issues will throw light upon the functioning of the major parties as
determiners of policies.

An economic issue which emerged in this campaign was the international trade policy of the United States. Secretary of State Hull
was influential in working out the trade agreement policy of the administration. Many eastern bankers, capitalists, and merchants supported Roosevelt because they thought that his Secretary of State
was sound in his ideas on international economic relations.

Since the Republican party was the party of the "outs," it spent
considerable energy in criticizing the Democratic administration. It
was charged that a party which disregarded its promises, as the
Democratic administration had, could not be trusted. Particular
reference was made to the unbalanced budget. The Democratic platform of 1932 had promised to reduce governmental expenditures
and to balance the budget. The Republicans viewed with alarm our
growing national debt, and expressed the fear that it might lead to
a disastrous inflation. The Democratic answer to this was that the
economic collapse of the nation had brought about such paralysis
of business that it was necessary to place the nation on a war basis.
This struggle against economic chaos required men and money. The
Roosevelt administration spent money to promote recovery, to prevent human suffering, and to aid the destitute. The budget could
not be balanced without eliminating relief expenditures. It was argued that the Republican party did not urge this drastic action.

The handling of relief funds became another issue in the struggle
against the Democrats. Republicans charged the administration with
"waste" and "extravagance." It was claimed that the people's money
was being squandered on "boondoggling projects." The Democrats
answered these charges by pointing out that while the gross cost of
WPA (Works Projects Administration) projects was greater than
straight relief or "doles," the value of the work done by WPA
offset this. By regarding this work as an asset, the New Deal accountants concluded that WPA was less expensive than direct relief.
Stress was placed upon such useful accomplishments as road build-

ing, buliding and improving schoolhouses, modernizing sewerage systems, supplying park facilities, and building airports. The New Dealers asserted that the administration of WPA never exceeded 6 per cent of the sum spent.

There were real differences between the farm programs of the two major parties. The Democrats promised to continue and improve the soil conservation and domestic allotment program with cash payments to farmers. The aim of the New Deal agricultural program was to establish a proper relation between agricultural production and effective demand. Republicans alleged that this plan involved destruction of food at a time when many people were going hungry, and that this resulted in a national deficiency in farm products which necessitated imports. The New Deal's answer to these charges was that the drought created the food shortage and that the pigs and cattle killed were made available for relief rations. Administration defenders pointed out that imports of all grains amounted to only 4 per cent of the United States production in the drought year. It was also claimed that farm cash income was nearly double the 1932 level. For the Republican scheme of subsidizing the dumping of farm surpluses in foreign countries, the Democrats had nothing but scorn. This was the scheme which Presidents Coolidge and Hoover vetoed with stinging messages. It would cost much more than the existing plan of soil conservation, and it would be unworkable because the world was no longer able or willing to absorb our surplus farm products as it once did, and because foreign nations would take steps overnight to prevent the unwanted commodities from coming in.

Perhaps the biggest issue which the American voters had to decide in 1936 was the question whether they wished to change personalities in the White House. The Democrats had pictured Roosevelt as the friend of the common man fighting desperately against tories and economic royalists. In the dark days of the bank crisis he had shown himself to be a man of great serenity in action. At that time his friendly voice over the radio speaking the words, "The only thing we have to fear is fear itself," gave the impression of great calm and assurance.[27] Judge Mack referred to him as a young Galahad

[27] Inaugural Address delivered in Washington, D. C., March 4, 1933. See F. D. Roosevelt, *Looking Forward* (New York, 1933), p. 261.

to whom the country had turned for relief, for aid and for help.[28]

The Republican opposition tried to present quite another picture of Roosevelt to the American public. Roosevelt was attacked as a dictator, a dangerous experimenter,[29] a wrecker, who surrounded himself with "brain trusters" of communistic leanings.

During the campaign President Roosevelt almost ignored the Republican candidate. The purpose of this was to belittle Landon. It was once said, "Bad publicity is better than none." [30] The attacks on Landon were made by the lesser lights of the administration, not by the head of the government. It is clear that the 1936 election marked the emergence of new issues in American politics. For better or for worse the New Deal has left its mark.

The next two elections were epochal in character in that they upset the American tradition that the presidency was limited to two terms of four years each. In 1940 President Roosevelt did not announce his candidacy until the eve of the Democratic convention. When it was known that he planned to smash the "no third term" tradition, the party organization fell in line, although there were murmurs from conservative Democrats. War had broken out in Europe in 1939, and foreign policy issues were topmost. The Republican party pulled out all the stops in its blasts against the third term. On the isolationist issue, the Republican party was divided. In one of the most dramatic rises to fame, Wendell Willkie, a dark horse of the early part of 1940, swept the public opinion polls and the Republican nomination in one of the most adroit preconvention campaigns that the country had ever seen. His high-pressure public relations, advertising, and mass media backers put on an unprecedented drive for the nomination. Willkie was the wonder worker, the Republican counterpart of "that man" in the White House, the miracle man who would "take the Champ," and the glamour boy who could out-glamorize F.D.R., the man who would snatch away from Roosevelt the leadership in foreign affairs.

After the campaign was over one of the isolationist Republican

----

[28] *Proceedings of the Democratic National Convention of 1936*, p. 212.

[29] For example, see H. I. Mencken, "Three Years of Dr. Roosevelt," *American Mercury* (March, 1936).

[30] Frank Kent, *Political Behavior* (New York, 1928), p. 252.

business executives said ruefully regarding the Democratic victory: "Roosevelt and his supporters, including powerful propaganda organizations, were out in front on foreign policy, which can now in retrospect be called 'international security,' telling the American voters they could have their lend-lease and *peace too,* that revision of the Neutrality Act would 'keep us out of war,' etc., etc."

The 1944 election came in the middle of the war period when we were bending every effort to defeat the Axis powers. President Roosevelt had already defied the tradition limiting the president to two terms. It is likely that he did not want a fourth term, but he felt that the exigencies of his position forced him to run again. This time the Republicans chose a candidate who had been thoroughly tested in earlier election contests, Governor Thomas E. Dewey of New York, who had won the governorship in 1942 in "the Champ's" own state. The campaign turned on the two term tradition, the question whether any man was indispensable, the efficiency with which the Washington civilian war effort was being led, the health of the candidates, and the economic and social plans for postwar America. Governor Dewey put on a shrewd campaign and he gave Roosevelt his closest run. If the war had ended before the election in time for the inevitable postwar reactions to set in, Dewey might have won. But this question was as President Roosevelt used to say, "iffy."

President Roosevelt died in office a little over three months after his fourth inaugural. Vice President Harry Truman became the thirty-second President of the United States and the leader of the Democratic party by virtue of his office. The popularity of the Democratic party fluctuated considerably during the following four years. A low point in the fortunes of the party was reached in the 1946 Congressional elections at which the Democrats lost control of both houses of Congress. This election was characterized by an extremely low poll. Further misfortunes came upon the party. The dismissal of Henry A. Wallace from the cabinet and his nomination as the Progressive party candidate meant the loss of some of the left wing elements of the party. President Truman's civil rights stand alienated some of the conservative elements of the party in the South who bolted the Democratic convention and formed a separate States' Rights Democratic party of their own headed by Governor Thurmond of South Carolina. On top of this, some of the northern city

Democratic organizations opposed President Truman's renomination before the 1948 convention but they could not agree upon a candidate. The President won a renomination and electrified the delegates by his fighting speech of acceptance during which he announced that he would call a special session of Congress to enable the eightieth Congress to act upon some of the Republican platform promises. During the campaign which he carried to all parts of the country he stressed the record of Congress, labor legislation, high prices, farm legislation, and other New Deal issues.

The Republican convention of 1948, contrary to the traditions of that party that a defeated candidate for the presidency should not be renominated, chose Governor Dewey again as its candidate for president. Thinking that he had an easy victory within reach, Governor Dewey waged a dignified campaign during which he and the Republican candidate for vice president, Governor Warren of California, stressed governmental efficiency, national unity, and harmony.

The election provided a stunning upset which surprised the pollsters, the party leaders, and the press. President Truman won 50 per cent of the popular vote and carried 28 states with a total of 303 electoral votes. Particularly noteworthy was his victory in the western farm and Pacific coast states. The votes received by minor party candidates were less than was expected. The election signified that the elements which were attracted to the Democratic party during the Franklin D. Roosevelt period were still in a majority in 1948. President Truman, undaunted by the misfortunes visited upon his party, refused to concede the existence of a Republican trend and confounded friends and foes alike by snatching victory from the overconfident Republicans.

In the forty-one campaigns, clean-cut party issues dividing the voters have been presented in some nineteen cases, namely, 1796, 1800, 1804, 1808, 1832, 1836, 1844, 1852, 1856, 1860, 1864, 1884, 1888, 1892, 1896, 1900, 1936, 1940, 1944. In some twelve cases the dividing line has been largely personal, as in 1789, 1792, 1812, 1816, 1820, 1824 (commonly called the "scrub race for the Presidency"), 1828, 1840, 1848, 1904, 1908, 1912. The campaigns of 1868, 1872, and 1876 were held in the shadow of the Civil War, under anomalous conditions. The other campaigns were based partly upon party tradition and record or upon a mixture of party record and personality of the candidates, as in 1880, 1916, 1920, 1924, 1928, 1932 and 1948.

The eighteen campaigns since 1876 may be classified as follows:

1880   Party tradition.

1884   Tariff (not fully outlined as an issue).

1888   Tariff.

1892   Tariff.

1896   Currency.

1900   Currency and imperialism.

1904   Roosevelt and party tradition.

1908   Roosevelt and party tradition.

1912   Roosevelt and social justice—Republican party tradition—Democratic party tradition and Wilson progressivism.

1916   Record of Democratic party and of Wilson.

1920   Record of Democratic party plus proposed League of Nations.

1924   Coolidge and "prosperity"—La Follette and farmer-labor program.

1928   Hoover personality and "prosperity"—Smith personality and "liberal" program.

1932   Record of Republican party and Hoover depression—Franklin Roosevelt personality.

1936   Roosevelt personality and New Deal program.

1940   Roosevelt personality, two term tradition, neutrality, keeping out of war, help to Allies.

1944   Roosevelt personality, two term tradition, efficiency in conduct of war, government controls in postwar world.

1948   Record of Congress, unity in government, inflation, farm legislation, labor legislation, price control.

CHAPTER IV

FORMULATION OF PARTY ISSUES

"The problem is how much of mind to use,
How much of instinct. . . ."
—Edgar Lee Masters

METHODS AND AGENCIES

PARTY CLEAVAGES ARE NOT DETERMINED WHOLLY BY PLATFORMS OR declarations but by:

(1) Questions of policy
(2) Personality of candidates
(3) General record of the party in power as compared with the party out of power—the ins against the outs
(4) Traditions of the party, general tendencies, and survivals

As a means of settling disputed questions of national policy, the national campaign does not carry the country far, although a host of significant issues may be implicit in the candidacy of an individual or the record of party performance. Tariff and currency have loomed large, but so have Cleveland, the Roosevelts, and Wilson. So has the "general genius" of the Republican and Democratic parties.

The standard platform is composed of certain general features and certain special features arising from the special situation. The standard features are:

(1) Elaboration of the record of the party
(2) Denunciation of the opposition party
(3) General declarations regarding democracy and the nation
(4) General reference to certain nonparty issues
(5) Expressions of sympathy
(6) Noncommittal reference to certain disputed issues
(7) Definite issues

Specific pledges are likely to be made in respect to certain nonparty questions, and are found in almost every platform. There will also be more general references to broader and more contentious questions, such as labor and capital, or foreign relations.

The competition between parties has often made these lists much longer than would otherwise be the case. The party does not wish to offend any large organized interest by omission of a friendly reference to any policy that is likely to be uncontested, or of evidence of sympathy that may not call for any action. There are of course certain taboos in the making of platforms. Adverse references to race (except the colored race in the South or the Chinese or Japanese in the Pacific coast states), to religions, to classes, to sections of the country are among these.

It cannot be assumed that there is any one principle upon which all members of a given party are united. Party platforms and principles are not endorsed in their entirety by those who vote the party ticket. On the contrary, an analysis of the party shows that it is a group made up of voters of widely differing views, who come together only upon some major issue and do not always agree upon that. Or they may not even agree upon any commanding issue, but may vote a party ticket for other reasons. Even in a sharp conflict like that of 1896 the parties were made up of diverse elements, as the analysis below shows:

Republicans	*Democrats*
Gold standard followers	Free silverites
Bimetallism followers	Bimetallism advocates
Free silverites	Gold standard advocates
High tariff advocates	Free trade advocates
Low tariff advocates	Tariff revision advocates
Reactionary as to corporate control	Reactionary as to corporate control
Liberal as to corporate control	Liberal as to corporate control

In the campaign of 1928 the major parties were made up of diverse elements, as follows:

Republicans	*Democrats*
Profarm relief advocates	Profarm relief advocates
Protariff	Protariff
Drys and wets (eastern and urban)	Drys (southern) and wets
Catholic (business) and Protestant	Catholic and Protestant
Progressives and reactionaries	Progressives and reactionaries
Important business interests	Important business interests

Thus the issues were so far obscured that a clear view of the result is difficult to obtain. The enormous majority back of Hoover was made up of elements so diverse that they could with difficulty coalesce. The same might be said of the Democratic combination which, under the direction of the wet elements in the party, attempted to make prohibition modification an issue, although many of the southern Democrats were ardent drys.

Even on the question of tariff revision, party divisions are no longer clearly outlined, and the diversity of party interests is plainly seen on tariff votes. Republicans and Democrats unite as geographical and industrial interests are involved, without great regard to party principle. The South, which was once the stronghold for the low tariff advocates, has now many interests seeking protection. In the North are manufacturers who support the reciprocal trade program.

Again in 1936 each party was made up of diverse elements which tended to interfere with the drawing of sharp issues.

Republicans	*Democrats*
Budget balancers and spending advocates	Spending advocates and budget balancers
Tariff advocates and reciprocal trade agreement advocates	Reciprocal trade agreement advocates and opponents
Crop control opponents and advocates	Crop control advocates and opponents
Work relief program opponents and supporters	Work relief program supporters and opponents

In 1948 the cleavages within the two major parties were as follows:

Republicans	*Democrats*
Price control opponents and supporters	Price control supporters and opponents
Tariff advocates and reciprocal trade agreement advocates	Reciprocal trade agreement advocates and opponents
Tax reducers and debt reducers	Debt reducers and tax reducers
Drastic labor curbers and labor defenders	Labor defenders and labor curbers
	Farm legislation defenders and nondefenders

It may and frequently does happen that the factional divisions within parties upon questions of public policy are far sharper than those between parties. Between the progressive or the reactionary wings of different parties there may be a closer bond of union than between different factions of the same party. Examples of this may be seen in the conditions in Wisconsin under the La Follettes, California under Johnson, Georgia under Arnal, and in many other places and times. In these instances the real lines of division upon broad questions of public policy do not correspond at all to the nominal party lines but run at right angles to them, as is shown in the diagram on the next page.

Under these conditions one or the other of the parties or neither may function as the real representative of liberal or tory sentiment, as the outcome of the nominating process may indicate; and a shift of voters may be made accordingly, subject of course to the limitations imposed by other factors in the composition of the party. The decisive factor here may be a personality rather than a declaration of principle—an attitude rather than definite program of action—the hopes or fears of opposing interests.

Under our biparty system the voter decides upon a major issue or issues and subordinates all else to them. To a considerable extent the compromises and concessions, which under the Continental system are made after the election by the various groups when the strength of the various factions is developed, are made here either in the nominating process or in the election itself. The voter may be obliged to choose between imperialism and currency, or between high tariff and the League of Nations, or between a policy and a personality, and so on through a long series of choices. Inevitably a constant struggle goes on between opposing interests for the possession of the party organization and name. In a campaign like that of 189 many liberal Republicans voted for Bryan, while many conservative Democrats voted for McKinley.[1] In 1904 many radical Democrats

[1] W. F. Ogburn and A. Jaffee, in their article, "Independent Voting in Presidential Elections," appearing in *American Journal of Sociology*, XLII (1936), 186–201, failed to recognize this. Their definition of party turnover was the difference between the Democratic percentages and the total vote in two successive elections. In 1892 Cleveland, the successful Democratic candidate, received 46 per cent of the total vote. In 1896, Bryan, an unsuccessful candidate, received 46 per cent of the total vote. According to the definition, there was no party turnover! If the Republican vote had been chosen, the result would have been as follows: 1892, 43 per cent for Harrison; 1896, 51 per cent for McKinley; difference, 8 per cent. If the minor party vote had been taken, the turnover would be relatively high. While Bryan received the same national percentage as Cleveland, an examination of the state and local returns shows that the vote for the two men was quite different.

cast their ballots for Roosevelt, while many conservative Republicans turned to Parker. It is evident, therefore, that the solidarity of the party is often more apparent than real, as far as principle is concerned.

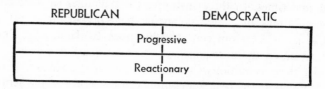

The frequent evasions, omissions, "straddles," "weasel words," and phrases of double meaning or phrases offset by others of opposite meaning are the outcome of the struggle to hold together elements that are difficult to combine within the ranks of any one organization. This balancing process may be carried to a point where the platform declaration loses all force and vigor. This may be offset again by the personality of the candidate, the power of the organization, or the favorable character of the situation.

A Gallup survey made right after the 1948 party conventions showed that nearly two-thirds of those interviewed had not read any portion of the Democratic platform and that nearly three-fourths had not read any portion of the Republican platform. The civil rights plank in the Democratic platform seemed to have attracted the most attention. Some observers thought that this plank helped precipitate the revolt of the States' Rights Democrats (Dixiecrats).

It is a serious, although common, mistake to assume that party principles may be ascertained solely by examination of party platforms. Convention declarations are often modified or developed, or occasionally even contradicted, by candidates in the course of a campaign. And many of the planks of the platform are obviously so drawn as to be capable of more than one interpretation. In national campaigns, the presidential speeches of acceptance are of very great value in shaping the campaign issues, and subsequent speeches of candidates and party orators, together with the campaign literature of the party, are very important in fixing the questions upon which the parties actually divide. The permanent differences in party policy or principle are more commonly reflected in the speeches of party orators or statesmen between campaigns, when the personality of candidates is not so much in evidence as in the utterances of the party press. Furthermore, many of the most important stands of the party are taken between conventions, as urgent occasions arise. International and internal situations develop unforeseen by the platform maker, or, if anticipated, are perhaps purposely avoided.

The platforms of the two major parties tend to be alike because they aim to attract a majority of the voters.

MINOR PARTIES AND ISSUES

As formulators of issues, the minor parties have often been more successful than the major parties.[2] As advance guards of new issues, the newcomers have been bolder than the established organizations. Thus the Free Soil party, the Populists, and the Progressives have formulated platforms and developed issues later accepted tacitly or openly by either one or both of the major parties. The Free Soil party raised the issue of slavery extension, which resulted in wrecking both the Whig and the Democratic parties, and finally compelled its acceptance as a national issue. The famous campaign of 1848 with Van Buren as the Free Soil candidate struck the death knell of the old parties.[3] The Populist party, after the campaign of 1892, was absorbed by the Democratic party, which adopted its fundamental planks in regard to free coinage of silver and the income tax, and in many ways breathed the general spirit of the Populist partisans.[4] The platform of the Progressive party in 1912 was also adopted in large measure by the Democratic administration of 1913–1917, and its principles applied in both the Republican and the Democratic platforms of 1916.

[2] See J. Kieran, *Information Please Almanac for 1948* (New York, 1948), p. 29; F. E. Haynes, *Third Party Movements since the Civil War* (Iowa City, 1916), and *Social Politics in the United States* (Boston, 1924), for excellent discussions of independent movements since the Civil War; also A. N. Holcombe, *Political Parties of Today* (New York, 1924), Chap. XI; and Paul H. Douglas, *The Coming of a New Party* (New York, 1932).

[3] The preamble of the Free Soil platform was as follows: "Whereas, the political conventions recently assembled at Baltimore and Philadelphia—the one stifling the voice of a great constituency entitled to be heard in its deliberations, and the other abandoning its distinctive principles for mere availability—have dissolved the National party organization heretofore existing, by nominating for the Chief Magistracy of the United States, under slave-holding dictation, candidates, neither of whom can be supported by the opponents of slavery extension without a sacrifice of consistency, duty and self-respect."

[4] See the opening paragraphs of the National People's platform of 1892, in K. H. Porter, *National Party Platforms* (New York. 1924).

Many other issues were developed by minor parties. For example, the eight-hour day is found in the Labor Reform platform of 1872 (for all government employees). Opposition to the use of convict labor appeared in the Labor Reform platform of 1872 and the Greenback platform of 1880. The attack upon excessive railroad rates was begun by the Labor Reform party of 1872. Universal suffrage for both men and women was demanded by the Prohibitionists in 1872. The income tax was urged by the Greenback party in 1880 and 1884, and by the Populists in 1892. The prohibition of child labor was asked by the Greenbackers in 1880. Attack upon monopolies was instituted by the Greenback party in 1880. Direct election of United States senators was found in the platform of the Prohibition party in 1876. Governmental ownership of telegraph and telephone systems was urged in the Populist party of 1892; the initiative and referendum in the Populist platform of the same year. The inheritance tax was urged by the Socialist Labor party in 1892, and social insurance by the Social Democratic party of 1900.

A careful examination of the minor party platforms for 1932 shows that the Socialist party came much nearer to anticipating the depression measures than did the major party platforms for that year. Among the Socialist planks were the following: a federal appropriation of $5,000,000,000 for immediate relief; another $5,000,000,000 for public works and roads, reforestation, slum clearance, and housing; free employment agencies; unemployment insurance; old age pensions; aid to farmers and small home owners against foreclosures; a constitutional amendment authorizing taxation of all government securities; increased federal aid to road building and education and social services for rural communities; abolition of injunctions in labor disputes, outlawing of yellow dog contracts and the passing of a law enforcing the rights of workers to organize into unions; recognition of the Soviet Union; complete independence of the Philippines. This Socialist program resembles the spending policies, the social security measures, the labor relations acts, the agricultural credit acts, the housing measures, the farm security acts, and other policies of subsequent administrations.[5] It is evident, then, that in many ways the minor parties are more active and more suc-

[5] David Lawrence, "Stumbling into Socialism," *Saturday Evening Post* (July 20, 1935).

cessful in the development of new and vital issues than are the older and major parties.

At the same time, of course, they may raise many issues which are never widely accepted but which pass into the limbo of forgotten social suggestions. Thus the Anti-Masonic party strove to make a national issue of Freemasonry. The Know-Nothings endeavored to found a party of nativism and Protestantism as against the newcomer and the Catholic. The Populists advocated the issuance of government certificates in exchange for warehouse receipts. In state campaigns grotesque issues are shaped by some of the minor parties, but the major organizations are not exempt from similar careless demands.

In some instances, in fact, the older parties, instead of making easier the formulation and decision of great issues, serve the function of suppressing them or of diverting attention from them. This was the case in the days of the slavery struggle, when the old parties refused to take a definite stand even upon slavery restriction. Again in the discussion of the currency problem the settlement of the question was evaded until 1896, when it unexpectedly became a national issue between the great parties, but only after the free silver movement acting through the Populist party had forced the problem to the front. Questions of equal suffrage and social and industrial justice were ignored until the Populist, Progressive, and Socialist parties, through popular discussion of them, required a more advanced position on the part of the older groups. The minor party may be created for the very reason that the major party cannot or will not take a definite stand on some broad question of national interest.

In 1948 the Progressive Citizens of America nominated Henry Wallace for President. During the campaign he denounced both major parties as tools of the "big-money boys" and blamed "superprofits" for inflation. He said: "Only a new party will expose the money-changers' control of the nation's economic and political life." [6] With regard to our foreign policy, he became an ardent advocate of peace and a bitter opponent of the stern attitude toward Soviet Russia.

On the whole, the significance and effectiveness of the third party

[6] *New York Times*, January 18, 1948.

movements are underestimated by the casual observer. As a matter of fact they have been very important factors in the actual shaping of national policies.[7] The Free Soil party played a very important, some would say the major role in the slavery struggle. The Greenback party and particularly the Populist party played a decisive part in the precipitation of the currency contest. The Progressive party of 1912 brought to the front the question of woman's suffrage and aided materially in achieving it; at the same time it forced action on various issues of social and industrial justice, notably that of child labor. In the case of prohibition, its advocates decided neither to concentrate on a separate party, nor to attempt to capture one or both of the major parties, but to operate through public opinion, the master of them all.

STATE PLATFORMS

If there are gaps in the platforms of the national party where no distinct issues appear, the platforms of the state parties are still more noticeable for this characteristic. As a rule there are no sharply defined issues of principle in state elections, but to this rule there are exceptions from time to time. Issues are occasionally joined upon the question of railroad or corporation control, more commonly in times past on the liquor question, sometimes on the efficiency or inefficiency of a given administration. In almost all states there have been party issues at various times arising out of local situations, as, for example, in 1890 when the so-called Bennett Law, requiring the teaching of English alone in the schools of Minnesota, Wisconsin, and Illinois, precipitated a storm which swept over those states. But in the main an examination of state platforms shows that there is a great lack of definite and concise principles dividing parties in state elections. State platforms, in fact, are taken much less seriously than are the national statements of principle, both during the campaign and afterward.

The platforms are occupied in great part with utterances upon national questions or contain more or less perfunctory promises or observations on local questions. The average voter could not identify state party platforms as Republican or Democratic in the absence of

[7] For a contrary view, see E. M. Sait, *American Parties and Elections* (New York, 1948).

that portion of them referring to national questions.[8] He would be a very good partisan who could select his own state party platforms of ten years ago, eliminating the national features from them. As a matter of fact, state campaigns, aside from their national elements, are often fought very largely around the personality of the candidates for governor, who represent various tendencies which may attract or repel voters. These tendencies may be personal, class, or sectional, or may represent differences in principle not reflected in the platform. Thus the Republican candidate may be a radical and the Democratic a conservative, or the Democratic may be radical and the Republican reactionary. This may be clearly understood, but yet may find no reflection whatever in the written words of the platform of either party.

During the period of the Farmer-Labor party in Minnesota and the Progressive party in Wisconsin, the party platforms in these states were more sharply drawn. Thus in Wisconsin, in the 1934 campaign for governor, Philip La Follette favored public ownership of central banks and public utilities but opposed further "nationalization," advocating instead the "conscious distribution of national income" through taxation and other governmental policies.[9] The Republican party vigorously opposed the Progressive policies.

In New York State the American Labor party was in advance of many of the policies of the national Democratic administration.

LIMITATIONS UPON PARTY AS A FORMULATOR OF POLICIES

In appraising the function of the party as a formulator of issues, it must be observed that there are notable limitations upon this faculty. Among the most important of these are: (1) the broad fact

[8] W. E. Henry, *State Platforms of the Two Dominant Parties in Indiana, 1850–1900* (Indianapolis, 1902); E. W. Winkler, *Platforms of Political Parties in Texas* (Austin, 1916); W. J. Davis, *History of Political Conventions in California, 1849–92* (Sacramento, 1893). Running commentary on the actual problems of states is contained in the messages of governors to state legislatures; also in the proceedings of the governors' conferences. Other material is found in various state histories, which are, however, of widely varying value.

[9] H. M. Groves, "Wisconsin's New Party," *Nation*, CXXXIX (August 1, 1934), 122; H. F. Gosnell. *Grass Roots Politics* (Washington, D. C., 1942), Chap. IV, "Progressive Politics: Wisconsin."

of nonpartisanship in local affairs; (2) constitutional limitations upon the policy determining agencies; and (3) the fact that there are large areas in which policies are decided without reference to parties, at the dictate of public opinion acting through both parties, or through agencies other than the political organization as such.

In local elections party issues have tended to disappear. Usually no party platform is adopted, and in any event there is no uniformity in party declarations. Neither Republicans nor Democrats have as a rule any distinctive local program. The Socialist party has also made little headway in the local field, partly because of its own weakness and partly because of a failure to secure the cooperation of labor groups.[10] When party lines survive in local elections, the campaigns are either reflections of the attitude of the voters on national questions, or they represent the struggle of the local party organization to strengthen itself by means of local spoils. The chief local issues have been those centering around regulation and ownership of public utilities, the wet and dry question, extension of public works programs, the size of the tax burden, entrance into such fields as low rental housing, and dominance of spoilsmen. In most cities either by law or by custom local elections are conducted upon nonpartisan or, more properly, upon nonnational lines. The party usually does not function as in state and national concerns. Other groups spring up, declaring principles and presenting candidates, effecting temporary organizations for campaign purposes. The ties of organization, obligation, and party allegiance may be relaxed while the local struggle proceeds. Even when party nominees are formally presented, the same process proceeds, and the actual election in a city like Chicago or Philadelphia, where party nominations are made, until recently bore little resemblance to a national or state election as far as party lines are concerned. Thus the great field of urban problems with the many significant questions involved is just beginning to enter into the party function. The rapid growth of cities, their great expenditures, their varied functions, their growing significance in the life of the nation give to this situation very great importance. That this large and increasing field of activity should have

[10] The city of Milwaukee under Mayor Hoan was a notable exception. See D. W. Hoan, *City Government: The Record of the Milwaukee Experiment* (New York, 1936).

been removed for so long from the immediate jurisdiction of the party is a fact of great interest and far-reaching significance. The depression had made the parties more aware of local problems and of their national importance, and both parties made some reference to them in 1936.[11]

Partly because of constitutional limitations and partly because of the power of public opinion behind both parties, many of the fundamental questions of public policy are not party questions at all. Large issues of our governmental organization have not been settled by party controversy; for example, direct election of senators, extension of the suffrage, the short ballot, the initiative and referendum, the merit system, the budget system, and administrative efficiency. The constitutional requirement of advice and consent of two-thirds of the Senate to treaties has meant that the major issues in foreign policy have to be settled outside of party politics. No one had a keener realization of this than the late President Franklin D. Roosevelt who as far back as 1940 began building bipartisan support for a postwar world organization. He was determined at all costs to avoid the mistakes of President Wilson in letting world organization become a partisan issue.[12] Nor have such questions as slavery, the drug traffic, or lotteries commonly been party issues. Rarely in the industrial field have workmen's compensation acts, child labor laws, the use of the injunction, railway control, antimonopoly legislation, the income tax, or social security been party measures. In short, the great body of state and national legislation is carried through without any party contest, or at any rate without any national contest. This is partly because the parties hesitate to take a position upon doubtful questions, but still further for the reason that the political parties under our system of government cannot enact measures which require amendment of the constitution of the

[11] The Republican platform mentions the following: "Federal grants-in-aid to the states and territories while the need exists, upon compliance with these conditions: (a) a fair proportion of the total relief burden to be provided from the revenues of state and local governments."

The Democratic platform says, "Where business fails to supply such employment, we believe that work at prevailing wages should be provided in cooperation with state and local governments on useful public projects."

[12] Frances Perkins, *The Roosevelt I Knew* (New York, 1946), p. 340; Eleanor Roosevelt, *This Is My Story* (New York, 1939), pp. 297–298; and Cordell Hull, *The Memoirs of Cordell Hull* (New York, 1948), pp. 1657 ff.

state or of the United States. The fact is that many important measures are of this class. Under our federal system of government, the national government has only limited powers. The parties must act through the federal government and through the forty-eight states. Neither party possesses under normal conditions the votes required for an ambitious program, and it must of necessity secure the cooperation of the other party if a result is to be obtained. Individual states may be completely under the control of some one party, even to the power of constitutional amendment, but a fundamental national program may require amending the Constitution of the United States.[13] In European states, including England, the party in power may as a rule carry through almost any project to which it may be committed, without regard to constitutional restrictions. It was Professor Dicey who said that the British Parliament can do anything except make a man a woman, and even in this case the legal capacities and disabilities of one might be transferred to the other by law. Under our system no party can hope to command and control for any length of time such a majority as would enable it to obtain a two-thirds vote of both houses of Congress and the favorable vote of three-fourths of the states. In 1936 the Democratic party nominally had a two-thirds majority of Congress and a three-fourths majority of the states, but in 1937 it was impossible for the party leaders to discipline this majority. The plan for the reorganization of the Supreme Court split the party wide open. Vital and far-reaching changes must in the main be effected by concurrent action of the major parties. If a powerful public opinion demands some significant change it may be carried through, even though the representatives of neither party favor it; indeed this is often the case in both state and nation.

Even where no constitutional obstacles intervene, a great amount of lawmaking is carried through without any reference to party lines or party affiliations. Only in exceptional cases is the party bugle sounded to rally the party members to the party standard, and even then they do not always respond.

The party as a formulator and advocate of measures is not without strong competition and formidable rivals in the field of social

[13] T. K. Finletter, *Can Representative Government Do the Job?* (New York, 1945); F. J. Goodnow, *Social Reform and the Constitution* (New York, 1911); W. Y. Elliqtt, *The Need for Constitutional Reform* (New York, 1935); E. S. Corwin. *The Twilight of the Supreme Court* (New Haven, 1934).

policy. There are many other organizations dealing with legislative problems, not only in the lobbies of legislative bodies, but before the electorate, and in discussions where public opinion plays so large a part. Some of these groups are organized for a specific purpose, more or less political in nature, and others assume these functions as a part of more general activities.

Of equal or greater significance is a long series of pressure groups which are from time to time interested in the programs of political parties and the course of legislation.

These take the form of the following:

I   General business groups
    National Association of Manufacturers
    Chamber of Commerce of the United States
    American Bankers' Association
II   Farmers' groups
    Grange
    American Farm Bureau Federation
    Farmers' Union
III   Organized labor and professionals
    American Federation of Labor
    Congress of Industrial Organizations
    Railway Brotherhoods
    American Bar Association
    American Medical Association
IV   Religious groups
    Federal Council of Churches of Christ
    Catholic Church
V   Women's groups, youth groups, groups for the aged
    League of Women Voters
    Townsend Clubs
VI   Other groups (cultural minorities, immigrants, intolerance movements, patriotic societies, etc.)
    National Association for the Advancement of Colored People
    American Legion, American Veterans Committee, Veterans of Foreign Wars [14]

[14] See Stuart Chase, *Democracy under Pressure: Special Interests vs. the Public Welfare* (New York, 1943) : H. B. Graves, *Readings in Public Opinion* (New York, 1928) ; H. L. Childs, *Labor and Capital in National Politics* (Columbus, 1929) ; E. P. Herring, *Group Representation before Congress* (Baltimore, 1929) ; E. B. Logan, "Lobbying," *Annals of the American Academy of Political and Social Science*, CXLIV (supplement, July, 1929), 1-89; and Belle Zeller, *Pressure Politics in New York* (New York, 1937).

All of these and others as well as often militant organizations which initiate proposals and carry on vigorous campaigns for their adoption. Practically all large groups have legislative committees or political action committees which pass upon questions of legislative policy, or in some cases on the personnel of candidates. In urban communities various groups practically take over the function of the political parties, as far as the shaping of issues is concerned.

These groups compete with the political parties, and often do so very effectively. They are often well organized, well financed and well led. They make up for lack of members in energy and aggressiveness, well systematized and steadily advanced, and their organizations are likely to be more ruthlessly pruned on the efficiency side than the parties themselves, which often fall into a form of dry rot, where nominal organizations are really ineffective.

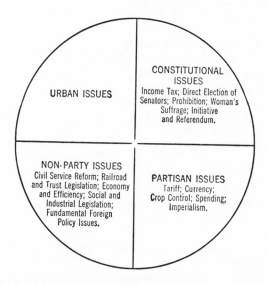

An analysis of legislation during the last forty years shows that many of the most significant measures have been initiated by such groups, and that a long propaganda has been carried on to bring about the success of these measures. The Suffrage Amendment and the passage and repeal of the Dry Amendment are conspicuous cases of such activity; the Federal Reserve Act, the Social Security Act, labor legislation, and in still larger measure the laws of the states and the ordinances of the municipalities are also the product of their enterprise in great measure. The fact is that much of the formulation of public policies goes on outside the political party. Some of the party leaders, of course, initiate measures, and the party groups in legislature pass upon the proposals presented to them; but after all much of the work in the formation of social policies is carried on outside the ranks of the party itself.[15]

The figure on the preceding page is designed to show roughly the limited number of political questions which are actually settled by political parties, and the large number of problems settled through but not by the parties. It is perhaps needless to say that the chart is not drawn to any exact scale.

Laws are enacted in state legislatures and in Congress by members of political parties, and are enforced mainly by members of parties; but partisans are influenced in their votes not so much by the party organization as by the innumerable quasi-public organizations of the type just described. They may have been pledged by these organizations before they were nominated or elected; they may have been persuaded or intimidated by them after they took their seats. The significant fact is that it is not the voice of the party as such but the voice of public opinion as expressed by some active agency to which they listen most of the time. They may listen to the voice of the party, but it does not often call upon them. It would be well if the party did call on the legislators more than it does since the party leaders are more likely to look out for the general interest of the public than are the leaders of pressure groups.[16]

TRADITIONS AND POLICIES

The parties are distinguished not so much by sharp division of opinion as by other features. Chief among these are: the rivalry between the ins and the outs; party traditions and historical tenden-

---

[15] A. L. Lowell quotes Redlich to the effect that England has a system of party government by a parliamentary cabinet, because she has no parties in the continental sense. *The Government of England*, II, 98.

[16] V. O. Key, *Politics Parties and Pressure Groups* (New York, 1947), p. 200.

cies; a differentiation of the parties by some general estimate of
their capacities, or possibilities, or probabilities.[17]

Every platform contains a recital of the record of the party and
a denunciation of the opposition, charts of the triumphs of the one,
and the failures of the other. Often the assertions are exaggerated
and sometimes they are clearly captious; but often they score telling
points. This function of mutual criticism is one of the important
functions of the party, but is often overdone in the platforms. If the
process does not degenerate into acrimonious wrangling, it is a very
great advantage to the public, and its educational value cannot be
easily overestimated. Neither party is ever in complete control of all
the agencies of all the governments, and hence both are on the offensive and the defensive all the time.

All platforms contain carefully calculated appeals to party names,
party traditions, party recollections. Great names and great deeds
adorn the pages of party history, and each party attempts to utilize
these memories to stir the emotion of the partisan, or to attract the
undecided.

Each party also endeavors to provide itself with a distinguishing
characteristic of a desirable quality, and to attribute the opposite to
the other. Thus the Republican party will be called the party of
"capacity" and "efficiency," and the Democratic party will be denounced as the party of "incompetence and unreadiness." [18] Senator
Beveridge drew the line between the "doers" and the "dreamers,"
between the "party of construction" and the "party of destruction
and opposition." Democratic platforms and speeches assert for their
party the prime representation of the common people and denounce
the opposition as the party of the rich—the tool of the trusts. They
point to the party of liberalism and progress, as against the party
of conservatism and reaction. It was President Wilson who once
said, "The Republican party has not had a new idea since the Civil
War." All of the arguments of all the special pleaders for each party
are, of course, never assembled; otherwise it would be found that

[17] In Japan before its defeat in 1945 concrete proposals were regarded as a sign
oi party weakness, according to Dr. U. Iwaski in *The Working Forces in Japanese
Politics* (New York, 1921), Chap. VII. See also H. S. Quigley, *Japanese Government and Politics* (New York, 1932).

[18] James Bryce's estimate as given in his *American Commonwealth* (New York,
1921), Chap. LVI.

some Republicans were contending that their party is "best for business" and others that it was most certain to regulate business effectively; or one set of Democratic partisans would be found declaring their party the sworn foe of Wall Street and another set quietly assuring Wall Street that it had nothing to fear from the Democracy, but that the real opponent was the Republicans.

In the 1948 campaign, Henry A. Wallace, the Progressive party candidate, denounced both the major parties. "There is no real difference between the Democratic and Republican parties on the important issues confronting the American people. Both serve the interests of big business. Both operate against the interests of the people. Campaign speeches and differences in party name simply conceal the fact that neither party represents the common people. The record of Congress and the administration on every issue vital to the welfare of the people reveals a clear pattern of service to concentrated wealth and privilege." [19]

The 1940 platforms of the two major parties contained some general statements about party differences. The Democratic platform said:

"Toward the modern fulfillment of the American ideal, the Democratic party, during the past seven years, has labored successfully—

1. To strengthen democracy by defensive preparedness against aggression, whether by open attack or secret infiltration;

2. To strengthen democracy by increasing economic efficiency; and

3. To strengthen democracy by improving the welfare of the people. . . .

The Republican party gives its promises to the farmer and its allegiance to those who exploit him. . . .

We condemn the Republican policies which permitted the victimization of investors in the securities of private power corporations and the exploitation of the people by unnecessarily high utility costs. . . ."

The 1940 Republican platform discussed the following general distinctions:

"The Republican party will put into effect such governmental policies, temporary or permanent, as will establish and maintain an equitable balance between labor, industry and agriculture by expanding industrial

[19] Henry A. Wallace, "Why a Third Party in 1948?" *Annals of the American Academy of Political and Social Science* CCLIX (September, 1948), p. 10.

and business activity, eliminating unemployment, lowering production costs, thereby creating increased consumer buying power for agricultural products. . . .

The New Deal policy of interference and arbitrary regulation has injured all business, but especially small business. We promise to encourage the small business man by removing unnecessary bureaucratic regulations and interference. . . .

To insure against the overthrow of our American system of government, we favor an amendment to the Constitution providing that no person shall be President of the United States for more than two terms."

PARTY AGENCIES FOR FORMULATING POLICIES

The agencies through which party principles are actually formulated are various. The most conspicuous of them is the convention, which is the official agency for the declaration of the policies of the party presenting the platform or program for that purpose. But there are also the declarations of the candidates either in the primaries or in the elections, the legislative caucuses of the party, the declarations of its responsible and unofficial leaders, and the pronouncements of the party press.

The platform of the national convention is the official statement of the party's position upon questions of public policy—the official declaration of the party creed. It is the quadrennial declaration of the political faith of the party, from which there may be no appeal, although there may be authentic interpretations by the party leaders. This important document is adopted by action of the convention on the recommendation of the committee on resolutions. This committee consists of one man and one woman from each state and territory, named by the delegates from such state or territory at the time of the convention. The wishes of prospective presidential candidates carry great weight with this committee. This was true of Theodore Roosevelt in 1904, of Wilson in 1916, and of Franklin Roosevelt in 1936, 1940, and 1944. The committee proceeds to organize and to give hearings to various groups requesting the right to appear before it, and then to formulate a platform. Of necessity both the hearings and the subsequent deliberation are all too brief for the very important measures with which they are charged. Hearings must be limited to a few minutes, perhaps fifteen minutes or half an hour, for a matter of vital importance to the welfare of the nation, perhaps a question of delicate foreign policy or one affecting the relations of classes and interests in the most significant fashion. Labor, business, agriculture, race, class, sectional, social, and industrial interests of all types appear in a hasty procession for perfunctory consideration of their claims upon the party. It is not a process that adds to the dignity of the national party system.

Nor is there time for adequate consideration of the claims of the various interests in the subsequent sessions where the draft of the platform is finally agreed upon by the committee. Here, however, animated discussion may be held over the most important issues, such as the tariff question, the currency problem, labor legislation, taxation problems, the wet and dry question, and the farm problem. In the Democratic convention of 1900 there was a spirited contest over the currency plank, in 1920 a prolonged battle over the League of Nations, in 1924 over the Klan, in 1928 over prohibition, and in 1948 over civil rights.

It would be easy to provide for preliminary hearings before the national committee or before some special committee appointed for the purpose, but little use has been made of such devices. In 1920 the Republican national committee appointed a large committee of well-known Republicans for the purpose of preparing a preliminary report on the platform. This body assembled a mass of information but did not materially affect the action of the resolutions committee finally selected for platform purposes. It is possible that the practice of preliminary inquiry may develop into a custom of considering more fully and deliberately the claims of the conflicting interests that come before the party. After the 1936 campaign, the Republican national committee appointed a special body to consider the program of the party. This agency held hearings, engaged in research, and published a report early in 1940. Four years later the Republicans again held preliminary conferences. The Republican declaration at Mackinac Island was an important pronouncement on foreign policy.

Final action on the report of the resolutions committee rests with the convention. Usually the platform framed by the committee is adopted without debate; in fact, with wild enthusiasm on the part of delegates and spectators. The intensity of the enthusiasm is in a way regarded as an evidence of party solidarity and a measure of the prospect of victory. But at times there have been violent struggles on the floor of the convention during the consideration of the party platform. Notable cases of this were seen in the conventions of 1896. In the Republican convention of that year, the Silver Republicans were headed by the venerable Senator Teller of Colorado who protested against the adoption of the gold plank and finally withdrew in tears from the floor of the convention. In the Democratic convention there was a famous contest between David B. Hill and William Jennings Bryan in which the young Nebraskan rose to party and national fame with his "cross of gold" speech.[20] In 1904 there was again a bitter contest in the Democratic convention over the currency question. In 1912 Mr. Bryan turned the Baltimore convention into a riot by the introduction of his resolution denouncing the activities of the friends of Wall Street in the convention.[21] The Democratic conventions of 1920 and 1924 were again the scenes of vigorous debate. Mr. Bryan was at both conventions the storm center, with the liquor question in 1920 and the Ku Klux Klan in 1924 as the objects of controversy. In 1928 Governor Smith wired the Democratic convention his position upon the liquor problem—varying from that of the platform. In 1948 there was a bitter debate on civil rights in the Democratic convention which ended in a bolt of some of the southern delegates.

Yet on the whole the convention floor is not a forum for debate and discussion of topics of national welfare. The number of delegates is too large, and the spectators take so lively a part in the proceedings that the situation is unfavorable to deliberation and careful consideration of grave questions of state. Party leaders will if possible agree upon a formula which will avert open discussion and avoid a breach in the solidarity of the party in the coming campaign.

[20] Compare George William Curtis' famous speech following the rejection of the Joshua R. Giddings plank inserting the equality clause of the Declaration of Independence, *Proceedings Republic Convention*, 1860; and Garfield's notable utterance in the convention of 1880 regarding the pledging of delegates to abide by the result of the balloting for President, *Proceedings*, 1880.

[21] *Proceedings Democratic Convention*, p. 129. This resolution pledged the convention to opposition "to the nomination of any candidate for president who is the representative of or under obligation to J. Pierpont Morgan, Thomas F. Ryan, August Belmont, or any other member of the privilege hunting and favor seeking class."

Attention has already been directed to the fact that in many campaigns there is no specific issue requiring careful and definite statement; and that in a number of instances it is the intention of the party management to avoid definiteness of commitment. Although the convention is the supreme authority of the party, it will be found necessary in most cases to seek elsewhere for an authoritative statement of the party's position upon the great questions of national policy.

In the national field the statements of the presidential candidate are frequently of greater significance than the platform itself. His speech of acceptance is of especial importance as an interpretation of the party position and will be more closely read than the platform itself; and probably greater significance will be attached to it by those who are carefully scanning the attitude of the particular party he represents. In 1904 the Democratic nominee, Judge Parker, declined to accept the nomination unless his views upon the currency question were held satisfactory by the convention, and this action was taken by the convention before he finally agreed to become the candidate of the party. After the convention adjourns equally significant changes may be made by the candidate if he desires to do so. Mr. Taft in 1908 accepted publicity of campaign funds after the convention had rejected it. In the 1920 campaign Mr. Cox definitely made the League of Nations a Democratic issue, although this was not so clearly indicated in the platform of the party, while Mr. Harding interpreted the Republican position upon this question in his own way. Governor Smith materially modified the platform position upon prohibition. The attitude of the candidate may be determined by his own personal position, by some shift in the general situation, or by the imperative requirements of party victory. In any event the candidates' declarations are of equal importance with the official party declarations. Statements of other prominent party leaders are also of great significance in ascertaining the party's real attitude, for the president standing alone cannot carry through any policy. Likewise the editorials and pronouncements of the party press are of great weight in fixing the actual issue. The recognized Republican and Democratic organs and the independents, affiliated for a campaign with a particular party, help to shape the party issue as the campaign goes on.

The state convention is also the official agent for the declaration of the party's principles in the state area. For two reasons, however, the major party state convention does not function as vigorously as the national. In the first place there are relatively few distinct state issues upon which the party cares to take a definite stand; indeed, in most instances there is no clear-cut state issue upon which the parties divide locally. The usual state platform will contain a declaration regarding national questions, a denunciation of the opposition party, a number of general statements, uncontested, in respect to state and local issues, and only occasionally will there be a definite disagreement upon some specific problem of state importance. In the next place, the direct primary has to a large extent supplanted the convention, even in the matter of party declarations. The candidate will be named before the convention assembles, and his preprimary declarations must be the platform. They have been openly made and the candidacy approved by the party voters. Hence the state convention cannot well undo them, and in any event it cannot change the candidate or his principles. The actual declaration then is likely to be that made by the successful candidate or a conference of those who are of his political belief. Much the same thing happened when nominations were made by the delegate convention, for in that case the successful faction controlled the convention for platform purposes as well as for nominations.

A number of methods have been devised for the statement of party principles under the direct primary. In some cases the state committee has been given this function. In Wisconsin the candidates for state office, acting with the holdover members of the legislature, are given the task of shaping the state platform. About half of the states make definite provision in their primary laws for the framing of the platform by a delegate convention, by the state central committee, by a party council or conference, or by some combination of these agencies.

In municipal campaigns the convention as a policy declaring body ceases to function altogether, with an occasional exception. The platforms are the declarations of the candidates, who are likely to submit a formal statement of their views and policies, either in one document or a series of statements. Occasionally, there is a platform declaration by some group or conference of citizens interested in municipal progress or reform of some sort. In general, however, in city elections the issues are not defined by regularly elected delegates to formal "conventions," but are much more informally and spontaneously put forward by far less highly organized groups of citizens. This is not because the issues are not as real and vital as in state and national campaigns, but because of the different electoral process which has been worked out in most of the municipalities.

A detailed study of particular campaigns shows plainly how within certain limits, and sometimes very wide ones, the issue shifts and sways about, before a final question ultimately emerges.[22] The tides of the campaign may readily be followed through the columns of the daily press or through the weekly organs, and these will show the groping for the issue which is so often characteristic of the electoral struggles.

In state elections the attitude of the candidate is of even greater significance than in the national election. The state platform is less important and the state issues are less defined than the national in general, though there may be distinct state questions of greater importance than the national campaign itself. Here the pronouncement of the Republican or the Democratic candidate for governor is of great significance, and will overshadow what the party platform may have said upon general subjects. Hence the governor and his group will in large measure make the party statement of local party principles.

The national convention meets but once in four years, and in the meantime many significant issues may arise, unforeseen in the party platform and wholly unanticipated. What is the party's position upon these new questions? And how is it determined? There is no official party declaration by which the most faithful devotee of the party may be guided. In these situations the party position is that taken by the responsible leaders of the party, in the first instance. For this purpose the president of the party in power and the congressional leaders of the opposition party are first in line of authority.

[22] H. C. Thomas, *The Return of the Democratic Party to Power in 1884* (New York, 1919), gives an admirable analysis of the campaign of that year; R. V. Peel and T. C. Donnelly, *The 1928 Campaign* (New York, 1931), and *The 1932 Campaign* (New York, 1935); P. Lazarsfeld, B. Berelson, and H. Gaudet, *The People's Choice* (New York, 1944).

They may take a position which is the party's position, for the time being at any rate. But in this process of determining the party attitude, where it is not covered by the party platform or the party traditions, unofficial party leaders also are or may be active in expressing and fixing opinion. The party press may be active. And innumerable groups within the party will begin to urge their views as the views of the party.[23] Following the 1932 election, President Roosevelt, the Democratic Congress and the Democratic state administrations proceeded to re-formulate the aims and policies of the Democratic party in the light of the problems of the depression.

There still remains, however, as a formal party agency, the party caucus. This may be invoked for determination of the party position where unity of action is desirable and possible. On legislative questions the party caucus is in a position to make an official statement of the party attitude, although this position may not be in fact the actual position of the bulk of the party. The technical agency through which congressional leadership is exercised is the party caucus.[24] In the early years of the Republic the joint congressional caucus held the unchallenged party leadership, but after a generation this institution was overthrown and was never revived in its old form.[25] The four separate caucuses of the two parties in the House and Senate still survive, and are the official organization of the parties in the legislative field. The House caucus for choice of the Speaker, and for determination of the rules of procedure, is of very great importance, as is the Senate caucus for the choice of committees. Yet neither in the House nor in the Senate are most matters of party position upon questions of broad legislative policy decided. The party leaders in Congress seem to get along without the caucus under ordinary conditions. The party platform, the attitude of the Presi-

[23] See Chap. VII on the subject of party leadership.
[24] See F. M. Riddick, *Congressional Procedure* (Boston, 1941); R. Heller, *Strengthening Congress* (Washington, D. C., 1945); L. Rogers, *The American Senate* (New York, 1926); P. D. Hasbrouck, *Party Government in the House of Representatives* (New York, 1927); H. Walker, *Law Making in the United States* (New York, 1934); and J. P. Chamberlain, *Legislative Processes* (New York, 1936).
[25] See H. A. McGill, "The Legislative Caucus," in A. C. McLaughlin and A. B. Hart, *Cyclopedia of American Government*; and P. D. Hasbrouck, "Caucus," in *Encyclopaedia of the Social Sciences*, III (1930), pp. 277–279; Floyd M. Riddick, "The First Session of the Eightieth Congress," *American Political Science Review*, XLII (August, 1948), pp. 677–693.

dent and party leaders, the party press, the individual interpretation of public or party opinion are of great weight in most cases. In the case of the party in power, administrative initiative is relied upon, while in any event the committee system tends to destroy party responsibility for action.

While the Legislative Reorganization Act of 1946 did not provide for the "policy committees" (one for the majority and one for the minority in each house) which were strongly urged by some, the Senate, on its own initiative, authorized such committees on an experimental basis for the Eightieth Congress. Senator Taft was the chairman of the majority policy committee and Senator Barkley was the chairman of the minority policy committee.

In a committee containing thirteen Republicans and ten Democrats, two Republicans combine with the Democrats to amend a measure or to report it out. With which party rests the responsibility? But this is just what is occurring every day in the actual course of legislation. In fact, the bulk of the measures passed are of this class, both in national and in state legislative bodies. Even on the old tariff bills it was impossible to reckon on the solid vote of the party either in committee or on the floor of the house. On the numerous amendments Republicans and Democrats would shift about as local interest or compromise dictated, and even on the final passage of the bill there would be notable breaks in the party ranks. The struggles of the Democratic party under Cleveland and of the Republican party under Taft are notable illustrations of the flexibility of party obligations even upon a fundamental platform issue.

The relative amounts of party and nonparty voting were clearly shown in an admirable study made some years ago by Lowell.[26] By a detailed study of legislative votings, counting all votes in which

[26] A. L. Lowell, "The Influence of Party upon Legislation in England and America," in *Annual Report of the American Historical Association*, 1901, I, 319–542. See also S. A. Rice, *Farmers and Workers in American Politics* (New York, 1924). A study of party cohesion in the British House of Commons in 1927 made by one of our students, Russell Jones, showed that 97 per cent of the votes cast by Unionists and Laborites were party votes according to Lowell's definition.

D. Hecock, "Social and Economic Interests Revealed by Political and Geographical Cohesion in Congress" (Columbus, 1931), cited by P. Odegard and E. A. Helms, *American Politics* (New York, 1947). For recent party votes in the House and Senate on principal bills and treaties, see J. Kieran (ed.), *The New Information Please Almanac 1948* (Garden City, N. Y., 1948), pp. 93–99.

nine-tenths of the voting members of a party were on the same side of the question as "party votes," he drew certain definite conclusions as to the solidarity of the party in legislative affairs. The amount of strict party voting is usually below 50 per cent. While this may seem a small percentage, other analyses have produced much the same result, and it is perfectly clear that the bulk of legislation is either nonpartisan or bipartisan in character. Even in the bitter partisan battles in the Congresses of Franklin D. Roosevelt's second administration, strict party voting was very rare. On such important legislation as the Taft-Hartley Labor Act, President Truman could not control his own party members in Congress.

It is true that the quantitative test is not wholly an accurate one, and that the significance of party measures cannot be gauged without taking into consideration the relative importance of the bills studied. A major issue determined by the party through party action may be of far greater importance than a score of minor issues where no party lines are drawn. Yet even then it will be found that the bulk of the more important laws are not enacted by anything like a party vote, and the party measures, as such, are often passed by seriously diminished party votes.

In the state legislatures the caucus is also the official organ for the expression of the party will. But here party lines are even less sharply drawn than in Washington, and the opportunity for party leadership is not great. The governor is relied upon, if he is a leader, to bring forward a program and rally around him a legislative majority from whatever party obtainable. Lowell's figures, readily verified by inspection of the work of any legislature, show the following percentages of party votes: Ohio, 3 per cent; Illinois, 3½ per cent; Pennsylvania, 2 to 3 per cent; Massachusetts, 1 to 6 per cent. Stuart Rice worked out ingenious indexes of party cohesion and party likeness which have been used to study trends in party discipline. His index of cohesion is the difference between the per cent for and the per cent against a given measure in a given party. Thus, if 50 per cent vote "aye" and 50 per cent vote "no," there is an absence of party discipline as 50 minus 50 equals zero. If 75 per cent vote "aye" and 25 per cent "no," the index of cohesion is 50. His index of likeness is obtained by subtracting the difference between the "aye" percentages of the two parties from 100. Thus, if the Republicans vote

80 per cent "aye" and the Democrats 10 per cent "aye," the index of likeness is 30 ($100 - [80 - 10] = 100 - 70 = 30$). Using this measure a number of investigators have corroborated Lowell's findings. Party discipline in American legislative bodies is low and it has shown no tendency to increase. The remaining part of the legislation is local, special, or nonpartisan in character. In states, too, may be found boss control reaching out to deal with the most important topics of state legislation, and reducing many of the ostensible lawmakers to the rank of pawns. The chief occasion for party leadership—the selection of a party choice for United States senator—no longer exists, since the senators are directly chosen.

In local legislative bodies such as city councils, county boards, or other similar bodies the caucus is little used; or it is as likely to be a bipartisan caucus as a party one. Such a caucus is seldom looked to for direction in party or public policy.

To the extent, however, that the caucus is employed it does give the stronger and more experienced congressman or legislator a position of strategic advantage which he may be able to utilize for personal or factional advantage. Party members may absent themselves from their party caucus, but at a heavy party disadvantage in the way of regularity; while if they come in they are likely to be outmaneuvered by the older and more crafty managers, more habituated to caucus methods of warfare.

It is possible that the caucus may be used in the service of the rank and file of the party and in the promotion of the public good, and there are instances in state and national affairs in which this has been the case. Examples of this are found in the use of the Republican caucus by Governor Lowden of Illinois in the advancement of party measures of importance and, in the national field, in the administrations of Presidents Wilson and Franklin D. Roosevelt.

It is not, however, the purpose of this study to appraise the value of the caucus, but to point out its significance as a means of formulating the position of the party upon public policies. There can be no question that for this purpose it still possesses great importance.

Nor is it within the scope of this inquiry to examine in detail the intricate processes of parliamentary procedure, as this would lead to the broad field of legislative methods and results. The tortuous ways of partisan and bipartisan leadership and direction offer an interesting and important study which cannot well be undertaken here [27] without a discussion of the parliamentary arrangements. Among the significant officials, however, are the steering committee, the floor leader, and the whip—all selected by the party caucus, directly or indirectly, by methods varying somewhat from session to session.

Of these the floor leader [28] and the whip are more nearly parliamentary officials. The floor leader is concerned with the immediate direction of the party forces in parliamentary struggles on the floor, and may or may not be directly concerned with the larger question of party policy. Practically he is likely to have a very significant influence upon the general direction of party strategy as well as the more specific problem of party tactics. The party whip is entrusted with the rallying of party members at times when party votes are taken—a task requiring diplomacy as well as energy. The steering committee is charged with the general supervision of party interests, and may at times take the place of the party caucus. But in such cases the leadership of the committee must depend upon the power and adroitness of its personnel, rather than upon the technical authority of the position.

Behind these arrangements, which vary somewhat from session to session, lies the power of the older, more experienced, and more powerful political leaders of Congress. At times they are overthrown, as in the uprising against Cannonism, but in the main their power over the legislative interpretation of the party position is very great. They are checked, however, by the great power of the President, by the force of public opinion, and by the threat of insurgency within their own ranks.

The power of the Speaker in the House of Representatives is a notable feature of the party development in Congress. Ample in the days of Henry Clay, it developed after 1899 under Republican Speaker Reed, Democratic Speaker Crisp, and Republican "Uncle Joe" Cannon, until the authority of the presiding officer of the House became second only to that of the President. Arbitrary use of this great power by Cannon led to its overthrow in 1910, but the speaker

---

[27] A general discussion of this topic is given in Riddick, *Congressional Procedure.*
[28] Walker, *op. cit.*

still retains a position of great prestige and significance in the party system, although shorn of much of his earlier power. In state legislatures the speaker still retains much of the older authority and continues to be a dominating figure in legislation.[29] Indeed in some cases he exercises power more arbitrarily, if possible, than the federal speaker in his palmiest days. In most states he still retains the power to appoint all committees.

In reviewing the function of the party as a formulator of issues, it appears that numerous limitations must be made upon the theory of the party's activity as a policy determiner. The party does serve to hold together men of like mind upon some broad question of public policy, such as the tariff, the currency, or regulation of business. It may sift and try out many issues and finally focus public attention upon some outstanding question. No other agency in the community is as actively engaged in this process of political expression as is the party. But the commonly neglected factors are of great significance in determining what the party actually does. Of these the most important are: (1) the large number of nonparty issues; (2) the activity of the nonparty groups in public affairs; and (3) the tendency of the party to appeal to its record, its general "character," rather than to specific promises regarding the future.

The two major parties find it very difficult to take a decided stand upon many important issues because such action might hopelessly divide their followers. On two issues alone, it is possible to have four different combinations. Take, for instance, reciprocal trade agreements, and aid to schools. There are the international trade advocates who favor aid to schools, those hostile to trade agreements who favor aid to schools, the international trade advocates who oppose aid to schools, and those who are hostile to both trade agreement policy and aid to schools. As the number of issues increases the more difficult it becomes to divide the voters into two distinct groups.

Most issues are not decided by the parties, but by public opinion. Nonpartisanship and bipartisanship (both as developed by the ma-

[29] See W. B. Graves, *American State Government* (New York, 1941); A. W. Bromage, *State Government and Administration in the United States* (New York, 1936); A. N. Holcombe, *State Government in the United States* (New York, 1931), Chap. IX.

chines and by their opponents) have deeply affected the whole party system. So true is this that we may conclude that the bulk of "political" problems are not decided by the parties as such. Here the activity of the nonparty groups is of prime significance, for it is clear that new groupings are taking the place of the political party at this point. Special and general organizations are doing the active work of preparing plans, conducting propaganda, and driving forward the movements for new social policies. Party leaders and organizations still play the most important roles in this process, but they have no exclusive place in the formation of national and local policies. Parties may be said to furnish the machinery of legislation and administration, but other organized interests supply most of the steam.

The party also tends to fall back upon its record of past performance rather than its promises for the future. It tends to attribute to itself and to its rivals certain general characteristics, certain tendencies of a somewhat permanent nature. A reputation of this type, as in the case of an individual, may save the labor of an elaborate argument as to intentions and capacities. If there is doubt regarding the proposed plan or disagreement in the party ranks, the tendency is to gloss over or compromise the troublesome issue and fall back upon the general record of the party, upon the specific character of its leaders, or the personality of its candidate or candidates. In about half of the campaigns this has been almost the only dividing issue, and at all times, even when there were sharp divisions of opinion upon some specific question such as the tariff, the general tendency or disposition of the party has been of the very greatest importance in the determination of the allegiance of the voters. The party achievements, real or fancied, are as often the basis of campaigns as are abstract questions of public policy. Records and tendencies may be at times a serious embarrassment to a party, but they are also valuable assets. New parties are weak because of the lack of these party habits which automatically lead the voter to support the ticket and program of the party.

In the party process, as in the larger political process, we may observe the appeal:

(1) To the advantage of individuals or groups
(2) To fundamental feelings, emotions, and predispositions

(3) To some rationalization of the proposed policy in terms of custom, tradition, religion, or general principle

Both the emotional appeal and the appeal to rationalization may be merely thinly veiled propaganda directed toward the evident self-interest of individuals or groups, sometimes both in primitive societies, and in modern times so thinly veiled as to be almost transparent, but still serving the useful purpose of advancing beyond avowed self-interest and open force. In these rationalizations there is a double tribute to:

(1) The group interest as paramount—in our day to democracy

(2) Knowledge or science in the effort to reach action through appeal to a "principle" or "law," which may be defective but is phrased in terms of logic and analogy, of reason even though diluted.

Thus the appeal is made to the special interest of a few and to the general interest of all or of many.

The analysis of the argument regarding the tariff, or currency, or labor legislation shows how these various elements are represented and combined. In each there is an appeal to the direct pecuniary advantage of special groups—the officeholding and certain industrial groups. In each there is an appeal to the general group-protective instinct in terms of national defense, honor, prosperity, prestige. In each there is a rationalization of the proposed policy in terms of some economic law or political principle which is asserted to be of universal validity.

CHAPTER V

ECONOMIC INFLUENCES
UPON PARTY PREFERENCES

"So strong is this propensity of mankind to fall into mutual animosities, that, where no substantial occasion presents itself, the most frivolous and fanciful distinctions have been sufficient to kindle their unfriendly passions and excite their most violent conflicts. But the most common and durable source of factions has been the various and unequal distribution of property . . . A landed interest, a manufacturing interest, a mercantile interest, a moneyed interest, with many lesser interests, grow up of necessity in civilized nations, and divide them into different classes actuated by different sentiments and views. The regulation of their various and interfering interests forms the principal task of modern legislation, and involves the spirit of party and faction in the necessary and ordinary operations of the government."
—James Madison, *The Federalist*, number 10.

MOTIVES

THE MOTIVES THAT INDUCE PARTY POLITICAL ACTION ARE MANY AND varied. Bryce enumerates four party forces which he terms sympathy, imitation, cooperation, pugnacity.[1] In the sweep of human interests almost everyone at some time or other becomes interested in some aspect of politics. But those who are continuously active may be placed in a group by themselves. They may be moved by some direct and personal economic advantages, as a job or a privilege; or by the advantage of their occupation or group, as the capitalist or the farmer or the union man; or they may look to some less direct economic advantage, as in the case of the lawyer who looks to the widening of his clientage. On the other hand there are considerable numbers of persons who are moved to political activity by an unusual socio-political sensitiveness—by a high sense of civic sympathy and responsibility, even though this may be accompanied by direct or indirect economic loss.

[1] James Bryce, *Modern Democracies* (New York, Macmillan Company, 1923), I, 112.

In the case of one moved primarily either by a direct personal economic gain or by the feeling of political responsibility, there will probably be found other factors of significance. There may be an element of social distinction or prestige; there may be a sense of power; there may be the joy of combat; there may be satisfaction in a wide area of human contacts; there may be satisfaction of the sense of organization on a large scale; there may be satisfaction of self-expression in oratory or argument; there may be the personal sense of loyalty to a leader who has inspired a follower to enthu- siasm. A long series of appeals may be made to qualities of human nature which lead men to group activity.

It must be observed, however, that politics must compete with others forms of activity in which similar motives may operate, as the social, the religious, the economic, the professional—all of which provide for somewhat similar types of gratifications. Party action is often the field of those who, as the phrase goes, "like the game," who consider it "the great game," who regard it as an interesting and absorbing form of activity. This may arise from no immediate economic or class advantage, although it is likely to be found ac- companying such advantage, apart from any particular sense of social or political responsibility. In fact, partisans of this type might quickly disavow any such feeling or purpose. They may be "tough- minded" rather than "tender-minded," and repudiate altruistic ideas altogether. They are to be sharply distinguished from those who shrink from human contacts, who have neither facility in expression or mass organization, nor joy in combat of this type; or who look upon the party forms of activity as relatively futile, or even regard them as common, corrupt on a low level.

A considerable amount of party activity is that of persons who are out to win for "our side," without regard to what the side is— for victory in the sporting sense of the term. Since the lines are drawn and the rules are fixed, they set out to win the contest, and often put a prodigious amount of energy into the struggle. They re- joice in the defeat of the enemy and are elated over their group vic- tory, although they may be fully aware that no particular issue is at stake or that one candidate may be as good as the other. They sup- port the party as they support the "team," hoping to win, but not disappointed if a good game fight is made. This is a feature of American party contests often overlooked by observers who take the attitude and expressions of the players more seriously than do the players themselves. If the apathy of the voters is at times inexplicable, their enthusiasm and energy is equally surprising on other occasions when an immense latent fund of interest is suddenly applied.

This attitude may often be distinguished from that of the intensely partisan voter, who takes no active part in the conduct of party affairs but religiously votes the party ticket, as a solemn rite. Many of these voters take the issues and the candidates most seriously, as distinguished from those who enjoy the "game," and gravely regard the success of the party ticket as closely connected with the welfare of the nation and of the social and political order in general. Here habit has deepened into conviction and the party activities have become a type of second religion.

The motives of party action, then, are numerous and varied, running a wide gamut of possibilities. In the main they are included under the following: personal or group interest, economic or otherwise, habit, family loyalty, response to leaders, the sense of community responsibility, the response to the appeal of the formula, specific gratification of desire for political-social contacts.

GROUPINGS

The broad basis of the party is the interests, individual or group, usually the latter, which struggle to translate themselves into types of social control acting through the political process of government.[2] Sometimes these interests work in the open and sometimes in the dark; they formulate principles and policies; they create an environment out of which comes the "hereditary voter"; they are the material out of which come leaders and chiefs, as well as the organizations and managing groups found in all permanent parties and indeed in all continuing groups.

Of great significance in the composition of any political party are the numerous types of social groupings. These are fundamental in

[2] A very useful discussion of this subject is found in A. N. Holcombe, *Political Parties of Today* (New York, 1924). See also V. O. Key, *Politics, Parties and Pressure Groups* (New York, 1947); V. B. Boothe, *The Political Party as a Social Process* (Philadelphia, 1923); W. B. Graves, *Readings in Public Opinion* (New York, 1928); and P. H. Odegard and E. A. Helms, *American Politics* (New York, 1947).

any scientific study of the political party, and too great emphasis cannot be laid upon them. Social scientists are just beginning to make an analysis of these groups, without a careful consideration of which we are likely to obtain an artificial picture of the political party, often far afield from the actual facts of party life.[3] The practical action is never guilty of omission of the study of social groupings, but the students of politics have sometimes proceeded as if parties were working in a social vacuum. It has even been assumed at times that in the United States there are no "classes" as in other countries and that therefore the necessity for considering such topics is absent. It is true that in the United States there are less deeply rooted class differences and less sharply defined types of class consciousness than in older nations, but social groupings are as universal here as anywhere.[4] The mobility of class ties and tendencies only makes their consideration all the more necessary to a fundamental knowledge of the party system.

Of great importance are the groupings that arise from common occupation, from common racial or national origin, from common religious belief, from common residence or localism.[5] What is the relation of these groups to the political parties? To what extent do they determine the allegiance of voters to the parties? Within broad

[3] Consult B. L. Smith, H. D. Lasswell, and R. D. Casey, *Propaganda, Communication and Public Opinion* (Princeton, 1946); C. E. Merriam, *Political Power: Its Composition and Incidence* (New York, 1934); H. D. Lasswell, *World Politics and Personal Insecurity* (New York, 1935), and *Politics: Who Gets What, When, How* (New York, 1936); A. N. Holcombe, *The New Party Politics* (New York, 1933), and *The Middle Classes in American Politics* (Cambridge, 1940).

Early studies of the significance of social groupings were made by the great political scientists, Johannes Althusius, *Politics Systematically Treated* (1609), and Jean Bodin, *The State* (1576); in later times by Otto Gierke in his notable treatise *Das Deutsche Genossenschaftsrecht* (Berlin, 1868). G. Ratzenhofer's study of this subject in his *Wesen und Zweck der Politik* (Leipzig, 1893) is freely interpreted in A. W. Small's *General Sociology* (Chicago, 1905), Chap. XXII, and followed by A. F. Bentley in *The Process of Government* (Chicago, 1908).

[4] See C. E. Merriam, *American Political Ideas* (New York, 1926), Chap. I; also his *Civic Education in the United States* (New York, 1934) and *The Making of Citizens* (Chicago, 1931). See also W. E. Binkley, *American Political Parties: Their Natural History* (New York, 1943).

[5] For an analysis of a variety of influences related to voting behavior in a metropolitan community, see H. F. Gosnell, *Machine Politics: Chicago Model* (Chicago, 1937), Chap. V.; H. F. Gosnell, *Grass Roots Politics* (Washington, D. C., 1942). For an earlier study, see W. F. Ogburn and N. S. Talbot, "A Measurement of the Factors in the Presidential Election of 1928," *Social Forces*, VIII (December, 1929), 175–183.

lines these questions can be answered, and the answers will throw light on the nature of the parties and on the meaning of the whole party process.

Common occupation is an important element in the composition of our parties. What, then, is the attitude of the agricultural, business, and industrial groups toward the party system? Or what predispositions or tendencies may be found among them? Obviously not all or any of these groups are members of any one party, but what general tendencies are found among them? [6]

Since the Civil War the dominant groups have been producer-minded groups, business, agriculture, and labor. The large-scale business group has been most aggressive and successful politically. While consumer groupings have been powerful numerically, they have not been able to organize permanently for successful political effort. Broadly speaking, these groups tend to follow the line of their interests, varying as situations vary; but certain habits, customs, and tendencies are established, which are revealed by an examination of the party activities of these groups.

Business

The larger business interests, centering in the northeastern section of the country, were identified with the Repubican party during the Civil War and have continued to follow the party in power since then. With the protective tariff and later the currency question, taxation, and the regulation of business and labor as national issues, they were strongly inclined to Republicanism. In the South they continued to be Democratic, because of the race question, but the bulk of the large-scale business was and is in the northern section of the nation.[7]

[6] A. N. Holcombe, "Present-day Characteristics of American Political Parties," in E. B. Logan (ed.), *The American Political Scene* (New York, 1936); D. Brogan, *Government of the People* (New York, 1933); S. Rice, *Farmers and Workers in American Politics* (New York, 1924), and *Quantitative Methods in Politics* (New York, 1928).

[7] G. Gallup, *The Gallup Political Almanac for 1948* (Princeton, 1948); B. J. Hendrick, *The Age of Big Business* (New Haven, 1921); H. L. Childs, *Labor and Capital in National Politics* (Columbus, 1930); J. T. Flynn, *Graft in Business* (New York, 1931); Odegard and Helms, *op. cit.*; S. M. Rosen, *Political Process* (New York, 1935); Matthew Josephson, *The Robber Barons* (New York, 1934); National Resources Committee, *The Structure of the American Economy* (Washington, D. C., 1939).

Yet these larger commercial interests were not at all partisan in nature. On the contrary they followed the lines of authority and power. As Mr. Havemeyer of the sugar trust testified before Congress: "In Republican States we contribute to the Republicans, and in Democratic States to the Democrats." And in doubtful states? "There," said he, "we contribute to both sides." Similar was the testimony of Mr. McCall in the New York insurance investigation, and that of Samuel Insull of Chicago before the Reed Committee investigating campaign expenditures in 1926. The national government being Republican, they tended to ally themselves with the ruling powers, but under Cleveland they were not hostile to Democracy of a conservative type. Particularly in recent years the bankers, brokers, iron and steel magnates, and large-scale manufacturers have contributed heavily to Republican campaign funds, whereas some oil, liquor, and tobacco interests have given financial support to the Democrats.[8] In Democratic states, the powerful corporate interests were Democratic, as in Virginia, Texas, Alabama, and other states, where railroad and other similar "combines" flourished in proportion to the material for their growth, rather than with relation to a particular party.

The fact was that the powerful corporations coming to life and strength struggled to control both parties and to make their will felt in both. In 1912 they were as strong in Baltimore when Mr. Bryan opposed them as they were in Chicago in 1932 when Mr. Roosevelt was opposing them. Party affiliations, attitudes, traditions, prejudices, and organizations were secondary to the prime purpose of the group at any particular time, and this group was also capable of quicker action than any of the other groups, quicker than the farmers, the laborers, or the middle class. The very fact that they were so powerful in the prosperous twenties made them all the more bitter about sharing power with agricultural and labor interests during the lean thirties.

Large-scale business was then predominantly Republican, except in the South where it was Democratic. Other business, although not of the very largest scale, was also likely to be Republican in

[8] Louise Overacker, *Presidential Campaign Funds* (Boston, 1946), and "Presidential Campaign Funds 1944," *American Political Science Review*, XXXIX (Oct., 1945), 899–925.

affiliation especially when the protective tariff was an issue or, the currency in question. It must be understood that reference is here made to a general tendency, not to a universal verdict. There were many notable personal exceptions to the broad drift described here. Of a hundred New England bankers not all are Republican, but the bulk of them are. And in the South they would be predominantly Democratic in affiliation. Perhaps of greater practical significance is the fact that they belonged to the conservative wing of both parties, and were more interested in conservatism in relation to business than in political parties. This conservatism of the business group was brought out dramatically in the 1936 campaign when two former Democratic presidential candidates, John W. Davis and Al Smith, joined the more conservative Republicans. Both were closely associated with Wall Street business interests at the time of their bolt, although Al Smith had, of course, been known as a liberal in his earlier days.

The salesmen, smaller merchants, clerks, unorganized salaried employees, and the professional groups tended to follow Republican lines in the northeastern and central states,[9] with very many exceptions, of course, and Democratic lines in the South, with the exception of the Negroes. In the West the lines are so confused as to make valuable generalization impossible. Here they have been inclined to follow insurgent or progressive leaders, whether Republican, Democratic, or representatives of the third parties, voting for Bryan or Roosevelt or Wilson or La Follette or Wallace, without great regard to party affiliations. They were against "monopolies," particularly the railroads at first, and later the trusts in general, or special representatives of them from time to time. Party habit looms larger in the political action of these groups than in the larger commercial interests which are capable of concentrating action much more quickly and adroitly than the unorganized groups under discussion. Yet at the same time it is from these elements that the intelligent

---

[9] H. D. Kitson, "Frequency of Republicans and Democrats among Eminent Americans," *Journal of Applied Psychology*, X (September, 1926), 341–345. On the basis of the examination of 1000 names from *Who's Who in America*, 1924–1925, he found that "among the eminent Americans who acknowledged party membership, Republicans are found to be more than twice as numerous as Democrats." In 1928 a poll of *Who's Who in America* was again made. Of the 9774 voting, 8510 or, 87 per cent were for Hoover.

"independent" vote has largely been recruited. There was no solidarity in the middle class, and they were pulled to the conservative and liberal wings of the larger parties and to independent movements.

The Gallup poll enables us to furnish certain sample breakdowns of the electorate that were formerly not available.[10] Gallup has indicated the following trends in the Democratic percentages of major party vote among professional and business groups: 48 per cent in 1936, 36 in 1940, and 41 in 1944. For the white collar workers he gives the following data: 61 per cent of major party vote Democratic in 1936, 48 in 1940, and 51 in 1944.[11] These figures indicate that the Democrats made some gains with business, professional, and white collar groups in 1944. These were wiped out, however, in the 1946 congressional elections.[12]

Our former colleague, Harold D. Lasswell, believes that the middle-income skill group, as he calls the middle class, has a definite mission in American politics:

"Plainly the middle-income skill groups have not yet found a common name; nor have they discerned the inner principle of sacrifice on which their unity depends; nor have they risen to the full comprehension of their historic destiny. In Europe their disunion has bred the politics of catastrophe; but in America there may be more time for the attainment of a common name, a common policy, and a common sense of political destiny." [13]

Agriculture

While the relative number and economic importance of the farmers have declined steadily since the closing of the frontier, the political importance of the group is still very great. The proportion of farmers among those gainfully employed shrank from over nine-tenths in Jefferson's time to about two-tenths in Franklin D. Roosevelt's time, but during the latter's first administration over half of the Congressmen came from rural districts.[14] Recently, with the

[10] See Chap. XVIII below.

[11] *The Gallup Political Almanac for 1948* (Princeton, 1948), p. 204; Wesley C. Clark, *Economic Aspects of a President's Popularity* (Philadelphia, 1943).

[12] National Institute of Public Opinion (Gallup poll).

[13] *Politics: Who Gets What, When, How* (New York, Whittlesey House, 1936), p. 173.

[14] Holcombe, "Present-day Characteristics of American Political Parties," *op. cit.*, p. 35.

passing of the hoe, the horse, and the buckboard, and the coming of the tractor, the combine, and the automobile, the farmers have been declining in absolute as well as relative numbers. The equal representation of the states in the Senate, however, and the general failure of the states to reapportion the congressional districts have entrenched agriculture in Congress.

The farmers as producers have a great variety of interests, many of which are conflicting. Thus the corn, wheat, and cotton growers produce more than this country can consume, and they are interested in the regulation of the total production and in the opening of new markets. On the other hand, the sugar and wool growers cannot meet the domestic demands and must compete with foreign producers in the absence of special governmental protection. In other words, the former groups are opposed to a high tariff and the latter favor such legislation. The dairymen, because of the perishable character of their product and its peculiar marketing problems, represent another set of interests.

In spite of their varied special interests, the farmers have certain problems in common. As purchasers of transportation services they have been interested in low rates; as sellers they have sought to increase their selling prices and diminish their selling costs; as borrowers they have worked for low interest charges and easy credit; and as individual producers they have been interested in the economic system of free enterprise. At various times the farmers have been attracted by wildcat banking schemes, inflationary monetary policies, cooperative marketing schemes, dumping, price supports, and plans for the restriction of total output. They are also highly tax conscious and are often willing to try substitutes for the general property tax.

The individualistic mentality of the farmer, fostered by the isolation in which he lives and works, has until recently retarded the development of farm organizations which could discover and promote common plans for action.

Among the farm organizations should be mentioned the Grange (National Grange of Patrons of Husbandry), founded in 1867 and now representing some of the more conservative-minded farmers; the Farmer's Educational and Cooperative Union of America, founded in 1902 and drawing its support largely from the more radical elements of the farm population; and the American Farm Bureau Federation, established in 1919 on the basis of pre-existing state and county farm bureaus which were interested in a vigorous but cautious farm policy. The political importance of the Farm Bureau Federation is revealed incidentally in the course of an administrative study made by one of our students, Dr. Baker,[15] who said:

"The rise of the county agent is an interesting and important development in the field of government. He serves at one and the same time as a representative of the federal, state, and county governments. In many states, he is also closely allied with a semi-private farm organization, the Farm Bureau, which he has in part built up. His function as an adult itinerant vocational teacher to carry forth and adapt the findings of the state agricultural colleges and the United States Department of Agriculture has been modified to enable him to assist in conducting national programs to meet major agricultural emergencies. The most recent of these emergencies, caused by the post-war depression, has necessitated drastic adaptations in county agent work to fit changing national objectives in agricultural policy. . . . Since 1933, he has served as a clearing house of information on the various federal programs available for farmers. In most sections he has also served as a promoter, adviser, semi-administrator, and even as an administrator of some of these programs in many counties."

Repeated efforts have been made to organize the farmers as a political party, but this has proved to be a difficult task.[16] The Greenback and the Populist parties were primarily agrarian movements, but their chief strength was found in the West and South. Although they carried counties and states, electing governors, legislatures, and senators, and at times choosing presidential electors, they were unable to develop qualities of solidarity and cohesion. They soon dissolved under the adroit attacks of the older parties who were able to absorb enough of their leaders and policies to leave the group helpless. Furthermore, the farming group never gave to these parties anything approaching unified support even in the West, while in the

[15] Gladys Baker, "The County Agent" (Ph.D. thesis, University of Chicago, 1938).
[16] See F. E. Haynes, *Third Party Movements since the Civil War* (Iowa City, 1916), and *Social Politics in the United States* (Boston, 1924); S. J. Buck, *The Agrarian Crusade* (New Haven, 1920), and *The Granger Movement* (Cambridge, 1913).

East the agricultural element remained indifferent to the efforts of their brethren in the other sections of the country.

The Progressive party of 1912 drew heavily upon the farming class, but failed to shake the party habit and allegiance of the rural sections in great areas of the country. Wilson in 1916 also was strongly supported by the farming constituencies for a variety of reasons, partly progressive and partly pacifist. The independent campaign of La Follette in 1924 drew much more heavily upon the farmer vote in the Northwest and the West, but was not strong enough to bring success in more than one state.

The prosperity of the twenties was not fully shared by the farmers, and the depression which started in 1929 found them in a weak position. So great was the disparity between the cash income and the real income of the farmers that by 1932 their plight called for desperate remedies. They were losing their farms at the time when their industry and skill were yielding the maximum production. Farm tenancy was growing by leaps and bounds. In a typical agricultural state the situation was described as follows: "There is imminent danger that Iowa will harvest this fall the biggest crop of farm mortgage closures, lost equities, and ruined farmers the state has ever known." [17] Farm strikes, mob violence, and a huge Democratic vote in 1932 and 1936 were some of the ways in which this discontent expressed itself.

The national administration under Roosevelt envisaged two solutions for the crisis of agriculture: (1) slashing tariffs, and/or (2) cutting total agricultural production. Since a gradual lowering of the tariffs would not regulate production at once and since the plight of the farmer was immediately pressing, the famous AAA (Agricultural Adjustment Administration) was put into operation. According to a public opinion poll this remedy was not popular with the voters as a whole,[18] but the other efforts of the administration to improve the lot of the farmer were received with greater favor. Roosevelt's popularity among the farmers was very high for a year following his second election, but in 1938, with the sagging of farm prices, it declined somewhat in the corn and wheat belts.

The outbreak of the war in Europe in 1939 brought a demand for American farm products which meant a rise in the price of those

---

[17] *Iowa Yearbook of Agriculture for 1932*, p. 6; Gosnell, *Grass Roots Politics*.
[18] Gallup poll of January, 1935, and August, 1937.

products and a period of relative prosperity for farmers. The Democrats in 1948 were still capitalizing on this prosperity in spite of a decline of their popularity as shown by a Gallup poll. According to Gallup's figures, the Democratic percentages in the farm vote were: 59 per cent in 1936, 54 per cent in 1940, 48 per cent in 1944, and 43 per cent in 1948.[19]

Labor

Although it has been estimated that there are more than thirty-five million nonagricultural employees in the United States,[20] it cannot be said that these wage earners are conscious as a group of their potential political power. In Great Britain, Australia, Belgium, and the Scandinavian countries the workers have organized powerful political parties which have from time to time held the balance of political power. American wage earners have been notorious for their disunity on economic as well as political questions. Lacking any well-defined political tradition, American labor has been divided along lines of industry, craft, section, color, immigrant heritage, type of organization, and skill.

One of the reasons for the relative inactivity of labor in American politics has been the slow growth of the trade union movement. In 1930 the largest of the labor organizations was the American Federation of Labor, a loose grouping of independent unions organized for the most part on a craft basis and containing altogether around three million members, or 10 per cent of the nonagricultural employees. While the years following saw a great increase in the strength of organized labor and the rise of a powerful rival organization, the Congress of Industrial Organizations, the combined membership of AFL and CIO did not bring the percentage of organized wage earners to that found in England and Australia.[21]

[19] *The Gallup Political Almanac for 1948*, p. 204. The 1948 figure was obtained from interviews in October and did not reflect later shifts to Truman.

[20] Leo Wolman, *Ebb and Flow in Trade Unionism* (New York, 1936), p. 116. See also H. A. Millis and R. E. Montgomery, *Labor's Progress and Some Basic Labor Problems* (New York, 1938), 3 vols.; Gosnell, *Democracy: Threshold of Freedom* (New York, 1948).

[21] J. R. Commons, "American Federation of Labor," in *Encyclopaedia of the Social Sciences*, II (1930), 26, estimates that industrial labor is 65 per cent organized in England and 60 per cent in Australia. If the reported figures for trade union membership in 1948 can be accepted (6,500,000 for the C.I.O., 7,500,000 for the AFL and 2,000,000 independents, totaling 16,000,000), this would be 45 per cent of the nonagricultural workers.

The older and more conservative section of labor as represented by AFL has not been vigorous in the unionization of the great mass of unskilled and semiskilled employees of the great production industries. It was not politically minded until recently. By and large the Federation has been a grouping of the better paid of the laboring classes, those highly skilled workingmen who could take advantage of their strategic position in the American economic system to demand special privileges for themselves. The building trades, the transportation workers, the skilled garment workers, the printers, and representatives of other highly trained trades and crafts have furnished the basis for the craft unions which make up the Federation. These craft unionists are so interested in their own welfare and in the preservation of their own special skills that they frequently quarrel among themselves in trying to claim this or that skilled occupation for their own group. The unskilled groups, which lack bargaining power and are more difficult to organize, have not been widely incorporated by the Federation. In the meantime, the growth of mass industries has made certain skilled trades obsolescent and has increased the number of semiskilled or unskilled operatives, which has reduced the relative magnitude of the number of employees who might possibly join one of the craft unions. In other words, the policy of the Federation has brought difficulties. This trouble was not unforeseen, since many labor leaders in the nineties and the early part of the twentieth century pointed out the need for industrial unionism, a type of labor organization which included all the workers of a given industry regardless of their particular skills.[22] The Industrial Workers of the World, which was formed in 1905, was committed to industrial unionism, and in certain industries it challenged the Federation with some success. IWW leaders have been persistent critics of the "capitalistic" Federation leaders on matters of doctrine, tactics and type of organization.[23]

The organization of Labor's Non-Partisan League in 1936 to aid President Roosevelt in his campaign for re-election marked a turning point in the attitude of organized labor toward participation in

[22] Daniel DeLeon and his associates organized the Socialist Trade and Labor Alliance in 1895. In 1898 the Western Labor Union proposed industrial unionism and independent political action.

[23] P. F. Brissenden, "Industrial Workers of the World," in *Encyclopaedia of the Social Sciences*, VIII, 13–18, and R. Chaplin, *Wobbly* (Chicago, 1948).

politics. Prior to that time the trade unionists had been guided in their political tactics by the "wobblies" (IWW), who eschewed all political methods, and by the philosophy of Samuel Gompers, who preferred the economic weapons of the strike, the boycott, and the union label to the uncertainties of American party politics. It is true that Gompers was very skillful as a lobbyist and that he worked hard to safeguard the interests of his constituents, but he was opposed to independent political action on the part of labor, and he limited the Federation's activities to those of the pressure type. The electoral motto of the Federation was: "Reward your friends and punish your enemies." An enemy was defined as one who voted in a hostile manner on legislation which concerned labor's right to organize, the conditions of work of certain special groups such as women and children, and other questions deemed important by the leaders.

The change in the political tactics of organized labor in 1936 was in part the result of the spectacular rise in the labor movement of John L. Lewis, president of the United Mine Workers of America. Contrary to popular opinion in the thirties, Lewis belonged as did Gompers and Green to the conservative wing of AFL.[24] While his union was more of an industrial union than some of the others in the Federation, this was the result of the peculiar conditions of work of the miners. Living in isolated communities, they have developed considerable class consciousness and depended less than other unions on the exploitation of particular skills. Lewis was never a "wobblie" and paid less attention to the radical labor movements of Europe than did Gompers. At the beginning of the New Deal the United Mine Workers union was in a very critical condition. Internecine warfare, unemployment, and development of new coal fields in the unorganized areas had reduced its membership to a low point. Lewis was the man who had the vision to take advantage of the labor provisions of the NRA (National Recovery Act), which recognized labor's right to organize. His men swept through the unorganized regions and for the first time brought the nonunion southern areas into the union fold. By the end of 1934 Lewis led the largest and most powerful union in the United States.

[24] Philip Taft, "John L. Lewis," in J. T. Salter (ed.), *The American Politician* (Chapel Hill, 1938), pp. 192 ff.

Encouraged by his success in his own field, Lewis reached out to organize the workers in the mass production industries which had been neglected by the Federation. Since the workers in these industries were largely semiskilled or unskilled, Lewis sought the privilege of trying to organize them on an industrial basis. The Federation leaders, however—William Green, Matthew Woll, and others—were not willing to relinquish the jurisdictional rights of the various craft unions which gave them the authority to organize certain types of workers regardless of industry. The struggle between the two points of view began within the ranks of the Federation, but it soon led to a split. In 1935 the Committee for Industrial Organizations (CIO) was established by Lewis of the United Mine Workers, Sidney Hillman of the Amalgamated Clothing Workers, David Dubinsky of the Ladies Garment Workers, and a number of other Federation leaders who felt that the time for decisive action had arrived. CIO unions were first suspended and then expelled from the Federation, but this did not stop their organizing efforts. Their determined drive on the unorganized workers in the steel, rubber, automobile, and electrical industries produced spectacular results which reached a climax in the famous sit-down strikes of 1937. The victories of that year made it possible for CIO unions to claim that their membership exceeded that of AFL.[25]

Labor's Non-Partisan League was organized before the split between AFL and CIO had been made definite, and it therefore appealed to both factions of the labor movement. Among the original founders of the League were AFL men. Lewis was also a founder, and after the election of 1936 his prominence in the League led the AFL executives to declare war on the League as well as on CIO. The attempts of the League to carry the municipal elections of Detroit, to control the nominations in Pennsylvania, and to set up other labor candidacies were unsuccessful, but in New York it seemed to hold the balance of power in state and municipal elections.

The executive committee of the Congress of Industrial Organizations established in July, 1943, the CIO Political Action Committee. PAC was formed in part as a protest against the antistrike Smith-Connally Act, which was passed over the President's veto, June 25, 1943. In its platform, *The People's Program for 1944,*

[25] *New York Times,* October 12, 1937.

PAC makes it abundantly clear that it regards political action as a duty. Said the *Program*:

"Everything must be done to mobilize nationwide support behind our Commander-in-Chief. It is our determination, as well as our duty, to make certain that the tears and blood of humanity shall not have been shed in vain. Ultimate victory, of which we are certain, must bring with it the assurance of lasting peace, the utter destruction of Fascism; the full realization of the Four Freedoms; and the development of an abundant life for the Common Man of this earth. The attainment of these goals will, in a great measure, be determined by the American people on November 7th, 1944 in the national elections. Those elections, will decide whether we can move forward with confidence to peace, freedom and security, or whether we will be thrown back into insecurity and want, imperialist conflict, Fascism, and inevitably, into a third World War. The CIO Political Action Committee has set itself the task of helping mobilize the American people to make that decision certain."

Among the public policies advocated by PAC in 1944 were the following in the foreign field: the ever closer cooperation among the governments and the peoples of the United Nations, the establishment of a general international organization open to membership by all peace-loving states, the establishment of international machinery to make long-term credits available to industrially backward nations, the extension of the right of asylum for persecuted minorities throughout the United Nations, adequate financing of the United Nations Relief and Rehabilitation Administration, and full labor representation on all international planning and administrative bodies. In the domestic field, PAC advocated that Congress adopt by joint resolution the President's New Bill of Rights contained in his message to Congress in January, 1944, that Congress establish a permanent National Planning Board, composed of representatives of industry, labor, and agriculture, and charged with the task of formulating plans to effectuate the New Bill of Rights, that the federal government endorse the principle of the guaranteed annual wage, that the full employment program be guaranteed by government with a prepared program of jobs at useful work, that the government take the necessary steps to assure every American a decent home at a cost within his means, that agricultural programs be designed to eliminate discrimination against rural areas, that an adequate program of government credits to small business be adopted, that practices on the part of monopolies and international cartels which restrict production, stifle fair competition, and hamper the full development of trade be outlawed, that the Wagner-Murray-Dingell Bill be passed, that equality of opportunity for education to every American be guaranteed, that a permanent Fair Employment Practices Committee with adequate appropriations and enforcement powers be established, that an anti-poll-tax bill be passed, and that the right to join labor unions of their own choosing must be guaranteed and protected for all wage earners.

A year before the 1944 election PAC set up its organization. Fourteen regional directors, responsible to the national headquarters in New York City, were appointed. The territory of each regional director covered several states; and in many states there were PAC organizations working out of the same headquarters as the state CIO councils. Local unions also had their own local political action committees.

In addition to PAC there was set up a National Citizens Political Action Committee which was "composed of a number of the leaders of the CIO and outstanding Americans outside of labor's ranks." Included on this new committee were political figures, authors, movie stars, farm leaders, educators, social workers, clergymen, and liberals of various shades. Honorable George W. Norris was honorary chairman and Freda Kirchway was one of the vice chairmen.

CIO endeavored to get the cooperation of AFL in its political endeavors, but it met with indifferent success. At its 1943 convention CIO declared:

"Whatever differences may divide labor on the industrial front, the overwhelming majority of the leadership and membership of every branch of the labor movement is in agreement upon our political program and objectives, and no barriers should be permitted to stand in the way of joint or parallel action in the political field with the unions of the AFL, the railroad brotherhoods, and unaffiliated organizations."

To this plea and others like it, President Green of AFL replied:

"We cannot afford to tie up with any political party or to become identified with a political party. Experience has shown that the interests of labor are promoted by supporting candidates for office whose records show them to be sympathetic with labor and supporters of labor's legislative program, and to oppose those who are known to be against us, regardless of party affiliation."

A number of AFL affiliates, however, international unions and state federations, endorsed President Roosevelt for re-election. Notable among these was the International Brotherhood of Teamsters, whose president, Daniel J. Tobin, was made head of the labor division of the Democratic national committee. Dan Tobin did not hesitate to cooperate with PAC.

John L. Lewis continued to oppose Roosevelt in 1944 as he had in 1940, but the rank and file of the miners did not follow Lewis' political leadership in 1944 any more than they did in 1940.

Before the election questions were raised as to whether the support of PAC would be a help or a hindrance to the Democrats. Sidney Hillman and PAC were subjected to vigorous counterpropaganda from the Republican Vice Presidential candidate on down which used anti-New York, antiforeign, and anticommunist slogans. Even some of the trade unionists joined in using such slogans. Said one labor weekly:

"Perhaps you would like to know the strongest antilabor force in America today. It is the C.I.O. Political Action Committee. The Communist affiliations of many of the key figures in the Political Action Committee will be thoroughly exposed."

When the election returns came in, it was apparent that the labor vote had been crucial in swinging the key states to the Democratic column. The margin between the two major parties was so close in the industrial states that any lack of enthusiasm on the part of labor would have been fatal to the Democratic chances. In New York State, where labor had parties of its own—the American Labor party and the Liberal party—it was clear to all that Roosevelt could not have won without the labor vote. In Michigan and Illinois the result hinged on the large vote piled up in the metropolitan centers. Once again John L. Lewis showed his inability to carry the members of his union with him in his political opposition to Roosevelt. In the mining areas of Pennsylvania, West Virginia, Kentucky, and Illinois, the Democratic ticket won as in 1940. The election showed that when labor leaders support a candidate who is popular with the rank and file of the unions, they can, with effective organization, help get out the vote and thus influence the result of a close election.

The Republican victories in the 1946 congressional elections meant that the Eightieth Congress was organized by the Republicans. While the Taft-Hartley Labor Management Relations Act of 1947 which was passed over President Truman's veto received many Democratic votes in Congress, President Truman made the passage of the law an issue in the 1948 campaign. So bitter was the opposition of labor leaders to this law that both AFL and CIO heads endorsed President Truman's candidacy. The Political Action Committee of CIO actively supported President Truman and so did Labor's League for Political Education, the political arm of the AFL. Organized labor undoubtedly contributed to President Truman's victory at the polls.

Various appeals have been made to labor by all the great parties. Republicans have declared that protective tariff meant high wages, that the gold standard signified prosperity, that the election of their party meant the "full dinner pail" and prosperity. In 1908 Gompers appeared before both of the major party conventions with Labor's Bill of Rights. An examination of the two platforms for that year shows that he got a sympathetic hearing in the Democratic convention but not in the Republican.[26] The Democratic party until 1928 held that the tariff was the "mother of trusts," that free silver meant higher wages, that Democratic rule meant better terms for the laborer. President Truman denounced the Taft-Hartley Act. Socialists have earnestly urged the importance of standing together as a class for the ultimate control of the government.

According to the Gallup poll the trend in Democratic percentages among labor voters has been as follows in recent years: 74 per cent in 1936, 66 per cent in 1940, 62 per cent in 1944, and 50 per cent in 1948. While according to the polls President Truman was less popular with manual workers and union members than was President Roosevelt, his vote among the labor element was equal to the combined Dewey and Wallace vote.[27]

[26] K. H. Porter, *National Party Platforms* (New York, The Macmillan Company, 1924).

[27] *The Gallup Political Almanac for 1948* and Public Opinion News Service, release for August 11, 1948.

The Socialist party has presented for many years a carefully prepared program, dealing with the industrial demands of the workers. Yet the platform of the Socialist party has been largely ignored by the working-class group, which has failed to respond to the appeal made specifically to industrial workers. Until 1936 the laborers in great industrial centers in states like New York or Pennsylvania or Illinois were quite as likely to vote the Republican national ticket as the Democratic, and they did not show great interest in the Socialist or Communist programs. However, in 1936 it became clear that the New Deal with its liberal labor program was attracting the labor vote.

We may assume that the geographical distribution of this strongly Democratic labor vote should resemble that of trade union membership. Organized labor is concentrated in the following states: New York, Illinois, Pennsylvania, Michigan, Ohio, Massachusetts, California. The politicians of industrial states must now reckon with this large labor element.

Repeated attempts have been made to unite the urban-industrial group with the agrarian in a political party, but thus far without success.[28] This was the aim of the Greenback party, of the Populists, of the Progressives, of the Farmer-Labor party, and of La Follette in 1924, but in none of these instances was the project carried through.[29] It has not been found possible to formulate a definite program upon which the various elements might unite. The Greenback issue was not sufficiently strong to win general support, and later, when the free silver idea became widely popular, the Democratic party took it up and absorbed the Populists.[30] Likewise the monopoly issue was a bond of union, but this was only perfunctorily taken up by both of the major parties. The passage of legislation providing for control of railroads and trusts prevented organization of a solid bloc of urban-industrial elements centering on this policy as a common issue. In 1920 another attempt was made by the Farmer-Labor

[28] Rice, *Farmers and Workers in American Politics.*

[29] The details may be followed in the interesting studies of the parallel movements of the farmers and the laborer in Buck, *The Agrarian Crusade*, and John R. Commons, *History of Labor in the United States* (New York, 1918).

[30] The Populist platform of 1892 looked to an effective union of the agrarian-industrial groups: "The union of the labor forces of the United States this day consummated shall be permanent and perpetual; may its spirit enter into all hearts for the salvation of the Republic and the uplifting of mankind."

party to combine the urban-agricultural groups into a political group. The program included special provisions regarding the promotion of agricultural prosperity and labor's bill of rights, while a bond of common interest was found in the declaration in favor of public ownership and operation of all public utilities and natural resources.[31] This program was worked out by representatives of organized labor, organized agriculture, and various liberals, and was carefully designed to bring about a fusion of the middle class and other groups with organized labor in the cities. The program was wrecked by disagreements in the convention itself, and was weakly supported by the voters in the campaign.

These groups have encountered great difficulties in attracting the leadership of a notable personality. The formidable names of Judge David Davis in 1872 and Judge Gresham in 1892 were canvassed, but they were not available. Even the Progressive party of 1912 under the notable leadership of Roosevelt was unable to make permanent progress, and after one campaign was dissolved. In 1924 another attempt was made to unite these elements, this time around a powerful and experienced personality in the shape of the elder La Follette. Five million votes were polled, but only one state was carried. In 1948 Henry A. Wallace tried to unite farmers and workers, but like his predecessors he had little success.

Thus far the diversities of interests between producers and consumers, in cities and on the farms, the different attitudes toward organization of labor, and the competitive programs of the larger parties have made it impossible for a farmer-labor political party to make headway. The common insurgency of these groups, however, makes a combination not impossible, given an issue and a personality as a candidate. They have in common a deep-seated antipathy to domination by plutocratic influences, whether in rural districts or in the urban community, and they constantly struggle to express this in concrete political results.

[31] In a letter to Will Hays (1918) Theodore Roosevelt said: "New issues are going to force themselves into American politics. . . . Transportation, price fixing, rigid public control if not ownership of mines, forests and water ways. And if the Republican party takes the ground that the world must be the same old world, the Republican party is lost. There can be no doubt but that labor must have a new voice in the management of industrial affairs."—J. B. Bishop, *Theodore Roosevelt and His Time* (New York, 1920), II, 446.

CHAPTER VI

NONECONOMIC INFLUENCES
UPON PARTY PREFERENCES

"For in the United States sectionalism has involved more than merely the control of the politics of each region by the strongest economic element in it. The further and distinctive characteristic has been the collaboration of diverse interests related by neighborhood."—Arthur W. Macmahon, "Political Parties in the United States," *Encyclopaedia of the Social Sciences* (New York, The Macmillan Company, 1933), XI, 598.

SECTIONALISM

SOCIAL INTERESTS, WHETHER ECONOMIC, RACIAL, OR RELIGIOUS, MAY center in particular territorial areas and thus add the sectional feeling to the group sentiment.[1] Where this is true the sentiment strikes its roots still more deeply into the party soil, and party action becomes more significant. If race, class, and geography combine, we have a very powerful political combination such as the "Solid South." Furthermore, our system of representation is based chiefly upon local or neighborhood representation, although it is differently developed in different sections and states.

There is a *jus soli* of the party as well as a *jus sanguinis*. Geography as well as race determine party adherence in many instances. Sectional analyses of parties show this plainly. There are well-defined territorial areas almost exclusively controlled by one party or the other. The most notable illustration of this is seen in the South, where eleven states, with over one-fifth of the total population, have been under Democratic control since reconstruction. On the other

[1] H. F. Gosnell, *Grass Roots Politics* (Washington, D. C., 1942), and *Machine Politics: Chicago Model* (Chicago, 1935); W. Diamond, "Urban and Rural Voting in 1896," *American Historical Review*, XLVI (1941), 281–305; F. J. Turner, *The Frontier in American History* (New York, 1920), and his "Sections and Nation," *Yale Review*, October, 1922; Ellen C. Semple, *American History and Its Geographic Conditions* (Boston, 1903); R. G. Wellington, *The Political and Sectional Influence of the Public Lands* (Cambridge, 1914).

hand, as Holcombe has ably demonstrated, there have been many elections in which there were more solid Republican congressional districts than there were Democratic.[2] In New England and in the Central West, examples of continuous Republican control for given periods are found. Maine, New Hampshire, and Vermont are almost steadily Republican. Republican traditions are also strong in Kansas, Nebraska, and the Dakotas. In the election of 1948, of the 531 votes in the Electoral College, 138 were practically decided in advance. This was an unusually low number and this fact made it hard to predict the election. In the absence of a political revolution the political complexion of these states could be predicted. Even "landslides" like the Democratic triumph in 1912, the overwhelming Republican victory of 1920, or the Democratic victory of 1936 do not change greatly the relative position of the states with reference to a given party. On the other hand, in 1932 many of the Republican strongholds in the North and West were captured by the Democrats. In this key election, twenty-six states shifted from the Republican to the Democratic column, to be followed by four others at the next election.

To some extent these sectional groupings are based upon local or sectional pride and rivalry. There is a type of sectional consciousness on a certain scale. There are great areas with a more or less developed local interest and pride, such as the East, the South, the West, and the smaller areas such as New England, the Middle West, the Northwest, the Southwest, the Coast. Within certain limits leaders or policies of any of these sections attract a degree of enthusiasm or interest as champions of the immediate locality. The eastern candidate or the western candidate is popular in the East or the West for local reasons; or the program or policy that is labelled "eastern" or "western" attracts a number of followers on the one hand and arouses a certain distrust on the other. Theodore Roosevelt was said to owe some of his strength to the fact that he was "an Eastern man with Western manners and ideas." Other leaders have been "western" men with "eastern ideas." East and West, North and South stand in contrast, and these contrasts often have a distinct political significance.

But sectionalism is strongest politically when it is not merely sen-

[2] A. N. Holcombe, *Political Parties of Today* (New York, 1924), Chap. IV.

timental but is allied with some specific issue which finds a local seat in a particular geographical location. The strongest case of this is seen in the South where a combination of circumstances—the race issue, bitter memories of the reconstruction period, the development of cotton as the chief crop of the region and a main item in our export trade, and religious homogeneity—has produced an intensity and solidarity of party interest which for the present eliminates the two-party system altogether. The rivalry between East and West is also based upon something more substantial than local pride, although this is a factor. There are differences in economic interest which in some cases may cause wide political differences. This was particularly true of the currency question for a generation. The West was inclined toward Greenbackism and free silver, while the East favored the gold standard. The larger element of the creditor class was in the East and of the debtor group in the West. The impulse to railroad regulation also came largely from the West, as producer and shipper, and the same may be said of the demands for corporate regulation and for tariff revision. In all these cases the economic interests of the East and the West conflicted to some extent. Or again the demand for the direct election of senators and for the income tax was in the main western in its origin, although neither of these measures was a distinct party issue at the time of its final passage.

At least three great campaigns, those of Jefferson, Jackson, and Wilson (1916), showed a fairly clear alignment of the West and Southwest against the East.[3] In these cases the territorial area, the interest of the smaller farmers and traders, and the Democratic program coincided.[4] The progressive movements have usually come from the West (although the definition of "the West" has varied in the last generation). Greenbackism, Populism, the insurgent Republican movement, the Progressive movements, all derived their main strength in the Mississippi Valley or west of it, where opposition to the "money power" and to Wall Street is most pronounced. On the other hand the urban industrial centers of the sections farther east

[3] See maps in W. E. Dodd, *Expansion and Conflict* (Chicago, 1915); also in C. O. Paullin, *Atlas of the Historical Geography of the United States* (New York, 1932); E. E. Robinson, *The Presidential Vote* (Stanford University, 1934), and *They Voted for Roosevelt* (Stanford University, 1947).

[4] Wilson also received strong support from certain urban-industrial sections.

may be centers of socialism and of economic doctrines more radical than those usually held by the western farmer group. Many of the workers in the industrial sections of the East find the "progressive" doctrines too mild for their taste.

A little analysis shows, of course, that there is no complete identity of economic interest in any of the so-called "sections" of the country. In New York there are the interests of the very rich and of the very poor in the urban communities, and again those of the farmers in the rural sections; while the same contrasts appear in a state of the type of Illinois. California in turn is a western state, but it has its urban capitalists, its poor, and its agricultural interests of varying kinds.[5] The eastern farmer may or may not be an owner or a tenant, prosperous or suffering; and the wage-workers of the East and of the West are not on the whole dissimilar in their position. Yet the geographical, sectional idea has material weight in political calculations, and must always be reckoned as one of the significant factors in the composition of the party.

An examination of the distribution of party votes in percentage form by states reveals the regional character of American politics. Figure 1 shows that even in such a landslide as the 1936 election there were five distinct patterns of party allegiance in the United States. While the Republican pattern included only two states, the smallest number it has contained in any election since 1865, the second and third patterns, including the states which the Democrats won by the smallest margins, extended in a wide band from New England westward to the middle of the Rocky Mountains. It was in this area that some of the most notable victories of the Republican party were won in 1938. The next pattern, which indicates the states the Democrats won by a ratio of two or three to one, is divided into two sections. One section includes the most northerly of the southern states—Virginia, North Carolina, Tennessee and Oklahoma—and the other includes the tier of states west of the Great Lakes bordering on Canada and extending to the Pacific where it moves south to Mexico. This is the area that proved to be fertile ground for various insurgent political movements. The 1936 map fails to reveal its volatile character. Two years later portions of it were swinging back toward the Republican party. The last pattern

[5] Gosnell, *Grass Roots Politics*.

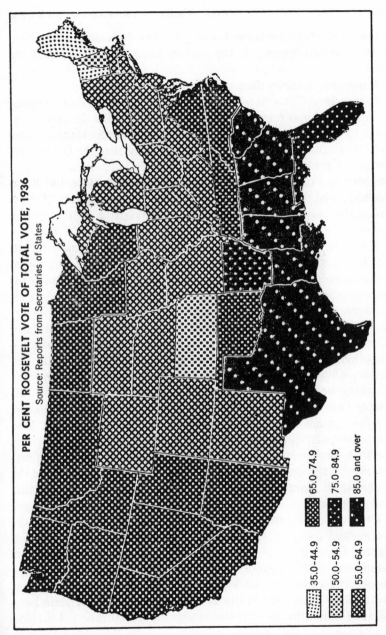

PER CENT ROOSEVELT VOTE OF TOTAL VOTE, 1936

Source: Reports from Secretaries of States

35.0–44.9   65.0–74.9

50.0–54.9   75.0–84.9

55.0–64.9   85.0 and over

Figure 1

is that of the Solid South, which has changed the least of any section in the past fifty years, but was split by the States' Rights party in 1948.

A map which shows the political complexion of the states does not indicate clearly how the inhabitants of the metropolitan regions vote. Figure 2 was prepared to give a general idea of the division of votes in the ninety-six metropolitan districts of the United States in 1936. In the North these districts were more strongly Democratic than the rural and other urban areas, except in the Northeast outside of New York City. The metropolitan districts of upstate New York, Pennsylvania, and New England showed a closer margin between the two major parties than in other parts of the United States.

The maps of the 1938 congressional elections are extremely revealing. Figure 3 shows the results by congressional districts, the shaded areas giving those districts which were carried by the Republicans and the other non-Democratic candidates (Progressives and Farmer-Laborites). In general, the Republicans staged their partial comeback in this election in those areas where the Democratic margin of victory was the lowest in 1936. There were a number of notable exceptions, however, which throw considerable light upon the persistence of party traditions in the United States. The northern tier of states, beginning with Wisconsin and moving westward to the Pacific Ocean, had been over two to one for Roosevelt in 1936 and yet they swung strongly back into the Republican column in 1938 and subsequent elections. This is borne out by Figure 4, also from the 1938 congressional elections but based upon the Democratic percentages of the aggregate congressional vote in each state. Could the violent shifts manifest in this area have been predicted by examination of previous voting behavior of the citizens living in its confines? We think that it could. As a matter of fact, an examination of the presidential vote of the states for the period of 1880–1924, not including the election of 1912, shows that the record of Wisconsin, Minnesota, South Dakota, and Oregon for refusing to support a Democratic candidate for President was without blemish. It was not until 1932 that the voters in these states swallowed their long-standing antipathy to anyone bearing the Democratic label. Holcombe's map of the American political climate, 1920–1932, tends to

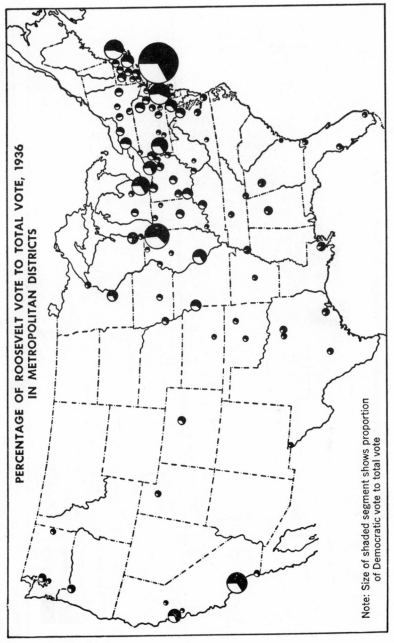

PERCENTAGE OF ROOSEVELT VOTE TO TOTAL VOTE, 1936
IN METROPOLITAN DISTRICTS

Note: Size of shaded segment shows proportion
of Democratic vote to total vote

Figure 2

113

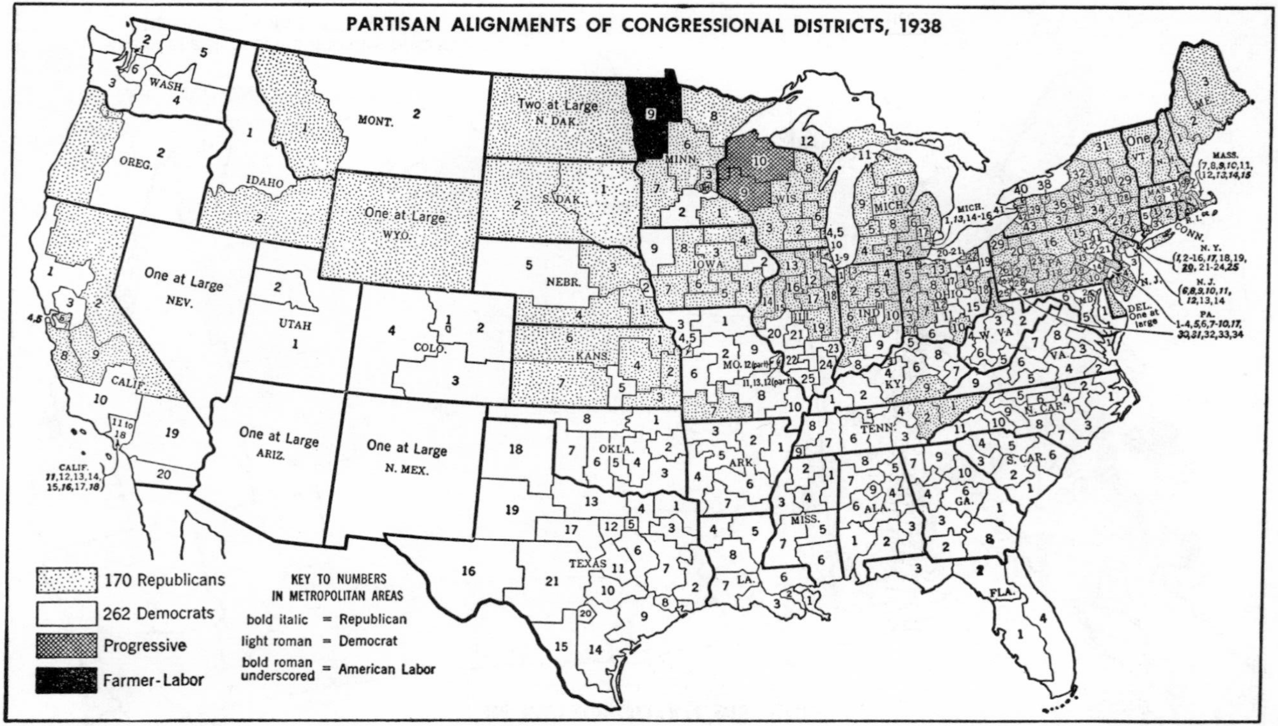

PARTISAN ALIGNMENTS OF CONGRESSIONAL DISTRICTS, 1938

KEY TO NUMBERS
IN METROPOLITAN AREAS

bold italic = Republican
light roman = Democrat
bold roman = Progressive
underscored = American Labor

170 Republicans
262 Democrats
Progressive
Farmer-Labor

Figure 3

(From *Congressional Directory*.)

114

PERCENTAGE DEMOCRATIC OF AGGREGATE CONGRESSIONAL VOTE BY STATES, 1938

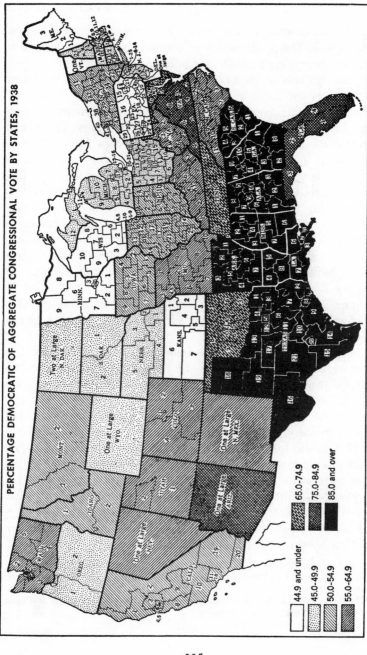

44.9 and under

45.0-49.9

50.0-54.9

55.0-64.9

65.0-74.9

75.0-84.9

85.0 and over

(Compiled from figures in *Congressional Directory*.)

Figure 4

bear out this conclusion,[6] but it presents some questions to be pondered as well. The period which he covered was not long enough to catch the underlying Republican fixation in Wisconsin and the relatively greater hold of Republicanism upon the minds of the voters of Oregon as compared with the other Pacific states.[7]

Turning to other parts of the United States, it is clear that Figures 3 and 4 represent a number of fundamental tendencies. The greater power of the Republican symbol in upstate New York, Pennsylvania, Ohio, and Michigan was not revealed by Figure 3, but it comes out very sharply in Figure 4. The rural character of the Republican vote in the more industrialized states may be brought out by comparing the results by congressional districts with the map showing the vote by metropolitan areas.[8] In addition to the states mentioned above, Maine, Vermont, Massachusetts, and Connecticut refused to support any candidate running under the Democratic banner during the years 1880–1924. Holcombe's map likewise reveals the Republican deviation of these states.

Figure 5 showing the percent Democratic by classes in the 1944 presidential election indicates how President Roosevelt was able to recover some of the losses which the party suffered in the 1938 and 1942 congressional elections. The Democratic gains were marked in the more populous states where the labor vote was rallied to the polls. On the Pacific coast, Oregon is shown to be the strongest Republican state.

When the 1946 Congressional elections came along, the magic name of Roosevelt was available only as a memory. The decline in the Democratic fortunes which began immediately after the 1936 presidential election was found to be in full swing again. Of the states north of the Mason-Dixon line only Montana, West Virginia, Maryland, and Rhode Island were carried by the Democrats, according to Figure 6, which shows the per cent Democratic of major party vote for the House of Representatives. In the southwest, Arizona and New Mexico were still in the Democratic fold.

[6] "Present-day Characteristics of American Political Parties," in E. B. Logan (ed.), *The American Political Scene* (New York, 1936), p. 23. See also Gosnell, *Grass Roots Politics.*

[7] L. Bean, *Political Behavior* (Washington, D. C., 1940), and *How to Predict Elections* (New York, Knopf, 1948).

[8] Gosnell, *Grass Roots Politics.*

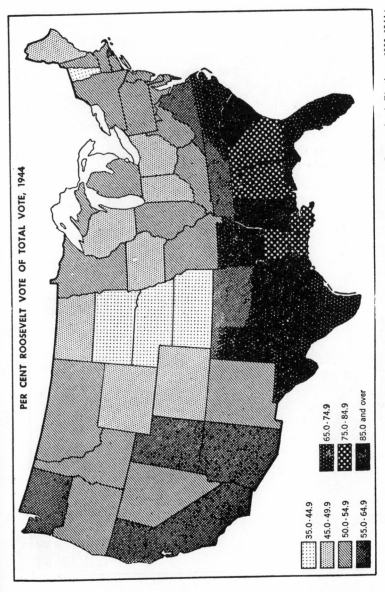

PER CENT ROOSEVELT VOTE OF TOTAL VOTE, 1944

35.0 - 44.9
45.0 - 49.9
50.0 - 54.9
55.0 - 64.9
65.0 - 74.9
75.0 - 84.9
85.0 and over

Figure 5

(From Bureau of the Census, *Vote Cast in Presidential and Congressional Elections, 1928–1944.*)

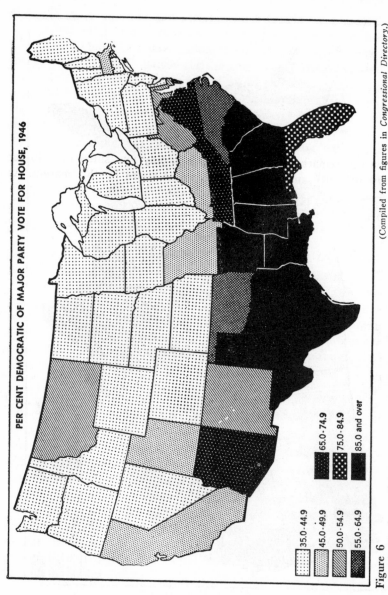

PER CENT DEMOCRATIC OF MAJOR PARTY VOTE FOR HOUSE, 1946

	35.0 - 44.9		65.0 - 74.9
	45.0 - 49.9		75.0 - 84.9
	50.0 - 54.9		85.0 and over
	55.0 - 64.9		

(Compiled from figures in *Congressional Directory*.)

Figure 6

The map for the 1948 presidential election is given in Figure 7. President Truman swept all but six states west of the Mississippi. Dewey carried Oregon, the Dakotas, Nebraska, and Kansas, and Thurmond carried Louisiana in this region. The two major party candidates divided the states bordering the Great Lakes. Contrary to expectations, President Truman carried Wisconsin, Illinois, and Ohio. While the President carried only Massachusetts and Rhode Island in the Northeast, he won the border and southern states except the four southern states which he lost to Thurmond. The election was remarkably close. Dewey won only four states by a 10 per cent plurality and Truman won twelve states by this margin. As compared with the 1944 election, the shift of the farm states of Wyoming, Colorado, Iowa, and Wisconsin to the Democratic party was remarkable. The principal Republican gains were in Oregon, Michigan and the northeastern states.

In view of the many shifts which have characterized American politics in the past two decades, it is clear that sectional balances may again be upset. The development of manufacturing and new methods of farming in the South, or the growth of industrial democracy in the East might make the South Republican and the East Democratic, or lead to the growth of some new type of political grouping not now on the horizon. These analyses are of value only as they call attention to the underlying factors upon which the development and activity of parties rest.

Neighborhoods

In many states, counties and cities there are found smaller areas or pockets appropriated by one party or the other and safely reckoned as one of party faith over considerable periods of time. Often this may be attributed to class, racial, or personal contacts and leadership. Or the general neighborhood sentiment itself may help to account for them. Political habits of allegiance to a party may be formed and may continue even though their original cause has disappeared. The neighborhood for local reasons becomes Republican or Democratic owing to some local advantage or burden attributed to one party or the other—a public building, an improvement, a privilege; and long after that benefit or burden has been forgotten by the bulk of the voters, its soul may go marching on. The party tradi-

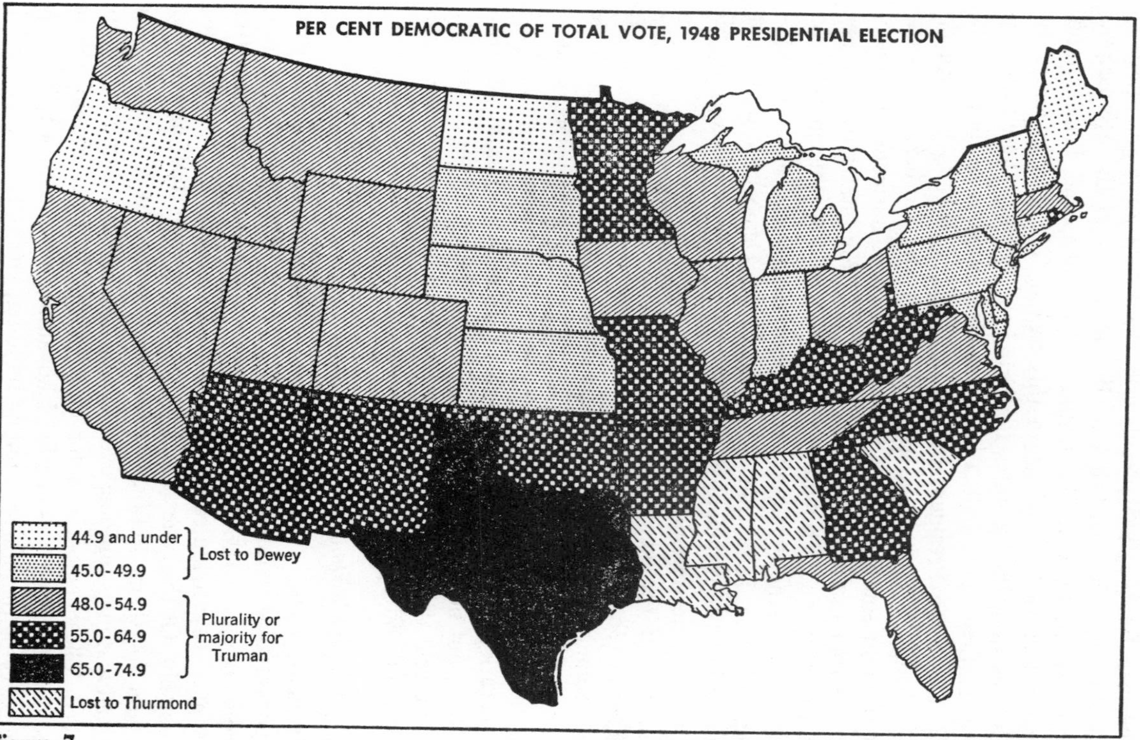

PER CENT DEMOCRATIC OF TOTAL VOTE, 1948 PRESIDENTIAL ELECTION

44.9 and under ⎫
45.0 - 49.9 ⎬ Lost to Dewey

48.0 - 54.9 ⎫
55.0 - 64.9 ⎬ Plurality or majority for Truman

65.0 - 74.9

Lost to Thurmond

Figure 7

(Compiled from figures given in U.P. release, December 6, 1948.)

tion may survive. With marked social or racial changes, or varied leaders, or shifting issues, the sentiment may change; but often it goes on for a considerable time, if it is once firmly set. An accurate political spot map would show, scattered over the state or county or city, these areas where definite political results may be predicted with reasonable accuracy under ordinary conditions. They form the basis of party cartography with which all practical political workers are familiar. This local or neighborhood sentiment, whatever may be its cause, will not long survive the heavy shocks of racial change or shift of industrial basis; but it possesses some resisting power, and the neighborhood habit will project itself for a substantial time. New interests, new industries, new issues, new leaders and organizers may shift its channel, but for the time being the neighborhood continues its party habits, with some degree of persistence. Just as residential or business districts or church districts change, so the political map alters with the new stream of forces, but the tendency to continue requires positive pressure to alter it.

Both the broader sectional differences and the narrower neighborhood situations and interests are of great significance in the composition of the political party. An understanding of them is fundamental to any comprehension of the theoretical or the practical side of party activities. They can be overlooked only at the peril of misunderstanding some of the basic forces in the party.

Race

Among the significant factors in the composition of the political party is that of race affiliation.[9] Sometimes this is the decisive element in determining party allegiance, as in the South, and often it is a secondary element. The most striking illustration is seen in the division between white and colored voters. Until after the 1934 election practically all colored voters were Republican, while in the southern states the overwhelming majority of the white race has

[9] H. F. Gosnell, *Democracy: Threshold of Freedom* (New York, 1948) and *Negro Politicians: The Rise of Negro Politics in Chicago* (Chicago, 1935); G. Mydal, *American Dilemma* (New York, 1944); S. Drake and H. Cayton, *Black Metropolis* (New York, 1945); H. L. Moon, *Balance of Power: The Negro Vote* (Garden City, N. Y., Doubleday & Co., 1948); W. F. Nowlin, *The Negro in American National Politics* (Boston, 1931); R. L. Morton, *The Negro in Virginia Politics, 1865–1902* (Charlottesville, 1919); P. Lewinson, *Race, Class and Party* (London and New York, 1932).

been Democratic. Where the margin between the Republican and Democratic parties was small or the Republican party was strong, the Republican leaders could count upon the unswerving loyalty of the Negro voters. Under no circumstances in these places would the Negroes desert the party of Lincoln, the emancipator. Disfranchisement, lynchings, Jim Crow laws, the cropping system, and other social and economic practices were laid at the door of the Democratic party. On the other hand, in cities where the Democratic party was normally in control, as in the city of New York, many Negroes voted with the Democrats even before the days of the Franklin Roosevelt New Deal. Beginning with the 1934 congressional elections large numbers of Negro voters were found supporting a Democratic administration in national politics.[10]

This racial division constitutes one of the most significant factors in American politics, of far-reaching importance in party organization and in national action. In a great section of the United States, the problem of race seems to overshadow all other issues. This division enables the southern group to exercise a powerful influence on Democratic national nominating conventions and Congresses. On the other hand, it enables the "administration," if the Republican party is in power, or the "organization" if it is not, to control a block of some 150 delegates from states where the party hardly has a real existence, and in this way to determine the control of the nominating convention where the result is otherwise close. Furthermore, the Negro vote in the doubtful border states has always been of great importance to the Republican party. Thus the southern section of the country, while removed from the ordinary divisions of national politics, exercises an important influence in the organization of both of the major parties.

Election returns in the United States are not kept by racial groups, but the concentration of Negro population in certain areas makes it possible to estimate the proportion of Negro voters and to study their general voting behavior. In the northern states Negroes have been segregated not as a matter of law but as a matter of fact. Hostile white communities, high-priced housing, and industrial property have constituted the barriers to the general spread of Negro residence in metropolitan centers.

[10] Gosnell, *Negro Politicians*; Mydal, *op. cit.*

An examination of the behavior of Negro voters in the border and northern states shows that before 1934 they were usually with the Republican party. Considering the fact that they are attached to this party by tradition and that this party was more willing than the Democratic to recognize their demands for representation, these tendencies were understandable. In some northern cities where the Democratic party occupied a predominant position and voting the Republican ticket was usually a futile gesture, the Negroes took a realistic attitude toward local politics and abandoned in large numbers their traditional loyalty to the Republican party. The success of Tammany Hall in winning over Negro voters by the same methods that it has used to win foreign-born voters is well known.[11] When the Democrats began to carry national, state, and local elections as a result of the reaction against the party in power at the time the depression started in 1929, Negro voters in the northern states shifted their party allegiance. It is true that they lagged behind all other groups in making this change, but once the spell was broken, the overturn was rapid. The relief policies of the New Deal administration hurried the process. Even before the economic depression and the overturn of traditional party alignments, Negro voters had shown remarkable independence when they felt some racial issue or favorite candidate was at stake. In the Chicago mayoralty election in 1923 over half of the colored voters were persuaded to desert the Republican candidate on the grounds that this candidate was hostile to the faction of the Republican party which had given considerable recognition to the Negro community in the form of jobs, favors and special privileges.[12]

The shift of the Negro vote toward the Democratic party in the four successive Roosevelt elections may be ascribed to the Democratic support of the Fair Employment Practices Committee, the relief policies of the Democratic administration, the impact of increasing urbanism upon the thinking of Negroes, and the absorption of Negroes in the local Democratic organizations of the North. In the South the Allwright decision brought increasing participation in primaries and elections on the part of Negroes. In Georgia some 100,-

[11] Colored Citizens' Non-partisan Committee for the Re-election of Mayor Walker, *New York City and the Colored Citizen* (pamphlet, 1929).

[12] Gosnell, *Negro Politicians*; Drake and Cayton, *op. cit.*; Mydal, *op. cit.*

000 Negroes took part in the primaries of 1946. In Texas about 75,000 colored voters took part in the primaries of the same year. Negro voters in other parts of the South showed the same signs of awakening.[13]

The Politics of the Immigrant [14]

In an environment which was none too cordial, the immigrant has often found the party precinct captain the one who was most willing to listen to his troubles regarding employment, naturalization, local police regulations, and political participation. Even though this party official might be a cog in a boss-ridden machine which was interested in exploiting the votes of the foreign born, he was at least human in his approach, and the very fact that he was asking for the cooperation of the despised "greenhorn" meant that the barriers between the new and the old world groups were being broken down. The political parties, then, have taken their place alongside the schools, the churches, the shops, and the factories in the process of assimilating the foreign born.[15]

The speed with which a given foreign-born group enters into the American party system varies with a multitude of factors. The size and distribution of the group, its language habits, its political heritage, the economic status of its members, its cohesiveness, its religious institutions, its educational level, and its leadership are all related to the rapidity with which it can make a place for itself in

[13] Gosnell, *Grass Roots Politics*, pp. 8–9; H. L. Moon, *Balance of Power: The Negro Vote* (Garden City, N. Y., 1948); O. Douglas Weeks, "The White Primary: 1944–1948," and Donald S. Strong, "The Rise of Negro Voting in Texas," in *American Political Science Review*, XLII (June, 1948), 500–522.

[14] See excellent discussion by Wallace S. Sayre, "The Immigrant in Politics," in F. J. Brown and J. S. Roucek (eds.), *Our Racial and National Minorities* (New York, Prentice-Hall, Inc., 1937), Chap. XIX.

[15] H. F. Gosnell, *Grass Roots Politics* and *Machine Politics: Chicago Model*; Edward H. Litchfield, *Voting Behavior in a Metropolitan Area* (Ann Arbor, Michigan, 1941); Abram Lipsky, "The Political Mind of the Foreign Born American," *Popular Science Monthly*, LXXV (1914), 397–403; R. A. Woods, *Americans in Process* (New York, 1902). See also the very useful Americanization studies made under the auspices of the Carnegie Corporation, especially, John Daniels, *America via the Neighborhood* (New York, 1920), Chap. XII; R. E. Park and H. A. Miller, *Old World Traits Transplanted* (New York, 1921); and John Gavit, *Americans by Choice* (New York, 1922).

the American party hierarchies.[16] The English, Scotch, Irish, and English-speaking Canadians were soon absorbed, since they had the advantage of familiarity with the English language. With the exception of the Irish, these same groups, plus the Scandinavians and a large proportion of the Germans, also had Protestant backgrounds. On the other hand, the Poles and the Italians took a longer time to make their influence felt in American politics because of their foreign language habits, Catholic faith, and lack of familiarity with American customs and institutions.

The process by which party allegiances were formed may be illustrated by considering some of the more important immigrant groups.

Irish

During the first half of the nineteenth century immigration from Ireland was larger than that from any other country. At present the Irish comprise one-fourteenth of the foreign white stocks in the United States. From as far back as Cromwell's time the Irish have flocked to America in order to escape the persecution of the British, the uncertainties of a one-crop system, and the evils of absentee landlordism.[17] Most of them stayed in big cities such as New York, Boston, and Philadelphia.

In the cities the Irish immigrants received a mixed welcome since they were poor, illiterate, Catholic, and spoke with a distinct brogue. The Democratic party since Thomas Jefferson's time, however, has welcomed the Irish. The party newspapers of those days were sympathetic, the party's stand on the Alien and Sedition laws was favorable to them, and the party leader was a believer in religious toleration.

As the number of persons of Irish extraction increased in the United States, the attachment of the group to the Democratic party grew closer. In the period before the Civil War the Irish could point

[16] Obviously, time is also an important factor. As B. Shrieke puts it in his *Alien Americans* (New York, Viking Press, 1936), p. 100: "But the member of the second generation knows how to play the game himself. At the same time, unconscious of any inconsistency, he can indulge in passionate oratory, consisting of a glorification of the lofty qualities of American democracy, for he has already assimilated Babbitt's unreflective conventional loyalty, ecstatic vocabulary, and specious humanitarianism." See also Harold D. Lasswell, *World Politics and Personal Insecurity* (New York, 1935).

[17] Edward F. Roberts, *Ireland in America* (New York, 1931).

with pride to the contributions of people with Irish blood to the success of the Democratic party. Jackson, Calhoun, Polk, and Buchanan were among those whose ancestors lived on the Emerald Isle.[18] The Whigs were contaminated by their unholy alliance with the Know Nothing party of the fifties which adopted an antiforeign, anti-Catholic stand. As far as the slavery issue was concerned, the Irish were willing to follow the southern leaders since they were not homesteaders but city dwellers, and they had some concern about possible competition from the labor of free Negroes.

The Civil War ended the dominance of the Democratic party and brought in a period of Republican control which lasted, except for two interruptions, until 1933. During this time the Irish were the mainstay of the Democrats in the North. The remarkable cohesion of the group was due to its loyalty to the Catholic church, its interest in Irish nationalism and the genius of its political leaders. In general, the Democratic national leaders adopted an anti-British (twisting-the-lion's-tail) policy, as exemplified in the Venezuela dispute during the Cleveland administration. However, the Irish were sorely disappointed in Wilson's failure to secure their independence in the League system, and they turned against his party with fury in the election of 1920.

It has been in local politics that the Irish have come to their own. Disappointed in the defeat of their hero, Al Smith, in 1928, they can still point to the city administrations which they control. New York City has had a long line of Irish Democratic bosses—Kelly, Croker, Murphy, Curry, Olvany, Dooling, Sullivan—and Chicago has had its Sullivan, Brennan, Nash and Kelly. The influx of newer immigrant elements from eastern and southern Europe has challenged the Irish supremacy in both the Catholic church and the Democratic party, but so far the Irish have kept most of their power and lived up to the motto: "Contention is better than loneliness."

Germans

About one-seventh of the persons of foreign white stock in the United States are of German origin. From 1850 to 1890 the German

---

[18] President Andrew Jackson was the son of poor Scotch-Irish parents. The Irish coming from Ulster during the nineteenth century were usually Scotch Presbyterians.

immigration was the largest from any single country. The inducements which brought the German immigrants to American shores have been political, religious, and economic.[19]

Some of the German immigrants who came to this country brought a burning love of freedom, others a faith in the revolutionary ideas of Marx and Engels; but probably the majority brought with them no very clearly shaped political attitudes. As far as their religious and occupational background was concerned, they fitted into the American picture fairly well, since roughly two-thirds were Lutherans, one-third were Catholics, and over half of them were agrarian.

Because of their love of liberty and their fear of the extension of the slave system to territories which were being opened to homesteaders, the "forty-eighters" were enthusiastic antislavery men and took an important part in the formation of the Republican party. However, most of the German Catholics joined the Democratic party. Toward the end of the nineteenth century many Germans were found in the labor movement and the socialist parties, but the majority were bourgeois in their outlook.[20] While it is true that a majority of those active in the Haymarket riot were Germans, there were also many Germans in the battles for sound currency.

In local politics the German-Americans were more likely to support Democratic than Republican candidates because of the dry stand taken by the latter on the liquor question.[21] They were also united in opposition to measures which limited instruction in German in their parochial schools, whether Lutheran or Catholic.

The Republicanism of the German-American elements in the United States was greatly strengthened by the events of World War I. American participation in the war on the side of the Allies was bitterly opposed by those of German origin, and their weight was cast in favor of Hughes in the election of 1916, apparently in anticipation of coming events. The war itself was a most trying period and left the group in a bitter mood which found its political expression in their swelling the tide of the Harding flood of 1920.

[19] A. J. Townsend, "The Germans of Chicago" (Ph.D. thesis, University of Chicago, 1927).

[20] An excellent discussion of the political attitudes of different German economic groups in the nineteenth century is found in P. Kosok, *Modern Germany: A Study of Conflicting Loyalties* (Chicago, 1933).

[21] Unpublished materials on the referendum in Chicago prepared by students of the authors.

In 1933 the persons of German extraction were confronted with a new crisis in America. In contrast with the Irish, the Germans in the United States had never been intensely nationalistic. However, the success of the Nazi revolution in Germany was to test the loyalty of the German immigrants, especially the recent ones, to the democratic ideas current in the United States. The antidemocratic, anti-Semitic bias of Nazi government in Germany brought forth a storm of criticism in the American press, and to counteract this a German-American Bund was founded which endeavored to spread the ideas of Nazi Germany and its leader, Adolf Hitler.[22] Most of the members of the Bund were born in Germany, and very few of the second generation were attracted by the movement. In opposition to the Bund there was established a German-American culture organization which tried to show the loyalty of the German immigrants to American political institutions. After World War II was over, it was revealed that the Bund was supported by the foreign section of the German Nazi party.

Scandinavians

The persons of Scandinavian extraction in the United States comprise about one-twelfth of all the foreign white stock. Typical of this group are the Swedes, whose political activities in the United States have been described by one of our former students.[23] Political oppression and proscription were not important in Swedish migration to the United States. But the industrial revolution, the disputes over land laws, the military services, were important in inducing many Swedes to seek their fortunes in the United States. They came to this country largely because they wished to improve their economic status.

The Swedes brought with them a strong tradition of independence, a faith in local self-government, experience with the jury system, and temperate habits. These characteristics tended to aid their assimilation. The fact that they had no sympathy for slavery contributed to their selection of the North as a place for settlement. As the feudal system never took root in Sweden, the Swedish peasants

---

[22] D. Strong, *Organized Anti-Semitism in America* (Washington, D. C. 1941).
[23] R. G. Hemdahl, "The Swedes in Illinois Politics" (manuscript, 1932).

were used to participating in government, and when they emigrated to the United States their faith in democratic ideals was merely transplanted to a new soil. The early Scandinavian immigrants were largely land seekers, and it was on the fertile western plains that they settled for the most part.

In the twentieth century socialism has won a number of followers among the Swedish immigrants—not a bitter, violent type of socialism which emphasizes class warfare and armed insurrection, but a revisionist brand of socialism which approaches British gradualism. It is undoubtedly this background which has influenced the politics of Minnesota in recent years.

The Scandinavians have been slow to assume the position in politics to which their numerical strength entitled them. However, following the Civil War a number of them began to busy themselves with town and county politics. Since the nineties they have been very active in state politics, holding legislative, administrative, and high executive posts.

The Swedes were strongly pro-Lincoln and they remained in the Republican fold for the most part. Within the Republican party the Swedes have been identified with the liberal elements represented by men like Governor Stassen of Minnesota. After the Progressive movement of 1912, some Swedish-American voters showed a tendency to support political movements which called for a relatively more rapid adjustment of governmental functions to changing economic conditions. In other words, the Scandinavian elements have furnished considerable support for such movements as the Progressive party of Wisconsin under the La Follettes and the Farmer-Labor party of Minnesota under Governor Floyd Olson and other Scandinavian leaders. In the thirties these political independents and insurgents of the Middle West formed an alliance with the new leaders of the Democratic party. Holding the balance of power, they have gained a strategic bargaining position.

Slavs

The Slavic groups, including the Poles, Czechs, Russians, Jugoslavs, and Lithuanians, make up one-fourth of those of foreign white stock. They are the most numerous of the recent immigration to this country. Like the Irish they were attracted to America because of political oppression abroad.[24] The Poles had been indifferent Catholics before the eighteenth-century partitions, but when the dominating governments began to coerce them they turned to the Catholic church as a means of preserving Polish nationality. They also turned to the Polish language as a means of keeping their unity. The Poles who have come to America have remained strong Catholics, and have clung tenaciously to their language even though their unfamiliarity with English has retarded their political advancement.

Farmers in Europe, the Slavic immigrants have become industrial workers in this country. They have been the men who do the rough work in the mines and factories of the North. At first, in such states as Pennsylvania and Michigan, many followed their employers' lead and supported the Republican party. Envious and jealous of the Irish, they derived some psychic satisfaction from this stand. The prohibition policy of the Republican party, however, the influence of the Catholic church hierarchy, the aid which Wilson gave to Slavic nationalities in Europe, and the liberalization of the Democratic party were all influences which drew them into the Democratic fold. In Chicago, Judge Edmund K. Jarecki, of Polish origin, and Mayor Anton J. Cermak, of Czech blood, were prominent in Democratic circles long before the days of the New Deal. The Polish National Alliance, the Czechoslovak Societies of America, the Yugo-Slav Council, and other Slavic societies have contributed to the cohesion of these groups in American life.

Latins

The Latin nationalities, Italian for the most part, constitute one-seventh of those of foreign white stock in the United States. They are the second largest group of the newer immigration. Most of those who came in the earlier period of Italian migration were from the southern part of Italy and from Sicily where illiteracy was high, poverty was widespread, and class distinctions were sharply drawn.

[24] E. G. Balch, *Our Slavic Fellow Citizens* (New York, 1910) ; Thomas Capek, *The Czechs in America* (Boston, 1920) ; Peter Roberts, *The Anthracite Coal Communities* (New York, 1904), pp 316–342, 355–358; J. S. Roucek, "The Poles in the United States," *Baltic Countries* (January, 1937), and his "A Study of Czecho-Slovaks in the United States," *Sociology and Social Research*, XVII (Sept.–Oct., 1932), 63–71; M. S. Szymczak, "Poles and Their Aptitude to American Politics," in *Poles in America* (Chicago, 1933).

The Italian immigrants, therefore, were somewhat slower than the older immigrant groups in adjusting themselves to American social and political conditions.[25] There was a marked tendency for the Italian immigrants to settle in segregated communities in the great cities and to live in isolation because of the language barrier, the strangeness of the new environment, and the hostility and indifference of the older Americans. New York, Philadelphia, Chicago, Boston, New Orleans, Cleveland, St. Louis, Baltimore, and Detroit have their Italian quarters, all of which are in overcrowded tenements teeming with children.

Many of the Italians who came to the United States planned to return to their home country as soon as they had made their fortunes. This attitude meant that they were preoccupied with Italian nationalism and imperialism, and paid little attention to American politics. Their entrance into American politics was therefore slow, as in the case of the Slavic groups. In the eastern part of the United States, particularly in Pennsylvania, they generally supported the Republican party because of pressure brought to bear upon them by their employers, the great steel and coal magnates. However, in New York City Tammany Hall had welcomed them as it did other foreign groups, and their leader, Generoso Pope, became an important figure in the party councils.

During the prohibition era certain undesirable Italians became important political powers in the larger cities of the United States as a result of their bootlegging activities. The names of Capone, Torrio, and Colosimo were blazoned in the newspapers throughout the land. "Scarface" Al Capone was immune to ordinary police prosecution, but he was caught in the mesh of the federal revenue agents who investigated his income tax.[26] After repeal, some of the Italian ex-bootleggers turned their attention to trade-union politics and gambling.

On the other hand, the best type of Italian political leader is exemplified in the picturesque figure of the late fighting mayor of

[25] R. F. Foerster, *Italian Emigration of Our Times* (Cambridge, 1917), pp. 399–400; E. C. Sartorio, *Social and Religious Life of the Italians in America* (Boston, 1918); John H. Mariano, *The Italian Contribution to American Democracy* (Boston, 1921).

[26] F. D. Pasley, *Al Capone: The Biography of a Self-Made Man* (Garden City, 1930)

New York, Fiorello La Guardia. Nominally a Republican, formerly a member of the Socialist party, the doughty mayor was not fettered by any party label when the interests of the public as he saw them were at stake.[27]

A number of other prominent Italians might be mentioned, such as Lieutenant Governor Charles Poletti of New York, Judge Ferdinand Pecora of New York, and Mayor Rossi of San Francisco.

Jews

Another group which has had to fight its way in American politics is the Jewish group.[28] While the Jews constitute only 3 per cent of the total population of the United States, in certain cities such as New York, the "New Jerusalem," they make up ten times that proportion.

For thousands of years Jews have been persecuted by Gentiles in different parts of the world. The prejudice against the Jews has gathered about itself a mass of tradition which has been handed down through the ages. The fundamental fact of the situation is that the Jews are fairly distinct in their physical appearance and in the spelling of their names from the run of American people. The mental picture of the Jewish trader, the Jewish banker, and the Jewish Communist is common to all cultures. Sharp trading is more noticeable among them than among other groups because they are conspicuous. Hostility to the Jews has increased in modern times because of the growth of nationalism. Jews have been persecuted because their religion, dress, dietary habits, and customs have been different from those of the country in which they have settled.

The Jews have been coming to the United States since the beginning of our history. At first they were not allowed to vote, but over a hundred years ago this disability was removed. Since they are traditionally urban dwellers, they had fewer adjustments to make to city life than some of the other immigrant groups. However, they showed a tendency to segregate themselves in ghetto communities because of the walls of prejudice sometimes erected against them and their strong group consciousness. As a group, the Jews have

[27] John Chamberlain, "Mayor La Guardia," *Yale Review*, XXIX (Autumn, 1939), 14. See also Paul J. Kern, "Fiorello H. La Guardia," in J. T. Salter (ed.), *The American Politician* (Chapel Hill, 1938), p. 46.

[28] Samuel W. McCall, *Patriotism of the American Jew* (New York, 1924).

shown no special party tendencies. Some have joined the Republican party, some the Democratic party, and still others have been active in the Socialist and Communist parties. Their allegiance tends to follow class lines or local group leadership. The Jewish banker is likely to be Republican in New York or Chicago. The labor agitator may be Democratic, Socialist, or Communist. The Ku Klux Klan, which was revived following World War I, drove many Jews into the Democratic party in the North.

In recent years the Jews have inclined much more strongly to the Democratic party. Governor Smith of New York had many Jewish advisers, including the able Mrs. Moskowitz. Franklin D. Roosevelt relied even more heavily upon Jewish brains. Prominent in his New Deal administrations were Justice Felix Frankfurter, Benjamin Cohen, Bernard Baruch, Judge Rosenman, Governor Lehman, Secretary Morgenthau, and other well-known Jews. With Jewish Democratic governors in New York and Illinois, Jewish voters continued to leave the Republican party.

The success of the Jews in business and politics has been one of the reasons why they have aroused so much animosity in certain circles. Anti-Semitism raised its ugly head in the United States in a variety of forms when Hitler was in power in Germany. The anti-Semitic organizations which sprang up like mushrooms after 1933 charged the Jews with conspiring to dominate the world and subjugate the Gentiles.[29] They alleged that most of the troubles of the modern world—communist revolutions, economic depressions, the degradation of morals by alcoholism, prostitution, the drug traffic, and obscenity—were to be blamed upon the Jews. Ridiculous as these charges were, there were some who were ready to believe and who found in them a gratifying explanation of their own misfortunes. The scapegoat function of the Jews is not a new one.

The role of the Jews in American politics has been well summarized by one of their own journalists:

"In American politics, too, the Americanization process has resulted in a political diversification as wide as that which exists among other citizens. . . . The proportion of Jewish radicals has been greatly exaggerated; it is very slight as compared with the large body of nonradical Jews in America. Moreover, with the Jewish group gradually developing

[29] Strong, *op. cit.*

from a working-class to a middle-class section of the population, this tendency to radicalism is decreasing. At the present time, Jews differ little from other groups in their wide political diversity, and Jews may be found in each of the important political movements, not only in their rank and file but also in their leadership." [30]

RELIGION AND POLITICS

A keen foreign observer has made the following comments on the relation between the church and the state in America:

"It is generally believed that the First Amendment to the American Constitution in 1791 assured complete religious equality, and the Americans were free to choose God, Jehovah, or Buddha as they pleased, or even to maintain that there was no God at all. This, however, is not the case, though it is true that there is no established church. It is nevertheless understood that America is a Christian nation and that Protestantism is the national religion." [31]

In the days of the Revolutionary Fathers religious differences and disabilities played a considerable role in our public affairs. During the Jackson era, provisions for state taxation in support of churches and religious disqualifications for office were removed. But to the present day there remain on the statute books of some states laws regarding Sunday observance, laws prohibiting the teaching of evolution in the public schools, and laws making blasphemy a crime.

Political sermons constitute a most interesting and significant part of our political literature, and the activity of the clergy is, of course, one of the patent facts of our political life. They have been most active in the discussion of "moral" issues, notably the prohibition of the sale of intoxicating liquors, but they have not neglected economic issues or broad questions of national policy. Indeed, as all large problems have been declared by one side or the other to be moral issues, the field has been open to consideration upon moral or religious grounds. Slavery, the currency question, the liquor problem, the "trust," the abolition of war—all were vigorously argued in the course of political campaigns by members of the clergy holding

[30] Harry Schneiderman, "Jewish Americans," in Brown and Roucek (eds.), *Our Racial and National Minorities* (New York, Prentice-Hall, 1939), Chap. IX.

[31] André Siegfried, *America Comes of Age* (New York, Harcourt, Brace and Co., 1927), p. 56.

different views and making different party applications. At times very solid and powerful ecclesiastical influence has been thrown upon one side of the scale or the other, notably in local and state elections. This has been particularly true in contests affecting moral issues, or in cases where the public school question was involved in some form. Specific instructions and injunctions are often given to members of the flock directly from the pulpit, but these are not uniformly followed, even in the case of moral questions where the influence of the churches is greatest. In the consideration of broad economic issues, the ecclesiastical group has often followed the general drift of the locality or class rather than undertaken the guidance of it on any religious basis. This is readily seen in the discussion of questions such as free silver, strikes, and slavery where the local interest colored the type of sermonizing. In more recent times the ecclesiastical groups have adopted striking types of industrial programs.

Since religious organizations have played a significant role in American politics, it is important to consider the size and distribution of church membership. According to the figures furnished by the federal government, over half of the adults in the United States are listed on the membership rolls of the churches.[32] It has been estimated that a much larger proportion, probably three-fourths, are in sympathy with a church denomination even though many of these are not officially registered as communicants.[33] An analysis of adult membership data by denominations shows that the Protestant bodies predominate, constituting almost two-thirds, as compared with three-tenths for the Catholics and one-eighteenth for the Jews. In no state do the Catholics or Jews constitute a majority of the total population, but in Rhode Island and New Mexico the Catholics come close to making up one-half of the adults. On the other hand, in nine southern states the Protestant church members are in a majority,

---

[32] The figures have been analyzed by C. L. Fry, "Changes in Religious Organizations," in President's Research Committee on Social Trends, *Recent Social Trends* (New York, 1933), Chap. XX.

[33] In November, 1937, the Gallup Institute of Public Opinion asked the question "Are you a member of a church?" and 78 per cent of the replies were in the affirmative. On January 10, 1948, the same organization reported that 94 per cent of its respondents in the United States answered "yes" to the question, "Do you, personally, believe in God?"

and in Utah the Mormons constitute four-fifths of the inhabitants.

The practical control of both parties is predominantly Protestant, since the Protestant South is widely influential in the control of the Democracy, and the Protestant Republicans of the North and West control the Republican party. It is not without significance that Presidents Cleveland and Wilson, the Democratic leaders of the last generation, and William Jennings Bryan as well, were all Presbyterians.[34] With the nomination of Smith in 1928 the Democrats embarked on a new venture which proved to be disastrous in the South.

While the leadership of the two major parties in the United States has been largely Protestant, no major party has dared to repudiate openly the Catholic or Jewish vote. However, there have been political movements founded upon Protestant nationalism. Just before the Civil War, when the Irish immigration began to be noticed, "Know Nothing" secret societies were established which, by means of passwords and secret ceremonies, endeavored to meet the growing "menace" of Catholicism. In the eighties an anti-Catholic American Protective Association was established to combat the Italian and Slavic immigrant invasions. This association was able to stir up religious prejudices and win many recruits in the Middle West.

Following World War I there was a brief period when the Ku Klux Klan was revived as an institutional form of chauvinistic Protestantism.[35] Unscrupulous adventurers, professional publicity agents, some Protestant ministers, returned veterans who could not find jobs, small merchants who were fearful of possible competition, and others combined to arouse the fears of the small-town middle-income groups regarding the "dangers" of Catholicism, atheism, evolution, European immorality, Bolshevism, alcoholism, and the challenge of the

[34] The religious affiliations of Presidents since 1860 are as follows: Lincoln, Unitarian; Johnson, Methodist; Grant, Methodist; Hayes, Methodist; Garfield, Disciples; Arthur, Episcopalian; Cleveland, Presbyterian; Harrison, Presbyterian; McKinley, Methodist; Theodore Roosevelt, Dutch Reformed; Taft, Unitarian; Wilson, Presbyterian; Harding, Baptist; Coolidge, Congregationalist; Hoover, Quaker; Franklin D. Roosevelt, Episcopalian; Harry Truman, Baptist.

[35] J. M. Mecklin, *The Ku Klux Klan: A Study of the American Mind* (New York, 1924); H. M. Kallen, *Culture and Democracy in the United States* (New York, 1924); Charles C. Marshall, "Open Letter to the Honorable Alfred E. Smith," *Atlantic Monthly*, CXXXIX (1927), 540–549; E. H. Loucks, *The Ku Klux Klan in Pennsylvania, a Study of the American Mind* (New York, 1936).

aliens and the Negroes to native white supremacy. In the South and in the Middle West the Klan as the champion of national morality was able to make some headway in cooperation with the Fundamentalists, the Prohibitionists, and the "Babbitts." Where the warnings of the fiery cross were not sufficient to intimidate or exile the aliens or other undesirables, the Klan members resorted to anonymous threats and at times to floggings, torture, kidnapping, and even murder. The disclosures of the *New York World* regarding the moral turpitude and financial greed of the leaders of the movement caused a break in its ranks, which was followed by a change in leadership and in tactics. In place of the former acts of violence, the movement employed the boycott, the membership drive, and familiar political machine techniques. In Texas, Indiana, and several other states, important state officers owed their selection to the Klan, and in Oregon the legislation passed against parochial schools was of Klan origin. Following the campaign of 1928, during which the Klan was again active, particularly in the South, this brand of American intolerance tended to disappear.

Religious attitudes are a factor in party division, but they are less significant than many other characters. They are frequently subordinated to race, class, and sectional differences, following these lines rather than independent ones. In the South the Democratic party is almost purely Protestant, except in Maryland, New Mexico, and Louisiana, where there is a strong Catholic element. In the North, however, the Democratic party includes many Catholics, particularly among the Irish and the Poles. The Republic party is probably more strongly Protestant in its composition in the North, but includes large numbers of conservative Catholics. The Presidential preferences of Gallup's respondents in 1936, 1940, and 1944 were broken down by religious groups. In all three elections Roosevelt was most popular with Catholics, Jews, and nonchurch members. He lost the Protestant vote in 1940 and 1944. Among the Jewish people, he maintained high popularity.[36]

The nomination of Alfred E. Smith, a Catholic, for president in 1928 by one of the two major parties increased the importance of religion as a factor determining party preferences. The question was

[36] *Gallup Political Almanac for 1948* (Princeton, N. J.); P. Lazarsfeld, B. Berelson, and H. Gaudet, *The People's Choice* (New York, 1944).

raised in a letter addressed publicly to Smith in 1927, which asked
whether it was possible for a Catholic president to observe the canon
laws and at the same time be loyal to his oath to support the Constitution of the United States.[37] Smith replied that he could not
"conjure up a possible conflict between religious principle and political duty in the United States, except on the unthinkable hypothesis
that some law were to be passed which violated the common morality
of all God-fearing men."[38] He said that if such a conflict were
conjured up he would resolve it by the dictates of his conscience.
Despite this answer and the efforts of the Democratic party to remove the question from the campaign, religious prejudices were
openly appealed to, and a vicious whispering campaign was carried
on as well. The loss of several of the states of the ordinarily solid
Democratic South showed the extent of this religious bias. In the
North there was a marked tendency for the Catholics to rally to
Smith.[39]

There are other religious minorities in the United States which
have been of political importance because of their concentration in
given areas. Mormonism is a political factor in the state of Utah and
in several of the adjoining states where the Mormon vote is significant. The Mormon church does not affiliate with either of the major
parties, as such, but in most cases has thrown its strength with the
winning group. Exceptions to this were observed in 1896 when the
strength of the Rocky Mountain silver sentiment carried Utah into
the Democratic column, and in 1912 when Utah remained faithful
to the Republican nominee, Mr. Taft. Senator Smoot stood for years
as one of the important members of the ruling group of Republican
senators, but this fact has no significance as evidence of the permanent alliance of the Mormon group.

On the whole, the significant feature of the American party system
is the relatively small part played by religions as such in party

[37] Marshall, *op. cit.* See also his *American Catholicism* (New York, 1928).

[38] Walter Lippmann, *Men of Destiny* (New York, 1927); H. F. Pringle, *Alfred E. Smith: A Critical Study* (New York, 1927); A. E. Smith, *Up to Now* (New York, 1929).

[39] Gosnell, *Grass Roots Politics*, and *Machine Politics: Chicago Model*; W. F. Ogburn and N. S. Talbot, "A Measurement of the Factors in the Presidential Election of 1928," *Social Forces*, VIII (December, 1929), 175–183. The zero order coefficient of correlation between the Smith vote and the percentage Catholic was .47.

activities, in comparison with the role of religions abroad in states such as Belgium, France, and even England. The large numbers of denominations, the absence of a state church or establishment, the tradition of religious toleration are all factors in this situation. Churches are not obliged to struggle for their ecclesiastical existence, and are not habituated to collective church action in politics.

SEX

While in countries which have strong ecclesiastical parties there is a pronounced tendency for the women voters to favor such parties,[40] in the United States neither of the major parties has shown any special powers of attracting the women's votes. Sex lines have thus far played no outstanding part in the determination of American party allegiance. Women's votes, like those of men, have followed lines of class, race, religion, section, rather than of sex.

In contrast with the election records of certain European countries, the American records have given scant attention to a separate analysis of the votes of men and women. Such figures, however, are available for the state of Illinois for the presidential elections of 1916 and 1920.[41] In the first of these there was a slight tendency for a larger proportion of the women voters to support Wilson, the Democratic candidate. Some women may have been attracted by the slogan, "He kept us out of war." In the 1920 election it was found that in all parts of the state the women were consistently more in favor of Harding, the Republican candidate, than the men. In both elections the Socialist candidates were more strongly supported by men than by women. In state and local elections the women voters of Illinois in the higher rental areas showed a more marked tendency to split their tickets and support reform candidates than did the men.

In a few American jurisdictions the figures for the registration of voters are kept by sex. On the basis of such figures one of the authors made a study of the voting behavior of women and other groups in the city of Chicago.[42] It was found that for the period 1928–1936 there was a tendency for the women to favor Republican

[40] H. Tingsten, *Political Behavior* (London, 1937).

[41] *Chicago Daily News Almanac and Yearbook* for the years 1914–1921.

[42] H. F. Gosnell, *Machine Politics: Chicago Model* (Chicago, University of Chicago Press, 1937), pp. 98, 109.

candidates. One reason for this was the fact that a larger proportion of the women registered in the higher rental areas where the Republican party had its greatest strength. The Republicanism of the women in Chicago and Illinois was in part the result of the failure of the party workers in the Democratic strongholds to get out their full quota of women voters.

Party registration by sex has been kept in certain states[43] for varying periods. Their figures show that the women are more timid about registering their party affiliations than are the men, and that during a period of changing party allegiances they lag behind the men in shifting their party loyalties.

Wherever woman suffrage and popular lawmaking have been combined, it is possible to make certain inferences regarding the measures or policies that women are more anxious to support than the men.[44] Prohibition has been such a policy. Women have uniformly voted drier than the men. There is also some evidence to indicate that women are more interested in economy measures and in measures designed to protect public health.

The public opinion surveys have thrown considerable light upon the voting behavior of men and women. Gallup has shown that in recent elections 53 per cent of the voters were men and 47 per cent women.[45] In his pre-election polls in 1948 he found that presidential preferences of women showed no difference from male vote. Lydgate concluded that there did not appear to be any such thing as the "woman's viewpoint" as distinguished from the male viewpoint when it came to voting for candidates of the two major parties in recent elections.[46] On the other hand, Lazarsfeld, Berelson, and Gaudet found that while there was almost perfect political agreement between husband and wife, the agreement between father and daughter was less, and the political disagreements between men and their mothers-in-law were marked.[47]

Where the specific interests of women and children have been affected women have carried through effective political programs for

[43] Gosnell, *Democracy: The Threshold of Freedom*, p. 300.

[44] Gosnell, *Machine Politics: Chicago Model*; H. Tingsten, *Political Behavior* (London, 1937).

[45] *Gallup Political Almanac for 1948.*

[46] W. L. Lydgate, *What Our People Think* (New York, 1944), p 117.

[47] *The People's Choice*, pp. 140–145.

legislation or for administration, but in this process the parties have been of secondary importance to them—a means to an end. It is of course possible that in the future women may develop specific forms of party or nonparty activity, and of this indeed there are some indications. Of these the National League of Women Voters is by far the most significant. Its nonpartisan educational and legislative activities have been of growing importance.[48]

PARTY TRADITION

How these political groups and areas tend to perpetuate themselves is clearly shown by an examination of the traditional party voter. When fully developed these tend to transmit their party allegiance to the next generation by a process of political baptism and party training.

An analysis of the leading political groups shows that a very large number of their members are born into families which took for granted allegiance to a given party. The child of Republican parents is not likely to be a Democrat. Statistical data on this point are not available, but from numerous tests we have made over a period of twenty years, the percentage of "hereditary" voters runs from 65 per cent to 85 per cent, averaging about 75 per cent.[49] These figures are confirmed by the observation and judgment of others, and may be considered reliable. This allegiance may be changed by particular persons or particular issues, or in the course of those revolutions which shake the party world from time to time; [50] but, after all, it is a powerful element in the party's composition. As General Hugh S. Johnson put it: "My father was a Democrat, my grandfather was a Democrat and my great-grandfather was a Democrat. They were all pretty good active and leading Democrats. So I am a Democrat by inheritance, conviction and belief and I have never given anybody cause to believe that I am anything else." [51]

The strength of party tradition may be studied by examining the

[48] Carrie Chapman Catt, *Woman Suffrage and Politics* (New York, 1923). Sketches of woman's work in the political field are given in *The Woman's Journal*, the organ of the League.

[49] Lazarsfeld, Berelson, and Gaudet, *The People's Choice.*

[50] J. Kieran, ed., *The New Information Please Almanac for 1948*, p. 117.

[51] *New York Times*, August 12, 1933.

extent to which the popularity of parties remains the same in given districts over a period of time.[52] If a county or a subdivision of a city remains loyal to a given party over a long period of time, it may be assumed that the traditional vote is strong in that area. To some extent the voting responses of the same people may be analyzed in this fashion. Furthermore, it is clear that the new voters in an area which does not change its affiliation over a period of time must be brought under the influence of a group tradition. Using this method, Ogburn and Talbot found that in selected counties from the northern part of the United States the relationship between the party percentages in the 1920 and 1928 elections was not very close.[53] In other words, party traditions were shattered in both of these elections. On the other hand, studies made of later elections show a much closer relationship.[54] In California, Wisconsin, Iowa, and Pennsylvania the general distribution of votes in the thirties resembled that of the twenties even though the party totals indicated that considerable shifting had taken place. In general, the New Deal strongholds were those areas which had developed the greatest Democratic strength before 1932. As one of the authors put it in describing an urban community:

"The elections held in Chicago during the New Deal administration show that party tradition, as measured by previous voting behavior, is the most important variable in explaining political attitudes. The main characteristics of party lines in Chicago, a typical American metropolitan community, were set long before the depression." [55]

The truth is that party opinions are frequently fixed at a very early age, long before rational discussion has been possible. Such early opinions are influenced by family affiliation or interests, by those of the local group, or sometimes by some very trifling incident.[56] Inquiry into the dawn of the party consciousness shows that it frequently appears as early as nine or ten years of age, and is changed with difficulty. A boy often participates in a Republican parade and is henceforth a Republican. He hears a famous Demo-

[52] Gosnell, *Grass Roots Politics* and *Machine Politics: Chicago Model.*
[53] Ogburn and Talbot, *op. cit.*
[54] Louis Bean, *How to Predict Elections* (New York, Knopf, 1948).
[55] Gosnell, *Machine Politics: Chicago Model*, p. 124.
[56] Lazarsfeld, Berelson, Gaudet, *op. cit.*

cratic orator or shakes his hand and henceforth is a faithful disciple
of Democracy. His playmates or friends are mostly Republican, or
Democratic; it is not good form to be a Republican, or vice versa
it is not the thing to affiliate with Democrats. Examination of a few
cases will reveal at what an early age party affiliations are formed,
will show how they are encrusted with family and social interests,
with associations, and with early recollections until it becomes an
exceedingly difficult matter to change them. Let the average voter
ask himself when and why he first became a partisan, and the non-
rational character of the process will at once become evident. Long
before the age of rational judgment and intelligent decision, most
persons have stamped upon them deep-cut party impressions to be
effaced only with great difficulty, and usually not at all. The individual may rationalize his party allegiance in later years, finding
reasons or interests that satisfy his desire for a reason; but the
initial allegiance is likely to endure. A wide variety of circumstances
may change this early attachment to a particular party, and frequently does; but the burden of effort is upon those who attempt the
change, for they are dealing with fundamental emotional tendencies
rather than with rational decisions.

The Republican or the Democratic or the Socialist party environment tends to perpetuate itself by attaching the voter by the ties
of early association and memory, which have a certain force in
holding the allegiance of the voter when all else is gone. Just as, on
the other side, they may develop the economic or social interest by
an appeal to a logical argument, or appeal to a moral principle as a
basis of action. These are, of course, the common ways and means by
which all organizations, party as well as church, bind their adherents
to them and endeavor to retain their continuing allegiance. They are
no more peculiar to political parties than to any other formal group,
but they are pointed out here because they are usually ignored in
descriptions of the nature and functions of parties. Group solidarity,
group adherence, idealized in group "loyalty" and anathematized as
group "disloyalty" or "treason," are the common equipment of all
societies, and find their justification in the necessities of group survival and growth. Their social value, however, depends upon the
significance of the group and the importance of its strength and its
functions.

It is also to be observed that the traditional party allegiance is much more evident in national issues than in state or local issues. The major parties are primarily national organizations, and they hold their members much more loosely in affairs of local importance. Thus the "hereditary" Republican who always votes the national party ticket is less careful in voting for the governor or other state officials, while in local matters he may be, or think he is, independent. Yet even in the smallest unit of the electoral process the "hereditary" element is a considerable factor and can never be ignored. Even in township and ward elections there is a considerable percentage of voters who can be safely credited from the beginning, regardless of candidates or issues, as Republican or Democratic.

Revolutions are caused, in many instances, not by a transfer of votes from one party to another, but by the failure of the hereditary voters in one party to rally to the standard of their organization.[57] They rebuke their party in many cases not by voting against it, but by failing to vote at all; or by failing to give its candidates their enthusiastic support and thus cooling the current of party ardor. In some cases the early party habit will be changed and another party adopted, or on some unusual occasion there will be a temporary bolt to the opposition, intended as a rebuke, but not a separation. In the campaigns of 1896, 1912, 1920, 1924, 1928, and 1932, great blocks of voters transferred their allegiance either temporarily or permanently. Racial, class, and sectional issues diverted them from the usual channels of party movement. The eastern businessman was hostile to free silver, the western farmer to the gold standard; the middle class rebelled against the "invisible government" at which Theodore Roosevelt tilted. Millions went to the support of the independent candidacy of the elder La Follette; other millions crossed the line to vote for Hoover in 1928 and later for Roosevelt in 1932 and the three following elections. In the rise and fall of parties may be seen the formation and the disintegration of political habits in response to social and economic interests.

Habits of party allegiance generated under one set of conditions

[57] In 1942 the Democrats nearly lost control of Congress. The total vote cast was only 28,043,748 or 59.8 per cent of the 1940 vote. In 1944 the vote was larger again and Roosevelt won the election. In 1946 the total vote fell to 34,400,742 and the Democrats lost control of Congress. The obvious explanation is that the Democrats lost in part because large numbers of their supporters stayed at home.

tend to persist after these conditions have passed away, but they may be and are adjusted to new situations as they arise. There is a limit to the persistence of the party habit, of which every party manager must take cognizance. The tendency toward party regularity is a powerful one, but not the only factor in the situation. Each presidential election brings millions of new voters whose habits are to be formed.

A party may be divided into various sections or circles. One is made up of voters who are fixed partisans, who can certainly be counted upon in national affairs, and indeed some in all cases. Another section includes those who are fairly strong partisans, who require strong pressure to overcome the party habit, but are not wholly immovable. They are partisans with certain reservations and conditions. Then there is a third group made up of voters nominally Republican or Democratic, but whose nominal allegiance is easily shifted by the issues or the personalities of a campaign. They are independently inclined, and the party habit rests lightly upon them. Here again we may distinguish between those who are partisan, predisposed to partisanship, and independently inclined, because of reflection and conviction. Partisanship may be based upon a theory of political action or upon prejudice and habit alone, and the same may be said of nonpartisanship or of independent tendencies. Here we enter into a field of political psychology thus far unexplored, but rich in its possibilities.

CHAPTER VII

PARTY LEADERS

"Let him know who knows, lead."—Plato, *Republic,* Book IX, Chap. VIII.

"If we take a hundred men at random, we shall find among them on the average, six wealthy, six eloquent, six learned, six having the gifts of eloquence, learning and fortune, and six having art, cunning and intrigue."—John Adams, *Works,* Vol. VI. 456.

"The final obstacle in the way of any aristocratic rule is that in the absence of an articulate voice on the part of the masses, the best do not and cannot remain the best, the wise cease to be wise."—John Dewey, *The Public and Its Problems* (New York, Henry Holt and Co., 1927), p. 206.

"The sublime man has the greatest value, even when he is most delicate and fragile, because an abundance of very difficult and rare things have been reared through many generations and united in him."—Nietzsche, *The Will to Power,* p. 996.

"National Socialism sees in the democratic principle a mistaken conception taken over in the west. It sets up against it the principle of the leadership of the elite (*Führerauslese*) from the highest to the lowest offices. Power from the superior responsible leaders; no majority decisions. The leading class arises on the base of the better race; it keeps itself worthy of domination and keeps power irretrievable." —Hitler, *Zwischenspiel,* p. 207.

E VERY SOCIAL GROUP HAS PERSONS WHO REFLECT GROUP ASPIRA- tions, embody group ideals, organize group activities, direct the social forces which emanate from the group, and divert the course of group sentiment into greater or less conformance with their personal desires. The party leaders perform these functions in connection with the electorate in a democracy, with the tacit population in absolute government. They must continually strike a balance between individuality and acquiescence to humdrum mentality. The study of political leadership must delimit the spheres of how far the group mind may be changed, of how much the individual possesses in common with larger social groupings, of to what extent the leader possesses characteristics not belonging to any particular group.

These three questions will be considered in order. Both the problems and the attempted solutions will be analyzed. First, the limits of personal dominance will be surveyed. To what extent does the leader actually lead the political party? Second, an analysis of party leaders on the basis of the larger social groups to which he belongs will be sketched. What does the political leader owe to birth and other accidental factors which place him in a position to grasp for political leadership? In the third place, we shall indicate what personality traits are peculiarly prevalent among political leaders, so far as studies have been made in the field.

THE EXTENT OF PERSONAL DOMINANCE

Depending upon the situation in which he finds himself, the leader must rely upon one or a combination of the three devices for influencing conduct: coercion, persuasion, and domination.[1] The structure of the society at the time is the important limiting factor in this case. A two-party system forbids the first measure to its political leaders, always in law and generally in practice. Therefore, the latter two are most important in the American party system.

Washington, Adams, and Hamilton held that leadership was of mystic origin and that the masses should be led rather than allowed to take the lead. This was the position commonly taken by the British aristocracy of the day, as is shown by the writings of Edmund Burke. In later periods of American development, when the influence of British customs had begun to wear off, there were still champions of the heroic interpretation of history. Calhoun, Emerson, William James, Wiggam, and others have stressed the "great man" theory of cultural advance.[2] On the other hand, Thomas Jefferson, John Fiske, Lester F. Ward, and John Dewey have upheld the more democratic theory of leadership which places stress on environmental influences rather than upon biology and unknown factors.[3]

[1] R. M. MacIver, *The Web of Government* (New York, 1947); Herbert Goldhammer and Edward A. Shils, "Types of Power and Status," *American Journal of Sociology*, XLV (September, 1939), 171.

[2] John C. Calhoun, *Works*, Vol. I, pp. 16, 24–25, 28; Ralph Waldo Emerson, *Representative Men* (Boston, 1876); William James, "Great Men, Great Thoughts, and the Environment," *Atlantic Monthly*, 46 (October, 1880), 441–459; Albert Wiggam, *The Fruit of the Family Tree* (New York, 1924).

[3] Jefferson wanted aristocratic rulers democratically chosen, *Works*, IX, 425; John Fiske, "Sociology and Hero-Worship," *Atlantic Monthly*, XLVII (January, 1881), 75–84; L. F. Ward, *Dynamic Sociology* (New York and London, 1915); John Dewey, *The Public and Its Problems* (New York, 1927); J. Ratner, *John Dewey's Philosophy* (New York, 1939).

Regardless of what theory of leadership is held, there is agreement upon the importance of the phenomenon of dominance and subordination in the field of politics as in other realms.[4] It is clear that personal leadership may attract or repel large numbers of followers, may raise or depress the morale of party forces, may carry the party through the "danger spot," where policy or interest is no longer effective or for the moment ineffective. Party "idols" of the type of Jefferson, Jackson, Clay, and Lincoln, or in more recent days Blaine, Cleveland, Bryan, the Roosevelts, and Wilson, have often proved the decisive factor in fixing the personal allegiance of the voter. Many persons are more definitely affected by the type of government represented by an individual human being than by any principle or policy, or within certain limits than by any ordinary social or economic interest. Enthusiasm for leaders is, of course, highest when it coincides most closely with the lines of personal or class interest. Then the leader furnishes at once the human personality, the formula or slogan of the cause, and championship of the definite interest to be served. If he moves far away from the lines of habit and interests, he cannot hold his following, although within certain relatively narrow lines he may carry them with him, and in the neutral field where established prejudices are not attacked or interests invaded he may bring them a long way with him. Thus neither the Roosevelts nor Wilson could have carried their followers to communism, nor could McKinley have led his friends to free trade, nor Debs his group to advocacy of the "open shop." Of course, a distinction must be made between those leaders who lead class, race, or local groups by intensifying and exaggerating these special interests or emotions, and those who make a more general appeal to the broader interest of the community. Thus there are leaders who lead certain groups by appeals to race prejudice alone, and others who lead by appeals to section alone as

[4] See C. E. Merriam, *Systematic Politics* (Chicago, 1945), *Political Power* (New York, 1934), *The New Democracy and the New Despotism* (New York, 1939), *Four American Party Leaders* (New York, 1926); H. L. Smith and L. M. Krueger, *A Brief Summary of Literature on Leadership* (Bloomington, 1933); A. A. Roback, *The Psychology of Character* (New York, 1927); G. W. Allport, *Personality* (New York, 1937); P. Pigors, *Leadership or Domination* (Boston, 1935); E. Bogardus, *Leaders and Leadership* (New York, 1934); O. Tead, *The Art of Leadership* (New York, 1935); T. N. Whitehead, *Leadership in a Free Society* (Cambridge, 1936); M. H. Krout, *Introduction to Social Psychology* (New York, 1942); and U. S. Army Service Forces, Research Branch, "A Check List of Leadership Practices," *What the Soldier Thinks*, April, 1945. No. 5, pp. 38–39.

its peculiar advocate; but these leaders do not as a rule aspire to or achieve national leadership except in a time when such an issue becomes a national question.

The element of personal leadership must also be considered with reference not only to the greater figures of the party, but also to all leaders from the smallest voting unit to the largest. On a smaller scale there appear the same qualities in kind as in the larger. In every walk of life there are types of men to whom, because of their intelligence or judgment or for special economic or social reasons, many others look for leadership in political affairs, just as there are other types pre-eminent in business or social or moral relations. These key men carry much weight with their fellows, and their enthusiasm, lukewarmness, or defection is of great significance. Often their personal judgment or advice is more effective than any other single consideration in determining party allegiance in their immediate circles of acquaintance. Numbers of their fellow voters follow them closely and many others wish at least to hear them before coming to a decision. Others listen with interest and attention, and if not influenced in regard to the vote itself, they are affected with reference to the degree of their enthusiasm for their party. When these leaders weaken or desert or divide or are indifferent, their party group is shaken and disaster is near. But if their interest is keen and their enthusiasm runs high, the effect is clearly evident in the party strength in the vicinity. To what extent these men sense or reflect public opinion, and to what extent they create or direct it, we do not undertake to answer exactly and completely here.

Theodore Roosevelt once commented upon his position as a leader as follows: "People always used to say of me that I was an astonishingly good politician and divined what the people were going to think. This really was not an accurate way of stating the case. I did not 'divine' what the people were going to think; I simply made up my mind what they *ought* to think; and then did my best to get them to think it. Sometimes I failed, and then my critics said that 'my ambition had overleaped itself.' Sometimes I succeeded, and then they said that I was an uncommonly astute creature to have detected what the people were going to think and to pose as their leader in thinking it." [5]

[5] J. B. Bishop, *Theodore Roosevelt and His Times* (New York, Hodder and Stoughton, 1920), II, 414.

SOCIAL STATUS OF AMERICAN POLITICAL LEADERS

In order to consider the peculiar characteristics of American party leaders, a brief analysis will be made of certain social data regarding American presidents. The presidency is the most important political office in the United States, even though it is not always held by the most outstanding political personality. A discussion of the kind of men who have occupied the White House will reveal considerable information about the American party system.

Of the thirty-two presidents, eighteen were born on farms and eight in small towns under 2500. In other words; although the United States at the present time is 56 per cent urban and although 34 per cent of the people live in cities over 100,000, only six presidents were born in urban communities, and just one in a great city. The failure of the cities to produce presidential material is a rather startling fact, but it became more understandable when one stops to think that Harry Truman was born in 1884, when only 30 per cent of the total population was urban, and there was but one city of over a million. All the other presidents were born before this. When the United States began its career as an independent nation it had not a city with as many as 50,000 inhabitants, and the overwhelming proportion of the people lived on farms.[6]

An analysis of the biographies of presidents shows that there was comparatively little change in their local environment until after they were sixteen years of age. Between the ages of sixteen and twenty-five a relatively large proportion of them moved to small towns or urban communities. Only four spent these years in purely farm communities. Most of them were going to school during this period of their lives, but some were wandering about trying to establish themselves. At the time of their election seven of the presidents were living on farms, and nine were living in cities of over 100,000. Thus it is apparent that the growing urbanization of the United States has had its effect upon the selection of presidents. Most prospective presidents may have been born on farms or in

[6] For a discussion of the growth of cities, see National Resources Committee, *Our Cities: Their Role in the National Economy* (Government Printing Office, June, 1937), and *Population Statistics, Urban Data* (Government Printing Office, October, 1937).

small towns, but they found it advantageous to move to cities early
in their political careers.

Another interesting fact to consider regarding the presidents is the
occupation of their fathers. This throws light upon the income and
prestige status of the future leaders during their early formative
years. Among American notables generally, Visher found that, in proportion to their numbers in the general population, professional
men contributed more than twice as many notables as businessmen,
nearly twenty times as many as the farmers, forty times as many as
the skilled laborers, and 1340 times as many as the unskilled laborers.[7] Of the thirty-two fathers of presidents seventeen were
farmers, three were clergymen, three were lawyers, and the remaining nine were in such scattered occupations as retailing, tailoring,
charcoal manufacturing, philanthropy, custodial service, and medi-
cine. The high productivity of the farmers in fathering presidents is
closely related to the above analysis of the birthplaces of the presidents. Farming was the main occupation of Americans at the time
that most of the presidents were born. Many of these farmers whose
sons later occupied the White House were quite well-to-do according
to the standards of their day. It is significant to note that only one
president was of what we might call working-class origin.

While the stories of persons with meager education who have risen
to the highest political post in America are featured in the school
textbooks, a cold analysis of the situation shows that only one president, Andrew Johnson, had no formal schooling and that only ten of
the thirty-two did not proceed beyond the common school. On the
other hand, two-thirds of our presidents have been college graduates.
The proportion of college graduates in the total population has
varied over the span of American history and is larger today than at
any preceding time.[8]

A closer examination of the education of American presidents
shows that practically all of them went to older institutions of learning in the eastern part of the United States. Only one president,
Herbert Hoover, graduated from a university west of Ohio (Stan-

[7] S. S. Visher, *Geography of American Notables, a Statistical Study of Birthplaces, Training, and Distribution, and an Effort to Evaluate Various Environmental Factors* (Indiana University Studies, XV, No. 79, June, 1928).

[8] John Kieran (ed.), *The New Information Please Almanac for 1948* (New
York. 1948). p. 317.

ford). All the presidents who attended college went to private colleges or universities, except James K. Polk, who attended the University of North Carolina. The great western state universities have yet to train a president of the United States. Time has been against them since many have been established in the latter half of the nineteenth century. It is likely, however, that the next hundred years will find the state universities playing a more important role in the education of presidents.

When a man is being considered for the presidency, one question is always asked, "How old is he?" If the person discussed is too young or too old, his availability is greatly lessened. An examination of the ages of presidents at the time of their inauguration shows that two-thirds of them were in their 50's, only six were over 60, and two over 65. Of these latter, William Harrison, age 68, died within a few months after his inauguration; but James Buchanan, just 65, finished his term. Theodore Roosevelt was the youngest man to be inaugurated president, being only 42 at the time of McKinley's assassination.

From what occupations have American presidents been recruited? While a majority of them were born on farms, two-thirds were lawyers at the time of their elevation to the presidency. Of the remaining third, three were farmers, two were soldiers, and the rest were scattered among the following professions: engineering, journalism, education, tailoring, writing, and public service. The preponderance of lawyers is more overwhelming than in the legislative branch of our government where the proportion has been around one-half.[9]

Looking at the skill and class analysis of American party leaders as a whole, it is clear that the profession of law is most largely represented. The legal group represents all types and shades of opinion —conservative, liberal, and radical. Agriculture and business are represented among the leaders of the parties, but by no means as largely as the lawyers. The medical profession is reflected among the leaders here and there, especially in local affairs, and sometimes on a national scale, as in the case of General Wood. More commonly their influence has been felt on the side of public administration in

[9] H. F. Gosnell, *Democracy: Threshold of Freedom* (New York, 1948); H. F. Gosnell and Margaret Schmidt, "Professional Associations," *Annals of the American Academy of Political and Social Science*, CLXIX (May, 1935), 25–33.

the great field of public sanitation. The same may be said of the engineering group, of whom Goethals and Hoover are conspicuous illustrations. Scientists and students, commonly called "professors," are found in the list of political leaders, although less frequently here than in any other country. A large number have also been "teachers" at some stage of their careers. Wilson and Butler are very conspicuous examples of the activities of the scholarly group in the American political field. During Franklin Roosevelt's first administration academic men were given a prominent place in the party councils and this led to the coining of the phrase "brain trust." [10]

The journalistic and "literary" group has supplied a notable series of political leaders, many of whom have held no public office but have directed party affairs or influenced them from a private station. Horace Greeley, Joseph Medill, George William Curtis are conspicuous cases in the period following the Civil War. At a later period came an extensive group ranging from the proprietors of metropolitan journals or series of them to the owners of the smaller journals, many of whom were widely influential. Here are found men of the type of Whitelaw Reid, Henry Watterson, W. R. Hearst, Scripps, Harvey, and a long line running down to Cox, Harding, and Colonel Knox. These journalists often made and unmade leaders, local, state, and national.[11] The ramifications of the journalistic group run so wide and deep in the political soil that they constitute almost a world by themselves, with attitudes, values, and techniques all their own, requiring separate description and study.

A striking feature of American political leadership has been until recently the small part played by the direct representative of labor. Men "carrying union cards" are found in local bodies, in state legislatures and in the lower house of Congress, but they are rarely elected as governors or senators, and they are just beginning to figure prominently in national conventions and in the inner circles of

[10] L. C. Rosten, *The Washington Correspondents* (New York, 1937), pp. 163–164.
[11] Interesting illustrations of the way in which journalistic power may be employed are given in Fremont Older's narration of his experiences in *My Own Story* (San Francisco, 1919); Melville E. Stone, *Fifty Years a Journalist* (Garden City, 1922); H. H. Kohlsaat, *From McKinley to Harding* (New York, 1923); S. Bent, *Strange Bedfellows: A Review of Politics, Personalities and the Press* (New York, 1928); and F. Lundberg, *Imperial Hearst* (New York, 1936).

party command. Notable labor leaders of the type of Gompers and Green have not taken a direct part in party management or direction, although they have engaged in various campaigns where the interests of labor were directly involved. In the United States, there have been few figures such as Keir Hardie or Herbert Morrison in England, or as Thomas or Jouhaux in France, or as other postwar leaders in the parties of Europe, who speak in the party circle directly for labor. This is in part due to the tactics of the leaders who until recently have deemed it wiser to avoid the field of party activity. It is probable, however, that with the growth of the labor movement there will be a larger direct participation of labor representatives in the party leadership and control. The late Sidney Hillman and his Political Action Committee marked the way.

At the same time it is to be noted that the great capitalists have not commonly taken a direct part in the leadership of parties. The Goulds, the Vanderbilts, the Rockefellers, the Harrimans, the Morgans have not undertaken the role of open leadership and management in either the parliamentary field or that of campaigns and management. Among the wealthiest presidents were George Washington and Franklin D. Roosevelt. When the latter died, he left an estate of $3,000,000. This is far from one of the great American fortunes, but it put him near the top of the income pyramid. Men of great wealth have occupied important positions in the President's Cabinet. Andrew Mellon's long career as Secretary of the Treasury is a case in point. Those at the apex of the income pyramid might and often did speak for large-scale capital, but the significant point is that the greater powers were rarely there in person.[12] Tilden was a man of wealth, but after all primarily an attorney rather than a proprietor. In later times Mark Hanna was a tentative candidate for president, and Lowden was an active candidate, but neither of these men could be ranked among the great industrial leaders of the day. As in the case of labor, the great capitalists have recognized the political weakness of their open leadership and have preferred the indirect method of operation through both political parties. Neither Morgan

[12] A possible exception is Senator Nelson Aldrich of Rhode Island, John D. Rockefeller's son-in-law. His nephew, Nelson Rockefeller, became Coordinator of Inter-American Affairs in 1940 and Assistant Secretary of State in 1944. Averell Harriman held diplomatic posts and became Secretary of Commerce in 1947.

nor Gompers would have been a strong candidate for the presidency. Both were busy with other affairs, and both brought all possible pressure to bear in critical cases upon both political parties. Yet there is a distinct tendency for the leaders of both labor and capital to enter more directly and openly into the field of party and parliamentary relations.

The military group has played a role in party leadership, but not on the basis of a class of professional soldiers.[13] From Washington to Theodore Roosevelt a military record has been a significant factor in party leadership. Sometimes this took the form of "celebrity" and "availability" with real management and control in the hands of managers, and at other times the military ability was coupled with real qualities of party chieftainship. Grant was an example of the first kind, and Theodore Roosevelt of the other. In contrast with the European systems, however, the professional army group possesses no great influence on the politics of the nation, and the military party leaders hold power by virtue of their eminence and prestige rather than the backing of a military class. They have also, of course, their appeal to the soldiers who were once a part of the armies they led or of which they were members. In spite of repeated denials of his candidacy, General Eisenhower showed remarkable popularity in the polls of 1948. So far as military celebrity is concerned, it may be regarded as an avenue of approach to party leadership rather than attainment and retention of it. The world-old prestige of the military chieftain must be pieced out with the other qualities of civic and party leadership to ensure permanent success.

LEADERSHIP TRAITS

Our knowledge of the human personality is only in its beginnings, as is our understanding of the social processes in which this personality is set.[14] Individual and social psychology is likely to make long strides forward in the next generation, perhaps indeed under some

[13] Albert Somit, "The Military Hero as Presidential Candidate," *Public Opinion Quarterly*, Vol. XII, Summer, 1948, 192–200.

[14] Both of the authors have in preparation studies of leadership. Mr. Merriam is working on a general study of leadership and Mr. Gosnell is studying the social and personal characteristics of successful and unsuccessful candidates for president of the United States.

other name and with some more effective technique than at present.[15]

The study of party leadership is inseparably bound up with the advancement of these subjects. The types of human differentials identified, their origin, are basic in the understanding of leadership, political or otherwise. We look confidently to physiology, to neurology, to psychology, and to psychiatry for aid.

A man such as Clay, Blaine, or Roosevelt may inspire personal devotion to a point where thousands "would go to hell for him." Others like Wilson have spoken like prophets, followed at a distance. Lincoln touched a deeper and more human chord in the hearts and sympathies of men. Types like Root and Hughes have been looked to as intellectual leaders, men who "knew what they were talking about." Leaders like Debs have awakened the sympathies of toilers and the human regard of others. Bryan's unchallenged sympathy with the democratic cause and his long and unembittered championship of the people's rule endeared him to thousands. Smith touched the emotional interest of great groups of persons. Closer analysis would of course show the specific qualities and technique in and through which each of these men functioned in the political life of the nation.[16]

On a smaller scale in states, counties, and cities, the same qualities of leadership are to be found, although, in many cases where the spoils system has held sway, overgrown by the special developments under the regime of boss rule.[17] A party leader cannot lead unless he has a general staff and officers, commissioned and non-commissioned, all along the line. In the personnel of the party's commanding offi-

[15] G. Murphy, *Experimental Social Psychology* (New York, 1937); C. P. Stone, C. W. Darrow, C. Landis, and L. L. Heath, *Studies in the Dynamics of Behavior* (Chicago, 1932).

[16] H. F. Gosnell, *Boss Platt and His New York Machine* (Chicago, 1924); C. O. Johnson, *Carte, Henry Harrison I* (Chicago, 1928); unpublished Ph.D. dissertations at the University of Chicago: Marietta Stevenson, "William Jennings Bryan" (1926); Roy Peel, "James Gillespie Blaine: A Study in Political Leadership" (1927); Pearl Roberston, "Grover Cleveland as a Political Leader" (1937); and the following master's dissertations at the University of Chicago: G. Routt, "Will Hays: A Study in Political Leadership and Management" (1927); L. F. Becker, "Alfred E. Smith: A Personality Study of a Political Leader" (1938). See also H. Zink, "A Case Study of a Political Boss," *Psychiatry*, I (November, 1938), 527–533.

[17] See Chap. IX. For a further discussion of these points, see also C. E. Merriam, *Political Power: Its Composition and Incidence* (New York, 1934), Chap. I.

cers are found much the same qualities and traits as in the larger leaders of the broader scale. Here too, in addition to the more specific qualities of leadership, there may be commanders who are followed because of great managerial and organizing ability, because of intellectual ascendancy, because of economic position, of military or other form of prestige, by reason of a series of qualities or combinations of qualities which induce men to follow. Sometimes, to be sure, the nominal leaders do not rule in their own right, but by reason of the strength of others.

There are certain outstanding features to which attention may be called, even though complete information is not available. Most leaders have been endowed with a powerful physique, as were Washington, Jackson, Lincoln, Theodore Roosevelt. They corresponded to the traditional leader as a man of great physical strength and endurance. Unquestionably they would have come through with honors in a searching all-round test of physical qualities. There were, of course, many exceptions to this.

The relationship between bodily structure and personality has been an attractive subject from earliest times. Shakespeare puts these words in the mouth of Julius Caesar:

> Let me have men about me that are fat;
> Sleek-headed men, such as sleep o' nights:
> Yon Cassius has a lean and hungry look:
> He thinks too much: such men are dangerous.
> —*Julius Caesar*, Act I, Sc. 2.

In recent times a German psychiatrist, Ernst Kretschmer, has presented the most elaborate analysis of this theme. In his book, *Physique and Character*, first published in 1925, he attempted to generalize on the basis of these clinical findings. In mental hospitals he found that dementia praecox patients were most frequently thin (aesthenic) and that manic-depressive patients were most frequently fat and rounded (pyknic). He postulated the theory that the difference between normality and abnormality was one of degree and not of kind, that temperament was largely a product of hereditary glandular structure, and that there were two main types of temperament, the schizoid (associated with thin or athletic physique) and the cycloid (associated with obesity). Schizoids were characterized as introverted, idealistic, formalistic, and romantic, and cyclothymic persons were likely to be extroverted, realistic, jovial, and objective. Applying these concepts to American party leaders, we would say that Woodrow Wilson was schizothymic and William Howard Taft cyclothymic. Kretschmer's work has been the subject of many spirited controversies, and it is easy to see that many exceptions must be made to his generalizations. However, he has stimulated research along these lines and some of his bold generalizations have been partially substantiated.

A notable contribution to the study of political personalities has been made by Harold D. Lasswell.[18] Emphasizing the relevance of material derived from intensive interviewing of individual persons, he has constructed theories of individual and mass behavior which are worthy of careful consideration.

The devising of new and better methods of intensive observation enabled Lasswell to consider the motives of political personalities from a fresh viewpoint. He gives the following formula for the development of the political man: The political man is one who "displaces" his private motives onto a public object and rationalizes his displacement in terms of public benefit. Thus a man who, by some circumstance, is without intimate friendship and feels the need for affection may displace this need by grasping the chance of becoming a political orator concerned with the underprivileged groups and thus be satisfied at least in part by the applause he receives.

Lasswell also generalized about the various types of personalities likely to be successful under differing environmental conditions. According to his analysis Lincoln rose to prominence in the early Civil War crisis because of conditions prevailing at the time. The North was then vacillating and disunited. Lincoln was not aggressive or demanding. Consequently, Northerners accepted his cautious leadership, whereas the South, united and determined, would not have accepted a leader of the Lincoln stamp.

[18] *Power and Personality* (New York, 1948); *Psychopathology and Politics* (Chicago, 1930); *World Politics and Personal Insecurity* (New York, 1935), and *Politics: Who Gets What, When, How* (New York, 1936). See also L. P. Clark, *Lincoln* (New York, 1933); J. Dollard, *Criteria for the Life History* (New Haven, 1935); L. K. Frank, "The Dilemma of Leadership, Psychiatry," *Journal of the Biology and Pathology of Interpersonal Relations*, II (August, 1939), 343; Zink, *op. cit.*

Following the work done in psychiatry, Lasswell developed a typology which is based upon the theory that personality is a latent system of reaction patterns finished shortly after birth or at least by the second or third year of the life of the individual. According to their aggressiveness, he classified political personalities as relatively uninhibited rage types, partially inhibited rage types and inhibited rage types.[19] The first category describes those who are extremely willful, domineering, violent, and egocentric. Andrew Jackson was such a type. Lincoln may be put in the second category as he had a strong structure of inhibition but also made some attacks upon his opponents. Calvin Coolidge illustrates the last type since he was not known to exhibit rage.

Another type of approach is the study of leadership through an examination and analysis of the several forms of skills, techniques, tricks of recognized political leaders—a behavioristic observation of what the leader actually does. Analysis might also be made of the words addressed to his audience, the various types of appeal used on various occasions. With all the facilities that might conceivably be employed it would be possible to obtain a realistic picture both of the speaker and of the audience, with sound and motion fully reproduced. With modern instruments it is possible to record a voice picture as well as the ordinary sound reproduction of the movies.[20]

It would also be possible to study closely other leadership situations as they develop: the conference, the administrative role, the judging situation, the various forms of adjustment and manipulation which make up the political process.

If nonleaders are also studied, it is possible to delineate clearly some of the attributes of the leader in contradistinction to the less skillful aspirant for power.[21]

[19] *Politics: Who Gets What, When, How*, Chap. VIII.

[20] Donald Hayworth, "Analysis of Speeches in Presidential Campaigns from 1884 to 1920," *Quarterly Journal of Speech*, XVI (February, 1930), 35–42; H. H. Higgins, *Influencing Behavior through Speech* (Boston, 1930). See also titles in H. D. Lasswell, *et al., Propaganda and Promotional Activities* (Minneapolis, 1935), "Oral Communication," pp. 338–340, and in B. L. Smith, H. D. Lasswell, and R. D. Casey, *Propaganda, Communication, and Public Opinion: A Comprehensive Reference Guide* (Princeton, 1946).

[21] From the standpoint of method, one of the most interesting studies of leadership is that by W. S. Cowley, "Three Distinctions in the Study of Leadership," *Journal of Abnormal and Social Psychology*, XXIII, No. 2 (July–Sept., 1928). In this study, twenty-eight psychological tests were given to leaders and nonleaders in

Broadly speaking, the common qualities of great party leaders have been: (1) Unusual sensitiveness to the strength and direction of social and industrial tendencies with reference to their party and political bearings.[22] (2) Acute and quick perception of possible courses of community conduct with prompt action accordingly. (3) Facility in group combination and compromise—political diplomacy in ideas, policies, and spoils. (4) Facility in personal contacts with widely varying types of men. (5) Facility in dramatic expression of the sentiment or interest of large groups of voters, usually with voice or pen—fusing a logical formula, an economic interest, a social habit or predisposition in a personality. (6) Courage, not unlike that of the military commander, whose best laid plans require a dash of luck for their successful completion. It was Theodore Roosevelt who said, "Only those are fit to live who do not fear to die," and Franklin D. Roosevelt who said on the dramatic occasion of the collapse of the banks in 1933, "All we have to fear is fear itself."

Not all leaders possess these qualities, but it will be found that a combination of them characterizes those who have attained and held eminent party position, and that many of these qualities are found in the minor leaders. It goes without saying that the leader must be adapted to those who follow, and that the opportunity and the environment must be favorable to the particular type of initiative and energy. It will also be found not infrequently that "celebrities" in nonpolitical fields may be transferred to party leadership, but in such cases leadership is likely to be nominal rather than real, unless latent qualities of the type above described are discovered.

In many respects the qualities of political leaders resemble those of other leaders in the world of ecclesiastical, economic, or social organization in any large-scale group where many contacts are involved. The magnate, the cardinal, the general have many points in common with the political head. Contacts between these various types of leaders offer one of the most interesting studies in the

---

three different face-to-face situations. It was an attempt to study leadership in army life, in student life, and in the criminal world. The tests differentiated between leaders and nonleaders in the same situation, but the leaders in the three different situations did not possess the same traits. This study was not based on a sufficient number of cases to make any generalizations but it suggests interesting possibilities.

[22] It was said of an important political leader that he kept both ears to the ground.

field of human affairs. The function of the political leader in the process of social control is, however, more complicated and difficult than any other of those who deal with large groups of men.

Analysis reveals many and varied forms and types of party leadership which call for different combinations of qualities. One is skillful in the contests of the forum; another in the field of written debate and discussion; another in the parliamentary conflicts of the council chamber; another in the formulation of constructive programs and policies; another in the qualities of the executive and the administrator; another in organization of party strength; another in finesse and intrigue. The leadership of the party, taken as a group, will include all of these elements and will use them; but the particular leader at any given moment may possess only one or several of them. Thus Blaine, Bryan, Wilson, the Roosevelts, Hoover, Root, Hanna, Smith, Truman, Dewey—all represent different qualities of leadership, or different combinations of qualities.

From another point of view we may distinguish other types. These would include: (1) the advocate of causes or principles; (2) the executive, dealing primarily with the mechanics and problems of technical management; (3) the spoilsman concerned primarily with graft and spoils. Sometimes two of these qualities are combined in one person, as manager-spoilsman, advocate-spoilsman, or advocate-manager. Theodore Roosevelt once drew a line between the leader and the boss as follows: A leader is one who "fights openly for principles and who keeps his position of leadership by stirring the consciences and convincing the intellects of his followers, so that they have confidence in him and will follow him, because they can achieve greater results under him than under anyone else." [23] The boss "is a man who does not gain his power by open means, but by secret means, and usually by corrupt means. Some of the worst and most powerful bosses in our history either held no public office or else some unimportant public office. They made no appeal either to intellect or to conscience. Their work was done chiefly behind closed doors, and consisted chiefly in the use of that greed which gives in order that it may get." [24]

Most of the greater leaders have been men of intellectual training

[23] *Autobiography* (New York, Scribner's, 1920), p. 148.
[24] *Ibid.*, p. 149.

and more than average ability. They were regarded as men of honesty, sincerity, and genuine democracy in their sympathies (aside from the few brief weeks of partisan campaigning when dishonesty, insincerity, and desire to betray the people were attributed to all of them). Of the great American political leaders it is evident that the larger number possessed the faculty of interpreting political forces either in oratorical or literary terms. Among the really great orators we may class Lincoln, Bryan, the Roosevelts, La Follette, Debs, Blaine, Schurz, Conkling, Johnson. Powerful speakers include men of the type of Smith, Hughes, Borah, Root, Reed, Garfield, Tilden, Altgeld, Clark, Weaver, Hayes, Harrison, McKinley, Dewey, and a long series of others. Among the leaders with high literary power for political purposes were Jefferson, Cleveland, Theodore Roosevelt, Wilson, Greeley, Curtis, Watterson, Hearst, Godkin. In all these cases ideas with a claim to universal validity were given formulation by representatives of various social and economic interests. These leaders supplied the formula, the phrase, or the program by means of which different groups might make effective their desires. Theodore Roosevelt once expressed their position clearly when he referred to himself as a "great sounding board" for popular ideas, declaring that he collected and reflected doctrines of the day.

Sometimes they spoke for narrow groups and sometimes for broader interests; sometimes for the nation, sometimes even for democracy in phrases that echoed around the world, as in the words of Lincoln and Wilson.

Often these leaders are identified with a "cause," which may be that of a class, a section, a race, a complex of interests, always interpreted, of course, in terms of the party, the nation, and the general good. All national leaders must make their appeal to the general interest of the community, even though in fact the appeal may be narrower in scope and primarily advantageous to a class or a section of the people. Many leaders have followed in this country a median line, holding to what Europeans call the Center, and avoiding the Right or the Left. To this our biparty system and our constitutional and judicial limitations upon government have contributed. No very radical program can be put through by any one party because constitutional change may be required before much progress has been made. Hence leaders in great social and economic movements have often been found outside the ranks of the parties, from the days of slavery to those of prohibition and the struggle against war. Neither the outstanding radicals nor the outstanding conservatives are found among our parliamentary or party leaders as commonly as in the European countries.

One of the main problems in the study of party leadership is the systematization of the material already obtained. A number of hypotheses are available which might be tested with the data at hand.[25] It cannot be too often reiterated that leadership cannot be studied as a thing apart, but only in its social setting, in its inter-relations with a wide variety of supporting situations. It is not divinity that explains the power of the leader, or some form of magic or occultism, or some mysterious magnetism which lies beyond the power of man to comprehend. When the forces that focus around the axis of what we call, for lack of a better term, personality are more fully understood, and when the forces that play around the axis of what we term mass, the group, and which we interpret in terms of social psychology are understood, it will be possible to set up an accurate description and explanation of what in earlier times was considered to be a mystery.

In the meantime we may progress by careful studies of the social and economic background of leaders, their family origins, their early life patterns and fixations, and the later problems of adolescence—the genetics of personality. We may study the constitutional background as intensively as modern and developing science permits; we may utilize such "batteries of tests" as are permissible; we may employ the techniques of psychiatry where feasible; we may scrutinize the intellectual and social traits or tendencies of leaders as far as they are susceptible of analysis. We may break down the acts of leaders as they become evident in overt behavior, and study their techniques as inferred from their conduct. On the other side, we may study the community itself with its many currents and trends of interest, sentiment, opinion, the specific types of situations that arise in such a type of community or in this particular community. Nothing is alien to the larger background which gradually focuses down to a specific situation in the spotlight of which the individual leader emerges.

[25] See Appendix for schedule containing items which are relevant to many different hypotheses.

CHAPTER VIII

THE ORGANIZATION OF THE PARTY

"There are more than 150,000 loyal men and women in this country who are connected with regular Democratic organizations ranging from 'bigwigs' like national and state committeemen, down through precinct and district captains and canvassers, to the local committee workers and other humble folk who pull the doorbells, distribute the literature, and haul the voters to the polls on election day. An army is seldom stronger than its infantry forces, and a political army is never stronger than its corps of workers."—James A. Farley, *Behind the Ballots* (New York, Harcourt, Brace and Company, 1938), p. 193.

AN ESSENTIAL ELEMENT IN THE COMPOSITION OF THE POLITICAL party is the "organization." This is composed of men who in large measure make politics their profession or occupation, and who constitute a governing group within the party group itself. The political practitioners, or "politicians" as they are commonly called, are the inner circle of the political or party group itself. They are the trustees or directors of the party, for the time being. Some have even called them the real party. This professional organization itself becomes an interest and helps to hold the party together and to ensure its continuity.

The members of the governing group have a direct and personal interest in the life of the party and in its prestige and success, for upon this hangs their economic and social position. They constitute, then, a solid inner core of voters who have been accustomed to common action in a campaign or series of campaigns, or in the actual work of legislation or administration, and who tend to continue their habit of concerted action, even after the occasion for their original concert of action has gone by. They are, therefore, powerful cohesive forces in the party system. They bridge over the spots where there may be no clear-cut issue between the parties, and hold the group together until "the next time." Without this group the nature of the party would be materially changed.

The bulk of the members of the "organization" are officeholders, although by no means all of them, and hence one of the chief elements of cohesion is the offices, either elective or appointive. Interest in the public service and adaptability to certain types of such service attract many men who possess some aptitude for group representation. Special industrial privilege, personal spoils, and graft also attract many, and not infrequently the spoils interest dominates or obscures all others. There is a common saying which has in it a grain of truth, although not the whole truth, that "there is no politics in politics." Under certain circumstances, hereafter more fully discussed, personal and private purposes overshadow public purposes, and then party control in the name of the public may become merely a mask for plunder and exploitation.[1]

As in all groups, the organization in the political party tends to master the group rather than to serve it, and if left unchecked by vigorous protest and counter action becomes irresponsible and unrepresentative of the party or public purpose.[2] Commercial organizations, churches, and societies of all types experience the same difficulty in holding their representatives to the straight line of the common interest. In the party this tendency is more highly developed than commonly, because of the highly specialized and exacting demands of party duties and because of a lack of intense common interest on the part of the mass of the party members at many periods of the party's life. The "organization" normally represents and often leads, but it also has a strong tendency to dominate and to impose its will contrary to the well-known opinions and interests of the mass of the party members. The competition of rival party organizations, the struggle between factional organizations in the same party, and the possibility of party revolution tend to check this tendency to dominate of the organization, and render it more amenable to the general will of the party or of the public.

The organization then is directly interested in party continuity and operates powerfully in holding together the loosely formed party. The continuing direct interest of the professional partisan

[1] See chapters IX–XIII on the spoils system.

[2] See R. Michels, *Political Parties* (London, 1915), on the oligarchical tendencies of the organization leaders of a political party. See also C. Berdahl, "Party Membership in the U. S.," *American Political Science Review*, XXXVI (February, April, 1942), 16–50, 241–262.

group, together with the continuing habit of the partisan voter, unite to give the party a continuing existence, an entity, a reality, which it would not otherwise possess. Leaders incarnate and dramatize it, and fresh issues vitalize the party from time to time.

THE COMMITTEE HIERARCHY

Party authority is vested, when conventions and primaries are not in operation, in a series of committees and committeemen.[3] If conventions and primaries are looked upon as legislative and policy-determining, the committees may be considered as executive or administrative in nature. They are the continuing organs of the party.

There are several ranks in the hierarchy of committees. The most important of these are the following:

National committee
Congressional committees
State or central executive committee
County committee
City, ward, township, or town committee
Precinct committee

In addition there are a number of other committees covering various types of districts to which they correspond.

Unlike the committee system of a British political party, the committees of an American political party are very poorly integrated. The heads of the national organization of the Republican party have few powers of compulsion to exercise over the lesser party managers. It is true that it may be easier to collect funds on a national basis, and the national leaders can then withhold funds from recalcitrant local party executives. But these local executives cannot be ruthlessly eliminated in the way that the British Conservative party can wipe out its local organizers. The local autonomy of state, county and city party committees in the United States is the product of our

[3] A good discussion of this subject is found in James A. Farley, *Behind the Ballots* (New York, 1938). See also E. J. Flynn, *You're the Boss* (New York, 1947). G. I Luetscher, *Early Political Machinery* (Philadelphia, 1903), discusses the beginnings of party structure, but a complete treatment of this subject is not available. See also E. M. Sait, *American Parties and Elections* (New York, 1948); F. R. Kent, *The Great Game of Politics* (New York, 1926); E. E. Schattschneider, *Party Government* (New York, 1942).

peculiar governmental institutions, our separation of powers, our federal system with forty-eight semiautonomous states, our relatively rigid federal and state institutions, our embalming of local units in constitutional provisions, and our multiplicity of local elective offices.

The National Committee

The national committee is composed of one man and one woman from each state and territory in the Republican party, and the same is true of the Democratic party except that there are also members from the Panama Canal Zone and the Virgin Islands.[4] These members are chosen for a term of four years, usually by the delegates from a given state to the national convention,[5] but sometimes in a direct primary by the party voters of the state, by the state convention itself, or by the state committee.

The principal powers of this committee center around the calling and organization of the national convention, and the conduct of the campaign after candidates are named. The committee fixes the time and place of holding the convention, which may or may not be a matter of strategic importance. It decides upon the method of apportioning the number of delegates to the various states. It also recommends the temporary officers of the convention, and makes up the temporary roll of the body. The latter power is one of prime importance, as the control of the convention may be determined by the temporary roll of its membership. This was clearly seen in 1912 when the action of the committee in placing Taft delegates on the temporary roll gave the control of the convention to the Taft forces. In the same way, in the Democratic conventions of 1896 and 1900, the power of the national committee was strikingly shown. Especially in dealing with the delegates from the southern states where the party organization is loosely thrown together, the power of the Republican committee is very large, and its decision may materially affect the relative strength of the factions and candidates.

At times the national committee has made suggestions on funda-

[4] See G. S. P. Kleeberg, *Formation of the Republican Party* (New York, 1911). The chairman of this committee is suggested by the presidential candidate, and the position is one of prestige in the party, especially in the case of success.

[5] The *Proceedings* of the Democratic committee are published as an appendix to the official convention proceedings.

mental questions of party organization. Thus the national committee of the Republican party presented to the convention of 1916 a plan for the readjustment of party representation; and in 1920 the Republican committee appointed a preliminary platform committee to aid in the consideration of the essentials of a party declaration of principles.

Following the 1928 campaign there has been a trend toward the establishment of a larger permanent staff on the part of the national committees. The success of the Democratic national committee's publicity bureau during the Hoover administration led the Republicans to copy this device. During the years 1929–1932 the so-called "Smear Hoover" campaign received part of its impetus from the central headquarters staff of the Democratic party.[6] With the advent of the New Deal, the Republicans established a similar continuing publicity bureau which has kept up a running-fire criticism of the Democratic administration. As a result of his experiences in the 1936 campaign, Republican Chairman Hamilton felt the need of a permanent and efficient staff so strongly that in 1937 he went to England and spent some time studying British party organization.[7] Since that time the permanent staff of the Republican national committee has been eight to ten times larger than it used to be in "off years."[8] The publicity division publishes a weekly clip-sheet, a weekly column of political comment, a news letter several times a month, and a compendium of editorial comments from leading newspapers. The research division issues from time to time studies on current problems. Although the national committee itself does not sponsor any regular periodical, it works in close cooperation with the Young Republican Federation which sponsors a national monthly magazine entitled *The Young Republican.*

An analysis of the personnel of the Republican and Democratic national committees in recent years shows that these party managers represent greater experience in terms of age than most public officials, that two-fifths of them had educational training of college rank, that one-half were recorded as members of fraternal orders,

---

[6] Charles Michelson, *The Ghost Talks* (New York, 1944).

[7] John Hamilton, *Memorandum on English Conservative Party Organization* (mimeographed, 1937).

[8] Information furnished by secretary to the chairman.

that their experience in public office averaged ten years, and that in both parties there was a preponderance of businessmen and lawyers.[9]

A key person in the committee hierarchy of a major party is the chairman of the national committee, whose task is to unify the party, to minimize differences, to emphasize and bring about agreements, and to secure coordinated action in the name of the party slogans. As a rule the chairman is a personal appointee of the party's presidential candidate. McKinley was so indebted to Mark Hanna for his nomination in 1896 that the selection of Hanna as chairman was a foregone conclusion. In 1920 Harding passed over his preconvention manager, Harry M. Daugherty, and continued Will Hays as the national chairman because of the universal acclaim of Hays's brilliant performance as chairman during the 1918 congressional campaign.[10] Usually an experienced and tried party manager is chosen for this post because of the heavy responsibilities which it involves. For instance, James Farley, Franklin Roosevelt's choice for the position in 1932 and 1936, had served ten years as a county chairman, four years as a member of the Democratic state committee of New York, and two years as state chairman.[11] When an inexperienced man is chosen the results are sometimes unfortunate, as Wilson discovered in 1912. His chairman in that year functioned ineffectively during the campaign and had to be relieved of his duties. An ideal national chairman should have great endurance, large reserves of nervous energy, and the ability to relax completely when necessary. He should be enthusiastic, optimistic, tactful, a good judge of personality, and he should have an excellent memory for names, faces, and speeches.

The relation of the national committee to the other party committees is not very sharply defined. During national campaigns the committee, through its control of funds, speakers, organizers, or through its powers of persuasion, may exercise a material influence

[9] Wallace S. Sayre, "Personnel of Republican and Democratic National Committees," *American Political Science Review*, XXVI (April, 1932), 360–363. A check of the national committeemen as of 1947 showed that the above generalizations were applicable. The later committeemen had attained an even higher educational level. A slightly larger proportion were lawyers.

[10] G. Routt, "Will Hays" (master's dissertation, University of Chicago, 1937).

[11] Farley, *Behind the Ballots* and *Jim Farley's Story; The Roosevelt Years* (New York, 1948).

over the other party authorities, state and local, but it has no specific powers conferred upon it for this purpose either by party rule or by law. In case a deficit is incurred during a national campaign, the chairman is usually charged with the task of seeing that it is made up. The managing committee of the victorious party will have material influence in the distribution of patronage, while the minority committee may be influential in organizing the party for the next campaign.

The Congressional Committees

The congressional committee is a committee of representatives dealing with congressional elections.[12] In presidential years it is overshadowed by the national committee but in the mid-term election it carries the burden of the battle. The old congressional caucus was once the dominant factor in national political life, but was overthrown in the days of Jackson and never revived. The present Republican committee was formed in the days of the struggle between President Johnson and Congress; from 1882 to 1894 it was not very active but since then has been more vigorous in its work.

The composition of the committee differs in the major parties. Republicans have a congressional campaign committee elected in a conference meeting of the Republican members of the House at the opening of each Congress. It consists of one member from each state having Republican representation in the House, nominated by the Republican members of that state. The Democratic committee includes one representative from each state and territory. Its members are selected by the respective Democratic delegations or by the committee chairman in states without a Democratic representative. Women who are not members of Congress are frequently appointed to membership on the recommendation of congressional committeemen. Money raising is the chief function of the congressional committees.

The function of this body is the oversight and conduct of the congressional campaign with the object of securing a party majority. The declarations of this committee in a way are a party platform, but they are likely to be overshadowed by the presidential candidate in presidential years, and by the president or party leader in other

[12] Kleeberg, *op. cit.*, pp. 224 ff.

years. The relation of this committee to the national committee is ill defined. In the dual scheme of things one represents the president and the other the House. Neither has authority over the other, and the general attitude is that of cooperation. Over the state and local committees the congressional committee has no authority except that of persuasion.[13]

The senatorial committee in both of the major parties consists of about half a dozen members who are appointed by the senatorial leader of the party.[14] The term of office is two years, but no senator serves during the two-year period when he is coming up for re-election. The committee has general charge of the election of senators in the various states. It has no official connection with the other party committees, but works in harmony and cooperation with them. Its chief function is to raise money for those senators who are running for re-election.

The State Committees

Each state has a central or executive committee, standing at the head of the state hierarchy of party organization. This committee completes the formal organization of the party in the various commonwealths, and is a significant part of the party mechanism. The size of these 96 committees varies from a dozen to several hundred, but averages 30 or 40. If the committee is very large the actual work devolves upon a small executive committee.

The unit of representation varies in different sections of the country. The congressional district and the county are the most commonly employed, but in a few cases the legislative district is used, and in some places a combination of various methods is found. Representation is usually based upon these units, rather than upon party strength or the size of the district; but in some instances allowance is made for the strength of the party vote in the given area. Recent rules or customs provide for placing women voters upon the official committees. Many states have the fifty-fifty plan of representation for men and women.

The term of membership is usually four years, although in many

[13] *Convention Manual for the Democratic National Committee* (1948), and information furnished by the Republican National Committee.

[14] In 1948 the Republican senatorial campaign committee had seven members.

states two years is the period, and in New Jersey three years. The tendency has been in recent years to increase the length of the term of the committeemen in order to give greater stability to the organization. Members are usually selected by delegates to the state convention from the area constituting the unit of representation, the county, if that is the unit, or the congressional district if that is the unit. In a number of states, the committeemen are chosen in party primaries by the party voters directly, and there has been a general tendency in this direction in recent years. There is no uniformity of method, however, and there are many exceptional ways in which state committees are constituted.[15]

The officers of a state committee are few in number. There are a chairman, a secretary, a treasurer, and sometimes a vice-chairman or so. These functionaries are generally elected by the committee itself, but they need not be and frequently are not members of the committee. In most of the organizations there are important subcommittees in which the active work of the committee is done. Of these the most significant is the executive committee, which is often the real center of power. Another very important committee for practical purposes is the finance committee. Of all the officers the chairman and the secretary of the whole committee are by far the most important. Indeed, the control of the campaign in many cases is turned over to these officials, or even to the chairman alone. The powers of the state central committee are seldom clearly defined, by either the written or the unwritten law of the party. It can scarcely be said to govern or guide the party in the formulation or execution of policies, for this is as a rule outside its jurisdiction. In a very few cases, however, the duty of making the platform has been transferred to the committee.[16]

As in the case of the national committeemen of the two major parties, the state chairmen are usually men of affairs in their respective states. An analysis of the occupations of recent state chairmen showed that over one-half of them were lawyers, about one-fifth held some sort of governmental position, national, state, or

[15] Berdahl, *op. cit.*; Stuart Lewis, "Composition of State and Local Party Committees," *National University Law Review* (1928).

[16] Illustrations of detailed regulation of party committees are found in the laws of such states as New York, Massachusetts, and Illinois.

local, and one-eighth were in private industry. Since the passage of the Hatch Act, federal officials have had to retire from party positions of this sort.[17] Only one state chairman could be found who gave farming as his principal occupation. Apparently the farmers prefer to leave the organization of their political affairs to the lawyers. Even more conspicuously absent are the representatives of organized labor. While the state chairmen are usually persons of considerable political experience who have climbed up the political ladder step by step, in recent years there has been a tendency for state committees to select younger men as their executives.

The informal steering or managing committee which really determines the party's line of action is likely to be another group of politicians, although the actual leaders, of course, control the state committee through their agents, and sometimes are found there in person.

The most important duties of a state committee, as of a national committee, center in the conduct of the campaign. Given the candidates and the platform, it is the function of the state committee to see that these particular persons and policies are endorsed by the voters of the state, or at least that the full party strength is polled for them. For this purpose the state committee raises funds, arranges meetings, distributes literature, struggles to bring about harmony, devises and executes the strategy and tactics of the campaign, and in short practices all the arts known to politicians in order to bring about the success of the party candidates. The state committee must be in touch with the national and congressional committees and candidates, on the one hand, and with the county and other local committees on the other. But its relations to neither are very clearly defined, and in fact vary widely in different campaigns. The state committee also determines the time and place of holding party conventions, issues the call for the convention, and sometimes fixes the ratio of party representation. It usually makes up the temporary roll of the convention, recommends temporary officers, and in general assists in putting the machinery of the convention in operation. But since the advent of the direct primary, these powers have become much less important than before. Even under the convention system

---

[17] In 1939 there were, acting as state chairmen, a collector of customs and a district director of the Federal Housing Administration.

of nomination, the general tendency is for the law to prescribe the details of the nominating process. An important surviving power in any event is the right of the committee to fill vacancies that may occur by reason of the death or disability of the party candidates. The laws of most states vest this authority in the state central committee.

In some instances the members of the state committee exercise an informal function of distributing patronage in their districts, or at least of being consulted in regard thereto. But this may be due to their local political strength more than to their membership on the committee. In Arkansas, the Republican rules provide that the committee shall recommend candidates for appointive office in the federal government, but this is not a customary provision.

The authority of the state committee over the county or other local committees is not very large, nor are their relations at all clearly defined. This problem is not as important now, however, as it was some years ago, in view of the fact that the state laws in many instances now provide in some detail for the organization and powers of the party committees both state and local. In some states the central committee is still entrusted with a wide range of authority over the local organization, and generally speaking in the southern states the power of the party committees is larger than elsewhere. These committees are as a rule given a wider range of power both in determination of the qualifications of party membership and in the regulation of the details of primaries and of party management.[18]

The real organization of the state party is not to be contained in the state committee, but is found in the actual distribution of political power in the commonwealth. The nominal control of committees is far less important than the location of the real power of leadership and direction. Party sovereignty is likely to center around a "federal crowd" of which a senator or some federal officer is the head; or around a "state crowd" of which the governor or some group of state officials will be the guiding spirits; or possibly around some combination of cities and counties, as a New York or Chicago group. All sorts of combinations and conflicts are, of course, possible, and as a matter of fact actually develop in the politics of the states. A boss or a leader may hold sway without very effective opposition, or there

[18] See Chap. XIV, below.

may be a long-continued state of factional warfare, with temporary truces to cover the election periods, particularly the national elections when party success and prestige may be at stake.

Local Committees

Below the state committees is a series of local committees, varying widely in different states. The list includes the county committee, the ward, township or town, or city committee, and the precinct committee. The county committee is composed of representatives chosen from towns, townships, or wards, or sometimes from the county at large. These members may be chosen by direct primary or in local caucuses or conventions, or by the county convention itself. The practice varies in the several states, but there is a strong tendency toward direct choice by the party voters.

The powers of these committees resemble those of the national and state committees, except that they operate on a smaller scale. They conduct campaigns, call conventions, and supervise local organizations. Generally they are not subject to the control of the state committee, although there are exceptions to this, and in turn they have little authority over the committees of inferior rank to them. The county chairman is likely to be an important figure in local affairs, and may wield great influence in party councils. If there is a county boss, he will control the whole organization and operate it as one piece of mechanism.

The unit cell in the party structure is the precinct or voting district committeeman, often called the precinct leader or captain. In some cases this authority may be organized in committee form, but even then one man is likely to be in actual charge. These committeemen constitute the working force of the party. To them are entrusted the execution of the extensive requirements of election routine and the detailed supervision of the interests of the party in the localities. They are in charge of naturalization, if need be, of the circulation of petitions, of the registration of voters, of the party canvass, of the distribution of party literature, of whipping up attendance at party rallies, of the task of bringing out the vote, of supervising the count. They are especially active in the party primaries, working for their district leader and the slate of candidates on which their faction has decided. They come in personal contact with the voters in a wide variety of ways, depending upon the character and needs of the neighborhood. In many places the captain is the "Little Father" of his community, holding local and political favor by fair means or foul as the case may be, and often expending for this purpose much time, energy and ability. Conditions vary so widely that it is difficult to generalize regarding the committeeman's duties beyond the routine requirements of the electoral system, but we may be sure that very few effective committeemen stop with the routine work that is absolutely necessary, most of them adopting whatever type of tactics is best suited to the needs and customs of their particular neighborhood. The wants of the very rich and the very poor are different in form, but for both the captain is likely to be an intermediary between the individual and the law—an interpreter of the state to the individual person, sometimes poorly translating the meaning of government, but in the main serving the same purpose of neighborhood representative of the government, whether for poor peddler or rich contractor seeking governmental privileges.

A considerable number of these committeemen are officeholders; a number serve without any direct personal interest; while others are the personal recipients of some privilege or represent some special interest group. In each well-organized voting district, there are from three to ten workers upon whom the committeemen can rely for a certain amount of assistance, paid or unpaid. At times there are subprecinct organizations extending to blocks or sides of blocks in the cities or to blocks of voters without much regard to geographical location.

A study of precinct captains in Chicago made over a period of time throws considerable light upon the character and activities of these party workers in a great metropolitan community.[19] While the original selection of some of these may have been somewhat accidental, their continued service during times of prosperity for their party depended upon one thing, success at the polls. A record of party loyalty was not always prerequisite, as in many cases when there was a shift in the fortunes of the two major parties the most efficient precinct captains were to be found gravitating to the winning side. The man who could carry his precinct possessed a skill

---

[19] H. F. Gosnell, *Machine Politics: Chicago Model* (Chicago, 1937), Chaps. III and IV; Sonya Forthal, *Cogwheels of Democracy* (New York, 1946).

which could be sold to the highest bidder. In England, where party issues are more clearly drawn than in this country and where aristocratic traditions are more deeply ingrained, a party agent would not dare to think of changing his party affiliation but in the United States no questions are asked of the deserter who can produce results for his new master.

While some idealistic party workers were found who performed the burdensome tasks of vote-getting out of loyalty to their party principles and without expectation of any concrete reward for themselves, they were the exceptions. About two-thirds of the precinct officials of the party in power had political jobs of one sort or another. An analysis of divisional leaders in Philadelphia by Kurtzman revealed about the same situation,[20] but in upstate New York cities Mosher found that the proportion of party committeemen who held jobs in the government service was smaller.[21] It was concluded by Mosher, however, that a majority of the committeemen were docile followers who could be counted on by those in control of the party because they came for the most part from the lesser employments such as clerical and unskilled work. In Chicago many professional men and businessmen—lawyers, contractors, insurance salesmen, and real estate agents—found that they could profit by political connections.

The Chicago study showed that in general the precinct captains were superior in their educational background to their constituents, but there was still a large proportion of local party leaders who had had limited educational opportunities. Mosher found that few persons with college training entered the field of party politics, and he contended that those who have enjoyed educational advantages are better equipped to determine the increasingly complex policies of a modern community than those who have not gone beyond grammar school.[22] While some college graduates who go into active politics may not live up to these expectations, it is possible in any large city

---

[20] D. H. Kurtzman, *Methods of Controlling Votes in Philadelphia* (Philadelphia, 1935). See also J. T. Salter, *Boss Rule* (New York, 1935).

[21] W. E. Mosher, "Party and Government Control at the Grass Roots," *National Municipal Review*, XXIV (January, 1935), 16–18; L. Weaver, "Some Soundings in the Party System: Rural Precinct Committeemen," *American Political Science Review*, 34 (1940), 76–84.

[22] Mosher, *op. cit.*, p. 17.

to find public-spirited college graduates who are actively engaged in party management.

The political and social activities of the precinct captains interviewed in Chicago and Philadelphia were varied. One-third or more of the Chicago party workers said that they were active in distributing food, coal, and rent money. Securing political or nonpolitical jobs, giving attention to complaints regarding streets and alleys, contacts with relief agencies, securing medical care, giving legal aid, giving help in naturalization, and attendance at funerals and weddings were activities listed in one-half or more of the cases. Less commonly noted in the more recent surveys were such benevolent services as advice regarding domestic difficulties, the adjustment of taxes, and the adjustment of traffic violations.

It is probable that there are between 130,000 and 140,000 election precincts in the United States.[23] This would make an army of over 130,000 precinct captains for each of the major parties, or around 260,000 for the two larger parties. There is usually an assistant precinct captain of the opposite sex so this figure might well be doubled. To this must be added something for the minor parties. Estimating the party workers at six per precinct, there would be around 800,000 workers in the party field. In times of great excitement and enthusiasm this figure may readily be doubled, reaching a total of over 1,500,000 active partisans occupied with the task of carrying on the campaign of the party.[24]

Not all of those active in a given campaign are a part of the permanent party organization. Some are a part of the standing army, and others are volunteers, or belong to the militia. The active workers, the inner circle of the organization, are those who, as the phrase goes, "do politics 365 days in the year."

URBAN ORGANIZATION

The party organizations in the larger cities operate under conditions where the urban-industrial factors in modern civilization are most evident, and also where the party as a local agency has largely

[23] Figures furnished by Republican national committee.

[24] Bryce's figure, now out of date, was 200,000 (*American Commonwealth*, Chap. LVII). Ostrogorski estimated the number of workers at 850,000 to 900,000 (*op. cit.*, II, 285). Farley's estimate of 150,000 Democratic party workers is given at the beginning of this chapter.

broken down, although it survives as a part of the national organization.[25]

An analysis of the turnover of ward committeemen in Chicago over a period of years showed a very high degree of stability in the office.[26] Out of some 500 ward elections, only 13 committeemen were defeated in straight contests for re-election. The other changes that took place were the result of deaths or voluntary retirements. In spite of political and economic upheavals the ward bosses are able to cling to their posts because of their power over the nomination of local officeholders, their control over the making of the boundaries of their own wards, their grip on the precinct boards of election and other parts of the election machinery, their power to invoke legal technicalities against their various and sundry rivals, their ability to grant special favors to many classes of voters, and the failure of the voters to appreciate the importance of the election of ward committeemen. This is not to say that a ward committeeman cannot be defeated. Rather it is to indicate that extraordinary efforts are required to accomplish such a defeat.

In many cases the ward or district committeemen serve as distributors of patronage in their jurisdictions. In a smoothly working organization, the local official will have a position something like that of the United States senator in respect to appointments to office. He will usually control the patronage of his area, or at least no appointments will be made without consulting him and obtaining his approval. He may also be a dispenser of favors and rewards of various types, depending upon the nature of the system in vogue and the nature of the committeeman. He is likely to be a center for the distribution of offices, contracts, perquisites, tax adjustments, favors, and sundry spoils, although there are many notable exceptions to this. His duties or functions, then, consist partly in looking after the interests of his party, and partly in protecting the interests of his particular party or factional organization.

[25] See Edward J. Flynn, *You're the Boss* (New York, 1947); J. S. Bruner and S. J. Korchin, "The Boss and the Vote; Case Study in City Politics," *Public Opinion Quarterly*, X (1946), 1–23; R. V. Peel, "The Political Machine of New York City," *American Political Science Review*, XXVII (August, 1933), 611–618; Gustavus Myers, *History of Tammany Hall*, rev. ed. (New York, 1917).

[26] Gosnell, *op. cit.*, Chap. II, "You Can't Lick a Ward Boss" and *Chicago Tribune*, April 14, 1948, for later returns on ward committeemen.

In the urban organization the political association often takes on certain social characteristics and functions.[27] This is notably true in the larger cities, and conspicuously so in New York where the social activities of Tammany have long been in existence.

In many districts there are headqua. ters which in some cases are really clubhouses of a certain type.[28] Here the active political workers may meet from time to time, and the place becomes a sort of clearing house for neighborhood political views of miscellaneous kinds. In addition there may be various types of social excursions, picnics, outings, clam-bakes, or other diversions for the benefit of the neighborhood, at the expense of either the boss or the organization, or at any rate with plenty of free tickets for all who care to come along. In cities there are also many less permanent clubs of a politico-social nature, some of them entirely law-abiding and some of them quasi-criminal. The Jolly Seven or the Colts or the Wide Awakes may include blocks of the younger voters associated for varying purposes. Sometimes they are thinly veiled devices for obtaining money from candidates, and in other cases they are more serious in purpose. In a Chicago district a candidate offered a barrel of beer to every club numbering not less than three members. Needless to say many of them sprang up, but the candidate stuck to his word and held the "parties" promised. Some clubs are chiefly interested in arriving at amicable relations with the police and the authorities. But many simply spring out of the natural desire of gregarious youth in congested centers to associate for amusement, with perhaps a little political activity as a side issue.

In many urban communities the local organization assumes more or less systematically the role of local protector and patron. Among the duties taken over are intervention for those charged with violation of the law, whether justly or unjustly; and general intermedia-

[27] See Charles Van Devander, *The Big Bosses* (New York, 1944); Myers, *op. cit.*—the best description of Tammany activities over a long period of time; D. G. Thompson, *Politics in a Democracy* (New York, 1893)—an old defense of the Tammany regime; and Lillian Wald, *The House on Henry Street* (New York, 1924). For a discussion of similar situations in Chicago, see Jane Addams, *Democracy and Social Ethics* (New York, 1913), Chap. VII; C. E. Merriam, *Chicago, A More Intimate View of Urban Politics* (New York, 1929); and Gosnell, *Machine Politics: Chicago Model*.

[28] Roy V. Peel, *The Political Clubs of New York City* (New York, 1935), pp. 128–129, lists the activities of political clubs.

tion between the individual or the group and the government at all points of contact where help can be rendered. But this list would not include systematic attempts to improve the housing of the neighborhood, its sanitation, recreation, street-cleaning, and similar features of the local administration.

THE SOCIALIST PARTY

The Socialist party organization differs somewhat from that of the major parties.[29] The official organization of the Socialist party rests upon the national convention which is held every even-numbered year and consists (in presidential years) of 250 or so delegates, one from each "organized" state and territory, and the remainder in proportion to the average party membership over the past year. These delegates are selected by a referendum vote of the members of the party. There is a convention fund accumulated out of dues payments which is never sufficient to pay full expenses of delegates, but is allocated to those farthest removed from the convention city.

The national platform is adopted by the convention, but it is subject to a referendum vote on petition of one-fourth of the delegates or upon request of the membership through the initiative provision of the constitution, and alternative propositions may be submitted when the referendum is held. Amendments of the party constitution are likewise adopted by any convention after three months' notice of the text of the amendment, or by referendum vote of the members.

The national organization is made up of a national executive committee which has varied in the last twenty years from seven to fifteen members, who are chosen by the national convention and who are subject to recall. This committee has general charge of the affairs of the Socialist party, and their active agent is the "Executive Secretary." It also acts as a court in cases of charter revocation or of suspension. This seems necessary because the Socialist party not infrequently purges itself of members or locals held not to be in sympathy with the purposes or policies of the main organization.

[29] See *National Constitution* of the Socialist party; for description of Socialist political activities see Morris Hillquit, *History of Socialism in U. S.* (New York, 1910); H. W. Laidler, *American Socialism: Its Aims and Practical Program* (New York, 1937); *Labor Year Book*, published by the Rand School of New York City. The proceedings of the Socialist conventions give the debates in full in *Proceedings* of these bodies.

There are a number of special features of the Socialist plan which require notice. Among these are the test of membership which definitely commits the applicant to the doctrine of the class struggle between capitalists and the working class, to political action for the purpose of obtaining "collective ownership, and democratic administration of the collectively used and socially necessary means of production and distribution," and to be guided in all political actions by the Socialist party.[30]

All elected officials are bound to carry out instructions given them by their appropriate governing bodies. In all legislative bodies members must vote as a unit and in support of all measures definitely declared for by the party. This follows the practice of most of the European socialist parties. Other significant features are the provision for election of delegates to the International Socialist Congress, and for Young People's Socialist Leagues.

In contrast to the major parties the Socialist party is a dues-paying organization, the membership of which is limited to those who are not delinquent in their fees. In states where the election laws require the popular selection of party governing committees, the party goes through the motions of electing such committees but keeps the control in the hands of those who have paid their dues.

COMMUNIST PARTY

To the left of the Socialist party stands the Communist party which, while insignificant in size and legally banned in ten states, presents some interesting organizational features. From the time of its origin in 1919 the Communist movement was openly a section of the Third or Moscow International until that body was dissolved in 1943. The following year the party disbanded as a political organization but maintained itself as the Communist Political Association. In 1945 it became a party again. While the roots of the movement may be traced to the extreme radicalism that was found among early

[30] National conventions have regularly for more than twenty years adopted resolutions indicating the willingness of the organization to cooperate with other groups seeking to establish a party ot the producing classes. In Wisconsin the Socialist party of the state was affiliated with and operated politically through the Wisconsin Farmer Labor Progressive Federation, an organized group within the Progressive party. In New York the Socialist party has endorsed independent labor candidates on the American Labor party ticket.

American syndicalists and socialists, its direction has been determined in Moscow. Although in the beginning this foreign control was used as a means of uniting contending factions,[31] it later led to the bitter quarrel between the Stalinites and the Trotskyites. It may also have contributed to the extremely high turnover which has been characteristic of the membership of the party.[32]

The Communist party is organized on a hierarchical basis with the central committee as the most important ruling body. This committee is elected by the national convention which meets every two years. The country is divided into twelve regions each of which is ruled by a district organizer. Each region is in turn divided into sections, each with its own section organizer and "agit-prop"—a "comrade" in charge of agitation and propaganda.[33] Sections are divided into units and these in turn into squads for the performing of specific duties. Earl Browder, former general secretary of the party, urged that "from top to bottom of our Party the predominance in leading personnel must belong to the native people most closely corresponding to the composition of the masses of the population for whom we are working in each particular city, factory, neighborhood, or mass organization."[34] It was admitted by the *Daily Worker* that the party is strongest in the eastern part of the country when it wrote: "The New York district organization is to the Communist party of the United States what Moscow is to the Soviet Union."

Membership in the Communist party is a much more serious affair than membership in one of the major parties. To remain in good standing the member must pay his monthly dues regularly, he must "assume the task of leading and educating at least one worker outside of the Party," he must submit to the iron discipline of the party which requires the burning out of "any tendency to irresponsible gossip with a red-hot iron," and he can consider "himself a real Bolshevik only when fifty or a hundred workers regularly look to

[31] A. B. Held, "The Launching of the Communist Party of the United States" (master's dissertation, University of Chicago, 1939); B. Moore, Jr., "The Communist Party of the USA," *American Political Science Review*, XXXIX (1945), 31–41; Irwin Ross, "It's Tough to Be a Communist," *Harper's*, June, 1945.

[32] F. C. Hanighen, "Foreign Political Movements in the United States," *Foreign Affairs*, XVI (October, 1937), 1.

[33] S. Browne, "Professor Quits the Communist Party," *Harper's Magazine*, CLXXV (July, 1937), 133–142.

[34] *Democracy or Fascism* (New York, International Publishers, 1936), p. 40.

him for guidance and leadership in the problems of the class struggle."[35] It has been the practice of the movement to establish auxiliary organizations to broaden the scope of its influence. Thus industrial unions, cultural organizations, legal defense organizations, Negro organizations, farm groups, foreign-language federations, and clubs of friends and sympathizers have been set up from time to time.[36]

LEGAL REGULATIONS

In recent years the party committee has become a subject of legal regulation, and many of its features are now determined by statute. This process began with the passage of the Australian ballot laws, when it became necessary to define "party" in order to determine what groups were entitled to a place on the ballot. With the process of legal regulation and particularly with the advent of the direct primary, the number, terms, and to some extent the powers of the party committees have been defined by statute and are no longer left to the option of the party. This legislation was due to the desire of the rank and file of the party voters to control the organization by choosing the officers directly. The exercise of these powers by the legislature has been sustained by the courts in repeated instances, and there remains no doubt as to the power of the state to outline and regulate the party organization. In New York the court has held that the Democratic committee could not expel from its membership a committeeman who had been elected by the party voters but no longer adhered to the party's principles.[37] In Wisconsin it was held that the decision of the Republican national committee regarding the regularity of contesting delegations was not binding as against the state law covering such cases. The La Follette delegation to the national convention was ousted in favor of the Stalwart delegation, but in the state courts the regularity of the La Follette convention's nominations was upheld in a decision rendered the same year.[38]

[35] Browder, *op. cit.*, pp. 38–40.

[36] H. D. Lasswell and D. Blumenstock, *World Revolutionary Propaganda* (New York, 1939); H. F. Gosnell, *Negro Politicians* (Chicago, 1935), Chap. XV, "Negroes and Communism."

[37] *People* v. *Democratic Committee*, 58 N. E. 124 (1900). Compare early cases cited by F. J. Goodnow in *Politics and Administration* (New York, 1900), Chap. IX. For the Democratic rule, see *Proceedings* National Convention of 1916, p. 148.

[38] *State* v. *Houser*, 122 Wisc. 534 (1904).

The right of the state to regulate the organization and powers of the party agencies has been strongly upheld by the judiciary.[39] Included in this power is the regulation of the relation between state and local committees. If there is no statutory regulation of these relations, the courts prefer to leave the settlement of the question to a party convention where this is possible, or to party rule or custom, if this can be determined. The decisions in these cases are by no means uniform, however, and it is necessary to scrutinize the judicial interpretations of each state to arrive at useful knowledge of the situation.

LEADERSHIP AND DIRECTION

The foregoing account of the technical organization of the party machinery does not explain the leadership and direction of the party forces, and it is therefore necessary to examine the various forms of party control not disclosed by an examination of this machinery. Here we may distinguish:

(1) Presidential leadership
(2) Congressional leadership
(3) Gubernatorial leadership
(4) Party control
(5) Unofficial leadership

Presidential Leadership

The leadership of the party in power is usually in the hands of the President. Party victory or success in opposition to the President is difficult to obtain, almost impossible on a national scale. The Executive is the party's chosen leader and to repudiate him is to jeopardize party success. Hence his leadership is not likely to be openly opposed, although it may be and frequently is subjected to sabotage by party associates.[40] Much of course depends upon the personal qualities of the executive, and at all times he must reckon with Congress. The nomination of Bryan by the Democrats in 1896 amounted to a repudiation of President Cleveland. The defeat of the Gold Democrats was costly to Bryan.

[39] Other cases are cited in C. E. Merriam and L. Overacker, *Primary Elections* (Chicago, 1928), Chap. VI, "Judicial Interpretation of Primary Elections."
[40] Franklin L. Burdette, *Filibustering in the Senate* (Princeton, 1940).

From the point of view of the party organization, furthermore, the president is the chief dispenser of the patronage that plays so large a part in the scheme of things as they are. He may make and unmake within large limits. Some of his appointments are subject to check by the Senate but many others are not. Even the senatorial suggestions are subject to his review; and his attitude is very important to the local organization. However remote the practical purposes of the local leaders may be from those of the president, the patronage is a weighty factor, and they are inclined to "go along" with him in order not to antagonize the great source of power. Further, the effect of a conflict with the executive may be disastrous in its influence upon local or state elections, and thus cause an indirect loss of power which may be equally serious. Thus the patronage-dispensing power is influential in obtaining for him the support of the technical organization under most circumstances, although not all. Aside from the power of appointment to office there are distinct advantages in the good will of the Chief Executive of the United States.[41] The arms of his administration reach far and wide through the country touching many areas of human life, and every organizer likes to be *en rapport* with the Great Chief, if he can.

But the president is more than the technical head of the party. He may appeal to public opinion in the party and outside of it also, and if he strikes a popular chord he is well-nigh irresistible. His selected policies are likely to become national issues, and battle is joined on the lines he marks out, within limits, of course. Thus the president becomes a leader, not only in the technical party sense, but in the broader significance of the term. He may lead by power of persuasion, by skill in popular appeal, by strengthening party morale, without which the most efficient organizer is helpless in a democracy. There are of course limits beyond which no president can go. Neither a Democratic nor a Republican president could lead his party to support communism. But within certain confines he may direct his party group. The prestige of the most powerful elective office in the world, the widespread publicity given his words and deeds, make the president the normal party leader. A great tribute was paid to the late President Franklin D. Roosevelt by the comment of a Republican precinct captain to the effect that the Roosevelt personality

[41] On the position of the president, see Grover Cleveland, *The Independence of the Executive* (Princeton, 1913), and the special discussions by Presidents Harrison, Taft, Theodore Roosevelt, Wilson.

had become real to his constituents, and had entered into their homes.

A major party which does not control the presidency is at a considerable disadvantage. Its defeated candidate is in no position to lead the party, as he is without official position in the national government. In countries having a two-party system and the parliamentary form of government the leader of the opposition has a regular position.

The president is in fact more than a party leader. He becomes an extra-party leader, undertaking the task of interpreting national, or even international sentiment. The party alone cannot furnish him with the support essential to carry out his program. An analysis of the figures shows clearly how dependent the president and even the party is upon the support of the opposition party for the execution of any comprehensive program, or even for carrying on the ordinary operations of the government. In the period from 1877 to 1949, 72 years, the Republican party held the presidency 40 years and the Democratic party 32 years; but during this time the Democratic party was in complete control only 22 years, and the Republicans, only 26 years. For 24 years, or two-fifths of the time, the president's party was not strong enough to give him the majority necessary for legislation. For the confirmation of appointments, requiring only a majority of the Senate, the president was in accord with the Senate for 56 years of the 72, but out of tune 16 years of this time. As far as foreign policy is concerned, only President Franklin D. Roosevelt had for a period of eight years the necessary two-thirds to carry through a treaty without securing votes of the other party in support of his measure, but he could not hold this party majority in line. The difficulties facing most presidents in carrying through their foreign policy were much greater than Roosevelt's, as, for instance, Grant's in his San Domingo policy and Wilson's in the Versailles peace treaty.

Table 2, on the following page, indicates the division of party control.

Our dual system of government divides authority between legislative and executive bodies, and Congress still retains significant powers.[42] This congressional authority may become the basis of party

[42] See George Galloway, *Congress at the Cross Roads* (New York, 1946); Roland Young, *This Is Congress* (New York, 1943); Paul D. Hasbrouck, *Party Government in the House of Representatives* (New York, 1927); and Lindsay Rogers, *The American Senate* (New York, 1926).

TABLE 2

PARTY AFFILIATION OF PRESIDENT, HOUSE, AND SENATE, 1877–1951

Years	*President*	*House*	*Senate*
'77–79	Rep.	Dem.	Rep.
'79–81	Rep.	Dem.	Dem.
'81–83	Rep.	Rep.	*a*
'83–85	Rep.	Dem.	Rep.
'85–87	Dem.	Dem.	Rep.
'87–89	Dem.	Dem.	Rep.
'89–91	Rep.	Rep.	Rep.
'91–93	Rep.	Dem.	Rep.
'93–95	Dem.	Dem.	Dem.
'95–97	Dem.	Rep.	*b*
'97–99	Rep.	Rep.	Rep.
'99–01	Rep.	Rep.	Rep.
'01–03	Rep.	Rep.	Rep.
'03–05	Rep.	Rep.	Rep.
'05–07	Rep.	Rep.	Rep.
'07–09	Rep.	Rep.	Rep.
'09–11	Rep.	Rep.	Rep.
'11–13	Rep.	Dem.	Rep.
'13–15	Dem.	Dem.	Dem.
'15–17	Dem.	Dem.	Dem.
'17–18	Dem.	*c*	Dem.
'19–21	Dem.	Rep.	*d*
'21–23	Rep.	Rep.	Rep.
'23–25	Rep.	Rep.	Rep.
'25–27	Rep.	Rep.	Rep.
'27–29	Rep.	Rep.	*e*
'29–31	Rep.	Rep.	Rep.
'31–33	Rep.	Dem.	*f*
'33–35	Dem.	Dem.	Dem.
'35–37	Dem.	Dem.	Dem.
'37–39	Dem.	Dem.	Dem.
'39–41	Dem.	Dem.	Dem.
'41–43	Dem.	Dem.	Dem.
'43–45	Dem.	Dem.	Dem.
'45–47	Dem.	Dem.	Dem.
'47–49	Dem.	Rep.	Rep.
'49–51	Dem.	Dem.	Dem.

Footnotes are on the facing page.

leadership when the party does not have the presidency or even when it does.[43] The senators in particular share the appointing power with the president, and may use this to block or circumscribe him and at the same time to build up strength at home. Custom has developed what is usually an amicable arrangement by which the senator, or representative, if his party is in power, is really given the federal appointments in his state or a generous measure of them; although the boundary lines of this power have never been carefully surveyed and are not clearly outlined even now, after a century of precedents. Neither president nor senator is willing to concede the unlimited authority of the other in matters of local appointments. A president is likely, however, to trade local appointments for support on questions of national policy. But bitter struggles have broken out at this point, such as those between Garfield and Conkling, Harrison and Quay, Cleveland and Tammany, Taft and the insurgents, Franklin D. Roosevelt and the conservative Democrats.

On questions of public policy the president is likely to be the leader, but his authority in this field may be challenged, and Congress may take or divide the leadership with him. This was true in the days of reconstruction when the president was impeached and almost ousted; in the Cleveland administration when the free-silver Democrats under Bryan broke away from the high-tariff Democrats under Gorman; in the Taft era when the insurgents seized control; in the closing days of Wilson's administration when opposition to the Paris peace treaty upon the part of the Republicans and Democrats won out; in Franklin D. Roosevelt's second, third, and fourth terms in the struggle between liberal and conservative party elements, and in the Truman administration when the Republicans won both houses of Congress.

Many congressmen have figured prominently as party leaders and as candidates for the presidency. Blaine received the Republican nomination, but failed of election; Garfield was nominated and

---

[a] Dem. and Rep. evenly divided plus two third-party men.

[b] Rep., 42; Dem., 39; third party, 5.

[c] Rep., 216; Dem., 210; third party, 9.

[d] Rep., 48; Dem., 47; third party, 1.

[e] Rep., 47; Dec., 47; third party, 1; 1 vacant.

[f] Rep., 48; Dem., 47; thir. party, 1.

[43] For a discussion of the role of Congress in the formulation of policies, see above, pp. 78-83.

elected while a prominent member of the House; McKinley had come into prominence as a member of the House and author of a tariff bill; Harding and Truman were members of the Senate.[44] Among the notable senatorial candidates were Conkling, Sherman, Morton, Edmonds, Logan, Depew, Allison, Thurman, Bayard, Payne, Gorman, Johnson, Underwood, Borah, Robert Taft. The frequent presidential candidacies of the senators, their power in foreign relations in particular and in matters of national policy in general, their length of term and frequent re-election, their control over state machines in many cases—all these factors help to place them in a strong position for party leadership. And they are not slow to avail themselves of it.

Likewise members of the lower house are influential in determining the direction of the party's action. The speaker of the House is second only to the president in political authority, and must always be reckoned with. Men of the type of Reed, Clark, and Garner have been conspicuous candidates for the office of president, and have played important roles in party management. Clark obtained a majority vote in the convention of 1912, and missed the nomination by only the smallest of margins. Garner was an important contender for the Democratic nomination in 1932 and 1940 and his great influence as vice president was in large part due to his reputation as a leader in legislative affairs.

Particularly when the party is not in power, the minority congressional group is in a position to assume leadership; for the immediate answer to the proposals of the president and his party comes from those in Washington, who are in a position to ascertain the facts and make an effective criticism, or propose some alternative policy. They do not commit the party to their ideas, but they occupy a strong position if they interpret public sentiment accurately. If they fail, the party may disclaim responsibility for their acts. The unofficial leaders are likely, however, to produce criticism upon broader grounds, as in the case of Bryan and Theodore Roosevelt. The congressmen, while aided by opportunities in the way of facts, are often embarrassed by their joint participation in the conduct of the government upon important matters. The committee system, with its

---

[44] Blaine had been Speaker of the House and later a senator; Garfield had been elected to the Senate, but had not taken his seat.

division of responsibility, and the frequent voting on nonpartisan lines often handicap them in the effort to differentiate their position from that of the dominant party. The need of local appropriations or local favors within the gift of the opposite party may render them more ready to compromise with the opposition.

Gubernatorial Leadership

Governors of the states may also be in a position to exercise a significant influence on the leadership of the party. The governorship has been in fact a frequent stepping-stone to candidacy for the presidency, as in the cases of Tilden, Hayes, Cleveland, Hill, McKinley, Theodore Roosevelt, Folk, Wilson, Lowden, Cox, Coolidge, Smith, Franklin D. Roosevelt, Landon and Dewey. The twentieth century has seen the rise of strong executive leadership on the part of many state governors, such as Johnson of California, Philip La Follette of Wisconsin, Wilson of New Jersey, Smith, Roosevelt, and Dewey of New York.[45] In breadth of opportunity for leadership the position of governor is far stronger than that of senator, but it is inferior in continuity, permanency, and close contact with national problems. The senator is elected for six years, and may be reelected for a number of terms, so that he may see presidents come and go. The governor's term may be two or four years, and he is not likely to have more than two terms—in fact, in a few states he is constitutionally ineligible to succeed himself. The senator often takes charge of the local state organization and becomes its leader or its boss for a long period of time, intrenching himself as it is not possible for the governor to do.

Of the present membership of the Senate about one-fifth have been governors at one time or another.[46] This list includes Bricker of Ohio and Saltonstall of Massachusetts, both of whom served as executive head and political leader of the state, but finally gravitated to the United States Senate. No commanding local position was open to them, except that of the unofficial leader.[47]

---

[45] Leslie Lipson, *The American Governor from Figurehead to Leader* (Chicago, 1939).

[46] Eightieth Congress. The total number is 19.

[47] The list includes Johnson of Colorado, Russell of Georgia, Wilson of Iowa, Capper and Reed of Kansas, Bridges and Tobey of New Hampshire, and Byrd of Virginia.

County Control

In the actual scheme of things the county looms large as a factor in routine political leadership and direction, especially on the organization side. There are some 3000 counties in the United States, electing some 45,000 officials, almost altogether on party lines. Of these 3000 counties, moreover, only some 200 have adopted any form of civil service merit tests, so that almost all of the appointive offices are open to the victorious party or faction.[48] In many of these counties public sentiment is not alive to the importance of vigorous county government, and the affairs of the county are often much neglected, in comparison with the interest given to national or city or even state affairs. It is only within recent years that light has been turned on the county as a governing agency.[49] County leaders who have depended on spoils of various types, such as interest on public funds, fees, contracts, patronage, have had practically a free hand, and groups of powerful leaders have combined to govern states, and to obtain immunity from regulation of their local affairs. The county boss and the county ring or rings have been factors of the first importance in the maintenance of a party system of state control.

On the other hand, the county government has given opportunity for personal contact with many voters, especially in the rural sections of the country, or the semirural semiurban counties, and as a consequence many vigorous and aggressive leaders have come to the front through the county offices. The office of prosecuting attorney of the county has been an avenue through which many ambitious and effective leaders have found their way to state or even larger leadership. Ring or boss control is precarious where the opponent may come into contact with almost all the voters of the area controlled. Men like the elder La Follette, Johnson, Folk, Whitman, Deneen, Gillette, Barkley, Dewey, and many others have started in this office and have gone on to significant positions of party leadership.[50] Nearly one-third of the United States senators in recent years started their

[48] Edward W. Weidner, *The American County—Patchwork of Boards* (New York, 1946).

[49] R. H. Wells, *American Local Government* (New York, 1939); John A. Fairlie and C. M. Kneier, *County Government and Administration* (New York, 1930); H. S. Gilbertson, *The County the Dark Continent of American Politics* (New York, 1917).

[50] See *Biographical Congressional Directory*, and any current *Congressional Directory*.

political careers as prosecuting attorneys.[51] In many states the county is the unit of representation in the state legislature, and many party leaders have come through this route to larger places of power and responsibility. In like manner the county judge has often found this position a stepping-stone to judicial promotion, and also to political advancement in other than judicial lines.

The county, then, deserves a larger place in the examination of political leadership than is usually accorded to it. The county attorney, the county judge, the county representative, the county boss, the county chairman, the local county leaders are likely to be factors of some permanence and to weigh heavily in the state convention or primary, or in the choice of congressmen or the choice of delegates to national conventions. On the sordid side of spoils, on the working side of organization, or as the basis of party principles and policies, they may be of great practical importance.

Unofficial Leaders

Important positions of party direction and control are also held by men with no official rank whatever. Bryan is the most conspicuous example of this sort, since he held for over a quarter of a century a place of very great authority in the councils of the Democracy. Although frequently not in the party majority, he was always able to command a hearing and was very influential even when defeated. Cleveland, Theodore Roosevelt, Taft, Root, Hughes were men of great force and influence whether in office or out of it—as is Hoover today. Independently of the attitude of their party in Congress or of the position of their party organization, they were factors to be reckoned with in all accurate party calculations. Well-known journalists, industrial magnates, professional leaders, and others must be placed in the group of those who influence and direct the action of the party, openly or quietly as the case may be. Neither the congressional group nor the "organization" could wholly disregard their views and policies.

Scores of less well-known figures influence the action of the party in state and local affairs and must be listed with those who determine the party's course in the more important matters where party action is taken. They compete with the technical or official leaders of the

[51] Tabulation made from *Congressional Directory*.

party for the confidence of the people as interpreters of sentiment and judgment and as advisers in the major questions. To ignore them in a view of the party leadership and direction is to take a wholly imperfect view of what actually goes on in the course of the party process.

Unofficial leaders of the boss type are Flynn of New York, Hague of New Jersey, Crump of Tennessee, O'Connell of Albany, and a number of others who have held local domains in their grip. These men have materially affected the direction and control of the party even in national questions. Their primary interest has not been in national policies, but in maintenance of local control; yet the national management is important for this purpose, and they have been active in the national as well as in the local field. They bring great groups of delegates to the national conventions, and they may determine the attitude of the doubtful state on which the national election hangs.

In combination with the senators who are also local bosses, these men wield far-reaching power in national conventions, and thereby become factors of the very first importance in fixing the policy of the party. Thus they defeated Theodore Roosevelt in 1912 and 1916. They were too powerful for Bryan in 1904, and almost overcame him in 1912, but for his masterful attack upon them in battle over the permanent chairman of the convention and his resolution. In 1944, they brought about the nomination of Truman for vice-president, thus paving his way to the White House. The local bosses and the senatorial bosses in combination with powerful social interests may readily control a convention, and are at all times of the very highest importance in matters of national policy.

Since the depression of the thirties there has undoubtedly been a decline in the influence of the unofficial leader of the boss type. In all parts of the country old city machines have been smashed and new bosses have been slow to rise.[52]

It will be evident, then, that party leadership and direction are somewhat loosely organized. The technical organization of various

---

[52] W. M. Reddig, *Tom's Town: Kansas City and the Pendergast Legend* (Philadelphia and New York, 1947); Anon., "Political Bosses' Creaky Chairs," *Literary Digest* (September 19, 1936); G. Creel, "The Complete Boss," *Collier's* (October 10, 1936).

committees, the presidential incumbents and candidates, the congressional group, the unofficial citizens, the bosses are all joint holders of the power and the direction of the party. The final action of the Republican or the Democratic party is a resultant of the action of all these forces. Sometimes the party enthusiastically follows a leader like Theodore Roosevelt, Wilson, or Franklin D. Roosevelt, sometimes they follow, but sullenly; sometimes there is no apparent leader, or none strong enough to command general agreement, and the result is confusion until some definite line of action emerges again. Of course, the process cannot be understood at all unless it is interpreted in the light of the social and economic forces that are playing upon both parties and are struggling to find expression through one or the other or both of the great organizations that deal in personalities and policies. What has been said of the national party is also true of the states, except that locally there is frequently, especially under boss rule, a very close-knit organization, sometimes almost military in its severity.

COUNTER ORGANIZATIONS

The great power of the "organization" as such as has been met by various counter movements, some within and some without the party. Of these the leading types are: independency; third-party movements; counter organization within the party.

Independency

"Independency," as it was called at first, was a movement in the direction of a new attitude toward the sacredness of party allegiance. It was a protest against blind adherence to a political party, against the persistence of party habits after their period of usefulness or reason for existence had gone by. Following the Civil War, the party adherence of many Republicans, in particular, had been sorely tried by the widespread corruption which was glossed over with the plea of party loyalty. "Independency" was voiced by many outstanding figures of the type of Lowell, Curtis, and Schurz, who threw the weight of their influence against the widely prevalent belief that party loyalty was a continuation of war patriotism which no loyal minded person could fail to appreciate. In many quarters partisanship had become so intense that the feeling of party attachment was intolerant of any challenge.

To assert that it was the right and the duty of intelligent men to leave the party in a crisis where some principle was involved was not popular in the early days of independency, but the sentiment gained strength as the echoes of the war died away. The Liberal Republican movement in 1872 marked its beginning. The Mugwump development of the eighties resulting in the election of Cleveland, the first Democrat chosen President in twenty-four years, was one of the triumphs of the independent voter. This development aroused the bitterest opposition from many party adherents who were likely to denounce the independent voter as a traitor and a deserter. But the idea made steady progress, until it attained a far wider degree of power than had been supposed possible at first.

The independent movement took deepest root, however, in municipal affairs. In urban and to some extent in rural questions national party lines had not been as sharply drawn as in other jurisdictions, and the development of strict national partisanship was not welcome. Independence was already established by custom, and the theory of local independency found a cordial welcome here. Whatever might be said of the desirability of party regularity in national affairs, it found relatively few defenders here and was rapidly supplanted by the independent theory and practice. Legal recognition of the desire for local independence was given by the change in time of holding elections so as to avoid confusion with the national, and in many cases by the passage of laws providing for a nonpartisan ballot from which the party designation was excluded. The stigma of "irregularity" did not attach to local independence. On the contrary, significant party leaders like Tilden, the Roosevelts, and Taft deliberately disregarded local party lines, and gave "aid and comfort" to the party's political enemy in the municipality from time to time.

Third Parties

The overdevelopment of "partyism" was checked from time to time [53] by the formation of other and competing party systems. Of these the Greenback, the Populist, and the Progressive movements

---

[53] See J. P. Cannon, *The Struggle for a Proletarian Party* (New York, 1943); Paul Douglas, *The Coming of a New Party* (New York, 1932); F. E. Haynes, *Third Party Movements* (Iowa City, 1916); and K. H. Porter, *National Party Platforms* (New York, 1924) for party declarations.

of 1912 and 1924 were the most important. These movements were in part protests against the machine and the boss, and in part against economic and social ills; partly directed against the power of the "organization" as such, and partly aimed at the failure of the party to function as a formulator of public policy. In the Progressive movements the combination of these factors, the political and the industrial magnate, was described by the phrase "invisible government"—a phrase employed to indicate the combination of the boss and special privilege in an offensive and defensive alliance. These movements as well as many state parties and bolts tended to break the continuity of party allegiance, and to familiarize the community with the shifting alliances of party leaders. In the thirties, third-party movements achieved outstanding victories in Wisconsin and Minnesota, while at the same time supporting Roosevelt for president.

None of these groups was strong enough to take the place of the older parties, but they forced material modifications in party policy and tended to make the party rulers more amenable to the party will. Without such developments, the ruling oligarchy in the party might easily have become much more autocratic than it actually was. Usually, after every such campaign, there was adjustment and reorganization of the party management and policy; and each served as a precedent to warn of future possibilities of revolt. They imperilled party victory, which after all was of vital significance to the organization, and to the partisan as well as the social interests they represented. This has been especially true of the American Labor and Liberal parties of New York State.[54]

Notable victories have been scored by the third parties. From 1896 to 1948 there were chosen by the minor parties some 15 governors, 213 senators and representatives, and many members of the various state legislatures. In addition to this many city and county and town officials were elected by the independent or minor groups.

Counter Organization within the Party

At all times there are bitter factional struggles for party control. Frequently there are rival organizations more or less completely equipped and duplicating each other in extent and activity. At times

[54] Hugh A. Bone, "Political Parties in New York City," *American Political Science Review*, XL (1946), 272–282.

there are rival spoils organizations. Sometimes there are "antimachine groups," aimed at the overthrow of the method and spirit of the dominant group and proposing the demolition of a spoils machine in power. The La Follette movement in Wisconsin, the Sinclair EPIC party in California, the Brookhart movement in Iowa, the anti-Tammany movement in New York, the anti-Kelly movement in Illinois, the anti-Long movement in Louisiana, the anti-Talmadge movement in Georgia, the anti-Pendergast movement in Missouri, and a long series of others are examples of the ferment within the party organization itself and the strenuous effort to check it by organized methods and activities.

These wars within the party laid bare to the public the facts of the party system, and at least possessed an educational value for the nation, the state, or the local community. In some instances they were crowned with substantial success, as in Wisconsin and California. In the course of these protracted struggles, tactics and leaders were developed that proved to be of great usefulness to the public life of the community in many instances. They tended constantly to keep the ruling group more closely in touch with the general opinion of the party, which, if unchecked, they are more prone to manipulate and dominate than to follow.

In the municipalities, especially, many organizations were formed for political action, independently of the regular party organizations. Some of these were utilized for purposes of publicity or of research only, without special reference to the work of primaries or elections. The citizens' league, the civic association, the city club often affected political parties very materially, even when they played no direct part in the choice of the official personnel. But there are still other organizations dealing directly with the problems of the selection and election of candidates. Types of these are the Citizens' Union of New York, the Civic Leagues of Cleveland and St. Louis, and the Charter Committee of Cincinnati. Such groups made specific recommendations regarding candidates and used their best efforts to bring about the election or defeat of candidates. Occasionally they took the form of distinct city parties, as in Philadelphia, Cincinnati, and New York. Usually, however, they did not function in this way, but passed in review the candidates of the political parties and made recommendations regarding them.

Like party organizations, these groups tend to rise and fall with the ebb and flow of events, and with the varying skill and success of their organizers and promoters. They often serve as training schools for civic recruits, rallying places for the unorganized, and aids in the organization of information for the community. They set up centers of political intelligence, interest, and capacity, other than are found in the regular party organization.

ORGANIZATION OF PARTY DIRECTION

A significant movement affecting party organization and direction is the effort to center power and responsibility more definitely upon particular agents or officials. This is commonly known as the "Short Ballot" movement.[55] The agitation has its origin in the states and in the local governments where the long ballot has its chief habitat. The long list of offices to be filled, in some cases running up to thirty or forty, makes it extremely difficult to locate responsibility for either good or bad conduct. Leaders of all parties, including Wilson, Theodore Roosevelt, William Howard Taft, Hughes, Root, Al Smith, and Franklin D. Roosevelt, agreed upon the desirability of shortening the ballot and centering attention upon the key offices by which the government is really controlled. The line would then be drawn between policy-determining and administrative officials, electing the former in order to ensure public control, and appointing the latter in order to obtain technical efficiency and relative permanency of tenure. In the states and counties some progress has been made with this idea and the rapid increase in the number of elective officials has been checked. In cities, however, the ballot has been materially shortened, and the number of elective officials actually reduced. Constitutional restrictions in the states and inertia as well as restrictions have been the cause of this condition in the counties.

Yet in the states the governor by common consent has often been made the party leader, and also the chief depository of official responsibility for state affairs. His veto power has been strengthened, as well as his appointing power and his power over state finances, and his general position has been made more formidable than ever

[55] R. S. Childs, *Short Ballot Principles* (New York, 1911).

before.[56] The voters have tended to cut through the other state officials, whether executive or legislative, and to fix responsibility upon the chief executive of the state. This has tended to give him not only public leadership, but to entrench his position within the party. As in the case of the presidency much depends upon the ability of the incumbent. It sometimes happens also that the governor is merely the tool of the boss or the machine.

Likewise in the national field, although no constitutional changes have been made in the legal position of the executive, his actual power and responsibility have increased. He stands above the congressional leaders, superior to the party machinery, in a position of leadership of the party itself. The press, radio, and television help cement this leadership. In the national field where the party really lives, its organization controls the party much less firmly than in the state and local areas in which the party is really only a reflection of the national agency.

Thus, the development of "conspicuous leadership" is an offset to the overdevelopment of the organization side of the party. Both the institutions and the common understandings which make this possible are the answer to the growth of the machine and the boss. Leaders of the type of Tilden, the Roosevelts, Hughes, La Follette, Johnson, Wilson, Bryan tend to bring the party back toward the line of group representation, where all party officials nominally stand, but often in name only. Without such rallying points the public would encounter even greater difficulty than at present in making its will effective.

The organization of the political party, then, is found in a complicated system, including the formal committees, the unofficial leaders, the bosses, the counterorganizations.[57] At times the boss or the leader emerges with the practical control of the whole machinery for the time being in his hands. The professional group, the party sentiment, the party machinery may at times operate harmoniously

[56] See A. N. Holcombe, *State Government* (New York, 1931) ; J. M. Mathews, *Principles of American State Administration* (New York, 1927) ; debates of New York Constitutional Convention of 1915; W. F. Dodd, *State Government* (New York, 1923) ; and ˮ. Lipson, *The American Governor: From Figurehead to Leader* (Chicago, 1939).

[57] The organization of the party in the form of the caucus, primary, and convention is considered elsewhere.

under a Roosevelt or a Wilson. In this case the party attains its highest degree of efficiency. But at other times there seems to be no effective direction, control, or leadership in the party, or there may be competing groups struggling for control of the party or even of both parties in a given area for a period of time.[58] The boss plays an important role in the national drama, but he does not control, as in the local agencies, although groups of bosses may do so. The most spectacular struggles have been those between leaders and bosses, as in the contest of 1912 in which Roosevelt and Bryan played so notable a part.

Over against the tendency of the organization to overshadow and control the group it nominally represents is the counter tendency to resist great centralization of power, to check the growth and power of oligarchies within the party. The appearance of independency, the spirit of revolt against arbitrary authority, the tendency to resist undemocratic centralization in rings or bosses or even leaders manifests itself with great strength, and at times a new party appears threatening the whole system of party control. The "machine" development produces the "antimachine" development. The array of efforts to prevent the representatives of the partisans from becoming their rulers is a long and formidable one. Ballot laws, detailed regulation of nominating processes, and of the organization of party committees, legislation against the spoils system, the appeal to independency and the formation of competing parties, the counter organization within the party itself, the effort to develop conspicuous leadership within Congress and within the government in general, sometimes by law, and sometimes by custom—all these have been characteristic of our time. To constitutionalize and democratize the party, to make it genuinely representative of the party will, has been the goal of a long series of energetic efforts within our generation.

[58] For an analysis of the spoils system, see Chaps. X–XIII.

CHAPTER IX

BOSSES AND REFORMERS

"The boss, on the other hand, is a man who does not gain his power by open means, but by secret means, and usually by corrupt means. Some of the worst and most powerful bosses in our political history either held no public office or else some unimportant public office. They made no appeal either to intellect or to conscience. Their work was done behind closed doors, and consisted chiefly in the use of that greed which gives in order that it may get."—*Theodore Roosevelt—An Autobiography* (New York, Charles Scribner's Sons, 1913), p. 149.

BOSSES

THE LEADERS IN THE WORLD OF SPOILS ARE COMMONLY CHARACTER-ized as bosses.[1] In a penetrating analysis of party decentralization in the United States, E. E. Schattschneider suggests that the word "boss" be defined as *an unofficial leader who exercises irresponsible*

[1] For sources, see H. Zink, *City Bosses in the United States* (Durham, 1930). See also W. M. Reddig, *Tom's Town: Kansas City and the Pendergast Legend* (Philadelphia and New York, 1947); D. D. McKean, *The Boss: The Hague Machine in Action* (Boston, 1940); Gustavus Myers, *History of Tammany Hall*, rev. ed. (New York, 1917); S. P. Orth, *The Boss and the Machine* (New Haven, 1921); James Bryce, *The American Commonwealth* (New York, 1921); M. A. Ostrogorski, *Democracy and the Organization of Political Parties* (New York, 1902), II, 367–440; Lincoln Steffens, *Autobiography* (New York, 1931); Judge Ben B. Lindsey, *The Beast* (New York, 1910); Walter Davenport, *Power and Glory: The Life of Boies Penrose* (New York, 1931); T. L. Johnson, *My Story* (New York, 1911), on Cleveland; and Brand Whitlock, *Forty Years of It* (New York, 1914), on Toledo; H. F. Gosnell, *Boss Platt and His New York Machine* (Chicago, 1924), and *Machine Politics: Chicago Model* (Chicago, 1937); D. T. Lynch, *Boss Tweed* (New York, 1927); and F. R Kent, *The Great Game of Politics* (Garden City, 1924).

Writers of fiction supply many facts and have illustrated the spirit of boss government in such works as P. L. Ford, *The Honorable Peter Stirling and What People Thought of Him* (New York, 1899); Winston Churchill, *Coniston* (London, 1906), *Mr. Crewe's Career* (New York, 1908), and *A Far Country* (New York, 1915); A. H. Lewis, *The Boss* (New York, 1904); W. L. Riordon, *Plunkitt of Tammany Hall* (New York, 1905); Theodore Dreiser, *The Titan* (New York, 1925), and *The Financier* (New York, 1912). A list of other titles is given in C. E. Merriam, *American Political Ideas* (New York, 1926), Chap. XIV.

power primarily to extract patronage from the government at all levels and for other private purposes.[2]

These rulers require rather different qualities from those in the field of party policy, and in certain positions of party management and administration. Their rise to power and their continuance in its possession are based upon a somewhat different set of political attributes personally, and upon a somewhat different environment. What are the qualities of the boss, and what is the social and political environment out of which he comes and which he must in a measure reflect? To these pertinent questions no very satisfactory answer has thus far been given. Righteous indignation has often taken the place of careful analysis of the actual conditions out of which boss rule springs. That the boss is a "bad" man, that he is a creature of the "slums," that he is unintelligent or illiterate, that he is a "foreigner," that he has no connection with the industrial or social development of the day, are common assertions or assumptions which have little or no basis in the actual facts. The boss may be personally "pious"; he may be found in the rural districts as well as in the cities; he may be highly educated; he may be a native-born American of the oldest stock; and finally he may be found in the most intimate connection with the leading business men of the community. William Barnes was a Harvard graduate; Croker was not. Senator Penrose wrote an erudite dissertation on the government of Philadelphia,[3] but Butler had no formal education at all. Abe Ruef was an honor man in philosophy and ethics at the University of California, and an able lawyer; Schmitz was a musician. Cox of Cincinnati was an ex-prize fighter; Quay was deeply interested in classic literature.

While bosses are not recruited from any particular class, creed, or nationality, the study made by Zink of twenty typical city bosses reveals certain tendencies.[4] One-half of those analyzed had Irish-born fathers and only one-fourth had native fathers. Of those of foreign stock, nearly one-half belonged to the nationality which, during the early part at least of their political careers, ranked first among all foreign-born groups in the city concerned. None came from the

[2] *Party Government* (New York, Farrar and Rinehart, 1942), p. 162.

[3] *Philadelphia, 1681–1887, Johns Hopkins University Studies,* extra Vol. II (joint author with E. P. Allinson).

[4] *City Bosses in the United States.*

families of the socially elite, although two of them were admitted into "society" after they had achieved financial and political power. All of them began life in moderate circumstances but without exception they were able to ascend to the upper part of the income pyramid.[5]

It is important that the critical examination of the traits and techniques of political bosses, rural and urban, be continued. In addition to the city bosses that Zink analyzed,[6] there are, among others: Maschke of Cleveland; Curry, Dooling, Sullivan, and Flynn of New York; O'Connell of Albany; Brennan, Cermak, Kelly, Nash, and Arvey of Chicago; Hague of Jersey City; Curry of Boston; Crump of Memphis; and Pendergast of Kansas City. Then there are the famous state bosses: Quay and Penrose of Pennsylvania; Barnes of New York; "Kingfish" Huey Long of Louisiana; Taggart of Indiana; and Brayton and Roraback of Connecticut. Studies of such bosses might cover their origins and development, their early history and training, their personality attributes, their methods of obtaining and holding power as well as their political decline, their relation to the social and class movements of their time and place, and their significance from the point of view of their role in the political and social process.[7]

The boss is a political leader, local or state in range, who uses chiefly the weapons of patronage and spoils. In addition to these he may make large use of favors or obligations of an indiscriminate character, reaching a large number of people. He may or may not use the tactics of the demagogue in making appeals to the general interest on specific issues, but at any rate he will be careful to preserve the appearance of popularity in his tactics. He will from time to time appear in the ranks of the regular party organization as the champion of party causes.

The powers of the boss include the nomination, election, and di-

[5] *Ibid.*, pp. 36–41. On the basis of estate figures, Zink estimates that over one-half of his sample amassed fortunes of at least a million dollars. "Doc" Ames of Minneapolis left a small estate, but it is clear that he at times enjoyed a big income. Furthermore, Ames may be classified as a demagogue rather than as a boss.

[6] Lomasney of Boston; Sullivan, Tweed, Kelly, Croker, Murphy, and Olvany of New York; McLaughlin of Brooklyn; McManes, Durham, and Vare of Philadelphia; Magee and Flinn of Pittsburgh; Cox of Cincinnati; Lundin and Sullivan of Chicago; Butler of St. Louis; Behrman of New Orleans; Ames of Minneapolis; and Ruef of San Francisco.

[7] See W. B. Munro, *Personality in Politics* (New York, 1924).

rection of legislative, executive and judicial officers; the appointment and removal of officials; the control and direction of the lawmaking process; the dispensation of a mass of accommodations or favors, related or unrelated to governmental duty—in short the concentration of the powers of government in a particular area, or, if the sway of the boss is not complete (and it seldom is), of a large group of such powers. In describing Senator Platt,[8] one of the authors made the following summary of the sources of a boss's power: "First, control over the nomination and election machinery through his coöperation with the state committee; second, control over the state legislature through his relations with the oligarchy ruling that body; third, control over the patronage through whatever influence he had with the president, the governor, and the federal, state, and local administrative officers; fourth, his control over the party campaign funds through the relations which he maintained with the directors of certain corporations who were high in financial circles; and lastly, control over the minds of the voters through his intimate relations with party editors and men of influence in the business and political worlds." In the exercise of these powers, the boss is irresponsible in the sense that as an unofficial leader there is no machinery for holding him accountable for the way in which he exercises his vast powers.

The personal equipment of the political boss contains something of the material found in the make-up of the manager of a large body of men and certain special requirements due to the political situation. Quick and accurate estimates of men, swift judgments of situations, skill in choice of tactics, and finesse in management are indispensable for continued success as a boss. For brief periods a man may exercise some of the powers of a boss without possessing all of these qualities in marked degree, but his fall is always imminent. Thus Ames of Minneapolis was not always a good judge of men, and his "reign" was insecure and culminated in disaster.[9] The boss deals with complicated political and social forces and forms and personnel, which he must know intimately and be able to organize and control if he is to survive.

Of particular significance to the boss are the balance of class relations, racial contacts, réligious prejudices, social customs, recreational

---

[8] Gosnell, *Boss Platt and His New York Machine*, p. 348.

[9] W. A. Frisbie, "The Minneapolis House-cleaning," *Proceedings of the Detroit Conference for Good City Government, 1903* (Philadelphia, 1903); Zink, *op. cit.*, p. 24 and Chap. XIX; Steffens, *op. cit.*

habits, and business ethics. If he is not at home here, he cannot succeed for long. Facility in intrigue, which in other circles might constitute diplomacy, is a prerequisite of the boss who holds on to power for any length of time. Zink did not find tact among the traits "possessed to any remarkable degree by the rank and file of city bosses," but on the other hand those who were deficient in this quality made up for it in other ways when they were dealing with groups.

The following keen observation regarding the personality attributes of a boss was made by A. F. Bentley:[10] "The power of the boss lies in his machine. The power of the machine lies in the boss only to the extent that the given boss is superior to the next best man (not in any attributed mental or other ability, but as a definite given man under the circumstances); and this superiority is much less than it is apt to be declared by close onlookers or by conversationalists of one sort or another."

As a rule the boss is strong if he has a good machine and he knows how to run it. The political intelligence bureau of such a boss is superior. His scouts and spies are everywhere, bringing him speedy and accurate information regarding the enemy's forces and plans, of the morale of the general public, and the attitude of all "powers" of importance in the community. He knows the community better than his rivals as a rule, and even while defying the "high-brows" he rules through superior organization of human intelligence.

He possesses a professional political army, made up of a following long trained in political warfare. His warriors are "soldiers of career." His general staff is composed of seasoned and skillful political fighters, intelligent, industrious, fit for their tasks as a rule. They govern inefficiently, but their governmental weakness is closely related to their political strength. The forces arrayed against them are usually the amateurs and the volunteers who must learn the art of war as they go, and suffer heavily in the process; although in recent years other group organizations have sometimes rivaled the machine in efficiency. The Charter Committee of Cincinnati overturned a boss system of long standing and it has continued its reform administration for over two decades.[11]

[10] *The Process of Government* (Chicago, 1908), p. 229.

[11] C. P. Taft, *City Management: The Cincinnati Experiment* (New York, 1933), "Cincinnati," *National Municipal Review*, XXXIII (September, 1944), 376–385; H. A. Stone, *et al.*, *City Management Government* (Chicago, 1940).

The morale of the boss's army is good. Discipline is strictly maintained and inefficiency and disloyalty punished. Failure is in the long run inexcusable. In no type of social organization is discipline more strictly observed than in a highly organized machine. Loss of position, demotion, and even criminal punishment may be employed.[12] Thus Governor Sulzer was ousted from his office by Tammany because he defied the organization and refused to obey its commands. Perhaps the most ruthless and thorough disciplinarian was the late Senator "Kingfish" Huey Long of Louisiana who stopped at nothing in whipping recalcitrant officeholders into line. Bribery, intimidation, military coercion without the formality of martial law, slander, trickery, ridicule, and social pressures were used to cow his followers and keep them meek.[13] Long warfare, with alternating victory and defeat, has made the machine leaders steady in disaster, tenacious, disposed to cling to positions in the expectation of relief. Firm in the belief that the general "system" will go on, they are not dismayed by temporary setbacks, but wait for the counteroffensive, certain to come.

As students of popular psychology, all bosses cultivate the doctrine that the machine is working steadily for the interests of the mass of the people. Adroit bosses have from time to time endeavored to supplement this by popular appeal on specific issues. Tammany favored Andrew Jackson and opposed the United States Bank, supported universal suffrage, opposed imprisonment for debt. Tammany opposed the Civil War, however, and the draft acts. In later years it supported home rule for New York City, nominally demanded municipal ownership of public utilities, and finally supported woman's suffrage in the campaign of 1917. Ruef and Schmitz were closely allied with the organized labor interests in San Francisco, and persistently professed friendship for the common man, although at the same time they were intimately related to the utility companies of the city. Thompson in Chicago professed to favor municipal ownership of the traction system and at another time pretended to stand for "America First." He posed as "Big Bill, the Builder," Chicago's greatest booster, the champion and "servant" of the people and the

---

[12] See T C. Platt, *Autobiography* (New York, 1910), Chap. XXV, "Discipline," and Gosnell, *Boss Platt and His New York Machine*, pp. 338–341.

[13] C. Beals, *The Story of Huey P. Long* (Philadelphia, 1935); W. Smith, *"The Kingfish"* (New York, 1933); H. T. Kane, *Louisiana Hayride* (New York, 1941).

defender of the weak. In the South Senator Long's rule was based in large part upon his success in building himself up as the champion of the poor whites, the "great unwashed," the "hillbillies, Cajuns and sapsuckers" as he called them. Long campaigned on the slogans "Every Man a King" and "Share the Wealth." [14] Instances of this kind might be multiplied, showing the effort to attract popular support on democratic measures, sometimes with sincerity and again with obvious hollowness and insincerity. Evidently the most effective arrangement is one by which the "interests" are publicly denounced and privately accommodated—a combination, unfortunately, only too common.

Bosses, stinging under newspaper criticism of graft, waste, and incompetency, sometimes strike a popular chord by denouncing *in toto* the "commercialized press" as the tool of business interests, unfriendly to the mass of the people. This coincides with the view of many voters, distrustful of modern journalism, and they thenceforth disregard even the truth regarding the machine's peculations of public property. Tammany bosses have held New York City when nearly all the newspapers were against them. In Chicago Mayor Thompson and his political machine won repeated victories in spite of the opposition of very powerful newspapers in the city. As one of the authors has put it: "In order to counteract the influence of his journalistic opponents, Mayor Thompson denounced them at every platform appearance, and sought an alliance with the two Hearst papers, the *Evening American* and the *Herald and Examiner*. He was most successful in recruiting supporters in the areas where there were many persons who read no newspapers and where the Hearst papers were relatively more popular." [15] On the other hand, the bosses have been aided by the fact that the newspapers are usually silent about the machine's relations with the public utility companies.

In like manner the boss assails "riches and reform," which he brackets together. The progressive character of the rule of certain

[14] H. F. Gosnell, *Grass Roots Politics*, Chap. VIII, "Long's Louisiana."

[15] H. F. Gosnell, *Machine Politics: Chicago Model* (Chicago, 1937), p. 180. The author goes on to point out that the Chicago papers which opposed the Thompson machine, *i.e.*, the *News* and the *Tribune,* were not without influence but that in the period 1919–30 this influence was not strong enough to defeat the machine. In 1931 Thompson was defeated for re-election, but the opposition newspapers were aided by the Democratic tide.

bosses was recognized by none less than Governor Gifford Pinchot in the tribute he paid to his former opponent, "Duke" Edwin H. Vare: "As I had followed the career of Senator Vare even before I knew him personally, there stood out of it his consistent championship of all humane measures. He was for workmen's compensation, he was for good child-labor laws. Point by point as you followed his career you found him standing on the side of those who had little, when the issue arose as against those who had much. It was the progressive tendency of his stand in the Senate which attracted me to him most before I knew him." [16] Reformers and reform organizations have been pictured as the creatures or tools of wealth, endeavoring to divert attention from the real evils of mankind, unsympathetic with the troubles of the hard-working man or woman. In this the bosses have been aided by the narrow views of some reformers, who have been little touched by the misery of the masses, and have been at times hostile to fundamental democratic reforms in politics or industry. Prominent reformers may oppose graft but also an eight-hour day for women; may fight waste of public funds, but also oppose a progressive income tax. The genuinely democratic body of progressive sentiment is thus classed with the pseudo-type, to the confusion of antiboss movements.

The internal weakness of the party organization is likely to be matched at this point by the internal dissensions of the opposition. Just as the machine may be split into factions, so the opposition may be split into groups with varied programs, some of which may be taken up by the machine. The strategy of the organization here is likely to be far superior to that of the amateur opposition, and if the forces are not too unevenly matched, the well-seasoned following and astute leaders of the machine are likely to win. If hard pressed, the organization can always adopt the central features in the reform program, thereby disarming their foes. After victory they may decide whether to make this new program actually their own, or to chance the short memory of the public.

Of course, there are always perils that beset the path of the organization. The law itself may seize upon certain of their leaders, as Tweed was taken in spite of all the resourceful resistance offered, as Mayor Schmitz was imprisoned, as the "invincible" Pendergast

[16] *Legislative Journal of the Commonwealth of Pennsylvania*, 1929, I, 1329.

of Kansas City was caught in the net of the federal income tax investigators, and as others have fallen before the criminal law,
wielded by a Tilden, a Johnson, a Loesch, a Milligan, or a Dewey.
There may be a general revolt occasioned by some unusual scandal
and revolution may run through the streets. Equally dangerous is
the revolt within the palace itself, the uprising of a rival leader,
who strives to seize the power of the boss and make it his own. Master of intrigue, the boss deals with other intriguers who may covet
his power and prestige and organize successfully against him. He
must always remember that there may be a combination between
some of his own followers and the outraged public, making common
cause for the moment in order to overthrow the power that is on the
throne.

The alliances made by the boss may cover a wide range of social
forces and groups. In cities he may effect a combination with the
underworld of vice and crime, in every community a powerful fighting force extremely effective in political warfare. He may ally himself with the leaders of sundry racial groups, particularly with the
newly arrived and less sophisticated politically. He may make terms
with religious groups. He may ally himself with territorial groups,
trading local support for improvements, buildings, parks, bridges,
or whatever may be desired locally. He may ally himself with class
groups, with labor either by appeals to the rank and file of the labor
constituency, or by direct relations with such of the leaders as are
open to money or political bribery. He may form working agreements with great corporate interests, particularly with public utilities, such as railways, traction companies, or any large or small
scale industrial interest that will pay for privilege or immunity. He
may ally himself with groups of contractors, purveyors of material
and supplies to the public, or with political bankers, all of whom
may contribute to the revenue of the realm in return for value received. He will always deal with patronage and in this way will
bring to his support many persons closely obligated to serve him.

The adoption of a more comprehensive system of social politics
will tend to diminish some of the evils of the party system in urban
centers. Nowhere was this more clearly illustrated than in New York
City in 1937 when, for the first time in this century, a reform mayor
was re-elected over a Tammany candidate. A negative policy on the
part of the government has justified some of the activities of the

urban boss in acting as local patron of his constituents. For example, proper treatment of unemployment and social insurance would tend to do away with job brokerage and political charity so often sought by or imposed upon the spoilsman. The defeat of the Republican machine in Philadelphia was brought about in part by the adoption of a more liberal attitude toward industrial problems by the Democrats. Broader governmental policies regarding care and protection of the immigrant would remove another source of the spoilsman's power in the immigrant centers.

In many instances the boss is doing, in a crude and enormously expensive way, work that the community itself should and can do much more effectively, and without betraying the government into the hands of organized agents of privilege. The spoilsman obtains "jobs" with the streetcar company for one hundred needy men, but his corrupt government will not be trusted with large power to deal with unemployment. He gives $100 to charity, but accepts $1000 for voting against an ordinance for better housing. He pays the funeral expenses of the man who dies because the boss killed the law to safeguard the machinery on which he worked. He helps the widow, whose suit for damages was blocked under a system he was paid to perpetuate. As the government broadens the range of its generally recognized social duties the occupation of the spoilsman is taken away and the interest of the citizen in his own government is stimulated.

The central factors in his organization will be, however, his control of the patronage and his industrial allies—one furnishing the army and the other the munitions. As cities, counties, and states vary, other factors may or may not be added, but in all cases these elements are common—the jobs and corporate connections.

We may now distinguish between various types of bosses. Thus there is the rural boss, the urban boss, the state-wide, rural or urban, or urban-rural boss. These rulers operate in different ways and often indeed have the most hearty contempt for each other, despising the means the other employs to purchase success.

The rural boss system is based chiefly upon patronage and minor spoils of various types, and it connects with the state organization through the state legislature, where votes are needed.[17]

[17] See Churchill's *Coniston*, for an early type of this. Similar groups may be found in the North and West, although the railway is no longer the base of supplies from which they operate.

The urban boss employs patronage, spoils of the underworld variety, contracts, race exploitation, and public utility alliances, and is likely to play upon class prejudice and demagogy, even though actually allied with the interests he assails.

The state boss may be either rural or urban, or a combination of both. In either case the foundation of the structure is the patronage and the superstructure is the industrial alliances with corporations or other interests willing to pay for protection of some sort.[18]

The powers of the boss, while in many ways greater than is generally supposed, are in many ways more circumscribed than is commonly assumed. The "nuisance value" of the boss is often very great, that is, his power to annoy, harass, and obstruct industrial or other progress through the interposition of obstacles carefully designed to make the maximum of trouble with the minimum of effort.[19] For this he often demands tribute on a surprising scale, of which the public hears nothing as a rule.

But the apparently arbitrary power of the boss has certain boundaries. The boss is the product of a system which has its limitations in the nature of its origin and powers. He may tyrannize over some of his allies, but not over all of them, or over too many of them; otherwise the breaking point is reached and revolt comes. A rival appears who may expose conditions and go to the aid of the public. Custom and common consent are the fundamental laws of his kingdom. The public must not be flaunted too far or it may turn, as it did against Tammany when the spread of protected vice to the homes of the poor in the crowded centers was exposed by Jerome and others; or when Sulzer was deposed from the governorship; or when Lorimer seized a senatorial toga and entered the banking field; or when Ruef became too arrogant for his principals, or when "Big Bill" Thompson became drunk with power; or when the Kelly-Nash machine tried to turn down Governor Horner in Illinois. Ordinary business interests enjoying no special privilege will submit to a cer-

---

[18] See Lynn Haines, *Minnesota Legislature of 1911* (Minneapolis, 1911), for the operation of a legislature under the control of a state "system." See also Gosnell, *Boss Platt*; Davenport, *op. cit.*; McKean, *op. cit.*; Reddig, *op. cit.*

[19] See Thorne's testimony in the N. Y., N. H. & Hartford R. R. case (cited by Myers, *op. cit.*, p. 315), showing some $15,000,000 paid to avoid these "obstructions"; also H. Morgenthau, *"All in a Life Time,"* Chap. II, "What I Learned from Tammany and Sulzer," *World's Work,* XLII (September, 1921), 465.

tain amount of tribute, but beyond that they may be baited far enough to fight, as many bosses discover. High taxes may arouse the property owners to organize action. Conspicuously ineffective service may irritate the public to a frenzy and crystallize opposition.

In short, the ancient maxims of Aristotle in his chapter on the maintenance of a tyranny and the better known and more subtle precepts of Machiavelli [20] must be observed, if the modern boss wishes to hold his power. Public opinion, like a sleeping giant, may be awakened to action by rude conduct. The social and industrial interests he serves are concerned with practical results, not with the boss personally; and they will prepare the way for his downfall, although not that of the system, unless he follows the general lines indicated by their substantial interests.

In the circle of officeholding and spoils perquisites, he may rule without much question, subject to the bombardment of the merit system and the criminal law, both of which often aim badly. He may command the ship and collect his tribute, but he must steer in the general current of his time. Bad judgment or bad luck will diminish his utility to the interests he serves, the officeholding group he supports and whose approval he courts. These, to be sure, are the limits of leaders as well as bosses, and of authority, always and everywhere, in democracy or in autocracy. Special application must be made to the boss in the light of the special conditions surrounding him. The key to understanding will be found in the analysis of the "system" in its social setting, in its relation to the social, industrial and political environment, as well as in its relation to our political mechanisms and our political *mores*. The pathological political developments are symptoms, not causes; they are evidences of disordered functioning of the body politic. We must look deeper for the causes of infection, the conditions of its continuance, the modes of reducing it.

Thus far there has been no national boss. Large powers have been held by small groups of men, such as those headed by Thaddeus Stevens at the close of the Civil War, by Conkling, Blaine, Gorman, Aldrich's "Old Guard," the Penrose group, and by the Ohio gang. But in no case did these powers approach the typical authority of the boss, and they are not technically comparable. Many of these

[20] Especially in Chap. XV of *The Prince*.

leaders were bosses in their states, but they were not able to effect a combination on a national scale of the kind they controlled locally. The country is too vast for a national boss.[21]

Mark Hanna more nearly approached the national boss than any other figure, but he was far from holding the position nationally that urban and state leaders held.[22] He held large powers in the Senate as a member of that body, he possessed much influence in industrio-political circles, and was on intimate terms with President McKinley with whom he had much influence; but he was by no means a dominant figure of the kind so frequently encountered in the smaller units of government.

Oligarchy has been found in the government of the nation, but thus far the combination of oligarchs has not taken on the typical boss shape. The great power of the presidential office, its conspicuous place in the life of the nation, the vigorous and independent character of many of its incumbents, the presence of notable party leaders with strong popular followings, all have tended to obstruct the general movement toward boss rule. Leadership to some extent has taken the place of boss rule, or where this was lacking or ineffective, the "Old Guard" has assumed the task of regency without, however, yielding to the rule of any one of them long enough to institutionalize the practice.

REFORMERS

"Reform" is in reality a term of varied and often conflicting meanings, used to cover all types of social change, whether industrial, ethical, or more narrowly governmental and political. "Reformer" likewise is a flexible term which may be applied to a wide variety of persons advocating some change in existing institutions.[23] Reform-

[21] See Herbert Croly, *Marcus Alonzo Hanna: His Life and Work* (New York, 1912).

[22] President Truman was "made" politically by Boss Pendergast but the "Boss" died 73 days before Truman was inaugurated as President. See Reddig, *op. cit.*

[23] See H. M. Kallen, "Reformism," *Encyclopaedia of the Social Sciences* (New York, 1934), XIII, pp. 194–195; Reddig, *op. cit.*; the chapter in Roosevelt's *Strenuous Life* (New York, 1918) on "Latitude ana Longitude among Reformers"; John J. Chapman, *Practical Agitation* (New York, 1909); W. B. Munro, *Government of American Cities* (New York, 1929), Chap. XIV; H. W. Farnum, "The Psychology of the Reformer and the Stand-Patter," in *National Municipal Review*,

ers may be persons who are normally of progressive tendencies, suggesting or advocating constructive changes; or those whose special interest leads them to demand some specific change; or those who are habitually incapable of cooperation in any organized system; or those whose ideals are incapable of practical realization in the immediate future. They range from the reformer *ad hoc* to the temperamental "neurotic," described in the vivid language of Theodore Roosevelt as the "lunatic fringe." And reform may pass over into the field of revolution and the more radical reconstruction of social or political institutions.

Reformers may also be grouped for purposes of convenience into these classes: those who favor administrative reform, moral reform, democratic reform, industrial reform. The first type is interested in such political changes as will promote economy and efficiency in the operations of government, restrain extravagance, corruption, and waste in expenditure and encourage prudence, foresight, and thrift in the management of public affairs. This is sometimes characterized as the businessman's type of reform.

The second type is interested in such changes as will make more effective certain ethical standards of conduct. They endeavor to bring about the prohibition of the sale of intoxicating liquors, the restriction of gambling and prostitution, the punishment of evil in the moral sense of the term. This is sometimes characterized as the clergyman's type of reform.

A third type is interested in such institutional changes as tend to promote democracy in public affairs. This group may include the expansion of the suffrage, the initiative and referendum, the direct primary, proportional representation, corrupt practices legislation, ballot reforms, demand for opposition to boss rule and to the spoils system, city manager plan, easier methods of amending constitutions. These changes affect the mode of popular control over the acts and the agencies of government.

XIII, 318; "The Psychology of Reform," in *Unpopular Review*, 24, 150; W. B. Graves, *Readings in Public Opinion* (New York, 1928), Chap. XXII; Munro, *Personality in Politics*, Chap. I; H. E. Broun and Margaret Leech, *Anthony Comstock* (New York, 1927); F. C. Howe, *Confessions of a Reformer* (New York, 1926); W. P. Lovett, *Detroit Rules Itself* (Boston, 1930); M. Seasongood, *Local Government in the United States* (Cambridge, 1933); and John Chamberlain, *Farewell to Reform* (New York, 1933).

A fourth type is interested in such institutional changes as tend to promote industrial or social democracy. This list may include public ownership, the single tax, corporation regulation, progressive inheritance and income taxes, unemployment, old age and health insurance, housing improvements, price control, and a series of measures for the protection of labor and for the advancement of what is termed industrial democracy.

Broadly speaking, the first of these types is favored by the business group and the middle class, the second type by the middle class with some support from the business group, the third by the middle class and by labor, and the last type chiefly by labor with some support from the middle class. It is the middle class that has dealt most directly with the political party system.

These conflicting ideals of reform are all found in active operation in the American political system. Most people favor reforms of some type, but few endorse the entire list that might be presented. The clash between them frequently results in the failure of all of them, or in groupings and adjustments, sometimes of a heterogeneous character. Not infrequently citizens are forced to choose between dishonest or incompetent democracy and honest, efficient, but undemocratic leadership; or between highly moral but undemocratic rule, and dubious morality with unquestioned democracy. These varied ideas of "reform" are the hope of the boss, who plays upon them in such a manner as to divide opposition and secure success for himself if possible. Unusual outrages or unusual personalities, however, often fuse all or many of these elements in successful struggles for political control, as in the cases of the La Follettes, Bryan, and La Guardia.

CHAPTER X

PATRONAGE

"Government work is so simple that anyone can qualify."
"Charity begins on the public payroll."
"Patronage is the price of democracy."
"The most efficient public servant is the worst one."
"Permanence of tenure is the cure for spoils."
"Home town jobs should go to home town boys."
"Public service is always less efficient than private enterprise."
—"Fallacies" collected by the Commission of Inquiry on Public Service Personnel, *Better Government Personnel* (New York, 1935).

IN THE ACTUAL OPERATION OF THE POLITICAL PARTY THE ELEMENTS of perquisites and emoluments play a considerable part, and it is therefore necessary to analyze the "spoils system" and make clear its methods and technique.[1]

The term "spoils" is used with many different shades of meaning. The "spoils system" may be used to indicate the selection of officials (chiefly administrative) on a party basis as distinguished from a merit basis—the use of offices as rewards of party or factional service, as in the well-known system adopted in the Jacksonian period and continued down to our own day. In this sense, the "spoils system" is contrasted with the "merit system" and refers to the practice of using political appointments, inefficiently it may be, as a means of building up parties or factions or individuals, or perhaps in return for support given to measures of public policy. Many organiza-

[1] W. M. Reddig, *Tom's Town: Kansas City and the Pendergast Legend* (Philadelphia and New York, 1947); V. O. Key, "Techniques of Political Graft in the United States" (Ph.D. thesis, University of Chicago, 1934); R. C. Brooks, *Corruption in American Politics and Life* (New York, 1910); H. F. Gosnell, *Boss Platt and His New York Machine* (Chicago, 1924); G. L. Hostetter and T. Q. Beesley, *It's a Racket!* (Chicago, 1929); W. B. and J. B. Northrup, *The Insolence of Office* (New York, 1932); Donald Richberg, *Tents of the Mighty* (New York, 1930); F. Kent, *The Great Game of Politics* (Garden City, 1924), Chaps. VIII, XVI, XVII; C. E. Merriam, *Chicago, A More Intimate View of Urban Politics* (Chicago, 1929).

tions are built up wholly or almost entirely from spoils of this type, and leaders have found it necessary or desirable to reckon with this system of official patronage.

There are also certain perquisites that fall to the party in office— honors, distinctions, preferments, preferences, favors. These may be dispensed upon a party basis. In any group, political or otherwise, there is a certain leeway within which the discretion of the governing official may be exercised, and within this field party preference or service may be the chief consideration. It is true that honors and distinctions are fewer here than in European countries, but they are not unknown in the United States, and they may be and actually are used for party purposes as the perquisites of those elevated to power. In addition to this, there are numerous preferences and favors of a legitimate type, accommodations and adjustments which are common everywhere, and which may be accorded in a governmental system for party reasons or purposes either in whole or in part.

PATRONAGE AND THE ORGANIZATION

Patronage is one of the essential and indispensable elements of the spoils system.[2] To the machine maker "jobs" are a *sine qua non.* They are the basic material out of which finished products are fashioned. The old-time spoilsman cannot conceive of a party or an organization in which this is not true. Politics without principles or policies he might understand, but politics without an organized system of patronage he could with difficulty imagine. An important party manager once said: "I simply do not understand Governor ————. He seems to take no interest in these appointments. He spends all of his time thinking about bills in the legislature, or about his speeches. He does not seem to care a damn about politics."

The attitude of a loyal organization man is well illustrated by a conversation between James Farley and Arthur E. Morgan, the first director of the Tennessee Valley Authority. Farley wrote:

[2] See Edward J. Flynn, *You're the Boss* (New York, 1947); L. D. White and T. V. Smith, *Politics and the Public Service* (New York, 1939); James A. Farley, *Behind the Ballots* (New York, Harcourt, Brace and Co., 1938), pp. 223–238; Raymond Moley, *After Seven Years* (New York, Harpers, 1939), Chap. IV; Commission of Inquiry on Public Service Personnel, *Better Government Personnel* (New York, 1935).

"I suggested it would be wise to avoid appointing people down there who would be unacceptable to the Senators and Representatives from that area, pointing out that simple things like that often bring about their defeat and that after all it was a smart practice in government to avoid antagonizing the men who vote the appropriations. . . . Dr. Morgan, however, got very exercised and promptly replied in what seemed discourteous fashion that he would appoint whom he liked and that he had no interest whatever in politics. I pointed out in turn that President Roosevelt would never have landed in the White House if someone hadn't thought about politics and that he himself was a political appointee. . . . However, when he got into trouble later, it was perfectly apparent that Dr. Morgan simply didn't understand how to get along with other people, and that's an indispensable quality in public life. Moreover, he never consulted Democratic Senators and at first they were not inclined to go to his defense or to give him a lift in presenting his side of the case to the public." [3]

On the other hand, Farley also wrote:

"I am convinced that with the help of a few simple ingredients like time, patience, and hard work, I could construct a major political party in the United States without the aid of a single job to hand out to deserving partisans." [4]

The effort of every boss, big and little, is first directed toward the task of building around him a group of loyal workers who owe their election or appointment to him, a group of men who may be rewarded by promotion or punished by discharge or other appropriate methods of discipline. To these men he looks for continuance of his power, and they look to him for opportunity and advancement. It is largely upon this basis that alliances are formed, re-formed and dissolved.

The members of the job-made machine constitute a seasoned army, accustomed to all forms of political warfare. They are schooled to obedience and habituated to service, held together by the direct bond of personal interest. They are the standing army against which the raw recruits are likely to be shattered, except in times of political revolution. Torn by jealousies which develop to an amazing degree in the atmosphere of politics, ready for far-reaching

[3] *Behind the Ballots* (New York, Harcourt, Brace & Co., 1938), pp. 232–233.
[4] *Ibid.*, p. 237.

intrigues against each other, or for open and bitter warfare, they constitute, nevertheless, a formidable army when united for action in a primary or election campaign.

With infinite patience and infinite skill this web is woven back and forth, until it covers every point on the political map. Every district, every county, every ward or township, every precinct is covered. But the division of patronage is not merely geographical. The various strata of social life are invaded. As far as possible, every interest is represented, whether racial, religious, territorial, business, fraternal, cultural, class, or other. Into every influential group the thread of patronage is woven. A representative of the "organization" is installed, if possible, in every center from which influence radiates, preferably, of course, an agent who can and does "deliver" votes and influence in return for his position.

The tendency of public service under such circumstances is inevitable. What shall it profit a man, the official may well say, if he make the most brilliant record possible, and lose his own precinct? For the spoils system places party service and success first, and public service second. The natural result has been more efficient organization of party service than of public service. Skill, courage, loyalty, industry, persistence, initiative have come in to build up the one and to exploit the other.

The seasoned politician does not always regard seriously the work of the volunteer or the amateur. He utilizes their efforts as far as possible in the heat of the campaign, but he expects little from them between times. In some cases the smaller leaders do not desire activity on the part of the outsiders, because it may give others experience and skill in party methods and warfare, and thus a rival may spring up and give battle for organization supremacy or at least make one more to be "taken care of." A local boss was once asked why he had discontinued the meeting of the ward club in his territory. "Because," he said, "it is only a nursery for upstarts, and I have too many statesmen on my hands now."

Under the patronage system many appointments are made of persons wholly or very largely unfitted for the duties of the particular

[5] In discussing his recommendations for positions, Farley said that he followed these rules: "First, is the applicant qualified? Second, is he loyal to the party and sympathetic toward the program of Franklin D. Roosevelt?" *Ibid.*, pp. 229–230.

position.[5] Preliminary qualification, permanency of tenure, promotion, and discipline are likely to be interpreted upon other than public grounds. Appointees may be unqualified to perform the duties of their public office, or too preoccupied to execute them efficiently. A system of "waivers" may be used to nullify promotional examinations.[6] In some instances it will be found that payrolls are padded outright by addition of fictitious names, and in other cases only half or part work is actually performed. Still more commonly the spoils pressure for appointments and yet more appointments operates against the establishment of practical and businesslike methods in public administration, through fear that some "jobs" may be lost in the process of reorganization of the service. In the long run this attitude is disastrous to the public service. It should not be concluded, however, that all party appointments are inferior in capacity or efficiency, for this would be a distorted view of the case.

From the point of view of the machine-maker the patronage serves as the basis for his whole campaign. It supplies him with the standing army, the retainers, and followers who are prepared to carry out the plans he may prepare. It places his followers in various strategic points within the government, where if desirable the many types of spoils practice can be undertaken. Patronage not only supplies them with the necessary personnel, but also places them in important tactical situations.

FEDERAL PATRONAGE

Beginning with the president, certain appointments are made by him with only nominal confirmation by the Senate, as in the case of the cabinet; a considerable number of presidential appointments are not subject to confirmation at all. The Senate usually accepts the president's nominations for these important posts without hesitation, for it is realized that if the chief executive is to be responsible for the administration, he must be given a free hand in choosing his immediate assistants. The Senate's rejection of Charles B. Warren, whom Coolidge named for attorney general in 1925, was a most unusual event and created a sensation.[7] More recently, the Sen-

---

[6] L. D. White, *Introduction to the Study of Public Administration* (New York, 1948).

[7] William Allen White, *A Puritan in Babylon* (New York, 1938)

ate rejected the nomination of Aubrey Williams for Rural Electrification Administrator.

Cabinet members are chosen upon a mixed basis in which are found the elements of personal equipment, party service, recognition of class, sectional and factional elements, friendship, and even campaign pledges or promises, perhaps unauthorized. As to other appointments, the president usually acts upon the recommendation of or consultation with the party senator from the state in which the appointment is made, if there is such a senator. In other cases he may consult the representative or the national committeeman in lieu of the senator. He may also consult the representative in case of major as well as minor appointments which may not require senatorial confirmation.

The presidential list is a long and important one, including certain positions in the diplomatic service, the district attorneys, the collectors of internal revenue, the federal judgeships, and a long array of miscellaneous officers, commissions, and special agencies.

Following the precedent set in the Harding administration, a resolution introduced by Senator McKellar of Tennessee was adopted on January 3, 1933, calling upon the Civil Service Commission to furnish "a full and complete list of all offices, positions, places and employments . . . with the amount of salaries of each attached, under the Government of the United States and *not under civil service rules* and regulations." The result was a document of over four hundred pages which served the party leaders as a catalogue of patronage.[8] "That document," said Republican Senator Vandenberg of Michigan, "became, probably, the most popular publication ever turned out of the Government Printing Office."[9]

The exact relation between the president and the senators and congressmen in the selection of these officials has never been determined, and must depend to a great extent on the relative strength and weakness of the officials concerned. A strong president or one closely interested in the placing of patronage will go much farther in the actual choices than a weak president or one less concerned with the official list. Again, a president may prefer the passage of

[8] U. S. Civil Service Commission, *Positions Not Under Civil Service* (Washington, D. C.).

[9] *Saturday Evening Post*, May 2, 1936.

legislative projects which have come to be called "administration measures" to official appointments, and may use his appointing power to secure the passage of laws otherwise difficult to obtain. There comes to be a process of jockeying between the executive and the members of the legislative body, in which, in dignified manner, of course, the relative merits of the law and the appointments are compared and appraised. There must be an agreeable amount of what Bagehot once called "illogical moderation" on both sides.

Notwithstanding the urgency of party harmony and the strong pressure to obtain an agreement, there have been constant clashes, some of them dramatic in their intensity. Of these the warfare between President Garfield and Senators Conkling and Platt over the collectorship of the port in New York City was the most notable. Senator McKellar's clash with the Tennessee Valley Authority over appointments was carried over to the nomination of David Lillienthal to the Atomic Bomb Commission. But there have been constant rivalries between Democratic presidents and Tammany, and between Republican presidents and various elements in their party.[10]

The policy of a strong and vigorous leader is stated by Theodore Roosevelt as follows: "In the appointments I shall go on exactly as I did while I was Governor of New York. The Senators and Congressmen shall ordinarily name the men, but I shall name the standard, and the men have got to come up to it." [11]

Sharing after a fashion in the appointing power of the congressmen are the local leaders upon whom these functionaries depend for their support in many cases. Suggestions or demands will come up for redemption, and must be met in some way. The local leader demands his post office or attorneyship, or other piece of patronage, and looks to Washington for favorable action on his expectation. In some

[10] See T. C. Platt's statement regarding his relations with President Harrison in his *Autobiography* (New York, 1910) and in Gosnell, *op. cit*. See also Grover Cleveland, *The Independence of the Executive* (Princeton, 1913).

[11] J. B. Bishop, *Theodore Roosevelt and His Time* (New York, 1920), I, 157. The same writer relates the following incident: Senator Bailey of Texas went to the President with a similar request, saying that the promotion which he sought was favored by the entire Legislature of Texas. "But," said the President, "it is opposed by all the man's superior officers." "I don't give a damn for his superior officers!" exclaimed the Senator. "Well, Senator," said the President, "I don't give a damn for the Legislature of Texas." I, 156. See also H. F. Pringle, *Theodore Roosevelt* (New York, 1931).

cases this has been carried so far that local primaries have been held for the purpose of recommending candidates for local post offices, although this has by no means been the general custom.

Whether a federal appointment is actually made by the local boss, or the federal representative, or the cabinet officer, or the president cannot be determined except by examination of the facts in the case. The personal strength of these competing factors, the degree of their confidence in each other, and the strategic situation in which they find themselves decide the matter.

The Commission of Inquiry on Public Service Personnel reported that in 1932 there were some 100,000 positions available for patronage purposes in the federal government.[12] This was only one-fifth of the total number of federal civil employees but it was large enough to weigh heavily with the party leaders. With the coming of the New Deal administration in 1933 there was a great increase in the number of so-called unclassified employees in the national service, due to the action of Congress in exempting the newer agencies from the merit system.

In principle, appointments to New Deal agencies not under civil service were made by the proper appointing authority. After his preliminary conversation with Dr. Morgan of the Tennessee Valley Authority, Farley said that he left the agency strictly alone. In many of the other agencies, however, applicants were required to secure "clearance" through the headquarters of the Democratic national committee. "Clearance" is an old custom and means obtaining a certificate of political endorsement, either that of a congressman, a state or local committee, or a county or ward party leader. In many cases "clearance" is easy to obtain and proves to be a formality, but for some important jobs and a great mass of clerical and minor positions it is often essential.[13]

Elaborate personnel files are maintained in the party headquarters.[14] Everyone holding office under the "clearance" system is listed with a complete record of his sponsors. New appointees and

[12] *Better Government Personnel*, p. 92.

[13] L. D. White, *op. cit.*, p. 283; Farley, *op. cit.*, pp. 223–238, and "Passing Out the Patronage," *American Magazine*, CXXVI (August, 1938), 20–22.

[14] Oliver McKee, Jr., "The Jobmaster General," *North American Review*, CCXXXVII (1934), 119–126; Drew Pearson and R. S. Allen, "The President's Trigger Man," *Harper's Magazine*, CLXX (March, 1935), 385–394.

their salaries are listed by location so that a fair division may be made among the various states, counties, wards, etc. Representatives of the national committee are sometimes located in key agencies where they can report vacancies or new positions and lessen the danger of friction between the party and the administrators.

The limitations of patronage in national politics were dramatically demonstrated by the so-called Hatch Act of 1939 which was aimed to eliminate federal office holders as political workers, and the amendments to that Act passed in 1940 which were aimed to eliminate state and local office holders supported in part or in full out of federal grant-in-aid funds. An avowed aim of this legislation was to reduce the power of the "federal machine." As E. E. Schattschneider pointed out, the legislation was based on the faulty premise that there was a "federal machine." [15] President Roosevelt's ability to win elections was not dependent on federal patronage, as the elections of 1940 and 1944 clearly demonstrated. Federal office holders and federally supported office holders were barred from political activity but President Roosevelt still won, thus showing that his power was based upon his substantive policies, his personality, and many factors other than patronage. The same generalization applies to President Truman's victory in 1948.

STATE AND LOCAL PATRONAGE

The governor of the state, like the president, has a long list of appointments to make. In only twenty states are there comprehensive civil service programs established by law. In the remaining twenty-eight states merit systems cover at least employees engaged in federal state assistance and employment security programs. There remains a long list of political appointments in the hands of the governor. The Commission of Inquiry on Public Service Personnel estimated that only 38 per cent of state employees were under civil service merit system rules.[16] While the number under the classified service has increased since this estimate was made in 1932, state patronage is still an important party consideration. Most states require the confirmation of appointments by the Senate, but the prac-

[15] *Party Government* (New York, 1942), pp. 166–167.
[16] *Better Government Personnel*, p. 92.

tice of senatorial courtesy has not developed in the states as in the federal government, and the governor does not turn over his patronage to the senators to dispose of as they will or subject to his check. As a rule appointments are confirmed without much discussion, although there are, of course, many exceptions to this practice, and at times the governor is hard pressed to carry his nominees through. Furthermore, an increasing number of gubernatorial appointments is made without the requirement of any confirmation by the Senate.

The governor must reckon, however, with the leaders of counties and districts upon whom he was dependent for nomination or election or both. Patronage must be divided with reference to their demands and the promises to or understandings with them. The governor in a boss-ruled state may be little more than a figurehead, in which case the actual appointing power is not in his hands at all, but in that of the ring or boss in actual control. If he is his own man he must still reckon with the leaders of his group, who present their claims for recognition, and are certain to urge them upon him with great assiduity, to put it mildly.[17]

Of the state governments still depending upon party affiliation as the chief basis of personnel selection, Missouri affords an outstanding example, and its records on the subject are more complete than in other jurisdictions. A shift in party control in the state during the twenties and thirties was followed by a large turnover in the administrative personnel. This happened in 1921 when a Republican administration replaced a Democratic, but in 1933 an even cleaner sweep was made by the Democrats. A study of the personnel situation in 1933 showed that in the office of the Secretary of State only one of the 148 employees had been employed prior to 1933, representing a turnover of 99.2 per cent.[18] There were no old employees left in the offices of the Treasurer, the Attorney General, the Adjutant General, the Building and Loan Bureau, or the Department of Labor. Only the State Highway Department and the Highway Patrol were exceptions to the rule, and in the former there is no doubt that the federal government exercised a restraining influence. In Missouri

[17] For an interesting account of the relations between Roosevelt and Platt in regard to patronage, compare the *Autobiographies* of the two men. See also Gosnell, *Boss Platt and His New York Machine*, pp. 204–216.

[18] Data compiled by Dr. M. L. Faust of the University of Missouri from the *Official Manuals, State of Missouri, 1931–32; 1933–34*.

during this period the patronage system was at its worst, and services suffered accordingly. Following the adoption of a new constitution in 1945, the state passed a new civil service law which implemented the merit system provisions of the constitution, particularly those referring to the eleemosynary and penal institutions.[19]

In the smaller districts, of which counties and cities are the chief forms, official appointments are made in much the same manner as on the larger scale, except that there is more likely to be a boss on the one hand or the merit system on the other. Where there is a boss in control, appointments are made by him acting through the nominal official. The boss in turn acts in consultation with his local leaders, who present their claims and demands for patronage. Patronage will be distributed roughly on the basis of the relative strength of the claimants, or their strategic importance at a particular time. Where there is no system of boss rule, or only an imperfect one, appointments are made by the officials in charge of the office. These officials again are governed very largely by the advice and demands of their friends or allies. They have to reckon with a type of "senatorial courtesy" not unlike in kind that which the President encounters on a large scale; and often much the same sort of bargaining process goes on between them as in the classic shade of the Capitol, substituting the ward or precinct committeeman for the senator.

In 1932 it was estimated that in the municipal field some three-fifths of the employees were under civil service rules, and that in the field of county, township and district government only 14 per cent were under the merit system.[20] While it might be laid down as a generalization that the most important patronage for the party machines is the local patronage, in rural communities the system is often very different, with an absence of bosses and with less emphasis on patronage elements in the party structure. It is in the urban counties that the patronage system is often at its worst. Paul Blanshard found the

[19] Reddig, *op. cit.* On the new constitution, see Martin L. Faust, "Reorganization in Missouri," *National Municipal Review,* XXXV (September, 1946), pp. 402–407; Tess Loeb, "New Constitution for Missouri," *ibid.,* XXXIV (April, 1945); Charlton F. Chute, "How to Get a New Constitution," *ibid.,* XXXVI (March, 1947), pp. 124–130; W. L. Bradshaw, "Missouri's Proposed New Constitution," *American Political Science Review,* (February, 1945).

[20] Commission of Inquiry on Public Service Personnel, p. 92. In 1946, out of 1,072 cities of over 10,000 population, 390 had substantially complete merit systems, while 600 had systems applying to part of the services

county offices in New York City to be "nests of the spoils system, reeking with incompetence and favoritism, and expensively operated by gentlemen of obvious unfitness." [21]

In most municipalities the practice of legislative confirmation has been abandoned, and the mayor is not obliged to secure the consent of the aldermen to his appointments. His most significant appointments, however, such as the chief of police and of health, are very carefully scrutinized, and their duties bring them into such intimate touch with the community that they must be made with great (political) discretion.[22] The development of the city-manager plan tends to emphasize the importance of professional standards of administrative service.[23]

PATRONAGE RULES AND REGULATIONS

The qualifications of the party personnel are determined by the party tests of fitness. In the main these run between the lines of public service on the one side and party or factional services on the other side. The ideal appointment would be that of an official who might render 100 per cent service to the public and 100 per cent service to the party or the faction at the same time. Practically all organizations make some appointments on the exclusive basis of public service, and some on the basis of party service. Most of them are somewhere between these two extremes.

Party or factional service may consist in the detailed and successful activity of the "worker" of the party, carrying the precinct, the ward, the township or the county, or making a strong showing there. But shrewd managers make appointments which appeal to a wide variety of social interests in the nation, the state, the county or the city. A judicious number of appointments will be made in recognition of race, of religion, of fraternal and social orders, of class, of

[21] *Investigating the City Government in the La Guardia Administration* (New York, 1937). Blanshard, as Commissioner of Accounts, followed up the Seabury Investigation.

[22] In Boston, important appointments by the mayor must be confirmed by the State Civil Service Commission.

[23] L. D. White, *The City Manager* (Chicago, 1927); Clarence Ridley and Orin F. Nolting, *The City Manager Profession* (Chicago, 1934); and Harold Stone, Don K. Price, and Kathryn Stone, *City Manager Government in the United States* (Chicago, 1940).

geography, [24] of eminence, or celebrity, for all these are strong factors in party or factional success. If certain elements are not included or "recognized," the cry of discrimination will quickly be raised, and overtures from the opposition quickly presented.

The appointment list is thus made up of those who will render direct party service in the form of party "work," of those who will indirectly benefit the party as representatives of various interests, and of those who possess special qualifications for public service.[25] It is of course possible that two or more of these qualities may be combined in the same appointee. If he can render distinguished public service, do active and effective party work, and at the same time represent some significant interest in the community, so much the better. But such a combination is not always obtainable, and then only one of the attributes may qualify the applicant for the position.

These qualifications and requirements are written on the largest scale in the choice of a cabinet, and the same principles may be found in the state, the county, the city, the smallest unit of civil organization. In the miniature as in the larger world, the same political standards are seen. In the larger field the factor of capacity for public service looms larger than in the smaller, but the difference is not as great as might be supposed at first thought. Among a hundred cabinet members there will be found several appointments made primarily because of high capacity for public service; there will be several dictated by sectional considerations; there will be several determined by factional considerations; there will be several determined by class or racial considerations; there will be a few appoint-

[24] An examination of the personnel records of the Missouri penitentiary showed that the staff of the institution was representative of almost every county in the state. See Missouri Association for Criminal Justice, *Missouri Crime Survey* (New York, 1926), p. 531. In an analysis of the legal residence of Illinois state employees as of 1928, made by I. M. Labovitz and Simeon Leland of the University of Chicago, it was found that the smallest number of employees credited to any one county was ten.

[25] There are some appointments made under the patronage system which do not serve either of these purposes. The practice of nepotism by Congressmen in filling their personal secretarial positions is a case in point. G. F. Nieberg, "All in the Congressional Family," *Atlantic Monthly*, CXLVIII (1931), 514–523, estimates that a considerable number of our national lawmakers appoint relatives to office jobs on Capitol Hill, sometimes for convenience and sometimes to supplement their income—admittedly low for Washington living. See C. E. Merriam, *Prologue to Politics* (Chicago, 1939), p. 41, on legislative salaries.

ments made for personal reasons. An analysis of a series of cabinets will readily show the constituent elements from which such appointments are made.

Minimum standards of efficiency and integrity will, however, usually be insisted upon. In the case of minor offices where political leadership is not at stake, and where minimum standards are not always obtained, the result is often disastrous. Administrative officials selected under this system are not in fact under the direction of their normal administrative superior, but of the political sponsor by whom they were appointed and by whom they may be promoted or demoted. Many officials thus owe a dual allegiance, and at times these rival allegiances may conflict. Strong and aggressive officials may insist, as the president may, that only fit men be sent them, but others will not be able to do this. Indeed, under a boss-controlled system they will be entirely unable to do so.

It is not commonly recognized as clearly as it should be that a great part of the paralysis in a spoils conducted office is caused not by the incapacity of the employees but by the fact that the office is disorganized, having a nominal head inside and an actual head outside, with a demoralizing division of authority. When the chief suspends a man, the employee turns to his local boss and he to the larger boss, and the larger boss back to the chief again. In this process organization, efficiency, and discipline may be badly shattered.[26] The fact that chiefs and heads are invested with the office amid public declarations that they are "entirely responsible" may usually be taken with at least "mild reservations," although at times when a clean-up or a record is sought this may be true.[27] Incoming city managers have often greatly increased the effectiveness of a municipal staff, with surprisingly few changes in personnel but with more sharply outlined responsibility.

Promotion, demotion, dismissal, and discipline are determined in

[26] J. T. Salter, *Boss Rule* (New York, 1935), p. 160, gives an excellent illustration of this division of responsibility. Nick, the precinct captain, had a city hall job, and when reprimanded for being late he appealed to his boss. Nick explained, "I never appeared again—except to get my pay check."

[27] The head of a great spoils system once decided to make a "feature" of the school trustees. He was found late one night in his favorite saloon, and was asked to make one of the customary types of appointments, but to the surprise of the solicitor he answered: "We ain't appointing no stiffs here. Give us a guy of some class."

much the same way as the original appointments are made, that is, upon the basis of public service, direct party service, and indirect party service.[28] To this will be added again the strategic necessity for the promotion of the individual at the given moment—the pressure there may be for an advance. Then too the organizing and combining ability of the official himself must be reckoned with, especially in the higher grades of the service. Discipline and dismissal are methods of maintaining morale often ruthlessly exercised by the appointing power. Disloyalty is perhaps the most serious offense, but party inefficiency and conspicuous public inefficiency are also causes for action. Faithfulness to the group or the leader and ability to "deliver," that is, to obtain practical results, are the great desiderata; and their absence cannot long be pardoned. Conspicuous inability leading to the embarrassment of the party, the faction or the leader may be found cause for dismissal, depending upon the attitude taken by the authorities responsible. Even in that case, however, a capable party worker may be "taken care of" in some other capacity. Just as the gambling house may be obliged to "stand for a pinch" if necessary, so dubious officials may be obliged to stand for a slap from the boss if necessary for the benefit of the group.

Of the party tests it may be said that they are eminently practical and adaptable. Is the applicant regular? Is he capable of performing the duties of the office? Is he an efficient party worker? Will he strengthen the faction or the party with some influential group, racial, sectional, or otherwise, in the community? How will he fit in with the given situation in which the appointing power now finds itself? [29] Sometimes, under these conditions, surprisingly good results are obtained for a time and in particular offices, but the general tendency inevitably is to subordinate the public service to the needs of the faction or of the party.

On the other hand it will be observed that there is little discrimination because of social considerations. Neither race, class, nor creed is

[28] L. D. White, *Conditions of Municipal Employment in Chicago: A Study in Morale* (Chicago, 1925), pp. 56 ff. See also *Report of Civil Service Study Commission* (Lansing, Michigan, 1936), p. 35.

[29] In corrupt systems the question may be asked: "Is he a 'right guy' or a 'wrong guy'?"—a "right guy" being dishonest and a "wrong guy" honest. Key, *op. cit.*, pp. 58–59, cites an excellent example of the appointment of a "right" man to a commission by Mayor William Hale Thompson.

tabooed. To some extent there has been in the past discrimination on account of sex, but this has tended to disappear with the advent of women's suffrage. No line is drawn between Jew and Gentile, between rich and poor, between the native and the naturalized citizen, or on any other "social" basis, such as characterizes the system of many other countries. The diplomatic service is an exception to this and is open usually to those of wealth, with general standards and requirements set thus far by courts and kings rather than by democracies.[30] There is also some discrimination against the Negro. [31] But in the main, whatever other faults it may have had, and they are numerous and glaring, the appointing system of the parties has not favored the cultivation of snobbishness and caste or class in the public service.

The substitution of party service for public service inevitably produces disastrous consequences in politics and in public administration. Politically, it tends to make the party leader more of a "job broker" than is desirable, distracting his time and attention from the responsibilities of his office, and thus lowering the grade of public service. It enables the professional patronage dispenser to form the nucleus of a powerful organization which may master instead of serve the party. It tends to keep or drive out of party life those to whom the task of patronage distribution is not congenial and those who possess no particular aptitude in this direction. The more powerful leaders have dealt with the "system" at arm's length, so to speak, making the best of it, pushing the lines ahead when they could, but often making terms with spoilsmen in return for support of their policies.

[30] R. Moley, *After Seven Years*, p. 131, says: "Once in the State Department, I found myself having a lot more to do with diplomatic appointments than I would have chosen. But Hull announced that he wasn't particularly interested and, except in one or two instances, proceeded to keep hands off. This left the ball to Billy Phillips, who soon showed a preference for Social Registerites and career boys ('cookie-pushers,' the newspaper men had dubbed them) so overpowering that Jim Farley raised the roof a couple of times and finally insisted that Phillips consult with me before he made any moves."

[31] H. F. Gosnell, *Negro Politicians: The Rise of Negro Politics in Chicago* (Chicago, University of Chicago Press, 1935), p. 196, says: "In these northern cities many white politicians, citizens, and visitors were not used to seeing colored persons in political jobs. Hostility to the appointment of Negroes might come from white factional leaders, appointing officers, employees, or citizens using the government services."

With the increasing competition for civil service positions, it has become more and more apparent that the patronage system wrongs the American philosophy of public education. The reward in education is given to those who merit it most, while patronage is distributed in many cases, with a total disregard of merit on an educational basis.[32]

The personnel of the administrative staff of the several governments is seriously affected by this method of selection, promotion, and removal. It tends to destroy continuity of tenure, or reasonable certainty of reward for meritorious service, which plays so large a part in the effectiveness and morale of a working force.[33] Political employment must in the long run compete with the professions and the skilled trades which in the last generation have tended constantly to develop standards of their own. These standards provide for recognition of special skill as the basis of employment, and for reasonable continuity of employment. Unions may provide for a standard and uniform wage, but even then the rule is a uniform one, and personal favor is eliminated. In many occupations the tendency has been to provide for efficiency systems, and to reward capacity and ability in special services, at the same time developing a degree of continuity of service. In that part of public administration now under the merit system, the same tendencies have been at work, and have been effective in many instances. The strictly spoils service suffers in comparison with competing occupations, placing skill in the background, and subjecting its working force to the gravest dangers as far as tenure is concerned. The "worker" never knows when the accident of party or even factional defeat may cause the loss of his position regardless of his own efficiency. His place is at the mercy of such whims of fortune as beset no other occupation. If he has faithfully performed the duties of his office for a considerable period, perhaps covering the best years of his life, the situation becomes all the more desperate, and his reliance on the boss and the machine all the greater. That under such conditions slackness, favoritism, inefficiency, and even graft develop is not at all surprising.[34] In fact, the conditions are the very formula for producing such a result. The passive resistance of

[32] White and Smith, *op. cit.*, p. 15.
[33] L. D. White, *Introduction to the Study of Public Administration.*
[34] White and Smith, *op. cit.*; Key, *op. cit.*

many employees to these tendencies and on the other hand the fear of defeat on the part of the leaders holds in check forces which would otherwise make public service almost impossible.

THE BATTLE AGAINST PATRONAGE

It is not the purpose of this study to trace the development of the "civil service reform" movement, but it is essential to summarize some of its features.[35]

Fifty years ago the nation began to be alarmed by the large powers conferred by the possession of great and growing patronage, and also by the incompetence and inefficiency displayed in many branches of the service. A program of civil service reform was advocated and was adopted by Congress in 1883. The proposal was to substitute merit tests for admission to, continuance in, and dismissal from the public service, in place of the tests of party or factional fitness. Leaders of independent tendencies like George William Curtis, Carl Schurz, Dorman B. Eaton, and others threw themselves into the battle, and were followed by many party leaders of the type of Pendleton and Garfield of Ohio. In 1880 the national conventions of the great parties endorsed civil service reform in somewhat guarded terms, but nevertheless effectively as far as the general movement was concerned. The assassination of President Garfield at the hands of one of a horde of disappointed office seekers helped to create the public sentiment which finally bore down the opposition and obtained the passage of a national law. The transfer of administrative positions from the party organization to the classified service was fought with great

[35] The history of the theory of this movement is given in F. Morstein-Marx (ed.), *Elements of Public Administration* (New York, 1946); C. E. Merriam, *American Political Ideas* (New York, 1920), Chap. X. See also Carl R. Fish, *Civil Service and the Patronage* (Cambridge, 1920); *Annals of the American Academy of Political and Social Science*, CLXXXIX (1937); W. E. Mosher and J. D. Kingsley, *Public Personnel Administration* (New York, 1941), Chaps. I–III; L. D. White, *Introduction to the Study of Public Administration*, Chaps. XVII, XIX; John M. Pfiffner, *Public Administration* (New York, 1935), Chaps. VIII–XII; and the President's Committee on Administrative Management, *Report with Special Studies* (Washington, D. C., 1937), especially "Personnel Administration in the Federal Service," by F. Reeves and P. David. See also the files and annual report of the Civil Service Reform League; the reports of the federal, state and local civil service commissions; *Public Personnel Review*; the organ of the National Federation of Federal Employees, *The Federal Employee*, and *The Public Administration Review*.

energy by some of the party managers, such as Senators Conkling, Foraker, Benjamin Butler, and others, who seemed to identify the spoils system with the life of the party system itself. Some of the opposition came from a sincere fear of the establishment of an aristocratic bureaucracy from which the average man might be excluded. But most of it was the resistance of machine leaders who feared a reduction of their personal or factional power. Strong party leaders, however, recognized the grave danger to the party from the possession of large quantities of the spoils of office. In the early seventies it is probable that the public attitude was favorable to the filling of administrative posts on a partisan basis, but the national and local scandals of that decade, the vigorous campaign carried on by a small group of zealous reformers, and the tragic death of the president were factors that produced a change of sentiment and brought about a reversal of the earlier attitude. Far-reaching modifications were made in the principle of administrative service by the act of 1883, and by the subsequent modifications of that initial statute.

Under the Roosevelt and Truman administrations the number of civil employees, both in the classified service and in the various temporary services, increased from 586,000 in 1932 to 1,766,000 in 1947. In the latter year, 45 per cent were under the Classification Act, 25 per cent under the Wage Board, and 26 per cent under the Postal Pay Act, leaving 4 per cent under other acts. Various unclassified services such as TVA had merit systems of their own. In 1937 President Roosevelt recommended sweeping extensions of the merit system. A Federal Personnel Council has been organized with representatives from the departments, and one of the president's administrative assistants has been made a special liaison official with the civil service. Broad extensions of the merit system have been made by Executive orders based upon congressional action.[36]

In the states and cities the progress of the merit system has been even more striking. According to recent figures there are 20 states, 607 cities over 10,000 in population, and 184 counties operating under some form of the merit system. As compared with thirty years ago this is a very distinct improvement and indicates that the patronage dispensers are in retreat.

[36] *Fifty-fifth Annual Report of the U. S. Civil Service Commission*; Ramspeck-O'Mahoney Postmaster Act (52 United States Statutes at Large, 1076).

The enforcement of existing laws leaves in some cases much to be desired. Laws may be wholly disregarded, or they may be poorly enforced by political civil service commissions. The power to make temporary appointments is frequently abused to avoid the entrance examination requirement.[37] Nevertheless, large sections of the public service have actually been transferred from unlimited party control to modified party control, and others to minimum control; some sections seem to stand almost entirely upon a merit basis. Even in the absence of any statutory requirement, the standards of service are rising because of the competition of other employments and the public disposition to apply "standards" of service attainment to office.[38] Of these facts the wise machine leader is not ignorant, whatever he may say, and gradually turns his attention from job brokerage to the deeper study of popular psychology.

Distinctly political aspects of the civil service laws are seen in the prohibition of questions touching the political affiliations of applicants for positions, in the forbidding of solicitation of assessments or contributions by civil service employees on the part of their superiors in office. In the federal law there are additional provisions forbidding the participation of officials within the classified service in partisan activities. Similar sections are contained in the state law of Illinois, but they are not usually followed in the state and local laws. Partisan activities are construed to be active and public participation in the work of a party organization—serving on party committees, presiding at party meetings, canvassing of voters, or other evidence of partisan affiliation and activity.[39]

Whether these restrictions on the freedom of activity among public employees are either theoretically sound or practically enforceable is open to serious doubt.[40]

Employees remain citizens, and if their livelihood depends on political considerations, they are no more likely than other groups to

[37] V. O. Key, "Methods of Evasion of Civil Service Laws," *Southwestern Social Science Quarterly*, XV (March, 1935).

[38] An admirable survey of this movement is given in G. A. Weber, *Organized Efforts for the Improvement of Administration in the U. S.* (New York, 1919).

[39] See L. D. White, *Public Administration*. For a discussion of the Hatch Act of 1939, see Chap. XVII, below.

[40] The political and industrial organization of public employees is an interesting and significant topic. but it is not intended to cover that subject in this study.

remain silent; and if there are numbers of them they are unlikely to remain without some form of association in defense of their common interests.[41] The equal interest of other groups and the paramount interest of the community are in the long run the safest reliance against unfairness or greed on the part of any particular set of men. Responsibility for the maintenance of the common weal is likely to be more effective than repression and restriction.

Does the partisan standard in administrative service tend to strengthen or to decline? Two tendencies are evident. On the one hand the number of positions in public employment increases rapidly with the extension of the functions of government. This is true not only when measured by numbers of employees, but also in the percentage of public employment to total employment. In view of the movement toward the public regulation or ownership of various industries, we may believe that this tendency is likely to continue for some time, with what limit no one can foresee. It is conceivable that a large number of these additional places in the public service may be filled in accordance with the tests and standards of party capacity and service.

On the other hand there are distinct offsets to this tendency. These may be classed as follows:

(1) The specialization of services and the development of professional organizations and standards among such groups as engineers, accountants, physicians, teachers, scientists. These groups tend to break the force of the political organization in the public service.

(2) The development of the trade union in many branches of the public service, in some cases following the lines of skilled trades outside the public service and in some cases recruited solely from special types of public servants. These groups also tend to restrict the political power of appointment and removal by the many means available to such associations where they develop a degree of solidarity. Many of these unions have affiliated with the national local unions for the purpose of strengthening their position.

(3) The number of positions in private employment open to political organization tends to decline. This is due to the greater publicity in regard to transactions once carried on in secrecy, and partly to the effi-

---

[41] Civil Service Assembly, *Employee Relations in the Public Service* (Chicago, 1942).

ciency movement in the corporations themselves and to their desire to escape political entanglements of this particular type.

(4) Large branches of the administrative service have been placed under the merit system by statute, demanded and supported by an active public opinion. The increase in the number and variety of positions in the public employment has tended to hasten this movement. The city-manager form of government has also strengthened the merit system.

(5) Since the coming of woman suffrage in 1920, women voters have exerted a steady pressure on behalf of the merit system which offers them better chances for public employment than the old patronage system.

(6) The widespread use of the grant-in-aid by the federal government in order to effect minimum standards of administration of national measures among the states has extended the merit principle. This action has been especially true in the field of social legislation, which requires national uniformity of administration. With the passage of an amendment to the Social Security Act, effective in 1940, the states had to install some form of merit principle in the selection of the employees to carry out the provisions of the Act within the borders of those states, and to obtain a slice of the federal "melon." The installation of scientific principles of personnel management will be a unique arrangement in many a patronage paradise and there will be a tendency for the other employees to demand the benefits of a sound personnel program.

On the whole, it may be concluded that the power of patronage in the party is on the decline, and will not in the future occupy as significant a position as in the immediate past and at present. Unionizing and professionalizing of the service, together with the general movement toward efficiency in public service, will tend to diminish the significance of the party test of public personnel in the administrative service. The spoils system in filling positions was a political or party attitude produced by a special set of conditions which is being displaced by another set of conditions to which it is no longer applicable, and another attitude appears likely to prevail.

CHAPTER XI

LEGISLATIVE AND JUDICIAL SPOILS

" 'An attack upon the principles for which we stand is an attack upon the government itself.' "—Franklin Griffith, president of the Portland (Ore.) Electric Power Company.

"Many public officials were won to the same point of view. In New York, H. Edmund Machold, Speaker of the Assembly and Republican State Chairman, was so much the slave of this doctrine that his successor in the party leadership complained: 'The trouble is not that Mr. Machold believes in the private ownership of public utilities but that he apparently believes in the private ownership of the State government.' "—Cited by David Loth, *Public Plunder: A History of Graft in America* (Carrick and Evans, Inc., New York, 1938), p. 376.

THE TERM "SPOILS" MAY BE APPLIED NOT MERELY TO A PATRONAGE or favor system, but to the use of public office in an illegal manner for personal profit or advancement. Here we find the exploitation of the public by the official sometimes assuming the most subtle and sinister forms of class and personal discrimination, or of open challenge to the fundamentals of law and justice commonly recognized in civilized society. Out of these elements arises the force which President Cleveland once characterized in his trenchant phrase as "the cohesive power of public plunder."

It is proposed to discuss the development of the spoils system in connection with the lawmaking machinery of the government, with the judiciary, with the administrative machinery, and certain special phases of the spoils system as seen in purchases and contracts, disposition of public funds, the underworld, and taxation. The spoils system involves both bribery and extortion. Examples of both of these practices will be presented in the following pages.

LAWMAKING MACHINERY

A significant legislative practice developed under the spoils system is that of "logrolling" in regard to appropriations. In cities, counties, states, and in the nation, appropriations for public improvements in various localities have been to a considerable extent affected and even controlled by deals, compromises, and adjustments on a spoils basis rather than in the general interest of the community, or sometimes even in the interest of the locality where the mon̄ey was to be spent. There are, of course, questions of policy as to the distribution of public funds, and there are many compromises to be made in any large appropriation bill, but in many cases the practice has gone far beyond the ordinary limits of reasonable compromise and concession, and has become frankly a struggle for public funds to be wasted or misapplied on local enterprises.

Federal funds came to be thought of as a barrel of pork out of which each Congressman was expected to get his share for his constituency, just as the head of each slave cabin in slavery days was expected to get his portion of pork when the barrel was opened in the planter's back yard. Leading citizens and congressmen talked both jokingly and seriously of "pork," but rarely with a sense of guilt. As a famous representative from Texas put it: "Every time one of these Yankees gets a ham, I'm going to do my best to get a hog." [1] The "pork barrel" in Congress has been reduced, but it still exists in spite of repeated denunciations of the most specific nature on the part of responsible critics. [2]

The more innocent forms of these raids upon the treasury are merely wasteful forms of public expenditure ensuring certain local support, but in other instances there is collusion with contractors and others to whom the money is finally paid. The beneficiary becomes a political supporter and an ally whose loyal assistance may be reasonably counted upon. [3]

This system is by no means confined to the national field, but is found in the states and in the local governing agencies as well, and everywhere with equally damaging effect. The pressure of the communities themselves, the desire of the representative for local pres-

[1] Cited by G. Milburn, "Statesmanship of Mr. Garner," *Harper's Magazine*, CLXV (November, 1932), 669–682. See also C. A. Beard, *American Leviathan* (New York, 1930), pp. 178–179, for a good account of the "pork barrel" and "logrolling."

[2] For an account of pork barrel appropriations for the army and war veterans see Raymond Clapper, *Racketeering in Washington* (Boston, 1933), Chap. X, "Preparedness and Pork," and Chap. XI, "Pensions and Politics."

[3] Raymond Moley, *After Seven Years* (New York, 1939), pp. 367–368.

tige, the more sinister forms of outright collusion between the representative and the beneficiary of the appropriation, all unite to support and continue the dangerous practice. Furthermore, with the "pork barrel" as with patronage, the official who dislikes and disapproves these methods may be forced or feel himself forced by competition to adopt and apply them, although he might rejoice to see them outlawed. He may not feel himself strong enough to ignore "pork" and "jobs" in the struggle for survival, where the machine plays so large a part in the determination of political destinies, and where these "perquisites" play so considerable a part in the maintenance of the machine. The "local" police station or school house, the local bridge or road, the local "institution," the local post office or canal are visible and tangible monuments remembered by the community and the organization alike, while cost and need may be minor considerations, relatively insignificant.

Logrolling may readily be extended to a series of trades and deals involving local or general legislation. In state legislatures this is a common practice, in view of the large amount of local and private bill making, while in Congress the making of the average rivers and harbors bill becomes a logrolling process.[4]

A part of this process is inevitable in the formation of such a bill, but the inevitability of some of it becomes an easy excuse for much more that is indefensible on any legitimate grounds of give and take or compromise and adjustment. The struggle of the local economic interests becomes the golden opportunity for those who are disposed to make politics the business of spoilsmen rather than of statesmen, as well as of such economic spoilsmen as are willing to join hands with them.

Under President Roosevelt and Secretary Hull the logrolling that usually accompanies tariff legislation was avoided by the reciprocal trade legislation which conferred powers upon the President to negotiate trade agreements.[5]

But the spoils system reaches beyond "pork" and partisanship in

[4] For a contrary view, see Propeller Club of the United States, *River and Harbor Improvements: How They Are Initiated, Authorized and Completed* (Cleveland, Ohio, 1938).

[5] Buel W. Patch, "Congress and Tariff Policy," *Editorial Research Reports,* May 19, 1948.

legislation, and in a larger sense becomes piracy and exploitation. Some of these aspects of the spoils system will now be discussed.

The spoils system obtains great strength through the manipulation of the various lawmaking bodies, local, state, and national. The theory of the party system is that control of legislative bodies is necessary to carry out the policies of the party, but control over the lawmakers may become a source of prestige or personal profit to the party group or individual in command. Under this system the power to make or unmake or refuse to make or to modify the law has a market value and may be bought and sold for the coin of the realm.[6]

The legislative power may be used either to grant privilege or immunity; to give away public property, or not to protect public property; or to withhold the control the public should properly have over private interests. The legislative power may be employed to grant a perpetual franchise to a corporation, or later to prevent adequate public regulation of a corporation which has secured such a franchise and which resists regulation. Under adroit direction, the whole network of parliamentary practice and procedure may be used, with infinite variety of method ranging from technical insistence upon legal forms to wide-open disregard of plain constitutional provisions. In the earlier days the grant of special privilege was most common; in later times immunity from regulation is more frequently demanded.[7] Land grants, loans of credit, franchises were the staples of the early lawmakers, but as time goes on the chief stock in trade is the power to prevent threatened social or industrial legislation.

The length of term of a franchise, the rate charged, the quality of service, the exclusion or inclusion of competition have all been given

[6] See P. S. Reinsch, *American Legislatures and Legislative Methods* (New York, 1913), Chap. VIII; Harvey Walker, *Law Making in the United States* (New York, 1934), Chap. XII; Matthew Josephson, *The Robber Barons* (New York, 1934), and *The Politicos* (New York, 1938); E. B. Logan, "Lobbying," *Annals of the American Academy of Political and Social Science*, CXLIV, Supplement (1929); Lynn Haines, *Your Congress* (Washington, D. C., 1915); and K. G. Crawford, *The Pressure Boys* (New York, 1939). The last-mentioned book gives an account of the efforts of the soap lobbyists to exempt soap from the Tugwell Act.

[7] For illustrations of early legislative tactics, see J. B. McMaster, *With the Fathers* (New York, 1917); and H. H. Klein, *Politics, Government and the Public Utilities in New York City* (New York, 1933).

careful consideration, and the commercial possibilities of each judiciously appraised and exploited. No accurate estimate can be made of the amounts paid lawmakers in return for these privileges, but the sum total has unquestionably been large. The benefits conferred were huge and the returns to the political promoters must have been correspondingly great. They have been large enough to serve as a basis for the city or state machine in many instances.

Taking the acts of Congress since the Civil War, it is clear that of the same nature was certain federal legislation respecting timber and mineral lands, Indian claims, water power rights, and a great group of other laws involving control over the property and rights of the United States Government. These acts need not involve direct corruption of representatives, but they make possible the distribution of enormous privileges. They help to build up and perpetuate the system of spoils.

The agitation regarding the passage of the Public Utility Act of 1935, the so-called "utilities death sentence," resulted in another senatorial investigation of lobbying. Stockholders and creditors of the utility companies were persuaded to flood the congressmen with appeals. On the other hand, the revelations of the investigating committee regarding the methods of private companies were used by the administration leaders to whip the congressmen into line.[8]

The legislative side of the spoils system is chiefly devoted to "preventive" legislation under present conditions. Within the last few years a flood of light has been thrown on our economic and social conditions, awakening both the public conscience and the public intelligence. The result has been a strong demand for new legislation to safeguard the public interest more completely and to protect the honest and scrupulous against the ruinous competition of the dishonest and unscrupulous. Public sentiment has been insistent in its demands for stricter regulation of public utility and other corporations, for laws to protect children and women, to fix standards of safety and sanitation in industry. Many bills have been presented to the various legislative bodies, some of them the work of the wise, others the handiwork of the unwise; some the work of the honest,

[8] *Hearings before a Special Committee to Investigate Lobbying Activities,* United States Senate, 74th Congress, 1st Session, pursuant to Senate Resolution 165 (July 12, 1935, to March 6, 1936).

and some of the dishonest. Some emanate from unbalanced minds and some from undeveloped conscience. Many are products of honest and mature deliberation based upon years of careful study and research.

Out of this confusion the spoilsmen have evolved an ingenious double-action system of revenue raising. On the one hand, they may rely upon delaying, defeating, and weakening legitimate measures under honest auspices—holding up the robbed—or, on the other hand, upon defeating reasonable or unreasonable measures introduced by spoilsmen for the sole purpose of spoliation—holding up the robber.

In fact, there are really three stages in the evolution of the modern system:

(1) Grant of privileges

(2) Protection against public desire to regulate privilege

(3) Introduction of "regulation" of the privileged to obtain what is commonly called "blackmail"

It is as if you were to charge a man for robbing a bank; then charge him for protection from the law; then threaten him with the law, so that he might feel the need of continuing protection. For example, a gas company pays to procure a perpetual franchise; then it pays to defeat an honest law permitting public regulation; then it pays and keeps on paying to kill the dishonest "regulator" introduced for the sole purpose of extorting revenue from a not wholly unwilling victim.[9]

The ramifications of this system are wide and deep. It covers the country and strikes its roots far down into the soil of industry. In city after city and state after state it has been laid bare. The Lorimer investigation in Illinois, the Allds inquiry in New York,[10] the Burns exposure in Ohio,[11] and the Pendergast investigation in Mis-

[9] Realistic and interesting are the recitals of Clifford S. Raymond in *American Magazine*, LXXIII, 469, 523, 651, and *McClure's Magazine*, XLIII, 19, 188. See also A State Senator, "Crooks in the Legislature," *American Mercury*, XLI (July, 1937), 269–275.

[10] *New York Senate Documents*, No. 28, 113th Session, Vol. I (1910).

[11] See *Outlook*, XCVIII, 45; *Cosmopolitan*, LI, 599. Compare "Great Cases of Detective Burns," *McClure's*, XXXVI, 386.

souri [12] are four striking illustrations in as many years in four leading states of the Union; while New York, Chicago, St. Louis, San Francisco, Pittsburgh, and Boston at the same time have exhibited the urban side of the same development.

The testimony before the New York Insurance Committee in 1905–1906 revealed the existence of a well-organized plan for the "protection" of the three large companies—the New York Life, the Mutual, and the Equitable.[13]

The corruption accompanying the election of William Lorimer led to a prolonged investigation by the Illinois Senate, by the Criminal Court of Cook County, Illinois, and by the United States Senate. In the course of these inquiries it was not only shown by sworn confessions and by corroborating testimony that money had been paid to members of the legislature for their votes for senator, but that there had been in existence for many years what was called a "jackpot."

The "jackpot," the testimony. showed, was a common fund, paid for the purpose of securing or of defeating legislation.[14] This sum was collected from various interests affected by legislation and was distributed at the close of the session to those entitled to participate. Most of those who shared in the "jackpot" did not know the total amount, by whom it was paid in detail, or the particular votes for which they were being paid. They only knew that if they "went along" with the others of their "crowd" and were "reasonable"— in other words, voted as they were told—at the end of the session they would be given a "share" of what had been collected by their leaders. The inquiry did not fully disclose who paid the money and for what specific purposes or who collected the money and to whom it was distributed. Special men were posted in different parts of the legislative hall to inform those who were "regular" how to vote on given measures. When the "high sign" was given, the regulars fell in line.

An estimate was made at the time of the sources and amounts of

[12] W. Reddig, *Tom's Town: Kansas City and the Pendergast Legend* (Philadelphia and New York, 1947)

[13] Legislative Insurance Investigation Committee, X, 23. An early narrative is given in H. C. Tanner, legislative stenographer, *The Lobby and Public Men* (New York, 1888).

[14] See testimony before U. S. Senate in the Lorimer Inquiries (1911–1912).

this fund.[15] We reproduce it (in Table 3) not because it is accurate, but because it represents what sometimes happens where the legislature is controlled by spoilsmen. In Missouri, the insurance investigation showed that the big money was paid directly to the boss.[16]

TABLE 3

ESTIMATED SOURCES OF ILLINOIS LEGISLATIVE CORRUPTION FUND

Senatorial contest	$250,000
Manufacturing bill	50,000
Bills inimical to employers and corporations	50,000
Antitrust bill	50,000
Cigarette bills	5,000
Mining bills	5,000
Anti-local-option bills	75,000
Street paving bills	40,000
Loan shark bills	3,000
Fish bills	3,000
Patent medicine bills	4,000
Osteopathy	2,500
Schoolbooks	20,000
Sleeping car regulator	25,000
Automobile regulator	5,000
Hotel regulator	4,000
Capital stock regulator	50,000
Railroad regulator	50,000
Insurance regulator	50,000
Banking regulator	25,000
Telegraph regulator	25,000
Gas, electric light and power regulator	40,000
Express company regulator	25,000
Stockyards regulator	25,000
Cold storage regulator	25,000
Employment office regulator	4,000
TOTAL	$910,500

Under conditions where laws are as loose and unscientific as they are in many cases, blackmailing legislation becomes easy. Our system of taxation, our laws governing corporations, our backwardness

[15] *Democratic Bulletin* of Chicago.
[16] Reddig, *op. cit.*

in social and industrial legislation present great opportunities to the rogues who ferret out the weak spots and prepare to make the attack there. It is not difficult to draw measures providing higher taxation, stricter regulation of public utility or other corporations, bills affecting sanitation and safety, and introduce them for no other purpose than to serve as a basis for a bargain. Since public sentiment probably favors the general purpose of the bill, its passage with gang support is no difficult matter. So the measure is introduced, goes to a favorable committee, is reported out; is passed by one house, introduced in the other, favorably considered in committee, passes the second house, goes to a conference committee, approaches a final vote, and the possibility of its enactment comes more closely home to the interest affected. The only solid defense is to appeal to public sentiment and prepare for reasonable adjustments of conditions, but it is often believed cheaper to pay the grafters' price and, securing temporary "protection," postpone the evil day of final reckoning.

These arrangements, deals and bargains are made through men prominent in the party organizations. The boss or bosses, depending upon the degree of centralization in the system, deliver their quota of voters and are paid in proportion to their influence and ability. The money and powers obtained by these machine voters become highly important factors in building up the party organization and in tightening the hold of the spoils system upon the politics of the city or state. The control of the lawmaking power, involving millions of persons and billions of dollars, is probably the strongest single element in the long category of perquisites belonging to the allied spoilsmen. It includes many forms of party assets, such as cash payments to lawmakers and bosses; thinly veiled forms of "honest graft," such as attorney's fees and business credits; campaign contributions which may not be expended; the influence of certain respectable citizens who mysteriously side with the machine when needed.

The line between extortion and bribery is a hard one to draw and it is likely that both are used in a situation involving huge business interests. In describing the downfall of the utility magnates in the thirties, Donald Richberg wrote: "Frequently they mask their effort by publicly asserting the need for 'protection' from political interference. Indeed, this is such a prevalent disguise for political aggression that doubtless most of the Insulls most of the time feel assured that they carry a sword only for defense and not for attacks when they lead a wealth-gathering foray." [17]

Profits in this field of action not only cause party interest to eclipse the interest of the state, but also cause personal and factional interests to obscure the party's interest. The spoils system, originally depended upon as a means of strengthening the party, leads to the destruction of the party itself, and indeed to the paralysis of the whole party system. Spoilsmen of both parties unite to maintain the system upon a bipartisan basis.

Lines are not drawn under these conditions between parties, but follow the spoils cleavage. In cities and states, and to a less degree in Congress, where the party spirit is more intense, party groups are dissolved and in their place appear the "special interests," the spoilsman's group or gang, the "gray wolves," the "blackhorse cavalry," the "owners' association." The "gang," by whatever name usually known, is made up impartially of representative spoilsmen of the theoretically hostile parties. Spoils Republicans join spoils Democrats and become true "spoilsmen" who control legislation. This becomes a living reality, while the party groups become mere fiction. The spoilsmen belong to an oligarchy of organized selfish interest, either political or economic, at war with the general interest of the community. Happily they are not everywhere or always in command.

In this way, the advantages of the party system are largely lost. Initiative in formulation of policies, and skill in administration, on the one hand, and counter initiative and free criticism on the other, may and do educate public opinion, produce a lively sense of responsibility on the part of those in authority, and stimulate the entire community. It is in these elements that the *raison d'être* of the party is found. With their disappearance, the value and effectiveness of the party declines. Furthermore, under such conditions the party oligarchies obstruct free formulation and vigorous expression of public opinion upon questions of public policy. They dam or divert the stream, clog or narrow the channel of public sentiment although they cannot permanently obstruct it.

[17] "Gold-Plated Anarchy: An Interpretation of the Fall of the Giants," *Nation*, CXXXVI (April 5, 1933), p. 368.

It is not to be concluded, however, that the public will is steadily defied, without compromise. When an overwhelming and sustained public interest demands particular pieces of legislation, spoilsmen will yield the particular points but retain the general life of the system. Conspicuous illustrations of this are the passage of the Australian ballot laws, the direct primary and corrupt practices acts, directed against the spoilsmen themselves. But under the spoils system these concessions do not destroy the effectiveness of the spoilsmen's program. They bend, but are not easily broken. They retreat "for strategic reasons," and regain at night the ground they yield during the day. In 1946, Congress passed the Federal Regulation of Lobbying Act which required individuals, corporations, and others seeking to influence legislation to register and file periodic reports of their receipts and expenditures. This law did not reach some part-time lobbyists whose main occupation did not necessarily imply appearances before Congress.

JUDICIAL MACHINERY

The last citadel to be assailed by the spoils system is the judiciary. Our courts have been unquestionably far less subject to open corruption than our lawmakers and our executives. Many decisions have been reactionary and some corrupt. Many others have been determined by the steady pressure of spoils influences and by prejudice or inertia. The corrupt judge is the exception, the political judge is not uncommon, while the ultraconservative or reactionary judge is not infrequently encountered.[18] Aristocratic and dogmatic the judge may sometimes be, but on the whole he is neither corruptible nor easily amenable to the rough discipline of the party boss. Too proud to take money or orders, he must be treated upon a wholly different basis. In many instances, our judges have been men of great ability

---

[18] James Bryce, *The American Commonwealth* (New York, Macmillan Co., 1921), I, 513. M. A. Ostrogorski says: "If the integrity of the judges is, in the main, fairly satisfactory, their independence is not intact in cases where the interests of the party are involved. In the administration of criminal justice, independence scarcely exists at all among the police magistrates in the large cities, and especially, the public prosecutors. . . . In matters pertaining to industrial relations and conflicts with labor, the independence of the judiciary has likewise been challenged for some time." *Democracy and the Party System* (New York, Macmillan Co., 1910), p. 376.

and of inflexible integrity. The "just judge" has been a figure of which many a community has been proud.

Here again we must distinguish between spoils as official patronage, as political piracy and as the perquisite of some special group using the party machinery for special class or group purposes. The courts have some value to the political machine, because of the official patronage they control and confer. The officers of the court are few in number but, such as they are, are generally appointed on a spoils basis, that is to say, with a view to strengthening the organization. The judge's bailiff is often expected to control his precinct, while more important officials such as the master in chancery "deliver" correspondingly larger political areas. In a considerable number of cases judges are given a very intimate relation to the pay roll, as in Cook County, Illinois, where the judges of the Circuit Court fix the number of employees (although not the salaries) in all the various county fee offices, including the important positions under the sheriff, recorder, and treasurer.

An illustration of the machine system was seen in 1927 in Chicago when the bosses refused to renominate certain judges who had offended them. In spite of the great effort made by the Bar Association, three valuable judges of the Circuit Court were thrown off the bench by local bosses.

Far more important than offices for patronage purposes are certain financial perquisites connected with the courts. The most valuable of these are the receivership, guardianship, and refereeship, which, in many cases, are determined by the judge, where not agreed upon by the parties in litigation. The Interborough receivership in New York City is an illustration of the vast power involved. The depression which started in 1929 brought an unprecedented number of receiverships, and in Chicago it was discovered by a committee of the Bar Association that many judges awarded these receiverships according to the dictates of their political sponsors. In eighteen months' time one receiver selected on a patronage basis received aggregate fees of $159,000.[19] Referees and guardians handling mil-

[19] E. M. Martin, *The Role of the Bar in Electing the Bench in Chicago* (Chicago, 1936), pp. 289–294. On court graft in New York State, see Luther Gulick, "The Shame of the Cities—1946," *National Municipal Review*, XXXVI (January, 1947), 20–21.

lions of dollars and receiving very profitable fees are not infrequently appointed for political reasons, on the recommendation of political powers or with a view of meeting their wishes. Bankruptcy cases are often lucrative, and appointments of referees are sometimes found on analysis to be on the machine's "list." Appraisers often fall in the same category. It is by no means to be concluded that all such appointments are made on a patronage basis, but so considerable a number are selected in this manner as to make them a political asset of material value.

A considerable number of judges do active political work for the machine, in some cases openly and in others quietly. Sometimes they are very active in matters of patronage, using their influence in every direction to secure additional "jobs" or to retain those already in possession. It was estimated that before 1933 about one-half of the sum appropriated for the New York magistrates' courts went either to political work or to waste and inefficiency.[20] On the other hand, there are judges who stand wholly aloof from practical politics, depending on their character, ability, and the support of the bar and the community for their continuance in office. In some instances, however, this dignified aloofness is purchased at the expense of occasional but important conferences with some powerful political boss or some adroit agent of special interests. Where "aloofness" is of this nature, it is, of course, far more dangerous to the public than the most active participation in the business of job brokerage.

The open prostitution of judges to spoils purposes is far less common than in the case of lawmakers and administrators. Instances are by no means lacking, however, and the extent of corruption cannot safely be measured by the number of impeachments. The most conspicuous cases of open abuse are found in the administration of criminal justice in the lower courts of our larger cities. The police magistrates of New York and the old justices of the peace in Chicago were notorious centers of political corruption. The alliance between the Tammany boss and the police judge was scarcely concealed from the public, as indicated by the presence of political magnates in the courtroom and the almost audible issuing of orders. During the Seabury investigation a number of New York magistrates

[20] Raymond Moley, *Tribunes of the People* (New Haven, 1932), p. 263.

testified that the district leaders asked favors of them.[21] In Chicago under the old system the term "justice shop" was commonly applied to the places where justice was bought and sold. Under such conditions, the underworld was guaranteed political protection even against the police, and masses of misdemeanors and more serious crimes were glossed over or inadequately dealt with. The police court was and to some extent still is the center of the metropolitan machine. "Influence" may take the place of orders or cash, but the net result of the process is the production of political power for those who pull the strings.[22]

Discussing the administration of justice in metropolitan districts, the American Judicature Society says: "Judges are not usually really elected but are designated by the leaders of the party political machine dominant in the district." It is further declared that "these leaders have the strongest motives for rewarding purely political service to an organization."

Open abuses of the judicial prerogative such as occurred in the desperate effort to free Tweed from the coils that were closing around him are no longer tolerated. Judges Barnard and Albert Cardozo issued writs and abused the powers of the court in a flagrant manner which could not happen today.[23] The record of the Sanitary District trials in Chicago following the 1928 graft disclosures shows the more subtle ways the judges may use to mitigate the rigors of the criminal law when important political personages are involved. There were delays in bringing the case to trial, delays in

[21] Samuel Seabury, *Final Report: In the Matter of the Investigation of the Magistrates' Courts in the First Judicial Department and the Magistrates Thereof, and of the Attorneys-at-Law Practicing in Said Courts* (New York, 1932).

[22] See Reddig, *op. cit.*; R. H. Smith, *Justice and the Poor* (New York, 1919); Cleveland Foundation, *Survey of Criminal Justice in Cleveland, Ohio*, 1921; report of the Illinois Association for Criminal Justice, *Illinois Crime Survey*, 1929. Federal Judge Martin Manton of New York was convicted and fined and imprisoned for criminal conspiracy. He had accepted money from the participants in a case of which he was the judge. The bar association disbarred him and he resigned therefore his office as a judge in the circuit court of appeals of New York. His conviction was upheld by the Supreme Court in 1940. See *New York Times*, February 27, 1940.

[23] See Gustavus Myers, *History of Tammany Hall* (New York, 1917), for account of this incident. Compare the anonymous works *Haunch, Paunch and Jowl* (New York, 1923), an account of a Tammany-controlled judge from the East Side of New York.

hearing it, repeated extensions of time in the preparation of the appeal, quashed indictments, the setting aside of convictions, and other devices.[24] In political controversies the judges have been from time to time grossly unfair and partisan in their rulings, evidently following the wishes or dictates of their political allies rather than the lines of justice. Fortunately, however, this has been the exception rather than the rule.

From another point of view, the courts may also be utilized by class or group interests for their special purposes, through the agency of the party machine, and may articulate with the spoils system when such interests are being so served. Interpretations of social and industrial legislation, attitudes toward the judicial use of the injunction and in personal injury cases have been very important in the general scheme of things. And the judicial position in these respects has been by no means neglected.[25]

Under a well-organized spoils system, the selection of judges, especially in the lower courts, is often made by the machine and the boss, and this power becomes an asset of great importance. A report submitted to the American Bar Association in October, 1932, by its section on criminal law and criminology stated that "Gangsters are often able to elect to judicial office their own attorneys and when charged with a crime, waive a jury trial and place their case before their own judge who acts as judge and jury." Judge Seabury's investigation in New York in 1930–1931 disclosed the bribery of police and police officers and the complicity of judges in shaking down criminal defendants, mostly women, on trumped-up charges. One magistrate was removed from office for acceptance of a loan of $19,600 from Arnold Rothstein, the notorious gangster. During his five years' service on the bench this judge had deposited more than $100,000 in his bank account in addition to his salary. Many of the magistrates admitted as a matter of course that their jobs were awarded them for considerations of service and that they gave special service to those who had had them appointed.[26]

The boss may render invaluable service to his allies by seeing to

[24] Martin, *op. cit.*, pp. 300–310.
[25] C. E. Merriam, *American Political Ideas* (New York, 1920), Chaps. VI, VII; Thurman Arnold, *The Folklore of American Capitalism* (New Haven, 1937).
[26] Mitchell Dawson, "Judging the Judges," *Harper's Magazine*, CLXIX (September, 1934), 437–448.

it that friendly judges are selected and retained. This action may signify merely a general point of view, for, as Lord Bryce has sagely said in this connection, "Virtue is compatible with a certain bias of the mind"; or the action may go farther in extreme cases and involve susceptibility to somewhat direct influences on the part of the machine. Happily, cases of the latter kind are rare, owing to a variety of forces, the strongest of which is the professional support of the lawyers themselves; but they are not wholly unknown.[27]

The effect of the slow and steady pressure of spoils politics upon the judiciary may easily be and generally is underestimated. In a spoils environment, the spoils type tends to develop and flourish. Brave men break through this mesh of circumstances, but the party monopoly over judicial selections makes this difficult, and the general tendency is depressing.

In a highly developed system, many judges are selected by either political or industrial magnates, and are expected to render fitting service in return. Recently an official refused to accede to the demands of an industrio-political magnate for certain patronage, to the great indignation of the latter, who exclaimed in wrath: "I will bring action to have the very law under which you operate set aside as unconstitutional; and I will bring the case before my own judge, too." And so he did. And so did the judge.

The usefulness of the courts to the spoils system may, then, be summed up under the following heads:

(1) Personal political service, labor and contributions
(2) Judicial patronage
(3) Police administration
(4) Political decisions, *e.g.*, elections, graft cases, civil service cases

[27] There has never been a careful sifting of the data available upon this question, and generally speaking the topic has been quietly ignored or uncritically examined. See C. P. Connolley, "Big Business and the Bench," *Everybody's Magazine*, XXVI, 147, 291, 439, 659, 827; XXVII, 116; and *Report of the United States Commission on Industrial Relations*, I, 38, especially pp. 44, 79. Gustavus Myers, *History of the Supreme Court of the United States* (Chicago, 1912), gives a socialistic interpretation of the federal judiciary. See also A. H. Hart, "Corrupt Judges and Political Bosses," *Current History*, XXXIII (November, 1930), 180–182; Anonymous, *Ex-Judge* (New York, 1930); and J. T. Salter, "A Philadelphia Magistrate Tells His Story," *National Municipal Review*, XXII (1933), 514–520, for the relationship between the judge and the politician.

(5) Decisions in cases involving industrial and social questions

(6) Legal graft in bankruptcies, foreclosures, and estates.

These are pieces of artillery of long-range carrying missiles with high powers of penetration and explosion. No practical organizer of faction or party on a spoils basis is ignorant of their importance in political war. No effort will be spared by him to obtain them, if he can.

CHAPTER XII

ADMINISTRATIVE SPOILS

"I don't like to admit it but an open town is far better for the Negroes than a closed town. An underworld boss with a little public spirit can do a lot of good too. The money that now goes to the police under Dan Jackson often went for charities and good movements. Of course these bosses make a lot of money, but while Jackson was in control he donated thousands to charities, the N.A.A.C.P., working girls' homes and the like. While Jackson was in power the colored people always had a friend to go to. If some old fellow got in jail and his son came down Jackson would sign his bond and send a note to the judge."—Negro journalist quoted by H. F. Gosnell, *Negro Politicians* (Chicago, University of Chicago Press, 1935), p. 132.

TREMENDOUS AS IS THE POWER OF SPOILSMEN THROUGH CONTROL over the lawmaking machinery and important as is the power to interpret the law, the power to enforce and apply the law through control over the machinery of administration is of the very greatest consequence in spoils politics. The riches or influence acquired in legislative affairs come only occasionally, but administration offers daily and even hourly opportunities to build up, little by little, the power of the group in control. Lawmakers adjourn, but administrators go on forever. No state has been able to dispense with the services of policemen, firemen, tax collectors, and other essential employees.

The laws passed by the legislators are stated in abstract terms regarding which there may not be universal agreement since legislative decisions are made by majority votes. Once a law is passed, however, every citizen is expected to conform to it in so far as it affects him concretely in his everyday behavior. The party spoilsmen are on the job ready to exploit the situations which arise from the discrepancies between concrete acts and abstract laws. This proposition is perhaps most clearly illustrated by the prohibition era during which the Eighteenth Amendment was the law of the land but bootlegging the practice. As Thurman Arnold has put it: "A fixed belief in the ideal of law enforcement hinders and delays the activities of public bodies, more than any other popular illusion.

. . . Our only recourse is the creation of a *sub rosa* organization which we call a political machine." [1]

Notwithstanding our traditional American aversion to strong administration, there are two reasons why administration is politically more formidable in our country than elsewhere. First, our laws are very detailed in their provisions, and, second, they are often very carelessly drawn. Our lawmakers do not usually content themselves with general propositions and directions. They often attempt to say in advance exactly how a thing shall be done, and the instructions are often loosely phrased and very often imperfectly considered. Hastily drawn enactments, full of minutely specified provisions, are likely to be difficult of practical application; in fact, to prove unworkable unless freely "interpreted" by the administration. To the spoils administrator such statutes are as manna falling from Heaven. He can interpret and apply them *politically*, defending himself on the safe ground that they are practically unworkable. The ill-drawn building code and the antiquated or ill-considered tax law have no terrors for the spoilsman. On the contrary, he welcomes them, for under these conditions favoritism takes the place of law. He takes down the spoils yardstick and metes out justice, where the legislative intent is doubtful.

Next, our governmental traditions have been against a strong administration. In early times this was caused by the fear of a hereditary king, the apprehension that a powerful administration would tend to become permanent, and perhaps gradually pass over into a monarchy. In later times the idea of rotation in office, a doctrine originally applied only to elective officials, was extended to administrators as well. Only in our own day have we come to recognize that the administration is the arm of the people, and that a weak arm will not be able to protect the public against the strong and well-trained arm of special interests. It is only recently that progress has been made in placing the administration on a basis where expert ability, permanence of tenure, and proper compensation are recognized as essential to satisfactory service.

Administrative services are subject to spoils considerations. Where "the system" is in full operation, the officials tend to use their office as a means of doing favors for friends, and in many cases as a

[1] *Symbols of Government* (New Haven, Yale University Press, 1935), p. 168.

means of indirect graft or outright fraud. The official, being a part of a huge machine built up on this principle, nominated and elected or appointed, as the case may be, by this machine, can scarcely escape the demand that he regard his party allies as entitled to special consideration in the operation of the service. In any event, he will be reminded of it by some of his allies, he will be crowded and pressed by them into courses of conduct contrary to his own judgment and will, and in the last resort he will be attacked, either as selfish and ungrateful or as useless to the band of which he is a member. With weak laws and fluctuating officials, the tendency becomes all the stronger and the power of resistance weaker. It is true that many deserving officials defy and disregard these influences, and that others bend only under strong pressure; but the political use of the administration persists.

In a city administration, for example, there are many points at which the public service may be used in the interest of the spoils system. The police, the building and health departments, the enforcement of franchise and ordinance provisions are all fertile fields to be cultivated by the diligent worker. A corrupt administration uses literally almost every law and ordinance as a means of building up either its power or its pocketbook.[2]

In a building code there are elaborate ordinances dealing with minute details of construction, methods of protection against fire, structural safety, and protection of inmates against unsanitary conditions. In a rapidly growing city with modes and conditions of construction also rapidly changing, it is difficult, even with the best intentions, for a building code to keep pace with the progress of events in the building trade. Hundreds of cases arise every year in large cities in which the discretion of the building department may be exercised. The question of interpreting the ordinance will arise and this may often be determined one way or the other, according to the political influence possessed by the person applying for a permit. With the backing of the local boss or alderman or some magnate of political influence, it is possible to secure not only a reasonable in-

[2] W. M. Reddig, *Tom's Town: Kansas City and the Pendergast Legend* (Philadelphia and New York, 1947); Luther Gulick, "The Shame of the Cities—1946," *National Municipal Review*, XXXVI (January, 1947), 18–25; Lincoln Steffens, *Autobiography* (New York, 1931).

terpretation of an ordinance, but even an unreasonable interpretation amounting to a gross violation of the spirit and purpose of the law. Without such influence, even an eminently reasonable interpretation of the rule may be refused, perhaps on the lofty ground of rigid law enforcement. Sometimes a system of downright corruption develops in a building department in which inspectors and others higher up levy a regular tribute upon individuals and upon contractors. The payment of money to employees of building departments for ignoring violation of building ordinances is too common in large cities. These conditions have been exposed over and over again in the larger cities by public prosecutors and special investigations.

Again the building operations of a city are so large and the force of inspectors relatively so small that it is impossible to cover properly the work which is under way. This leads to a general laxity and carelessness of inspection which makes it practically useless for many purposes; and, what is still more serious, in many cases to the practical persecution of individuals who are selected for inspection. One who is active against a political machine may easily find himself a mark for their hostility. In his case, all the minute details of the building and zoning ordinances are scrutinized with the utmost care and are faithfully applied with strict and rigid interpretation.[3] If his building is not properly equipped with fire escapes, he may be compelled to install them, although his next-door neighbor passes unnoticed without them. If his doors swing inward when they should swing out, he may be compelled to alter them although the doors of a hundred of his neighbors swing inward. In short, the instrument designed to protect the people may be invoked in his particular case and disregarded in a thousand other cases. The whole purpose of such activity is, of course, to enforce conformity with the dominant spoils organization. The more drastic the ordinance the greater the opportunity for persecution. In fact, it is sometimes said with a show of truth that spoilsmen favor the enactment of unreasonably rigid laws in order that they may have a wider range of discretion.

[3] Norman Thomas and Paul Blanshard, in *What's the Matter with New York* (New York, 1932), p. 48, assert that "In a city like New York the right to change the zoning laws may make or break a man's fortune."

In country and other local governments, the avenues of administrative influence are many. They include, in many instances, the valuation of property, the care of the poor, the prosecution of crime, the control of offices such as those of the sheriff, recorder, and coroner. The use of the power to value property will be considered in a later section.

The state's attorney's office is an important cog in the spoils machine. The prosecuting official is, theoretically, not only the protector of the community against crime in general, but also the special watchdog of the public against political corruption and crime. But if the prosecuting attorney is politically controlled, graft and corruption enjoy practical immunity from prosecution. Conviction for political offenses is extremely difficult to secure, even where the intentions of the people's representative are unimpeachable. The least trace of unwillingness to prosecute vigorously and effectively in such cases is sufficient to ensure the freedom of those engaged in political plunder. Further, the prosecuting attorney has a wide range of discretion as to indictments, vigor of prosecutions, nature of penalty, and other incidents of criminal trials. In many instances, this discretion is used on the basis of political influence. Crime or particular kinds of crime may be ignored. The prosecuting attorney may, in these relations, either levy money tribute or merely use his office in order to strengthen the political organization of which he is a part. It was estimated that in New York and Chicago over one-half of the felony cases were eliminated by the prosecutor in the preliminary hearings.[4]

In the same way the office of sheriff, the office of recorder, and sundry other county offices are often shot through and through with political favoritism.[5] There is scarcely a procedure or process which may not be bent in the wrong direction under a highly organized spoils system, whether it be the treatment of prisoners, the service of processes, the handling of official documents, or other points where the public may come in contact with officialdom. In numerous county jails the sheriff's ill-treatment of his charges is the result of the fee system of compensation. Under this plan the jailer is per-

[4] Raymond Moley, *Politics and Criminal Prosecution* (New York, 1929).
. [5] See O. T. Schultz and E. M. Morgan, *The Coroner and Medical Examiner* (Washington, D. C., 1928).

mitted to keep any money he can save out of that allotted for the feeding of the prisoners. As a result, few, if any, can resist filling their pockets by keeping the inmates on a starvation diet.[6] Judge Seabury, during his investigation of graft in New York City, discovered that the sheriff had a "wonderful tin box" from which he took $360,000 in a period of six years. The Register of Kings County, James A. McQuade, was found to have a bank account of over half a million dollars which he said he borrowed to help the other thirty-four McQuades, whose troubles he related in the minutest detail— but when asked where he obtained the money, he could not remember.[7]

One of the most glaring cases of spoils in county government is the famous Sweitzer case of Cook County (Chicago), which has been described by one of the authors in the following words:

"Early in May, 1935, there were rumors that this audit showed a shortage in the funds of around $400,000. The audit was finally made public; and on the basis of it the county board removed Sweitzer from the office of county treasurer, to which he had recently been elected. A most extraordinary series of events followed. By his own admission, it was obvious that he regarded the tax-redemption fund which had been in his charge, as county clerk, as 'nobody's money,' to be handled as he pleased—in his vest pocket or even in the stocks of questionable companies which were about to make fortunes manufacturing coal bricks, monkey wrenches, or what not, but never did. It was also obvious that this fund was a kind of 'self-service' money reservoir for politicians, who were free to dip into it at any time with no thought of paying any of it back."[8]

The state administrative service offers a wide field for political exploitation.[9] The maintenance of state institutions constitutes one side of this and the enforcement of state law the other. It might

[6] J. F. Fishman and V. T. Perlman, "Let's Abolish the County Jail," *Survey Graphic*, XXVIII (January, 1939), 26–27.

[7] Walter Chambers, *Samuel Seabury: A Challenge* (New York, 1932), pp. 330 ff.

[8] H. F. Gosnell, *Machine Politics: Chicago Model* (Chicago, University of Chicago Press, 1937), p. 20. Sweitzer was acquitted of the criminal charges brought against him, but a civil suit was brought against his bonding company and the court awarded damages of $269,126 to Cook County.

[9] The ramifications of a state spoils system are discussed in C. Beals, *The Story of Huey P. Long* (Philadelphia, 1935); H. F. Gosnell, *Grass Roots Politics* (Washington, D. C., 1942).

seem that the care of the defective, dependent, and delinquent charges of the state would be the last field for the political free-booter. On the contrary, experience has shown that nowhere has there been a ranker growth of political favoritism than in the dark spots of penitentiaries, hospitals for the insane, and homes for the care of the unfortunate. It has been shown that these institutions have often been permeated with favoritism and fraud, to say nothing of the cruelty and inhumanity with which inmates have often been treated. The criminal, the insane, the helpless red man, and other wards of the state have frequently been regarded as legitimate prey of the spoils system. Contract labor of prison inmates has been a perquisite of loyal henchmen. Supplies to state institutions have been notoriously defective in quality and quantity, until the recent changes in state administration of charitable and correctional institutions. The blind could not see, the deaf could not hear, the dumb could not complain, the feebleminded and the insane would not be considered, the convict would not be believed; and so these helpless ones have been the favored subjects of political exploitation. Not the least of the contributions to the spoilsmen's fund is that coming from the bridewell, the jail, the penitentiary, the asylum, from dungeons and hospitals, but recoined in political influence, power, and respect-ability, in delegates, votes, and contributions, in precincts, wards, cities, and states.

Even the sheltered corridors of state educational institutions have not been free from the spoilsmen. The activities of Governor Bilbo in Mississippi, Governor Huey Long in Louisiana, and of Governor Talmadge in Georgia show how far the politicians may carry this form of exploitation.[10]

The enforcement of most of the law of the state is local in its nature, but there is a considerable field of state action. Supervision over insurance companies, public utility and other corporations, enforcement of factory and labor laws, medical inspection and supervision are very largely in the hands of state officials. Every one of these is open to political use. One of the most notable illustrations

[10] J. F. Hudson, "The Spoils System Enters College," *New Republic*, September 17, 1930. In 1939 President James Monroe Smith of Louisiana State University was convicted of embezzlement in connection with the handling of the funds of the university. President Smith was a product of the Long regime. See *Time*, July 17, 1939.

of this is the relation between insurance companies and state officials, illustrated in the investigations made by New York and Wisconsin on insurance methods and practices. The enforcement of factory, mine, labor, and liquor laws leaves wide play for the exercise of discretion. As in the case of many branches of the city's administration, so in these instances the inspecting force is generally wholly inadequate to do what is expected of it. The Centralia, Illinois, coal mine disaster is a case in point. This condition is, of course, an invitation to select certain persons for purposes of inspection and to ignore certain others; and with a spoils administration it is absolutely certain that the selection will be made for political reasons. A manufacturer or a mine operator who is politically strong may be laxly inspected, while much more rigid tests will be applied to those who are weak in political influence.

Nor has the federal government been lacking in illustrations of the use of the spoils system in public administration. On the contrary, its history from time to time has been stained by exploitation on a great scale, and in a systematic manner. Although the merit system was earlier and more generally adopted in the service of the United States, and although there has usually been a higher degree of dignity and efficiency in the administration, nevertheless important branches of the federal service have been paralyzed from time to time by spoils influence; and at all times the efficiency of the United States Government has been impaired by the influence of spoilsmen. Whiskey kings, timber kings, sugar kings, cattle crowds, coal and oil interests have all made heavy inroads on the integrity and efficiency of the administration, while contracts, for anything from printing to public works, have often been sources of the most serious loss. Fortunes have been coined from the customs and excise services, while public lands, forests and water rights have been likewise exploited.[11] The oil scandals which occurred during the Harding administration are a great blot on our national record. The Secretary

---

[11] For customs frauds, see United States Senate Reports, No. 1990 (1886, 49th Congress, 2nd Session). Report of Public Lands Commission, 1905, Senate Document 154, 58th Congress, 3rd Session. The Teapot Dome episode is described in M. E. Ravage, *The Story of Teapot Dome* (New York, 1924). See John T. Flynn, "Graft in Business," *New Republic*, LXVII (August 5, 1931), 304–307, in which he asserts, "The average politician is a rank amateur in the gentle art of graft compared with his brother in the field of business."

of the Interior leased two valuable naval oil reserves to two separate oil magnates under very suspicious circumstances. In a civil trial, the United States Supreme Court annulled the leases as fraudulent and corrupt. While the criminal trial against the culprits failed, one of them was sentenced to jail for failing to answer questions before a Senate investigating committee. The income tax amendment has also brought rich opportunities for the spoilsmen. It was inevitable that the huge spending programs of the thirties and forties, first for relief and then for military purposes, would be accompanied by charges of spoils and inefficiency in the administration. The Senate investigating committees disclosed that federal funds had been administered in a fashion that was open to criticism.[12] The federal agencies endeavored to correct these situations when they were brought to light.

It is not to be presumed that any government will be wholly free from loss by dishonesty or inefficiency, any more than any large business enterprise; and on the whole the federal government has maintained distinctly higher standards than the state and local units. This is all the more significant in view of the fact that our political parties are strongest in the national field and weakest in the local situations. In other words, the spoils influence is least prominent where there are sharpest differences upon questions of policy, and most pronounced as we go farther from genuine party differences. As party principles and policies arise, the spoils system sinks. The party system and party spirit do not need spoils. On the contrary, they are incompatible; and the stronger the one is, the weaker is the other.

It is unnecessary to catalogue all the devious means by which the unscrupulous turn the public service to their private ends. The list is limited only by the ingenuity and the opportunities of the partisans who control the system. New and unsuspected forms of favoritism or graft constantly come to light.

It is difficult to make a satisfactory classification of methods employed for spoils purposes in the various branches of the administration, because of the wide range of interest and activities covered.

[12] *Investigation of Senatorial Campaign Expenditures and Use of Governmental Funds*, 76th Congress, 1st Session, Senate Report, January 3, 1939; "Relief and Politics," *Social Service Review*, XIII (March, 1939), 111–113; U. S. Congress, Senate, Committee to Investigate National Defense, *Report*, 78th Congress.

Roughly speaking, however, they fall under the following general heads:

(1) Acquiescence in habitual violation of law and ordinance, known or suspected

(2) Political interpretation of terms of obscure or unworkable law or ordinance, almost equivalent to violation

(3) Reasonable interpretation of unreasonable law or ordinance, granted as a political favor, not as a right

(4) Inadequate enforcement of provisions as to service or material in contracts, purchases, franchises

(5) Inadequate prosecution for violation, deferred prosecution, perfunctory prosecution, inadequate penalty or conviction

Taken together, they constitute a formidable array of weapons, which may be employed for financial blackmail, official oppression, and personal, factional, or party support.

PURCHASES AND CONTRACTS

The purchase of supplies and materials by the government has been for many years a rich source of revenue for a corrupt machine in control.[13] Roughly speaking, one-third of the total expenditures of governing bodies are made for these purposes. The purchases of coal, of machinery, of lands for various uses, of institutional supplies, and of a great variety of miscellaneous materials offer a fertile field for the political exploiter. The letting of contracts for public works of various kinds, paving, etc. is of still greater importance. The construction of great water, sewer, and street systems, the erection of city halls and school buildings in cities, of bridges and courthouses in counties, of capitol buildings and institutional structures in states, of post offices and a wide variety of construction works in the federal government, are illustrations of the different kinds of opportunities open to followers of the spoils system.

The waste and graft in public works and purchases are probably no greater than in any other branch of the government where politi-

[13] See J. E. Finegan, *Tammany at Bay* (New York, 1933), for a detailed account of Tammany's activities in connection with purchases and contracts. Numerous examples and techniques drawn from the Chicago scene are given in W. Ligget, "The Plunder of Chicago," *American Mercury*, XXV (March, 1932), 269–279.

cal control is found. They appear to be worse because the waste is more easily measurable and the losses may be more graphically shown. It is more impressive to show that a building which should have cost $100,000 actually required an expenditure of $200,000 than to show that a bureau which should have been maintained for $100,000 cost $200,000, or at a cost of $100,000 was only 50 per cent efficient. There is an added element of personal interest if it can be shown, as occasionally happens in the case of public works, just who received the superfluous $100,000.[14]

Illustrations of this side of the spoils system are abundant. The capitol building at Albany and the state capitol at Harrisburg are classic cases of riotous waste, fraud, and theft under the auspices of the busy spoilsman. Scandalous losses in the federal service have been notorious from the Civil War with its shoddy blankets to the Spanish War with its "embalmed beef," and on to the scandalous abuses in the Veterans Bureau after World War I, with a long trail of land and building scandals lying between. It is not proposed to recount these transactions, but to point out the typical ways in which losses are sustained by the public and gains accrue to the managers of the system.

The different cases may be summed up under several heads:

(1) "Gift" contracts
(2) Unfair specifications
(3) Unfairness, laxness, or fraud in enforcement of specifications
(4) Unfairness in payment of bills

The chief evil, however, is failure to enforce contract provisions. It matters not how honestly the specifications may be drawn if knaves are in charge of their execution. Indeed, the more rigid they are, the greater the opportunity of the spoilsman, for the exacting specifications may exclude the honest man who assumes their enforcement and makes his bid high accordingly, while the "inside"

[14] A large amount of material indicating the practical effects of the spoils system is given in the reports of research and efficiency bureaus, such as those of New York, Chicago, and Philadelphia; and (less critically handled) in periodical literature. In A. Michie, "Huey Long's Heritage," *Nation*, CXLIX (July 29, 1939), 120–123, the case is cited of a swindling scheme in which the furnishings of a hotel belonging to a friend of the president of the Louisiana State University were twice sold to the university.

man with the "pull" knows in advance that the enforcement in his case will be lax and accordingly he makes a low bid. At one time it was reported that the specifications for certain paving in Chicago could not be honestly executed with a fair margin of profit to the contractor for one-third greater price per square yard than the price specified. Information of this kind travels quickly through the trade, and it is little wonder that competition for public business is often not more active.

Under the spoils system the enforcement of contract provisions becomes a political question, and out of this situation there is likely to develop favoritism or outright fraud. In extreme cases all safeguards seem to be utterly destroyed and the public contract becomes a wild riot of fraud and reckless waste. Philadelphia's Art Museum, "an enormous stone pile" contracted for at a cost of $3,500,000, was finished for $25,000,000. The bosses and contractors discovered additional "necessary" expenses.[15] If this were an isolated instance, little attention need be given to it. But the construction of other public projects gives ample evidence of the same procedure.[16]

TRIBUTE FROM THE UNDERWORLD

One of the great sources of strength of the political organization in many cities arises from its power to levy tribute on vice and crime in return for immunity from the law. The so-called "underworld" exists by toleration of the local authorities, and particularly by the favor of the police force. Operating at all times under the ban of

---

[15] Allan Frazier, "Philadelphia: City of Brotherly Loot," *American Mercury*, XLVII (July, 1939), 275–282; Gulick, *op. cit.*

[16] Prior to the clean-up in Montclair, New Jersey, in 1939, contracts for road oil had been so drawn that only one company could supply it. When competitive bidding was introduced the price dropped from 12 to 8 cents a gallon. Similarly, crushed rock for roads sank from $2.36 to $1.04 a ton. Cited in W. Hard, Jr., "From Garbage to Good Government," *Current History*, L (September, 1939), 19–20 ff. After investigation of purchases in Massachusetts the state now secures wastebaskets for 75 cents instead of $10. See M. A. Rose, "Yankee Tax Revolt," *Reader's Digest*, XXXII (March, 1938), 56–59. In New York City investigation disclosed that the charter provision that any contract over $1000 must be let competitively had been evaded in 37 cases by splitting up the contracts into open market orders of less than $1000 each and then awarding them to favored concerns. Cited in W. Waldron, "City Watchdog," *Survey Graphic*, XXVIII (March, 1939), 210–211.

law, vice and crime are easy prey for those who control the law-enforcing machinery.

Reports of a series of inquiries in various cities extending over a period of fifty years have shown in documentary form concrete evidence of actual conditions. The connection between certain political organizations and the vice industry is no longer a matter of speculation or conjecture. The testimony before investigating committees and in courts of law, and in numerous instances actual criminal convictions, have established the knowledge of these conditions in the realm of fact. It is possible to outline this system scientifically, to describe its framework, its ramifications, its modes of operation and its relation to the party system of which it is an integral part.[17]

The center of this wealth lies principally in the control of the police force, with the coroner's office and the prosecuting machine of secondary importance. Professor Goodnow says: "There has never been invented so successful a get-rich-quick institution as is to be found in the control of the police force of a large American city." [18] It was estimated by the foreman of the grand jury, as long ago as 1894, that the annual revenue from this source in New York City alone was approximately $7,000,000. The report of the Chicago Vice Commission in 1911 estimated that the annual profit from vice in that city was $15,000,000, of which $3,000,000 was the amount to be allotted to police graft. According to Pasley, federal investigators estimated the sources of revenue commanded by the Capone gang from illicit liquor, gambling, vice, and business "rackets" at $105,-000,000 annually.[19] Few corporations pay larger dividends than the vice and crime trust.

[17] See reports of following investigating bodies: "Lexow Committee," New York State Senate (Albany, 1895); New York Committee of 15 (1902); New York Committee of 14 (1910); "Curran Committee," New York Board of Aldermen (1913); Chicago Commission on Social Evil (Chicago, 1912); Chicago City Council Committee on Crime (1915); *Illinois Crime Survey* (1929); National Commission on Law Observance and Enforcement (Washington, D. C., 1931); Samuel Seabury, *In the Matter of the Investigation of the Magistrates' Courts* (New York, 1932). See also Raymond Fosdick, *American Police Systems* (New York, 1920); E. D. Sullivan, *Rattling the Cup on Chicago Crime* (New York, 1929); F. D. Pasley, *Al Capone* (Garden City, 1930); and Reddig, *op. cit.*

[18] F. J. Goodnow, *City Government in the United States* (New York, 1904), p. 232. See also V. O. Key, Jr., "Police Graft," *American Journal of Sociology*, L (March, 1935), 624–636; and "Unholy Alliance," *Survey Graphic*, XXIII (October, 1934), 473.

[19] *Al Capone*, p. 60.

So profitable is this enterprise that it has followed the general tendency of other great businesses and has taken on the form of a syndicate or trust in many cases. Vice and crime have been commercialized and have assumed the organization and the aspect of large business institutions.

One of the items in the series of police revenue is that derived from the social evil. Regular tribute is exacted from the unfortunates whose lot has fallen into the swamp of prostitution, and upon all those in any manner profitably connected with it. No branch of activity pandering to the sexual appetite escapes taxation in a well-organized spoils system. The roll of those who contribute includes the street walkers themselves, the houses of prostitution, houses of assignation, disorderly flats, or apartments. It embraces many of the saloons in which vice mongers are harbored, some of the restaurants where they have rendezvous, the shady hotels, and all the other collateral agencies. The Seabury investigation in New York showed that the vice squad not only accepted money for the protection of prostitutes but extorted money from innocent victims by actual or threatened false arrests.[20]

Nor does the possibility of profit stop here. Under a completely organized system, profits from various side lines are distributed to political favorites. The sale at exorbitant prices of special brands of beer, wine, whiskey, and champagne to houses of prostitution, the supply of cigars and cigarettes, the furnishing of food, clothing, jewelry, furniture, and even medical advice to inmates of brothels or protected resorts are privileges which may be allotted to those whom the machine favors. The profits are enormous, and the purchases may be made compulsory.[21] Beneficiaries also include owners of real estate obtaining high rents for property used for immoral purposes, lawyers employed in defense of these properties, purveyors to prostitutes, dope peddlers, and a great group of hangers-on who get the crumbs that fall from the lavish tables of the underworld.

In the same group belong the abortionists, the midwives, and the

[20] *Intermediate Report* to Hon. Samuel H. Hofstader, Chairman of the Committee appointed pursuant to Joint Resolution (of Legislature of the State of New York) by Samuel Seabury, Counsel to the Legislative Committee (New York, January 25, 1932).

[21] W. C. Reckless, *Vice in Chicago* (Chicago, 1933); F. D. Pasley, *Muscling In* (New York, 1931); Lloyd Wendt and Herman Kogan, *Lords of the Levee* (Indianapolis, 1943).

baby farmers, who carry on a thriving business in many centers. Their activities must fit in with those of the police, the coroner, or the prosecuting attorney, and consequently they are likely to become parts of the political machine to an extent determined by the measure of their profits. Skirting the frontiers of murder, their charges must be high, and the tariff on their business correspondingly strict.

Closely connected with this source of revenue is the income derived from tribute levied upon alliances and understandings of various descriptions with those who trade in chance. Unquestionably one of the most profitable connections of a well-oiled political machine is its control over various forms of gambling.[22] This relationship extends from the "small games" to the "big game." It may cover merely crap games (dice throwing), slot machines, "numbers," and various other minor games, or it may extend to the well-equipped modern "place" with up-to-date gambling devices where fortunes are won and lost in an hour. It will always include policy, race track gambling, bookmaking, and protection of various "clubs" in which games of chance are carried on. The racing racket alone runs into billions of dollars annually. From time to time in some cities, as in New York and Chicago, gambling has apparently been placed upon a syndicated basis. The "big men" have found it advantageous not only to exact tribute from those engaged in the business of gambling, but also to apply the monopoly principle to this industry. Assuming control of the games, they have been able to use the police force to prevent competition. The "outsider" who endeavors to begin the profession of gambling for himself finds it necessary either to make terms with the gambling trust or to be subjected to frequent raids and arrest. The enormous profit in the ordinary game of chance, which for the house, bookmaker, or track is not a game of chance at

[22] Earl Brown, "The Racing Racket," *Life*, XXII (May 5, 1947), 112–126; Carleton Beals, "Sharing Vice and Votes," *Nation*, CXLI (October 2, 1935), 377–379. J. T. Flynn, in "Too Much Fun," *Collier's*, CIV (October 7, 1939), 14–15 ff., points out that in this decade the source of the underworld's revenue has shifted from liquor to gambling and other forms of commercial vice. The relation between gambling and politics is illustrated by the activities of San Antonio's late city boss, Charlie Billinger, who died in 1937. Billinger started his career in gambling, branched into the banking and real-estate business, and thus used his wealth to swing city elections. See R. Maitland, "San Antonio: The Shame of Texas," *Forum*, CII, (August, 1939), 51–55.

all but an absolute certainty, makes the supervision of this phase of activity one of the most lucrative in the entire field of machine operations. In'every large city it will be found that the gambling group contains in its ranks men of great political influence and far-reaching political power. Sometimes these men are openly identified with the political machine, but in other cases they stand in the background and their real connections and purposes are not generally understood by the public. The gambling "fraternity," exercises very material political power.

The political machine has also a direct connection in many proven instances with criminals of various sorts. The protection of crime is a part of the spoils system and a source of political revenue which cannot be ignored in a comprehensive review of the subject. Crime in its most primitive and brutal forms, naked assault upon persons and property, as well as in its more refined and modern shapes, has been arrayed, sometimes openly and sometimes secretly, with our political organizations.

All this might seem incredible but for the records. The clean-up of Cleveland's police department in 1937 revealed that a police captain had deposited $139,000 in gifts which he had received from notorious gangsters.[23] The history of New York, San Francisco, Los Angeles, Minneapolis, Chicago points in the same direction.[24]

But this does not exhaust the list, for we must still reckon with revenues derived from desperate criminals fleeing from justice, with "fences" of all sorts, with dealers in the tools of crime, and with an army of minor violators of law, federal, state, and local, with "hang outs" and rendezvous of criminals, professional bondsmen, and crooked lawyers. All are likely to be known, and as they are recognized, to be fitted into the needs of the dominant organization, as active or contributing members, or in both capacities. This combination is sometimes called the "big fix."

Dealers in intoxicating liquor are usually liable to payment of

[23] Stanley High, "Cleveland Versus the Crooks," *Current History*, XLIX (October, 1938), 22–24.
[24] *Report of Chicago Council Committee on Crime*, p. 163 (1915); also *Report of Illinois Association for Criminal Justice*, 1929. See W. B. and J. B. Northrop, *The Insolence of Office* (New York, 1932), for an account of the Seabury investigation in New York. Chap. XXIII reveals the intimate relationship of the police and the rackets.

tribute. This was especially true during the prohibition era under the Eighteenth Amendment. Conditions now vary widely from city to city and state to state, but on the whole it is clear that in many cases the liquor dealer, for one cause or another, is obliged to pay for the privilege of carrying on his business.[25]

There is an intimate connection between prostitution, the use of habit-forming drugs, the sale of intoxicating liquors, and crime. These activities, taken together, form a system which cannot flourish without the protection of political influence, for which cash, votes and political support are rendered in return. Their directorates are frequently interlocking, not only with each other, but with the political machines of both parties.

Whatever the precise sum paid into the party treasuries from the underworld, it is clear that this is one of the mainstays of the spoils system in our great cities. Prostitution, gambling, habit-forming drugs, bootlegging, racketeering are a part of the system as it prevails in certain of our metropolitan communities. The rays of the red-light district reach far, and the "tenderloin" influence, when thrown in the balance, is heavy in national and state as well as in local affairs. It carries with it cash, votes and delegates—important weapons of political warfare.

RACKETEERING

Closely connected with the political tribute levied upon the underworld is the toll which the spoilsmen exact from the racketeers. Racketeering has been defined as "the activity for profit (in connection with the sale of goods and services) of an organized group which relies upon physical violence or an illegal use of group pressure to accomplish its end." [26] It is a form of extortion which has flour-

[25] *Hearings on National Prohibition Law before the Sub-Committee of the Committee on Judiciary, U. S. Senate, 69th Congress,* April 5–24, 1926, 2 vols. Testifying before this committee, Lincoln C. Andrews stated that there was "astonishing corruption" among prohibition agents, that 875 of them were dismissed for cause, and that 121 of these dismissals were extortion and bribery. Investigations in Atlanta disclosed that police officers had forced upon the bootleggers an elaborate profit-sharing set-up involving 40 per cent of the local police. Illegal liquor dealers were allowed to operate freely after paying bribes that ranged from $25 to $100 a month. See "Atlanta Clean-up," *Newsweek,* XI, (June 13, 1938), 11–12.

[26] Murray I. Gurfein, "Racketeering," in *Encyclopaedia of the Social Sciences,* XIII (July, 1934), 45–49.

ished in the foodstuffs, trucking, building, clothing, cleaning, and liquor industries of the larger cities of the United States since the beginning of the twenties. Sometimes it has been parasitical and at other times it has served the function of acting as a stabilizing influence in a given industry. It may take the form of a monopoly set up by the racketeers simply with the aid of protection from the politicians, or it may take the form of an association, the members of which are given "protection" against violence to person or property in return for the payment of dues. The goods of those who fail to pay may be destroyed or their persons may be assaulted.

There is no doubt that organized racketeering could not exist without the acquiescence or tacit approval of the police and the politicians in control of the law-enforcing machinery. As one writer has put it: "No racket of any size could operate longer, than seventy-two hours without the O.K." [27] Undoubtedly racketeering exacts a heavy toll in the United States, but only the roughest estimates can be made of its costs. Losses by extortion are not reported as fully as are thefts. Furthermore, such indirect costs must be considered as increased insurance rates on plate glass, burglary, and bombing risks, and increased police and prosecuting expenses. The national tribute to racketeers was estimated by the Attorney General of the United States in 1933 to be $1,000,000,000 annually, but the New York State Crime Commission estimated in 1931 that the racket costs to the nation were many times that much.

Not only does business at times engage in practices akin to racketeering, but it may also actually employ racketeers, whose reputations may be highly questionable. The combination of the businessman, the labor racketeer, and the underworld figure is an all too familiar one in some of the larger American cities. Many businessmen would, of course, prefer to deal with neither honest nor dishonest unions, but given the chance, some businessmen choose the latter, encourage them, and frequently make them an essential part of their labor policy.

While political corruption of the racketeering sort was greatly stimulated by federal prohibition, the repeal of the Prohibition Amendment turned the energy of the ex-bootlegger into business

[27] T. J. Haggerty, "Spoils and the 'Racket,'" *Annals of the American Academy of Political and Social Science*, CLXXXIX (January, 1937), 17–21.

racketeering. The step from political protection of illegal liquor rackets to other forms of criminal racketeering was an easy one. As the sanction of force became routine it was an easy matter to find subsidiary fields of action, as, for example, where law enters the frontier of regulations.

The suppression of racketeers is primarily a matter for local law-enforcing authorities, but in some instances the federal government has been much more effective than the state or local governments. The national officials rely upon the income tax and the antitrust laws, the laws forbidding extortion by use of the mails, and the federal statutes dealing with kidnapping, white slavery, and stolen motor vehicles.

The ability of all levels of government to combat racketeering is related to the success of a democracy. As one writer has put it:

"A real danger to our institutions lies in the fact that as criminals and racketeers become more powerful, through their close alliances with influential politicians and office holders, law-abiding people will eventually lose confidence in our system of government and, in desperation, will seek other means of procuring for themselves the security and self-respect to which they have every right to feel entitled as citizens of a civilized country." [28]

TAXING MACHINERY

An important asset of a spoils machine is control over the assessment and taxation of property. The loose and unscientific character of our taxing system makes political exercise of this power easy and precise location of blame difficult. The general tax on real and personal property commonly in use is altogether antiquated and has been abandoned in every civilized country except our own. In early days when industry was largely agricultural in its character, there was no great difficulty in assessing with accuracy both real and personal property; but with the growth of large cities, the rise of manufacturing industries, the development of corporations and intangible values, great obstacles have been encountered in the way of accurate assessment, especially of personal property. It is relatively easy to

[28] Smedley D. Butler, "Making War on the Gangs: A Plan to Take Police Out of Politics," *Forum*, XXXXV (March, 1931), 134–141.

see what the taxable property of the farmer is by looking at his land and equipment, but it is difficult to tell whether he or any other person possesses stocks, bonds or mortgages. The development of intangible property has made the present system of personal property taxation in many respects a farce.[29]

Evidence upon this subject has been piled mountain high. It is more than half a century since the absurdities of our system were clearly set forth.[30] Commission after commission in state after state has investigated and reported on the inequality and injustice of our system. Numerous changes in tax laws and in tax administration have been made since then, but in the main the taxing system is still in a backward state.

Illustrations of the power of the assessor and of the injustice often inflicted will readily occur to anyone at all familiar with the taxing system. In many instances the rates are such as to call for an income tax on personal property of from 30 to 50 per cent, and in some cases the rate of taxation is higher than the return from the property.[31] The tax rate may be, for example, as high as 6 or 7 per cent when the ordinary return on the property is 3 or 4 per cent. Even with the best of intentions the practical administration of such a system is a matter of very great difficulty, and under a spoils system its possibilities are limited only by the imagination of the administrators.

Injustice with respect to valuation of real property is easier to ascertain, but the most glaring discrimination in the field of personal property may occur with small possibility of detection. The assessment of real property itself has not in most instances been placed upon a scientific basis. It has been made as a rule in a political fashion, by assessors appointed or elected for political reasons and retaining their power for the same reason. They have not been able to make an accurate, just, and scientific valuation of land itself or of the improvements upon land.

[29] See Reports of National Tax Association, 1907 to date; and H. D. Simpson, *Tax Racket and Tax Reform in Chicago* (Chicago, 1930).

[30] Professor Seligman said: "The general property tax sins against the cardinal rules of uniformity, of equality and of universality of taxation. . . . Its retention can be explained only through ignorance or inertia."—*Essays in Taxation* (New York, 1895).

[31] See *The Assessment of Real Property in the United States*, Special Report of the New York State Tax Commission, No. 10 (Albany, 1936); and R. E. Untereiner, *The Tax Racket* (Philadelphia, 1933), pp. 118–127.

In assessing personal property on the present basis, a scientific method is practically out of the question. In the absence of any such possibility, taxing officials have been given practically a free hand in valuing the personal property found in every community. It has remained within their power to make a high valuation or a low valuation, a just assessment or an unjust assessment, to exempt altogether the favored individual and to assess his neighbor to the full limit of the law.

The possibilities under this system of unscientific assessment of real property and absolutely chaotic assessment of personal property have not escaped the eye of the practical political machinists. They soon learned and took pains to teach their friends that it lay within their power to undervalue property, and their enemies discovered that it was in their power to overvalue property, not, it is true legally overvalue, yet practically and relatively to other property. This power has been used, therefore, to build up the political machine by placing under obligations to it lists of favored persons. The situation is even worse than this, for so wholly unjust is the existing system that an average, common, or current undervaluation of personal property frequently may not be had as a matter of right, but must be obtained as a matter of political favor. Thus the individual who desires nothing more than to pay his fair share of taxes is placed in the position of a suppliant who must beg for justice from the political power in control of the taxing machinery.[32]

The far-reaching influence of this authority is generally but little understood, yet to those who are familiar with the inner workings of the political machine the significance of this control over taxation

[32] The log book of an unscrupulous organization would read something like this:

1. Widow James: Inherited $10,000. Fixed valuation at $1,000. Three sons. Fixed by B.
2. Widow B. Left $10,000. Fixed valuation at $10,000.
3. John Smith. Personal property $25,000; fixed at $2,500. Will vote right.
4. R. D. Personal property $25,000; fixed at $25,000.
5. Wm. J. Manufacturer. Value of plant $100,000; fixed at $50,000. Campaign contributor.
6. A. F. Anti-machine. Manufacturer. Value of plant $100,000; fixed at $90,000.
7. Gas Co. Plant worth $1,500,000; valued at $500,000. $5,000 check.

D. C. Andersen, "Tax Collecting as a Fine Art," *Commonweal*, XI (February 5, 1930), 391–393, cites the case of a Pennsylvania precinct worker who offered to secure voters tax receipts if they supported his candidates.

can scarcely be overestimated. This power goes into avenues and channels which are otherwise unapproachable. It reaches spots that cannot be approached in any other way. It terrifies those who would otherwise be unterrified. It strikes a certain fear into the heart of every man, especially those engaged in a competitive business where accurate or just taxation is of prime importance.[33]

In the course of a generation, men learn that resistance to the political organization may meet with punishment in the form of increased taxation, while quiet neutrality will be rewarded with low taxes if desired, or with average taxes if this is asked. The precinct captain, or the ward committeeman or some higher power who "takes care" of assessments for his constituents wields tremendous influence. He and the organization of which he is a part readily build up in this fashion secret lists of friends or favored ones who are under obligations to them for lower taxes and who may be relied upon either to give support, or at least not to attack them.

In the case of financially important persons, these lists may be further used in case contributions are desired for campaign funds. The assessor has in his possession not only the lists of those who pay taxes, but what is more important for his purposes, the lists of those who would pay larger taxes if the provisions of the law were enforced. It is an easy thing for him or some agent of the organization to obtain campaign contributions from some of those who are exposed to higher taxes.

While this influence operates in a small way throughout many communities, it reaches its climax in dealing with the large combinations of capital in the form of corporations. The public service corporations and particularly railroads have been especially vulnerable at the point of taxation. The huge investments in city utilities and in railroad properties throughout the country make the assessment of their property a matter of grave importance, while the loose character of the laws regulating the taxation of such corporations makes the task of collecting funds all the easier. These corporations, in many instances, therefore, become attached to the political machine through the taxing power. Other large industrial corporations may,

[33] *The Nation*, February 5, 1938, cites the case in which the Board of Tax Appeals reduced the 1933 valuation of a Chicago newspaper's capital stock from $4,023,619 to $1,447,006; *Fortune* placed the 1933 valuation at $53,600,000.

for the same reason, ally themselves with the dominant party or faction. They may either make direct contributions to individuals who are parts of the political machine, or they may make their contributions in the more delicate form of campaign gifts to the treasury of one party or the other, or both.

It is true that the development of a more scientific system of taxation with reference to public service corporations, municipalities, and the railroads has to some extent eliminated this system of graft, but in many places it still continues to be an important part of the spoils system. Our whole system of taxation is still so loose and unscientific that the fear of blackmail or the desire to escape fair taxation makes corrupt use of the taxing power only too common. A system which, at its best, makes equitable taxation almost impossible, when operated by political machinists becomes a brutal instrument of extortion and injustice, swinging from confiscation to total immunity, as political expediency dictates.

No political machine is complete, therefore, without the taxing power. No political organization can afford to overlook, or does overlook, this tremendously powerful weapon. Its intimidating power is enormous. It makes possible untold tribute upon huge aggregations of capital and petty graft upon the whole industrial world. It makes it easy to build up a clientele of favored friends. Taxation is one of the most powerful weapons in the well-equipped arsenal of the "invisible government." "The power to tax," said Chief Justice Marshall, "is the power to destroy," and the power to administer a loose and unscientific taxing system is not to be despised.

With the development of more objective techniques of making assessments and with the growing strength of citizens' tax associations, the use of the taxing machinery for spoils purposes is declining. A political machine which abuses its control over the taxing machinery will find business and industry moving away from its bailiwick.

SUMMARY

The following analysis of the powers of a local boss in a city of 100,000 illustrates the scope and method of the fully developed system. It is assumed that the boss or machine is in complete control of the situation and dominates all lines of organized governmental activity in the given area, whether municipal, county, state, or federal. This would involve the control of all these agencies by the same party and the same faction. Any reader may compare his own local situation with this outline, making such additions, subtractions, or corrections as the case may warrant.

Of the different elements enumerated, one or more may be lacking or unused in a given situation. One or more may be wholly neutralized, or in the hands of a hostile machine, or wholly or partly devoted to the public service, and therefore immune from spoils influences. Happy is the community where none is known. The purpose of this outline is to show a situation in which all the varied factors are assembled under one central control.[34] Here the full possibilities of the spoils spirit and methods are developed and unfolded, subject only to such checks as may be imposed either by the moderation of the authorities, or a successful political revolution on the part of the community.

I Administration
  A Pay roll of, say, 1500, including municipal, county, and state patronage, plus positions obtained with private or quasi-public corporations, contractors, and others seeking or holding political privileges. The time and energy of these men and an assessment of perhaps 5 per cent on their salaries; surety company for bonding officials.
  B Administrative control, city, county, state, and federal (as far as possible). Of especial significance are:
    (1) Police department and prosecuting attorney—
        yielding tribute from the underworld of vice, gambling, bootlegging, racketeering, and crime; useful in traffic violations, elections, and strikes; guaranteeing immunity from prosecution
    (2) Health, fire, and building departments—
        useful for rewarding friends and punishing foes; for supplying tribute or securing political allegiance from those concerned with unsanitary tenements and workshops, fire traps, impure food and drink
    (3) Public utility supervision—
        giving large powers over traction, gas, electric light, and telephone companies, capitalized at, say, $10,000,000

[34] See Reddig, *op. cit*.

    (4) Highways (streets)—
        covering a network of privileges and immunities, including
        street obstruction and occupation
    (5) Education and recreation—
        giving wide power in favoring localities and persons
        (See also pay roll and purchases.)
    (6) Relief, welfare, charities, hospitals and corrections—
        with wide range of favoritism among the unemployed, defec-
        tives, dependents, and delinquents
    (7) Trade supervision—
        enforcement of a wide range of regulations regarding the con-
        duct of business—a sweeping power

C   Purchases and contracts, including lands, buildings, machinery, sup-
    plies, printing, amounting to, say, $1,000,000 a year. A rate of
    10 per cent on this amount would yield $100,000.

D   Taxation Property valued at say $150,000,000, which might legally
    be valued at $200,000,000 or $250,000,000, giving opportunity
    for favoritism or cash collection.

II   Legislative Machinery

This would include control over the city's legislative body, over the
county board, the local members of the state legislature, and of Congress. Franchises, street vacations and locations, police power ordinances, contracts, bond issues, and appropriations depend upon this
power, and hence large revenues and influence have been derived there-
from.

III   Judicial Machinery

Naming of judges, judicial patronage; control of police courts, receiverships and court plums, influence on decisions in election, graft, and certain industrial cases

IV   Election Machinery

Power to name election officials and designate polling places, to control
registration, canvass and count votes; power to nominate candidates of
all parties, frame platforms, elect officials, collect and disburse campaign
funds

V   Favors

A long list of favors, accommodations, adjustments, legitimate and illegitimate, within the power of the boss These touch almost every walk
of life, sooner or later.

The consequences charged to the prevalence of the spoils system in
party affairs have been of the most serious character. They include
breakdown of representative government over large areas and long

periods of time, destruction of the party system itself in cities and elsewhere through bipartisan combinations which supplant the opposition and rivalry of the parties, enormous waste and inefficiency in the conduct of government, failure to protect industrial and political democracy, obstruction of comprehensive and constructive plans for social and industrial betterment. Some of these, it must be conceded, are defects characteristic of modern democracy or of modern government in general; others are peculiar to the rapid development of social and industrial conditions in our country. But there still remains a formidable array of counts against the operation of the spoils system in our political life.[35]

[35] On offsets to spoils, see below, Chap. XXII.

CHAPTER XIII

ROOTS OF THE SPOILS SYSTEM

"As I reviewed all this that day, for the purpose of questioning Croker about his boss-ship, I asked myself suddenly what was the difference between a political boss and a banker boss. None that I could see, except that one was a political, the other a financial, boss. Both political government and business government were run on the same lines, both had unofficial, unresponsible, invisible, actual governments back of the legal, constitutional 'fronts.' "—Lincoln Steffens, *The Autobiography of Lincoln Steffens* (New York, Harcourt, Brace and Company, 1931), p. 235.

THE CAUSES OF THE GROWTH OF THE SPOILS SYSTEM ARE COMPLEX. There is no simple explanation of the pathological conditions that have arisen in our political life. Some of the reasons lie on the surface of things, and for others we must dig down deeper into the soil of national characteristics, and into the social order itself.

Two great facts of our national growth stand out as conditions which would try the temper of any governmental system. These are the rapid territorial expansion of our country and the rapid growth of its population. Within the limits of a century our population has increased from twelve million to one hundred and forty million, and at the same time this population has been spread over a vast geographical area. This expansion has involved great readjustments of economic, social, and political life which must always accompany a migratory and expansive movement of this character. It has imposed a tremendous strain upon the flexibility of the government, testing to the utmost its organization and its functions. At the same time, such a movement, intensely absorbing in its activities, distracts the attention of the population from the problems of government to those of the conquest and exploitation of nature. The isolation of the communities, the preoccupation of individuals, and the shifting of movements within the nation tend to prevent formation of mature public opinion on questions of public policy. These difficulties, to be sure, are not insuperable, but they are formidable; and they can be overcome only by an expenditure of greater energy than would be necessary under ordinary conditions. Similar difficulties have not been encountered by such nations as Germany, France, and England.

During the last fifty years our problem has been still further complicated by the tremendous concentration of population in urban centers.[1] The urban population of the United States in 1790 was 130,472, or 3.4 per cent of the total population. In 1850 the urban population was 289,758, or 12.5 per cent of the total population. Then began the enormous urban movement. By 1880 the urban population was 14,772,438, or 29.5 per cent. In 1890 the urban population was 22,720,223, or 36.1 per cent of the population; in 1900, 30,797,-185, or 40.5 per cent of the total poulation. In 1910 it reached the figure of 42,623,383, or 46.3 per cent of the total population; in 1920, 54,816,209, or 51.9 per cent; in 1930, 68,954,823, or 56.2 per cent, and in 1940, 74,423,702 or 56.5 per cent. Figures 8 and 9 show graphically the development of cities in the United States.

The rapid growth of these great centers of population imposed burdens upon city governments which they were unable to carry and under which they broke down. Furthermore, in great metropolitan communities many of the citizens most likely to be interested in civic reforms moved out of the city limits into the suburbs where their influence in politics operated in a much smaller sphere. The growth of the city also decimated the rural district from which its population was in great part drawn. The breakdown of city government and the degeneration of many rural governments profoundly affected the state government and helped to bring about subnormal political conditions there. The enormous plunder in the capture of cities made them centers of the spoils system and materially helped to confuse and demoralize the political situation throughout the land. Thus the corruption of certain rural districts in communities in northern New York and New England, combined with the corruption of great centers like New York, Boston, and Philadelphia, brought about the condition which was the exact formula for the growth of the spoils system. Without the disturbing in-

[1] National Resources Committee, *Our Cities: Their Role in the National Economy* (Government Printing Office, June, 1937). On spoils in cities, see Luther Gulick, "The Shame of the Cities—1946," *National Municipal Review*, XXXV (Jan., 1947), 18–25.

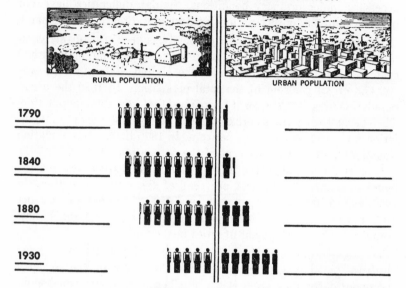

PROPORTION OF RURAL AND URBAN POPULATION

Each figure represents 10 per cent of total U. S. population

Figure 8   [From National Resources Committee, *Our Cities: Their Role in the National Economy* (Washington, D. C., 1937), p. 1.]

fluence of this urban concentration and rural loss of population, the problems of American government would have been far more simple and easy to solve.

A further condition complicating the situation was the heterogeneity of population. The great immigration movement beginning about the middle of the nineteenth century gave us a cosmopolitan population recruited from Ireland, Germany, the Scandinavian Peninsula, Italy, and later, from the eastern nations of Europe. The cooperation of these different races was inevitably a difficult problem from every point of view—the economic, the social, and the political. It is, of course, inevitable that the formation of a common political consciousness and of a common agreement upon questions of public policy should be more difficult in proportion as the population is more diverse, and easier in proportion as it is more homogeneous. Each race brings its own standards, customs, and ideals,

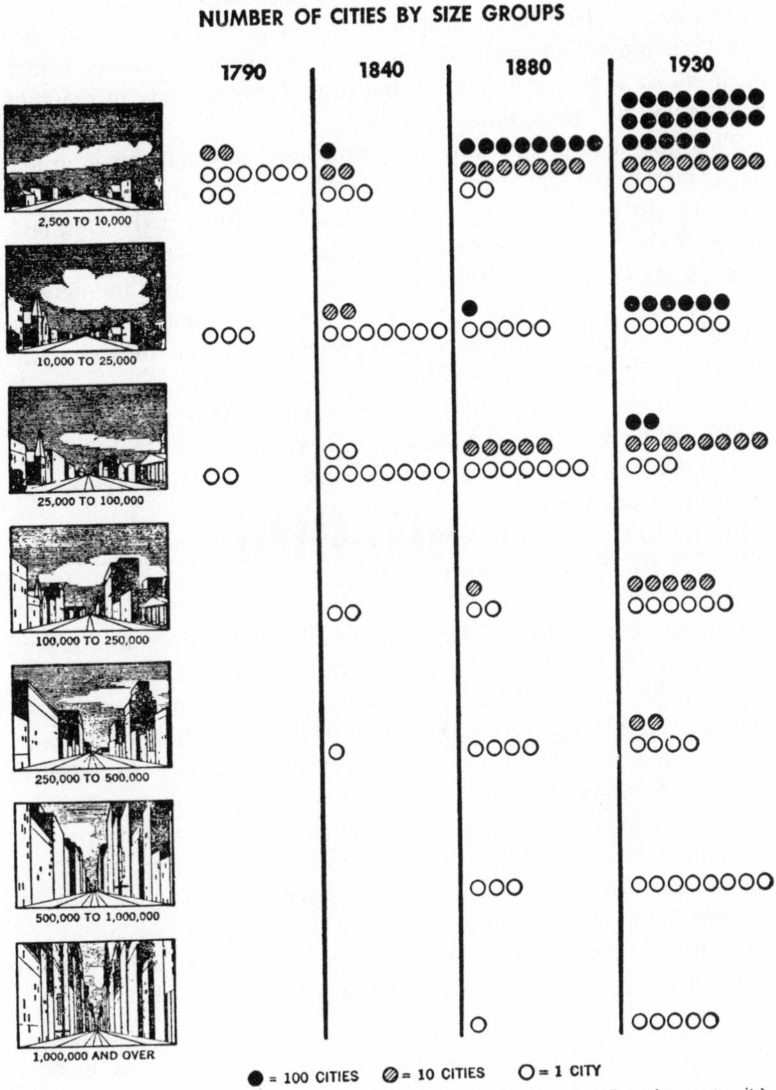

NUMBER OF CITIES BY SIZE GROUPS

● = 100 CITIES   ⊘ = 10 CITIES   ○ = 1 CITY

(From National Resources Committee, *op. cit.*)

Figure 9

and these must first be blended before a common understanding can be reached. In the meantime, appeals to race pride and race prejudice will be made with more or less success by various interests, selfish or unselfish as the case may be, and in this way the day of reaching a consensus will be so much delayed.

This does not involve any reflection upon any particular group, but is merely the statement of the simple fact that it takes time for strangers to reach a common understanding. As a matter of fact, many of the newly arrived people rendered signal service in the development of our national life. For example, the German immigrants and the Irish were intense Unionists and without them it is doubtful whether the Union could have been preserved.[2] In the long run, this blending of cultures may result in a higher and finer culture, but in the meantime the possibility of misunderstandings offers a fertile field for the spoilsman and the political leader whose stock in trade is an appeal to, or a combination of, selfish and private purposes. An analysis of great urban communities like New York, Chicago, Detroit, Philadelphia, and Boston shows that the party machine is strongest in the areas where there is the largest percentage of foreign-born.[3]

It must be remembered that this rapid territorial expansion and the growth under urban conditions, with a mixed population, were made at the time of the greatest influence of certain theories fixed upon our population during the period of the Jacksonian democracy. One of these was the idea of rotation in office already discussed in previous chapters. As was there stated, rotation in office was originally applied only to elective positions and was designed to prevent permanent tenure of office with a possible relapse into hereditary government. In the Jacksonian era, however, the policy of rotation was applied to all positions, administrative as well as legislative, and the political maxim "To the victor belongs the spoils" was definitely adopted as a party principle and a public policy. That this idea

[2] See W. E. Dodd in *American Historical Review*, XVI, 787, showing that the election of Abraham Lincoln was due largely to the support given by the newly arrived immigrants.

[3] H. F. Gosnell, *Machine Politics: Chicago Mode* (Chicago, 1937), p. 109. The coefficient of correlation between straight party voting and the percentage foreign born was .66. See also J. K. Pollock, *Michigan Politics in Transition* (Ann Arbor, 1942); Edward H. Litchfield, *Voting Behavior in a Metropolitan Area* (Ann Arbor, 1941).

should have been adopted just before the enormous expansion of the duties of government began was extremely unfortunate, for it placed the whole growth of cities particularly and of all branches of government under the influence of the spoils philosophy. At the very moment when expert servants appointed on a permanent basis were most necessary, the policy of rejecting the expert and permanent servant of the public was definitely fixed.

Equally damaging was the policy also adopted at this time of electing as many public officials as possible. In the early days, the ballot had been an extremely short one. But at this time the plan of electing by popular vote a long list of administrative officials was put into force as a means of securing greater popular control over the government. At the time this plan was adopted, it may have had that effect; but, as in the case of the spoils system, the effect of this plan was generally detrimental because it occurred at the very time when the number of officials began to increase, particularly in cities. The effects of the wholesale elective process were seen later in the confusion caused by the independent election of long lists of coordinate officials and by the consequent destruction of governmental responsibility. It has taken many years to break the force of this idea and the opposite practice has gained slowly. The widespread movement for a short ballot has found quickest expression in cities, but in states and counties it has made hardly an impression.

A further cause of difficulty has been the weakness of the administration in the beginning of our government. In their fear of a monarchy the founders of our government gave the executive little strength in the several states, although the office of president was materially stronger than the contemporary state governor. For the first generation, the popular theory was that the executive branch of the government was something to be feared and distrusted; and, in view of the strong leaning toward monarchy on the part of many conservatives, it is not surprising that this idea lingered in the public mind.[4] Under Jackson, the power of the executive was revived as far as public leadership was concerned, but the administration as such was fatally weakened by the adoption of the spoils idea. By a curious coincidence, the same influences that created "King Andrew"

[4] L. Lipson, *The American Governor: From Figurehead to Leader* (Chicago, 1939).

with autocratic political power, at the same time assailed the principle of expert and permanent service. The rehabilitation of the executive power in the Jacksonian period, as seen alike in the national, state, and local governments, did not mean organization of a powerful administrative service, but rather exaltation of the executive power in terms of political leadership and of legislative strength. This tradition of suspicion toward the administration continued for many years, and its practical effect in all forms of government was to prevent the building up of efficient public service. This gave our administration its political character, the looseness, laxness, and inefficiency which made it so adaptable to the later purposes of the more predatory spoilsmen.[5]

Under quickly changing conditions, the powers and duties of the administration were bound to expand at a very rapid rate, and the politician took full advantage of it, relying upon the public prejudice against the creation of expert public service. It is only within the last generation that this idea has been overcome and that the opposite practice has slowly been adopted. The long-continued campaign for the merit system has had a profound effect in modifying the public idea of what "administration" should be, and the citizen is now coming to see that a strong administration is the surest defense against exploitation by the political machine or by private interest.

Furthermore, the conditions of modern life are such as to force upon the community the idea of expert service.[6] It becomes clear that the work of the engineer, the chemist, the bacteriologist, the technical inspector can no longer be performed by anyone not specially trained for that work. The need for special services and the appearance of men with the special training to meet them have combined to create a new public sentiment that will soon close the door upon the spoilsmen in the great structure of public administration.

American public life has suffered severely from lack of a tradition of public service on the part of men of wealth and leisure.

---

[5] See Luther Gulick, *op. cit.*; F. J. Goodnow, *Politics and Administration* (New York, 1900), for an interpretation of the boss's power in terms of lack of official responsibility in government. See also Elihu Root, "The Function of Political Parties as Agencies of the Governing Body," in *Addresses on Government and Citizenship* (Cambridge, 1916), p. 20.

[6] L. D. White and T. V. Smith, *Politics and Public Service* (New York, 1939), Chap. IV.

During the first generation of our national life, conspicuous work was done by men of this type. Their aristocratic tendencies, however, led to the overthrow of this system, and the obligation to public service has only slowly revived. The generation following the Civil War witnessed a great expansion of business and a remarkable absorption of energetic men in the work of trade development. It was also a period of sharp conflict between private interest and public interest, so that men of wealth and leisure often found themselves arrayed against the government, and therefore unable to co-operate heartily with the common enterprises as a whole. Thus the community has lost the valuable services of the types that in England, France, and Germany have contributed much to the solution of governmental problems in those countries. On the other hand it must be recognized that until recently aristocratic traditions in Great Britain have made it difficult for nonaristocrats to rise in politics.[7]

A fundamental cause of this condition must be sought deep down in the soil of industrial and social conditions of which political life is a part. The lack of proper organization of governmental machinery and the lack of sufficient public interest to ensure effective political action are themselves the result of some underlying cause. The graft and spoils system may be explained by defective organization and public apathy, but the inquiring mind will still ask why there is not an adequate organization, and why there is not a livelier public interest in the affairs of the community.

Unquestionably one reason for the development and power of the spoils system in the United States is the wide discrepancy between the industrial and the political balance of power.[8] The "equilibrium" between property and political power, to which Harrington referred years ago in his *Oceana,* powerfully affects the character of every government. It is difficult to maintain a genuine political democracy in the face of oligarchy or of aristocracy in the industrial world, for

[7] H. F. Gosnell, *Democracy: Threshold of Freedom* (New York, 1948), p. 45; H. J. Laski, "The Personnel of the English Cabinet, 1801–1924," *American Political Science Review*, XXII (February, 1928), 14–20. Since the Labour party has come to power in Great Britain, more nonaristocrats have been elected.

[8] See the notable chapter LIX in Lord Bryce's *Modern Democracies* (New York, 1921), on "The Money Power in Politics"; also his comparative estimate of the power of wealth in the United States, II, 454. See also A. B. Cruikshank, *Popular Misgovernment in the United States* (New York, 1920) ; and C. F. Adams, *Chapters of Erie* (New York, 1886).

economic power inevitably tends to translate itself into political power. It is quite clear that if a few men own all or most of the property, while the mass of the people have all or most of the votes, disturbance and corruption are bound to ensue. Those who control the property will inevitably try to turn their dollars into votes and their property into political power. The substance of wealth will not be content with the shadow of power. Under these conditions, political corruption will continue to exist until industrial oligarchy has crushed out effective opposition to its control over the agencies of government; until it has made democracy a shell, preserving its forms but destroying its spirit and essence; or until democracy has definitely established control over great combinations of wealth and placed them in a position where they cannot challenge the popular will. This antagonism disturbs the political as well as the industrial world. It is the irrepressible conflict of our day beside which all minor questions are dwarfed into insignificance. The party system cannot be understood without observing the effort of certain groups of concentrated wealth with only a few votes to control a democratic form of government in which there are many votes.

We must take cognizance of the fact that the limited franchise of the Fathers has been greatly widened, while the wealth and financial control of the nation have passed into fewer hands. The control of huge industrial interests centers in extremely small groups of men, and these men in large measure dominate and direct the industrial life of the country.[9] The great special financial interests, endeavoring to obtain or maintain some special privilege, are not interested in the use of patronage to build up a political machine, or tribute levied on vice and crime, or the use of public funds for political purposes, or in the plunder derived from public works. Those who hold some special privilege are interested, however, in the control over legislation, administration, judicial interpretation, taxation. And in order to obtain this control over lawmakers, executives, and courts, it is necessary to tolerate incidental and often objectionable developments of the party system. In order to maintain the system by which they benefit, they must permit a certain profit to the political pirates who man the ship. They may, and unquestionably do, hate and de-

[9] A. A. Berle, Jr., and G. C. Means, *The Modern Corporation and Private Property* (New York, 1932); Lincoln Steffens, *Autobiography* (New York, 1931).

spise these tools, who are willing to pilfer and plunder the public in order to maintain a political machine. They recognize the moral debasement involved in connection with tribute upon vice and crime in our great cities; they recognize the humor and tragedy in the political management of institutions; they appreciate even more keenly than the average citizen the inefficiency of our city, state, and national governments when administered by these groups of modern spoilsmen. But in order to obtain what they want, which is control over the machinery of the government, they must permit their agents these incidental profits, these minor spoils that go to fill the pockets of the political bosses and bosslets who do their bidding. The great utility corporation, whose power will enable it to prevent adequate rate regulation and thereby to make, let us say, an annual profit of from five to ten millions of dollars, cannot afford to war with the Democratic boss or the Republican boss for having too many men on the public pay roll. Privilege holders cannot afford to remonstrate with the Democratic or the Republican boss because of the impropriety of collecting money from gambling, prostitution, or crime in cities, for this very tribute helps to maintain the organization which controls the government which makes the privileges possible. They cannot afford to enter into a controversy with the Republican boss or the Democratic boss who profits by scandalous contracts in the field of public works, by printing jobs, by paving scandals, by state capitol buildings, or by government supplies, for this plunder is the perquisite of men who control the organization that controls the power that permits the making of the millions. So they must tolerate inefficiency, spoils, and corruption by bosses and machines because through these organizations they are enabled to capture and control the government and thus secure by virtue of wealth what they could not obtain by virtue of votes. It cannot be presumed that all persons of great wealth are interested in preserving the spoils system. On the contrary many of them are bitterly opposed to it and struggle against its tendencies. But it is idle to ignore the intimate connection often found between concentrated wealth and political corruption.[10]

It is not necessary, and it is historically incorrect, to assume that this system has been built up consciously and designedly for the pur-

[10] Matthew Josephson, *The Politicos* (New York, 1938).

pose of obtaining control over the government. The fact is that most of the system was in existence before the great industries grew to anything like their present power.[11] The spoils system took its modern form, as far as patronage is concerned, in the days of Andrew Jackson, while the graft system developed when cities sprang into something like their modern proportions, in the years immediately following the Civil War. Finding the spoils and the graft system in existence, certain interests have utilized to the full its enormous possibilities; they have organized it; they have systematized it; they have standardized it; they have placed it upon a business basis comparable with other parts of the great industrial machine that business enterprise has built up. The vice trust, the gambling trust, the jackpot, the bipartisan alliance, the boss are all devices to systematize and organize what was formerly individualistic, anarchistic, unrelated political activity. Instead of an indefinite number of minor lords of gambling, it has been found more economical and efficient to syndicate gambling in a great city. Instead of allowing individual members in the legislature to carry on a guerrilla warfare, each man for himself against corporations, it has been found more economical and efficient to systematize and organize this peculiar industry into definite understandable form. Instead of having two political parties, or two machines fighting each other, in a competitive way, it has often been found more economical and efficient to institute a working agreement between them to limit the field of warfare, to prevent the destruction of the system, to underwrite the interests of all concerned.

It may be said that the struggle for industrial and political democracy, far from being confined to the United States, is common to all modern states; but the characteristic features of the spoils system are peculiar to our government. Why not a spoils system in Switzerland, France, or England?

Among the causes for the absence of spoils in Great Britain should be mentioned the lack of a frontier atmosphere, the limited natural resources of the British Isles, the aristocratic tradition which includes the monopolization of the higher civil service positions by the

[11] See Gustavus Myers, *History of Tammany Hall* (New York, 1917); H. L. McBain, *DeWitt Clinton and the Origin of the Spoils System* (New York, 1907); and D. R. Fox, *The Decline of Aristocracy in the Politics of New York* (New York, 1919).

graduates of the older universities and the virtual prohibition of candidatures on the part of election agents of the older parties, the absence of immigrant groups demanding recognition in the form of public offices, the prohibition of all candidatures by civil servants, and the concentration of responsibility in the cabinet. Conservative and Liberal party agents who do all the work that precinct captains and ward committeemen do in the United States are forbidden by unbreakable traditions to run for elective office themselves, to expect any appointive governmental positions, or to look for any compensation outside of their somewhat meager salaries paid by the party.[12]

Another and deeper reason for the spoils system in America is the prodigality of nature and a favorable geographical position, rendering us until recently almost immune from war. Millions of acres of free land and the mineral wealth of an untouched continent long eased the otherwise urgent demands for governmental organization and action to meet the problems of social and industrial justice. The governments of states like Germany and England have been compelled for generations to face the problems of poverty and social distress from which we thought that we were free. Free land was our answer to poverty and unemployment for many years, with even free gold for the more fortunate pioneer. The tremendous shock of the Civil War was necessary to complete our national unity, but a generation of feverish economic activity and political apathy followed. The lofty war spirit of sacrifice was succeeded by a reaction toward private interest, and none of the military organization and efficiency of the national government, purchased at such appalling cost, was transformed into civil efficiency and organization. On the contrary, civil corruption and scandal followed with sickening rapidity. A similar reaction followed the idealism of the World Wars.

Out of all these varied forces came the party system as it has been here described—a resultant of many influences playing upon American public life. Our great territorial expansion, our vast increase in numbers, the amazing urban concentration of population, the het-

[12] H. F. Gosnell, *Why Europe Votes* (Chicago, 1930). On the reasons for the absence of spoils in Europe, see also Bryce, *op. cit.*; R. C. Brooks, *Civic Training in Switzerland* (Chicago, 1930); and J. K. Pollock, ed., *Change and Crisis in European Government* (New York, 1947).

erogeneity of our population, the adoption of the spoils idea in the Jacksonian era, the long list of elective offices, the traditional suspicion of strong administration and its consequent weakening, the absorption of men in industry after the Civil War, the unfriendly attitude of many city dwellers toward the moralistic and Puritanical legislation forced upon them by rural-dominated lawmaking bodies, the naïve faith of these lawmakers in the power of positive legislation to change our habits, the lack of well-defined traditions of public service and obligation, freedom from military and industrial pressure—all these combined to create a spoils environment of the familiar type. The spoils idea was well established before 1850, but its disastrous consequences did not become evident until there was placed upon the government the heavy strain of vastly greater duties. The havoc wrought, especially in cities, by direct application of the crude principle that the public service belongs to the dominant party, and the party to the "machine," aroused the public to the fearful dangers of the situation and sounded the alarm. But the lingering "spoils idea" permeated the public mind, and the desired change of conditions is coming only slowly and with the very greatest difficulty. Over eighty years have elapsed since the Tweed exposé startled New York City and the whole nation, but the battle still rages.

It may be asked: Who profits by the workings of the spoils system? In whose interest or by whose sufferance does it endure? How shall we account for the tenacity with which this apparently indefensible order of things clings to its hold upon our public affairs?

None of the genuine interests of any political party is permanently advanced by spoils methods. At the point where the spoils system is strongest—in cities and states—the parties are actually weakest, and in fact in many instances in cities the national parties have been excluded by law from the local ballot. Our parties are primarily national parties, but it is precisely in the national field that the spoilsmen have been severely, although by no means effectively, checked. The climax of the spoils system in party affairs is the bipartisan combination in which party differences are merged and the party really vanishes. The enormous profits to the spoilsmen make it eminently desirable that warlike tendencies, except in the common cause against the "outsider," be restricted, and the area of conflict limited. The apotheosis of spoils methods in the party is the elimination of party differences altogether, the cessation of the conflict of principle and policy, commonly characteristic of the party system. Jobs and graft and spoils do not make the party possible; the party makes them possible, and it is often unmade and undone by the very opportunities afforded its notorious partisans.

It may be maintained that certain groups or classes profit by the perpetuation of spoils methods; that they use the spoils machinery to obtain privilege and immunity on a huge and profitable scale; that these forces protect and defend spoilsmen in order to continue the exploitation of land and labor, out of which vast fortunes are built and enormous revenues coined.

On the whole, however, a spoils regime is not favorable to legitimate industry and trade. The field of special privilege is necessarily small, and those outside this little area are not favored. The smaller producers and tradesmen have not been a part of the system or its beneficiaries. On the contrary, they have been in many instances its earliest victims. "Jackpots" have not helped them, but have given advantages to their competitors on the basis of their financial size and their political unscrupulousness. In many instances, smaller stockholders in the spoils combination have discovered that they were really pulling out of the fire the chestnuts of the "insiders" who controlled the springs of action, and profited by the results of others' efforts.

Uncertainty in policy and unfairness in method are weak foundations for trade, and in the long run both expensive and dangerous. The spoils brand upon a tariff, a timber law, the industrial code of a state, and the police ordinances of a city does not inspire public confidence in their durability. In the end, adjustment must be made. In comparison with social and industrial policies, based upon broad foundations of integrity, maturity of deliberation, and soundness of administration, the spoils product is incomparably inferior—an expensive substitute for genuine policies.

After all, the chief beneficiaries of the spoils system have been a few persons who have amassed fortunes under its flag. A small number of political bosses and industrial magnates under this regime have been able to reach the heights of wealth and power at heavy costs to their fellow men. But only a few have been helped. The great mass of the citizens have suffered.

Nor can the party system or the spoils aspect of it be charged with all of the evils arising from the struggle for industrial control. The modern struggle has cut across all the strands of social life, has weakened or destroyed established standards of action and set up others in their stead. It has profoundly affected the whole *mores* of our day, social in the broader sense of the term, as well as political in the narrower.[13] Politics presupposes certain established customs, certain ideas of right and wrong; but if these are confused or lacking, the political group suffers just as other groups suffer in the period of transition. Industrial ethics, legal ethics, medical ethics, social ethics have all been sadly confused by the rapid changes in industrial and social processes and organization;[14] and political ethics, standards, and methods have been affected by the same general tendencies.

We must recognize that often those who have participated in the processes of political corruption have been rated among the strongest, the most intelligent, and sometimes even the most honest in the community. They have found themselves enmeshed in a system from which there seemed to be no easier way of escape than the muddy and malodorous one of bribery and corruption. But graft and corruption were not peculiar to the political system. They were found widespread in the business and labor worlds where the earlier standards of honor and fair play were often rudely shattered in the processes of consolidation and in the vast new economy of modern trade. Corrupt practices were as common in industry as in politics; that is, corrupt in the sense of being unusual, uncommon, contrary to the earlier code of business conduct.[15]

---

[13] Cf. R. C. Brooks, *Corruption in American Politics and Life* (New York, 1910); E. A. Ross, *Sin and Society* (Boston, 1907); and D. Loth, *Public Plunder: A History of Graft in America* (New York, 1938).

[14] See J. H. Tufts, *The Real Business of Living* (New York, 1918); and "The Crises of Democracy," *Annals of the American Academy of Political and Social Science*, CLXIX (September, 1933); also J. T. Flynn, *Graft in Business* (New York, 1931).

[15] See Brooks, *op. cit.*, Chaps. II–IV. Corrupt commissions acts were passed in a number of states, penalizing gratuities to influence agents in purchases, sales, etc., in Massachusetts, New York, and other states. Cf. Virginia laws of 1906, Chap. 260. See also F. R. Kent, *Political Behavior* (New York, 1928), Chap. XXVIII; Walter Lippmann, *Drift and Mastery* (New York, 1917), Chap. I; and H. F. Gosnell, *Boss Platt* (Chicago, 1924), Chaps. I, XIV.

The vigorous men who were found in control of large-scale industry often stopped at nothing. They were little restrained by codes of laws, whether enacted by the state or proceeding from any other group, if these rules came across their path in their struggle to destroy competitors or to extend trade and profits. The unwilling legislature, the stubborn competitor, the corrupt labor leader, were all so many obstacles to be brushed aside—to be bought out and removed from the pathway.

The party weakness was symptomatic of a community weakness, a tendency to obtain by favor, influence, or money that which could not be obtained in strict accordance with the established codes of action. Thus business espionage, corruption of purchasing agents, purchase of trade secrets or lists, squeezing of competitors, underselling through local price cutting, inaccurate labeling, carelessness as to weights and measures and standards and specifications, and a long series of unfair trade practices led to the conclusion that political obstacles were likewise to be brushed aside or bought away, regardless of what might be indicated by the codes or customs of the times. Likewise, blackmailing, extortion, graft, and corruption in the labor world developed on a large scale, the measure of which was taken by the country from time to time. Notable illustrations are seen in the revelations in New York and Chicago, showing collusion between labor leaders, contractors, politicians, bankers, and material men. Graft in business, graft in labor, graft in politics were all intimately associated, for they were all parts of the same social and economic process; all sprang from the same environment. The observer of political affairs could not fail to note the presence of two standards of political judgment: the one conventional, hostile to all forms of graft, favoritism, and corruption; and the other much more tolerant toward practices theoretically condemned.

From the class point of view, there were also factors of great significance during the period of industrial expansion. The middle class was increasing in numbers but was poorly organized, while the commercial group, especially large-scale business, was very greatly strengthened. The labor group was just coming into a position of strength, but not yet politically conscious and active, and often infested by parasitic grafters. Middle-class standards, the product of earlier conditions, were universally agreed to in theory, but were not universally applied either by business or by labor.[16] While nominally they remained in effect, in practice they were often quietly disregarded by either the enterprising promoter on the one hand, or the business agent on the other. The boss and the machine were found to be convenient agencies for the brokerage of privilege or immunity as the case might be, and they were readily taken over by the large interests whom they could so readily serve. The offensive and defensive alliance of the powerful business machine and the powerful political machine proved too strong for the community in only too many cases, and broke through the thin line of public defense, weakened in a transition period by many subtle social and economic causes, as well as by political traditions hostile to vigorous government and administration.

As to the actual working of the spoils system, it may be truthfully said, "The half has never been told." History will paint the picture in still more lurid colors than have yet been used. It will not be assumed that the "grafters" or the "politicians" were a type apart from their kind, but they will be treated as part of a common form of social life. The "grafters" include all those who were willing to accept the advantages of the social inheritance, and assumed none of its responsibilities, or who took more than they gave. In business, in labor, in politics, an underlying spirit was often seen, shifting to others the heavy burdens of social responsibility, refusing the labor of democratic cooperation in the great fellowship of democratic society.

It may be asked, then, how under such a system it is possible to carry on the ordinary governmental functions of order, justice, and public welfare. The answer is that the real governor in America is not the party, powerful as it may seem, or its rulers, however imposing their rank and station and apparently illimitable the range of their power, but public opinion, which dominates all political parties, and all politicians and leaders. When the public is sufficiently insistent, its will prevails; when public sentiment is clearly and sharply defined, opposing parties compete with each other in feverish haste to be the first to express or to execute the public's will. This is the paradox of American politics which many foreign observers and

---

[16] See the interesting studies by Sinclair Lewis in *Main Street* (New York, 1920), *Babbitt* (New York, 1922) and *It Can't Happen Here* (New York, 1935).

many pessimistic Americans have not seen themselves. The truth is that we govern through parties, but often against the party's will. They are master in some things upon the fundamental condition that they shall obey the public will when the public speaks. The personnel of candidates or the type of legislative policy proposed may not represent at all the desire or the hope of the spoils group. Nevertheless, we observe this group, sometimes with an admirable show of cheerfulness, nominating and electing the undesirable candidate, enacting the unwelcome bill, and enforcing the obnoxious law. The real sovereign is public opinion, and when that voice is heard, all parties stand at attention and salute their superior officer. They do not surrender their system, but they yield on the specific occasion to the specific command of their undisputed sovereign. Over and over again this significant phenomenon may be observed in city councils, in the legislatures of states, and in the halls of Congress.

When the general public is indifferent, a powerful interest group may often overcome a political group. Agriculture, or labor, or business, or the Anti-Saloon League, or women, or others may persistently besiege the party until capitulation follows.[17] The most stubborn resistance is that made when the special interest of the party organization, as in the case of civil service reform, is involved, or that of some close party ally is granted; but even here the party will not battle to the death, but will yield, slowly perhaps and not willingly, to powerful pressure by determined men.

Not only is this true, but within each party group there are a number of party patriots who oppose the tendencies of the "spoils system" both in the narrower and in the larger sense in which that term is used. High-minded men and women are found in all party organizations, and their voices must be heard. They struggle to raise the level of party action and improve its standards, to better its morale. And from time to time they are aligned in support of measures of distinct public interest and advantage. If the only influence in political parties were that of the exploiter or of the patronage

[17] B. L. Smith, H. D. Lasswell, and R. D. Casey, *Propaganda, Communication, and Public Opinion: A Comprehensive Reference Guide* (Princeton, 1946); P. H. Odegard, *Presssure Politics, the Story of the Anti-Saloon League* (New York, 1928); H. D. Lasswell, *et al.*, *Propaganda and Promotional Activities: An Annotated Bibliography* (Minneapolis, 1935), and continuations in *Public Opinion Quarterly.*

brokers, the party course might be far different. But in truth the final action of the party is a resultant of the action of many diverse and competing forces—a compromise which is a balance of opposing forces. Potentially, if not always actually, the party is an instrument for serving the general interest. To continue in the confidence of the people, a party must be more than a conglomeration of special interests.

CHAPTER XIV

STATE NOMINATING SYSTEMS

"Primaries are really the key to politics. There is no way for party candidates to get on the general election ballot except through the primaries. Primaries are the exclusive gate through which all party candidates must pass. Control of that gate in any community means control of the political situation in that community."
Frank Kent, *The Great Game of Politics* (Garden City, New York, Doubleday, Page & Company, 1923), p. 7.

ONE OF THE MOST IMPORTANT FUNCTIONS OF THE POLITICAL PARTY is the selection of public servants filling various official positions, either by election or by appointment. In no country are there as many official places not under some form of merit system, and in no place is so large a part of the time and energy of the party managers and leaders, as well as of the rank and file of the party, consumed in the task of selecting the personnel of the official service. Accordingly a careful analysis of this process is indispensable to an understanding of the nature and function of the political party.

The subject may be divided into three main parts: nominations, elections, appointments. As indicated in an earlier chapter, appointments are largely the work of the inner circle of the party organization. In nominations the organization shares its power with the voters of the party or at least submits its results to them after a fashion, and in the electoral process the party must reckon with the entire voting constituency. Yet in all cases the process is one of the choice of the personnel of government largely through the party groupings.

The number of elective offices usually selected upon party lines is very large—probably exceeding 800,000.[1] Table 4 presents the estimates by level of government.

[1] Estimates made by a group of our students. These estimates were necessarily very rough since accurate figures could be collected only at prohibitive costs. There is no clearing house for this type of information. Some careful studies have been made of units of government in the United States, but these fail to reveal how many

TABLE 4

ELECTIVE OFFICERS IN THE UNITED STATES

Federal officers	533
State officers	10,000
County officers	54,000
City officers	66,000
Miscellaneous, town, rural and school	750,000
Total	880,533

Many of these offices are regularly filled on a strictly partisan basis. These offices form the backbone of the active party force. Filling them is one of the regular tasks of the party organization, and one which occupies a large part of its time and energy.

NOMINATIONS

European observers are always impressed by the elaborate legal and party machinery which is employed in the United States for the purpose of making nominations for elective offices.[2] They are used to much simpler devices for limiting the choices of the party voters and they find it hard to understand why such technical procedures are necessary in America. A petition signed by a few voters or a decision by a local party association is all that is usually required to make a nomination in a European democratic country.[3] Foreigners have to be told that American nominating methods are the product of the country's historical traditions, faith in democratic dogmas and positive law, and peculiar social and political conditions, of which the one-party system in the southern states is one.

In the early period of our history the nominating process was a relatively simple one. The number of elective offices was very small,

---

elected officers are chosen from each unit. In many cases a unit has no elective officers. See U. S. Bureau of the Census, *Elective Offices of State and County Governments* (Washington, D. C., December, 1946) ; W. Anderson, *Units of Government in the United States* (Chicago, 1945) ; and Illinois Tax Commission, *Atlas of Taxing Units* (Springfield, Illinois, 1939).

[2] Dennis Brogan, *Government of the People* (New York, 1933) ; H. F. Gosnell, *Democracy: Threshold of Freedom* (New York, 1948).

[3] E. M. Sait, "Nominations," in *Encyclopædia of the Social Sciences*, XI (New York, 1933), 392–395.

and the number of voters was not very large, judged by present-day standards of suffrage. Means of communication and transportation were poor, and party affairs were largely in the hands of a very few. At this time local nominations were often made either by the announcement of the candidate himself, or by his friends, or perhaps at a meeting called for the purpose.[4] Where there were elective state offices—and in many cases there were not—the legislative caucus of the party presented the party candidates for governor or other state position. At the end of a generation, however, the legislative caucus lost its hold upon the public favor and rapidly declined. After passing through the transition stages of "mixed" or "mongrel" caucus, made up partly of legislators and partly of delegates, it took new form in the nominating convention. This process was completed in the states about 1820. The convention was regarded as a material advance over the older legislative caucus, and undoubtedly was at that time a more democratic method of party nomination than that which it succeeded.

With the Jacksonian Democracy the number of elective offices was materially increased, and the importance of the nominating machinery became greater than ever before, both in the state and in the localities. Under the spoils system the number of appointive offices was also very largely increased. The principle of adult (male, white) suffrage was also recognized at this time, and the number of voters was enlarged. No serious suggestions of change in nominating methods were made for another generation, however.

After the Civil War the scandalous corruption in the great cities like New York, to say nothing of states and local governments, led to the demand for various forms of adjustment of the nominating procedure in the great parties.[5] From California to New York arose the cry for some more effective procedure in the nomination of party candidates, some method that would put an end to the fraud, bribery, trickery, and corruption that had come to be characteristic of the nominating methods in many parts of the country.

In surveying the field of primary legislation, certain broad tend-

[4] F. W. Dallinger, *Nominations for Elective Office* (New York, 1897), gives a good account of early nominating methods.

[5] See C. E. Merriam and L. Overacker, *Primary Elections* (Chicago, 1928), Chaps. I–IV.

encies are apparent. The most striking feature is the gradual regulation by law of the affairs of what was originally regarded as a purely voluntary association. Step by step the advance has been made until the party is now almost completely encompassed by legal restrictions, often of the most minute type. From the optional statutes, first respectfully tendered to the party, the legislatures advanced to the passage of mandatory acts for special localities. From local laws the legislatures went on to cover the entire state with a network of regulations which now envelops the party.

But the primary movement did not stop with the legal regulation of the party election. The next stage in the development was the substitution of the direct for the indirect method of nomination. A generation of primary legislation may be summed up as follows: starting with unregulated primaries, the advance was made to the prohibition of a few flagrant offenses, or to optional local regulation; then to compulsory regulation; then to the direct primary. The direct primary development began as far back as 1867, when the Crawford County plan was adopted in Pennsylvania. Following this time many counties in various states of the central and western sections of the country, as in Ohio, Indiana, Iowa, Kansas, adopted the direct system by party rule and put it into effect. In the southern states the direct primary was also used under voluntary party rules. In the South the nomination was equivalent to an election as a rule, and hence the primary became the real election at which it frequently happened that more votes were cast than in the regular election itself.[6]

About 1900 the movement for the direct primary began to develop much more rapidly and within ten years spread widely over the western and central parts of the country. Robert M. La Follette, Sr.,[7] was

[6] See G. Myrdal, *An American Dilemma: The Negro Problem and Modern Democracy* (New York, 1944); Merriam and Overacker, *op. cit.*, Chap. V; E. C. Meyer, *Nominating Systems* (Madison, 1902); and a brief summary by Louise Overacker entitled "Nominations" appearing in E. B. Logan (ed.), *The American Political Scene* (New York, 1938)). On the origin of the movement, see J. H. Booser, "Origin of the Direct Primary," *National Municipal Review*, XXIV (April, 1935), 24.

[7] See A. F. Lovejoy, *La Follette and the Establishment of the Direct Primary in Wisconsin*, 1890–1904 (New Haven, 1941); *University of Chicago Record*, I (1897), 587; Robert M. La Follette, *Autobiography* (Madison, 1913); and A. O. Barton, *La Follette's Winning of Wisconsin* (Madison, 1922).

one of its earliest advocates, but it included supporters in the ranks of progressive elements of all parties. Bryan, Hughes, Cummins, Roosevelt, and Wilson were among the advocates of the new method of making party nominations. The chief motive for the demand was the revolt against the political machine in alliance with industrial privilege in various forms, corporate chiefly. The movement was in part a democratic one, animated by a desire for wider popular participation in government, but it was also a part of the protest against social and industrial conditions. The party system was regarded as an element in these conditions, and popular opposition converged upon the machine as the source of much of the evil it was desired to eliminate. Startling disclosures of the betrayal of party trust by party leaders aroused the people to a crusade for responsible party government.

It was believed that the direct primary would bring out a larger vote than the delegate system and that the choice would therefore be a more democratic and representative one than that obtained under the caucus system, where often only a handful of party voters selected and instructed delegates. Other arguments were that a superior type of candidate would be selected if the choice were made directly by the voters of the party, or if it were known that all choices must be ratified by the voters; and that the direct vote would tend to break up the power of the boss and the machine and to make the party management more responsible to the will of the rank and file of the party.[8] Finally, it was hoped that the direct system would aid in the overthrow of the industrio-political machine against which the insurgent movement of the time was really directed. Friends of the direct primary argued that the "invisible government" or "trusts" and "bosses" would not survive the new form of party government, or at any rate that their rule would be more easily overthrown than before.

On the other hand, vigorous opposition was made to the direct nomination plan. It was contended that the ballot would be crowded with an impossible array of candidates; that the urban districts would outvote and overwhelm the rural sections; that the expense of

[8] A strong statement of the popular argument is given in Governor Hughes' message to the Legislature of New York, 1910; also in his article in the *National Municipal Review*, X (1920), 23, summing up the argument for the direct system.

campaigning would be prohibitive to all except the very rich. It was believed by some that party unity and harmony would be impossible and that party responsibility would be utterly destroyed.[9]

The practical operation of the direct primary is still a subject of general discussion in which wide variation of opinion is expressed.[10] In spite of strenuous opposition, however, the primary system remains intact with a few exceptions. The passage of a direct primary law by New Mexico in 1938 left only Connecticut and Rhode Island as the two states that select all party candidates by party convention. However, New York and Indiana have limited the use of the direct primary to local nominations, employing the convention for all state-wide offices.[11] Where there has been a direct vote on the proposal to repeal the direct nomination law, the popular verdict has been in favor of the retention of the law.[12] On the whole the direct primary seems likely to stay for some time.

An examination of actual developments under the direct primary shows that many of the arguments urged by the advocates of the new system and many of those advanced by its bitterest opponents were not wholly valid.[13] On the other hand, there were many effects not generally anticipated. It was frequently charged that the direct primary would destroy the party system. Some even expressed the fear that representative government would be undermined and over-

[9] See W. H. Taft, *Popular Government* (New Haven, 1913), Chap. V, and *Representative Government in U. S.* (New York, 1921); A. B. Hall, *Popular Government* (New York, 1921), Bibl., 274–277. Elaborate argument against the direct primary is cited in R. Boots, *Direct Primaries* (New York, 1917).

[10] See A. Harris and C. Uhr, *Direct Primary Elections* (mimeo., Berkeley, Calif., 1941); J. K. Pollock, *The Direct Primary in Michigan* (Ann Arbor, Mich., 1943); Merriam and Overacker, *op. cit.*, Chaps. IX–X; Boots, *op, cit.*, a discussion of the New Jersey system; A. Millspaugh, *Party Organization and Machinery in Michigan* (Baltimore, 1917); N. H. Debel, *The Direct Primary in Nebraska* (Lincoln, Nebr., 1914); *Third Conference of Governors* (1910), pp. 117–142; "The Direct Primary," *Annals of the American Academy of Political and Social Science,* March, 1923; ○ E. Norton, "The Direct Primary in California" (unpublished); W. Schumaker, "The Direct Primary in Wisconsin" (unpublished); O. McKee, "Direct Primary, a Failure and a Threat?" *Atlantic Monthly,* CXLVIII (August, 1931), 185–193.

[11] Overacker, "Nominations," *op. cit.*, and "Direct Primary Legislation in 1928-29," *American Political Science Review,* XXIV (1930), 275.

[12] Merriam and Overacker, *op. cit.*, p. 271.

[13] Statistics of primary elections are often given in state manuals or handbooks (see Merriam and Overacker, *op. cit.*, Appendix B, p. 423), but nowhere is there a complete collection of the figures for the several states. See also U. S. Bureau of the Census, *Election Data in State Documents* (Washington, D. C., October, 1944).

thrown. It is perfectly plain that parties still survive and the organization still goes on; and it is no longer seriously contended that party management is incompatible with this particular form of nomination. On the contrary, we frequently encounter the argument that the direct primary strengthens the machine and should therefore be repealed, although this must be taken with a grain of salt when coming, as it frequently does, from members of the organizations said to be so strengthened.

It was believed by many that the direct primary would result in discrimination on the part of the urban districts against the rural; that the mass vote of the cities would uniformly and inevitably overwhelm the more widely scattered rural vote; and that the agricultural sections would lose their influence in the selection of party candidates. This has not come true.[14] There have been instances where the cities have taken more than their share of candidates and also vice versa, but as a rule this has not been the case; and the old argument from this point of view is now rarely encountered.

On the other hand, the preprimary slate has appeared more frequently than was anticipated by either the advocates or the opponents of the new primary plan.[15] The possibility of this was pointed out by some students of the subject, but it was not generally realized that the organization or the machine might name the candidates in advance and then obtain the ratification of the slate proposed by them. In some cases this possibility has become a fact and a custom; the primary has then ceased to function as intended by its proponents. In many other instances there have been no slates at all, or if framed they have not obtained a uniform or even an encouraging success.

Sometimes there have been two or more slates and the honors have been divided between them. When there is a long list of candidates to be chosen with much patronage at stake, it has been more easily possible to form and carry through a slate. The direct primary has not made automatically impossible the control of the nominating system

[14] O. C. Hormell, "The Direct Primary with Special Reference to the State of Maine," *Bowdoin College Bulletin No. 13* (December, 1922); "The Direct Primary Law in Maine and How It Has Worked," *Annals of the American Academy of Political and Social Science*, CVI (March, 1923), 128.

[15] S. Wallace, "The Preprimary Convention," *Annals of the American Academy of Political and Social Science*, CVI, 97. See also William M. Reddig, *Tom's Town: Kansas City and the Pendergast Legend* (New York, 1947).

by a ring or machine, even of the corrupt type. The machine slate wins easily where independency is weak.

To what extent the new system has influenced the choices made by the organization which still nominally controls is a question much more difficult to answer. The character of nominations is determined not only by open and successful resistance to organization nominees, but also by the possibility and the probability of resistance which is anticipated or discounted or thwarted by the character of the nominations made by the organization itself. A wise machine will make many concessions in order to prevent the raising of the standard of revolt by an opposing faction or by unorganized insurgents. Resistance is more readily made under the direct primary than under the convention system. There is always a certain protest vote, and there are always groups within the apparently united machine that are ready to take advantage of any insurgency for the sake of advancing their own ends. Such resistance is much more effectively registered by the popular vote than by the number of delegates elected.

The question whether "better" candidates are obtained cannot easily be answered, chiefly because no sufficiently elaborate inquiry has been made to cover all the facts in the case.[16] There can be no question that such an inquiry would be eminently useful. Very bad candidates have been selected under the direct primary system at times, and also very good, competent, honest, and representative ones. That more than usually unfit candidates are selected because no one is directly responsible is not true as a general thing, although it may happen occasionally. But incredibly bad candidates have also been chosen by "responsible" conventions under adverse conditions, to phrase it mildly. On the whole it is difficult to see how the "bad" man would find it easier to obtain a nomination under the direct system than under the delegate plan, while it is clear that a "good" man may win a primary fight when he would be wholly lost sight of in a struggle for delegates and the collateral control of a convention nominating a whole series of other candidates. That many competent candidates are excluded from office because of their unwillingness to go through a primary is a pleasant fiction without much basis in the actual facts of political life. Yet no judicious and impartial observer

[16] Pollock, *op. cit.*; Schumaker, *op. cit.*; and Norton, *op. cit.*, have made some comparisons with respect to age, education, and experience of candidates.

will contend that the new nominating system has revolutionized the character of candidates with reference to their ability, their integrity, or their representative character.[17] This is a part of the great problem of democracy which cannot be so simply solved, and which will not be determined by either directness or indirectness in methods of selection.

That the expense of campaigning tends to exclude the worthy and favor the undesirable types of candidates in the direct system can scarcely be sustained.[18] It will be found that in the case of a candidate of great efficiency or one who stands for some broad general policy in which a large number of voters are interested, it is possible to raise the funds necessary for the reasonable conduct of the campaign; and if these funds are raised upon a democratic basis so much the better for the party and the candidate and the general public. Occasionally a candidate is available because of his "barrel," yet the machine can always raise the necessary funds through the application of its own peculiar system of revenue. If no insurgent candidate is available except one who conditions the use of his funds on his own candidacy, little is lost for the community. Nor can it be forgotten that conventions have often been controlled by small groups of men representing directly or indirectly wealth and privilege in concentrated form. If money was not spent, it was ready for spending.

Furthermore, elaborate and reckless use of funds is not beneficial to candidates; it may even be positively harmful, and often disastrous. The personally financed campaign of Governor Lowden in 1920 and his related defeat for the presidential nomination is a striking illustration of the deceitfulness of riches. There is much insincerity and ignorance in the discussion of campaign funds, but there is little evidence to show and none to demonstrate that the use of wealth in direct primaries is more effective than in the capture and

[17] See an interesting but inconclusive attempt reported in *Transactions of the Commonwealth Club of California*, XIX, No. 10 (December, 1924), 553.

[18] In the Pennsylvania senatorial primary of 1926, $800,114 was spent on behalf of Vare and $1,804,979 for Pepper; in the Illinois senatorial primary $354,616 was spent by McKinley and $253,547 by Smith. Pepper and McKinley were defeated Smith was nominated and elected but he surrendered his credentials after being excluded by the United States Senate. He was defeated for renomination in the primary of 1928. See C. H. Wooddy, *The Case of Frank L. Smith* (Chicago, 1931). In 1930 Mrs. Ruth Hanna McCormick spent over $440,000 for her successful campaign in the Republican primary but she was defeated in the election.

control of conventions. The abuses of the use of money should be checked and there should be publicity in regard to receipts and expenditures, but too great confidence should not be placed in automatic devices for this purpose. They will not include the expensive services of the "organization" or outside associations, or of the press. The confiding electorate that trusts to a statute for fencing out money or economic power from primaries and elections deserves its certain fate.

It is also to be observed that some confusion has been caused by attributing the expense of public regulation of primaries to the direct system. If the primary is to be supervised by the state, whether it is direct or indirect, the public expense will be about the same in either case. The outlays for rent of polling places, the payment of election officials, the printing of ballots, the provisions for canvass of votes are as great in one system as in the other. If all direct primary laws were repealed and the regulated delegate system retained, the public expense would not be materially reduced. And if there are real contests under the delegate system, as Mr. Hughes has pointed out, the expense of the campaign is not much altered. Some money might be saved by having no primaries, conventions, or elections, but more would be lost.

One of the unforeseen tendencies observed by Godkin in his incisive study of democracy was the small vote under universal suffrage in many elections. In some states this is still more true of party votes than of general elections. The direct primary has not always drawn out as large a vote as was predicted by its most enthusiastic advocates in the first days of its introduction. In the New England states and in the Middle West as shown by Figure 10, the ratio of the primary vote to the total vote at the following election was below 45 per cent.[19] In other cases, however, the primary vote has been much larger, rising several hundred per cent in the case of the southern states. Thus, in the case of South Carolina in 1942 some 980 per cent or nearly ten

[19] See figures in Merriam and Overacker, *op. cit.*, p. 273. The ratios for forty-three states of the total number of votes cast in the primary to the total number of votes at the general election in 1942 given in Figure 10 were based upon U. S. Department of Commerce, *Statistical Abstract of the United States, 1946* (Washington, D. C., Government Printing Office, 1947), pp. 306–307. Percentages have been calculated in V. O. Key, *Politics, Parties, and Pressure Groups* (New York, 1947), p. 362.

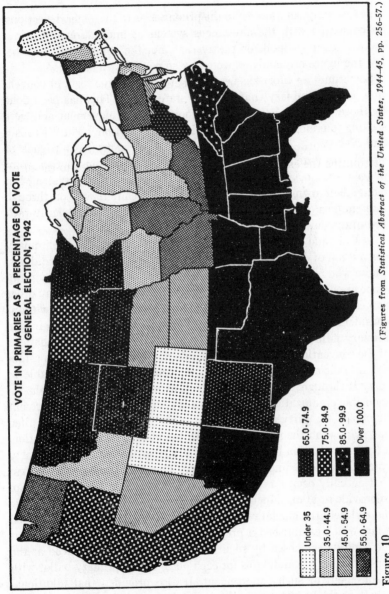

VOTE IN PRIMARIES AS A PERCENTAGE OF VOTE
IN GENERAL ELECTION, 1942

Under 35

35.0 - 44.9

45.0 - 54.9

55.0 - 64.9

65.0 - 74.9

75.0 - 84.9

85.0 - 99.9

Over 100.0

(Figures from *Statistical Abstract of the United States, 1944-45*, pp. 256-57.)

Figure 10

times as many voters came to the primaries as to the general elections. As compared with the old caucus system, it unquestionably brings more votes to the polls on the average, but the number still falls below the figure originally expected by some of its champions.

Sometimes an effort has been made to retain some form of convention or a preliminary conference in state affairs. This has been done by those who were hostile to the whole primary movement and were seeking to undo it in the interest of the organization, as in Wisconsin and New York, but in other cases the move came from friends of strictly regulated primaries on the direct basis. From another point of view the Socialists paid little regard to the primary system, but made their own nomination through their conferences or through referendums of dues-paying members, which were subsequently ratified in the official primary.

In Colorado a law was passed in 1910 providing for a preliminary convention of delegates to consider and recommend party candidates. Those who receive at least 10 per cent of the convention vote for any office are placed upon the regular party primary ballot, but any other names may be put upon the ballot by petition, either with or without consideration by the convention. The action of the party in the primary is final, and may follow or disregard the recommendations of the convention. Governor Hughes made a strenuous effort to establish an official "designation" plan in New York, but was unable to carry it through. The theory of his measure was, briefly, that the responsible organization in charge of the party should meet and present its choice for party office, but that other names also might be filed and printed on the ballot along with the choices of the organization. The final selection of candidates would then be made by the party voters in a succeeding direct primary. This is not unlike the process that actually occurs in many places, but it was sought by this plan to provide legal machinery for it and if possible to bring home a little more closely the official responsibility. In 1932 Massachusetts passed a law which established a preprimary convention and provided that the candidates chosen by such a convention should be placed at the top of the list of candidates for each office on the primary ballot with a statement of such endorsement. It also provided that additional names could be placed on the ballot by petition and other names could be written in at the time of voting. While this law was designed to fix party responsibility, the bitter factionalism of Massachusetts politics of the thirties hardly gave it a fair trial, and it was repealed in 1937.[20]

Official preprimary designation has also been suggested as a desirable amendment of the primary law, with the provision that if there are no opposing nominees there shall be no primary.[21] Selection of party slates of candidates before the primary is now a common practice in many places.[22] But it has not changed the general character of the candidates or the party, as may readily be shown in concrete cases.

In South Dakota the Richards law was adopted after long discussion in 1917. This was an elaborate statute providing in great detail for the calling of a preprimary convention, for the selection or recommendation of candidates, for the conduct of the primary itself, including provision for joint discussion by candidates, for the recall of party officials, and other interesting features. It was an ingenious, detailed, and somewhat complicated system, by far the most elaborate attempt to organize party leadership and popular party control through a statutory system that has yet been proposed or attempted.[23] This law was repealed in 1929 and replaced by one which provided for a "short primary ballot." Under the new law the nominations for only a few key positions are made directly, the rest being left for conventions.[24]

On the whole, there seems to be in state politics a widespread desire to retain some of the features of the party conference, but at the same time a still stronger desire on the part of the 'rank and file to make sure that they possess in the last analysis the right to name the candidates. The reconciliation of these elements has nowhere been

[20] Overacker, "Nominations," *op. cit.*, p. 253.

[21] See *National Municipal Review*, December, 1921.

[22] C. H. Wooddy, *The Chicago Primary of 1926* (Chicago, 1926); C. E. Merriam, *Chicago* (New York, 1929); H. F. Gosnell, *Machine Politics* (Chicago, 1937).

[23] See description by C. A. Berdahl in *Annals of the American Academy of Political and Social Science*, CVI (March, 1923), 158. The Richards law was deprived of some of its novel features by the legislature of 1921, which repealed several provisions, including the one regarding joint debates, but most of the original plan remains.

[24] Overacker, "Direct Primary Legislation in 1928–29," *op. cit.*, p. 371; C. A. Berdahl, "New South Dakota Primary Law Applies Short Ballot Principle," *National Municipal Review*, XIX (April, 1930), 235–238.

worked out in such a form as to command a general acceptance by the various elements in the major parties. There is some discontent with the direct primary, although this is stronger in the East than in the West, and is not pronounced in the South. The organizations would repeal the law, if they had the power, and would not imperil their position thereby; but the mass of the voters are very dubious about returning to the old delegate system with which they were familiar forty years ago and under which they suffered grievous misrepresentation. The difficulties and disappointments of the direct primary system are conceded, but the evils of the old convention system do not present an attractive alternative. The gerrymandering of districts, the logrolling for nomination, the bribery and undue influencing of delegates, the domination by combinations of bosses and special privilege, the helplessness of the average voter under the old convention plan have been for the moment obscured. When comparison is made of the old nominating system with the new, it is unlikely that there will be general acquiescence in a quiet abandonment of the direct primary and return to the old method of indirect and unregulated choice. Modifications and compromises seem more likely.

Fundamental to any satisfactory progress in the development of desirable nominating systems is the short ballot.[25] As long as voters are required to pass upon thirty or forty offices, it will not be possible for them to make intelligent choices. Some of these officers are important and others are unimportant. The combination of the two merely confuses the voter and at the same time increases the power of the machine, which profits by the ability to trade and bargain in the make-up of a slate. To provide for the popular choice of a large number of insignificant officials does not increase but on the contrary diminishes the power of the voter. A long array of elective offices means control by the few rather than by the many. Popular control may better be secured by adjusting the number of offices so that the requirements of the candidates for each position may be carefully scrutinized, and the most discriminating choice be made.

The sound principle is that the people should select all officers concerned with the formulation of public policies but that they need not choose men engaged primarily in the administration of policies. The making of law may be partisan, but the enforcement of it should

[25] Pollock, *op. cit.*

be nonpartisan. The administration may be controlled through the elected representatives of the people, who may supervise and direct them in the way they should go to carry out the public will.

Unless the short ballot is adopted, it is not likely that either the direct primary or the delegate system or any other plan will work with satisfaction to the electorate. The complications and confusions of the long ballot will entangle the voters to the advantage of the machine, which understands its intricacies far better than the individual voter can.[26]

Another fundamental necessity to reaching better nominating systems is a sounder type of political education.[27] A more thorough-going political education, both preparatory and adult, is therefore an indispensable prerequisite to the improvement of the choices made in nominating systems, whether direct or indirect. This cannot, of course, be accomplished by legislative enactment. It necessitates a readjustment of social point of view and training, and in the nature of the case requires a long time for its development. One need not urge any patent process for this purpose, but only emphasize the underlying necessity for the cultivation of a more adequate form of discernment and discrimination which will serve as an antidote to demagoguery and propaganda.

PROBLEMS OF THE PRIMARY

Whether the primaries are to be direct or indirect in nature, there are certain problems which they have in common. Two of the most important of these center around the question of party allegiance tests and the ever-present topic of expense.[28]

What constitutes a Republican or a Democrat? And how shall a

[26] A thoroughgoing, detailed study of the practical operation of the primary system, with constructive suggestions, is urgently needed; but this must obviously be a cooperative undertaking. See Pollock, *op. cit.*; Merriam and Overacker, *Primary Elections*, Chap. XI.

[27] Franklin L. Burdette, *Education for Citizen Responsibilities* (Princeton, 1942); C. E. Merriam, *Civic Education in the United States* (New York, 1934); Merriam and Overacker, *op. cit.*, pp. 287–295. On the limitations of education for this purpose, see Walter Lippmann, *The Phantom Public* (New York, 1925).

[28] Clarence A. Berdahl, "Party Membership in the United States," *American Political Science Review*, XXXVI (February, April, 1942), 16, 241; Merriam and Overacker, *op. cit.*, Chap. VIII.

satisfactory legal test be made? Or shall any test be made? These are questions that are of importance whether the primary is held for the election of delegates alone or for the nomination of candidates. At first the whole question of party tests was left to the party organization to determine and to some extent it still is in the southern states. But it was found that in many instances these tests were arbitrary and unfair, as in New York where only a member of Tammany Hall in good standing (this to be determined by the organization) was eligible for the primaries; or in the South where arbitrary tests aimed at the Negro were and still are imposed.[29] Hence the problem was taken over by the legislatures who undertook to find a basis for party membership. Two systems are in use: the closed primary and the open primary. In the closed primary there is some form of party test; in the open primary there is none. Of the closed primary there are two principal types, the enrollment or registration system, and the challenge system. The registration system provides for an enrollment of party voters, usually at the time of the regular election, and from the lists of registered party voters the primary lists are made up. No one is then eligible to vote in a primary of a party unless he has previously registered with that party. This system is used in New York and in some other states, principally in the eastern section, but not wholly confined to that part of the country.[30] Provision must be made, of course, for supplementary registration, for transfers from one precinct to another and for change of registration from one party to another. The figures show that a good percentage of voters declare their party affiliation and qualify as party voters, but in times of excitement in one party they tend to shift to the point of great interest.

Under the "challenge" system there is no preliminary party enrollment, but the voter may be challenged at the polls when he asks for a party ballot. In that case he must swear that he is a Republican or

[29] See party rules of South Carolina, providing that "Every negro applying for membership in a Democratic Club, or offering to vote in a primary, must produce a written statement of ten reputable white men, who shall swear that they know of their own knowledge that the applicant or voter voted for Gen. Hampton in 1876, and has voted the Democratic ticket continuously since." Sec. 6. A few of these were found in 1930.

[30] See A. N. Holcombe, *State Government* (New York, 1931), p. 214, for figures on enrollment in certain states.

a Democrat, as the case may be; or in some states he must be more specific regarding his intention to support the party candidate or his sympathy with the principles of the party, or his previous support of party candidates. Having voted in the primary of a party, he cannot change within a fixed period, which may be two years. If he votes in a Democratic primary, he cannot vote in a Republican primary until two years have elapsed, or whatever the time may be in the particular state. This system prevails in Illinois and is more common than the registration system.

In the open primary system there is no test of party affiliation either by registration or by challenge. The voter may cast in secret the ballot of any party. This is sometimes called the Wisconsin plan from its early adoption there in 1903. A similar provision in the laws of California and Oregon was declared unconstitutional. However, there are now some eight states which employ one form or another of the open primary system.[31] The slowly growing popularity of this device may in part be the result of the increasing power of organized labor in American politics. The trade union leaders look upon it as a means of lessening the employer pressure on labor to vote in the primary of the party which is held to be more favorable to the employers.

It is urged in behalf of this plan that it gives complete protection to the secrecy of the ballot; that it makes intimidation and undue influence impossible; that the requirement of a partisan test is both unnecessary and useless; and that a test of allegiance excludes only the scrupulous citizen while admitting the dishonest and unscrupulous. It is objected, however, that without some form of party test the responsibility of the party for platforms and candidates is broken down, and that the party system cannot be maintained without some restriction in the way of a party affiliation test.

A perfectly working system would have sufficient flexibility to allow voters to pass from one party to the other as issues change or as individual opinions change, and at the same time would prevent the shifting of machine controlled or other voters to the primaries of another party without any intention of supporting the party. It is clear that none of the systems in use meets exactly all of these requirements, and it is not easy to see just how they may be met. The

[31] Overacker, "Nominations," *op. cit.*, pp. 248–249.

solution will depend not so much upon ingenious systems for squaring this circle, as upon the general tendency of the party system as it develops during the next generation. Party membership is not a fixed quantity.

In the so-called "blanket" primary law of 1935, the state of Washington extended the freedom of the voter in the open primary to a new limit. The primary is so wide open that the voter can express his choice for any party's candidate for any office without a declaration of allegiance to any party. A uniform ballot is given to all voters which has the names of all the various parties' candidates on it grouped under each office. It is possible then for the voter in the same primary to express a choice for the nomination of a Democratic candidate for United States senator and a Republican candidate for governor.[32] Here we have a curious mixture of nonpartisanship and party labels.

The expense of primaries, whether direct or indirect, is a problem of great public interest and importance.[33] Originally the whole burden was laid upon the candidate, who was obliged to pay certain fees or assessments to cover the cost of the party election. But in time it came to be seen that the primary was in reality a public affair rather than a personal contest between ambitious aspirants for office, and the entire expense of the conduct of the primary was thrown upon the government, state or local. This was an important step forward. In some states "publicity pamphlets" are circulated at public expense in the interest of educating the public regarding the candidates. These pamphlets contain a brief statement regarding the record and platform of each candidate, and they are placed in the hands of every voter at a nominal expense to the candidates. In this way, every person entering the primary contest may bring to the voters at a slight expense a minimum statement of his qualifications and his program. It is also possible to allow candidates the use of public buildings, such as schoolhouses, or perhaps to secure other meeting places and permit their use by the candidates. A limited amount of billboard space or radio time may be provided, or other devices employed for

[32] C. O. Johnson, "The Washington Blanket Primary," *Pacific Northwest Quarterly*, January, 1942, pp. 27–39; Louise Overacker, "Direct Primary Legislation in 1934–35," *American Political Science Review*, XXX (1936), 281.
[33] Louise Overacker, *Money in Elections* (New York, 1932).

securing to the candidates a minimum of publicity. Unquestionably the candidate should not be subjected to the necessity of mortgaging his political future in order to obtain a nomination, whether at the hands of the delegate convention or the voters directly.

Underlying the whole question is the democratic financing of campaigns which is a prerequisite to the solution of the problem. If there is a reasonably large group of persons interested in a particular candidacy, there should be no difficulty in providing an adequate fund for the advancement of the cause. If there is no such general interest, the chance of a successful candidacy is very small, and little is lost by its failure to start.

The party, after all, is in sharp competition with many other social groups, and cannot hope to survive them without careful consideration of their methods and results in the competitive field. What steps are the parties taking in this direction? [34]

It is evident that the delegate convention presents many serious problems of organization, action, and temper. The convention is designed partly for deliberation and partly for demonstration, and alternates between these moods and tensions. At one moment it is seriously considering the merits of complicated questions of tariff, or currency, or finance, or corporate regulation; in the next moment it is a tumultuous sea of emotional demonstration in behalf of some symbolic hero or tradition. Now it is a personnel-selecting agency, passing upon the qualifications of a governor or a president, and in the next moment an Indian war dance; returning hoarsely, however, to its sober choice of an executive manager and leader. Now it is dominated by its lungs; now by its brains; now they are in conflict. No one knows when it will become a parliament and when it will become a mob.

Under these unique conditions the task of the convention requires the most thoughtful consideration if its merits are to be developed and its weaknesses avoided. It is believed that the following suggestions will help to operate the convention plan more successfully, if and when it is desired to continue it in operation. An equitable basis of convention representation, an orderly and direct choice of delegates, a mechanism for dealing with contests, a minute regulation of

[34] Material on the convention quoted from Merriam and Overacker, *op. cit.*, pp. 331 ff.

convention procedure, more adequate systems of platform-making—all these might be useful in preserving the values of the convention plan where it is desired. More than that, however, the level of the convention must be raised through thoughtful consideration of its significance in the party life and in the political order of which it is a part. Only as the temper of the convention is lifted above chicanery and spoils and as its results reflect a different spirit can it hope to gain the confidence and respect of the political community.

Many of the purposes of the convention would be better served by a smaller body than now ordinarily assembles. If it is desired to foster acquaintanceship among the party members, the number is now far too large; and this particular function of the body is largely, although not wholly, submerged in the crowds that go milling about. A group of 2000 or even 1000 is altogether too large for purposes of friendly encounter between various sections of the state, especially if the session lasts for a few hours only. Likewise, a body of such a size is not well adapted to the exercise of the function of deliberation, if it is hoped to revive this aspect of the convention's work. Bodies one-half or one-fourth the present size would be far more effective in carrying out the theoretical purposes of the convention, upon which emphasis is so often placed. They would increase very greatly the possibility of friendly intercourse among the party representatives, and make serious consideration of significant party problems more probable. The smaller size would tend to make the convention less an instrument of demonstration and more an agency of deliberation.

After all, a living and growing convention system must be genuinely representative of the party and of the community in another and broader sense. The convention began to go down when its personnel fell into the hands of spoilsmen, who put forward their own interests and those of their privilege-seeking clients. Their failure to represent the spirit and temper of the party begot a lack of party confidence and a lack of public confidence in the delegate convention process which endures down to this day. The difficulties of the direct primary have tended to distract attention from the abuses of the convention plan; but they are real and important, and they must be met if it is hoped to restore the convention plan to a position of public esteem.

PROBLEMS OF THE DIRECT PRIMARY

The direct primary has certain special problems of its own. The style of the ballot is not uniform in the different primary systems. In some states the names are arranged alphabetically; in others in the order in which nominating petitions are filed; and in still others the names are rotated in such a way as to place each name first an equal number of times. There is a distinct advantage in position on the ballot, both first and last place being desirable, as against the middle position.[35] This is especially true where there is a large field of candidates. In many cases, however, the assignment of place upon the ballot is purely arbitrary and hence a matter of favor on the part of the officials in charge of this particular branch of the election machinery. The alphabetical order gives an advantage to the candidates whose name begins with A, and hence this order meets with objections. Arrangement in accordance with the order of filing or of receipt by mail is wholly unworkable and is the least desirable of all the systems in use. It has been found possible to rotate the names on the ballot in such a way as to give each candidate first place an equal number of times with every other candidate; and while this system is somewhat cumbrous it is now coming into general use.

The method of framing the platform under the direct primary is frequently a topic of discussion, and various methods have been devised to meet the situation. The various plans are as follows:

Adoption by a convention following the primary
Passage by a joint convention and party council
Adoption by a party council made up of candidates for state office and legislative candidates and hold-over legislators or other officials (Wisconsin)
Making of a platform by the winning candidate or a conference of the supporters of the winning candidate [36]

The usual method is to adopt a state platform through a state convention meeting after the primary has been held, and in practice the

[35] Pollock, *op. cit.;* Schumaker, *op. cit.*, estimated that the first position on the ballot before provision was made for rotation gave the favored candidate an advantage of about 15 per cent in Wisconsin.

[36] See above, p. 76. See also Merriam and Overacker, *op. cit.*, pp. 85 ff.

platform adopted will be that of the successful candidate. If the candidate's views are not those of the convention, they can with difficulty repudiate their standard bearer, for he has already been named by the voters of the party, although perhaps by a minority vote. But as a matter of fact, if serious differences of opinion develop in a primary contest, there are likely to be only two factions, and the vote will indicate which of them is in the majority. It must be borne in mind that in many state contests there is no definite demarcation of issues and no alignment upon which they take a definite stand.[37]

In case definite machinery is desired, the party council plan possesses much merit. The party program is made under this system by those who, if elected, are to carry it out; and the majority might be held to bind the minority. But even here the platform is made after the candidates are selected, and in the case of a recalcitrant candidate there is no way of securing acquiescence in the party declaration either before or after the election except by his defeat. The same difficulty would be present under the convention system.

At the outset there was much discussion regarding the percentage of the total party vote necessary for a nomination, but in general the present tendency is to rest with a plurality vote. In the southern states, however, a majority is often required, and in case no nomination is made on the first trial a second or "runoff" primary is held in which the two highest candidates compete. Here, however, the primary is really the election, and the primary choices are practically final. Minimum percentages have been tried in a number of states, and the system is still found in Iowa where there is no nomination unless the highest candidate receives 35 per cent of the party vote in the primary. In that event nominations are made by the party convention. Yet most of these arrangements have been abandoned and there are only a few survivals. Experience shows that where there is a sharp division upon a question of principle, the number of candidates will be small and the contest is likely to resolve itself into a struggle between two of them. But if the battle is a personal contest between individuals with no particular principles at issue, there is no

---

[37] The Oregon law allows the candidate twelve words to state any measure or principle he especially advocates, and this brief platform may be printed upon the ballot.

great harm done by allowing the one receiving the highest vote to take the nomination.

In some places experiments have been made with the preferential voting system, as in Wisconsin, North Dakota, Idaho, and other states.[38] Difficulty has been found in persuading the voters to make use of the preferential vote, and not all the predictions of the promoters of the new plan have been realized. Many of the systems used were defective since a voter might injure his first choice by expressing second and other choices. Preferential voting has been abandoned, but the alternative vote, an application of the Hare rules to majority elections, might have possibilities. The alternative vote system would eliminate the necessity for a runoff primary and would thus effect considerable savings.

LEGAL REGULATION

In the process of legal regulation of the political party, some judicial obstacles have been encountered, but on the whole the courts have been friendly to the primary laws enacted by the legislatures.[39]

Registration laws and the Australian ballot laws had settled certain broad principles regarding the right of the state to regulate elections and thus the way was paved to primary regulation. No particular property rights were involved, the pressure of public opinion was strong and steady, the judges have been intimately conversant with the facts and the philosophy of the party system; and hence relatively little difficulty has been found in sustaining the primary laws.

At first it seemed as if the judiciary might take an adverse position. In Michigan the courts held that a law requiring registration commissioners to be selected from the two leading parties was unconstitutional because parties "cannot be recognized as having any legal authority as such." [40] Vigorous attacks were made upon the principle of legislative regulation of party affairs. Such legislation, it was said, would "stretch the arm of the criminal law to an unwarranted extent

[38] O. Douglas Weeks, "Summary of the History and Present Status of Preferential Voting in State Primary Systems," *Southwestern Social Science Quarterly,* XVIII (1937–1938), 64–67; A. N. Holcombe, "Direct Primaries and the Secret Ballot," *American Political Science Review,* V, 535.

[39] See Merriam and Overacker, *op. cit.,* Chap. VI.

[40] *Attorney General* v. *Detroit Common Council,* 58 Mich. 311 (1885).

over the citizen, in derogation of the constitutional right of citizens to assemble together for their common good; for what is a convention or primary meeting but such an assemblage?" [41] It was contended that the parties have a natural right to carry on their internal affairs, and that the state could not interfere except to prevent fraud, intimidation, corruption, or other crimes.

But this view of primary legislation did not prevail, and in general the laws were sustained when contested. Primaries, said the judges, are matters of public interest, not merely the private affairs of individuals.

"Primary elections and nominating conventions have now become a part of our great political system, and are welded and riveted into it so firmly as to be difficult of separation. . . . In the conduct of the primaries there have arisen evils of the very gravest character, which are patent to every observer. These evils more than anything else have weakened our whole system of government. To say that the legislature may not lay its hand upon a public evil of such vast proportions is to say that our government is too weak to preserve its life." [42] Such was the decided stand of the judiciary.

The right of the legislature to regulate the test of party allegiance has generally been upheld. In 1905 the Nebraska Supreme Court in upholding a party test provision declared that "an indiscriminate right to vote at a primary would tend in many instances to thwart the purposes of the organization and destroy it." [43] In Oregon it was concluded that the closed primary system was not a denial of any constitutional privilege and it did not interfere with the freedom of elections.[44] On the other hand, the state legislatures cannot provide for tests of party allegiance which discriminate against particular races. The United States Supreme Court decided in the case of *Nixon* v. *Herndon* [45] that the Texas "white primary" law which aimed to exclude Negroes from the Democratic primary elections in Texas was unconstitutional because it violated the Fourteenth Amendment.

---

[41] *Leonard* v. *Commonwealth*, 112 Pa. State, 607. See dissenting opinion in *People* v. *Democratic Committee*, 164 N. Y., 335 (1900); also *State* v. *Michel*, 46 So. Rep., 430.

[42] *Leonard* v. *Commonwealth*, 112 Pa. State, 607.

[43] *State* v. *Drexel*, 105 N. W. Rep., 174 (1905).

[44] *Ladd* v. *Holmes*, 66 Pac. Rep., 714 (1901).

[45] *Nixon* v. *Herndon et al.*, 47 Sup. Ct. Rep., 446 (1927).

The state then gave power to the party state committee to determine the qualifications for party membership. Acting under the statute the state committee barred Negroes from party membership, and in the case of *Nixon* v. *Condon* the United States Supreme Court declared this act unconstitutional on the ground that the state could not delegate a power which was unconstitutional.[46] The legislature then repealed the law regarding party membership and the Democratic state convention passed a resolution limiting membership to white citizens. In the case of *Grovey* v. *Townsend* the Supreme Court refused to interfere with the action of the party convention on the ground that it was the action of the party and not the state.[47] But the Supreme Court in the *Classic* case of 1941 upset the belief that the federal government had no power to regulate primaries held under state authority.[48] It held that: "Where the state law has made the primary an integral part of the procedure of choice, or where in fact the primary effectively controls the choice, the right of the elector to have his ballot counted at the primary is . . . included in the right protected by" the constitutional provisions regarding the election of the House of Representatives.

In 1944 the Supreme Court overruled the *Grovey* v. *Townsend* case in the case of *Smith* v. *Allwright*.[49] It held that the primary in Texas was an integral part of the machinery for selecting officials. The Court found that discrimination against Negroes in the primary was prohibited by the Fifteenth Amendment even though the party convention acted on its own authority. Following this decision the South Carolina legislature repealed all the acts relating to the conduct of primaries and left nominations completely to the party authorities.

On the whole, the courts have sustained the constitutionality of primary legislation of the last forty years with few exceptions. In California and in Illinois [50] considerable difficulty has been experi-

[46] *Nixon* v. *Condon*, 286 U. S. 73 (1932).

[47] *Grovey* v. *Townsend*, 295 U. S. 45 (1935).

[48] *United States* v. *Classic*, 61 Sup. Ct. 1031 (1941).

[49] *Smith* v. *Allwright*, 321 U. S. 649 (1944). See R. E. Cushman, "The Texas 'White Primary' Case—*Smith* v. *Allwright*," *Cornell Law Quarterly*, XXX (1944–1945), pp. 66–67.

[50] In Illinois seven primary laws have been declared unconstitutional, in the following cases: *People* v. *Board of Election Commissioners of the City of Chicago*, 221 Illinois, 9 (1906); *Rouse* v. *Thompson*, 228 Illinois, 522 (1907); *People* v

enced in securing the passage of a law that would meet the approval of the courts, but elsewhere the judicial veto has been very sparingly exercised. In no field of legislation has the judiciary shown itself more friendly to experiment than in the regulation of political organizations. The law of registration, the Australian ballot system, the legal regulation of the primary have all been treated with the greatest consideration. There has been unusually little of the "law's delay" to hinder the advance of primary legislation. If primary laws are not perfect, the courts cannot be blamed.

The objection of "special legislation," of unfair discrimination between political parties, of interference with the freedom and equality of elections, and of unwarranted invasion of the rights of political parties as voluntary associations have all been met and overruled. The theory of the party as a voluntary association has been completely overthrown by the contrary doctrine that the party is in reality a governmental agency, subject to legal regulation and control. The element of public concern in the making of nominations has been strongly emphasized, and the right of the legislature to make reasonable regulations to protect and preserve the purity and honesty of elections has been vigorously asserted. The police power has been invoked against the unregulated party. The absence of any constitutional prohibition or regulation has been advanced in behalf of the law-making body of the state and made a part of the general argument in behalf of laws attacked. And finally the privileged position of the party upon the ballot, under the official ballot system, has been used as a means of justifying all manner or restraints and regulations in return. As Justice Holmes said, "the legislature has a right to attach reasonable conditions to that advantage, if it has a right to grant the advantage." [51]

Strassheim, 240 Illinois, 279 (1909); *People* v. *Deneen*, 247 Illinois, 279; *People* v. *Fox*, 294 Illinois, 263 (1920); *McAlpine* v. *Dimick*, 157 N. E. Rep., 235 (1927); *Kreeger* v. *Sweitzer*, Circuit Court of Cook County, B-153251, reversed in *People* v. *Kramer*, 328 Illinois, 512 (1928). See G. A. McCleary, "The Constitutionality of Primary Legislation in Illinois," *Illinois Law Review*, XXIII, 265–275 (1928).

The California cases are: *Marsh* v. *Hanley*, 43 Pac., 975; *Spier* v. *Baker*, 52 Pac., 659; and *Britton* v. *Board of Election Commissioners*, 61 Pac., 1115. After three acts were declared unconstitutional, a constitutional amendment was adopted.

[51] *Commonwealth* v. *Rogers*, 63 N. E. Rep., 421 (1902).

NONPARTISAN PRIMARIES

In urban affairs the nominating tendencies have been somewhat different from those developed either in the state or in the national field. In many cities, especially in the smaller ones, national party lines have long been disregarded, usually by common consent. "Citizens" or "taxpayers" or other informal groupings have presented candidates without much regard to the national parties. In the larger cities where elections were held on a national party basis, various efforts were made to regulate the election of delegates and in some instances the direct primary was introduced, although the advocates of the direct system had always pointed out the difficulty of applying the direct primary to the urban situation. Most cities, however, have not attempted to regulate the party process, as such, in the local elections, but have endeavored to provide for some form of so-called "nonpartisan" elections. In such cases the party form of ballot has been abolished by law, together with the party emblem, circle, column, and designation. Nominations are then made by petition only, without any party designation whatever, and the election goes to the candidate receiving the highest number of votes, whether this constitutes a majority or not.[52] In some cases the preferential vote has been provided.

The form of minority representation which has gained the widest recognition in this country is the single, transferable vote, or the Hare system of proportional representation.[53] This system is used in multimembered districts and the voters are given the opportunity to mark their first, second, and other choices. The first step in the count-

[52] See W. B. Munro, *Government of American Cities* (New York, 1929), Chaps. VI and VII; and discussion of political parties in city government in *National Municipal Review*, VI (1917), 201. See also T. H. Reed, *Municipal Government in the United States* (*New York*, 1926), pp. 244–259; W. P. Lovett, *Detroit Rules Itself* (Boston, 1930) and *Municipal Year Book, passim.*

[53] Ashtabula, Ohio, which first adopted the system in 1915, used it for eight elections and repealed it in 1927; Boulder, Colo., (1917, repealed 1947); Kalamazoo, Mich. (1918, two elections); Sacramento, Calif. (1920, one election); West Hartford, Conn. (1921, one election); Cleveland, Ohio (1921, five elections, repealed 1931); Cincinnati (1924); Hamilton, Ohio (1926); Toledo, Ohio (1934); Wheeling, West Va. (1935); New York City (1936, repealed 1947); Yonkers, New York (1939); Cambridge, Mass. (1940); Lowell, Mass. (1943); Marshfield, Ore. (1944); Long Beach, New York (1945, repealed 1947); Worcester, Saugus, Medford, Quincy, and Revere, Mass. (1947); Hopkins, Minn. (1947); and Coos Bay, Ore. (1946).

ing process is the determination of the quota. The total number of valid ballots is divided by the number of candidates to be elected, plus one, and the quotient is completed to the next round number. In New York City where the system was in operation from 1937 to 1947, the fixed quota plan was employed, with the quota fixed at 75,000 votes. The campaign for repeal emphasized the antiminority, particularly the anticommunist sentiment in the United States. Under the Hare plan, all candidates whose first choice ballots equal or exceed the quota are at once declared elected. The surplus ballots of those candidates who had more than the quota are then transferred according to the next available choices marked on them. After all the surplus ballots are transferred, the candidate with the fewest ballots is defeated and his ballots are transferred accordingly to the choices marked on them. This process continues until the proper number of candidates have been elected.[54] While the first choices give a general idea of how the election is going to come out, the transfers sometimes bring about important changes. In Cincinnati the counting of the ballots usually take a week, but in some of the boroughs of New York it took more than a month. The city of New York considered the use of tabulating machines to speed up the count before it abandoned the plan.

The chief criticisms of the proportional representation system are that the system is complicated and results in the spoiling of many ballots; that large numbers of the voters do not avail themselves of the privilege of using the second and other choices; that no substantial improvement is obtained over the earlier and more common systems; that the plan promotes racial and religious blocs; that it helps extremists; and that it makes it hard to secure a majority and fix responsibility. In the campaign against it in New York City, particularly potent was the argument that under the plan two Communists were elected to the council.

On the other hand its advocates contend that it gives the voter wider command over the political situation than does the straight

[54] See G. H. Hallett and C. G. Hoag, *Proportional Representation* (Washington, D. C., 1937) ; C. G. Hoag and G. H. Hallett, *Proportional Representation* (New York, 1926) ; F. A. Hermens, "The Trojan Horse of Democracy," *Social Research,* V (November, 1938), 379–423; G. H. Hallett, "Is Proportional Representation a Trojan Horse?" *Social Research,* VI (September, 1939), 415–419; H. F. Gosnell, *Democracy: The Threshold of Freedom* (New York, 1948).

and inflexible vote; that it gives a more genuine representation of the community than is otherwise possible; that it does away with the rotten borough and the gerrymander; that it avoids the expense and trouble of a primary; that it permits and encourages the representation of live interests and groups instead of outgrown sections or units which in urban communities have no real existence for political purposes. It is maintained that a body chosen under the proportional system presents a more real and genuine picture of the community than is obtained under the ward plan.[55]

A large number of cities, however, have adopted the "nonpartisan" primary system. This is in effect a double election system, with the party ballot eliminated and the national party spirit discouraged or subdued. As a rule candidates receiving a majority of all the votes cast are held to be elected, and if none receives such a majority a second ballot is held in which the two highest candidates contest. In cities adopting the council-manager form of government during the last ten years, this has been a very common device. It will, of course, in many instances obviate the necessity of holding a new election.[56] In 1920 this plan was adopted in Chicago for aldermen, but not for the mayoralty.[57]

In other instances the nonpartisan ballot has been applied to the choice of school officials where elective, to the selection of judges, to the election of county officers in California and a few other states, and to the election of the state legislators in Minnesota and Nebraska. In the last-mentioned state no party designations are given on the ballot and the names of all candidates for the unicameral legislature are rotated. The names of the two highest are then placed on the final election ballot.[58]

[55] See J. P. Harris, "The Practical Workings of Proportional Representation in the United States and Canada," *National Municipal Review,* XIX (May, 1930); H. F. Gosnell, "Proportional Representation," in *Encyclopaedia of the Social Sciences,* and "Proportional Representation: Its Operation in Cincinnati," *Public Affairs,* II (March, 1939), 133–135, and "Motives for Voting as Shown by the Cincinnati P. R. Election of 1929," *National Municipal Review,* XIX (July, 1930), 471–476.

[56] For a list of the council-manager cities, see *Public Management, passim,* and *Municipal Year Book.*

[57] On the operation of the nonpartisan system, see Merriam and Overacker, *op. cit.,* p. 91.

[58] Overacker, "Direct Primary Legislation in 1934–35," *op. cit.*

Some of the larger cities, such as New York, Chicago, and Philadelphia, still retain the national party primary for mayoralty elections.[59] But it is difficult to maintain anything like a solid party front, and in practice this is not done. A study of recent mayoralty elections in Chicago shows that the party lines have usually been almost completely shattered.[60] On the other hand, mere adoption of the "nonpartisan" ballot does not automatically eliminate the national parties, and in a number of cases party nominations are still made, as in Boston.[61] Of course, the party label cannot be used in these cases, but the campaign may be conducted as a party campaign to all intents and purposes. The mere shift in the form of the ballot alone will not change the whole situation. It will take away a psychological advantage in favor of party voting, but there must be other tendencies at work in order to offset the aggressive tendencies of the party organizations. Actually the local groupings do not follow national lines, but the national party organizations tend to override the local differences in the interest of national party advantage. Under a spoils system the groups of men who profit by municipal misrule will endeavor to maintain themselves in power under the protection of some national party flag where this is possible. If they can capture both party organizations and nominations, they are reasonably secure. But even under the nonpartisan system they will still remain in existence, and will be active in the pursuit of their interests, combining and campaigning for that purpose. If the public interest and sentiment that secure the nonpartisan law continue to be effective, the efforts of the partisan groups will not accomplish much; but if the public interest flags, as it often does, the partisan groupings will re-enter and reclaim the field from which they have been driven.

The elaborate nominating methods used in American state and local elections give the citizens an opportunity to repudiate the party . . . but to use this opportunity the citizens must themselves organize effective forces of opposition. They must develop leaders of their own.

[59] In New York, however, the parties may fuse under the law, and one candidate may receive a number of nominations and appear in various columns on the ballot.

[60] Gosnell, *Machine Politics*, p. 173, shows that the relationship between the vote for Cermak, Democratic candidate for mayor in 1931, and the Democratic vote for President in 1932 was very low. In 1947, many Republicans voted for Kennelly.

[61] See discussion reported in *National Municipal Review*, VI, 201–237.

CHAPTER XV

PRESIDENTIAL NOMINATIONS

"The delegates even showed signs of being ashamed of their own immoderate antics. They wondered whether the way to run a great political party is to get drunk and ride donkeys into hotel lobbies."—Herbert Agar, *Pursuit of Happinesss* (Cambridge, Houghton Mifflin Co., 1938), p. 132.

BY FAR THE MOST IMPORTANT NOMINATION MADE BY THE PARTIES IS that of the presidential candidates.[1] The quadrennial nomination of the party leader who may also become the national leader, and may even pass over into the ranks of world leaders, is a political event of prime significance. It arouses the intense interest of leaders, managers, bosses, and deeply stirs the public opinion of the nation. It brings to the surface both the best and the worst qualities of democracy in general, and of our own particular system of nomination and election.

Presidential nominations have been made in three ways: (1) by the congressional caucus; (2) by the national delegate convention; and (3) by the combination of delegate convention and direct primary. At the outset candidates for the presidency were named by a congressional caucus, consisting of all the numbers of each party in the House and Senate.[2] However, only one caucus was held by the Federalists, namely, that of 1800. From 1796 to 1824 (with the ex-

---

[1] See James Farley, *Behind the Ballots* (New York, 1938); John Kieran, ed., *The New Information Please Almanac 1948* (New York, 1948); Louise Overacker, *The Presidential Primary* (New York, 1926), and "Nominations," in E. B. Logan (ed.), *The American Political Scene* (New York, 1938); E. M. Sait, *American Parties and Elections* (New York, 1939), Chaps. IX, XVII, XVIII; R. C. Brooks, *Political Parties and Electoral Problems* (New York, 1933), Chap. XI; M. Ostrogorski, *Democracy and the Organization of Political Parties* (New York, 1902), Vol. II; James Bryce, *The American Commonwealth* (New York, 1921); and J. A. Woodburn, *Political Parties and Party Problems in the United States* (New York, 1924).

[2] See P. D. Hasbrouck, "Caucus," *Encyclopaedia of the Social Sciences*, III (December, 1930), 277-279; M. Ostrogorski, "The Rise and Fall of the Nominating Caucus," *American Historical Review*, V, 253.

ception of 1820) the Republican caucus was held every four years. This was at first a secret caucus but later was thrown open. Madison and Monroe were both named in this way.[3] From the beginning objection was made to the congressional caucus; by 1824 it was sadly weakened; and in 1828 Jackson was ready to make an issue of the overthrow of King Caucus.[4] Increasing ease of transportation and communication, the fact that there was only one party after the disintegration of the Federalists, the antagonism of the western Democracy to an institution which they regarded as a relic of aristocracy— all combined to effect the downfall of the caucus as a nominating agency. The intention of the framers of the Constitution clearly was that the president of the republic should not be named by Congress, yet in the first generation of our history the presidential candidates were named by the parties in Congress, and two Presidents—Jefferson in 1800, and Adams in 1824—were actually elected by the House of Representatives. This led to the common belief that the congressional caucus was helping to do indirectly what the Constitution had intended to forbid. When after a long period of struggle Crawford finally obtained the caucus nomination in 1824, he therefore found it to be a hindrance to his campaign instead of a help. As the caucus nominee he received only 41 electoral votes in a total of 261.

In the interval between the old caucus system and the new, convention nominations were made in a variety of ways. Sometimes this was done by a huge mass meeting; sometimes by a joint resolution of the state legislature; sometimes by a legislative caucus of a party.

In 1831 the ephemeral Anti-Masonic party held a national delegate convention at Baltimore.[5] This was made up of 112 delegates from 13 states, nominating a candidate for President and adopting an extremely long platform.[6] In the same year a Whig convention was held, although no platform was adopted. The Democratic party also held a national convention in 1832 to nominate a candidate for vice-

---

[3] Monroe received the caucus nomination by a vote of 65 to 54 for Crawford, but there was no contest made in spite of the narrow margin of victory.

[4] See debates in United States Senate, March 18, 1824, *Annals of Congress,* 18th Congress, 1st Session, I, 354 ff., for vigorous attacks on the system.

[5] See account of the Federalist Conference of 1812, by some classed as the first convention, in *American Historical Review,* I, 680.

[6] See *Niles Register,* XLI, 83, 166, for description of meeting and for platform.

president as a running mate for Andrew Jackson in his campaign for re-election. In 1836 the Whigs held no convention, but in 1840 both of the major parties held delegate conventions and since then this has been the regular practice of all parties.[7]

At first there was great irregularity and laxity as to the delegate representation. In 1835, for example, there were some 600 delegates in the Democratic convention, of whom about 200 were from Maryland and over 100 from Virginia.[8]

Soon, however, a definite basis of one vote for each electoral vote was adopted in both parties, although sometimes double the number of delegates were sent. After the Civil War the number of votes per state was changed to twice the number of electoral votes. Territories have been admitted with some variations as to the vote allowed.

This system, which makes population rather than party strength the basis of representation, has been subjected to severe criticism, especially in the Republican party. The lack of an organized party in the South and the large number of delegates sent by a relatively small number of voters from states certain to return a Democratic electoral vote, together with the frequent contests and charges and countercharges of fraud and corruption in the choice of delegates, caused discontent with the system and created a demand for a reorganization of the basis of representation.[9]

In 1912 southern states which in 1908 had cast 50,000 Republican votes (and in the election no electoral votes) were represented by 88 delegates or one for each 600 voters, while other states such as Ohio, Illinois, and Indiana were represented by one delegate for 10,000 to 15,000 voters. When the party was in power, the patronage was used to influence the selection of delegates, and when out of power there were great temptations to employ undue influence in a situation where there was only the semblance of a regular organization.

Since the ill fated 1912 convention, the Republicans have gradually changed the basis for apportioning delegates. In 1916,[10] they provided

---

[7] The Whigs had no platform on this occasion, other than that supplied by the slogan "Tippecanoe and Tyler too."

[8] See *Niles Register*, XLVIII, 226.

[9] See *Proceedings*, Convention of 1900, pp. 95–97.

[10] *Proceedings*, p. 9.

for four delegates at large for each state, one delegate for each congressman at large, one for each congressional district, and one additional for every district polling more than 7500 Republican votes in the last election. The effect of this rule was to reduce the southern representation from 33 per cent to 16 per cent of the whole. In 1921 they gave one delegate to districts casting 2500 votes for Republican electors, and two if 10,000 were cast, again somewhat reducing the representation of certain southern states. The 1923 rule provided for one district delegate from each congressional district, one additional district delegate from each congressional district casting 10,000 votes or more for any Republican candidate in the last election, and three additional delegates at large from each state casting its electoral vote for the Republican nominee in the last preceding presidential election. In 1940 the rule was again changed so as to reduce the southern vote. A district must have a Republican vote of 1,000 or more before it is entitled to any delegate.

CHOICE OF DELEGATES

Delegates are chosen by congressional conventions, or by state conventions, as in the case of delegates at large, or by the voters in party primaries. In some cases the delegates are nominally selected by the state convention, although actually recommended by the district convention. Since 1892 the rules of the Republican party have required choice of district delegates by districts, but there was no uniform rule governing this point in the Democratic party until 1912 when the right of the district to choose a delegate in the direct primary was officially recognized.

Contested cases are decided by the national convention after preliminary hearings first before the national committee and again before the convention's committee on credentials.[11] In the Republican party many of these contests originate in the southern states, where the irregular character of the organization makes regularity a difficult matter to decide in some cases. In 1912 the seating of a block of delegates whose seats were contested determined the control of the con-

---

[11] See Republican convention *Proceedings* of 1892, 1908 and 1912, and Democratic conventions of 1896 and 1904, for abundant illustration of the type of contests arising in each party

vention by the Taft forces and prevented the nomination of Roosevelt. In 1936, 57 seats in the Republican convention were contested, most of them being Negro v. white delegates from the states of the Solid South. In accordance with the "lily white" policy of the party in recent years the latter were seated in every case. Unfortunately these contests are not always decided according to the standards of impartial justice but by the strategy of rival factions struggling for control. In many instances where no general principle or factional advantage is involved, the contesting delegations are both seated and the voting power divided between them.[12]

CONVENTION ORGANIZATION

The temporary officers of the convention are recommended by the national committee, and their suggestions are usually adopted by the convention. This does not always follow, however, as the committee slate is sometimes rejected. This was true in the Republican convention of 1884 when the committee recommendation was rejected by a combination of the anti-Blaine forces. Again in 1896 the committee of the Democratic party recommended a "gold" man for temporary chairman, but the delegates substituted a "silver" man. In 1912 the choice of the candidate turned on the selection of the temporary chairman and the struggle at this point was the central feature of the convention. The dramatic contest a few weeks later in the Democratic convention at Baltimore was fraught with significant consequences in the choice of a candidate. The refusal of the Clark forces to back Mr. Bryan's policy in the selection of chairman resulted eventually in the nomination of Wilson.

Committees are appointed on credentials, permanent organization, rules, and resolutions. The delegation from each state and territory is represented by one member on each of the first three committees and in the case of the resolutions committee by one man and one woman. Of these committees the most significant are those on credentials and on resolutions. In the latter the struggle over the platform

[12] The decision of the convention as to the regularity of contesting state delegations is not binding upon the state. See *State* v. *Houser*, 122 Wisc. 534, where the La Follette convention in the state, although held irregular by the national convention, was subsequently held regular by the state Supreme Court.

is carried on. Hasty hearings of various interests are given before this committee, and a draft of a platform finally appears. Before this committee in rapid succession may come the representatives of business, of labor, of agriculture, of women, of professions, of the wets and the drys, of all the various shades of organized interest affected by the platform declarations.

PROCEDURE

The procedure of the two parties is similar in nature, but there are important exceptions to this general statement. The Democratic party uses the "unit rule" in voting under certain circumstances. The whole vote of the state may be cast by the majority of the delegates from the state as a unit, where so instructed by the state convention.[13]

This rule was adopted by the Whigs but was not employed by the Republicans, although attempted at times. The most notable case was the attempt of the Grant delegates in 1880 to establish the unit rule, which would have effected the nomination of Grant in that instance.[14] The rule was used by the Democracy from the first, although opposition developed from time to time. In its bitter fight against Cleveland, Tammany opposed the rule in 1884, as they were bound under the regulation to vote for their opponent. Their effort was defeated, however, by a vote of 332 to 463. With the advent of the direct primary a grave question was raised as to delegates instructed by their districts to vote for a particular candidate. Could a delegate so instructed be bound by the majority of the state delegation to vote against his instructions? To meet this situation the unit rule was so modified [15] as to read that the convention would enforce "a unit rule enacted by a state convention except in such states as have by mandatory statute provided for the nomination and election of delegates and alternates to national political conventions in congressional districts, and have not subjected delegates so selected to the authority of the state committee or convention of the party, in which case no such rule shall be held to apply." On the other hand, in a case like that of California where delegates are instructed by the vote of the

[13] See Carl S. Becker, "The Unit Rule in National Nominating Conventions," *American Historical Review*, V, 64.
[14] See *Proceedings* of 1880, p. 420.
[15] *Proceedings*, 1912, p. 76.

entire state, Republican delegates are in one sense voted as a unit in the convention.

The Democratic party until 1936 required a two-thirds vote for the nomination of candidates. This was construed as meaning two-thirds of the delegates voting. This rule was attacked in 1833, but was then sustained (231 to 210) and held until 1936. In the national convention of that year the Roosevelt forces were strong enough to put through the repeal of this rule. They had tried to do this in 1932 but met with great opposition. The decision of the rules committee to increase southern representation in the convention helped to override southern opposition to the change.[16] During the period that it operated, the rule defeated a majority candidate on only two occasions, Van Buren in 1844 and Clark in 1912. However, it gave one-third of the delegates a veto in advance of the naming of any candidate and it increased the power of minority blocs.

The actual organization of the conventions is more complicated than appears on its face. Its elements include:

The inner circle of leaders, including delegates and magnates
The delegates
The galleries
Party and public opinion

Nominally and technically, control rests absolutely with the 1000 convention delegates,[17] who hold the sovereignty of the party in their hands. Whatever they may do is the supreme law of the party. They are, in a partisan sense, omnipotent. But they are grouped in series or blocks which are led by a relatively few men. There are leaders of leaders and bosses of bosses, finally reducing the actual direction of the convention to a small number of men, although this does not mean that they may be absolutely arbitrary in their conduct. Within limits their writs of authority run; beyond those come murmurings and revolt. If these leaders and bosses, not all of whom need be members of the convention, agree upon a line of policy, it is likely to be carried through. Conflicts come when they do not agree, and declare war upon each other.

[16] Everett S. Brown, "Presidential Campaign and Election," *American Year Book*, 1936.

[17] In the 1948 Republican national convention the number was 1094 and the Democratic 1234.

An analysis of the factors of control shows the following elements as the principal centers of power: the administration (of the party in power), the congressional group, the bosses, the leaders. If the party is in power, the president, his cabinet, and his appointees will be in a commanding position. This will be particularly true of the Republican president, who will have the southern delegates almost solidly, largely for reasons of patronage. The administration will also carry with it a certain part of the senatorial and congressional group, always strongly represented in conventions. When the party is out of power the senatorial group may take the leading position, or at any rate an important position in determining the lines of action. The bosses (some of whom may be senators) will control considerable blocks of votes and will figure largely in the proceedings. In many cases their chief interest will be local rather than national in scope. They are powerful factors in the party organization of large and perhaps doubtful states, and they may also be allied with special industrial interests, not to be ignored. The groups of unofficial leaders are also of great and sometimes of chief significance. Here we may find important figures of the type of Bryan, the Roosevelts, Taft, Hoover, or leading journalists from Horace Greeley to William Randolph Hearst and Col. Robert R. McCormick. These leaders are to be consulted, even if their suggestions are not to be followed. Either Bryan or Franklin D. Roosevelt, single-handed, was a host in himself with a following not to be despised. Prominent candidates with a large and compact following also become influential in the course of a prolonged struggle for power. Within limits they may determine the course to be taken by their delegates. The centers of actual authority are usually the administration in the case of the party in power, and a group made up of the organization and the leaders in the party out of power.

The galleries or the spectators, now greatly multiplied by television, do not have a vote, but they have considerable influence on the convention. The enthusiasm, or the degree of it, on the part of these nonmembers, often affects the convention, either by directly impressing the delegates themselves, or by affecting sentiment outside which in turn affects those inside. A deliriously enthusiastic gallery influences the party and the public, and indirectly the delegates. The ominous cry of "We want Teddy" in the Republican convention of 1908 improved the prospects of Mr. Taft, Roosevelt's favorite at the time; and again in 1912 and 1916 the same slogan raised by the spectators was not without its grave influence. Irrational as demonstrations may be, they are impressive, and they may affect courses of action either by warnings of consequences if they are unheeded, or by holding out hopes of favor and success if they are followed. Demonstrations, in which the spectators as well as the delegates participate, have lasted over an hour—a triumph of crowd demand. In these prolonged outbreaks there is, of course, an element of artificiality and organization often evident. The lady in the gallery who waves the banner or the man who unfurls the picture when the excitement begins to lag are not necessarily accidents. But the freshness and spontaneity of genuine demonstrations are unmistakable, and are certain to influence all of those present. The nomination of a candidate for president of the United States on the basis of the volume of crowd applause would seem to be impossible or undesirable, but the effect of these huge demonstrations is undeniable. Delegates are not "stampeded" by it, for they are likely to be "hardboiled," capable of holding their wits in exciting moments, but they are likely to be influenced by the clamor, even while they smile at it.

Outside, party opinion and public opinion watch and wait. Radio and television bring to every part of the land each movement of the president-makers, and literally millions watch with the keenest interest the process by which the next ruler of the land is being chosen. Over the wires may come the lightnings of the party and the public, and they may presage sunshine and victory or they may forecast a storm. Editorial and other comment comes back to delegates and leaders of the party, and if pronounced may help to shape their course. Direct messages from constituents are not wanting and not without their influence. In Mr. Bryan's famous fight for the control of the Baltimore convention in 1912 [18] perhaps the greatest triumph of his spectacular career—it is said that 110,000 telegrams from members of the party were sent to delegates during the struggle.[19] In a long contest delegates are very likely to hear from the "folks at home," who may express themselves with force and effect regarding

[18] *Proceedings*, 1912, p. 129.
[19] W. J. Bryan, *Tale of Two Conventions* (New York, 1912), p. 152. Mr. Bryan himself received 1128 telegrams from 31,331 persons in 46 states.

the convention's action. There is little question that the prolonged deadlock between the McAdoo and Smith forces in the Democratic convention of 1924 reacted against the fortunes of the party. The bitter struggle left both factions dissatisfied, and the rank and file of the party showed little enthusiasm during the election.

It is true that public opinion has expressed itself chiefly in the course of the prenomination campaign, where its decided preferences, if any, have already been fully developed. But if the issue is still undecided, and the contest is long drawn out, there is still wide opportunity for renewed statement of the party or the public will and judgment.

Murmurs against the nomination of Blaine in 1884, against Parker in 1904, against Taft in 1912, against Smith in 1928 were unheeded, but they forecast disaffection in the party ranks, and party disaster at the polls. Cleveland, Bryan, the Roosevelts, Wilson were opposed by powerful forces, usually dominating and actually holding the necessary votes to defeat them, but not daring to act against the evident demand of the general opinion of the party.

This opinion is made up of the organized and unorganized demands of various interests and ideals: business, agriculture, labor, professions, women, propaganda groups of all types, and the less organized and less articulate general feeling of the community, which intelligent party leaders strive to catch, whether they wish to follow it or avoid it. In this process, curiously enough, citizens participate without much regard to party, mingling in the general stream of influence. Partisan Republicans "hope" that the Democratic party will nominate this or that one, while partisan Democrats "hope" that the Republican party will nominate one or another of the candidates suggested. To the extent that they give expression to that "hope" they influence the selection actually made. In this formative process, of course, class, race, and section play their parts, but often the preferences have little basis other than the broad verdict as to the personality of the man or his general attitude on national problems. And it is true that small minorities well equipped with funds and publicity may artifically create a "demand" or "sentiment" for a candidate which might equally well have been created for a thousand others with no greater qualifications.

The convention process of nominating has at its core definite interests, cold calculation of party and class prestige, of managerial skill and prudence; at its surface, fever heat and pandemonium. There are tropical and arctic zones where torrid enthusiasm or cold cunning rules, each in its own appointed sphere.[20] A great event in a great democracy, it is set and staged on a great scale. An eloquent nominating speech has not yet secured a nomination for the candidate named, but at least two convention speeches have led to the choice of the orator. Garfield's nomination of Sherman in 1880 and Bryan's "cross of gold" speech on the platform in 1896 brought the nomination of the speaker in each case.[21]

The choice of party standard bearer is a question of "availability" for party victory or class purpose or both in most instances. For this reason a "compromise" candidate may be selected who has not been among the recognized leading candidates for the nomination. Polk in 1844, Pierce in 1852, Seymour in 1868, Hayes in 1876, Garfield in 1880, Harrison in 1888, Bryan in 1896, Harding in 1920, and Davis in 1924 were all "dark horses," whose names appeared prominently only after the others were deadlocked and evidently unable to command the requisite votes for nomination.[22]

The choice of candidates is determined by a wide variety of factors which are by no means constant, but which contain a number of quantities that change but little. Such questions as these are always important. What are the chances for party victory with this candidate? Or, what disposition will he make of the party patronage? Or, what is the nature of this candidate's personality? What would be our probable relations to him? Or, what are the principles for which he stands? What is his record of public service in relation to this campaign? Behind these are the constantly recurring questions raised by class, race, religion, social group, each deeply affected by the answer to their particular inquiry. Victory is not the only considera-

---

[20] For a description of conventions, see Kieran, *op. cit.*; Edward Stanwood, *History of the Presidency* (Boston, 1898); A. K. McClure, *Our Presidents* (New York, 1905); J. B. Bishop, *Presidential Nominations and Elections* (New York, 1916); and James A. Farley, *Behind the Ballots* (New York, 1938).

[21] For famous nominating speeches, read Ingersoll on Blaine, Republican *Proceedings*, 1876, p. 295; Conkling on Grant, 1880, p. 550; Garfield on Sherman, 1880, p. 554; Bragg on Cleveland, 1884, Democratic *Proceedings*, p. 176; Franklin D. Roosevelt on Al Smith, 1928, pp. 98–104.

[22] Nominated on the following ballots, Polk, 9th; Pierce, 49th; Seymour, 22nd; Hayes, 7th; Garfield, 36th; Harrison, 8th; Bryan, 5th; Harding, 10th; Davis, 103rd.

tion as is sometimes erroneously said. Otherwise Theodore Roosevelt would have been the Republican nominee in 1912 or in 1916, or Hoover in 1920. In the one case defeat and in the other case a doubtful outcome were preferred for reasons that affected the organization and various interests. Patronage is not the only consideration, for if so Clark would have been named at Baltimore in place of the uncertain quantity in the form of Woodrow Wilson, the professor in politics.

The outstanding feature in availability is location in a large and doubtful state where party successes may turn the tide toward victory. This is clearly shown by the list of nominations for president and vice president from 1876 to 1948 given in Table 5.

Of 76 major candidates for the offices of president and vice president in the period from 1876 to 1948 New York has supplied 23 (17 presidential and 6 vice presidential); Ohio, 10 (8 presidential and 2 vice presidential); Indiana, 9 (2 presidential and 7 vice presidential).[23]

Of 164 presidential candidates, 55 have come from three states, and 48 from two states, New York and Ohio. One of the objections to the proposed direct vote for the president was that such an arrangement would work to the advantage of the large states, but as a matter of fact the largest states under the present plan have indirectly obtained an advantage probably greater than would be possible if the vote were directly cast.

In a number of instances a military record has been reckoned an advantage, notably in the case of Grant, Hayes, Garfield, Hancock, Harrison, McKinley, and Theodore Roosevelt—a total of 9 of the 42 major candidates for the presidency since the Civil War. In 1948 just when he was running at the top of the public opinion polls, General Eisenhower dramatically removed himself from the presidential competition.[24] Powerful campaigning ability was a distinct consideration in the cases of Blaine, Garfield, Bryan, and Smith, while almost all of the candidates have been men of more than average ability as public speakers.

[23] This does not include the Socialist candidates, all of whom have come either from Indiana, the state of Debs, or New York, the home of Hillquit.

[24] New York *Times*, February 1, 1948; in the earlier period, Washington, Jackson, Harrison, Taylor, Scott, McClellan. See above, p. 155.

TABLE 5

PRESIDENTIAL AND VICE PRESIDENTIAL NOMINATIONS BY KEY STATES

New York		Indiana		Ohio	
Tilden	'76	Hendricks	'76	Hayes	'76
Wheeler	'76				
Arthur	'80	English	'80	Garfield	'80
Cleveland	'84	Hendricks	'84		
Cleveland	'88	Harrison	'88	Thurman	'88
Morton	'88				
Cleveland	'92	Harrison	'92		
Reid	'92				
				McKinley	'96
T. Roosevelt	'00	Fairbanks	'04	McKinley	'00
T. Roosevelt	'04				
Parker	'04				
Sherman	'08			Taft	'08
T. Roosevelt	'12	Marshall	'12	Taft	'12
Hughes	'16	Fairbanks	'16		
F. D. Roosevelt	'20	Marshall	'16	Cox	'20
Smith	'28			Harding	'20
F. D. Roosevelt	'32				
F. D. Roosevelt	'36				
F. D. Roosevelt	'40				
Willkie	'40				
F. D. Roosevelt	'44			Bricker	'44
Dewey	'44				
Dewey	'48				

There are also certain broad limits of availability in the national field—the customary limitations upon candidates. Since 1876 all candidates of the major parties, except in 1928,[25] have been white, male, Protestant, have lived north of the Mason and Dixon line, and most of them have lived east of the Mississippi. With the exception of Hoover and Truman no successful presidential candidate has been chosen from west of Indiana. All but two of the popular choices have thus been made to the east of the center of population, and

[25] The nomination of a Catholic by the Democrats and the nomination of a westerner by the Republicans in 1928 broke party precedents of long standing. The vice-presidential nominations of that year also failed to conform to party practice. They were western men in both cases.

somewhat near the financial center of gravity. No distinct representative of agriculture or of labor has been nominated by the major parties, nor has any businessman been selected for president, although there have been exceptions in the case of the vice-presidency. The legal profession has claimed by far the largest number of candidates, although in many instances the candidates were not active practitioners.

PRESIDENTIAL PREFERENCE PRIMARIES

In 1905 Wisconsin provided for direct election of delegates to national conventions.[26] In 1910 the state of Oregon provided for direct election of delegates to the national convention from congressional districts and of delegates at large by the party voters of the whole state, accompanying this by provision for a direct vote on candidates for the presidency.

This method was taken up by the progressive element in the Republican party and in the Democratic also. The powerful support of Theodore Roosevelt was given to the plan, and state after state took up the new system. Public opinion pressed hard for a direct vote upon candidates, and in that campaign some 12 states operated under some form of presidential primary. These states selected 360 delegates in each party. Roosevelt was apparently the popular choice among Republicans for the nomination, but in the bitter convention struggle following the primaries, Taft was named as the candidate. Clark obtained a majority of the votes cast in the Democratic convention, but was unable to secure the two-thirds vote required by the rules of the party, and the nomination eventually went to Wilson.

In 1913 President Wilson strongly urged the passage of a national primary law in his message to Congress. The presidential suggestion for a convention called for a body made up of senators, candidates for senatorial vacancies and for the House, members of the national committees, and presidential candidates. Similar measures have been introduced from time to time, but have made no progress in the congressional field. Strong objections were urged upon constitutional

[26] See Overacker, *The Presidential Primary*, "Nominations," *op. cit.* and her "Direct Primary Legislation," 1936–1939," *American Political Science Review,* XXIV (June, 1940), 499–506; B. W. Patch, "Presidential Primaries," *Editorial Research Reports* (January 14, 1948).

grounds, and many were also made as a matter of policy and opinion. It was strenuously asserted that Congress is given no power under the Constitution to regulate the choice of electors in the several states, as this is an exclusive power of the individual common-wealth.[27]

In 1916 there was little opportunity for trial of the direct vote plan, although in the 22 states having mandatory laws and the two states having optional laws there were altogether about 600 delegates chosen in each party. In the Democracy there was no opposition to the renomination of President Wilson, and the convention was a triumphal procession for him. Colonel Roosevelt, still a Progressive, could not allow his name to go before the Republican voters,[28] and Justice Hughes on the bench could not well make a campaign.

In 1920 there were again 20 states having some type of direct presidential primary, electing about 600 delegates in each party. There were a number of factors entering into the 1920 situation, notably, the fact that the greatest of the party leaders were out of the field and none had risen to take their place. Roosevelt, in all probability, would have been the Republican standard bearer, but his death left the progressive wing of the party leaderless. The con-servative element of the party preferred the delegate system to the direct primary. President Wilson, the leader of the liberal wing of the Democracy, was stretched upon a bed of illness and incapacitated for leadership, although still the nominal head of the party. Further-more, shrewd observers forecast almost certain Democratic defeat.

In the Republican presidential primaries of 1924, Coolidge re-ceived some 2,500,000 votes and Johnson about 1,000,000 votes. This entitled Coolidge to over a majority of the delegates in the entire convention and he was nominated on the first ballot. In the Demo-cratic presidential primaries of this year McAdoo was far ahead of any of the other candidates in the matter of total votes secured, but this vote entitled him to only 194 delegates. The convention failed

[27] See *Newberry* v. *U. S.*, 256 U. S. 232. As shown above, p. 325, this position has been reversed.

[28] In the Massachusetts Republican primaries of 1916 one set of delegates at large was for Roosevelt and the other set was unpledged. The Roosevelt set received about 43 per cent of the total vote cast. This discouraged Roosevelt and may have been responsible for his refusal of the Progressive nomination. See Overacker, *The Presi-dential Primary*, p. 169.

to follow the popular verdict and chose Davis, a dark horse. McAdoo had been discredited by his connections with an oil magnate, and his candidacy was bitterly opposed by the Smith supporters.

In 1928 the presidential preference primaries foreshadowed the action of the two major party conventions but it cannot be said that they operated in a smooth fashion. While Hoover clearly amassed the most preference primary votes of all the Republican candidates, he won only in those states where he was unopposed, or where he ran against other than favorite sons. Smith, on the other hand, had fewer favorite sons to contend with, but when he entered a contest against one, he likewise came out second best. Both men, however, were clearly the leading national contenders in their respective parties.[29]

Hoover's renomination by the Republican convention in 1932 was a foregone conclusion. Since he was sure of the convention states and since there were only 17 states which used the presidential primary, he did not authorize the use of his name in any of the state primaries. Where he had no opponent and his name was written in, he won with ease. On the other hand, in the Democratic preconvention campaign, there was vigorous battle between Al Smith and Franklin D. Roosevelt. Both candidates entered the state contests where they were sure of victory, and either kept their names out or sought uninstructed delegations where victory was doubtful. Roosevelt won in 12 states, and the delegates from these states plus those from convention states who were pledged to him made up a majority of the convention, but not the two-thirds majority which was then necessary for the nomination. On the other hand, Smith did not win the minimum one-third of the delegates which would have been necessary to block Roosevelt's nomination.[30]

In 1936 a new situation developed in the presidential preference primaries which bids well to contribute further to the decline in the use of this device. Since Roosevelt's renomination was a foregone conclusion there was little interest in the Democratic primaries. In the Republican party there might have been some spirited contests, but one of the leading contenders, Governor Alfred Landon of Kansas, deliberately chose to keep out of the primaries and to rely upon

[29] Roy Peel and T. C. Donnelly, *The 1928 Campaign* (New York, 1931), pp. 14–15.

[30] Roy Peel and T. C Donnelly, *The 1932 Campaign* (New York, 1935).

other methods to build up his convention support. Since he had important newspaper support, this proved to be adroit strategy. Senator Borah took the opposite view and entered most of the presidential primaries. Taken by themselves, Borah's primary votes looked impressive, but they failed to make allowance for a new factor which was now operating in the situation, namely, the public opinion polls which were being conducted by a sampling method all over the United States. In these unofficial polls, based upon a small sample from all the states and not simply upon the sixteen states which used presidential primaries, Landon showed a steady growth in popular strength.[31] His manager, John Hamilton, used this information

TABLE 6

POPULARITY OF REPUBLICAN PRE-CONVENTION CANDIDATES 1936

	Dec.	Feb.	Apr.	May
Landon	33%	43%	56%	56%
Borah	26	28	20	19
Hoover	12	17	14	14
Knox	8	7	5	5
Vandenberg	3	4	4	5

and other well-known devices to win the convention delegates. When the convention met, Borah's "pledged" votes disappeared and it was a walk-away for Landon.

The weaknesses of the presidential preference primaries was never more clearly illustrated than in the 1940 preconvention campaigns. In the preliminaries to the Democratic convention President Roosevelt did not indicate his intention to smash the no-third-term tradition until the last minute before the nominations. In the Republican presidential primaries, Governor Dewey outdistanced the other contestants, and until a few weeks before the convention he led in the public opinion polls. A group of journalists and high-powered advertising executives then put on one of the most whirlwind preconvention campaigns for Wendell Willkie that the country had ever witnessed, and they were able to put their man over in the convention itself. They made a mockery of the presidential preference primary machinery.

[31] *Time*, May 18, 1936. The five-month record of the American Institute of Public Opinion (Gallup) poll is given in Table 6.

In 1944 the presidential primaries were able to indicate more clearly the course of events, at least in the Republican party. Wendell Willkie was again one of the candidates but this time he entered some of the primaries and his relatively poor showing in Wisconsin against Governor Dewey effectively eliminated him as a candidate. Governor Dewey again ran ahead of all the other Republican contestants in the other primaries and in the public opinion polls. This time the convention followed the mandate of the Republican voters and nominated Dewey.

Four years later the Republican presidential primaries were again of considerable importance in determining the result of the nominating convention. The ups and downs of the two leading candidates— Governor Thomas E. Dewey and Harold E. Stassen—are shown in Figure 11 put out by the Gallup Public Opinion News Service on

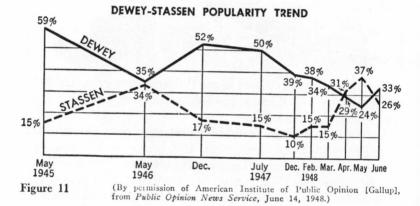

Figure 11   (By permission of American Institute of Public Opinion [Gallup], from *Public Opinion News Service*, June 14, 1948.)

June 14, 1948. Following his success in the Nebraska and Wisconsin primaries, Stassen surpassed Dewey, but Dewey again forged ahead when he won over Stassen in the Oregon primary. The highly publicized Dewey-Stassen radio debate on Communism may have also been a contributing factor to Dewey's regain of his popularity. Figure 12 shows the estimate of the delegate strength by states as given by the *New York Times* on the eve of the convention. The roll call on the first ballot showed that the estimates were excellent.

Between one-third and one-fourth of the states have mandatory

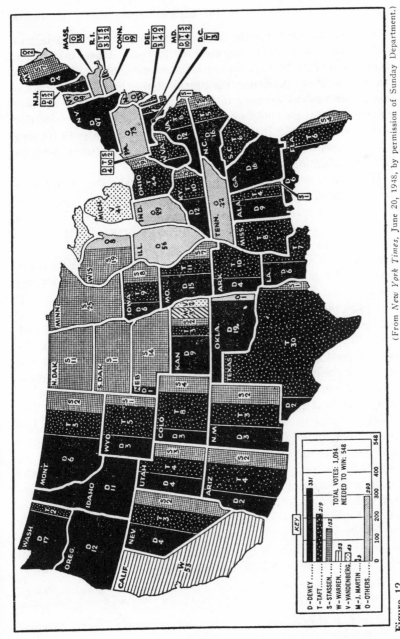

(From *New York Times*, June 20, 1948, by permission of Sunday Department.)

Figure 12

349

laws, providing either for the direct election of convention delegates or for presidential preference votes or for both. Since 1916, when there were twenty-two mandatory laws and two optional laws, there has been a steady decline in the presidential primary.[32] Among the reasons for this decline may be listed the immunity of the national convention from the control of the state laws, the lack of uniformity in the laws, the difficulties national candidates encounter in running against favorite sons, the ineffectiveness of existing statutes and their limited application.

The larger number of states that still retain the presidential primary are in the western and central sections of the country, although the East is not without representation. The New York law which merely provides for direct election of district delegates gives the voter little control over their action in the convention. On the other hand, those laws which provide for a preference vote for president and for selection of delegates by state conventions have not given satisfaction. On several occasions state conventions have ignored the popular verdict completely.[33] The most common type of presidential primary law combines direct election of delegates with the preference vote. The difficulty with these laws has been that the two methods have sometimes given contradictory results. In a few states the preference vote has been eliminated and provision is made for direct election of delegates whose preferences are stated on the ballot. While this system is better than the others, none of the laws affords a complete opportunity for free expression of opinion. In fact the machinery for the preferential presidential primary has never been set up in such form as to give the system anything like a fair chance to function. It is possible to express a popular party verdict in the great Republican states, as in 1928, but it is not possible to carry that verdict into effect, as was clearly shown by the primaries of 1912 when it was obvious that Roosevelt was the choice of the generality of the Republican voters in states where there was a direct vote. At present there is no clear line of tendency regarding use of the direct vote in presidential nominations.

[32] L. Overacker, "Direct Primary Legislation, 1936–1939," *American Political Science Review*, XXXIV (June, 1940), 499–506. In 1948 there were fourteen mandatory laws.

[33] See C. E. Merriam and L. Overacker, *Primary Elections* (Chicago, University of Chicago Press, 1928), p 151.

There are several alternatives. The direct primary for presidential candidates may be extended until the convention is either abolished or reduced to the work of ratifying an accomplished fact; or the direct vote may be abandoned altogether and the entire choice of the candidates left to the convention; or the present system of votes advisory to the convention may be continued. A consideration of the fundamental questions involved is of great importance, and an examination of some of them will be undertaken here.

Certain special difficulties stand in the way of the presidential direct primary which are not found in state primaries. First, there is the fact that the election of the president is not based upon a direct vote, but upon a federal system in which territory and population are combined in determining the electoral vote. If the president were chosen by direct vote, the primary would be somewhat simpler. In recent Congresses the sentiment for a constitutional amendment which would abolish the Electoral College and provide a system which would approximate a popular vote has been growing. The fact that the States' Rights Democrats nearly threw the election into the House of Representatives in 1948 gave an additional impetus to the demand for a new system.

In the next place, both parties are to some extent sectional, and the distribution of the party vote is very unequal. This is conspicuously true of the Republican party, which is almost unrepresented in one large geographical area. The South furnishes delegates to the Republican convention, but few electoral votes to its candidates since 1876. These delegates may determine organization control, platform policy, and candidates, but they will not supply the electoral votes necessary for success. Many congressional districts in the South have no Republican candidate for Congress, but these districts send delegates to the national convention. In less marked degree, the same thing may be said of a few northern states which rarely cast a Democratic electoral vote, although the certainty is by no means as great as in the case of southern states. Assuming that conventions are strictly representative of the party vote, what allowance, if any, shall be made for the probability of securing electoral votes from any particular territory? In the naming of candidates, of course, the states with a positive complexion, whether surely for the party or surely against it, are discounted, while the doubtful states have a significance of which they cannot be deprived by any rule or regulation. This is one of the puzzling points in the present system, but after all, it is equally difficult of adjustment whether we make use of the delegate system or of the direct vote.

To some extent the question of expense is involved, but it must be said that much of the discussion regarding the cost of primaries is not very closely related to the facts or primary practice. The public in times past has been unfamiliar with the outlays involved in electoral campaigns, and is easily aroused by the charge that great "slush funds" have been wickedly expended when, as a matter of fact, much greater sums have been spent without comment under their eyes in city or county or state contests.

Considering the size of the country and the great possibilities in the way of expenditure of a type no one would question, it cannot fairly be said that any presidential candidate has yet expended alarming sums of money. Of course, the type of the expenditure, the source of the funds, and the interests, connections, and purposes of the contributors are another matter and deserve the closest scrutiny. There is no reason to believe, however, that a reasonable campaign cannot be made for the presidential nomination without excessive and undesirable expenditure. There is no reason to suppose that with enlightened public opinion regarding the necessary costs of campaigning, with democratic financing of campaigns, and with a reasonable amount of public aid to campaigns, any candidate representing any large group of persons may not present his case and that of his group to the electorate in adequate fashion, whether in a campaign for delegates or for instructions to them in a preferential primary.

If the direct system is to be retained and developed, and we believe it should be, it is clear that various changes should be made by common consent, by party rule or by statutory or constitutional action. These changes are necessary for successful operation of the system. In the first place, it is desirable that primaries be held upon the same day, or at least within a very short span of time. Experience has shown the value and necessity of this in local and state elections, and it is even more urgent in the national field. Our elections and, as a rule, our primary choices of delegates are based on the theory of simultaneous expression of opinion by all members of the given group. It is believed that this is a fairer test of opinion than the type of election which is spread over a considerable period of time with shifting battlefields and scattering returns, with varying issues and situations arising as returns from one state are made available in another about to vote. The inevitable tendency has been to hold some primaries so early that the issues have not yet been clearly formulated, and for others to be too long delayed. The North Carolina primary in the Republican party, for example, was held in 1948 shortly before the convention, and the Illinois primary of the same year was held nearly three months before that date.[34]

It will be desirable to define more clearly the relation between the primary vote and the delegate vote, to outline more sharply the obligation of the delegate under the preferential system. At present there is no common custom or agreement upon this point, and much confusion has arisen in consequence. The delegate who is announced as a supporter of A may be chosen for local reasons, and at the same time may find the preferential vote of his district strongly in favor of B. Assuming, however, that the preferential vote is to govern, and assuming that the district is the unit for all except delegates at large, the question arises as to the nature and extent of the delegate's obligation to vote for the candidate receiving the highest vote in the preferential contest.[35] Does his obligation then extend to the organization of the convention in the interest of his candidate, to the selection of a platform in accordance with the beliefs of his candidate, if they are available, and how long must he support the man for whom he is instructed? For one ballot, a few ballots, until released by his candidate, or under some other conditions? Some of these questions may be settled by custom, some by party rule and others by legislation; but in the interest of securing efficient machinery, the practice should be standardized as rapidly as possible. The common custom in other conventions has been for delegates to vote as instructed until "released" by the candidate.

If the direct primary is further developed, what form should a decision finally take? Should it be a plurality vote, a majority vote,

[34] For table of dates, see J. Kieran, ed., *The New Information Please Almanac for 1948* (New York, 1948), p. 128.

[35] In the Republican primary in 1920 in the tenth Illinois district (Chicago) one delegate was elected who had run as an avowed Johnson delegate, but cast a preference vote for Wood. The presidential preference vote of the state at large that year was for Lowden.

or should the count be made by states, each state being given the same weight as its delegate strength in the convention? In the later case, should a plurality, a simple majority, or a two-thirds vote be required for a nomination? Should the action of the convention be simply a ratification of the preliminary preferential vote, or should the convention formally and legally retain its right to an independent choice of a candidate? Thus far there is no agreement upon these points, and the various bills introduced for national systems show a wide divergence upon many questions of principle and detail. As the situation now is, under universal use of the direct vote, the choice of candidate would be made on the basis of instructed delegates rather than by preponderance of mass vote without regard to state or district lines. The experience of states using a combination of the delegate and direct system, as in Illinois, was that the aggregate vote was more impressive than the delegate vote, and that the candidate having the largest vote was likely to demand the nomination even against a candidate receiving a smaller vote but having more delegates. But this might not follow in the federal field, where the state is the unit of electoral choice. Yet under any circumstances to override the claims of a candidate who received a substantial majority of all of the votes cast, assuming a large participation in the primary, would be very difficult and almost impossible in view of the demand for party harmony.

In any thoughtful reconsideration of the direct primary in national affairs, consideration should be given to the subject of second or third choices and the other devices for qualifying the individual vote, or for rendering it more flexible in its application. In Ohio the voters have a choice between delegates whose second as well as first choices for president are given on the ballot. The delegates, however, have always given as their second choice some native son whose chances for the nomination were small. It is possible that more extensive use may be made of preferential voting in presidential nominations.

In this connection the suggestion of Dr. Boots is an interesting one. He proposed that the vote be taken by states, that each candidate be given his proportionate share of the delegates, and that he be allowed to select his own representatives.[36] Thus if candidate A re-

---

[36] See *Supplement to National Municipal Review,* September, 1920.

ceived 200,000 votes as against 100,000 for B, and there were 21 delegates, A would select 14 of them, and B, 7 of them. In this way there would be no question about the loyalty of the delegate to the candidate on all convention questions, and no such incidents as occurred in the 1920 Republican convention when some delegates deserted Johnson or gave him half-hearted support.

Dr. Overacker proposes that the relationship between the preference vote and the election of delegates should be clarified.[37] "The following two plans are suggested as carrying out these ideas. In Plan I it is proposed to eliminate the preference vote, electing all delegates at large. Provision should be made for proposing these candidates in groups, and these groups should be arranged in lists upon the ballot with the name of the presidential preference of the group, or 'For an Uninstructed Delegation,' at the top of the list. The voter would then be called upon to make but one decision and cast but one vote in order to vote for the list. By providing for proportional representation no geographical or political minority need be barred from representation. In Plan II the presidential preference vote would be retained and popular election of delegates eliminated. The law should provide that the names of presidential aspirants be placed upon the ballot upon the request of five proposal-men, eligible voters of the state, who should at that time file a list of delegates, equal to the whole number of delegates to which the state is entitled, who might represent the candidate in the convention. There would be no reason why the same presidential aspirant might not be proposed by more than one group of proposal-men or why a group of proposal-men should not support 'An Uninstructed Delegation,' with the names of the proposal-men (if any) sponsoring such a proposition. The voter should be called upon to cast a vote for the presidential aspirant he favored or for the uninstructed delegation. After the primary each presidential candidate should be allotted a proportion of the whole delegation equal to the ratio which his vote bears to the whole vote cast. The secretary of state should certify as elected the requisite number of names from each of the lists filed with him, beginning at the top of the list as prepared by the proposal-men. The writer believes that such a plan would secure a short

[37] Merriam and Overacker, *op. cit.*, pp. 188–189. See also page 193 for a method of carrying out the national preference vote for President.

ballot, proportional representation, a direct vote for the presidential candidate, and responsibility for candidacies."

PARTY CONFERENCE

On the whole, there seems to be a general desire to retain some form of a party conference, but at the same time a pronounced distrust of recent methods and results. In the cities the party convention seems to have no root, in the counties and states somewhat more general support, and in the national field its chief support. Not only the party convention, but the party itself to a considerable extent has been driven from the city field; in the county and state the convention still retains a tentative position of interest and power; and in national affairs the party parliament is materially stronger in the degree of general interest in its acts.

In an effort to find the key to the present situation it may be useful to analyze the elements of present party control.

The agencies of party government are numerous and loosely organized. They include:

Party committees, national and state and local
The congressional committees
The party caucus, Senate and House, and the legislative caucus in states
Party leaders in executive positions, as the president, governors, etc.
Party leaders holding no official position
Party primaries, national and state
Party conventions, national and state

Somewhere in these various agencies may be found the control and direction of the party. The various elements of leadership in policies, of technical management, of responsible governmental leadership, are all expressed here, in somewhat indefinite form. The president is practically the only agency through whom they are all united, as there has never been a national boss who could claim sovereignty over all these various domains of party power. This organization is the result of growth rather than design, of the struggle for power rather than any desire for logical symmetry. Yet the serious study of the party organization is not out of the question in a nation where large-scale organization and efficiency have been unsurpassed in their recent development.

It would be possible to establish an agency in the nature of a party council, as a mean of supplementing and unifying the present party mechanism. Such a council, like the British party conferences, might be held annually for the consideration of party questions relating both to management and to policy. The great leaders and managers of the party might be brought together for purposes of acquaintance, of conference, and of public and private consultation. To some extent this council might serve as a testing place for plans and personalities, in that respect helping in the formulation of conclusions regarding policies and candidates. It might serve to bring together the scattered threads of party control or party leadership and to that extent aid both the party and the public in forming conclusions on public questions and men.

Such a council might well include:

The president and vice president and cabinet (of dominant party), and leading candidates at previous primaries (candidates of minority party)

Party members of Congress, say 200

Party governors and runners-up, 96

Party national committeemen and chairmen of state committees, 200

Prominent party leaders chosen by national or state committee, or by party leagues or associations, say 200

This would make a council of about 600 members, bringing together the leaders, the managers, the responsible officials in a conference on party and public questions.

Such a body might discuss the problems of party organization and management, receiving reports on such subjects as party primaries, corrupt practices acts, improvements in party machinery, finances, propaganda, or other problems, primarily of management. It might consider questions of party policy and, if desired, receive reports from special committees or commissions. It might hear great leaders on the questions of the day, giving them a forum for the elaboration of their plans and purposes. A Republican council of this day could hear men of the type of Martin, Hoover, Dewey, Taft, Landon, while a Democratic council could listen to Truman, Rayburn, Barkley. The great women of the parties might also be heard. If, as Dr. Lowell says, the party is a "broker" of policies and personalities, the council could afford a convenient occasion for the display of their wares. Party managers and technicians might also be heard on the problems of party administration and practical operation. What the real powers of such an assembly might be is conjectural. They might remain largely persuasive and educational, or they might become authoritative or directive in nature, or they might be purely perfunctory.

In this connection it is important to recall the suggestion made by Justice Hughes, and also by Dr. Boots,[38] that a party conference might designate candidates for office in state and local affairs, subject to approval by the voters of the state or other district.[39] It would, of course, be possible to apply the same plan on a national scale, assuming that such conferences were in existence in the states and could be built upon to make a national conference; and it would be possible to submit the recommendations of such a body to the party voters in a presidential primary. The action of the voters in such a primary might be made final, or there might follow a national convention of the present type for ratification of the results of the primary or for further deliberation in the light of the primary indications of party sentiment.

It might be said that such a conference would not be welcome either because discussion of policies would show party dissensions that would weaken it, or that discussion of managerial problems would reveal the secrets of the organization. But as to policies few are deceived by the artificial appearance of unity and harmony often presented by the party, and this may become a weakness if the public thinks that a party stands for nothing, or that it dodges an important issue on which the nation wishes to vote at that time. The open discussion of differences often tends to clarify views and reconcile diversities of opinion. In any event, party divisions are not likely to remain state secrets in a democratic community.

Party strategists and tactics in particular campaigns may be re-

[38] Much earlier (1902) by Dr. Judson and Dr. Whitten. See Merriam and Overacker, *op. cit.*

[39] *National Municipal Review*, X (1921), 23; VIII (1919), 472

garded as war measures, but the general managerial methods of the parties are not secrets from anyone who cares to inquire into them. Each party manager knows intimately and minutely the methods of the other party; and hence public discussion of methods could have no terrors for the party administrator. On the contrary, the general discussion of party management and technique might have the most helpful effect upon both parties by opening up such subjects as party representation, primary methods, party finances, party propaganda, and related topics belonging to the side of management rather than to that of policy.

It may well be asked whether parties are not already organized to an unwarrantable and undesirable extent, and whether further organization would not merely intensify the existing evil. In some ways it is true that the party suffers from an excess of organization, not only in the quantity and quality of the machinery, but in the predominance of the machine over the men served by it. In every association the organization has and must have large authority. It is looked to for initiative and for administration and commonly furnishes much of one and all of the other. In all associations of a permanent nature there is complaint from time to time of the abuse of power by the organization in authority. This may be seen in a church, in a business organization, in a labor union, or in any other group. When this feeling reaches a point where it interferes with the morale and the efficiency of the group, it becomes serious. In the political party that point has been reached and passed, so that there is frequently rebellion and very commonly a sense of hostility to or suspicion of the organization. This is sometimes unwarranted and undiscriminating, based upon ignorance of the needs of leadership and of concerted action among large groups of men, but unfortunately often documented by specific evidence of actual betrayal both of public and party trust, and gross dishonesty. The organization will always arouse distrust and suspicion, but the corrupt organization will arouse these feelings to a point where the effectiveness of the whole group is seriously weakened and its primary purposes imperiled.

The difficulty is still greater when it happens that an organization is allied in its corruption with a particular class and that constituting a minority of the community. The frequent combination of the boss with special privilege seeking interests has aroused the deepest concern and has cost the party much of its natural and normal strength. In a party group in a democratic nation the unpardonable sin is the betrayal of the chief purpose of the group—the undermining of its foundation and the denial of its goal—that of popular government. The leaders in the church who are not loyal to religious ideals, the labor leaders disloyal to labor, the chamber of commerce betraying business, the agricultural associations unfaithful to the interests of the farmers can with difficulty maintain their position, and if they do, they weaken the whole group of which they are in command. In the same way similar results follow in the political party which is, after all, not exempt from the principles that govern the action of other groups. If it were not for striking exceptions in the shape of great party leaders and for the faithfulness of many managers, the party system would have suffered even more than it has.

While, then, the party is in some ways overorganized, in other ways its organization is defective, and would not pass an efficiency test on the technical side. And on the side of organization for the consideration of party policies and party techniques it is singularly defective. The leaders, the managers and the responsible officials are not brought together for consultation as they would be in almost any other form of organization. They have neither the personal contact which is so valuable in all groups, the comparative study of management, nor the interchange of ideas regarding national or party policies, as in other groups.

CONCLUSIONS AS TO NOMINATIONS

In comparison with the nominating processes of other democracies, those of the United States are unique. No such elaborate system is known either on the Continent or in England, where party conditions more closely resemble those in America.[40] Not only is there no direct primary, but there is no formal delegate convention, and no legal regulation of the nominating process. Party "diets" and con-

[40] H. F. Gosnell, *Democracy: Theshold of Freedom* (New York, 1948); Frederick A. Ogg, *English Government and Politics* (New York, 1936); W. L. Middleton, *French Political System* (London, 1932); Walter R. Sharp, *The Government of the French Republic* (New York, 1938); Robert C. Brooks, *Civic Training in Switzerland* (Chicago, 1930); Thomas Reed, *Government and Politics of Belgium* (Yonkers, 1924); James Bryce, *Modern Democracies* (New York, 1921); Charles Seymour and D. P. Frary, *How the World Votes* (Springfield, Mass., 1918).

ventions are frequently held, especially on the Continent, for the purpose of discussing questions of party policy, and at times these are of very great significance in fixing party attitudes or even national attitudes on important questions. But the selection of candidates is left either with the local clubs or societies, or with the national committee or the national leaders.[41] Under the various forms of parliamentary systems, there is, of course, no such significant official as the president of the United States; and almost the only party candidates are candidates for parliament. Our system is as incomprehensible to the European seeing it for the first time as the European system is to us.

What actually goes on in the primaries is a sifting process, in fact a preliminary election under the nominal forms of the party, but in reality much more than a party affair. Personalities and programs must run the gantlet twice—in the preliminary and in the final election. Social and economic interests may carry on their struggle first within the party, and then before the whole electorate; somewhat as in the party caucus the legislative proposal must first secure the favorable party vote and then the favorable legislative vote. In some instances this will enable the minority to rule, as in a case where there are:

	Republicans	Democrats	Total
Progressive	200,000	300,000	500,000
Conservative	250,000	100,000	350,000

In this case the conservative interests having control of the majority party may control the election, although in a minority of the electors. But of course this may be adjusted in the election, provided the desire for a progressive candidate or policy is strong enough to overcome the cohesive force of party heredity or other considerations holding the voters within the party lines.[42]

[41] In Belgium the Worker's party and the Liberal party have adopted by party rule methods of nomination which resemble American methods before the days of legal regulation.

[42] The American Institute of Public Opinion in April, 1938, asked the following question: "If there were only two political parties, one Conservatives, the other for Liberals, which party do you think you would like to join?" The replies revealed the following preferences:

	Republicans	Democrats
Liberal	15 per cent	64 per cent
Conservative	85 per cent	36 per cent

If one party is in full control, as the Republicans in Vermont or the Democrats in Texas, the primary becomes in effect an election. More votes may be cast and greater interest shown under these conditions than in the regular election itself.

In the primary contests the concentrated units of power, whether economic or social or political, have the advantage over the unorganized groups and are in a position to dominate. Where the professional political machine allies itself with some powerful group of special-privilege interests, its strength becomes very great and can with great difficulty be defeated in a primary fight.[43] The inertia of a mass of voters, the expert use of propaganda, of machine methods, the aid of the press, the appeal to hereditary allegiance on the one hand, and the appeal to immediate class or personal interest on the other—all combine to make possible a state of affairs in which direct democratic control is destroyed, and there remains only the indirect appeal to the powerful group in actual control of the machinery of the party. This often tends to be a plea rather than a command, an entreaty rather than an order. Here the difficulty dips below the surface and enters the stratum of social and industrial and political *mores*.

The power of the organization is checked, however, by the veto of the party voters in the primaries and the veto of the electorate in the final choice—by party opinion and by public opinion. The ruling group frequently divides, and if fusion with the independent or insurgent party voters offers promise of success, a break in the ranks of the organized machine is not impossible. The possibility of such a revolution always has a restraining influence on the powers that be, and tends to hold them back from the extremes of arbitrary conduct. Sometimes popular dissent may crystallize into an effective counterorganization, which may be built from the ground up and may overthrow the old guard for long periods of time. Of this type is the organization effected by the La Follettes in Wisconsin and Johnson in California.

What actually occurs is a struggle on the part of various community elements to capture one or if possible both of the major

[43] W. Reddig, *Tom's Town: Kansas City and the Pendergast Legend* (Philadelphia and New York, 1947); Walter Davenport, *Power and Glory: The Life of Boies Penrose* (New York, 1931).

parties, and commit them to their program, their candidate, or their general attitude. The most disquieting phase of the nominating process has not been the power of the organization as such, but the evident alliance of the organization on many occasions with compact industrial groups representing large corporate combinations. This alliance has been the source of the very gravest discontent, and lies at the bottom of the restless experiments with nominating machinery and the attempts to make popular control over the party more effective. From another point of view the apathy of the voter in regard to primary and regular elections has been the source of grave misgivings on the part of serious students of democracy the world over. It may safely be said, however, that both the power of the boss, with his sinister relations to corrupt industrial leaders, and the indifference of the voter show signs of disappearance from our public life.

CHAPTER XVI

WINNING ELECTIONS

"When you are attacked never defend yourself. If your opponent calls you a liar, call him a thief. Raise him.

"Never attack a woman or a preacher. When a woman attacks me, I say nothing. The women are always right.

"When a man is heckled at a political meeting, he should never lose his temper. That is fatal.

"I believe with the elder Harrison that bad publicity is better than none."—The late William Hale Thompson, former mayor of Chicago.

"Keynoting implies the ability to . . . give the impression of passionately and torrentially moving onward and upward while warily standing still."—Edward G. Lowry, *Washington Close-ups* (Boston, 1921).

A LEADING PARTY PROPAGANDIST RECENTLY REMARKED THAT THE political campaign is no longer a struggle between fundamental policies but "a race for the best positions, for flashlights." [1] Historical research shows that the American political campaigns where fundamental policies were determined are few and far between. So we might say that modern techniques of communication have made these political battles almost continuous struggles to steal an advance on the enemy by some new mechanical or psychological device.

Once nominations are made, the party concentrates its efforts on success in the election. [2]

Organization, propaganda, and finance are the central considerations in the campaign. The backbone of the organization for cam-

[1] R. D. Casey, "Party Campaign Propaganda," *Annals of the American Academy of Political and Social Science*, CLXXIX (May, 1936), 96–105.

[2] Paul Lazarsfeld, B. Berelson, and H. Gaudet, *The People's Choice: How the Voter Makes Up His Mind in a Presidential Campaign* (New York, 1944); Cortez A. M. Ewing, *Presidential Elections from Abraham Lincoln to Franklin Roosevelt* (Norman, Okla., 1940); R. D. Casey, "Republican Propaganda in the 1936 Campaign," *Public Opinion Quarterly*, I (April, 1937), 27–44; James A. Farley, *Behind the Ballots* (New York, 1938); R. V. Peel and T. C. Donnelly, *The 1928 Campaign* (New York, 1931), and *The 1932 Campaign* (New York, 1935); H. F.

paigning is the "regular" party force, ready at hand for the struggle. This is supplemented by an auxiliary organization which reaches far beyond the limits of the usual standing army. The regular organization has its standard routine duties to perform, including registration of voters, conduct of the canvass, execution of the party propaganda, manning of the polls, supervision of the count, and the canvass. In an electorate of some 80,000,000 this task is of no light proportions, and requires concerted effort on a large scale. In times when popular excitement is at fever heat there will be many willing hands to aid in this operation, but in the "off" years, when popular interest is relatively slight, it will be much more difficult to obtain the force necessary to carry through the task vigorously and effectively.

The leaders of the organization will direct their efforts toward completion of the machinery, filling in the inevitable gaps and reinforcing the weak spots as far as possible. They will endeavor to bring the organization to the highest possible degree of efficiency. They will strive to bring about harmony between clashing factions and personalities. They will labor to strengthen the morale of the workers by creating confidence in a victorious outcome—the "illusion of victory," or at any rate a memorable "showing" where victory is out of the question in a particular territory. Battles may be won or lost by the skill and energy shown at this particular point.

The "regulars" will be supplemented, however, by various classes of organizations, hastily improvised for the occasion or carried over from some previous campaign in skeleton form. These will include groups of all types and kinds where there is a prospect of adding to the party's strength. The types will vary somewhat in campaigns and from section to section. Nationalistic committees will include

---

Gosnell, *Boss Platt* (Chicago, 1924); E. Stanwood, *History of the Presidency* (Boston, 1928); A. K. McClure, *Our Presidents and How We Make Them* (New York, 1905); J. B. Bishop, *Presidential Nominations and Elections* (New York, 1916).

Election statistics are often given in the reports of the secretaries of states. Compilations are found in *Appleton's Encyclopedia* (1861–1903); E. E. Robinson, *The Presidential Vote 1896–1932* (Stanford University, 1934); *The Presidential Vote, 1936* (Stanford University, 1940); *They Voted Roosevelt* (Stanford University, 1947); the *American Year Book*; the *World Almanac*; and U. S. Bureau of the Census, *Vote Cast in Presidential and Congressional Elections, 1928–1944*. The best running accounts of election processes are found in the columns of the daily and weekly press.

Italian, Polish, Czech, Swedish, German, Negro, Lithuanian, Greek, Jewish, and other group representatives, often with separate headquarters, speakers, and literature, and with a special campaign organized to fit their peculiar needs.

Other types of organizations are designed to attract economic groups, such as business, labor, and agriculture in their various branches. There may not be special committees for groups as broad as these, but there are separate organizers or chargés who specialize in party canvasses of this description. In certain campaigns there may be a high degree of specialization, and very intensive efforts made in special fields of the occupational and professional groups. Lawyers, physicians, retailers and wholesalers in special lines of industry, bankers and brokers, real estate and insurance men, and many other groups may be organized in local campaigns or in national contests. In the field of labor, similar subdivision will be made.

The farming constituency is so large and so widely distributed and operates under such widely differing conditions that no special form of committee organization is devised as a rule, but each state and locality develops its own method of procedure.

With the advent of women's suffrage new machinery has been devised for dealing with women's votes. For this purpose special committees and special campaigns have been started. These agencies undertake to deal with the problems of swaying the woman's vote from one party to the other through special organizers, literature, speakers, and all the direct and indirect methods of influence that the occasion may require.

In national contests, the East, New England, the Middle Atlantic Coast, the West, the South, the Middle West and their subdivisions may all require special methods of campaigning which must be studied by the management. In 1940 the Democratic party maintained four regional headquarters to supplement the national headquarters in New York. The arguments, speakers, literature, and spot broadcasts adapted to vote-getting in one section may not fit well in another, and a judicious variation of the basic tune may be advisable. While the broad lines of the party's campaign must be uniform, yet frequently the party position is a flexible one, and arguments may be emphasized differently here and there to meet local situations. In 1928 the Republicans did not urge prohibition in the East or in the cities; nor did the Democrats emphasize wetness in the South or in the rural North and West. In 1948 President Truman did not press his civil rights program as hard in the South as he did in the North. The same principle of regional application is found on a smaller scale in state and local campaigns.

A special appeal is sometimes made to new voters who may be organized as clubs of various descriptions.[3] College clubs are formed from time to time for the same purpose. The first voter not only is of help to the party in the particular election, but he is likely to continue voting as he began; his initial ballot therefore possesses an unusual significance. Its importance has never been fully realized by the party managers, who have often failed to sense the psychological significance of the establishment of the party habit.

Elaborate campaign committees are also set up, consisting of various types of citizens of various forms of prominence. These lists include men and women whose names are influential in their neighborhoods, whether the range is large or small, strictly local or nationwide. On these "committees" are placed thousands of citizens who are not parts of the regular working organization and are not actively interested in politics, but who constitute a great reserve army now thrown into action at the critical moment. Some are traditional members of the party; some are new recruits; some represent accretions from the independent group or from the traditional foe; some are moved by general interest and some by very definite and specific special and personal interest in the outcome of the campaign.

The party organization at the height of its activity consists of thousands of workers, regulars and volunteers, spreading the propaganda of the party, with its traditions, its policies and its candidates. At the center is the core of seasoned veterans, led by commanders skilled in the strategy and tactics of political war, the general staff in whose souls the noise and confusion and shock of battle raise no panic or dismay. Many of them sniff the battle from afar and rejoice in it. Around them are the large numbers of the volunteers whose enthusiasm may be great, although in all probability of short dura-

[3] In 1948, the Young Democratic Clubs of America were the official youth organizations of the Democratic party.

tion. Men and women of all classes and races and sections are arrayed in a hastily improvised army of propaganda led by skilled and seasoned chieftains. No definite figures are available, but a fair estimate of the number of workers in the last few weeks of a great national campaign is over a million, doing "more or less" in the interest of the party cause. The amount of latent interest available for this purpose is very large, and the amount of time, thought, and money contributed in this way is beyond all calculation. There are times of great excitement when political issues crowd all others into the background, while the great problem of self-government comes to the fore as the major subject of human interest.

PROPAGANDA CHANNELS

The chief media or channels of propaganda are the printing press, films, demonstrations, radio, public address systems, television, the canvass.

The party press includes here dailies and weeklies as well as other periodicals, party pamphlets, leaflets, clip-sheets, boiler-plate, press clippings, cartoons, auto stickers, posters, and pictures—all designed to spread the doctrines of the party to the voters. The great metropolitan dailies and the country weeklies unite in the drive for victory. Some of these papers are moved by traditional party interest or by the issues of the particular campaign; others are owned by party leaders or the interests affiliated with them; still others are influenced in various ways by printing or other more direct subsidies. They constitute powerful weapons of offense and defense, not only during the campaign but in the more quiet intervals between battles. Presidents Franklin D. Roosevelt and Harry Truman won elections in spite of the overwhelming opposition of the daily newspapers. Especially striking was the lack of support which President Truman received in the daily press in 1948.

In national campaigns the parties have emulated the newspapers, and have publicity bureaus which resemble the editorial staffs of the large metropolitan dailies. The personnel of the party publicity bureaus is usually recruited from the ranks of newspapermen. Special publicity agents prepare releases suitable for publication in all papers, including the opposition press, producing just the shade of opinion that the occasion calls for in the particular situation.

Skillful writers endeavor to cover all the various shades and types of journals, trade and industrial, both in the form of open appeal and in the subtler form of indirect propaganda. The foreign language press is carefully cultivated.[4] Specially prepared material is sent out to the various newspapers, and in many cases a "plate" service is sent out to the rural papers, ready for insertion.

Material in general use includes the platform and policies of the party, criticism or defense of the party record as the case may be, information regarding the personality of the candidates, statements by the party leaders, and above all the expressions of opinion made by the candidates themselves, outlining their principles and projecting their policies. Of value are the statements of independents, known to be free from party dictation, or of those who have been hostile but now support the party. No pains are spared to spread broadcast the party ideas and sentiments through every section and class in every langauge and in every conceivable style, wherever they will be useful in the great enterprise of vote getting.[5]

In connection with the work of the publicity bureau are other features of party advertisement. The billboard still survives as an instrument of publicity, blazoning the faces of the candidates, and perhaps carrying some slogan of the campaign designed to catch the attention of the voter. Pictures of candidates are circulated by the million, and where possible are placed in private homes. They serve a useful purpose in suggesting the party idea to the passer-by, although a variety of different pictures tends to confuse him. Further, a strong predominance of the party pictures on one side or the other helps to create the much coveted "illusion of victory," which may itself bring victory.

The use of motion pictures in political campaigns offers many more possibilities than the old-fashioned still pictures.[6] In recent

---

[4] See Robert E. Park, *The Immigrant Press and Its Control* (New York, 1922).

[5] The campaign textbook issued by each party in presidential years is an excellent compendium of party arguments, although it does not exhaust the repertory of appeal. An interesting study has been made of propaganda methods by R. Casey in his *Propaganda Technique in the Presidential Election of 1928* (unpublished, Madison, 1929), and his "Republican Propaganda in the 1936 Campaign," *Public Opinion Quarterly I* (April, 1937), p. 29.

[6] On the role of motion pictures in American life, see Ruth Inglis, *Freedom of the Motion Pictures* (Chicago, 1947); Morris Ernst, *The First Freedom* (New York, 1946).

campaigns various "news events" have been screened in order to familiarize the motion picture public with the candidates, their supporters, and their views. Franklin Roosevelt's first campaign for governor of New York State was greatly aided by a series of sound pictures which were sent into all parts of the state. In some local campaigns candidates have used a fleet of trucks equipped with sound motion picture machines which would back up to convenient walls and attract street crowds. In California in 1934, at the time of Upton Sinclair's EPIC campaign, the cinema companies contributed to Sinclair's defeat by faking pictures of "bums" and "riffraff" and hoboes flocking into the state because of his promised Utopia. The national committees of the two major parties used a number of special short reels to appeal to such groups as the farmers, the Negroes, and the workers. In 1948 television became an additional means of communication during the campaign.

MASS MEETINGS

The meeting or demonstration is a standard form of party warfare. The accompaniments of the barbecue and the parade are less frequent than in earlier days, but the party mass meeting still flourishes in undiminished vigor. In some places it is accompanied by a modified form of vaudeville entertainment.[7] Meetings are intended partly as appeals to reason but largely as appeals to emotion. They assemble and encourage the faithful; they may attract the independent or undecided voter; they intimidate the enemy by a show of strength and enthusiasm. In most campaigns they are attended largely by the regulars who come to learn why rather than whether, but in times of stress thousands of undecided voters are reached in this manner.

Political meetings are an important means to develop and maintain party morale. Some political meetings may take over the patterns of religious revivals or camp meetings. When a real master of the art of political oratory addresses such a meeting, he may be able

In local campaigns the "entertainment" feature of the "meeting" may readily take first place, and the "smoker," "stag" or "show" may crowd everything else to the rear. The candidate himself may entertain the audience by singing, by swinging Indian clubs, by a hillbilly band, by juggling tricks, or other amusing devices to lift the act of voting out of the realm of personal choice into the area of impersonal service for the country. A successful political meeting appeals to local consciousness, party loyalty, and civic pride. The leading spellbinders are adept at the art of mass mesmerism, and may bring their audiences to an emotional frenzy.

Campaign oratory is a type of party warfare almost universally employed but varying widely in its application, purpose, and effect. Some speakers arouse the regular to renewed enthusiasm; others may reach the independent voter; some carry with them chiefly the weight of a record and a name of value to the party. The greatest significance attaches to the utterances of the candidate or leading candidates, and in less measure to the deliverances of well-known leaders of the party. The candidate not only expounds a view, but also expresses what may be more important—a personality. The voter asks not only, what does he stand for; how does he state his case; but also, what manner of man is he? Regulars will probably support him in any event, but the fervency of their enthusiasm will be to some extent determined by his personal characteristics; and upon that magnetism or lack of it will often hang the outcome of the battle.

The importance of oratory in American presidential campaigns is difficult to evaluate. Bryan, the Roosevelts, Taft, Smith, Wiilkie, Truman, and Dewey made extensive speaking tours, but McKinley, Wilson, Harding, Coolidge, and Hoover did not. The long speaking tour is exhausting and less care can be taken in the preparation of the speeches.[8] On the other hand, it is clear that President Truman by his vigorous campaign in 1948 won substantial support.

The mass meeting is nevertheless a significant factor in party success, radiating waves of electrical enthusiasm, strong or weak as the case may be. It is not merely the oratory or the argumentation that is effective, but the generation of impulse to action, of enthusiasm and determination, sending out men who become advocates of the party cause, spreading the contagion of their interest through their own immediate groups and points of contact. The organization utilizes enthusiasm, but the successful meeting generates it. This is

[8] H. R. Penniman, Sait's *American Parties and Elections* (New York, 1948), Chap. XXII. On the other hand, Farley believed that Franklin Roosevelt gained by his tour in 1932; James Farley, *Behind the Ballots* (New York, 1938).

as true of the small house meeting where a few neighbors are gathered as of the meeting in some great auditorium where thousands are assembled.

RADIO

The most important technological advance in political campaigning in recent years has been the extensive use of the radio. It was first employed in the presidential campaign of 1924, but it was not until later campaigns that huge funds began to be expended on this form of publicity. "Radio voice" has become an important consideration in connection with the question of availability, and many attribute Franklin Roosevelt's phenomenal success as a campaigner to his voice quality and voice control before a microphone.

J. Carlile in *Radio Amusement Guide* said, "One of the finest voices over the radio is that of President-Elect Roosevelt, it is pleasant and clear with a pleasing inflection." [9] On the same point the New York *Times* said, "Mr. Roosevelt, with his 'all American' voice, so-called because it has no drawl or twang that would stamp it sectional as was the voice of Calvin Coolidge, deftly handles aerial speech so that his personality 'lives' on the air with every word. 'He is a natural,' whether addressing both visible and invisible audiences at the same time or in the quiet of his study during a 'fireside' chat." [10]

Stuart Chase in his book, *A New Deal*, which appeared in 1932, predicted that some time in the not-so-distant future a presidential campaign would be fought in which one candidate would be favored by the greater majority of the newspapers and the other candidate would have to resort to radio as his chief means of disseminating his propaganda. He further predicted that the candidate using the radio most successfully would win. According to some observers, his prediction was fulfilled within four years.

In 1948 Dr. Gallup conducted a survey on the question as to which presidential candidate was regarded as the best radio speaker. Governor Dewey received in this poll more than twice as many votes as President Truman, and almost four times as many as Henry

[9] Cited by Belle Moses, *Franklin D. Roosevelt* (New York, 1933).
[10] November 8, 1936.

A. Wallace. The 1948 election returns show that the voters did not prefer in this year the man with the best radio voice. In the 1944 campaign a similar survey showed that almost six out of ten voters thought the late President Roosevelt was the best radio speaker. In that year only one out of five named Governor Dewey as the best radio speaker.

A party which does not have a candidate with an outstanding radio voice may employ others to use this medium. Well-known radio commentators have been known to appear as many as five days a week for a national campaign committee. "Spot announcements" and short skits have also been used to drive home the views of the party and its candidate. Broadcasts in foreign languages have been employed extensively by both of the major parties.

Especially in state campaigns the power of the radio has been demonstrated a number of times. In Kansas, Dr. John R. "Goat Gland" Brinkley was able to obtain nearly a third of the votes in the Republican primaries of the early thirties by employing the radio as his exclusive means of publicity.[11] Senator Huey Long's power in national politics was in large part a product of his extensive and skillful use of the radio. The national broadcasting chains gave him free time on the air to rake the administration and to recruit members of his "Share Our Wealth Society."[12]

When the radio was first used in political campaigns, some expressed the view that it would reform political oratory and rationalize campaigning. Since the listeners could dial out any speech which was not appealing, it was claimed that mass mesmerism and spellbinding were things of the past. Unfortunately, this has not been so. The homeliness and earthiness conveyed by Huey Long on the air; the powers of vituperation, of condemnation, and of innuendo demonstrated by Father Coughlin in his broadcasts; and the old-fashioned evangelistic techniques employed by Gerald Winrod show that the radio may be a means for multiplying the audience of the demagogue.

The importance of the radio in American politics has made the question of the control of broadcasting a fundamental democratic

[11] *Christian Century,* June 15, 1932, p. 755

[12] Paul Hutchinson, "Heretics of the Air: Huey Long," *Christian Century,* March 20, 1935, pp. 365–368.

issue. Since the radio industry is a private one in this country, based upon the profit motive, and not a public enterprise as in most European countries, the party which can buy the largest amount of radio time and the most extensive hookups has an advantage over its rivals. While it is true that the major party utilizing the largest amount of radio time in the first three campaigns in which radio was important did not win the presidency, yet the effect of this new medium on minor parties has been discouraging. Only in such a state as Wisconsin where there is a state-owned radio station has some attempt been made to lessen the power of money as far as this new campaign device is concerned.[13]

The development of television has brought the candidates even closer to the voters. In the 1948 Democratic national convention the dramatic acceptance speech of President Truman was the high light of the proceedings. Those with television sets who stayed up to see him were rewarded by hearing and seeing a fighting candidate who brought new hope to the delegates.

CANVASS

An essential feature of the campaign is the canvass, or personal solicitation of voters. This may be conducted either by the candidates or by the workers of the party, regular or volunteer. The personal canvass is intended to give the bulk of the voters a personal impression of the candidates, where the electorate is small enough to permit it; or groups of them where the electorate is too large for personal contact with any considerable percentage of the voters.[14] Not all candidates are equally adapted to this undertaking, but every successful official who faces the electorate must possess a certain facility in the art of personal contact with the mass of the voters. The sensitive electorate will inevitably detect any symptoms of shrinking from mass contact, and will respond in kind.

Canvassing techniques must necessarily vary with the type of the

[13] Elton D. Woolpert, "Wisconsin's Broadcasting System," *National Municipal Review*, XXIII (September, 1934). On the ownership and control of American radio, see Morris Ernst, *The First Freedom* (New York, 1946); L. White, *American Radio* (Chicago, 1947).

[14] See M. Ostrogorski, *Democracy and the Organization of Political Parties* (New York, 1902), I, 454, 641, on the British method of canvassing. See also Frank Gray, *Confessions of a Candidate* (London, 1925).

district. In some of the exclusive high rental areas of the metropolitan centers of the United States it is not possible for a political
worker to get past the doorman or the butler without a proper introduction. On the other hand, in poorer urban areas and in country
districts canvassers may be welcomed. Women have proved to be excellent house-to-house workers for the parties and for independent
political movements. As one of the authors has put it:

"At a ward meeting the workers were addressed as follows: 'Go into
homes again and again. Let them know the facts of the case. If sister is
washing go down into the laundry and help her wash. If cleaning, get
yourself a feather duster and talk.'

"The canvassers learned by experience to adapt their appeals to their
listeners. One precinct official boasted that he could talk with any of his
constituents. He could pray with an old woman, talk craps with a gam-
bler, and talk with men about their women or anything they wanted to
talk about. He could also talk 'highbrow.' " [15]

The worker's canvass may be designed to ascertain the preferences
of the voter, or may be an effort to enlighten or persuade him. To
the trained worker, a preliminary canvass quickly reveals the strong
and the weak spots of the campaign, and upon these vigorous work
is commenced. The local canvasses are reported to central points
where they are carefully analyzed, and their revelations may direct
the character of the campaign. They should show the run or drift
of public opinion, and the apparent causes for the movement. To
check or aid these tendencies active work may be begun. Errors in
strategy may be corrected as "bad spots" are discovered, and general
or local tactics materially modified. These early reports are the
myriad "feelers" of the party, showing where advance is easy or
difficult.

Canvasses are valuable as indications of tendencies only in the
hands of experienced and skilled readers of their meaning, for so
many voters are either unconsulted or undecided or refuse to indicate their preferences as to mislead the careless observer. Thus a
canvass showing Republican 150, Democratic 100, doubtful 150 sig-
nifies little, unless it is definitely known what changes are taking
place in party alignments. But in the hands of the worker who has

[15] H. F. Gosnell, *Negro Politicians* (Chicago, University of Chicago Press, 1935),
p. 140.

canvassed the same voters for many years and knows his lists intimately the result may be very valuable. He will watch the significant changes or the significant silences of the key voters, as the signals that indicate the strength or weakness of the party cause. In a hotly contested battle doubtful voters may be canvassed two, three, or more times, and every effort made to influence each one who is undecided or wavering. No pains are spared to "reach" every voter, not merely through the local party representative, but by whatever route or way he may be most effectively approached. The canvasser who is a local officeholder uses the "bread and butter" or "crying towel" argument. He solicits votes on the ground that his job depends upon his carrying the precinct.[16] Among those voters who hold the ballot lightly this argument has some effect. The skillful worker employs a network of social, business, fraternal, religious, racial, personal lines of influence to bring over the doubtful or even the hostile voters. Great ingenuity and energy are often shown in this process, for in a close contest the five or ten votes per precinct that may be gained by this intensive process may readily snatch victory from defeat. It is precisely in this inner technique that the professional surpasses the amateur, and in the long run often wins his victories.

For the most part the canvass must be made by ringing doorbells and climbing stairs. However, the telephone has come into greater and greater use in putting the finishing touches on the canvass. In fact, the telephone may be used with telling effect as in the case of the Wheeling charter reform campaign of 1935.

The radio has revolutionized the canvass, however, for radio appeals and their timing may be very effective. The canvasser cannot keep up with the broadcasters, who are in contact with their audience every day and almost every hour. On the other hand, personal contacts are still a very important campaigning technique. While Gallup and his associates play down the importance of the precinct captain and the canvass, Lazarsfeld and his colleagues felt that their study of Erie County, Ohio, showed that the personal element was very important.[17]

[16] S. Forthal, *Cogwheels of Democracy* (New York, 1946).
[17] Lazarsfeld, *et al., op. cit.*, and American Institute of Public Opinion, release of November 9, 1940.

From one point of view the effort of the campaigners may be classified as follows:

Arousing the enthusiasm of the regulars—maintaining the morale of the group [18]
Detaching previous opponents from their party allegiance
Securing the adherence of the independent voter
Recruiting the new voter without definite party ties

But the objects may also be classified as:

Logically effective statements of party programs,
Exploitation of the candidate's personality
Completion and energizing of the organization
Skillful conduct of party propaganda, both logical and psychological

It may all be summed up in the creation of a state of mind in the electorate which will find expression on a specific election day.[19]

A successful campaign may be focused or timed to meet the occasion when the photograph is taken of the community, and to produce a certain favorable attitude or expression at that particular time. An adroitly and successfully conducted campaign will often be "timed" to run not too rapidly or too slowly, but to catch the psychological moment when the high point of enthusiasm is reached —not too soon or too late.

PARTY SYMBOLISM

Party success at the polls is in part due to the skill of the candidate and his supporters in the manipulation of symbols. Social scientists have paid increasing attention to the role of symbolism

---

[18] See G. S. Hall's interesting study, *Morale* (New York, 1920).

[19] Frank Kent in his *The Great Game of Politics,* and his *Political Behavior* (New York, 1928) has endeavored to formulate some of the rules for political campaigning in this country. His cynical rules seem to be the following: Every candidate in every campaign is confronted with situations in which he has to choose between losing votes and humbugging his audience. Acquire the fine art of seeming to say something without doing so. Give them a good show. Ignore charges of corruption. Voters are indifferent to party misdeeds, since material welfare has a vastly greater appeal than any moral issue. Give them hokum. Even bad publicity is better than none at all. In order to serve the people, you must fool them first.

in the election process.[20] Symbols, whether verbal or nonverbal, are those representations consisting of sounds, marks, objects, or expressions which exert influence in social life because of the emotional content which they have come to have. The process of winning votes for a given party involves the conditioning of persons to react in a favorable way to the symbols of that party and unfavorably to those of the opposition. The symbols, key words, phrases, tunes, or objects chosen to elicit specified responses must conform to the predispositions of the largest possible number of voters. While there is no question that the conditioning of the voters to respond in a certain way toward given symbols begins at a very early age, the process may be made a continuing one by the constant association of new symbols with familiar ones.

Let us take for an example the way in which certain citizens have been conditioned to respond to the familiar party labels. A study made of some political concepts of a group of adolescents in a junior high school showed that the party names had already acquired significant but varied meanings.[21] A word-association test was given to these pupils and they were instructed to put down a single reaction to each stimulus word. In response to the label "Democratic party," a few put down such answers as "bums," "no good," "cutthroats," "dirty politics," and a few were at the opposite end of the scale with such replies as "good party," "leading party," "good principles," "strong party," and "best party," but the majority wrote down words of a more neutral character such as "special party," "politics," "donkey," and "voting." The responses to the term "Republican party" ranged from such unfavorable ones as "awful," "gypp,' "blah blah," to "expresses my ideas of government," "good

[20] For detailed references consult *Propaganda and Promotional Activities: An Annotated Bibliography,* compiled by H. D. Lasswell *et al.* (Minneapolis, 1935) ; B. L. Smith, H. D. Lasswell, and R. Casey, *Propaganda, Communications and Public Opinion: A Comprehensive Reference Guide* (Princeton, 1946) ; and notes in the *Public Opinion Quarterly.* The most elaborate content analysis which has yet been made of a political campaign is the one by Douglas Waples and Bernard Berelson, *Public Communications and Public Opinions* (Graduate Library School, University of Chicago, 1941, mimeographed). This study uses some of the methods of content analysis suggested by H. D. Lasswell, Nathan Leites, and others. For other studies see reports of Experimental Division for Study of Wartime Communications, Library of Congress.

[21] J. Donald Kingsley, "Some Political Concepts of a Group of Adolescents in the Public Schools of Albany, N. Y." (Ph.D. thesis, Syracuse University, 1933).

party," and "leading party," with such noncommital answers as "politics," "dry," "election," "elephant" in between.

Attachment to a party symbol becomes a fixation in some cases. This is the situation in certain minority groups which have been closely bound by historical ties to a given party. Some older Negroes in the United States have what might be called a reconstruction fixation. In their case the tradition of Abraham Lincoln as the emancipator and their bitter disappointment at the collapse of the reconstruction regimes have conditioned them against any association with the Democratic party. Disfranchisement, lynchings, Jim Crow laws, the cropping system, and other social and economic practices are laid at the door of the Democratic party. Some Negroes have asserted that under no circumstances would they support a candidate bearing the Democratic label. The qualifications of the candidates and the issues become irrelevant when the party symbol has become such a target for hostile feelings. While the Negroes in the northern industrial areas are getting over their Republican fixations, there still remains a considerable body of dyed-in-the-wool Republican sentiment among them.

Political attitudes boil themselves down to key words, slogans, phrases, or objects which may be called symbols. The process by which these symbols are encrusted with meanings may not be a logical one. In the physical sciences and mathematics, symbols are not emotionally charged, but in politics many symbols are employed which arouse respect or hatred toward a person, group, or policy. The emotional states of rage, fear, and affection are powerful stimulants to action and the task of civilization has been to prevent these impulses from becoming antisocial and to sublimate them along socially useful lines.

According to H. D. Lasswell, political symbols may be classified as symbols of demand, of identification, or of fact.[22] A symbol of demand is one which embodies a commitment to action. Thus the campaign slogans, "Make the World Safe for Democracy," "Turn

[22] *World Politics and Personal Insecurity* (New York, 1935), p. 7; "The World Attention Survey," *Public Opinion Quarterly*, V (Fall, 1941), 456–462; Lasswell and associates, "The Politically Significant Content of the Press: Coding Procedures," *Journalism Quarterly*, XIX (March, 1942) 12–42; and mimeographed studies, Library of Congress. Experimental Division for the Study of Wartime Communications.

the Rascals Out" and "Balance the Budget" are symbols of demand. Symbols of identification refer to persons or groups in the name of which statements of fact and demand are made. For example, certain persons who classify themselves as "Americans," "Protestants," "Nordics" may attack other persons as "Communists," "Foreigners," "Jews," or "Fascists." A symbol of fact is a statement about past, present, or future conditions for which no overt preference one way or the other is expressed in the sentence in question. "Prosperity Is Just Around the Corner" and "He Kept Us Out of War" are examples of symbols of this sort.

The language used by political propagandists tends to reflect the interests and habits of the voters. Because personal achievement and business success are so prized in the United States, it is not surprising to find the politicians using the terminology of business in order to win favorable collective responses. The Republican slogan of 1896 is an illustration of this tendency. "Sound Money" was a cry difficult to meet, because it tended to put the opposition on the defensive. "Protection" was also an effective cry. In the twenties the Republicans exploited the "Prosperity" appeal, asserting that prosperity was more secure under Republican than under Democratic rule. In the thirties and forties the Democrats were successful in using "Social Security."

There is also a tendency for American politicians to employ theological and legal language. Clergymen and lawyers have played an important part in the development of the symbolism of American politics.[23] The discussion of such issues as slavery, prohibition, the degradation of morals in the great urban centers, and of the place of the home and the school in American life has been carried on in Biblical terminology. It is significant that the champion of fundamentalism in the Scopes trial involving the teaching of evolution in the public schools of Tennessee was William Jennings Bryan, three times candidate for president of the United States, former Secretary of State, and a leading figure in American politics for forty years. Bryan was also a lawyer and so were over half of the presidents of the United States. "Constitutionalism," "Judicial Supremacy,"

[23] André Siegfried, *America Comes of Age* (New York, 1927), Chap. III, "The Religious Aspect"; H. D. Lasswell, *Politics: Who Gets What, When, How* (New York, 1936).

"States' Rights," "Bill of Rights" are the terms used to discuss political issues by all parties. Measures designed to meet economic needs are discussed not on the basis of their merits but on the basis of their conformance to the canons of American legalism.

Since the voters pass upon candidates as well as issues, the party propagandist must build up favorable pictures of his own organization candidates and unfavorable pictures of those of the opposition. The vocabularies of encomium and vituperation in American politics are particularly rich. Elaborate myths are constructed regarding the superior qualities of a candidate who is being promoted. Thus in 1928 Hoover was pictured as a superman, a practical idealist, a humanitarian, a great engineer, a veritable miracle worker, and a master of emergencies. In 1936 Franklin D. Roosevelt was painted as a warmhearted statesman, a calm, hard-working executive who kept cool in the country's greatest peacetime crisis; and Landon was presented to the American public as a great economizer, a Kansas Coolidge, a typical American, and a second Lincoln. In 1944 Roosevelt was pictured as the master world statesman whose continued presence in office was needed to win the war and formulate the peace. At the same time the opposition is attacked by means of countermyths. In 1928 the Republican propagandists did everything they could to destroy the picture of Al Smith as the "Happy Warrior," and they presented him instead as the wise-cracking city clown, without dignity or reserve, a Catholic, a Tammany man, a drunkard, a tobacco-chewing city smart alec, a politician devoid of education and the virtues, and a city-bred lowbrow, whose wife did not possess the social qualifications for the White House.[24] In four elections the opposition to the New Deal tried to "smear" Roosevelt as the dangerous idealist, the foe of business, the fickle executive, the warmonger, the dictator, the incompetent administrator, the friend of the Communists, the helpless invalid, who would not live through another term.[25]

Fortunate or unfortunate phrases of candidates or their friends may become campaign incidents of great import. Thus the Rev. Burchard's phrase characterizing the Democracy as a compound of

[24] Casey, "Party Campaign Propaganda," *op. cit.*
[25] H. A. Bone, *Smear Politics: An Analysis of 1940 Campaign Literature* (Washington, D. C., 1941); T. M. Black, *Democratic Party Publicity in 1940* (New York, 1941).

"Rum, Romanism, and Rebellion" carried consternation among the friends of Blaine, and perhaps cost him the election of 1884, in view of the fact that New York, the pivotal state, was carried by Cleveland by a bare 1000 votes. Mr. Bryan's declaration in the campaign of 1912 that "If Roosevelt thought he was the Moses of the Progressive movement, he must have mistaken the voice of Perkins for the voice of God" circulated with deadly effect.

The language of reproach and vituperation affords a wide vocabulary of phrases aimed at the foe. This list has included such terms as mugwumps, reformers, copperheads, goo goos, gangsters, grafters, bolters, crooks, soreheads, double crossers, bipartisan dealers, tax eaters, stoolpigeons, racketeers, and a long series of variations upon the basic theme of the unfitness of the opposition for any position of public trust. In 1948 President Truman characterized the Republicans as reactionaries, gluttons of privilege, old moss-backs, mealy-mouthed double-talkers who uttered "G. O. Platitudes."

The party seeks to find a basis for party allegiance in the deep roots of the common life, down below the surface of the political storms, in nationalism, democracy, morality, justice, economic security or advantage where possible, adding to this, of course, whatever the arts of manipulation and management have already obtained. All groups and all interests appeal to the general good which they all profess to serve. All aim to promote the material good of the whole nation and to advance its loftiest ideals of democracy, efficiency, morality, however special their real purposes may be.[26]

Each campaign consists of two parts. One is based upon an appeal to the common interest, on the theory that there are no classes, no races, no religions, no sections, no special interests, but that the common interest of all will be the criterion by which each voter will decide his party allegiance. The other section of the campaign is based upon the opposite theory that the whole electorate is made up of a long series of special interests which must be shown their special advantage in the support of the particular party and its candidates in order to obtain their support.[27]

[26] Cf. Graham Wallas, *Human Nature in Politics* (New York, 1921).

[27] Speaking of modern parties, Lord Bryce says: "They must sometimes wish that it was possible for them to address their own followers in one tongue, and their opponents in another, each uncomprehended by the other, as shepherds in the Scottish Highlands are said to shout their orders to one dog in English and to

CONFERENCE

The campaign management does not rest with organization, speeches, literature, and canvasses. It undertakes the tasks of influencing groups of interests of various types by various means.[28] Nowhere does the ability of the skillful manager show itself more clearly than here. The active and tactful promoter here finds a wide and inviting range of possibilities open to him, and often he produces remarkable results. He seeks to find the key men in large or small groups, who are widely influential in political affairs, whatever the cause may be. He searches for disaffection or insurgency in the ranks of the opposition, and when found he encourages and fosters them. He plays upon local pride; he seizes upon racial groupings and their leaders; he attempts to obtain the open or tacit support of religious leaders; he seeks alliance in social and fraternal organizations; he scours the field of industry and labor for useful points of contact and support, in all types of groupings, in all gangs from high to low. If he cannot win a group or leader, he attempts to soften or neutralize the opposition; if he must attack he makes the most of it among rival and competing groups. His feelers reach a great, intricate network of social interests which he endeavors to influence in behalf of his party or candidate by flattery, promises, cajolery, plans general and special, arguments *ad hominem* and *ad hoc*, inducements ideal and material. But both energy and diplomacy are required, for the movement is swift and there is no time for long drawn out *pourparlers*. Action is urgent. The election is imminent. Delay is fatal.

From the precinct worker to the national manager, a concerted effort is made to reach the nests and groups of voters through their leaders great and small, and by means both direct and devious, as occasion may require. The expert sees what the amateur often does not, the significance of the blocks or groups of voters; and he bends

---

another in Gaelic." *Modern Democracies* (New York, Macmillan Co., 1921), I, 118. The radio makes it harder to make purely local appeals. In the 1948 preconvention campaign, Stassen was criticized for making statements in different localities that were hard to reconcile.

[28] P. Odegard, *Pressure Politics* (New York, 1928); Graves, *op. cit.*, Chap. XXV.

his efforts to capturing as many of these as possible in the limited time he has. In this struggle, superior acquaintance with men and interests, quick and accurate valuation of them, untiring energy, diplomacy, shrewd judgment, prompt decision, coolness, and balance amid wild confusion will often prove of decisive value, other factors being equal. In popular uprisings all these qualities of finesse are often of no avail, for then the mass weight of the public bears down and wears down the best tactics of the defense.

The general strategy of the two larger parties differs somewhat. The Democratic party builds upon the Solid South, a block of almost a third of the electoral vote (176 of 531 in 1944) and then aims at the East, Center or West. In 1948 the Dixiecrat movement made it impossible for President Truman to count on this block of votes. More commonly the attack is made upon the Center and the West as the chief objectives, although New York has been a bone of contention for many campaigns. Tilden, Cleveland, and Franklin Roosevelt alone were successful in making a combination including certain eastern states. Bryan, Wilson, and Cox built on the South and hoped for the Center and the West. Smith hoped to retain the South and to gain the East.

An analysis of campaigns showing the principle, class, or personality relied upon, and the geographical points of attack, illustrates these differences and their variations in recent years:

	Republican		*Democratic*	
1916—				
	Anti-Wilson adm.	East	Wilson	South
	Efficiency	Center	Progressive	West
	Business	West	Democracy	Center
			Farmer	
			Labor	
1920—				
	Anti-Wilson	East	League of Nations	South
	"Normalcy"	Center	issue with anti-	West
			Wilson-manage-	Center
			ment	
	Business-pro-	West		
	gressive-farmer			
	Nationalistic			

	Republican		*Democratic*	

1924—

	Republican			
Business	East	Republican	South
Prosperity	Center	Corruption	West
Fear of	West		Center
"radicalism"			

La Follette

	La Follette		
Farmer-Labor	Center	
Opposition to		
special interests	West	

1928—

Hoover	East	Smith	East
Business	Center	Farm Relief	
Prosperity	West	Labor	South
Dry, Protestant,	South	Wet (local option)	Cente⁻
anti-Tammany		Progressive	

1932—

Hoover	East	Roosevelt	South
Business	Center	Emergency	Center
individualism		relief	West
		Farm relief	East
		Labor	
		Anti-Hoover	

1936—

Business	East	Roosevelt	South
Extravagance		Social security	Center
and corruption		Relief spending	West
Constitutionalism		Farm program	East
Anti-Roosevelt		Labor	

1940—

Business	East	Roosevelt	South
Isolationism	Center	Preparedness	Center
Two term		Labor	West
tradition		Lend lease	East
Anti-Roosevelt			

	Republican		*Democratic*	

1944—

Business	East	Roosevelt	South
Efficiency	Center	Win the war	Center
Two term		World leadership	West
tradition		Labor	East
Anti-Roosevelt			

1948—

Business	East	New Deal	Center
Efficiency	Center	Anti-Congress	South
Truman incom-	West	Anti-inflation	West
petent		Labor	East
Dewey		Farm program	
Unity			

Except in unusual years such as 1928 and 1948, the Republican party has had little hope of the South, but pins its faith on New England and a division of the western and central states. The Republican tactics are traditionally based on the northern and eastern manufacturing and business group, with the central farmer, and a division of the middle class and of the labor vote in the great industrial centers.

The Democracy, barring unusual events such as the nomination of a Catholic or the bolt of a states' rights faction, counts upon the white vote in the South without regard to class, but in the other sections of the country strives to secure the support of the farmer, especially in the West, of the middle class and of labor. It makes less serious efforts to obtain the manufacturing and commercial element of the North and East, although by no means without strength here.

ELECTION STATISTICS

One of the surprising facts regarding national elections is the tendency toward an equilibrium between the great parties. In the 18 elections between 1876 and 1944 there were 12 in which one party received a majority of the vote, and 11 in which the difference in the percentage of the vote received by the major parties exceeded 5 per cent.[29]

Figure 13 shows the ups and downs of the fortunes of the Democratic party in winning the presidency and in winning seats in the House of Representatives. While in general the party strength in the House of Representatives tends to follow the party vote for president, there are fluctuations in the congressional elections which come between presidential elections. A party which controls the presidency is likely to lose seats in the House of Representatives in the midterm elections. Putting it in another way, a party which wins the presidency is likely to carry with it a majority in the House of Representatives. Looking at the entire period from 1858 to 1948 the curve shows that there have been political cycles, the exact period of which has varied.

The "avalanche" and the "landslide" were relatively rare before 1896, but since that time they have been more common. Congressional and state elections show wider ranges of party vote, and reversals of form are not uncommon here. But in the national elections where the parties function most vigorously there has been a remarkable uniformity in the vote of the major parties. In the election of 1890 following the passage of the McKinley tariff bill the Republican party was almost wiped out,[30] but in the election of 1896 it was back to its usual vote. In 1904 the Democratic party under the leadership of Parker was overwhelmingly defeated, but rallied in four years to almost its normal strength. The Republican party in 1912 carried only four states, but in 1916 was again on its usual footing. The Democracy was overwhelmed in 1920, but before the inauguration of the new president was planning the battle of 1924 with high hopes of return to full party strength at that time. In 1928 the Democracy

---

[29] A. L. Lowell, "Oscillations in Politics," *Annals of the American Academy of Political and Social Science*, XII (1898), 69; F. S. Chapin, "The Variability of the Popular Vote at Presidential Elections," *American Journal of Sociology*, XVIII (September, 1912), 222–240. In the latter article the view is expressed that the variability of the presidential vote between states has been growing greater. See also a criticism of the Chapin study in H. F. Gosnell, "Statisticians and Political Scientists," *American Political Science Review*, XXVII (June, 1933), 392–403. For recent election figures, see U. S. Bureau of the Census, *Vote Cast in Presidential and Congressional Elections, 1928–1944* (Washington, D. C., 1946); and George Gallup, *The Gallup Political Almanac for 1948* (Princeton, 1948).

[30] Eighty-eight Republicans survived in the House.

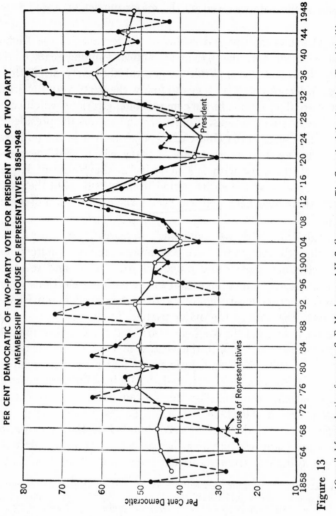

PER CENT DEMOCRATIC OF TWO-PARTY VOTE FOR PRESIDENT AND OF TWO PARTY MEMBERSHIP IN HOUSE OF REPRESENTATIVES 1858-1948

Figure 13

(Compiled from election figures in S. E. Morison and H. S. Commager, *The Growth of the American Republic* (New York, 1942) for the period 1858-92 and from the *Statistical Abstract of the United States* for the period 1896-1944. Figures on House from Office of the Secretary of the United States Senate, *Factual Campaign Information* and *Congressional Directory*.)

388

was again overwhelmed, and had losses in the Solid South for the first time since 1876, but four years later it staged its most impressive comeback since the Civil War.

Table 7 shows the electoral vote of four sections of the United States in the last fourteen campaigns: the Northeast, the Center, the South and the West. The Northeast includes ten states, namely, Connecticut, Delaware, Maine, Massachusetts, New Hampshire, New Jersey, New York, Pennsylvania, Rhode Island, and Vermont.

TABLE 7

ELECTORAL VOTE

	Northeast		Center		South		West		Total	
	R	D	R	D	R	D	R	D	R	D
1896	120	0	110	0	26	130	15	46	271	176
1900	120	0	110	0	14	142	48	13	292	155
1904	129	0	116	0	26	140	65	0	336	140
1908	129	0	116	0	27	146	49	16	321	162
1912	4[a]	102	27Pro.	94	0	183	4[b]	56	8	435
1916	140	4	97	24	7	176	10	73	254	277
1920	144	0	121	0	56	127	83	0	404	127
1924	144	0	121	0	47	136	83[c]	0	444	87
1928	121	23	121	0	119	64	83	0	382	136
1932	59	85	0	121	0	183	0	83	59	472
1936	8	136	0	121	0	183	0	83	8	523
1940	8	136	53	69	0	183	21	62	82	449
1944	8	136	61	60	0	183	30	53	99	432
1948	121	20	32	86	8	133[e]	28	65	189	303

[a] Prog., 38.   [b] 23 Prog.   [c] 13 Prog.   [e] 39 Thurmond

The Center includes seven states, namely, Illinois, Indiana, Iowa, Michigan, Minnesota, Ohio, and Wisconsin. The South includes sixteen states, namely, Alabama, Arkansas, Georgia, Florida, Kentucky, Louisiana, Maryland, Mississippi, Missouri, North Carolina, Oklahoma, South Carolina, Tennessee, Texas, Virginia, West Virginia. The West includes fifteen states, namely, Arizona, California, Colorado, Idaho, Kansas, Montana, Nebraska, Nevada, New Mexico, North Dakota, Oregon, South Dakota, Utah, Washington, Wyoming.

STATE CAMPAIGNS

State campaigns are usually overshadowed by national issues. But at times there may be distinct and direct state questions at stake. It is even possible that state issues may overshadow the national question, but this is unusual. State campaigns are fought upon national issues modified by the records and qualifications of the candidates, by factional, class, racial, or religious conflicts, and sundry local differences. Railroad and corporation control, the wet and dry question, boss rule, extravagance, and incompetence have often been the dividing issues in states, but usually the national aspects overshadow all others and give the prevailing color to the contest, especially if the state and national elections coincide.

In the political history of all states there is the story of struggles in which the regular party lines have been badly broken. In New York the rivalry between Conkling and the "Half-breeds" was of nationwide significance, while the antagonism between Tammany and the anti-Tammany forces is historic. The clashes between Tammany and Tilden, Cleveland and Hill are well-known episodes in our national history. In Wisconsin the "Half-breeds," calling themselves "Progressives in the thirties and forties," led by the La Follettes, father and sons, have carried on a battle with the "Stalwarts" or Republicans for almost half a century. Bryan and anti-Bryan factions divided half of the states of the Union for the same period of time. The Smith campaign split the ᴊouthern states wide apart. The annals of every state contain the record of bitter struggles within the ranks of the party, whether we look south or north or east or west.

Analysis shows that the chief factors in the various contests are: (1) the struggle for control of the machinery of the party, leading to personal or factional feuds without regard to issues or policies; (2) the struggle of public interests against special interests, of which railroads were once the chief type, but where local public utilities, liquor, insurance, mining, manufacturing, and a wide variety of other interests have entered into the situation. Industrial and political barons with large resources in the way of men, money, press, and propaganda have fought over many states like feudal lords, sometimes against each other and sometimes banded against some common foe who has championed the cause of the general public.

The task of campaigning in states is even more complicated than in the national field. Personal, factional, class, sectional, racial, and religious antipathies and attractions are found in more intense form; and the compromises of national politics are often unavailing in the smaller local field. In a national situation many of these conflicting interests offset each other and may produce an equilibrium or compromise; but in the state, class or sectional or racial factors may assume controlling proportions. Agrarian interests may dominate, or manufacturing; or urban-rural rivalries may prove conclusive; or geographical considerations may be all-important. Race questions may come to the fore where one or more races dominate. At the same time the bonds of party loyalty rest much more lightly upon the state voter than upon the national voter, for the national Republican or Democrat may have many reservations in affairs involving only the state.[31]

It is in state campaigns that some of the most important innovations have taken place in American politics. In the early twenties the Non-Partisan League, with its far-reaching program, got its start in the primary campaigns of the Western states. With the prolonged period of economic contraction which began in 1929, many new state political movements sprang up. Huey Long started his "Share the Wealth" movement in his home state of Louisiana. Upton Sinclair, former Socialist writer, put on a whirlwind campaign in California under the slogan EPIC (End Poverty in California). Olson built up the Farmer-Labor party in Minnesota, and the La Follettes started their Progressive party in Wisconsin.[32] In these states class lines have been more sharply drawn than in some of the other states, and the activities of the party propagandists have been much more ruthless than elsewhere.

Are elections won or lost in accordance with the skill or lack of skill of the party propagandists? This is a difficult question to answer since vigorous promotion may be offset by counter promotion. In the party primaries and in local campaigns it is likely that superior

[31] For an interesting description of a state campaign, see Paul H. Douglas, "Running for Political Office," *New York Times Magazine*, September 5, 1948.

[32] See Gosnell, *Grass Roots Politics*.

campaigning techniques may be decisive, but in presidential elections, where the floodlights of national publicity are focused on both of the major candidates, it may be that the direction of the tide of public opinion is more important than the skill of the party propagandists. When the tide is running strongly against the party which has held the presidency, as in the campaigns of 1920 and 1932, it appears doubtful if any technical devices could have stemmed it. Adverse economic conditions, an accumulation of latent animosities, and a general lack of confidence are obstacles which overwhelm the party managers from time to time. Under these circumstances the function of the organizers is to hold the ship together and wait for better times. Lazarsfeld and his associates showed that party propaganda is most likely to be read by those whose minds are already made up. Party publicity has a reinforcing influence. It is necessary to get out the party vote. On the other hand, the conversion effects of party promotion are most likely to be seen in those citizens subjected to cross pressures. President Truman showed in 1948 what could be done by a whirlwind campaign. Commentators are agreed that he won many last minute votes.[33]

[33] *Report of the Social Science Research Council Committee on Analysis of Pre-Election Polls and Forecasts* (New York, 1948).

CHAPTER XVII

THE INFLUENCE OF MONEY
IN ELECTIONS

"I'll take money from any man," said Penrose. "You can't run a party on nothing and when you need money the place to get it is from them that have it."—Walter Davenport, *Power and Glory, The Life of Boies Penrose* (New York, G. P. Putnam's Sons, 1931), p. 177

IT HAS BEEN INDICATED THAT A STRONG POLITICAL ORGANIZATION IS needed to educate the voters regarding issues and candidates and to induce them to perform their duties as citizens upon election day. Such an organization must have a well-trained personnel to perform the routine tasks so necessary in politics, such as canvassing, opening their homes for neighborhood meetings, addressing envelopes, distributing literature, making public speeches, and looking after the technical details of the election process. It is necessary to have persons who are willing to do these things and who know how to meet the tactics of the opposition. They must be willing to work long hours and to withstand harsh criticism.

It is conceivable that the elements of a political organization which have been mentioned so far could be supplied on a volunteer basis. The workers and leaders might be fired with a zeal for their cause. Mass meetings might be held in the open or in donated halls and the general newspapers might carry all the political news that was necessary to inform the voters. In some local campaigns in the United States most of these functions have been performed on a voluntary basis. In the 1944 and 1948 campaigns a large amount of volunteer help was furnished the Democratic party by the Political Action Committee of the Congress of Industrial Organizations (PAC of CIO). It is a well-known fact, however, that neither of the two major parties in a national election in recent years has relied primarily upon voluntary efforts. Money furnishes the backbone of American major party organizations in a presidential campaign.[1] Such items as printing, the use of the mails, newspaper advertisements, billboards, the use of auditoriums and office space, telephone service, radio broadcasting, television, public address systems, lithographs, and sound motion pictures are not available without large expenditures of money. Money can also buy practically every other type of political service needed should the supply or zeal of the volunteers run low. Speakers, clerical helpers, canvassers, professional publicity men, professional organizers, legal experts on election affairs can all be hired for a consideration. Thomas Jefferson could run his first successful campaign for the presidency with a personal expenditure of fifty dollars, but in the twentieth century the party expenditures run into millions. The increase in the size of the country, the spectacular growth of the electorate, and the rapid invention of mechanical devices for mass impression have multiplied campaign costs a hundred thousand fold.

American economic enterprises are so organized that a considerable proportion of their budgets is devoted to advertising and salesmanship. A party organization during a political campaign is largely a promotional and sales organization. It is selling its candidates and its issues. Without a huge budget it would be unable to acquaint the voters with its wares. The 1944 presidential campaign, coming as it did when we were concentrated on winning the war, involved a reported expenditure of over $20,000,000 on the part of the major organizations.[2] The actual monetary outlay was much larger than this. In absolute numbers this is a large figure, but it should be remembered that it is only about 42 cents for each of the 48,000,000 votes cast. When it is recalled that it costs about 10 cents to send a single letter to a voter, this cost per voter does not seem excessive. A page advertisement in a leading metropolitan daily costs over $3000 and a national hookup on the major radio stations costs $195,000 an hour. It is surprising that the parties can put on extensive publicity campaigns for 42 cents per voter.

[1] Louise Overacker, *Presidential Campaign Funds* (Boston, 1946) and *Money in Elections* (New York, 1932) ; J. K. Pollock, *Party Campaign Funds* (New York, 1926), and his chapter on "The Use of Money in Elections" in E. Logan (ed), *The American Political Scene* (New York, 1936).

[2] Overacker, *Presidential Campaign Funds,* p. 34.

Most of the campaign expenditures are legitimate and necessary for the successful operation of the electoral process. However, in hotly contested local elections or party primaries it sometimes happens that excessive outlays are made for the so-called election-day expenses. These involve payment for transportation, payment of workers, "treating" expenses, and outright bribery of voters. The line between bribery and payment for election-day services is a hard one to draw since the services required are sometimes very nominal. In the famous or infamous Pennsylvania Republican primary of 1926 the expenditure of $60 per precinct for election-day workers by a single faction seemed unduly high.[3] On the other hand, if the money went to persons who had made a genuine canvass, if it went to checkers and watchers who put in a twenty-four-hour day, who is to say that the expenditures were not justified? It is possible to use that sum of money in each precinct in a highly honorable way.[4] For the most part, campaign expenditures are legitimate.

SOURCES OF CAMPAIGN FUNDS

From the standpoint of the future of democracy, the question of how the campaign funds are raised is more important than the one of how they are spent. If the funds are contributed largely by wealthy persons who have special interests at stake, then the fiction of equal suffrage has been destroyed and democracy has degenerated into plutocracy.

In the United States the chief sources of party revenue have been:

(1) Contributions from officeholders
(2) Contributions from candidates
(3) Contributions from citizens with general interest in view
(4) Contributions from special group interests (including the underworld) and individuals with direct personal interest
(5) Services of public employees
(6) Services of volunteers
(7) Support of the party press or favorable press
(8) Support from various organizations not classed as party agencies

[3] Overacker, *Money in Elections*, p. 40.
[4] H. F. Gosnell, *Machine Politics: Chicago Model* (Chicago, 1937), p. 59.

(1) Officeholders holding positions by reason of party election or appointment are liable to assessment in most cases. Their contributions may be voluntary in form or more or less mandatory, but they are expected and are usually forthcoming. Sometimes a regular scale is fixed in the form of a percentage on the salary of the incumbent. A common figure for this purpose is 5 per cent of the annual compensation. The figure may be higher or lower, or there may be no assessment at all, as the case may be. In Illinois, in the 1928 primary, a graduated salary assessment was levied upon state employees which varied from one-sixth to four-fifths of a month's salary.[5] The investigation of the appointment of postmasterships in the South by the Brookhart Committee showed that various coercive practices had been employed to collect campaign funds from federal officeholders.[6] Following the 1936 campaign, selected persons in the government service in Washington, D. C., were invited by the Young Democratic Clubs of the District of Columbia to attend a Democratic Victory dinner at ten dollars per person. The invitation was accompanied by an explanatory note which said: "Two dollars and a half of this amount covers cost of the dinner; the remaining seven dollars and a half is to be contributed to the Democratic National Campaign Fund to help wipe out the deficit."[7] As President Roosevelt said at a Jackson Day speech in 1940, "The $100 pays for a $10 dinner with all the fixin's free—no cover charge, no tips—nothin' to sign and nothin' to jine—and a ring-side seat at a plate-side chat."[8]

It may safely be concluded that the average incumbent of office held through the party tenure does not escape the payment of a material contribution to the party exchequer. Assessment of civil service employees is now forbidden by statute where the merit system is found, but this does not stand in the way of voluntary contributions from the officials. Nor is the law itself rigidly enforced.

(2) Assessment of candidates is another source of income, especially in state and local campaigns. Here again the percentage system is commonly used, and the figure may run to 5 or 10 per cent of

[5] *Chicago Daily News,* March 13, 1928, cited by C. H. Wooddy, *The Case of Frank L. Smith* (Chicago, 1931), p. 164.

[6] United States Congress, Senate Report No. 46, 71st Congress, 2nd Session.

[7] The charge for the Jackson Day dinner ranged from $100 a plate (in Washington) to $5 a plate in other sections.

[8] *New York Times,* January 9, 1940, p. 14.

the salary, which may be computed as the salary for one year, or in some cases as the salary for the term of office. Well-to-do candidates are of course expected to contribute in large amounts, and in exceptional cases may bear the whole financial burden of the campaign. In a county election, if there are thirty candidates whose aggregate salaries amount to $100,000 a year, and a 5 per cent assessment is levied on an annual basis, the proceeds would be $5000 for the purposes of the contest. For important offices like those of governor and senator, candidates frequently contribute much larger sums for election purposes, depending upon their means and upon their willingness to "plunge." In hotly contested elections in such populous states as Pennsylvania, Illinois, and Michigan, a wealthy candidate may put up several hundred thousand dollars.[9] In the national elections the contributions of the candidates are not usually a significant factor. However, in some preconvention campaigns well-to-do candidates have made very sizable donations to their own campaign funds.

(3) In all campaigns considerable sums are contributed by citizens whose chief interest is a general one—perhaps in the particular candidate in the race, perhaps in the particular issue at stake, perhaps in the general welfare of the party as an exponent of national welfare. An examination of the contributions to national funds shows large sums of money contributed on this basis with no apparent desire except for the general good—contributions "with no strings on them." The large contributions made by automobile manufacturers in 1928 might be put in this class. In state and local campaigns, although the actual figures are not as readily available, the same situation is found in many places and at many times. In recent years an organized effort has been made to obtain small sums of money from large numbers of citizens, and some success has been achieved. Outstanding has been the success of organized labor in its "a buck for Roosevelt" campaign. The Political Action Committee (PAC) raised $757,217 in 1944 from individual contributions. The respondents on a recent Gallup poll indicated that some 14 million voters or more than one-fourth of the electorate would be willing to contribute $5 to the party of their choice.

Table 8 shows that while there has been an increase in the rela-

[9] Ruth Hanna McCormick contributed almost half a million dollars for her primary campaign in Illinois in 1930 Overacker, *Money in Elections*, p. 65.

tive importance of contributions under $100, particularly in the case of the Democratic party, both parties, but especially the Republican party, rely upon contributions of over $1000. In 1936 over half of the Republican contributions came from this source.

TABLE 8

PERCENTAGE DISTRIBUTION BY SIZE OF CONTRIBUTIONS TO DEMOCRATIC AND REPUBLICAN NATIONAL COMMITEES, 1928–1940 [10]

	1928		1932		1936		1940	
	Dem.	Rep.	Dem.	Rep.	Dem.	Rep.	Dem.	Rep.
$5,000 and over	52.7	45.8	43.7	40.1	26.0	24.2	13.1	3.8
$1,000 to $4,999	17.0	22.6	14.4	24.8	19.4	26.8	19.6	38.3
$100 to $199	16.3	21.9	14.5	23.4	18.0	23.9	17.3	30.7
Less than $100	12.5	8.2	16.0	9.1	18.5	13.5	23.3	13.4
Impossible to allocate	1.5	1.5	11.4	2.6	18.1	11.6	26.7	13.8
Total	100.0	100.0	100.0	100.0	100.0	100.0	100.0	100.0

(4) Of great significance are the contributions made by various groups with specific interests at stake. This list includes railroads, corporations of various types, banks, protected industries, mining interests, or other industries with a somewhat direct interest in the outcome of the election. One of the most notorious examples of contributions of this sort was the contribution or "loan" made by Harry F. Sinclair, the oil magnate, to make up the deficit in the Republican campaign fund of 1920. In some cases such contributions are doubtless made with the general interest also in mind, as in the campaign of 1896, or in the belief that one party or the other tends on the whole to promote business prosperity.

On the basis of the reports filed with the clerk of the House of Representatives by the two major parties, it is possible to make a rough estimate of the proportion of the total campaign fund contributed by different economic groups. Dr. Overacker's studies of large campaign contributions furnish the basis for Table 9.

A number of startling tendencies are revealed by this table, particularly as far as the Democratic party is concerned. In the pros-

[10] Table from Overacker, *Presidential Campaign Funds* (Boston University Press, 1946), p. 14.

TABLE 9

PERCENTAGE DISTRIBUTION BY ECONOMIC INTEREST OF CONTRIBUTORS OF $1000 OR MORE TO NATIONAL COMMITTEES, 1928–1944 [11]

Group	Democratic					Republican				
	1928	1932	1936	1940	1944	1928	1932	1936	1940	1944
From bankers	25.3	24.2	3.3	3.1	5.2	28.2	20.5	14.7	13.7	16.7
Manufacturers	16.1	10.5	13.6	7.4	8.1	24.4	26.3	29.6	34.0	24.2
Mining and oil	4.5	4.4	6.9	5.3	—	9.0	9.7	5.3	5.9	—
Brewers, distillers	—	—	5.7	3.9	—	—	—	0.2	0.7	—
Railroads, airways	9.7	6.1	2.5	1.8	—	4.2	4.1	3.5	1.3	—
Professional men	—	12.2	12.7	8.6	—	—	7.4	4.4	4.1	—
Publishers, advertisers	—	7.1	2.6	4.5	—	—	1.4	3.3	1.8	—
Organized labor	—	—	10.2	15.9	—	—	—	—	—	—
Retail stores	2.4	2.4	2.3	1.9	—	5.0	2.2	1.9	2.6	—
Officeholders	—	—	12.6	19.3	—	—	—	—	—	—
Unclassified or unidentified	42.0	33.1	27.6	28.3	—	29.2	28.4	37.1	35.9	—

perous twenties the Democratic party received over half its financial support from the bankers, the manufacturers, and the mining and oil interests, but in the 1940 and 1944 campaigns it received only one-seventh of its campaign funds from this source. These losses were made up by large contributions from the liquor interests, organized labor, and officeholders. On the other hand, the Republican party in 1940 still derived half its funds from the banking, industrial, and extractive industries. These figures undoubtedly show the beginning of sharper class lines in American politics. A closer analysis of the contributions from the manufacturers shows that the Democratic party gets some financial aid from the tobacco manufacturers, whereas the Republicans enjoy the confidence of the iron and steel and chemical manufacturers.[12]

If it were possible to examine the sources of state and local campaign funds as closely as national funds, there is no question that a

[12] Overacker, "Campaign Funds in the Presidential Election of 1936," *loc. cit.*, and *Presidential Campaign Funds.*

[11] From studies by Louise Overacker, in (for 1928) *Money in Elections*, p. 162; (for 1932) "Campaign Funds in a Depression Year," *American Political Science Review*, XXVII (October, 1933), 776; (for 1936) "Campaign Funds in the Presidential Election of 1936," *op. cit.*, p. 485; and (for 1940 and 1944) *Presidential Campaign Funds.* The 1928 figures are for contributors of $5000 or more.

large proportion of the campaign moneys would come from real estate interests which feared the power of the local taxing authorities, and from the underworld interests which were concerned with the powers of the local law-enforcing officers. In the metropolitan centers of the United States, which now contain about one-half the voters, the underworld interests are often important.

In the big urban centers where the wet sentiment predominates and where there are many persons with liberal views on prostitution, gambling, and other organized vices, the existence of a powerful underworld, ready to supply the services which are banned by the puritanical code of morals imposed on the unwilling populace by state legislatures dominated by rural interests, can be taken for granted. The combination of businessmen and politicians which can give immunity from the blue laws is called the "Big Fix." [13] Bootleggers, racketeers, gambling-house keepers, panderers, thieves, and other hoodlums cannot operate unless they secure certain immunities from interference on the part of the law-enforcing agencies. Gangsters and other criminals realize that this freedom from restraint depends upon how useful they can make themselves to the politicians. When asked to make campaign contributions, the leaders of the underworld cannot very well refuse. If they should be so rash as to turn down the local powers that be, they would find their places of business closed by the police within a remarkably short time. The Seabury investigation in New York showed the deep ramifications of this system of raising local campaign funds. [14] A little probing into the campaign secrets of any other city where there was a powerful political machine would show the same tie-up. [15]

(5) Each party can call upon its army of local noncivil service public employees for campaign services, and can reckon upon work from most of them. If these men were paid for their time, the total sum required would be very large. There are some 300,000 precinct captains whose time at $5 per day would make a bill of $1,500,000

[13] C. E. Merriam, *Chicago* (New York, 1929), p. 26.

[14] William B. and John B. Northrop, *The Insolence of Office: The Story of the Seabury Investigations* (New York, 1932).

[15] United States National Commission on Law Observance and Enforcement (Wickersham Commission), *Report on Prosecution* (No. 4), p. 15; C. O. Johnson, *Carter Henry Harrison*, I (Chicago, 1928), pp. 186–187; Gosnell, *Machine Politics*, p. 42.

a day, and many days are consumed in campaigning. Of course, not all of these committeemen are officeholders, but many of them are. To some extent this work is done on the public's time, to some extent outside of public service hours.[16] Some of the work is partly paid for, and some of it entirely unrecompensed. In any event, this is the largest single factor in party revenue, but an item that does not and cannot enter into statements of party expenditures.

(6) A large amount of party service is rendered by volunteers. Many contribute their services cheerfully for the good of the party or the cause. On the whole, in campaign times there is an astonishing amount of work done by men and women who are enthusiastic about the party in general or about some personality or special cause which has touched them deeply. Others are taking a hand in an interesting game. Amid many sordid features of political campaigns the whole-souled enthusiasm and energy of the volunteers, men and women, is often a refreshing sight. But at what value are these unpurchasable services calculated in the party financial statements?

(7) An element in the revenue of the campaign is the service rendered by the party press, or by the press favorable to the candidate or the party for the particular campaign. The value of the political advertising contributed in this way is difficult to calculate, although it is sometimes placed upon the market and sold to the highest bidder. Political advertising which must be purchased is very expensive, and where this is done the bills of the party or the candidate are very large. But the party or personal organ, or the friendly paper, may contribute space and support which could not be bought. The party newspapers in the United States are of great significance.[17] They constitute one of the most powerful divisions of the party's strength.[18] Their services need not and do not enter into

[16] In Chicago, the Sanitary District pay roll disclosures of 1928–1929 showed that the number of employees dropped four days after the presidential election of 1928 was 1147. See *Chicago Tribune*, November 22, 1928. On page 178 above, the number of precinct captains for the major parties was given at 260,000. There are at least 40,000 precinct captains for the minor parties.

[17] In England regular party organs of propaganda are maintained, such as *Gleanings and Memoranda* (Conservative), the *Labour Magazine* and the *Liberal Magazine*, each an official agency supported by the party for the use of the workers and the friends of the party. This resembles a periodical edition of an American campaign textbook. A present type is the *Republican News*.

[18] Robert E. Park, *The Immigrant Press and Its Control* (New York, 1922).

statements of campaign expenditures (unless cash payments are made for advertising), but they are nevertheless one of the great assets of the party in the conduct of the party hostilities. To the regular party organs are joined in times of stress the accretions from the independents and from the wide range of trade or labor or other journals of all descriptions which are interested in the outcome of the election and are disposed to take a hand in it.

(8) Another source of revenue consists of the party aid given by various kinds of organizations which are not primarily political, but which are interested in the particular candidate or the particular campaign. The number of these is as varied as the social interests of the country itself. Business, labor, agriculture, races, religions, and sections, classes, and subclasses of all types may lend their powerful aid to the conduct of the campaign; or they may carry on their activities beyond the campaign into the quieter period between times. The Anti-Saloon League urged prohibition, the woolen manufacturers may preach protection, the brewers and distillers may plead the merits of stimulants, the labor organizations may steadily contend for their policies. For such purposes, which may run closely parallel with the activities of some party, they may strive year in and year out. They may expend large sums of money in the advocacy of ideas which may be the policy of one party or of neither. Such items will not enter, of course, into any party statement, and in fact cannot well be there incorporated, as they may be only collateral activities from the point of view of these organizations themselves; although from the point of view of the party they may be a very direct aid. What disposition shall be made of these items in an estimate of the receipts and expenditures of parties? Clearly they can neither be accurately known nor reckoned in the campaign budget, but just as clearly they are of fundamental significance in estimating the actual resources of the contending parties in the election. Since the 1936 election when organized labor made a huge contribution to the Democratic party campaign chest, increasing attention has been paid to this source.

All of these items taken together constitute the budget for the party campaign. In the aggregate the amount reaches a high figure in local, state, and national elections. The ordinary statements of campaign expenditure give no clear idea of the amount of social energy actually appropriated for party purposes in the great struggles that from time to time shake our communities. Table 10 shows the nominal outlay of the national committee alone in the campaign for the presidency. This does not include large amounts expended by state or other organizations in the locality, or the out-

TABLE 10

SUMMARY OF EXPENDITURES INFLUENCING PRESIDENTIAL ELECTIONS
1928, 1940, AND 1944 [19]

(*In Thousands of Dollars*)

	National Committees [a]	State and Finance Committees	Independent National and Intrastate Agencies	Total
Democratic				
1928	$3,157	$ 2,445	$1,550	$ 7,152
1940	2,198	2,786	872	5,856
1944	2,056	2,033	3,352	7,441
Republican				
1928	4,065	4,762	607	9,434
1940	2,243	9,111 [b]	3,587	14,941
1944	2,829	9,261	1,106	13,196
Total				
1928	7,222	7,207	2,157	16,586
1940	4,441	11,897	4,459	20,797
1944	4,885	11,294	4,458	20,637

[a] Exclusive of transfers to states, included under "State and Finance Committees."
[b] Exclusive of transfers from finance committees to state committees.

side expenditures of other organizations of the class previously described.

Expenses in state campaigns may also run high, and in a state of average size, say 3,000,000, may easily reach $100,000, not including expenditures in county and local campaigns carried on at the same time. The expenditures in municipal campaigns may be even more extensive. The campaign expenses in cities like New York and Chicago may run from $200,000 to $1,000,000. Even in ward campaigns it is not uncommon for $25,000 to be spent, while in certain cases this figure has been exceeded. No figures are available regarding the

[19] Table from Overacker, *Presidential Campaign Funds*, p. 34.

total annual expenditures in party campaigns, although this is obviously important. In recent elections the total outlay for the major parties has been over $40,000,000. This would not include the cost of the election system or of the primaries. Election costs would amount to many millions more, and the aggregate costs of the various primaries cannot be estimated by any method available to the writers. Generally speaking, the expense of the urban campaigning is higher than the rural, and the outlay in the North is, of course, much greater than in the South, where the primary is usually the election.

REGULATION OF CAMPAIGN FUNDS

Within recent years an effort has been made to regulate the expenditure of funds in campaigns by statutory measures.[20]

At the outset regarded as a purely private affair, the cost of elections has become increasingly a matter of public concern. On the one hand the expense of elections has been made more and more a public charge, and on the other hand the expenditures of and on behalf of candidates have been more and more closely subjected to public supervision and regulation. Public supervision has taken the following forms: [21]

(1) Requirements of publicity as to campaign revenues and expenditures

(2) Restrictions on sources of expenditures

(3) Restrictions on the character of the expenditures

(4) Limitation of the amounts to be expended

(1) The purpose of the publicity requirement is to give to the public full information as to the donors of funds and the purposes to which they are applied. In earlier times such information was

[20] S. S. Minault, *Corrupt Practices Legislation in the 48 States* (Chicago, Council of State Governments, 1942) ; Overacker, *Money in Elections*; Pollock, *Party Campaign Funds*; E. R. Sikes, *State and Federal Corrupt Practices Legislation* (Durham, 1928) ; Perry Belmont, "Abolition of the Secrecy of Party Funds," 62nd Congress, 2nd Session, Senate Document, 495; also 64th, 2nd Session, S. R. 898, S. D., 640; and R. C. Brooks, *Corruption in American Politics and Life* (New York, 1910), Chap. VI.

[21] Compare the British system as described in J. K. Pollock, *Money and Politics Abroad* (New York, 1932).

usually wholly inaccessible and was considered to be the private information of the candidate or his manager. Publicity may, of course, be obtained by voluntary agreement between the parties, as was the case in the national campaign of 1908,[22] but as a rule no such arrangement is effected, and the figures are not forthcoming unless required by the law of the state. Even here the question may arise whether the publication of receipts and expenditures shall be made before the election or after, or both; and the still more serious question whether the returns made correspond to the actualities. All but a few of the states now require the filing of statements of campaign receipts and disbursements. In three-fourths of the states, both candidates and parties must file such statements; in the remaining states only candidates must file. Where candidates alone make statements it is easy to evade the law. An obvious weakness in most of the laws is the failure to provide for official inspection of the statements filed. Many of the statements made under the laws are obviously absurd, and possess no significance whatever.

Effective publicity provisions must call for pre-election as well as postelection publicity. The voters have the right to know before they cast their ballots how much money each candidate is spending, from what sources he derives his financial support, and in what ways he is using money to win votes. If it is known before election day that a given candidate spent a huge fund collected from sources which expect a *quid pro quo*, then the voters who support that candidate cannot later complain that they were deceived regarding the nature of his campaign.[23] On the other hand, postelection publicity is just as essential for another set of reasons. A candidate may borrow money extensively in order to finance his campaign and the most important aspect of his campaign fund is the method employed to make up the deficit. Dr. Overacker has pointed out a number of other considerations of considerable importance in this connection.[24]

"The real difficulty arises when one attempts to go behind the face of the returns, to provide an analysis of their salient points, and to dissemi-

[22] Later required by the federal laws of 1910, 1911, 1925, 1939, 1940, and 1944. See U. S. Congress, Senate, *Report of the Special Committee to Investigate Senatorial Campaign Expenditures, 1946*, pursuant to S. Res. 224 (79th Congress), January 31, 1947, Washington, Government Printing Office, 1947.

[23] Wooddy, *op. cit.*

[24] *Money in Elections*, (New York, Macmillan Company, 1932) p. 354.

nate this information. Nowhere is the existing machinery adequate. If it is to be made adequate candidates and treasurers of political committees must be given access to the books of their political opponents; the custodian of reports must be empowered to prescribe a uniform system of accounts and to supervise political reports continuously; machinery for informal summary investigations during the campaign, as well as after the campaign, must be provided; and it must be made the duty of the officer in charge of the reports to issue an analyzed summary of them just before the primary or election, and embody a more comprehensive comparative study in his annual report."

Pre-election statements especially suffer from the fact·that they are incomplete and that there is not sufficient time to examine them.

(2) A second provision of these laws is aimed at the source of revenue. The most significant features here are the prohibition of contributions by corporations in federal elections (1907) and in over two-thirds of the states and the prohibition against trade union contributions enacted in 1943 and re-enacted in 1947. The immediate cause of the first prohibition was the disclosures in the course of a legislative inquiry in New York regarding large payments made by various companies from the funds of the stockholders. This was notably true in the campaign of 1896 when various insurance companies contributed large sums of money. Other large contributions became known in the course of inquiries made about the same time. Nearly three-fourths of the states now prohibit contributions from corporations. One of the recommendations made by the Lonergan Committee which investigated the campaign funds of 1936 was that the federal Corrupt Practices Act be amended so as to prohibit contributions from trade unions.[25] The prohibition on contributions from organized labor originated as a rider on the Smith-Connally Anti-Strike Act passed in 1943. This law was challenged in the courts in 1948.

The provisions which have prohibited contributions from corporations have reduced, but have not eliminated, funds from this source. It is an easy matter for the directors of a corporation to make *individual* contributions and to recover their payments in the form of bonuses from the corporation. In the famous Kohler case in Wiscon-

[25] U. S. Congress, Senate, *Report of the Special Committee to Investigate Campaign Expenditures in 1936*, 75th Cong., 1st Sess., March 4, 1937, p. 135.

sin, it was shown that certain expenditures of the Kohler company which were in the nature of campaign outlays were charged to the corporation originally but after the primary were charged to members of Mr. Kohler's family.[26]

The methods used to finance PAC were sharply criticized during the 1944 campaign. At first PAC was financed by pledges from the international unions, aggregating a little under $700,000. Each of the four largest CIO unions—the Amalgamated Clothing Workers, the United Automobile Workers, the United Electrical Workers, and the United Steelworkers—contributed $100,000 each. Money paid on these pledges came from the various union treasuries.

In August, Sidney Hillman, president of the Amalgamated Clothing Workers and also chairman of PAC, told the House Committee on Campaign Expenditures that PAC had spent $371,086, of which only $67,320 went for federal primary or state election campaigns. Most of the money had been paid out for rent, furniture, running expenses, salaries, travel, publications, and publicity. Mr. Hillman also told the House committee: "We froze our trade union contributions account immediately after the conclusion of the Democratic convention. No funds will be expended from that account except for contributions to or on behalf of candidates in primaries or state elections or for such other purposes as are unquestionably permitted under the terms of the Corrupt Practices Act. All other expenditures will be made from the committee's individual contributions account."

From July 23 on, and until the election in November, the national and regional activities of PAC were financed by individual contributions. Members of CIO were asked to contribute $1 each to the fund. "A Buck for Roosevelt" was the slogan used. It was reported to the House committee that $56,922 was received in this fashion.

Experience showed that the part-time PAC services of persons who were both union and PAC officers could not readily be segregated. In California it was especially difficult to separate the state PAC from the state CIO council.

The activities of the two committees were designed to promote the political program of CIO without violating the Federal Corrupt

[26] *Money in Elections*, p. 336.

Practices Act. Before the Democratic convention, PAC carried on an educational program which included distribution of literature bearing on the issues of the campaign and on the voting records of candidates; the endorsement of candidates for the presidency and vice presidency, and the endorsement of congressional and local candidates; radio programs; a campaign to induce people to register as voters; and the holding of meetings and sending out of speakers. After the Democratic convention, PAC used funds derived from the contribution program to engage in the same range of educational activities, but it refrained from making money contributions to candidates or to political committees. On the other hand, the National Citizens Political Action Committee, operating on funds derived from individual contributions not confined to labor circles, engaged in educational activities and also made money contributions to candidates in their campaign for election.

The assessment of officeholders was one of the first abuses of party campaign fund financing which Congress attempted to regulate. In 1867 an act was passed which was designed to protect the employees of the navy yard from political assessments. The Civil Service Reform Act of 1883 went much further than this and forbade the solicitation of campaign funds from any officer or employee of the United States by a fellow employee; it also protected employees from discharge for refusing to make political contributions. This legislation was reasonably successful in reducing the pressure upon federal civil service employees, but many federal political appointees were still expected to make "voluntary" contributions. Table 9 given above shows that nearly one-fifth of the Democratic campaign fund in 1940 received from contributors of $1000 or more came from officeholders. About one-third of the states prohibit the assessment of officeholders. This leaves a large proportion of the state and local employees without any protection against this form of tribute. The so-called Hatch Bill, enacted in 1939 and as amended in 1940, forbids all officers and employees of the executive branch of the federal government and all state employees part of whose salaries comes from federal funds to take any active part in political management or political campaigns. Legislative, judicial, and state and local government employees are not included, nor are federal officials in policy-determining positions. Expressions of opinion are allowed and membership in political and civic organizations is permitted, but soliciting funds, working for a candidate or party, and acting as an officer in a political organization are forbidden by the act.[27]

(3) A third set of provisions is directed at the character of the expenditures made in the course of the campaigns. Some of these laws prohibit certain types of expenditures. Payment of money for the purchase of votes had long been prohibited in most states, as had been expenditures for meat, drink, and entertainment of voters as an incident of campaigning. To this list there was now added a long and varying series of forbidden items, differing materially in different states. Among the items included were payment of poll taxes, payment of naturalization fees, payment for transportation to and from the polls, payment of workers on election day, and many other types of campaign outlay. In the state of Wisconsin the abuse of excessive expenditures for workers on election day has been practically eliminated by the prohibition of any payment of any election-day worker by any candidate or committee..

In nearly two-thirds of the states expenditures are limited by the enumeration of what are legitimate expenses. All campaign expenditures are prohibited except those specifically allowed by law. In the Pennsylvania act, for example, a series of such items was set up, and no others were permissible under the law. This included printing, traveling expenses, stationery, advertising, postage, dissemination of public information, meetings and demonstrations, rent and furnishing of offices, payment of clerks, janitors and messengers, election watchers, transportation to and from the polls, bona fide legal expenses. It must be said, however, that no little difficulty was found in discovering a legal form that would permit all necessary expenditures without at the same time admitting into the legal fold types of

[27] See H. Eliot Kaplan, "Political Neutrality of the Civil Service," *Public Personnel Review*, I (1940), 10; L. V. Howard, "Federa. Restrictions upon the Political Activity of Government Employees," *American Political Science Review*, XXXV (1941), 470–489; J. R. Starr, "The Hatch Act—An Interpretation," *National Municipal Review*, XXX (1941), 418–425. The Hatch Act declared it "unlawful for any person employed in the executive branch of the Federal Government, or any agency or department thereof, to use his official authority or influence for the purpose of interfering with an election or affecting the result thereof. No officer or employee in the executive branch of the Federal Government, or any agency or department thereof, shall take any active part in political management or in political campaigns. All such persons shall retain the right to vote as they may choose and to express their opinions on all political subjects and candidates."

outlay that would gladly have been prohibited. As a matter of fact, such provisions may be highly objectionable. If they are too narrow and detailed, they may fail to keep up with new inventions in the field of communication. A strict construction of many of the laws would bar the use of the radio, the sound truck, television, and the movie.

(4) In some instances a limitation is placed upon the amount of expenditure during a campaign, or the amount to be contributed by the candidate. The federal law of 1925 as amended by the Hatch Act of 1940 restricts the individual expenditure for the election of senators to $10,000 and of representatives in the House to $2500, or an amount equal to the amount obtained by multiplying three cents by the total number of votes cast at the last election for the office the candidate seeks but in no event exceeding $25,000 if a candidate for senator or $5000 if a candidate for representative and it restricts the expenditures of national party committees to $3,000,000.[28] A public return of receipts and expenditures is required of candidates and committees, but this does not include personal expenditures of candidates, expenditures by candidates for printing and for distribution of material and various other services; expenditures by state and local committees, and in fact very large expenditures are possible under this law. Nor are other individuals or groups forbidden to contribute to the campaign or to make expenditures on behalf of the party except in the case of trade unions and corporations. In most cases, the itemized statement of the candidate's expenditures includes only those items falling outside the excepted classes. Thus, the candidate may spend large sums for letters, circulars, and telegrams, and leave no hint of his total outlay in his report. His friends may spend huge sums for workers on election day, as long as they keep him blissfully ignorant of what they are doing.

The reports of the party committees also have serious limitations. In 1944 the Political Action Committee of the Congress of Industrial Organizations showed how a group could spend money to elect a presidential candidate without coming under the $3,000,000 ceiling

[28] H. M. Megill comp.), *Federal Corrupt Practices Act and the Hatch Political Activity Act* (Washington, D. C., Government Printing Office, 1946) ; L. Overacker, *Presidential Campaign Funds* (Boston, 1946). See also Clayton Knowles, "Campaign Is Costliest in History of Nation," *New York Times*, October 24, 1948.

or the ban against trade union contributions.[29] In fact, the law has accomplished little except to decentralize campaign finance and to make effective publicity of campaign expenditures more difficult. The figures in Table 10 show expenditures in excess of the $3,000,000 by each of the major parties in 1940 and 1944.

In over three-fourths of the states laws have been enacted placing limits either upon the candidate's expenditure or on the sum total to be spent in his behalf.[30] But as a rule the more drastic limitations apply only to expenditures on the part of the candidate. The amount which may be expended may be a fixed sum or it may vary with the salary of the office or the size of the electorate. Where the sums are fixed they are usually ridiculously low. The same is true of the sums which depend upon the salary of the office sought. It would be impossible in many states for any kind of campaign to be put on if the limitations were strictly observed.

A distinction must be made between limitations imposed upon the candidate personally and the total amount available for the conduct of the campaign—a consideration not infrequently overlooked and a common cause of confusion. Most of the laws, it appears upon careful scrutiny, are not designed to restrict the total amount expended in a campaign, but merely the amount given by the candidate—often a wholly different matter. In Massachusetts an attempt has been made to concentrate the responsibility for the raising and spending of money in campaigns in the candidates, their agents, and political committees. While expenditures by individuals are prohibited by law, they have not been eliminated, and the law is not vigorously enforced.

The Kohler case in Wisconsin illustrates many of the difficulties involved in any attempt to fix responsibility for the financing of a given candidate's political campaign. A very competent observer had indicated that he regarded the Wisconsin law as an example of comprehensive and thoroughgoing regulation. According to this law no candidate was allowed to make any disbursement except under his personal direction or through a party committee or a personal cam-

[29] The ban on use of union funds for political purposes was declared unconstitutional in a test case in Washington, D. C., in March, 1948, by a federal district court.

[30] Minault, *op. cit.*; H. R. Penniman, Sait's *American Parties and Elections* (New York, 1948), p. 563.

paign committee. The acts of every member of a personal campaign committee were presumed to be with the knowledge and approval of the candidate, until proved otherwise. The law also limited the expenditures "by or on behalf of" a candidate for governor to $4000. In the trial following the 1928 primary, Mr. Kohler's attorneys did not deny that over $100,000 had been spent in the interests of their client. They did deny, however, that he had authorized any expenditures in excess of the legal maximum although some of the money was spent by members of his family, by members of his company, and by the treasurer of the state Republican committee, who was a close associate. The jury held that Kohler could not even be held responsible for entertainment of voters in his model village.[31] In other words the limitations limited no one but the candidate.

The corrupt practices acts have not been particularly effective in curing the evils at which they were aimed. In the first place, the machinery for enforcement is often very defective, and as a result the regulation regarding publicity becomes a sheer farce. Returns of ridiculously small expenditures, and often no returns at all, reduced the laws in many cases to a dead letter. The early acts passed in the nineties may be said to have died of neglect, but after 1904 there was much closer attention given to the practical execution of the laws. But even when public opinion was awake to the possibilities of these measures, the machinery for enforcement was so clumsy and ill-contrived that no vigorous application of them was possible. Fines and imprisonment are the most common penalties for violation of state corrupt practices acts. It is difficult to get conviction under these acts. A greater use of forfeiture of office and disqualification to hold office might have a beneficial result. In Arizona, Arkansas, Florida, and Oklahoma persons violating certain parts of the corrupt practices act are disqualified from holding public office.

Sanctions and penalties may be provided for by the law, but this does not mean that they will be utilized. A striking example of this is furnished by the defiance of the publicity provisions of the Michigan law by Governor Comstock of Michigan in 1932. As the governor put it, "Purposely, I did not file any statement of expenses in my campaign because I wanted to show the people of Michigan how easy it was to evade the present corrupt practices act. There was no

[31] *State ex rel. La Follete et al.* v. *Kohler,* 200 Wis. 518 (1930).

way or any agency that could get at the fellow who deliberately sat back and said, 'I won't do it.' " [32] Although the law stated that the name of a candidate who had failed to file an account was not to be certified and placed on the ballot, that such a candidate if elected should not be allowed to take the oath, and furthermore that he should receive no salary until the law had been complied with, yet Comstock and the public officials concerned paid no attention to the provisions of the law.

Regarding the Hatch Act of 1940 and its operation, a special assistant to the Attorney General said:

"We respectfully submit that in our opinion the present existing federal laws relative to contributions and expenditures of political parties are fatally defective in accomplishing the purposes intended by Congress, and are, in our opinion, unenforceable under the conditions which have been presented in this investigation." [33]

Difficulties also have arisen from the various ways of evading the law. In an election where there are many candidates, say 30 or 40, it is not easy with the best of intentions to allocate precisely the expense chargeable to each of the candidates. And it is not difficult to shift the burdens about so that the expense of one may be proportionately large and of another proportionately small, particularly if some of the candidates are subjected to rigid laws and others are not. In an election where there are national, state, and local candidates, this situation presents serious difficulties.

More questions arise regarding types of expenditures in behalf of candidates which are not easily controllable by the law, such as the services of the party organization, the services of the party press, the services of associations indirectly political but directly involved in a particular campaign. What is the position of the candidate who has no organization, but must employ workers, or ot the candidate who does not have with him a friendly press as against one who owns a string of newspapers, or of the candidate who has no economic groups behind him as opposed to one who is backed by powerful and active organizations whether of labor or of capital? In these cases the continuous advocacy of a principle, year in and year out,

[32] Cited by Pollock, "The Use of Money in Elections," *op. cit.*, p. 199.
[33] Report dated February 26, 1941.

helps a candidate, or a party or a faction, but it is not chargeable to any campaign account. Yet in the broad processes by which public opinion is shaped and electoral events in large measure determined, of what great significance are these widespread activities which sit so lightly upon a campaign expenditure statement?

The chief value of these laws has been the education that has accompanied the general discussion of the sources and the applications of campaign funds. This has affected the political morale of the community more deeply than the actual enforcement of the laws. A generation ago the question "Who is paying the bills?" was not even raised. Attention has been called to the large contributions by private interests and to the obligations directly or indirectly incurred by the candidates. Interest has been awakened in the democratic financing of campaign funds, and the individual sense of responsibility for the party budget has been aroused in many persons who in earlier days never questioned the source of campaign funds. The democratization of party finances has been urged, and some progress has been made in this direction by popular subscriptions which shift the burden of the campaign from a small number of directly interested persons to a larger number only indirectly concerned in the outcome of the campaign. This of itself is a distinct gain for the political *mores* of a democratic society.

Finally the discussion regarding corrupt practices acts has directed attention to the interest of the government itself in campaign expenses, and has led to steps in the direction of public payment of many election expenses by the state. All ordinary expenses incidental to voting have long since been taken over by the state. For a long time, however, the expense of primaries was borne by the candidates themselves. For this purpose fees were required of the entrants and the sums so raised were devoted to the payment of the cost of the primary. An effort has likewise been made to shoulder a part of the candidate's usual burden by providing for a "publicity pamphlet" in which the statements of the various contenders are printed and circulated by the government at a nominal cost. Oregon led the way in this movement and a few states have followed. These measures give to every candidate a minimum amount of political publicity at a cost below the expense to an individual of printing and circulating his own material.

President Theodore Roosevelt in his message of December, 1907, urged the payment of campaign expenses out of public funds as a means of obviating some of the evils of campaign fund collections.

A law was enacted by the state of Colorado in 1909 authorizing appropriation of state funds for campaign expenses. Twenty-five cents was to be allowed on the basis of the last party vote for governor, and of this sum 12½ cents was to go to the state committee of the party and the other half to the county committee. This law was held to be unconstitutional, however.[34]

It has been proposed that the franking privilege be extended to all candidates for public office. In England and France each candidate for the lower house of the national legislature is allowed one free mailing to all of his constituents. This provision puts the wealthy and poor candidates on more of a plane of equality. Another suggestion that has been made concerns the distribution of radio time. Where there are government-owned radio stations, as in the state of Wisconsin, it is possible for all parties to be given an opportunity to present their views to the electorate over the air.

On the whole the neglect, evasion and nonenforcement of the corrupt practices acts left them without much effect on the actual conduct of the electoral process. In national politics the senatorial investigating committees have made up for many of the deficiencies in the law. The publicity sections of the acts were the most helpful features, while the limitations and restrictions upon amounts were more honored in the breach than in the observance. But, as has been shown, the publicity acts omitted many features of expenditure indispensable for a thorough knowledge of the real expense of the campaign. The chief value of the laws was educational, and in this field they served a useful purpose by focusing public interest on the source of campaign funds and on the obligations incident to meeting the requirements of the party budget.

[34] In the case of *People ex rel. Bradley* v. *Galligan and Kenehan*, demurrer upheld October 10, 1910, in which no opinion was rendered.

CHAPTER XVIII

PUBLIC OPINION POLLS

The people's voice is odd
It is, and it is not, the voice of God.
—Alexander Pope

SOME FIFTY YEARS AGO JAMES BRYCE STATED THAT THE NEXT STAGE in the development of democracy would be reached "if the will of the majority of citizens were to become ascertainable at all times."[1] He was unaware at the time of the possibilities of statistical sampling, market analysis, and social psychology.

Beginning in 1935 a group of psychologists and social scientists demonstrated in dramatic fashion the potentialities of the sample survey based on the quota or area method. Sampling techniques were not new.[2] Nineteenth century statisticians had discovered the basic elements, journalists applied them to elections early in the twentieth century but social scientists were slow in recognizing the practical applications of these methods to public opinion analysis. They also did not know how to finance these applications. In 1936 Dr. George Gallup, psychologist and advertising executive, predicted the presidential election with considerable accuracy using a very small sample. Mr. Elmo Roper of *Fortune* Magazine, also appeared to do a good job of forecasting.[3] These and other market analysis experts showed that such surveys could be made self-supporting.

From 1916 to 1936 the *Literary Digest* conducted mail ballot polls. The directors of this magazine made no attempt to use sampling techniques but sent their ballots to all the names on selected lists such as automobile registration lists and telephone directories. These lists were biased in favor of the upper income groups. In some cases,

[1] *American Commonwealth* (New York, 1888).
[2] C. Robinson, *Straw Votes* (New York, 1932).
[3] H. F. Gosnell, "How Accurate Were the Polls?" *Public Opinion Quarterly*, I, (1937), 97–104.

the *Digest* used lists of registered voters, but even here the mail ballot gave an erroneus result because the lower income groups did not respond in as large numbers as the upper income groups. The mail ballot method was not the answer to Bryce's hope. It was expensive, slow, cumbersome, and inaccurate, as shown by the ridiculous results obtained in the 1936 prepresidential poll. The *Literary Digest* poll in that year predicted that Landon, the Republican nominee, would win! Gallup and others had warned the *Digest* that their methods overweighted the vote of the upper income groups, but the *Digest* was adamant. One of the results of the fiasco was the collapse of the magazine.

Gallup and the others making public opinion surveys avoided the errors of the *Digest* by quota sampling. After a careful analysis of the characteristics of the American electorate they directed their investigators to see individuals who answered certain descriptions.[4] Thus, an investigator in town A would see so many men and so many women; these persons would be distributed in a prearranged pattern according to income level, color, previous voting behavior, place of residence, place of birth, and other relevant factors. The interview schedules would be checked against certain known factors. Quota sampling was not new. Sociologists and political scientists had made surveys using this method.[5] But it had not been applied on a national scale to a pending election. Its superiority to the *Digest* methods was patent to all in 1936. It forecast President Roosevelt's re-election by a comfortable margin.

The quota or representative sample method has now been used in four presidential elections and in many minor contests. The polls using this method have varied in accuracy but those conducted in a careful fashion gave reasonably good results except in 1948. Since the President is elected by a majority in the electoral college, which body is chosen by the states voting at large, the state-by-state polls are the only ones which can safely be used to forecast the election. Gallup and Crossley have presented state figures. Their errors in percentage points (percentage differences between the election and the poll for a given candidate) have varied from 0.1 to 17.0 for the four

[4] The method of quota sampling is elaborately explained in National Opinion Research Center, *Interviewing for NORC* (Denver, 1945).

[5] C. E. Merriam and H. F. Gosnell, *Non-Voting* (Chicago, 1923).

times that the forty-eight states have been polled.[6] For the 1944 elections Gallup's and Crosley's average state-by-state errors were 2.5 and 2.4 respectively, but for the 1948 elections they were 5.2 and 4.6 respectively. Improvements need to be made in this technique. The errors have been in the direction of underestimating the Democratic vote. In the close presidential election of 1948 the polls were not sufficiently accurate to avoid missing the result in the electoral college by a substantial margin. Gallup, Roper, and Crossley have reported only percentages. They have not given full information regarding adjustments. Fuller reporting will be necessary if polling is to be put on a sounder statistical basis. The sources of bias in the public opinion polls have been the following: a lack of knowledge regarding the exact characteristics of the electorate so that true quotas could be described; a lack of training on the part of the interviewers; a lack of random sampling within the quota limits defined; an unwillingness on the part of some elements of the electorate, particularly the lower income groups, to cooperate with interviewers; a possible small amount of cheating on the part of the interviewers; defective questions; a failure to estimate the size of the vote cast and the nature of the party division among those who come to the polls; a failure to catch last minute shifts in sentiment; a lack of knowledge of how to combine elements needed for a prediction; and other human elements which have not yet been isolated.[7] The polling organizations have been trying to solve these problems.

The quota sampling method is relatively cheap and fast, and its accuracy, at least as far as a pre-election poll is concerned, can be improved. It is a flexible tool which can be adapted to many uses.

Quota sampling, however, was still beyond the means of ordinary investigators. Gallup, an advertising executive, solved this problem by selling his polling service to newspapers. The results of his survey were handled by the press in a manner similar to a syndicated column. *Fortune* magazine made its surveys one of its exclusive

---

[6] Gosnell, *op. cit.*; D. Katz, "The Public Opinion Polls and the 1940 Election," *Public Opinion Quarterly*, V (1941), 52–78, and "The Polls and the 1944 Election," *Public Opinion Quarterly*, VIII (1945), 468–482.

[7] H. F. Gosnell and S. De Grazia, "A Critique of Polling Methods," *Public Opinion Quarterly*, VI (1942), 378–390; *Report of the Social Science Research Committee on Analysis of Pre-Election Polls and Forecasts* (New York, 1948).

features. In this fashion was the problem of financing such surveys solved. More recently, private foundations, universities, and governments have entered this field.[8]

Federal government public opinion surveys probably started in the Department of Agriculture, although the Bureau of the Census had been working on sampling methods for many years. In 1936, the Bureau of Agriculture Economics began on a small scale some informal studies of the public reaction to some of the farm programs. During the war public opinion research was undertaken by the Office of Facts and Figures, the Office of War Information, the Office of Price Administration, the War Production Board, the War Department, the Navy Department, the State Department, the Treasury Department, and other agencies.[9]

Government public opinion surveys have been more exact in their methods than the private surveys. The Bureau of the Census and the Department of Agriculture have made improvements upon the sampling methods employed by market research men. Instead of the quota plan which gives the interviewer considerable freedom in selection of respondents, these two agencies have worked out a system of area sampling which conforms much more closely to the requirements for random sampling as defined by the mathematical principles of probability.[10] The methods are more expensive and slower than quota sampling but they yield more accurate results.

The polls have been used to predict election results and also to sample sentiment on various political issues. The major parties have been intensely interested in the findings of the polls, and a congressional committee made an investigation of the various polling organizations.[11]

One of the most penetrating surveys was that of the 1940 presidential election campaign in Erie County, made by Paul Lazarsfeld

[8] See Quinn McNemar, "Opinion-Attitude Methodology," *Psychological Bulletin*, July, 1946.
[9] J. L. Woodward, "Making Government Opinion Research Bear Upon Operation," *American Sociological Review*, IX (1944), 670–677.
[10] M. H. Hansen and P. M. Hauser, "Area Sampling—Some Principles of Design," *Public Opinion Quarterly*, IX (1945), 183–193.
[11] U. S. Congress, House, Committee to Investigate Campaign Expenditures, *Hearings on H. Res. 552*, Part 12, 78th Cong., 2nd Sess., Dec. 28, 1944 (Washington, D. C., 1945).

and associates for the *Life* magazine and the Office of Radio Research of Columbia University.[12] The Roper polling organization did the interviewing, and a number of social scientists cooperated in analyzing the results. The so-called panel technique was employed which called for re-interviews of the same respondents at regular intervals. These expressions of voting intentions were analyzed by means of many different breakdowns. A thorough content analysis was also made of mass media to which the voters in the area had been subjected during the campaign.[13] This involved a detailed classification of the party appeals. The voters were asked what things helped them make up their minds regarding the election. The analysis showed that if a voter's predispositions were known his behavior could be predicted within limits. The most important predispositions as far as the Franklin D. Roosevelt-Wendell Willkie contest was concerned were religion, economic level, and residence. A voter who was Catholic, poor, and lived in a poor urban neighborhood would be likely to vote for Roosevelt, whereas a voter who was Protestant, well-off, and lived in a high-class neighborhood or in the country, would be likely to vote for Willkie. In this study the investigators checked voting behavior (going to the polls) against intentions to vote. In 1948 a follow-up study employing the panel technique was made in Elmira, New York, by a group of cooperating universities and research organizations.

In general the polling organizations have used single-answer questions or very simple multiple-question forms. Considerable discussion has been going on regarding the relative merits of the fixed-question interview as opposed to the open-ended, intensive interview where the respondent is given a chance to express himself freely. It appears that the pre-election polls of 1948 did not detect the ground swell for President Truman. A more searching interviewing technique was needed. Psychologists have generally favored multiquestion schedules which have been rationalized by some scaling technique.[14] Beyle applied one of these techniques to the construction of

[12] P. Lazarsfeld, B. Berelson, and H. Gaudet, *The People's Choice* (New York, 1944).

[13] D. Waples and B. Berelson, *Public Communications and Public Opinion* (mimeo., Graduate Library School, University of Chicago, 1941).

[14] McNemar, *op. cit.*

a scale on attitudes toward candidates.[15] Thurstone has shown recently how such a questionnaire might be used to predict the voter's choice.[16]

Heated controversies have arisen over the theoretical implications of the polling devices. Is there a band wagon vote? Do the polls undermine representative government and substitute an unofficial direct democracy in which only a few citizens take part in a hit and miss fashion? Can the private polling organizations be trusted to do an honest job? Should our legislatures and parties follow the uniformed views of the voters as expressed in a private poll?

Gallup has taken the view that the polls are the "pulse" of democracy and the fulfillment of Lord Bryce's dream.[17] Others have taken exception to this view and expressed alarm at the potentialities of the polls for damaging democracy and the party system.[18]

The present writers refuse to be alarmed at the calamity howls of the most ardent detractors of the polls. They have confidence in the skepticism and common sense of the American voters. The polls will have to stand or fall on the confidence of the public in their accuracy and honesty. No polling organization could stand another *Literary Digest* fiasco. Following the 1948 elections the polling organizations were under heavy fire. The commercial polling organizations check each other and in turn are checked by the final election results and studies made by nonprofit polling organizations.[19] While some psychologists would like to see more work done on the validity of the polls, slow progress is being made in this direction.

Some sociologists have taken the view that public opinion polling, as currently conducted by many of the polling organizations, forces a treatment of society as if it were only an aggregate of disparate individuals. They contend that this view neglects the process by which public opinion is formed. When a poll is used to predict an

[15] Herman Beyle, "A Scale for the Measurement of Attitude Toward Candidates for Elective Governmental Office," *American Political Science Review*, XXVI (1932), 527–544.

[16] L. L. Thurstone, in C. W. Churchman (ed.), *Measurement of Consumer Interest* (Philadelphia, 1947).

[17] G. Gallup and S. F. Rae, *The Pulse of Democracy* (New York, 1940).

[18] "Public Opinion Polls: Dr. Jekyll or Mr. Hyde?" symposium in *Public Opinion Quarterly*, IV (June, 1940), 212–284.

[19] McNemar, *op. cit.*

election, polling methods now commonly used are justifiable since the vote of each citizen has the same weight as that of any other citizen. In situations where this is not so, where there is wide variation in the influence of different citizens, the usual polling sample may not be appropriate. A British public opinion research organization, Mass-Observation, places emphasis upon the technique of the participant observer. In the United States, surveys have been made of leadership opinion as well as of general opinion. The surveys of general opinion based upon the principles of random sampling might be said to present a cross section at a given time of some of the influences which have been at work on the public. They may reveal ignorances and blind areas. Psychologists are of the opinion that the surveys should place more emphasis upon the open-ended interview and the multiquestion survey so as to gain as much as possible of the dynamics of opinion forming. If the polling organizations are to make pre-election polls, the 1948 results showed that they must get at the dynamics of the election process. They must do more than ask citizens what their voting intentions are. They must have an intelligence system in the party organizations which will furnish a clue as to what types of voters will take the trouble to go to the polls and cast their ballots.

American major parties can no longer afford to lag behind currents of public opinion. The polls are here to stay as long as we retain the democratic system of government. Polls are not permitted under a dictatorial form of government. While the public may be uninformed on some questions, the poll can show areas of ignorance which should be corrected. The polls also tear the veil away from the false representations of selfish pressure groups. A one-sided letter and telegram bombardment of Congress can be put into proper perspective by a public opinion survey.

While the administrative agencies of the government have been quicker to recognize this new tool of democracy, the legislators are gradually waking up to the possibilities. A recent study of the attitudes of a group of congressmen showed that they thought that the public opinion polls less useful to them as a way of discovering public opinion than personal mail, visits to the public, newspapers, and visits from the public.[20] One of the drawbacks of the national polls

[20] M. Kriegsberg, "What Congressmen and Administrators Think of the Polls," *Public Opinion Quarterly*, IX (1945), 333–337

has been that the small sample did not permit breakdowns by congressional districts. A member of Congress could always say that the national sentiment might be so and so but in his district it was different, and he had to think about his re-election. A few congressmen have been using public opinion polls in their constituencies.[21] As more and more congressmen utilize such methods, the nearer we will come to Bryce's ideal of government by public opinion.

Public opinion survey methods can also be used to test the effectiveness of party propaganda. If the experimental method with a proper control group is used, the effectiveness of propaganda, written or orally delivered in person or via radio, can be examined. Different media and different types of appeal could be tested. Some small beginnings have already been made with experimentation in this field.[22] Party leaders are not fully awake to the possibilities. They have failed to realize that a science of politics is almost within their grasp. The Research Branch of the Army showed during the war what could be done in testing motion pictures, analyzing morale, and improving training techniques.

Public opinion survey organizations can never take the place of representative assemblies, popular law making devices, election booths, and political parties. The precinct captain and his house-to-house canvass can never be replaced by the interviewer with a quota to fill. Even in anticipating election results, the analysis of preceding election returns furnishes a basis which the poll takers cannot afford to ignore. Figure 14 shows how voting trends in the states is related to national voting trends.[23] The need for legislators cannot be eliminated by substituting public opinion analysts. Constitutional amendments should not be ratified by an opinion survey. The theory of democratic suffrage demands that all qualified voters have the chance to participate in electoral decisions. Many voters may fail to exercise their chance, but their power to do so, though latent, is still there. Representative government and popular law making de-

[21] Congressman Corbett of Pennsylvania and McGregor of Ohio use public opinion reports.

[22] H. F. Gosnell, *Getting Out the Vote* (Chicago, 1925); P. F. Lazarsfeld, 'The Change of Opinion During a Political Discussion," *Journal of Applied Psychology,* 1939, XXIII, 131–147.

[23] Gosnell, *Grass Roots Politics.* See also L. Bean, *How to Predict Elections* (New York, 1948).

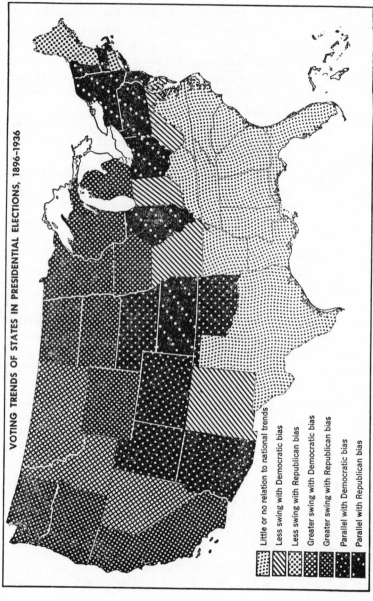

VOTING TRENDS OF STATES IN PRESIDENTIAL ELECTIONS, 1896-1936

Little or no relation to national trends
Less swing with Democratic bias
Less swing with Republican bias
Greater swing with Democratic bias
Greater swing with Republican bias
Parallel with Democratic bias
Parallel with Republican bias

Figure 14   (From H. F. Gosnell, *Grass Roots Politics*, p. 12, by permission of American Council on Public Affairs, Washington, D. C.)

vices are themselves political inventions which made possible the operation of democracy or a larger scale. The public opinion survey is another invention which should enrich the potentialities of democratic institutions. It should assist in the selection of party candidates, the clarification of party issues, and the guidance of popularly elected representatives.

CHAPTER XIX

BALLOT AND ELECTION LAWS

USE X ONLY IN MARKING BALLOT

| DEMOCRATIC TICKET | REPUBLICAN TICKET |

"Now all you fellows have to do to vote right is to put your cross under the rooster with the short legs." Cincinnati Republican precinct captain to his voters.

IN THE IDEAL REPUBLIC WHERE EVERY VOTER IS HONEST AND WHERE the elected officials have only the public welfare in mind, there would be need for few election laws. As in the elections conducted by many private societies, only those qualified would take part, any slips of paper could be used for ballots, and everyone would be sure of an honest count. Unfortunately, these ideal conditions are not found in the United States, nor in any other large political community. In this country, the widespread character of the spoils system as described above means that there is a large body of persons whose daily bread depends upon their carrying their particular election districts by fair means or foul. If the election law is loosely drawn and its enforcement is lax, the ward heelers find it easier to win votes by corrupt than by honest means.

What are the types of fraud which an election law musι guard against? In the United States every conceivable type of corruption has been practiced at the polls. There are two steps in the voting process which must be watched with extreme care. Ballots which are otherwise good may be cast by persons who are not qualified to vote; or the counting of the ballots may be manipulated, sometimes with and sometimes without the collusion of the election officials. The first type of fraud arises where there is no adequate method of identifying the voters at the polls. Its most common forms are repeating, personation, and colonization. In some cities defective registration systems have commonly meant repeating.[1] While the moving of gangs or colonies of voters from place to place is less common than it was, it is not unknown. The second type of fraud is found where there are corrupt election officials or where there is no adequate means of safeguarding the distribution of the ballots and the making of the count. Its most common forms are ballot box stuffing, the endless chain fraud, short penciling, stealing the ballot box, and making false returns. When none of these methods works, the corrupt politician may use a gang of thugs to go about from polling place to polling place intimidating the opposition.[2]

REGISTRATION FOR VOTING

The growth of large cities, the increasing mobility of the population, the influx of immigrants and the broadening of the franchise have made it harder and harder to see that only the legally qualified vote upon election day. The method which has been most widely adopted to secure this end has been the establishment of a system of registration for voting.[3] The registration laws have aimed to make it

[1] William B. Lex, "Election Frauds Go Unchecked," *National Municipal Review*, XXXIII (May, 1944), 228; W. M. Reddig, *Tom's Town: Kansas City and the Pendergast Legend* (Philadelphia and New York, 1947); D. R. Castleman, "Louisville Election Frauds in Court and Out," *National Municipal Review*, December, 1927; D. H. Kurtzman, *Methods of Controlling Votes in Philadelphia* (Philadelphia, 1935), p. 122.

[2] "The Kelly-Nash Political Machine," *Fortune*, August, 1936, p. 117.

[3] The most careful study of registration for voting in this country has been made by J. P. Harris. See his *Registration of Voters in the United States* (Washington, D. C., 1929); also J. P. Horlacher, "The Administration of Permanent Registration in Philadelphia," *American Political Science Review*, XXXVII (Oct., 1943), 829–838; Helen M. Rocca, *Registration Laws* (pamphlet, 1925); "A Model Regis-

possible to investigate the actual qualifications of the persons seeking to vote and to provide some means of identifying the voters at
the polls. These laws have invariably been state laws, as the control
of elections is a state function in this country.

A registration law was passed in Massachusetts in 1800 providing
for a "correct and alphabetical" list of all qualified voters to be made
up annually by the assessors in each town and revised by the select-
men. This is the type of registration system which is found in Great
Britain today. A number of the New England states followed the
example of Massachusetts, but there was no general extension of
registration until after 1860. The peculiar American form of registration found its origin in the California and New York laws of 1866
which provided for personal registration. Under these laws each
voter was required to appear in person before the election and prove
to a registry board that he was qualified to vote. The example of
these states has been followed by most of the other states. At the
present time some form of registration is required for voting in
almost all the states. In most of the states registration is made compulsory; that is, no one can vote who has not previously registered.[4]
In Wisconsin, Oregon, and Nebraska compulsory registration has
been declared unconstitutional by the courts.[5] This means that un-
registered voters can swear in their votes on election day. The courts
in most of the state, however, have upheld this obligatory registration.[6] One-fourth of the state registration laws apply only to cities.
In Arkansas and Texas the poll tax receipt is used as a means of
identifying the voters at the polls instead of a system of registration.

Unlike most European countries which have uniform registration
systems all over the entire country, the registration systems in the
United States vary from state to state. Only some of the main
characteristics of the American systems can be described here. There
are still a few nonpersonal registration systems which, like the

tration System," supplement to *National Municipal Review*, XVI (January, 1927),
45–86; and Chicago Bureau of Public Efficiency, *A Proposed System of Registering
Voters and Canvassing the Registration Lists in Chicago* (pamphlet, 1923).

[4] Harris, *op. cit.*, p. 110.

[5] *Dells* v. *Kennedy*, 49 Wis. 555 (1880); *White* v. *Multonomah County*, 10 Pac.
484 (Oregon, 1886); *State* v. *Moorehead*, 95 Neb. 80 (1914).

[6] *State* v. *Butts*, 31 Kan. 537 (1884); *People* v. *Hoffman*, 116 Ill. 587 (1886);
and many other cases.

original Massachusetts system, lay the responsibility for making up the list upon the officials. In half a dozen states this type of registration is used exclusively. Official or nonpersonal registration is the rule in Europe, but it works better there than it does here because we do not have anything like the continuous police censuses such as are kept in Europe. In the absence of adequate information on the basis of which the lists of voters may be kept up to date, the lists become cluttered up with the names of persons who have died or moved.[7] The most successful registration systems now in operation in the United States require personal application. Where new registrations are not required too frequently, this requirement is not unduly burdensome.

When personal registration was adopted in the large cities of this country, it was felt that it should be periodic. The requirement of a new personal registration at frequent intervals would automatically clear the lists of those who had died or moved away. Registration was made annual in New York and a number of states, while it was made biennial or quadrennial in other states. There is no question that the periodic systems of registration are burdensome upon the voters and virtually disfranchise many qualified persons. Within the past fifty years there has developed a new type of permanent registration which is less expensive, less burdensome and which seems to be more effective in eliminating fraud. J. P. Harris has summarized the features of this system as follows: "Registration is conducted at a central office throughout the year, instead of in the precincts on particular days. Outside offices may be used at times, but not in each precinct. Some form of individual records (loose-leaf, cards, or visible) takes the place of the cumbersome bound volume precinct registers. The work of keeping the registers clean of dead weight is not left to precinct officers, who are apt to be negligent and sometimes corrupt, but is performed by the clerical employees of the central office. The corrections are made upon the basis of routine information instead of relying upon challenges. Official death reports, cancellation because of failure to vote within a two-year period,

---

[7] In the rural parts of New York this system is used. In the non-urban parts of Monroe County the registration exceeded the number of citizens over 21 years of age, according to the 1920 census, by 25 per cent. See "A Model Registration System," *op. cit.*, p. 57.

transfers, and a house-to-house canvass of all registered voters are used to purge the registration books. The voter who moves from one address to another within the city may transfer his registration to the new address upon request, and in some cities this is done for him on the basis of gas and electric removals, and other reliable information. Ordinarily the voter under permanent registration remains registered, and registered from one address only, as long as he continues to reside within the same city." [8]

Some sort of permanent registration system is now used in four-fifths of the states either in part or in whole. It applies to all areas in twenty-eight states and to some areas in eleven.[9] Among the large cities having permanent registration, Boston has had the longest experience, its system dating from 1896. The essential feature of the Boston system is the annual verification of the registration lists by the police, who make a complete census of all adult persons. The census is used for the purpose of striking off names and for making transfers. The Milwaukee system adopted in 1912 has many commendable features. The individual card record, the police house-to-house canvass before each important election, the continuous opportunity for registration at the city hall, and the simple method of effecting transfers make this system convenient to the voters, low in cost, and effective in preventing frauds. Omaha adopted a system of permanent registration of voters in 1913, similar in the main to those above, which has given complete satisfaction. The Oregon permanent registration law of 1915 introduced the novel feature of cancellation for failure to vote within a two-year period, as a means of keeping the lists up to date. Many other states have adopted permanent registration systems modeled after the plans outlined above. The Wisconsin registration law, which applies to all cities of 5000 population or over except Milwaukee, has many unique provisions. It has been described as follows: "The records may be either loose-leaf or cards, and contain an affidavit which is signed by the

[8] J. P. Harris, "Permanent Registration of Voters," *American Political Science Review,* XXII (1928), 349. The same author has described the permanent registration systems of various cities in a series of articles in the *National Municipal Review:* Minneapolis, September, 1924; Milwaukee, October, 1925; Boston, September, 1926; Omaha, November, 1926; and in his *Registration of Voters in the United States, op. cit.*

[9] Council of State Governments, *Book of the States, 1945–1946* (Chicago, 1946).

registrant. An unusual feature of the Wisconsin law is that the city clerk is required to secure each month from the gas and electric company a list of removals of service, and from this make the proper transfers within the city. The voter is to be sent a form notice of the transfer. It is anticipated that most removals will be taken care of without any bother to the voter." [10] A system of permanent registration, if it is carefully worked out, has many advantages over periodic registration. It is cheaper and it lessens the burden of the voter. But permanent registration itself, without the most approved records and the best methods of checking the lists and keeping them up to date, is ineffective in preventing frauds. The experience of Indiana and Kentucky before 1933 clearly shows this.[11]

Whether registration is permanent or periodic it does not secure its principle purpose if there is no adequate method of identifying the voters. The information required for registration varies from state to state, including such items as name, address, age, naturalization record, length of residence, height, color of eyes, occupation, name of employer, exact location of residence, and many other items. The use of the signature as a means of identification of the voters at the polls was started in California in 1895. New York followed in 1908 with very beneficial results.[12] The Committee on Election Administration of the National Municipal League made the following comments on the value of this device: "The use of the signature is the ideal method of identification. It is positive, can be applied readily to every voter, and gives rise to no sound objections. It unquestionably should be a feature of every system of registration. Even in rural sections where normally every applicant to vote is personally known by the members of the precinct board it would be a good practice. A permanent record is made when the vote is cast; a signature must be written on the poll books. The requirement that each voter sign his name in the poll book when he votes would put a stop to practically all fraudulent voting which is still carried on in rural sections. In cities of any considerable population the signa-

[10] Harris, *Registration of Voters.*
[11] Castleman, *op. cit.* See also F. H. Riter, "Permanent Registration for Elections Unsuitable for Large Cities," *National Municipal Review,* XIV (September, 1925), 532–535.
[12] J. A. Lapp, "Identification of Voters," *American Political Science Review,* III (1909), 62.

ture identification is almost indispensable to sound registration."[13]

The use of the signature makes it possible to employ a more economical and convenient registration procedure. Where no such means of identification is used it is felt that the registration should be done in the voting precincts. Actual experience in many places has shown that precinct registration is very costly and that it does not eliminate fraud.[14] Where the signature is used registration can be continuous at the central office until thirty days or so before an election, as in Boston, Providence, Milwaukee, and Omaha, or it may be conducted by field workers as in some of the cities of California. The house-to-house canvass conducted by field workers in Los Angeles results in registration of a high percentage of the qualified adults.

BALLOT LAWS

The voters may be properly identified at the polls but if proper safeguards are not placed around the act of voting, the whole election process may be vitiated by intimidation, bribery, violence, and fraud. With the growth of large-scale industry and great urban populations it becomes increasingly easier for the large employer of labor and political corruptionist to bring pressure to bear upon certain classes of voters. Complaints regarding voting frauds led to the adoption of the secret ballot method of voting.[15] The use of ballots or voting tokens by legislative assemblies is an ancient custom which can be traced back to classic Greece and Rome, but it was the American colonies of England which led the rest of the world in the use of voting papers for the election of representatives. The use of ballots was made obligatory in several of the state constitutions adopted in 1776.

[13] "A Model Registration System," *op. cit.*, p. 85.

[14] Harris, *Registration of Voters*, p. 187; J. B. Johnson and I. J. Lewis, *Registration for Voting in the United States* (Chicago, Council of State Governments, 1946); J. P. Horlacher, "The Administration of Permanent Registration in Philadelphia," *American Political Science Review*, XXXVII (1943), 29–37.

[15] Spencer D. Albright, *The American Ballot* (Washington, D.C., 1942); E. C. Evans, *A History of the Australian Ballot System in the United States* (Chicago, 1917); E. B. Logan, *Supervision of the Conduct of Elections and Returns with Special Reference to Pennsylvania* (Privately printed, Lancaster, Pa., 1927). See J. P. Harris, *Election Administration in the United States* (Washington, D. C., 1934).

The success of a ballot law in lessening intimidation and corruption at elections depends in large part upon the extent to which voting is made secret. By the middle of the nineteenth century the ballot was used in practically all the American states, but it was not a secret ballot. All of the parties or candidates furnished their own voting papers, and complaints were common regarding intimidation, bribery, and ballot box stuffing. In Massachusetts and Rhode Island an attempt was made in 1851 to secure secrecy by an official envelope system, but compulsory use of this device was abandoned after a short trial. The party managers, whose control over nominations and elections was made secure by the unofficial ballot system, opposed all reforms aiming to give secrecy.

Widespread political corruption following the Civil War led to demands for thoroughgoing ballot reforms. The successful operation of a new ballot system adopted in Australia in the late fifties led a few farsighted persons to agitate for similar changes. Under the Australian ballot system, only the official blanket ballot furnished by the state can be used, the nomination of candidates is regulated by law, the ballots are distributed by sworn representatives of the state, the ballots are marked in secret by the voters, the casting and counting of the ballots is regulated by law, and any abuse of the law can be remedied by an appeal to the courts. The cooperation of reform associations and labor organizations brought about the first adoptions of this system in the United States in Louisville, Kentucky, and in Massachusetts in 1888. The unprecedented use of money in the campaign of 1888 brought many other states to adopt the same reform within the next few years. At the present time some form of the Australian ballot system is found in all the states of the union but three, namely, Georgia, South Carolina, and Delaware. Of these three states South Carolina alone has none of the essential features of the Australian ballot system. Georgia has an optional law, and Delaware has an official blanket ballot but the law does not require that the ballots be marked by the voters in the secrecy of the polling booth.[16]

The ballot form which was introduced in Louisville for municipal elections in 1888 was the same as that which is used in Great Britain and the British dominions. It contained the names of the candi-

[16] Albright, *op. cit.*

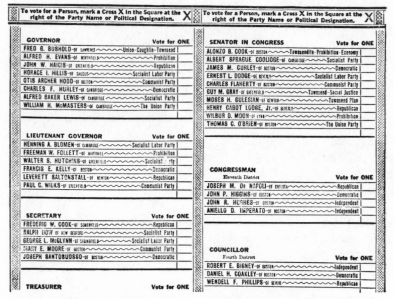

dates without party designations, grouped alphabetically under the appropriate offices. The state-wide Massachusetts ballot law adopted in the same year applied to many more offices than the Kentucky law. The same general arrangement was followed, but in addition the name of the party that nominated each candidate appeared after his name. This form of ballot has been called the Massachusetts or office group ballot. Whether an elector votes a straight party ticket or splits his vote, he must put a cross mark in the square opposite the name of each candidate whom he wishes to support. It was felt that the length of the ballot made it necessary to add the party names as a guide to the voters. Needless to say, the politicians welcomed this modification of the Australian ballot system. At the present time about one-third of the states have the office group form of ballot.[17] In all of these states but Florida, Mississippi, Tennessee, and Virginia the party names appear. The four southern states men-

[17] In 1948 Arkansas, California, Colorado, Florida, Kansas, Maryland, Massachusetts, Minnesota, Mississippi, Nebraska, Nevada, New York, Oregon, Tennessee, and Virginia. Consult C. O. Smith, *A Book of Ballots: Representative Facsimile Ballots of Local, State and National Governments* (Detroit, 1938).

tioned omit the party names in order to confuse those Negro voters who want to support the Republican party.[18] The names of the Democratic candidates appear first on the ballots of these states, except in Tennessee. In most of the other states the names of the candidates are rotated when there is more than one candidate for an office. On the New York ballots the party emblem appears as well as the party name, the emblem serving as a guide to illiterate voters. In the course of time the New York literacy test for voting will eliminate any need for party emblems on the ballot.[19]

When Indiana adopted the Australian ballot in 1889 it introduced a different form from the one used in Massachusetts. The ballot was a blanket one but each party was given a separate column with its name and emblem at the top. In order to vote a straight party ticket with the Indiana ballot the voter simply places a cross mark in the circle at the top of the party column. A split ticket can be voted either by putting a cross in one party circle and a cross opposite the names of candidates favored in other columns or by a cross opposite the name of each candidate preferred. It is obvious that this form of ballot favors straight party voting as opposed to independent voting. Where there are many officers to be elected and several parties have nominated candidates, this arrangement makes the ballot very unwieldy.[20] The Indiana or party column type of ballot has been adopted by more than 50 per cent of the states, half of which use both the party name and the party emblem. The eagle for the Republicans and the rooster for the Democrats are the most common devices. All of these states follow in general the Indiana method of marking the ballots, except several of the southern states where the voter scratches off the names of all the candidates for whom he does not wish to vote. In some states the party circle is used only for voting a straight ticket.[21] The long ballot and the cult of party regularity are the main causes for the popularity of the Indiana type

[18] Evans, *op. cit.*, p. 43.

[19] This law, which was passed in 1923, is not retroactive. Any illiterate person qualified to vote before the law was passed is not deprived of his right to vote.

[20] The Chicago ballot used in the presidential election of 1924 measured 36 by 29 inches. In 1927 the presidential electors were taken off the ballot so the 1928 presidential ballots measured only 24½ by 21½ inches.

[21] In Michigan, Idaho, Utah, Vermont, and Rhode Island the voter who splits his ticket must cross out the name of the rejected candidate in his own party's column.

of ballot. In Chicago the use of the party circle varies from about 28 per cent in sections where rents are high and high school education is general, to 87 per cent in depreciated residential areas inhabited by voters who have had limited educational opportunities.[22] Party bosses may from time to time cut the party ticket, but they know that it is dangerous for them to undermine party regularity. The press and civic organizations are the agencies which encourage independent voting.

There are half a dozen states which do not have either the office-group type or the party column types in their first forms. In Pennsylvania the names of the candidates are grouped under the appropriate offices but facilities for voting a straight ticket are also furnished. There a single cross mark in the party circle or square designated for that purpose is sufficient for voting a party ticket. This arrangement defeats the purpose of the Massachusetts ballot as it makes it harder to vote a split ticket than under the party colmun type of ballot. With an Indiana ballot the independent voter can run his eye down the column and pick out his favorites, but with the Pennsylvania ballot the independent voter has to look over all the candidates. In the remaining states the party column type of ballot is used but there is no provision for voting a straight ticket.[23] This form is not as favorable to independent voting as the Masssachusetts form but it is more so than the Indiana form. Cross marks must be put opposite the names of all the candidates favored by the voter whether or not they are in a single column.

Casting and Counting of Ballots

The Australian ballot system also provides for careful regulation of the handling of the ballots. While the ballots are being printed, watchers are posted to see that none is stolen and that the proper number is run off. After they are printed and sealed in packages of one hundred or so, they are taken by the proper authorities who distribute them to each of the local election boards in time for the opening of the polls. The local officials are held accountable for all ballots in their possession and must return the voted and unvoted ballots at the close of the count.

[22] H. F. Gosnell, *Machine Politics: Chicago Model* (Chicago, 1937), pp. 95–109.
[23] In 1948, Montana, New Jersey, and Wyoming.

If adequate means are not furnished for identifying the ballots at the polls, there is danger that a ballot will be stolen and the endless chain fraud started. This is sometimes called the Tasmanian dodge, from the place where it was first practiced. The corruptionist obtains in some way an official ballot early on election day. Where an official endorsement on the back of the ballot is the only means used of checking the ballots this is possible even with an honest election board. For instance, in Chicago a well-dressed woman went into a polling booth to vote, simulated fainting, and in the excitement which ensued an official ballot was carried out with her.[24] The corruptionist marks the stolen ballot and the voter whom he has bribed substitutes it, in the polling booth, for the ballot that was given to him by the election judge. The unmarked ballot is brought out to the corruptionist who marks it and uses it with his next voter. This process is continued during the day. In nearly one-half of the states a detachable numbered stub is used on the ballot to guard against this fraud and to prevent ballot box stuffing. A record is kept of the number of the stub on the ballot and a check is made before the stub is detached to see that each voter casts the ballot which was given to him. In a few states there are two stubs and the ballots are bound together in books as an additional check against fraud.[25] Where both stubs are detached, this system does not impair in any way the secrecy of the ballot.[26] In Nevada and Missouri the coupon device apparently furnishes anyone who makes a check of a voter's number a means of identifying his ballot during the count as the ballot and stub bear the same number. In Colorado this danger is guarded against by pasting down the corner of the ballot on which the number appears, so that the ballot cannot be identified except in the case of a recount. The Colorado provision preserves secrecy and enables a court in case of a contested election to throw out tainted ballots.

The original Louisville act which introduced the Australian ballot system in this country did not provide any means by which illiterates could get aid in marking their ballots. A leading decision handed down by the Kentucky Court of Appeals made it necessary

[24] *Chicago Daily News*, April 16, 1928.
[25] Among them are Arizona, California, Kentucky, Nevada, Ohio.
[26] As in Ohio.

to insert a provision in the act permitting assistance to be given to illiterates,[27] and to those who by reason of physical incapacity are unable to mark their ballot. Such a provision was contrary to the spirit of the Australian ballot system but like provisions are now found in most of the American states.[28] Experience has shown that a loosely drawn provision allowing assistance to illiterates results in widespread abuses. It is often used to destroy the secrecy of the ballot and to exert pressure upon the voters.[29] It offers corruptionists an opportunity to see whether the votes which have been bought are delivered. The Pennsylvania law is very poorly drafted in this regard. Assistance is given on the voter's word alone and he may select "any qualified voter of the election district to aid him." The party precinct leaders are on hand to perform this service and in some places they force their attentions upon the voters.[30] The Pennsylvania legislature of 1927 made a slight improvement in this section of the law when it made the records of assisted voters more available for later examination. In New York and California the need for assistance must be declared at the time of registration. An oath of illiteracy or physical disability is required. If the number seeking assistance appears unduly large, the election officials have the time and opportunity to investigate. Assistance must be given by election officers of different political faith. In Missouri the ballot of the assisted voter is marked by the election officers in the presence of all the persons at the polls. These different devices for eliminating abuses of the instructions provisions have had varying success. The model system, already referred to, advocates that "no assistance should be given to the illiterate voter." [31]

The huge blanket ballots used in the United States have encouraged the development of mechanical voting.[32] In 1892 the city of

[27] *Rogers* v. *Jacob*, 11 S. W. Rep. 513; *American Law Review*, XXIII, 719.

[28] Voters unable to read the English language are denied assistance in Massachusetts, Nevada, Arizona, South Dakota, Tennessee, Florida, Maryland, Ohio, Delaware, Connecticut, Vermont, and Michigan.

[29] At one election in Chicago nearly all the voters in a certain precinct asked for assistance. They did not take the oath as required. When asked why they called for assistance, they claimed that they had washed their eyes in a peculiar kind of soap and could not see.

[30] Logan, *op. cit.*, p. 98; Kurtzman, *op. cit.*, p. 134.

[31] Specification 28. Reproduced in Harris, *Election Administration in the United States*, p. 48.

[32] *Ibid.*, Chap. VII; T. D. Zukerman, *The Voting Machine* (Political Research Bureau of the Republican County Committee, New York, 1925).

Lockport, New York, initiated the use of voting machines in this country. The voting machine is a mechanical device which, like a cash register or an adding machine, gives the total number of times that each lever has been pulled down and registered. On the most common type used, the ballot is the face of the machine on which appears the name of each candidate under a lever. In order to vote for a given candidate, the lever over that candidate's name is pulled down. The machine is enclosed in a curtain so that no one besides the voter can see how the levers are arranged.[33] In states where there is provision for voting a straight ticket on a voting machine, there are party levers or pointers in addition to the candidate levers. It is impossible for a voter to spoil a ballot as the latest machines have an interlocking device which makes it impossible to register more than one choice under a given office title. If a voter pulls down a wrong lever in arranging his choices, this does no harm as his vote is not registered until he leaves the curtain enclosure. None of the levers can then be removed until the next voter closes the curtain. The counters are concealed behind plates which cannot be seen while the voting is in progress. When the polls are closed, these plates are unlocked and the results of the election are read off.

It is obvious that use of such a machine has many advantages. Secrecy is preserved better than under any paper ballot system. There is no danger of the endless chain fraud. Defective votes are practically eliminated. There is no long and tiresome count after the polls are closed during which ballots may be spoiled or changed by the short pencil device. The chances of deliberate or careless falsification of the returns are minimized. Experience has shown that the voting machine has other advantages. It lessens the time required for voting and it brings about considerable savings of public money. Where machines have been introduced, the number of polling places has been lessened, the number of election inspectors cut down and their hours of work considerably reduced.[34]

In spite of the obvious advantages of the voting machine, it is actually used at the present time in only ten states, although one-

[33] An observer reported to the writers that secrecy was destroyed in certain parts of Utica, New York, by placing a mirror on the ceiling over the booth. A discerning voter could insist upon the removal of any such contraption.

[34] Zukerman, *op. cit.*

half of the states have voting machine legislation.[35] In no state has the voting machine entirely supplanted the paper ballot. In New York State about 86 per cent of the total population is served by voting machines; in Connecticut about 63 per cent, in Washington about 50 per cent, and in Indiana about 45 per cent. In the other six states where machines are used much smaller percentages are served. In the state of Michigan some 389 machines were listed in a survey made of the election administration.[36] In Iowa 27 out of a total of 99 counties use mechanical voting. In Wisconsin, Maryland, and California voting machines are used only in occasional counties. The machines in use in Minnesota were discarded when changes in the election laws nullified their advantages.[37] Authorizing legislation has been passed in nine other states [38] but no machines have as yet been introduced.

A number of obstacles have prevented a wider use of the voting machine. In some cities like Chicago, grave scandals accompanied the efforts to introduce them many years ago, but in 1947 machines were bought and a few were used for the city election.[39] It has been shown on some of the older machines that it is possible to manipulate the count where the election inspectors and watchers are in collusion. Legal obstacles have stood in the way in some states. In Ohio a law authorizing their use was declared unconstitutional in an early decision, but the court later reversed itself and legislation was passed permitting the use of voting machines.[40] While the machines effect

[35] H. R. Goslee, *Election Administration in New York State Cities* (Albany, 1931), p. 28; Zukerman, "The Voting Machine Extends Its Territory," *American Political Science Review*, XXI (August, 1927), 608. The New York law has some safeguards against the abuses which have arisen in connection with the use of voting machines. It provides that there must be an automatic canvass of the counters so as to prevent misreading (transposing) of results and that all devices for destroying the secrecy of voting are illegal. In Albany it was discovered that the curtains were sandpapered so that they would be transparent under a very powerful light. Now such powerful lights are forbidden.

[36] J. K. Pollock, "Use of the Voting Machine in Michigan," *Bulletin No. 5* (1926), and "Election Administration in Michigan," *National Municipal Review,* XXIII (June, 1934), 356–357.

[37] Paper ballots were also prescribed.

[38] Massachusetts, Illinois, Maine, New Hampshire, Virginia, Arkansas, Arizona, Oregon, and Maryland.

[39] Zukerman, *The Voting Machine*; Harris, *Election Administration*.

[40] *State ex rel.* v. *Superintendent of Elections,* 80 Ohio State, 471; *State ex rel.* v. *Miller,* 187 Ohio State, 12. *State ex rel. Ammerman* v. *Sprague,* 117 Ohio State, 289 (1927).

ultimate savings in most cases, their initial cost is high, each machine selling for about a thousand dollars. In small rural communities where there is only one polling booth, the machine cannot bring great economies. The prevailing types of machine are not suited for preferential voting. As machines have not yet been devised which will make a record of how each vote has been cast, there is a general feeling of distrust regarding their reliability. In communities which have a genuine short ballot, mechanical voting is not a great necessity. Finally, the greatest obstacles have been the inertia of the electorate and the determined opposition of the politicians. The political corruptionists do not want to see such devices as chain voting and fraudulent counting made difficult or impossible by introduction of voting methods which are much surer to register the real choices of the voters.

The counting of huge blanket ballots in states which refuse to introduce machines presents many serious problems. In precincts where five hundred or so votes are cast it is not uncommon for election boards to be on duty for more than twenty-four hours at a stretch. Fatigue makes it impossible for them to perform their functions efficiently. There are many chances for the ballot crook to change the ballots by means of a piece of lead attached to a ring or some other device on the inside of his hand. Where there are thousands of election precincts, as in such cities as Chicago or New York, it is extremely difficult to organize a corps of watchers to keep track of the count in each precinct. In the counting of proposition votes a tired board may be especially careless, and the ballot crooks may be unusually active. A private recount of the proposition ballots cast in 56 precincts in a Chicago election showed that one-fourth of the precincts had enormous errors. On one proposition the recount lowered the proportion of the favorable vote by nearly 9 per cent.[41] In order to safeguard the counting process a number of states have provided for special counting boards.[42] The members of the counting board appear some time after the voting has started and begin tl ir work in separate quarters while the voting is still going on. The drawbacks to this system are the necessity for maintaining two sets of watchers,

[41] David M. Maynard, "Fraud and Error in Chicago Referendum Returns," *National Municipal Review*, XIX (March, 1930).

[42] Colorado, Idaho, Iowa, Kansas, Michigan, Missouri, Nebraska, Oklahoma, Oregon, Texas, Utah, and West Virginia.

the difficulty of getting the necessary rooms, the trouble in securing qualified counting officials, and the danger of the early returns' leaking out and influencing the result. Some use has been made of a central count which has many commendable features.[43] In the cities which use the Hare system of proportional representation and in the cities of Rhode Island a central board of canvassers makes the official count.[44] In Cincinnati, Toledo, and the other cities employing this system there have been no complaints regarding the accuracy and honesty of the count. In Rhode Island, where a preliminary count is made by the precinct officials, the clerk of the board of canvassers of Providence reports that the precinct returns are sometimes hundreds of votes in error.[45] It would seem that a better practice would be to abandon the precinct count altogether. The ballots cast in a British parliamentary election are always brought to a central counting place within each constituency.

SELECTION OF ELECTION AUTHORITIES

No matter how carefully the registration and ballot laws are framed, if honest and efficient officials are not secured to administer them, the chances for error and fraud are very great.[46] The common practice in the United States is to have the conduct of both the registration and the election in the hands of a precinct election board which varies in size from two to ten inspectors. In Pennsylvania and some of the southern states there are separate registration and election boards. Where central registration is used there is no need for precinct registration boards. However, the precinct election boards are still universally required. The precinct is the smallest electoral unit, containing from 200 to 2000 voters, the average being around 400 voters.[47] This is a much smaller unit than is found in European countries. The small size of the American election unit makes election costs very high and makes supervision difficult. The precinct

[43] J. K. Eads, "Indiana Experiments with Central Ballot Count," *National Municipal Review*, XXIX (August, 1940), 545–548.

[44] Laws of Rhode Island—Providence, Pawtucket, Central Falls, and Newport.

[45] Logan, *op. cit.*, p. 113.

[46] M. H. Shusterman, "Choosing Election Officers," *National Municipal Review*, XXIX 'March, 1940), 188–193; *Municipal Year Book* (current issue).

[47] C. A. Crosser, "Registration by Precincts," *Toledo City Journal*, VIII (September 15, 1923), 447.

election board is usually of a bipartisan character appointed by some local authority upon the recommendation of the local committee of the two major parties.

The Citizens' Association of Chicago estimated that there were at least 250 precincts in the city of Chicago in which vote frauds are habitually committed.[48] One of the causes of this is the requirement that the judges and clerks must be chosen from the residents of the precinct in which they are going to serve. In Missouri and Michigan the appointing power can select the inspectors from any of the residents in a given ward, and in New York and New Jersey they are limited only to residents of the city. St. Louis has the power to compel service as election officers. As new officers are needed, a panel of citizens living or working in the ward is drawn up. These people are then interviewed by some representatives of the election commissioners. The plan has worked well. In Milwaukee election officials have been chosen on the basis of a civil service examination since 1936. In Michigan the requirement of bipartisanship is also omitted. This greater latitude in choosing election officials has resulted in the selection of a higher type of official, especially in the city of Detroit. Mr. Distin, the chief superintendent of the Detroit Election Commission, makes the following statement regarding the appointment of inspectors in his city:

"There are times when there is a very spirited contest that citizens of considerable prominence in the industrial and financial life of Detroit volunteer for the work from the standpoint of doing their bit towards good citizenship, and along that line presidents and other officers of banks, industrial and commercial institutions help to maintain clean elections. The majority of the election inspectors are bank clerks and people who are doing some branch of accounting or clerical work in some of our large industries. The bank and manufacturers' associations have assisted wonderfully in placing many of their men at the disposal of the Commission on election days, allowing the men to take the day off with pay." [49]

In all the states but Pennsylvania the election inspectors are appointed. The elective system used in Pennsylvania, coupled with the

---

[48] "New Election Law Needed," Citizens' Association of Chicago, *Bulletin No. 75* (1928), p. 4. See also Harris, *Election Administration*, pp. 142–143.

[49] Logan, *Supervision of the Conduct of Elections and Returns with Special Reference to Pennsylvania* (Lancaster, Pa., 1927).

requirement of bipartisanship, works very poorly. The constitution provides for annual election of the judge and two inspectors and for appointment of a clerk by each inspector. The certificates of election for the judges and inspectors indicate almost invariably that the board is divided politically, but a check on the registration books where the party affiliations of the voters were given showed that many of the certificates were inaccurate.[50] The ability of the election inspectors in Philadelphia does not compare well with that found in Detroit.

Where the appointive system is used, the question comes up as to what authority should do the appointing. The best practice seems to be to put this in the hands of a single authority, selected without regard to his party affiliations. This plan has worked very successfully in Omaha, Nebraska, in Los Angeles, California, and in Rochester, New York.[51] The usual practice in large cities is to have a bipartisan commission controlling electoral matters. Only where this board hands over the actual administration to a chief clerk or superintendent divorced from party control are the affairs of the office efficiently managed. Economical and honest elections will be secured in the United States only when the party workers are deprived everywhere of their mastery of the electoral machinery.

The long ballot, the multiplicity of elections, the small size of the election precincts and the lack of adequate safeguards against fraud are all factors which play directly into the hands of the political bosses. These trappings of an archaic rural democracy, which assumed the existence of omnicompetent citizens, function badly in the great metropolitan centers of the United States. It is no wonder that the voters get lost trying to mark their jungle ballots and are willing to be led by the suave representatives of the political bosses who take the time to show them sample ballots and to explain the mysteries of the slate. One of the best illustrations of cultural lag in the field of politics is the slow pace at which positive law is catching up with the unanimous recommendations of political scientists for several generations in reference to the short ballot.

Electoral corruption and petty graft weaken the faith of the masses in democratic methods, and consequently it is necessary to eliminate

[50] *Ibid.*, pp. 61–63; Kurtzman, *op. cit.*, p. 117.
[51] "A Model Registration System," *op. cit.*, p. 52.

these evils if the democratic ideology is to survive. In the fight against the vote thieves it should be recognized that legal regulations are necessary, but they alone are not sufficient. We have a naïve faith in the power of legislation—constitutional, statutory, and local —to change our habits and keep us good. The colossal failure of the "noble experiment," with its constitutional prohibition of the manufacture, sale, and transportation of alcoholic beverages, has to some extent weakened this faith. A legal device designed to purify politics is workable only if someone is concerned with seeing that it works Even the most perfectly drafted election law can be manipulated by unscrupulous politicians who are not carefully watched. The best that positive law can do is to create a legal framework which makes the perversion of public office for private profit risky and which facilitates the expression of civic points of view.

CHAPTER XX

VOTING AND NONVOTING

"In the ideal democracy every citizen is intelligent, patriotic, disinterested. His sole wish is to discover the right side in each contested issue, and to fix upon the best man among competing candidates. His common sense, aided by a knowledge of the constitution of his country, enables him to judge wisely between the arguments submitted to him, while his own zeal is sufficient to carry him to the polling booth. Though it is usually assumed in platform speeches that the audience ad dressed are citizens of this attractive type, everybody knows that in all communities, not only in Chicago, but even in Liverpool, let us say, or in Lyons, or in Leipzig, a large proportion of the voters are so indifferent, or so ignorant, that it is necessary to rouse them, to drill them, to bring them up to vote."—James Bryce, Preface to M. A. Ostrogorski, *Democracy and the Organization of Political Parties* (New York, Macmillan Co., 1902), I, xliv.

IN THE DAYS WHEN BULLETS INSTEAD OF BALLOTS WERE EMPLOYED to settle political disputes, the opposing parties amassed their greatest strength as a matter of course. Today the use of the ballot box in democratic countries to decide who has won the struggle for power does not always mean a full mobilization of the eligible citizens on election day. The individual voter seems to play such a small part in deciding the result that he often neglects to cast his ballot unless the matter is brought to his attention in a striking way.[1] In Australia the significant function of seeing that the voters come out on election day is performed largely by the government. In the United States the persons who have been most concerned

[1] C. E. Merriam and H. F. Gosnell, *Non-Voting: Causes and Methods of Control* (Chicago, 1924), p. 112; J. K. Pollock, *Voting Behavior: A Case Study* (Ann Arbor, University of Michigan, 1939); Edward H. Litchfield, *Voting Behavior in a Metropolitan Community* (Ann Arbor, University of Michigan, 1941); Paul F. Lazarsfeld, Bernard Berelson, and Hazel Gaudet, *The People's Choice* (New York, Duell, Sloan and Pearce, 1944); G. M. Connelly and H. H. Field, "The Non-Voter—Who He Is, What He Thinks," *Public Opinion Quarterly*, VIII (Summer, 1944), 175–187; George Gallup, "Don't Stay Home on Election Day," in John Kieran (ed.), *The New Information Please Almanac 1948* (Garden City, N. Y., 1948), p. 114. H. F. Gosnell, "Mobilizing the Electorate," *Annals of the American Academy of Political and Social Science*, CCLIX (September, 1948), pp. 98–103.

with getting out the vote have been the party workers who expect some immediate gain if their candidates are successful at the polls. The precinct captain who carries his district is usually rewarded with some petty office or sinecure. He is really interested not in getting out all the voters, but merely in arousing those who will vote his way. The party workers have been aided in this task by the newspapers and by various organizations, but the main brunt of the work has fallen upon them. How well have they performed this function in recent times?

EXTENT OF POPULAR PARTICIPATION IN ELECTIONS

It is difficult to determine the number of eligible voters in the United States because of the great variety of suffrage provisions and the inadequate character of the election records. In any of the European democracies, such as France, Belgium, or Great Britain, the official lists of voters contain practically all the names of eligible voters. In the United States, each of the forty-eight states has a separate election law, and only about a dozen states record the number of registered voters. The lists in these states are far from complete, since, as has been explained in the preceding chapter, registration is usually a personal matter. All estimates of the number of eligible voters must therefore be based upon the census figures. Adult citizenship is the first prerequisite for voting in all the states. The number of adult citizens in the United States as given by the census does not furnish an entirely accurate idea of the number of eligible voters.[2] Taking all of the disqualifications together, it is necessary to make a correction of the census figures for adult citizens in order to arrive at the number of persons actually qualified to vote in the United States, even in a census year.

One method of estimating the number of eligible voters in this

[2] In his *Why Europe Votes* (Chicago, 1930), H. F. Gosnell tried to make allowance for lack of residence in estimating the number of eligibles in the United States because he wanted to make the figures as nearly comparable as possible to European election statistics. When the main purpose is to study the trend in American political participation, it is not necessary to make any estimates as to mobility. The figures presented by C. E. Merriam in the President's Research Committee on Social Trends, *Recent Social Trends* (New York, 1933), II, 1507, are calculated without reference to mobility.

country is to leave out the southern states where the Negroes are largely disfranchised. A careful study of the participation of the voters in twenty-one typical northern states at the 1920 presidential election showed that about 56.3 per cent of the adult citizens voted.[3] As this was a census year these figures only slightly exaggerate the number of eligible voters in these states. The problem of estimating the number of eligible voters in noncensus years is a very complicated one, but there have been a few bold enough to attempt it.[4] Estimates for years other than those when presidential elections and census coincide must be based upon interpolations and extrapolations. A number of attempts of this sort have been made. All agree that the low point in American popular interest in voting was in 1924. A study of the official returns in Great Britain, France, Belgium, and Switzerland since 1919 shows that the participation in national elections has not fallen below 70 per cent of the eligibles in any one of these countries.[5] The highest polls have been over 76 per cent of the registered voters in all these countries. It is obvious that the American record for voting efficiency in the period immediately following World War I was considerably inferior to that of a number of European democracies, some of which have more liberal suffrage provisions than the United States. The first election held after the advent of the New Deal (1936) brought the highest poll of the twentieth century, both in relative and absolute numbers. In thirty of the states the record was as good as in the European democracies. This high participation was maintained in the later Franklin Roosevelt elections with only a slight decline in 1944 when many eligible voters were overseas. In the 1948 presidential election there was again a slump in voting interest. Only about one-half of the potential voters came to the polls.

Between 1876 and 1900, popular participation in American elections was about the same as in the British, German, and French parliamentary elections. During this epoch the margin between the two leading parties was a very narrow one, the combined vote of

[3] S. A. Rice, *Quantitative Methods in Politics* (New York, 1928), pp. 243–247.

[4] A. M. Schlesinger and E. M. Ericksson, "The Vanishing Voter," *New Republic,* XL (October 15, 1924), 162–167; C. A. M. Ewing, *Presidential Elections* (Norman, University of Oklahoma Press, 1940) ; *Editorial Research Reports,* II (August 6, 1943).

[5] Gosnell, *Why Europe Votes*; Gallup, *op. cit.*

the losing parties never falling below 50 per cent of the total vote cast except in 1896. A close margin between the two major parties was found in many of the states as well as in the country as a whole. In view of the fact that the presidential electors are chosen at large by states, this condition accounts in part for the large vote in those days. The switch of a few votes one way or the other was a matter of great importance to the party managers, and in the doubtful states they put forth great efforts to see that all their supporters come out to vote. A grouping of states by the proportion of eligible citizens that voted in 1940, shows that the doubtful states were those with the highest voting records.

From 1896 to 1932 the margin between the two major parties was not so even, except in 1912 and 1916. Until 1932 the Republicans, and from 1932 to 1948 the Democrats, maintained a majority of all the votes cast. During the period of the preponderance of the Republican party there was a tendency on the part of many voters in this country to stay away from the polls.[6] This tendency was arrested in the presidential election of 1936, in which some 69 per cent of the estimated number of adult citizens in the entire country took part.[7] At this election Landon received the second largest absolute vote of any Republican candidate for President, but Roosevelt was over eleven million votes ahead of him. The highest vote was cast in 1940 when nearly 50 million came to the polls, or 71 per cent of the estimated eligible voters.

CAUSES OF NONVOTING

Can the indifference of the voters really be laid at the door of the one-sided party situation in recent times? The Republican party first enjoyed a period of unprecedented prosperity during the first three decades of the twentieth century, which tended to dampen

---

[6] See H. F. Gosnell, "The Voter Resigns," *New Republic*, October 21, 1925, and *Why Europe Votes*.

[7] According to *Statistics of the Congressional and Presidential Election of November 3, 1936* (compiled by the clerk of the House of Representatives), the total vote cast in 1936 was 45,646,817. The census estimate for the total population of the United States in 1936 was 128,429,000. For purposes of calculating the above percentage it was assumed that the ratio of adult citizens to the total population was the same in 1936 as in 1930. See *Editorial Research Reports, loc. cit.*

interest in politics.[8] The attention of the voters was absorbed by many competing interests, such as the cinema, the radio, and the automobile. The politicians in both of the major parties were anxious to obscure issues because they feared the consequences of a split-up in the existing alignments. In 1928 the Democratic party managers raised the prohibition issue and also the issue whether a Catholic could aspire to be president of the United States. These were issues which really engaged the emotions of the masses, and the result was the highest relative vote we had had in this country since 1916. There was no falling off of this level of interest in the 1932 election, but it required the election of 1936, with the burning issues arising out of the policies inaugurated by the New Deal, to raise this level.

The effect of the one-sided party situation in the United States can further be studied by a close analysis of election results by states. The voting records of the adult citizens in Indiana, Delaware, and West Virginia are about as high as that of the British and French voters. A study of the state returns for the elections from 1896 to 1944 shows that the proportion of the adult citizens who come to vote tends to vary directly with the strength of the losing parties in that state. In short, as the ratio of the vote cast by the minority parties in a given state approaches one-half, the higher is the total poll in that state. Thus, in 1928 in the state of West Virginia approximately 41 per cent of the vote cast went to the minority parties and 75 per cent of the estimated number of adult citizens voted, whereas in the state of Pennsylvania only 34 per cent of the total vote went to the minority parties and 61 per cent of the estimated number of adult citizens voted. When the result became closer in Pennsylvania in the thirties and forties the participation rose also.[9] In the Solid South the supremacy of the Democratic party has had a similar effect except in the election of 1928. In the six southern states which were carried by the Democratic candidate for president in 1928 this tendency was still marked. In the southern states which Smith lost by a narrow margin, the proportion of the estimated eligibles that voted was much larger than in 1920 and 1924. It may be said in general that the proportion of the vote cast

[8] Walter Lippmann, *Men of Destiny* (New York, 1927), Chap. III.
[9] H. F. Gosnell, *Grass Roots Politics* (Washington, D. C., 1942).

by minority parties is a rough measure of the element of uncertainty in the election. Where it is felt that the result of the election in the state is practically certain, the party managers and the voters tend to be indifferent. Previous voting records and straw votes indicate to the party leaders whether or not they have to work to keep a given state in line. Funds, speakers, and workers are then concentrated in the doubtful states.

The party situation and the method of choosing presidential electors at large in each state are among the factors which have a marked influence upon popular participation in American elections. Woman suffrage was one of the important causes of the relatively low poll in 1920.[10] In most of the states the women were voting for the first time and they had not yet become accustomed to the use of the franchise. Separate returns were not kept for the men and women in this year except in Illinois, where it was shown that some 46.5 per cent of the adult female citizens took part as compared with 74.1 per cent of the adult male citizens. Since 1920 there has been a gradual trend toward equal participation by men and women.[11]

In order to understand thoroughly the problem of nonvoting it would be necessary to have many more facts regarding voters and nonvoters than their sex. It would be useful to know to what extent nonvoting was prevalent among the various age groups, the different economic and occupational groups, the manifold religious groups, and the diverse educational groups. Unfortunately, official statistics on this subject are lacking in this country.[12] However, private studies made in a number of cities throw some light on this problem. Two field surveys made in Chicago,[13] a survey in the town of Delaware, Ohio, surveys made in Detroit and Ann Arbor, a panel investigation in Erie County, Ohio, and the survey by the National Opin-

[10] Rice, *op. cit.*, p. 246.

[11] H. F. Gosnell, *Democracy: Threshold of Freedom* (New York, 1948).

[12] In urban Basel a study of popular participation in a cantonal election among occupational groups was made by the canton in 1911. See *Statistik der Grossratswahlen vom 6/7 Mai 1911 im Kanton Basel-Stadt* (Basel, 1911). See also E. Bock, *Wahlstatistik* (Halle-Salle, 1919); H. Tingsten, *Political Behavior* (London, 1937); and A. Senti, "Die Nichtwähler in Zurich," *Züricher Statistiche Nachrichten*, 1926, No. 4, pp. 160–170.

[13] Merriam and Gosnell, *op. cit.*, and H. F. Gosnell, *Getting Out the Vote* (Chicago, 1927).

ion Research Center should be mentioned.[14] The first Chicago study was made shortly after the mayoralty election held in April, 1923. The nonvoters interviewed were taken from all parts of Chicago, and as far as sex and race were concerned constituted a fair sample of the entire adult citizen population of the city. A comparison of the characteristics of the nonvoters with those of 5000 registered voters showed that newness to the city, unfamiliarity with local surroundings, foreign-language habits, and derivative citizenship were all factors which were related to electoral abstentions. The second Chicago study and the Delaware study were both made in connection with the presidential election of 1924, and both were based upon a nearly complete census of all adult citizens within the selected areas studied. The Chicago study was based upon twelve selected districts and the Delaware study upon the entire town. These two studies showed that the highest participation was found among the residents of the well-to-do neighborhoods, those who had the most education, those who had lived in the city more than ten years, and those in managerial, governmental, professional, or skilled mechanical positions.[15] The lowest voting records were found among the women, the colored persons, the residents of the poor districts, those with little or no education, and those in domestic or unskilled work. The voting records of the states of Illinois and Ohio are above the average of the country as a whole, and the studies made in these two states were on a small scale. Nevertheless, these studies indicate that education and improved economic status are stimulants to interest in elections.[16]

[14] B. A. Arneson, "Non-voting in a Typical Ohio Community," *American Political Science Review*, XIX, 816–825. See also R. C. Martin, "Municipal Electorate," *Southwestern Social Science Quarterly*, XIV (December, 1933); J. K. Pollock, *Voting Behavior* (Ann Arbor, 1939); Lazarsfeld, *et al.*, *op. cit.*; Connelly and Field, *op. cit.*

[15] Unpublished figures collected in connection with the second Chicago study (Gosnell, *Getting Out the Vote*).

[16] Later studies made on a more extensive scale, but utilizing only available statistical material, appear at first sight to be at variance with these results except as far as the women are concerned. A more refined analysis of these data, however, shows that when the complicating factor of mobility is removed these influences are still apparent. The participation of the Negro voters is about the same as that of other groups when this same allowance is made. See H. F. Gosnell, *Machine Politics: Chicago Model* (Chicago 1937), Table 10, p. 109, which gives the relationship of interest in voting, as measured by the percentage of

In the first Chicago study the authors hunted for specific causes of nonvoting by questioning the persons who had failed to vote as to their reasons for not voting. A recheck upon this method was made in the second Chicago study. Since those citizens who fail to take the trouble to register are the most typical nonvoters, Table 11 showing the results of the two studies is given.[17]

The similarity of the results of the two investigations shows that the conclusions reached in the earlier study regarding the quantitative importance of the various reasons given by the nonvoters for their electoral abstentions are fairly accurate. In both years, one-third of those who failed to register said they were indifferent to elections, one in every six or seven said they were detained by sickness or absence, one in every seven or eight expressed disbelief in women's voting, one-tenth professed ignorance or timidity regarding elections, and so on. "The analysis of the sex, color, nationality, registration status, voting experience, age, term of residence in city, and economic status of the nonvoters that gave particular reasons for not voting brought out more clearly the close relationship that existed between the social situations and the peculiar characteristics of the nonvoters. For instance, illness kept at home on election day many elderly housewives and a few elderly gentlemen. Absence from the city on election day was most common among the registered, native white, middle-aged, well-to-do businessmen. Fear of loss of business or wages was a significant cause of nonvoting among the registered males, some of them colored and some of them foreign born, who lived in poor neighborhoods and who were employed in manufacturing, construction work, or in the small retail business. Many middle-aged poor people insisted that one vote counted for

---

the adult citizens registered in Chicago, to such variables as percentage of the women in the total number of registered voters, percentage of the foreign-born in the total population, percentage of persons of Catholic origin, median rental, home owners, unemployed, mobility, doubling up, and education, as shown by coefficients of correlation calculated on the basis of units obtained by dividing the city into 144 parts. When mobility is held constant by the method of partial correlation, the results are not so contradictory to the earlier Chicago studies. H. F. Gosnell, *Negro Politicians* (Chicago, 1935), p. 347; G. Mydal, *An American Dilemma; The Negro Problem and Modern Democracy* (New York, 1944).

[17] Gosnell, *Getting Out the Vote*, p. 9. Compare with results obtained in Greencastle, Indiana, reported by H. Zink in his *Government of Cities in the United States* (New York, 1939), pp. 148–153; Connelly and Field, *op. cit.*

TABLE 11

REASONS FOR NOT REGISTERING GIVEN BY SELECTED NONVOTERS IN THE 1923
AND 1924 ELECTIONS: PERCENTAGE DISTRIBUTION

Reasons for Not Registering	Adult Citizens Not Registered for the Mayoralty Election of 1923	Adult Citizens Not Registered for the Presidential Election of 1924
All Reasons:		
Number	3369	649
Percentage	100.0	100.0
Illness	7.7	12.3
Absence	6.2	4.2
Detained by helpless members of family	1.6	1.1
Insufficient legal residence	7.6	6.6
Fear of loss of wages or business	2.9	3.3
Congestion at the polls	0.5	0.5
Poor location of polling booth	0.7	1.1
Fear of disclosure of age	0.3	0.0
Disbelief in woman's voting	11.3	13.4
Objections of husband	1.6	1.8
Belief that one vote counts for nothing	1.6	2.2
Disgust with politics	4.9	6.0
Disgust with own party	0.6	0.0
Belief that ballot box is corrupted	0.7	0.0
Disbelief in all political action	0.5	0.0
General indifference	33.4	33.8
Indifference to particular election	2.3	0.3
Neglect: Intended to register but failed	5.0	2.9
Ignorance or timidity regarding elections	9.6	10.0
Failure of party workers	1.0	0.5

nothing, that the candidates were equally bad, that the ballot box was corrupted, and that the whole election system was a sham and a fraud.,. . . General indifference was very prevalent among the white females of foreign parentage who were not registered, who lived in poor sections of the city, and who were engaged in housework. . . . The educational opportunities of many of these people had been so limited that they did not even know how to mark a ballot, and they hesitated to go to the polls for fear of being ridiculed." [18] The investigation by the National Opinion Research Center showed that the nonvoters to a greater extent than the voters were satisfied with the way most people who held political office were doing their jobs. Fewer of them thought that the Constitution should be changed. Stated positively, voting was associated with a desire for a change.[19]

We have been principally concerned up to this point with the consideration of popular participation in presidential elections, which is almost always higher than that in any other type of election in this country. Even in presidential years, the total vote cast for members of the House of Representatives is less than that cast for President. For instance, in 1944 the congressional vote was 94 per cent of the presidential vote. The system used to elect representatives in this country resembles that used in Great Britain and France at the present time, and that used in Germany prior to 1918. It is the so-called single member district system under which each electoral district elects a single representative on the basis of a majority or plurality vote. As in the European countries mentioned, so in the United States this system tends to depress interest in voting in districts where one party is sure to win. Thus in the First Congressional District of South Carolina 92.6 per cent of the total vote cast was obtained by the winning candidate, and only 6.4 per cent of the adult citizens went to the polls.[20] The voting record at congressional elections is always higher when they coincide with a presidential

TABLE 12

CLOSENESS OF ELECTION AND PARTICIPATION

Percentage of Votes Cast Which Were Received by Winning Candidates	Number of Votes Cast	Total Number of Adult Citizens	Percentage of Adult Citizens Who Voted
50– 59.9	2,176,780	3,545,461	61.4
60– 69.9	405,787	811,770	50.0
70– 79.9	787,702	1,811,198	43.5
80– 89.9	179,364	568,518	31.6
90–100.0	65,737	774,966	8.5

[18] Merriam and Gosnell, *op. cit.*, pp. 253–255.
[19] Connelly and Field, *op. cit.*
[20] This tendency is illustrated in the following table based on the Congressional elections in Delaware, Indiana, Pennsylvania, and South Carolina for 1920.

election than when they do not. Thus, in 1946, the congressional elections brought out only 34,400,742 voters, or 76 per cent of the presidential vote in 1944. A study of other nonpresidential years will show that this is typical.

The multiplicity of elections in the United States puts a great strain upon the attention of the voter. An examination of the ballots used in the 1944 presidential election shows that over one-third of them contained twenty or more offices to be voted for, to say nothing of the propositions to be voted upon. A study of the election returns for the states of New York, Nebraska, and California reveals that there was a considerable falling off in the size of the vote for minor offices as compared with that received by the head of the ticket.[21] For example, in 1946, 10 per cent of those who came to the polls in New York did not vote for state assemblymen, in Nebraska 20 per cent of those who voted for United States Senator did not vote for state superintendent of public instruction, and in California in 1944, 26 per cent of those who came to vote did not register their choice for state assemblymen. Where minor officers alone are chosen at an election the decline in the size of the poll is even more striking.

The ballot used in Indianapolis in 1932 was especially formidable. It contained 319 printed names and was so huge that it required special machines.[22]

STIMULATING INTEREST IN ELECTIONS

There is difference of opinion at the present time as to the importance of the problem of nonvoting in the United States. There are those who believe that indifference upon the part of a large portion of the electorate is a dangerous tendency.[23] On the other hand, there are those who think that the slacker vote is not a menace.[24]

[21] Compare with this C. T. Titus, "Voting in California Cities, 1900–1925," *Southwestern Political and Social Science Quarterly*, VIII (March, 1928), 383–389, and *Voting Behavior in the United States* (Berkeley, 1935).

[22] See also Merriam and Gosnell, *Non-Voting* (Chicago, University of Chicago Press, 1924), p. 190.

[23] "A New Get Out the Vote Movement," *Literary Digest*, LXXXII (August 23, 1924); Gallup, *op. cit.*

[24] W. B. Munro, "Is the Slacker Vote a Menace?" *National Municipal Review*, XVII (February, 1928), 80–98; P. Herring, *The Politics of Democracy* (New York, 1940), pp. 31–35; Francis G. Wilson, "The Inactive Electorate and Social Revolution," *Southwest Social Science Quarterly*, XVI (1936), 73–84.

Which of these two opposite points of view regarding electoral in-difference is the correct one? Sufficient evidence is not at hand at present to answer this question in any definite fashion. It is usually assumed in a democracy like ours that the persons who do not vote are willing to abide by the decision given by those who vote. Conse-quently, it is highly improbable that any violent revolution will be started by the great body of nonvoters. If nonvoting means satisfac-tion with things as they are, it is not a dangerous sign. On the other hand, there are certain types of nonvoting which indicate that our political institutions are not functioning properly. The methods em-ployed to choose the president and the Congress of the United States are such that they discourage many intelligent people from voting in one-party districts. Indifference caused by the overburdening of the ballot reveals another serious defect in our governmental system. The electoral arrangements are so inconvenient in some states that many are deterred from voting. Electoral indifference due to other causes may or may not be serious. We have no evidence to show that more or less intelligent decisions are rendered when the fullest pos-sible number vote. Some have attacked the indiscriminate get-out-the-vote movements. After all, there are few, if any, indiscriminate ones. The Chambers of Commerce concentrate on getting out the business vote, and the Leagues of Women Voters confine their efforts largely to the better-class residential districts. The illiterate non-voters are not reached by these movements. The real danger of the present system is that we are not sure that those who do take the trouble to vote do so for the best of reasons.[25] In fact it is clear that many voters are enticed to the polls by favors or promises of favors from precinct captains and other representatives of the party ma-chine. This is especially true at primary elections where the machine vote is likely to be a more potent factor than at national elections.[26]

The study of elections abroad shows that where the voter is called to pass upon a few important positions and the issues are sharply

[25] W. B. Munro, *Government of the United States* (New York, 1936), p. 583.

[26] In the Chicago primary elections of 1924 and 1926, the percentage of the registered vote cast was much higher in the wards showing the highest number of vote frauds than in the wards showing the least fraud. Thus in the First, Twentieth and Twenty-seventh Wards, all in poor neighborhoods, over 60 per cent of the registered vote was cast in 1924, while in the Fifth, Forty-eighth and Forty-ninth Wards only 45 per cent of the registered vote was cast.

drawn, the participation in elections is usually high. In Europe the voter is not overwhelmed by a huge blanket ballot as he is in many American cities.[27] In Great Britain the voter is usually called upon to select one candidate from two or three nominees for the House of Commons in his district. Local elections do not coincide with national elections, and the task imposed upon the local electorates is comparatively light. In France the voter has about the same functions to perform as in Great Britain. In Holland, Belgium, and Switzerland the voters at national elections are required to choose between a number of rival lists of candidates. In Switzerland, where there are many local elections, the voters show the same indifference toward the choosing of minor officers that is manifested in the United States. This is the old lesson of the need for a short ballot in most parts of the United States. The simplification of the government and the concentration of power in the hands of a few important elective officials would remove one of the important causes of nonvoting in this country.

The system of choosing the presidential electors at large in each state tends to discourage voting in the sure states. In Germany under the Weimar regime the president was chosen by a direct popular vote, and the participation in the 1932 election was over 86 per cent of the electorate. It would be possible in the United States for each state to provide that its presidential electors be chosen on a proportionate basis without a constitutional amendment. But a more thoroughgoing solution of this problem would demand an amendment to the United States Constitution providing for the direct popular election of the President.[28] Such an amendment would stimulate interest in voting in the states that are now regarded as one-party states. The Democrats in South Carolina would feel that their support was needed just as much as that of the Democrats in New York. The discussion of such an amendment might also bring up the question of the suffrage qualifications and the question of presidential nominating methods. There is no doubt that it would

[27] There are many other factors which contribute to the high polls in European parliamentary elections. Among these should be mentioned the class and social divisions found in politics. See Gosnell, *Why Europe Votes*; *Democracy: The Threshold of Freedom*; and H. Tingsten, *Political Behavior* (London, 1937).

[28] "Should the Electoral College Be Abolished?" (symposium), *Cong. Digest*, XX (March, 1941), 67–96.

have far-reaching implications, but it is also clear that the present machinery for choosing the President needs overhauling.

The single member district system which is used to elect congressmen and state legislators tends to discourage voting in certain districts. The introduction of some form of proportional representation might stimulate popular interest in these districts. The list or general ticket plans of proportional representation, such as are used in Holland, Belgium, Switzerland, and other countries, make practically every vote count. A number of representatives are chosen from each district and each voter indicates his preference for a given party list of candidates. The rules for assigning the seats to the various lists take into account the size of the vote cast for each list. The party managers realize that the larger the vote of their party, the larger will be its representation in the legislative body. The Hare system of proportional representation has been tried out in a dozen cities in this country and so far it has not increased popular interest in municipal elections where it has been used. The experience of Cincinnati shows that the election of a council under the single transferable vote has not brought out as large a vote as mayoralty elections did. Was this decline in popular interest caused by the council-manager plan or by proportional representation? It is hard to isolate these two factors but it is likely that the election of a city council alone lacks some of the dramatic qualities that are usually attached to the election of a mayor. It also seems that a dissatisfied electorate is more active than a satisfied one.[29] The voters of Cincinnati thought that things were going well. The city of Dayton, Ohio, has the city-manager plan with a council elected at large by a plurality vote. The size of the vote cast in municipal elections in Dayton under this system has been much smaller than that in Cincinnati under P. R. Theoretically, the Hare system should stimulate interest in voting as it makes a much larger proportion of the votes count toward the election of representatives than any plurality or majority system. Actually, the various list systems of proportional representation seem to be more effective in this respect. In Switzerland the introduction of a list system brought a large increase in the size of the vote, which has been maintained at subsequent elections. Such a system might be used in the states to elect mem-

[29] Connelly and Field, *op. cit.*

bers of the House of Representatives. It would do away with gerry-mandering, give full recognition to minorities, and at the same time encourage voting. These advantages would have to be balanced against the strong preference of the American people for the two-party system and methods of representation that favor that system.

It has also been shown that failure to register is an important cause of nonvoting in this country. It has been estimated that there were 60,000,000 registered voters at the time of the 1944 presidential election. This was 75 per cent of the estimated number of adult citizens in the country at that time. Partial registration statistics for prior elections show that this condition is not a new one. The Chicago study was an attempt to measure the success of an unofficial nonpartisan canvass to increase registration in selected districts.[30] It was based upon a complete survey of all the adult citizens in twelve districts taken from different parts of the city. A series of nonpartisan notices regarding registration were mailed to one-half of the citizens interviewed in each of the twelve districts and not to the other half. The purpose of leaving half of the citizens in each district untouched was to establish a control for the experiment. If in any given district a larger proportion of the citizens who were sent notices registered than of those who were not sent notices, then it was assumed that the canvass had had some effect. For purposes of convenience, the two groups of citizens studied were called the stimulated and the nonstimulated citizens. A comparison of the characteristics of the 3000 stimulated citizens with those of the 3000 nonstimulated citizens showed that as far as such matters as the ratio between the sexes, the proportion of foreign born, and the length of residence in the city were concerned, the two groups were almost alike. In other words, the method of random sampling was used to keep constant the factors that vary with the extent of popular participation in elections. Seventy-five per cent of the citizens who were sent registration notices registered, as compared with 65 per cent of the nonstimulated citizens. The difference of 10 per cent between the registration response of the stimulated and nonstimulated citizens is a fairly accurate measure of the value of mailing registration notices. There are many other municipalities like Chi--

[30] Gosnell, *Getting Out the Vote.*

cago where the registration system is unduly burdensome upon the voters. The adoption of a form of permanent registration such as has been described in the previous chapter would undoubtedly increase the proportion of adult citizens registered.

Compulsory voting has been suggested as a means of keeping up the interest of the voters in elections.[31] Where it has been tried, as in Belgium, Australia, and parts of Switzerland, it has done away with the need for partisan efforts to rally the voters to the polls.[32] In Belgium small pecuniary fines, public reprimands, and disfranchisement were the penalties inflicted upon citizens convicted of electoral negligence. In actual practice, very few nonvoters were brought to trial. The success of the system is not dependent so much upon the penalties as it is upon the fact that the whole process of election is organized by the government. Each voter receives an official summons to every election, and he does not have to rely upon the party workers for information regarding his duties.

What are the possibilities of introducing such a system in the United States? The first obstacle in the way of its adoption would be the inadequacy of the lists of registered voters kept in this country. It would be necessary to know the names and addresses of all the eligible voters if compulsory voting were to be successful. Otherwise, the negligent citizens would simply fail to register. In the second place, there are a number of legal obstacles which would have to be surmounted. American courts are likely to follow the precedent set by the Supreme Court·of Missouri when it declared the obligatory voting provision of the Kansas City Charter unconstitutional.[33] Lastly, popular prejudices against governmental pressure in connection with voting would have to be overcome. The voters in the state of Oregon showed a decided dislike to compulsory voting

[31] Gosnell, *Why Europe Votes*; S. Spring, "The Voter Who Will Not Vote," *Harper's Magazine*, November, 1922; W. T. Donaldson, *Compulsory Voting and Absent Voting with Bibliographies* (Columbus, 1914); *Massachusetts Constitutional Convention Bulletin No. 24* (Boston, 1917); P. Deeter, *Prize Essay on Compulsory Voting* (Philadelphia, 1902); W. A. Robson, "Compulsory Voting," *Political Science Quarterly*, XXXVIII (December, 1923), 569–577; C. E. Merriam, "Compulsory Voting in Czecho-Slovakia," *National Municipal Review*, XIV (1925), 65–68; T. T. Smyth, "Compulsory Voting," *Municipal Review Canada* (April, 1944), 9–11.

[32] J. Barthélemy, "Pour le vote obligatoire," *Revue du droit public et de la science politique en France et de l'étranger*, XL (1923), 101–167.

[33] *Kansas City* v. *Whipple*, 126 Mo. 481, and the *Harvard Law Review*, X, 43, 9–40.

when they voted on the question in 1920.[34] Obligatory voting is made permissive by the constitutions of North Dakota and Massachusetts but no legislative action has been taken in either state. The agitation that would be necessary to secure the enactment of such a scheme might have in itself a stimulating effect upon voting.

The system of obligatory voting which would come the nearest to fitting American conditions is the one which is found in Australia. This law makes registration compulsory as well as voting. In the words of the law, "Every person who is entitled to have his name placed on the Roll for any Subdivision whether by way of enrolment or transfer of enrolment, and whose name is not on the Roll upon the expiration of twenty-one days from the date upon which he becomes so entitled, or at any subsequent date while he continues to be so entitled, shall be guilty of an offense. . . . "[35] A later section of the law states that every elector who "fails to vote at an election without a valid and sufficient reason for failure" or who gives a false reason "shall be guilty of an offense."[36] The Australian law would get around the fact that no American state has an official and complete system for registering voters.

Compulsory voting requires the government to make complete and orderly arrangements for the notification of the voters regarding pending elections. The second Chicago study showed the marked difference that such notification made in the size of the vote.

When taken together with a number of other fundamental changes needed in the American electoral system, the device of fines for non-voting might perform a very useful function.[37] American politics has been corrupted at its source. Too frequently the motive power which brings the voters to the polls is the selfish interest of a minor party worker which is linked with the selfish interests of the higher party officials. The vote has been regarded as a commodity which could be bought and sold.[38] If democracy is to survive troublesome times,

[34] J. D. Barnett, "Compulsory Voting in Oregon," *American Political Science Review*, XV, 255–256.

[35] "Commonwealth Electoral Act, 1908–1929," in B. J. McGrath and G. J. O'Sullivan (eds.), *The Laws of the Commonwealth of Australia, 1901–1931* (Australia, 1932) Part VII, Section 42.

[36] *Ibid.*, Section 128A.

[37] This view is Dr. Gosnell's only.

[38] D. H. Kurtzman, *Methods of Controlling Votes in Philadelphia* (Philadelphia, 1935) ; J. T. Salter, *Boss Rule* (New York, 1935) ; Gosnell, *Machine Politics.*

like the present it will need to have a firmer foundation than the cohesive power of public plunder. If an aroused electorate could see in such devices as compulsory voting, fairer systems of representation, more equal opportunities for campaign publicity and better safeguards against fraud, a chance to break the shackles of the party machines, we might be moving in the direction of a party system which would function on a higher intellectual and administrative level. Such a new party system would place the contenders for public office on a more equal basis as far as mere organization was concerned and it would compel them to appeal more to reason. Elections would turn less on such considerations as the relative number of payrollers and more on such considerations as the relative drawing power of the candidates and their programs.

CHAPTER XXI

FUNCTIONS OF PARTIES

"How were the people to know about the proceedings of Congress and the work of their Congressman?

"I thought it all over. It was clear to me that the only way to beat boss and ring rule was to keep the people thoroughly informed. Machine control is based upon misrepresentation and ignorance. Democracy is based upon knowledge. It is of first importance that the people shall know about their government and the work of their public servants."—Robert M. LaFollette, *A Personal Narrative of Personal Experiences* (Madison, Wisconsin, 1913), pp. 64–68.

THE PARTY MAY BE LOOKED UPON AS A TYPE OF SOCIAL GROUP, primarily concerned with social control as exercised through the government.[1] It rests upon fundamental psychological tendencies, upon social, political, or economic interests, develops its own organization and attracts its personnel, acquires its professional standards and professional technique, and in time its traditions, tendencies, predispositions. Like other groups its momentum may carry it on, after its immediate purpose has been achieved. Group solidarity, personalities, traditions, ambitions will have been obtained in the struggle, and those who have been acting together, in the narrower circle as governors and in the broader circle of those interested for wider social and economic reasons, may go on acting together for other purposes.

The party system may be regarded as an institution, supplementary to the government, aiding the electorate in the selection of official personnel and in the determination of public policies, and in the larger task of operating or criticizing the government. In this sense the party may be regarded as a part of the government itself, an extension of officialism, shading out from very definite responsi-

[1] Robert Michels, *Political Parties* (New York, 1915); H. F. Gosnell, *Democracy: Threshold of Freedom* (New York, 1948); E. Pendleton Herring, *The Politics of Democracy* (New York, 1940).

bility for official acts to the less definite responsibility of shaping and guiding the course of public opinion.

The party contains at its core a central group of active leaders, the inner circle, in whose hands rests the leadership of the group; next comes the much larger outer circle of those who make a profession of politics or take a lively and practical interest in it; then comes the area of those who are strongly partisan, immovable by any ordinary issue, the irreducible minimum of party strength; then comes a large group of men and women who are partisans as a rule, who are predisposed to the party, and in general approve of its leaders and its policies, but who are capable of independent action and cannot be relied upon to follow the party leadership under all circumstances. Still farther from the center of the circle are those who are feebly disposed to follow the party, shading over into the group of voters who are largely independent of party affiliations, and will readily be drawn one way or the other by the issue or the candidates of the campaign. In between are those voters who are torn by conflicting predispositions.

The most significant factors in the party are:

(1) A mass of persons predisposed through traditions, tendencies, habits, principles to act as Republicans, Democrats, Socialists, or otherwise;

(2) The active leaders, a relatively small group of persons who are politically conscious and active—the initiating and managerial group, the urge to political activity, the struggle for mastery and power, the desire for fame, the spirit of service, the concrete ambition for money and privilege produce a group actively interested in the perpetuation or reconstruction of party groups;

(3) Economic, racial, religious, political interests desiring party action or inaction; railroads, steel, coal, oil, land, labor, women, the innumerable groups and interests of which the state is made up and whose constant interaction produces a resultant through the political process;

(4) Logical forces or tendencies, giving rise to formulas, platforms, creeds, policies, ideas, with their corresponding attractions and aversions; and also the somewhat blinder feelings, tendencies, reactions, dispositions, emotions, which are the product of the experience and training of the society and which constitute the back-

ground of social activity; personalities, memories, formulas are like signals flashing signs of action, differently interpreted of course to thousands of persons.

What we really have is a series of groupings roughly cooperating to produce the result of government. These include:

(1) The government
(2) The political parties, major and minor
(3) Nonparty political organizations
(4) Social organizations, secondarily political and nonparty in form, but politically active at times
(5) Social organizations, only faintly or occasionally political

Under the third head are such groups as the League of Women Voters and many other types of local or civic leagues active in municipal affairs. These groups are political in character and method, but nonparty in character, though at times they pass over into the party class.

Of the fourth type are such organizations as the representatives of the great occupational groups, agriculture, labor, and business, with their large number of subdivisions and subsections. These are nonparty in form and nonpolitical in theory, but in actual fact they are often very active in public affairs, and widely influential in shaping the course of elections and of legislation.

Of the fifth type are the groups which have only an occasional interest in the problems of parties, although the interest may be very intense at times. Of these the churches in the United States are good examples. Others are the social clubs and organizations not directly concerned with the outcome of the party or political struggle. At times they may awake and engage most actively in the political or party struggle, but as a rule they remain outside the area of conflict.

The same individual may of course be a member at one time of all of these groups. He may be a public official, an active member of a party, a member of various nonparty political leagues, and of all the other types less pronouncedly political. He will normally be a member of several of them, and may exert an influence through all of them, or none of them, depending upon a variety of circumstances. His sentiment may be in the ascendancy in all of them or in none of them at all; or more commonly in some and not in others. In all cases, the pattern is a complex one. Sometimes the individual finds himself the victim of conflicting tendencies, and this may delay his choice or create indecision.[2]

The party in short has no monopoly in the shaping of public opinion or the selection of the official personnel of the government, although laws are made by the votes of partisans, and administered in great part by them, and officials are (outside the merit system and frequently in local elections) named by them. Yet the party is not merely a reflector of the general process. The party is itself a part of the process and itself a social and economic interest, often an important one. In the long run the party will not misinterpret the dominant social and economic interests of the time, but in the short time period it may exercise a considerable range of choice and judgment in selection of men and issues. In times of crisis, of acute stages in the relations of nations or of classes, the party or its leader may determine the course of the nation; or may delay, obstruct, or hasten the course of legislation and administration at all times.

Usually, however, what looks like the vast power of a party leader, or boss, will upon more careful analysis be found to be the visible part of a larger process not at first seen because below the surface of things. Below the surface lie the habits, tendencies, and forces which condition the action of the party as guided by its apparently all-powerful leaders.

Sometimes the pressure groups take over the party openly or cover it, sometimes they go around it, sometimes they form irregular alliances with the party or with parts of it, as occasion or the tactics of these interests may dictate. Their relations to the parties constitute one of the most interesting phases in the intricate process of social control and of the special form of democratic society and government.[3]

It may also happen that one or more groups exercise control over both of the parties permanently or for certain periods of time. Under the multiparty system of the Continent the relations between class or group and the party are clearer than in the biparty system, but

[2] P. Lazarsfeld, G. Berelson, and H. Gaudet, *The People's Choice* (New York, 1944).

[3] V. O. Key, *Politics, Parties, and Pressure Groups* (New York, 2nd ed., 1947); H. W. Jones, in *Safe and Unsafe Democracy* (New York, 1918), criticizes the "partisan party" and advocates the formation of "political leagues" in its stead.

the process is not difficult to follow even here.[4] It is easy to trace in our party history the influence of the East and the West, of the business group and the farmer. It is as the interpreter of these interests, special and general, that the party really functions in the great political process of which the party system after all is but a part.

In the understanding of the interplay of these interests with the technical organization and the party mass held by habit and predisposition, the most interesting and significant phases of the party life are to be found; and here we approach most nearly the central problems of the great process in which the state, the party, and the other social groupings are elements. In the problems of mass organization, mass morale, mass leadership, mass psychology, and propaganda, lies the technique of the party as an instrumentality in the great struggle for power and adjustment that constantly goes on under the veneer of formulas and phrases.

The party habit or predisposition is a definite factor in the process of government, and must always be reckoned with in an appraisal of the tendencies of social and political organization. Men acquire strong partisan allegiances because of early conditioning, feel themselves to be members of parties, adjust their political conduct to the party's action within certain limits; a part of their life energy goes into the mold of party expression. Rooted in habit, in formula and theory, in social interests, in the psychology of leadership and of the mass, the party is a significant factor in the life of modern democracy. Those who abandon one party are likely to go into another. They do not abandon the system, although they may protest against it. When the cords of habit fail to hold the individual, he may enter another party, or he may become an extraparty man—an independent; but when new interests or personalities enter the field he is likely to make use of the party again as a means of expressing his desire and his conviction.

The party has been most seriously weakened by: (1) overdevelopment of the organization to a point where the equilibrium of mass and leaders has been lost; (2) the general feeling that the party has been seized by small groups of men representing predatory privi-

[4] H. F. Gosnell, *Grass Roots Politics* (Washington, D. C., 1942); A. N. Holcombe, *Political Parties of Today* (New York, 1924).

lege; and (3) the general conviction that because of the influences just enumerated the party does not function as effectively in the public interest as it should, and that at times its mechanism serves to hinder rather than to help the expression and the execution of the public will and judgment.

In the two-party system the party is so loosely held together, especially on the side of policies and of definite social and economic interests, that it is less homogeneous than in the multiparty system where the party represents fairly definite class or economic interests. In our system the "organization" becomes correspondingly strong, and the normal tendency of the group agents to dominate their principal becomes very evident. Organization and leaders carry along the party when interests and issues are less actively engaged. This tendency has led some observers to characterize the party in terms of the organization itself, as if the essence of the party were this feature of it. An organization alone, however, is not a party, any more than is the mass of the voters who are disposed to party activity but not organized as a party. A group of active and skillful men might conceivably create a party, but the unorganized mass will produce its leaders just as certainly; and the economic or social interest will produce its formulas, its programs, its organizations and its leaders.

Fundamentally, the party process is one through which various interests express their desires and secure their satisfaction. In this they resemble the state itself, but the party is not the state. It is the portal to the state. It makes or helps to make the men who make the will of the state, who formulate and execute it in concrete and specific ways, vocal and real. All groups and classes therefore struggle for representation there, for the protection or promotion of their interests. Commerce, labor, agriculture, all strive to influence the government through the party. And the many cross sections of social groups which cut through the lines of business and labor and agriculture likewise carry on their conflicts to capture the party as a means of carrying through a policy. This is not true in all cases for there are many measures which never become party issues, and where party control is not desired. In fact, no intelligent interest desires to see its program adopted by one party exclusively and made a partisan issue, if the concurrent endorsement of both or all parties can be obtained. But, of course, endorsement by one party may be the means by which endorsement of the other party will be obtained.

Parties cannot be regarded merely as combinations of isolated individuals, but as they are in reality, aggregations or groups of persons reflecting certain interests, either general or special. These groups speak in general terms, and perhaps believe that their measures will benefit all alike, even if actually they are selfish and special. The tariff, the gold standard, the workmen's compensation act, the labor relations law, are all presumed to be for the general good.

If both parties are convinced of the desirability of a program, its success is almost assured. If one party agrees and not the other, the lines are drawn for an issue, but of course there may be some other overshadowing issue, in which event the party commitment may mean relatively little.

The party then is one of the great agencies through which social interests express and fulfill themselves. From time to time a distinct group may assume the control of the party, and again there may be present conflicting groups or compromise programs. The professional organization, the traditional voter, the "disinterested" citizen, the special interest group, all play their parts in determining the ultimate line of action of the party as a whole.

Analysis of the party process shows that it performs functions in the broader political and social process of which it is a part. These may be grouped as follows:

(1) Selection of official personnel
(2) Formulation of public policies
(3) Conduct or criticism of government
(4) The party as a nationalizing and educational agency
(5) Intermediation between individual and government

SELECTION OF OFFICIAL PERSONNEL [5]

The political party functions in the choice of officials, both elective and appointive. In caucus, primary, convention, election, it is busy

[5] Herring, *op. cit.*; E. Schattschneider, *Party Government* (New York, 1942); A. L. Lowell, *Public Opinion and Popular Government* (New York, 1913), *Government of England* (New York, 1908), I, 455, II, 97, and *Public Opinion in War and Peace* (Cambridge, 1923). See also A. C. McLaughlin, *The Courts, the Constitution and Parties* (Chicago, 1912).

with the selection of officers, and in the appointive group it is almost equally active in influencing the choices of the nominal appointing powers. The party works as a huge sieve through which the competing types of personnel are sifted and choices are finally made. Public choice is often controlled or even checked as well as facilitated, but in the main the party machinery serves as a tryout for the prospective officeholder. In this sense the party is really a section of the general election machinery, and in fact has been so recognized by the law in the various statutes regulating party procedure.

Appointive positions are also largely filled by the party group, although nominally and sometimes actually appointments are made by the official charged with the power of appointment. From United States senators down, the party officials play an important role in the selection of the personnel of the appointees. Sometimes appointments are made after consultation with or with due deference to party leaders, and sometimes the selections are turned over to them with little or no pretense of concealment.

Two important exceptions to the selective power of the party must be made, however. These are the many urban nonpartisan positions, and the administrative positions placed under the merit system. Urban choices and rural also are often made on a nonparty basis, while the merit system removes the influence of the party, to the extent that the law is actually carried out. In most instances a margin of party appointment still appears even here.

FORMULATION OF PUBLIC POLICIES

The party sifts and tries proposals for public action or policy. To each party a multitude of competing issues are presented as possible planks in a party platform, as possible policies to which the party group might be committed. These are explained, expounded, discussed, urged, and opposed from the point of view of party expediency and public advantage, and finally a decision is reached, rejecting, postponing, mildly approving, enthusiastically endorsing. Out of this process a dominant or dividing issue may come. This process is most acute in primaries and elections, but in reality it goes on incessantly without regard to these events, for the party leaders in responsible positions and the unofficial leaders are constantly assuming attitudes toward all sorts of public questions. They follow the public opinion polls and from time to time take polls of their own. The regulation of business and labor relations and the balancing of the budget have been important issues with which the major parties have been concerned in recent years, but many others have been sifted and rejected or avoided and compromised. And in many cases significant issues have been endorsed by both of the parties, as in the case of the merit system, and hence no conflict has been precipitated. On the other hand, both of the major parties have shied away from the issue of the heavier taxation of lower incomes as a means of meeting increasing national expenditures.

Exceptions must also be noted here. In local and state affairs the party has not been as active in formulating a policy as in national affairs. Further, there are many competing agencies at work in the formulation of issues. These agencies may be more active and more efficient than the party itself. The party group is limited by the strong pressure for immediate victory, while the other groups are not so circumscribed. Ideas or attitudes on which the party may look with suspicion, other groups may encourage and advocate till the idea comes within the magnetic field of party "availability," when it may be taken up by one party or by both. Notable illustrations of this are woman's suffrage, social security, and an international world organization.

Governments act not merely in accordance with instructions given at election times, but in response to continually operating forces coming from outside organized political parties. The primary, the convention, and the election are by no means the only points of contact between the public and the party, or between the public and the government. Pressure is brought to bear upon the agents of government at many points and on many occasions by all sorts of interests and organizations bent on the enactment or administration of law, or upon some other governmental purpose. The elections are the dramatic events, but they decide relatively few questions, except the personnel of the government and general satisfaction or dissatisfaction with the governing group. What the rulers shall do when chosen is determined in some ways by the party platform or position, but in many more ways by nonparty influences. On the whole, more acts of government are the result of pressure from special groups or from public sentiment than from party platforms or party guidance. The personnel of officialdom and a few of its policies are partisan in great part, but most of its activities are due to the operation of forces which the regular parties by no means direct or control. Unless this is borne in mind, the significance of the party system in relation to the American government is not seen in its proper perspective.

In view of the fact that much legislation is enacted without the approval of any particular party as such, the activity of nonparty groups is all the more significant. The formulation of public policies is then by no means an exclusive function of the party, but one which it shares with other competing groups in the community— with the American Legion, with the labor organizations, with the United States Chamber of Commerce, with the National Farm Bureau Federation, and scores of other organizations bent upon certain types of public policies. The party, however, represents the public interest more generally than any of these pressure groups which are likely to represent a narrow producer's interest.

CONDUCT OR CRITICISM OF GOVERNMENT [6]

Parties function in the general operation of the governing process, in which personalities, group policies, traditions, administration, foreign and domestic affairs are all blended to make a type of government upon which the citizen may finally pass judgment. A major party is either the conductor or the critic of the government, or the administration as it may be termed. The party "in power," Republican or Democratic, presents a "type" of governing which the opposition criticizes (where the party system is working), and presents another possible "type." This "type" is a composite of officials, policies, leadership, lawmaking, administration, and even judicial interpretation—an *ensemble* which is brought before the community, state, or nation as the case may be, for its ratification or rejection. Is the rule of the party in power desirable on the whole, or is it time

[6] H. J. Ford, *The Rise and Growth of American Politics* (New York, 1900); Woodrow Wilson, *Constitutional Government in the United States* (New York, 1908); T. K. Finletter, *Can Representative Government Do the Job* (New York, 1945); E. P. Herring, *Presidential Leadership* (New York, 1940); H. Hazlitt, *A New Constitution Vow* (New York, 1942); and R. Young, *This Is Congress* (New York, 1943).

to change to the opposing major party? This is the question constantly raised by the citizen, and with special interest as the quadrennial election approaches and it becomes necessary to make another choice of "types." It is the record of the party as a whole, its leaders, its policies, its traditions and tendencies, its promises and its performances, that stands over against another set of leaders, policies, tendencies and traditions, promises and performances. These types are defended and developed in electoral processes on a great scale, chiefly in national affairs, less frequently in state and local matters.

The rough function of constructing and criticizing a type of rule is then an important function of the political party, if we confine ourselves to the major groups. The minor groups of course limit themselves to the formulation of policies and to criticism of the given type or both types of political rule.

Certain limitations must be observed in this connection. No party is ever in complete control of the government from policeman to president. Neither the Republican nor the Democratic party is ever entirely out of power. Even in the national government no party is in complete control for a very long time, and about half of the time the authority is divided. Further, most measures are not party measures. In the states the same situation is found, emphasized by the fact that most state governments are greatly decentralized, and the local governments have important groups of powers over which the state government has little actual control. In the urban governments the parties do not as a rule assume responsibility for conduct of government, except in a few instances.

We may say, as frequently happens in political campaigns, that the party is "responsible" for conduct of government, but this must be carefully qualified in view of the fact that many fundamental issues involving constitutional change and judicial interpretation are rarely party matters, that many important matters are settled upon a nonpartisan or bipartisan basis, and that most of the time no party is in a position to carry through a complete legislative program. In a limited sense only, the Republican party may rightly be held responsible, or the Democratic party may rightly be held responsible for the government at a given time, since the government is so decentralized and political power so diffused. In a real crisis the voters holds the two parties together responsible. The system, or the "politicians," the guild of those who are "in politics," is called to account when things go wrong. These men constitute a group of exceptionally well-informed individuals with experience in government and a certain *savoir faire* in political management; and it is to them that the community looks for the conduct of the government, rather than to either party.

THE PARTY AS A NATIONALIZING AND EDUCATIONAL AGENCY [7]

The party also functions as a political educator. One of the great foes of democracy is the apathy of the voter and the failure of the individual to realize and act upon his responsibility for the common interest. The party's advocacy of personalities and of policies involves elaborate instruction which is carried on through press, forum, and personal contact. The party activities are dramatic and appeal to the mass of the community, often arousing an interest which is the beginning of a political education. Some may be repelled by the party methods, but in the main this is not true. The process is often crude and superficial, often an appeal to prejudice, instinct, hatreds, class rivalries, and jealousies, but often it is stimulating and socially useful. The appeal of the great party leaders of the type of Jefferson, Jackson, Lincoln, Cleveland, Theodore Roosevelt, Wilson, Bryan, Hughes, Smith, Hoover, Franklin D. Roosevelt has often been inspiring in its effect upon the community morale. Great exponents of statesmanship have exerted an influence the effect of which it is difficult to calculate, for in no other circumstance would such words have carried as far as in the party contest. With less skill

[7] Gosnell, *Democracy*: F. L. Burdette, *Education for Citizen-Responsibilities* (Princeton, 1942); Council for Democracy, *America's Free Schools* (New York, 1941); Citizenship Clearing House, *The Citizen's Participation in Public Affairs* (New York University School of Law, New York, 1948); Jesse Macy, *Political Parties: Party Organization and Machinery* (New York, 1904); W. M. Sloane, *Party Government* (New York, 1914); Woodrow Wilson, *Constitutional Government* (Boston, 1885); C. E. Hughes, *Addresses and Papers* (New York, 1908). Cf. Albert Shaw, *Political Problems* (New York, 1907), Chap. VI, "Party Machinery and Democratic Expression"; Moorfield Storey, *Problems of Today* (Boston, 1920), Chap. I; and New York University School of Law, *The Citizen's Participation in Public Affairs* (New York, 1948).

and success many others have contributed to the training of the political society.

There are, it is true, many competing agencies at work in political education. The schools are foremost in this work; but the press, the forum, the pulpit at times, innumerable civic societies, and interest groups are also active in political affairs.[8] Sometimes these agencies are more aggressive and frequently more efficient than the party, but they lack the large-scale enterprise of the party, and its claim upon human interest in the dramatic struggles which it stages.

It is also true that some of the training given by the political party is not socially useful and may even be pernicious. The work of the demagogue is harmful rather than helpful, and the example and precept of the local grafter and gangster are often educational in the wrong direction. They may train men and habituate them to an attitude toward the political and social organization which may be anything but useful to the community.

The party unquestionably functions as a nationalizing agency of great importance. In the early period of our history the national party system aided materially in the formation of bonds of contact, sympathy, and eventually, tradition. The Federalists and the Jeffersonians, and later the Whigs and the Democrats, were national parties when the nature of the Union was a subject of serious and continued controversy. The party convention, the party caucus and conferences, the great party demonstrations brought together men of all sections on occasions that were essentially nationalistic in their character and tendencies. It is a notable fact that one of the last bands to snap in the days before the Civil War was the party tie.

Since the Civil War and the beginning of the more recent tide of immigration, the parties have aided in the nationalization of the newly acquired citizens of the Republic. They have assisted the naturalization of the immigrants and encouraged them to affiliate with the political parties. Teuton and Celt, Latin and Slav have been welcomed into the party. They have attended meetings, served upon party committees, marched in party parades, acted as party candidates, functioned as party leaders. The party allegiance has been one

[8] See series on the making of citizens, especially C. E. Merriam, *The Making of Citizens* (Chicago, 1933); B. L. Pierce, *Civic Attitudes in American Textbooks* (Chicago, 1930); and the series on social studies, especially C. E. Merriam, *Civic Education in the United States* (New York, 1934).

of the easiest to acquire in the new country. The doors of the party were wide open and the party duties simple. There were no barriers, economic or social or religious, to prevent immediate membership. So the Italian or the Slav became a partisan Republican or Democrat as the case might be, taking on the color and traditions of the party. In no other association except that of labor was the mingling of people so common and so easy as in the political party.[9]

There were many nationalizing influences at work—the school, the intercourse of labor and trade, intermarriage, the party. Of these the influence of the party was the smallest, but still it was not negligible, and must be included for full measure in an accurate survey.[10]

INTERMEDIATION BETWEEN INDIVIDUAL AND GOVERNMENT [11]

The party performs another function which may be defined as that of the intermediary, the buffer, the adjuster between society and the individual. The political worker aids his constituents in their dealings with the government, sometimes in the interest of justice and sometimes not; and he often acts as a general "adjuster" for a large or small community.

Many laws and regulations of the government are complicated and difficult to understand. The party representative may explain and interpret. Many laws and regulations are unworkable or work with difficulty. Perhaps the community except in moments of great enthusiasm does not care much for them. Or the administration may be unsympathetic and of little understanding. At all such points the party representative may come in as an equitable intermediary, breaking the rude force of the law, which was not intended to carry with it the idea of detailed and relentless enforcement. In many instances there may be established a relation something like that

[9] See Macy, *op. cit.*

[10] See John Daniels, *America via the Neighborhood* (New York, 1920).

[11] J. J. Ingalls, *A Collection of the Writings of J. J. Ingalls* (Kansas City, 1902), p. 309; M. K. Simkovitch, "Friendship and Politics," *Political Science Quarterly*, XVII (1902), 189; W. L. Riordon, *Plunkitt of Tammany Hall* (New York, 1905), Chap. I, "Honest Graft and Dishonest Graft"; R. C. Brooks, *Corruption in American Politics and Life* (New York, 1910); Sonya Forthal, *Cogwheels of Democracy* (New York, 1946); H. F. Gosnell, *Machine Politics* (Chicago, 1937).

between patron and client, especially among the weak and helpless in the urban centers, or the rich and powerful who wish to evade certain provisions of the law. If a free license to peddle or an escape from a fine of $5.00 and costs may appeal to one, the automobile speeding ordinance and the antitrust law have terrors for the other. Both may appeal to a political patron, each in his sphere giving what he has to offer in return. The amount of this adjustment or inter-mediation, legitimate and illegitimate, is greater than is commonly supposed, and in fact forms a great part of the stock in trade of the politician. It is as significant an element in party success as the skill in organization, or the graft and spoils too often found in connection with the controlling group. Adjustments and favors have a peculiar appeal to all groups in all places, and the political group has not been slow to appreciate this fact.

There are many shades of this activity, ranging from the impart-ing of information regarding governmental services and personnel to personal favors of an innocuous type, to dubious privileges, to illegitimate spoils and graft of a systematic nature. Theoretically the public official or the party official has nothing to do with these un-official acts, but practically he has much to do with them; and in many cases the greater part of the time of the official is taken up in performing various types of services for his constituents or others. The congressman or his secretary is quite as likely to be occupied in solicitous attention to these affairs as in deep research on the funda-mental problems of the nation.[12] In much the same situation are the other solons of high or low degree and other public officials and party leaders, not excepting the judges in many cases. They are presumed to "go to the front" for their friends and supporters, or their neighbors, or their group; and on the whole a very material portion of their time and energy is occupied with these affairs. Nor are these favors or services confined to the poor and the weak, as is sometimes supposed. The millionaire is quite as likely to appear as the man out of a job; the wealthy club or church as the simplest type of local society. The form of favors asked is different, but the general type is much the same.

[12] See George Galloway, *Congress at the Crossroads* (New York, 1947); and Bryce's description of a similar system in France, in *Modern Democracies* (New York, 1921), I, 257.

In a broader sense the party serves as an intermediary between the citizen and his government. Graham Wallas [13] points out that "The party is, in fact, the most effective political entity in the modern national state." Croly also calls attention to this when he argues that the party requires a higher type of allegiance than should be given to any but the state. There is a real sense in which the party is more human than the state, more approachable, more intimate in its relations than the government, even though the party may be the possessor of the government or of the machinery for the time being. A major party is in a sense a political church which does not require regular attendance or have a very strict creed; but still it provides a home and it "looks after" the individual if he pays the minimum of party *devoirs*, consisting in acquaintance with and occasional support of some one of its lords, even though a minor one. Or, changing the metaphor, the party is a sporting interest, like a baseball team in which the individual is intensely interested from time to time. Party language has taken many words from sporting games of chance such as "square deal," "new deal," "raw deal." An immense void would be left if all reading and writing and speaking about parties and their candidates and policies were dropped out of our life. Political conversation is legal tender, acceptable throughout the realm, a common leveler of all class distinctions for the time being.[14]

These various party functions are not uniformly exercised by all the different elements within the party. The managerial set in the professional party circle is chiefly occupied with the tasks of selecting officials either by election or appointment, with the dispensation of favors and accommodations, and only secondarily with the shaping of policies and the conduct of the government in its larger aspects. Others, however, are primarily concerned with the broader questions of policy and administration, and only secondarily with patronage and favors.

The political society as a whole looks upon the parties as standing for certain policies and for broad tendencies in the management of

[13] *Human Nature in Politics* (London, 1908), p. 82.

[14] Graham Wallas says, "Something is required simpler and more permanent, something which can be loved and trusted, and which can be recognized at successive elections as being the same thing that was loved and trusted before; and a party is such a thing." *Ibid.*, p. 83.

government. Party tradition, personal interest and a general theory of the public good are likely to be intermingled in the interpretation of what the party actually stands for. Special groups and classes in the community identify the party with special advantages, and endeavor to control it for the sake of such special gains. Manufacturer and miner, banker and farmer, labor and the professions tend to attach themselves to or detach themselves from parties as their interests are affected favorably or adversely. In most instances, although not in all, they identify their own interest with the benefit of the whole country. Theoretically all parties are for everyone's interest, although practically they represent at times sharp differences in economic and social advantage.

It is of course possible that the voters might choose members of legislative bodies and executives pledged to carry out various policies without any parties or party organization of any formal type. But differences of policy divide voters from time to time; inevitably organization arises; traditions of common action develop and maintain groups for other purposes than those that first brought the voters together; political impulses and ambitions develop in the form of rival leaders with their groups of followers. The party group or guild itself becomes an interest and continues its concurrent action. Out of all this comes a party and a party government organized to capture, control, or exploit the regular government for a combination of individual, group, and general purposes. Sometimes this group holds the government and sometimes it does not; more often it is partly in possession of government and partly outside of governmental control. But the party, even when in complete control, is usually an "easy boss" permitting laws and plans to become effective if they do not encroach upon the selected preserves of the ruling dynasty in the party leadership.

What the party really does is often obscured by the complexity of the socio-political situation. Not only is the party one among many competing social groups, but it is one among many scattered governmental groups. Our government is divided between federal and state organizations; in each of these the power is divided among three departments; the local governments are often largely independent of the state government, and many are nonparty or partly so. The parties move in and out among these social and governmental groups and mechanisms in what may seem a mysterious way. Bipartisan and nonpartisan arrangements and agreements at times efface party lines or blur them almost beyond recognition. Through it all, however, the party habit, party attitude, party institution persist, rendering a service to the political community. Like fire, the party is a good servant, but often the party means becomes an end itself, the guard becomes the ruler, the actual function of the party is overcast by a secondary function; and in the course of time the party functions in a dual capacity, or in the many capacities heretofore described.

CHAPTER XXII

THE FUTURE OF PARTIES[1]

"Every year, if not every day, we have to wage our salvation upon some prophecy based upon imperfect knowledge."—Justice Oliver Wendell Holmes.

LIKE ALL OTHER INSTITUTIONS, THE POLITICAL PARTY IS IN CONSTANT process of reconstruction and must justify itself to each succeeding generation; otherwise it is likely to be destroyed or superseded by competing institutions. An appraisal of the value of the party finds many serious liabilities charged against it. Among these are:

(1) The dominance of the party by a small group or oligarchy ruling by the use of spoils and graft in a manner harmful to the general interest

(2) The dominance of this organization oligarchy by another industrial oligarchy, and the consequent control of the government in the interest of economic privilege

(3) As a consequence of the combination of the boss and the trust, the weakening of the collective confidence in the nation's capacity for achievement—the undermining of the morale of government. This brings grave losses in efficiency, in the narrower sense of financial damage and "leaks," and in the broader sense of constructive community conservation—in the weakening of the sense of the justice and utility of the whole political order.

That the machine has exercised undue influence over the party, that the money power has exercised undue influence over the machine, that the nation has suffered from the paralysis induced by the parties in many times and places are charges so frequently made by such accepted authorities as Theodore Roosevelt, Taft, Root,

[1] H. F. Gosnell, "The Future of the American Party System," in L. D. White, ed., *The Future of Government in the United States* (Chicago, 1942). L. Bean, *How to Predict Elections* (New York, 1948); C. C. Rohlfing and J. C. Charlesworth (eds.), "Parties and Politics: 1948," *Annals of the American Academy of Political and Social Scienc* CCLIX (September, 1948).

Wilson, Bryan, and by impartial observers of the type of Bryce and Ostrogorski, that it is unnecessary to confirm them by evidence additional to that already adduced. We may proceed to inquire, therefore, what agencies and methods are most active in bringing about a reorganization of the party system and bringing it into closer accord with the undoubted interests of the nation. Here we find a group of tendencies operating in the party and political processes themselves; another group in the larger field of economic and social relations; and another group affecting the underlying foundations of the party in the *mores* of the people.

PARTY AND PATRONAGE

The party process itself is being slowly changed and party activities fundamentally modified in various directions. Among these are the decline of patronage as a prime factor in the party. The gradual substitution of the merit system for the spoils system in public administration profoundly affects the character and course of the party. It weakens the standing army of the machine, it opens a way to public service outside of party channels, and it leads to the development of public administration upon a scientific basis. With this domain recognized by public opinion, the party organization must seek other fields of enterprise where its activities will less seriously interfere with the public service. The spoils system wins battles, but it steadily loses the war to neutralize the field of public administration. Notwithstanding the increasing number of governmental functions and the correspondingly larger number of public employees, the influence of "patronage" tends to decline perhaps more rapidly than is generally perceived. This is due not only to development of public sentiment against the spoils system in public office and to enactment of statutory requirements regarding the merit system, but to other and still more powerful forces. These are the increasing specialization of activity, the appearance of professional and skilled groups with their vocational organizations which tend to set standards of attainment and to protect their members against arbitrary and unreasonable treatment. Teachers, physicians, engineers, scientists, and technicians constantly tend to form groups with special qualifications and specific powers of such a nature that it may not be "good politics" to treat their group as the spoils of political office. Furthermore, the skilled trades have perfected organizations of such a nature as to destroy much of the arbitrary power once possessed by the political leader or boss. Large areas of the public service are thus taken away from the once undisputed field occupied by the triumphant party manager.

It is these forces as much as the civil service laws that have tended and now tend toward restriction of the practice of political patronage in public administration. It is not impossible that politics may return to the domain of administration, but it is more likely to be in the form of organized activities of groups of public employees assuming certain political powers, than in the form of unorganized blocks of public servants subject to the will of the party boss and bound to do his bidding under penalty of discharge or discipline.

The dark view of American politics which a consideration of the spoils system gives should be counterbalanced by taking stock of some of the long-run trends and countertrends in the methods and objects of graft.[2] Certain privileges which used to be obtained by bribery and corruption are now sold in a legitimate fashion by the government in accordance with rules which are aimed to safeguard the interest of the general public. The vacation of a street, a license to sell alcoholic beverages, a franchise to operate a utility monopoly used to be privileges, which were sought by corruption, but now the procedures for obtaining them have been institutionalized. The administrative tribunals which regulate the utilities have been comparatively free from scandals, in part because they have been guided by general principles which endeavor to reconcile the interests concerned.

Widespread improvement in the methods of governmental accounting has reduced the danger of embezzlement of public funds. The adoption of sounder budgetary practices has lessened the amount of pork-barrel and logrolling legislation.

The experience of Cleveland and other cities shows that a determined and skilled public safety director can break up the system of tribute from the underworld and thereby cut away one of the foundation stones of a spoils machine. The advances that have been made in police administration make it possible to challenge the lawless elements.

[2] See V. O. Key, *The Technique of Political Graft in the United States* (Chicago, 1936).

The economic depression which began in 1929 brought to light the incompetence of the spoils machines to handle the problems of unemployment and relief.

Finally, there is no question that the dismal thirties brought with them a citizens' revolt against corrupt politics that has been unprecedented in its scale. Not only in New York, but also in Boston, Cleveland, Kansas City, Los Angeles, St. Paul, Chicago, and many other cities a wave of indignation swept the spoilsmen from office and replaced them with clean administrations.[3] The patronage system is clearly on its way out, while competent public administration is rapidly coming in. Wide ranging advances in the direction of administrative competence are seen in city, state, and nation; merit and efficiency are indeed the order of the day.[4]

PARTY AND RESPONSIBLE LEADERSHIP

While the task of the party in the selection of appointive personnel is being lightened by the merit system and the development of technical standards and vocational groups, the party duties in the election of public officials are also being slowly reduced. The general tendency is toward reduction of the number of elective offices, or, more cautiously stated, the tendency toward increasing the number has been checked. A considerable number of municipal and local officials have been taken away from the party list and may be removed from the party assets. In county and state the tendency is toward limiting the list of elective offices to those concerned with the determination of public policies rather than with the administra-

[3] W. M. Reddig, *Tom's Town: Kansas City and the Pendergast Legend* (Philadelphia and New York, 1947); Luther Gulick, "The Shame of the Cities 1946," *National Municipal Review*, XXXVI (January, 1947); Anon., "Civic Virtue: Municipal Reform Forces of Nation in Full Cry," *Newsweek*, XII (December 12, 1938), 12–13; M. A. Rose, "Yankee Tax Revolt," *Reader's Digest*, XXXII (March, 1938), 56–59; Stanley High, "Cleveland Versus the Crooks," *Current History*, XLIX (October, 1938), 22–24, and "St. Paul Wins a War," *ibid.*, XLIX (September 1938), 18–20; E. R. Schauffler, "End of Pendergast," *Forum*, CII (July, 1939); G. Creel, "Unholy City," *Collier's*, CIV (September 2, 1939), 12 ff.

[4] F. M. Marx, ed., *Elements of Public Administration* (New York, 1946). See President's Committee on Administrative Management, *Administrative Management in the Government of the United States* (Washington, D. C., 1937); publications of the Public Administration Clearing House located in Chicago; *Public Personnel Review, passim.*

tion of them. The short ballot is likely to prevail in the long run, although it is far from being established at present. Judges are likely to continue in the elective lists as long as their policy-determining functions continue or until more sparing use is made of this power. Yet in a broad review of tendencies, we may reasonably look forward to a time when the list of elective officials with which so large a portion of the party activity is now taken up will be materially reduced, especially in the county and in the state. This process is certain to affect the general character of the party system, reducing the available patronage at this point, and freeing a large element of party energy for other tasks than nomination and election of officials such as coroner or surveyor or secretary of state who have nothing to do with the purposes or policies of the parties.

In these two foregoing respects, then, the duties of the party are likely to be lightened, as the selection of certain classes of official personnel is transferred to the field of technical administration. At the same time it is to be observed that the simplification of the structure of government and the tendency to unify power and responsibility are developing responsible leadership within the government. The tendency is to combine governmental and party leadership. At present they are often separated, and the party boss is outside the government, while the nominal ruler is inside the government but actually helpless. Even when no structural changes are made, the tendency is for power to center around a few officials, as the president or the governor, who become party and public leaders as well as governmental chiefs. This enables the nominal leader to assume the initiative and responsibility, and to appeal more to public and party opinion than to the organization. The excuse for the boss as the necessary "coordinating agency" disappears when the elected public official is able to take the leadership with reasonable power of action. Subordination or subservience to an outside boss is not easily reconciled with the role of a powerful leader within the government.

The parliamentary plan as developed in the European countries ensures complete control over the government to the party in power, and the party leaders usually are at the same time the responsible governmental leaders or its open critics. But no such system has been seriously supported in the United States, and our concentration of authority has been obtained largely through the independent executive, who can secure support for his policies only through the cooperation of the legislative bodies and the strong approval of party and public opinion. There has been strong support for a plan permitting cabinet members the freedom of the floor in Congress, but no action has been taken thus far.

Unquestionably the shortening of the ballot and the strengthening of the hands of governmental leaders either by law or custom will tend to sharpen the lines of leadership and develop a somewhat different type of party politics, in which the power of the boss will not be as easily developed as that of the leader or the demagogue. Croly, indeed, contended that the two-party system "cannot survive the advent of an official representative system, based upon direct popular government." [5] Whether this is true or not, it is apparent that the development of responsible government tends to alter the general character of party politics by giving wider scope to the party leader and less to the party boss. Even here, however, without a high level of public attention and appreciation the demagogue may crowd the leader aside and press forward, perhaps supported by the organizing power of the boss and an extensive propaganda based upon abundant spoils.

PARTY, DIRECT LEGISLATION, AND THE POLLS

The American party system operates primarily through the devices of representative government. However, in those states which have the initiative and·referendum it must reckon with popular reversals.[6]

[5] H. D. Croly, *Progressive Democracy* (New York, 1914), p. 341; Secretary Cordell Hull reported on his trip to Moscow in 1943 to a joint session of the two houses of Congress.

[6] See H. F. Gosnell, *Democracy: Threshold of Freedom* (New York, 1948); U. S. Bureau of the Census, *State Proposals Voted Upon in 1940* (Washington, D. C., 1947); C. O. Johnson, "The Initiative and Referendum in Washington," *Pacific Northwest Quarterly,* XXXVI (January, 1945); H. F. Gosnell and M. J. Schmidt, "Popular Law Making in the United States," in New York State Constitutional Convention Committee, *Problems Relating to Legislative Organization and Powers* (New York, 1938), vol. VII. See also V. O. Key and W. C. Crouch, *The Initiative and Referendum in California* (Berkeley, 1939); James Bryce, *Modern Democracies* (New York, 1921); J. D. Barnett, *The Operation of the Initiative, Referendum and Recall in Oregon* (New York, 1915); and A. B. Hall, *Popular Government* (New York, 1923), Chap. VI

The initiative and referendum take away from the legislature its monopoly upon the passage of laws. They make it possible for other groups to place upon the statute books various measures reflecting public policies. The voter may return the party's representative, but at the same time approve a measure disapproved by him or disapprove a measure which he favors. From one point of view this might strengthen the party, for in case of a serious dissension in the party, a reference to a referendum might be a welcome escape from a perilous situation, as was often seen in votes upon the liquor situation. From another point of view the party might be weakened by the growth of other agencies of popular action. Here again our experience is confined to state or local governments; and in these cases the party did not function vigorously. In the states where most commonly used, as in California and Oregon, the initiative and referendum have not changed the character and activities of the parties, and there is no ground for predicting that they will do so. They do, however, make it possible for organized groups, outside the regular political parties, to carry on campaigns for or against various measures of public policy, and to carry through or defeat legislative projects. But a considerable part of modern legislation is already secured in this manner. These groups lack the powerful aid of party habit, of the appeal to tradition, pride and regularity, and the services of the skilled army of the organization. On the other hand, they are relieved from the maintenance of a standing army such as the party possesses, from the conduct of electoral processes, from the pressing requirements of party victory.[7] Figure 15 shows what use is made of the popular law making devices in the different states.

But many groups desiring the passage of laws prefer to undertake their own propaganda rather than the task of capturing the control or the consent of the official party organization. Vigorous action by well-organized groups, nonpolitical in character, has come to be a common mode of obtaining governmental action upon questions of public policy, and the parties already have strong rivals as molders of public sentiment and directors of political action. When the

[7] For an interesting study of the effect of the initiative and referendum upon parties in Switzerland, see R. C. Brooks, *Civic Training in Switzerland* (Chicago, 1930), and *Government and Politics of Switzerland* (Yonkers-on-Hudson, 1918); also A. L. Lowell, *Governments and Parties in Continental Europe* (New York, 1900), II, 313.

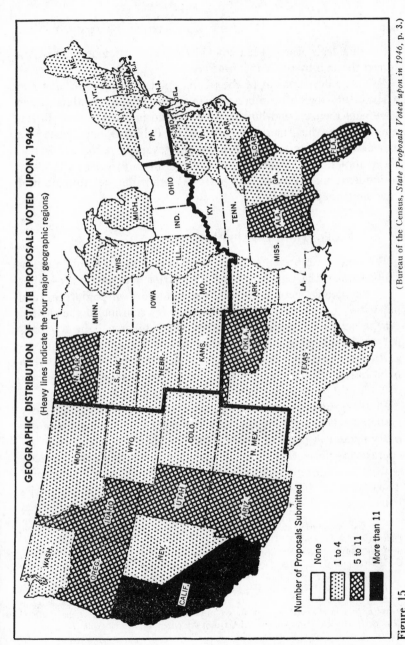

GEOGRAPHIC DISTRIBUTION OF STATE PROPOSALS VOTED UPON, 1946

(Heavy lines indicate the four major geographic regions)

Number of Proposals Submitted

- None
- 1 to 4
- 5 to 11
- More than 11

(Bureau of the Census, *State Proposals Voted upon in 1946*, p. 3.)

Figure 15

489

California legislature failed to make a reapportionment, this was forced through by popular initiative.

With the development of the public opinion surveys we may find a substitute for the cumbersome initiative and referendum which have held their ground but have not spread in recent years. Beginning in 1935 the American Institute of Public Opinion began an extensive survey of attitudes on a great variety of economic and social topics. As the survey technique gains in prestige it is likely to influence more directly the party leaders in the determination of governmental policies.[8]

PROPORTIONAL REPRESENTATION

Proportional representation is another device which might materially modify the party system.[9] Proportional representation aims to bring about more equitable representation of majorities and minorities, particularly to prevent complete exclusion of the smaller groups unable to muster sufficient strength to prevail in any ordinary geographical unit of representation. The Hare system of proportional representation secures a greater degree of flexibility in balloting by allowing second, third, and other choices. It shades over into the system of occupational representation.

Proportional representation would not, of course, destroy the party system as such, but it might have the effect of developing a multiparty system in place of the biparty plan. It might conceivably encourage the formation of smaller groups, rewarding their tenacity with occasional representation if not with responsibility and power. Thus far it has been applied chiefly in the cities. In other countries it has been extensively employed for all elections. It is notable that

[8] Current summaries of the public opinion surveys are given in *Public Opinion Quarterly.* See Chapter XVIII above.

[9] See above, p. 298. See also H. F. Gosnell, *Democracy: Threshold of Freedom*; G. Hallett and C. G. Hoag, *Proportional Representation: The Key to Democracy* (Washington, D. C., 1937); C. G. Hoag and G. Hallett, *Proportional Representation* (New York, 1926); the files of the publication called *Equity* down to 1920 when it was merged with the *National Municipal Review* and *American Proportional Representation Review.* The latter publication is now a section of the *National Municipal Review.* Unfavorable views are presented by G. Horwill, *Proportional Representation* (London, 1925); and F. A. Hermens, *Democracy or Anarchy: A Study of Proportional Representation* (Notre Dame, Indiana, 1941).

many European countries have adopted some form of proportional representation, including France, Italy, Belgium, Switzerland, Holland, and the Irish Free State. In all of these the party system is built upon the group system with a series of parties running up to ten or twelve, but with at least three or four of major importance.

Thus far in the United States as in England the two-party system has dominated, although there have been periods when third parties were important all over the country, and there are now states in which they are factors to be reckoned in the practical calculations of party leaders. As labor becomes more politically conscious and politically active, either alone or in connection with elements of the agricultural electorate, a third party of considerable strength may appear.

It would seem that proportional representation is more likely to be the consequence than the cause of multiparty groupings, although its general influence would be in the direction of the multiparty plan. As a means of obtaining fairer representation between majority and minority, or as a means of providing a preferential vote, it might find a place even in a two-party system. At the present time proportional representation makes most rapid strides in the urban centers, where in addition to the weakness of the national parties great difficulty has been encountered with the ward system of representation. In general, the American people are so attached to the two-party system that they cling to methods of representation which favor that system. Proportional representation might undermine the two major parties and therefore it makes little headway outside of a few cities.

CONSTITUTIONALIZING THE PARTY

Some progress may be made through legislation affecting the form of the ballot and the election practice and procedure. The Australian ballot system was a notable step in the direction of democratic control over the electoral process, prior to that time deflected by the fraud and corruption often practiced by political managers. A complete and thoroughgoing enforcement of the law has not yet been attained here, however. Furthermore, the party emblem, circle, and column still operate as artificial inducements to nondiscriminating voting, and it is probable that these absurd forms of ballot will be altered in the near future to conform to the Massachusetts or office group form. Other changes in registration procedure, in the methods of counting the ballots and in the selection of election officials have been made which have definitely removed some of the artificial advantages of the professional manipulator of election devices. The rapid spread of sound systems of permanent registration, with adequate safeguards for identifying the voter in the form of the signature requirement, have greatly limited the election corruptionists who used to rely upon repeating and personation. In some jurisdictions where the long ballot has remained, the use of voting machines has markedly reduced fraud and error in the count. The experience of certain European countries and Australia shows that it would be worth while considering some form of compulsory voting as a means of reducing the importance of the officeholder as a vote getter.

Most of the abuses in nominating methods that used to be flagrant under the old unregulated convention system have been practically eliminated by the primary laws. The direct primary legislation has made its contribution to outlawing the packed convention run by steam-roller methods. However, neither the direct primary alone nor any form of regulated convention system, nor any mixed type, can be expected to alter the party process fundamentally. Such legislation may remove hindrances to popular control and open more democratic channels of party government, but it cannot be relied upon to revolutionize party leadership and responsibility automatically. The convention system was a protest in its beginnings against the narrowness of the legislative caucus; the regulated convention system a protest against the iniquities of the "soapbox" caucuses where fraud and force played so large a part; the direct primary was again a protest against the unrepresentative character of cliques and rings controlling conventions and dictating nominations.

These mechanical devices, often unwisely heralded as "panaceas," are significant in the development of the party system, and they mark important stages in the evolution of democratic control. They are subject of course to the same charges that are made against democracy itself—that the voter does not always use the ballot when it is conferred upon him and that he does not always use it wisely or effectively. But these are not accepted as conclusive arguments for abandoning universal suffrage or giving up the attempt to obtain responsible government.[10]

The problem of constitutionalizing and democratizing the party, however, of ensuring genuine popular control over genuinely democratic leaders, of maintaining an adequate organization which is the servant and not the master of the party—cannot be solved by legislative enactment alone. The answer to this problem will be found in the deeper study of democratic society and its yet unsettled questions regarding the balance between technical knowledge, political leadership, and popular control. The problem of democratic control is also dependent upon the growth of political consciousness, interest, and *savoir faire* on the part of large elements of the community which have hitherto shared only slightly in the responsibility for the conduct of the common affairs of the state. This process is in reality just beginning, speaking broadly, and we may reasonably look forward to great advances in this direction in the immediate future. The entrance of women into the political field, the awakening of labor, the shorter working day, the development of universal education, the general advance of adult sophistication in affairs of state— all these point toward more general appreciation of the methods of conducting common affairs, hitherto the private possession of those who guarded them as professional mysteries, or as their own private opportunities or responsibilities. Through their organizations and societies, labor and women especially are receiving an education in parliamentary and public practice and procedure such as was formerly the possession only of the elder statesmen.

In this connection attention may be directed again to the great significance of the development of numerous types of groupings, political and semipolitical, in our present society. Organizations, societies, leagues, unions spring up all around us and become centers of political power, influencing policies and affecting the selection of official personnel. These groups did not exist on the same scale a generation ago, but now they rival the party and the "machine" at many points. The problem of party leadership and control must be viewed in the light of these new centers of authority which tend to alter the character of the party system of control. Conceivably these new

[10] In Italy under Fascism such arguments were used against the parliamentary system. See H. Schneider, *Making the Fascist State* (New York, 1928).

groups will destroy the parties, but more probably they will extend their influence and control them. The party managers must reckon with the facilities of these powerful organizations in the way of finances, publicity, propaganda. The party must now deal not only with organized business, but also with agriculture, labor, trades, and professions.

If the parties themselves desire to reorganize their methods, it would easily be possible for them to make many significant changes, either by custom or by party rule. In the generation just past many changes have been made in the attitude of party leaders toward practices at one time openly or tacitly approved. The general position of the leaders toward bribery and corruption in elections, contributions from special interests, appointment of incompetent partisans, "honest graft" of various types, has shifted notably; many practices are now openly condemned or quietly opposed which a generation ago were looked upon as necessary evils, or perhaps not as evils at all. It is not impossible that important changes may be made in the organization and procedure of the parties themselves under the stress of present-day criticism and suggestion. The development of the party conference [11] as a clearing house for the consideration of party policies and the technique of management would be an easy point of departure. Out of such conferences might develop significant modifications of organization and procedure as well as the broader discussion of the questions of party policy.

Among these changes might be a standardization of the nominating process, especially in the national field where it is most sadly needed; repression of corrupt practices in nominations and elections; more democratic methods of financing campaigns; development of more desirable methods of organizing party leadership and responsibility; closer study of the technique of large-scale organization as adapted to the special needs of the political party; effective cooperation in election and ballot reform, in the establishment of the merit system, in the organization of efficient government; and in general the adoption of standards and customs in harmony with public-policy politics rather than with spoils politics, and in harmony with the terms and conditions of the developing industrial and social democracy now in the course of realization. In short, the party might be made a more

[11] See above, p. 356.

effective instrument in the service of the democracy in whose name it assumes to act.

Yet it must be conceded that it seems improbable that any such step will be taken, with the situation as it now is and with forces now at work in continued action, unless the parties become more homogeneous than they now are; unless there is an earnest desire for genuine conference on matters of common interest to the party; or unless the democratic interest of the mass of the party develops to a point where it might demand and enforce such changes. Of these conditions there is some indication at present, but this interest takes the common form of regulating in detail the party process and procedure until it approaches the nature of the standardized machinery of elections. What further form the democratizing and constitution-alizing process which has been so notable in the parties during the present century may take in the future it is impossible to predict. It is possible that with the wider diffusion of political knowledge, with the entrance of women into political life, with the possible appearance of labor in the leadership of parties, a spirit of change may come over the whole party system and it may be transformed in its methods and purposes.

It is important to observe that the political party is now hard pressed by other groups competing for public interest and favor. Other agencies are carrying on much the same functions as the party is presumed to perform, with perhaps less friction and waste, and are attracting the interest, the enthusiasm, and support of many citizens who remain indifferent to the demands of active partisan work. If the party is to maintain a position of leadership in the community, it will be necessary to alter materially the methods which have often been followed, and to adopt others more in keeping with the spirit of the new time.

PARTY SYSTEM AND THE ECONOMIC ORDER

The relation of party organization and party process to the economic organization has already been considered, and it must be reckoned as one of the prime factors in the future adjustment and adaptation of the party system. The swift rise in economic power of the corporate authority was a conspicuous feature of the last generation, and the rush of this newcomer captured the party at many times and places. But although the voters were overwhelmed by a new group whose organization and methods they did not understand, the rank and file resisted valiantly, and in fact carried the struggle into the enemy's camp. Railroads and trusts were fought with the Interstate Commerce Act and the Sherman Anti-Trust Law, while the combination of boss and privilege was exposed and everywhere denounced. Perhaps history will say that the surprising feature of the last generation was not the power of concentrated wealth in the party, but the tenacious and often successful resistance against corporate combinations by the unorganized mass of the community. That small groups of powerful economic leaders should capture the machinery of government is no new thing in the chronicles of mankind. It is indeed the commonplace of politics, but that the mass should resist and make successful headway against a strikingly powerful "invisible government" is noteworthy in the record of democratic progress.[12]

No one can forecast the process of development of the economic order, but apparently the tide has turned in the direction of industrial democracy. Apparently the power of concentrated wealth will be less in the future than in the past. The middle class has gained in numbers and at the same time the power of organized labor has been very greatly strengthened, and that power seems likely to increase rather than diminish in the near future. The skilled trades and the professions alike increase the strength of their organizations, and they constitute important centers of resistance to autocratic economic control. Neither has shown great power thus far in party warfare, but in the nonparty struggles for legislation and social policies both have been very active and effective. Organized labor has entered the political field in the United States as in England and other modern states, although it is as yet far behind the British labor movement. The control of either or both of the parties by small groups of wealthy men will thus tend to become increasingly difficult.[13]

The agricultural group was for many years dominant in party affairs, and since the Civil War has retained great authority, although its position has been greatly weakened by the rapid rise of cities, the

[12] See W. B. Munro, *The Invisible Government* (New York, 1928).
[13] Holcombe, *Political Parties of Today*, and *The New Party Politics* (New York, 1933); "The Changing Outlook for a Realignment of Parties," *Public Opinion Quarterly*, X (Winter 1946–1947), 455–469.

development of the great corporations, the depopulation of many rural districts, and by the recurrent and prolonged agricultural depressions. The Granger movement of the 1870's the Populist party in the 1890's, the Insurgent and Progressive movements in the 1910's, the Farm Bureau movement which blossomed in the 1920's, and the Progressive and Farm-Labor state parties of the dismal 1930's— all were given powerful support in the country districts. The relative strength of the farming group in numbers and in wealth has diminished greatly, however, and furthermore there is a growing division between the owner and the tenant class of farmers, which is likely to increase rather than diminish in the future as the period of free land disappears. Movements like those of the Progressives and Farmer Laborites suggest the possibility of powerful organizations wtih political influence emerging from the middle group of farmers with average means. Likewise the Farm Bureau Federation and the Farmers' Union suggest other possibilities in the way of organized activity on the part of the farmers in the domain of party or politics. The agricultural "bloc" formed in Congress is another evidence of the same tendency toward organized agricultural activity. The indications point to strongly developed vocational groupings among the agricultural population with marked political activities, although these activities may not be of the party type but may take the shape of nonparty struggle for legislation.

The unorganized middle class in the towns and cities and the unorganized workers constantly tend to organize and professionalize, and thus to become stronger centers of activity than they have thus far been. At present they constitute the weakest of all the groups in political influence, although one of the largest in the aggregate of their voting power. Consumers' leagues and an occasional tenants' association have endeavored to meet the situation, but thus far with little success. The power of the press and propaganda is especially strong over this group, which is not guarded by the special protective devices of the better-organized classes in other fields. Their leaders and their press rest upon a much less secure basis than others, and can with great difficulty maintain themselves through long periods of time.

On the whole, the power of plutocracy in the political parties seems likely to be curbed in the future by developing forces in the economic field. The great corporations were the first to organize on a large scale, taking advantage of the new order of things made possible by transportation and communication, and they reaped the advantage of their swift mobilization for a period of thirty years after the Civil War. Since then other types of organizations have arisen to challenge them; labor, agriculture, the professions, consumers, innumerable groups have sprung up and begun to play their part in the struggle for social and political control as never before. The dreadnaughts and superdreadnaughts of the commercial world have been met by similar fighting craft manned by other groups and quite capable of doing battle in case of parliamentary or juristic warfare. The corporation can no longer shoot down the wooden craft of the opposition as in the early days when there was none strongly enough armored to oppose the new type of fighter. And there is a strong sentiment in favor of industrial peace.

It may be asked whether these new social organizations will enter into the contest for control of the political parties. This makes little difference in the long run. If they undertake to influence party action directly, they will make a material impression, and will modify the results hitherto obtained. They will ensure more democratic control of the parties, and will jeopardize the position of the oligarchies which have often controlled the party struggles. Whether they confine their efforts to the election, or the lobby, or the courts, or the referendum, or the influencing of public opinion, the new groups will be felt in this field. In either case they will tend to check the power of the small groups of politico-industrial magnates so mighty in the party system for the past half century. It is quite evident that it is far easier for the trust and the boss to plow their way through an unorganized community than to advance over territory covered with a network of powerful counter organizations, compactly constructed and well financed and led.

The organizing tendency in almost all occupations and the democratizing tendency especially evident in large-scale industry seem likely to check the power of the few, in the party as in the government. If these groups care to enter into the parties, they will vitalize and strengthen them. If they care to remain out of the contest for party control, they will weaken the hold of parties upon the public and diminish the importance of the party in the process of political and social control. In either case they will no longer leave the field of organization to the makers of political machines and their allies.

PARTY SYSTEMS AND POLITICAL MORES

Finally, it must be recognized that the character of the party system is dependent upon the political *mores* of the community, upon the standards, the appreciations, the values found in the mass of the political people. The party will not rise very far above or sink very far below the custom or habit of the voter in estimating and acting upon things political. What is called the tone, the temper, the spirit of the electorate will determine the character of the party system in the long run. Class and group conflicts are inevitable in the struggle for economic and political power, but what is the common standard in the war? What is the degree of community interest, and what are the generally accepted standards of legitimate partisan activity? Is the tendency toward deeper interest in common affairs, toward sharper and more critical analysis of conflicting claims of personnel and policy? Does science or knowledge tend to set higher minimum standards for parties and their leaders and managers? [14]

There is discernible a keener sense of social or of civic obligation in the narrower sense of the term. This has sometimes been a vague expression of impractical idealism, but it comes to have a definite place in the practical adjustment of public affairs. Democracy after all is new—new to labor, new to women, new to the world. The consciousness of common responsibility for common direction and control is recent in the history of the race. Time is necessary for the full operation of the democratic system in which all are admitted to equal rights and duties in the political scheme of things, and to a share of the common responsibility for the common heritage.

Civic responsibility tends to develop in our day.[15] In a transition

[14] See J. T. Shotwell, "Democracy and Political Morality," in *Political Science Quarterly*, XXXVI, 1; T. V. Smith, *The Promise of American Politics* (Chicago, 1936), and *The Democratic Way of Life* (Chicago, 1926); C. E. Merriam, *The New Democracy and the New Despotism* (New York, 1939); R. M. MacIver, *The Web of Government* (New York, 1947); and C. E. Merriam, *Systematic Politics* (Chicago, 1945).

[15] See C. E. Merriam, *Civic Education in the United States* (New York, 1934), and "Citizenship," *University of Chicago Magazine*, III (1911), 275; James Bryce, *Hindrances to Good Citizenship* (New Haven, 1919); and D. Snedden, *Civic Education* (Yonkers-on-Hudson, 1922).

stage where we pass from an era largely military in its political activities to an era largely or wholly industrial in character, the process of developing responsibility is of necessity slow. We still think of liberty as if won chiefly on the battlefield; of human rights as protected mainly by the sword; of free institutions as if maintained by the army of the soldier. The quiet processes by which thousands of citizens formulate public opinion and provide for its execution have never been dramatized as have the scenes of war. The poet, the painter, the historian, the dramatist have portrayed the conflicts of war in masterpieces that are immortal, but the new obligations incident to citizenship are not yet fully realized. Hence we find that men who are willing to suffer and die for their country in war may be unwilling to serve it in time of peace, or remain indifferent because they do not see the connection between effort and effect in public affairs as in military affairs. The action of the bullet, the bayonet, or the sword is direct and perceptible. The citizen's part in molding public opinion is difficult to trace, although none the less mighty in effect. The difficulty in our present situation lies in transferring the old types of military enthusiasm to new conditions.[16] The citizen has the spirit and virtue of the soldier, but he does not see the necessity of applying these qualities to social and political conditions.

We may reasonably look for a stronger growth of the feeling of political and social obligation with the broadening of social and industrial democracy, and with the broadening of the basis of education. A quickened political and social consciousness would tend to rise the morale of public affairs and improve the fundamental conditions under which parties operate. The result should be a quicker perception of the needs of the community, greater readiness in organization and action to secure the desired ends, and a superior type of party activity.

Other groups may attract the interest and claim the loyalty of the individual as against the broader political interest, but the tendency is toward the larger group loyalty and allegiance. It may be contended that the sharpening of class lines, if continued in increasing measure, will have the effect of substituting class allegiance for state allegiance. Organized labor, organized capital, organized agri-

[16] See the suggestive study of "Pluralistic Behavior" by F. H. Giddings in the *American Journal of Sociology*, XXV, 385, 539; and H. D. Lasswell, *World Politics and Personal Insecurity* (New York, 1935).

culture may develop a solidarity which will challenge the public interest and overwhelm it with the pressure of narrower group interests. It is of course impossible to foresee the course of development that may be taken by the state in the future,[17] and for our immediate purpose it is not necessary to do this. The development of group consciousness on a larger scale may for a time operate against interest in the commonwealth of groups taken together, and may even embarrass the state for a time; but in the long run it is likely to be beneficial rather than harmful, notwithstanding its temporary inconveniences. Powerful forces impel us toward larger and larger units of social, economic, and political interest and sympathy, and we may reasonably look forward to a period of increasing civic interest and sympathy.

It may be expected that with the growth of education and experience the standards of public appreciation and criticism of political action will rise, and the tone of party action will improve. An increasing degree of sophistication on the part of the voters will make many of the tricks and artifices of the earlier day impossible and compel an increasing degree of intelligence in the discussion carried on by the political parties. The farcical and the insincere will tend to become less useful and therefore less valuable to the partisan organizations. Compulsory education and the shorter working day are powerful influences in the democratic process. Invention as well as tradition comes to play an important part in political affairs, and a constructive attitude appropriate to a world of rapid change.

Yet the way is not by any means clear, and never will be. Great dangers lie across the path in the shape of the recently discovered possibilities of organized propaganda, in the misuse of the far-reaching power of the modern press, in the appearance of the demagogue accomplished in the arts of dealing with the psychology of the crowd. New mechanisms of control are in process of creation through which the interest of the few may be made to master that of the many. Particularly formidable would be a combination of plutocratic influences with propaganda and the press, headed possibly by an ingenious and accomplished demagogue.[18]

[17] See the interesting theory of Miss M. P. Follett in *The New State* (New York, 1918).

[18] See upon this point the significant comment of Bryce in *Modern Democracies*, *op. cit.*

Not much imagination is required to frame subtle forms of control through education, press, and propaganda. It is not improbable that such types of conquests over the democracy will be projected and attempted, and that in some instances they will succeed.[19] And one of the avenues of control may be the political party and the party system.

But the tendency is steadily in the direction of closer analysis of party positions, of party allegiance, of the utility and the application of the methods of partisan action. Popular education is likely to do more than provide the antidotes for its own poisons; it should develop the knowledge, skill, aptitudes for social and political control appropriate to a democratic society. We do not know this, but it is a reasonable working hypothesis, based upon experience and upon an analysis of democratic social organization.[20]

As far as the political parties are concerned, so many other and competing channels of public activity are being opened to those who have a political interest that the party cannot hope to maintain itself on the older basis, except at a very heavy cost in public confidence and esteem. With entrance into the public service through the technical and scientific avenues, and with the shaping of public policies opened to those who take no part in the party activities, it will be necessary for the party organizations to raise the standards of party action and appeal more directly to the intelligence of the community. Partisanship cannot continue to be a synonym for unfairness, insincerity, exaggeration, and intemperance of feeling, but must tend toward more intelligent division of the voters upon more rational lines of cleavage.[21]

Genuine political education, or, more broadly, social education, is just in its infancy, and we may reasonably look for far-reaching

[19] Very suggestive studies are those of Walter Lippmann in *Liberty and the News* (New York, 1920); H. D. Lasswell in *Politics: Who Gets What, When, How* (New York, 1936); *Technique of War-time Propaganda* (New York, 1927); *Democracy Through Public Opinion* (Menasha, Wis., 1941).

[20] See the admirable discussion of democracy by John Dewey in his *Democracy and Education* (New York, 1923) and *Reconstruction in Philosophy* (New York, 1920); also his *Freedom and Culture* (New York, 1940).

[21] Ratzenhofer says, "The science of politics, however, is primarily a psychopathology of human beings, and with reference to such a science the truth is always rather of a depressing than of an exhilarating nature." Cited by A. W. Small in *General Sociology* (Chicago, 1905), p. 319.

he future of the party is bound up with that of the
of which it is a part, and in a larger way with the
ustrial order, with the social and political psychology
ith the attitudes, the precesses seen in the larger whole
a part. The political party will not be reconstructed
than the reorganization of the political order, or de-
ts and tendencies more rapidly than the development of
c *mores* or the social ethics of its day. The two great
r day—that furiously raged for political and industrial
nd that more quietly fought between ignorance and
e ordering of human life—condition the nature of the
as of all the social processes of our time.

progress at this point in the next generation.[22] A thorough understanding of the nature of the social, the economic, and the political
order, and of the social, industrial, and political processes, and their
relations one to the other, will provide a basis for constructive participation in these processes by the individual of the next generation.
Men will not be the victims of prejudice or chance environment or
contacts, but will be grounded in social and political science and
prudence, as up to this time they have never been. It is as true now
as in the days of Jefferson that education is the foundation of democracy; only we now come to recognize that this must be a social
education, including the business of living with others in the great
cooperative enterprise of democracy, and that it must begin early.
Social and political education must begin in the schools, not at the
polls. If this education stops with the schools, it is likely to be sterile,
but it can be continued through the adult period, and it doubtless
will be in a certain measure, not in the formal style of "schooling,"
but in the broader process by which society educates itself—through
discussion, criticism, construction and reconstruction, organization
of community intelligence. Without this, the dangerous powers of the
demagogue and propaganda are likely to work greater mischief in
social life in the future than the boss and the grafters have in the
past. An open mind, an eye for the facts, a tendency to analyze them
and to reconstruct them, to make them a part of the individual's
life, shrewdness in penetrating the sham in personalities and policies,
intelligent reconstruction and adaptation of the old to the new—
these qualities the schools may teach, and the broader school of adult
society may fruitfully expand and develop them.

In the busy life of individuals will it ever be possible for men and
women, with all the cares of business, of family, of church, of social
relations, to attain practical intelligence and judgment in political
affairs more extensively than they now have? We do not know; but
only to the extent that such faculties are developed will they be able
to meet the challenge of those who profit by ignorance and inatten-
tion to organize schemes of profiteering and to exploit the common
man.[23] There is no panacea, no philosopher's stone, no shortcut to

[22] See C. E. Merriam, *A Prologue to Politics* (Chicago, 1939); *New Aspects of
Politics* (Chicago, 1931); *On the Agenda of Democracy* (Cambridge, 1941).

[23] See C. E. Merriam and L. Overacker, *Primary Elections* (Chicago, 1928),
Chap. VIII, "Analysis of Primary Forces."

self-government. We have reason to believe that the future holds for each individual some precious part in the unending process of social reconstruction, some really creative role in determining and modifying the conditions under which he lives, and in transmitting the social heritage to posterity. But that far, certainly, we cannot consider ourselves to have progressed.[24]

We cannot speak with certainty of what the future holds. But assuming there are no radical changes in the political or social order, it seems likely that a party system will continue for an indefinite period, but that fundamental changes will slowly be wrought in the party process. The modifications in our political organization, both by statute and by custom, the alterations in the economic and social basis of the party system, the gradual change in the political *mores*, the infiltration of science into human life will all have their weight in determining the form and activities of the future party system. The surviving parties will be weaker in organization and stronger in morale, with less of patronage and more of principles, with less of the spirit of spoils and more of the desire for community service, released from the domination of the small groups of bosses and special privilege interests, and following more closely the general judgment of a larger and more democratic group of supporters. Yet there can be no guarantee against successful raids upon the general interest by powerful, well-organized, and aggressive special interests.

Whether a biparty system will continue or a multiparty system will develop has often been a subject of speculation. If economic, racial, and religious differences are sufficiently vivid and continuing, they tend to take the form of parties, as in France and Switzerland, but thus far in the United States the two parties have cut across the lines of such divisions in such a way as to attract the political interest and loyalty of voters and prevent the crystallization of social groups in party form. Blocs and combinations, economic and sectional, appear from time to time and sometimes occupy strategic positions of great importance, but thus far they have yielded to the superior attractions of the major parties. To this the strong emphasis on executive leadership has contributed, and further the social divisions, while at times vivid, have not been fixed and permanent enough to

[24] Compare John Dewey, *The Public and Its Problems* (New York, 1927); Walter Lippmann, *The Phantom Public* (New York, 1925).

provide a sure basis for party
possible that these conditions
the lines and types of party c
interesting illustration of str
mains dubious as far as form

Agrarian or labor groups o
as a new basis of a new party
might serve as a rallying point
goals. Such alignments and al
will be made again. They ha
national parties. Thus far the
the diversity of races and so
means uniformly produced tv
denominators of heterogeneou

The succession of economic
years has brought many harsh
the multiple-party systems. 1
there was a world-wide trend
World War II the Communists
form of totalitarianism is the v
has commented on this situat

"Pestilence, war, famine, flo
moments when decisionism is co
who may act before it is too late
when the crisis is over; but in
any immediate occasion has gon
outcome of an international sit
jural order, and an internal situa
its peace with economic and po
solution of these problems, the
tion might recede and disappea
would be a weary bureaucracy
position against the rising dem
common affairs." [26]

[25] See A. N. Holcombe, *Political I
American Politics* for a brilliant discu
Charlesworth, "Is Our Two-Party S
Academy of Political and Social Scien
[26] Merriam, *New Democracy and N
pp. 236–240.

Obviously
political orde
social and inc
of the time, w
of which it is
more rapidly
velop new tra
the democrat
struggles of o
democracy, a
science for th
party system,

CHARACTERISTICS OF SUCCESSFUL CANDIDATES AS COMPARED WITH UNSUCCESSFUL CANDIDATES

Election_____Investigator_____

Successful Candidate_____

Unsuccessful Candidate_____

(In the space provided, indicate by a plus sign if the item is related positively to the successful candidate; indicate by a zero sign if the item is related negatively to the successful candidate.)

I. CULTURAL BACKGROUND

A. *Birthplace*

___ 1. Nearer to geographic center of population of the United States

___ 2. A larger community

___ 3. More urban culture pattern

___ 4. Nearer to metropolitan center

___ 5. A larger proportion of native white of native parentage

___ 6. More temperate climate (greater range between extremes)

B. *Place of residence during the modal average of years from 16 to 25*

___ 7. A larger community

C. *Actual place of residence at time of election*

___ 8. Nearer to center of population

___ 9. A larger community

___ 10. More urban culture pattern

___ 11. Nearer to metropolitan center

___ 12. A larger proportion of native whites of native parentage

___ 13. More temperate climate

D. *State of legal residence at time of election*

___ 14. Larger population

___ 15. More urban

___ 16. Larger proportion of native whites of native parentage

___ 17. Greater wealth

___ 18. Greater inequality of distribution of income

___ 19. Greater density of population

___ 20. Older

___ 21. Larger proportion of persons in agricultural pursuits

___ 22. Closer margin between major parties at preceding presidential election

II. PERSONAL DEVELOPMENTAL HISTORY

A. *Culturally conditioning factors*

___ 23. Birth closer to a depression, war, revolution, or any generalized mass movement utilizing counter-*mores* activity in an area as large as a state

___ 24. Childhood spent in community with more rigorous control of counter-*mores* acts

___ 25. Mother older at birth of subject

___ 26. Birth closer to date of last sibling

___ 27. Birth closer to date of parents' marriage

___ 28. More siblings closer to the same age

___ 29. More parental affection toward another sibling

___ 30. Mother and/or surrogates have a larger share of the early educating and disciplining of the subject

___ 31. More affectionate relations between parents

___ 32. Father more strict

___ 33. Mother more strict

___ 34. Father more reserved about exhibiting affection

___ 35. Mother more demonstrative in granting affection

___ 36. Parents' wealth and income greater

___ 37. Parents' prestige greater

___ 38. Parents' health better

___ 39. More political symbols used in home

___ 40. Higher grade attained in school

___ 41. More limited strata contacts in school

___ 42. More political symbols used in occupational group

___ 43. Earlier assumption of economic responsibility

___ 44. Wife more reserved in exhibiting affection

___ 45. Wife's social prestige greater

___ 46. Wife's wealth and income greater

___ 47. Wife's health better

___ 48. Wife resembles subject's mother more

___ 49. Wife with more political interests

B. *Characteristics of interpersonal relations*

a. INFANCY

___ 50A. More indulgences granted by mother and/or surrogates

___ 50B. Greater attention paid to training habits

___ 50C. More aggressive tendencies toward mother

___ 51. Better health

b. CHILDHOOD

___ 52. More identification with father

___ 53. More identification with mother

___ 54. More aggressive tendencies toward father

___ 55. More affectionate tendencies toward mother

___ 56. More deprivations with reference to demand for affection

___ 57. Greater anxiety at occurrence of disciplinary measures

___ 58. Better health

c. JUVENILE ERA

___ 59. More aggressive tendencies toward siblings and playmates

___ 60. More competition with siblings for parental affection

___ 61. More cooperation with teachers

___ 62. Easier adjustment to extra-family relationships

___ 63. Better health

d. PREADOLESCENCE

___ 64. More affection for male playmates

___ 65. More collaboration with groups

___ 66. More aggressive tendencies toward siblings and playmates

___ 67. More willingness to assume responsibilities for leadership.

___ 68. More social contacts through relatives

___ 69. More indulgences from school activity

___ 70. More pyknic or lateral in body structure

___ 71. Better health

e. ADOLESCENCE

___ 72. Greater ambitions

___ 73. More heterosexual deprivations

___ 74. More deprivations from school activity

___ 75A. More rebellious toward authorities

___ 75B. More aggressive tendencies toward associates

___ 76. More anxiety with parents and surrogates due to acts not in conformity with family standards

___ 77. More adjustive activity upon occurrence of deprivations

___ 78. More pessimism, brooding, etc., upon occurrence of deprivations

___ 79. Better health

f. ADULTHOOD, PREPOLITICAL

___ 80. More deprivations from occupational activity

___ 81. More inhibitions about occupation with money matters

___ 82. More heterosexual deprivations.

___ 83. More emotionless relations with people

___ 84. More anxiety with wife

___ 85. More rebellious toward superiors

___ 86. More adjustive activity upon occurrence of deprivations

— 87. More pessimism, brooding, etc., upon occurrence of deprivations

— 88. Younger age of marriage

— 89. More children

— 90. More use of more competitive and strenuous sports

— 91. Presence of more "nervous" symptoms, and psychic "peculiarities"

g. ADULTHOOD, POLITICAL

— 92. Transition to politics more abrupt

— 93. Younger age of marriage

— 94. More children

— 95. More indulgences from early political activity

— 96. Greater generosity

— 97. More affection granted in intimate relations

— 98. More loyalty and affection for superiors

— 99. More affection granted to electoral supporters

—100. More affection granted to party workers

—101. More readiness in listening to advice and complaints in an "understanding way"

—102. More refraining from "rational" acts which temporarily diminish followers' support or loyalty

—103. More commission of "irrational" acts which temporarily conserve or increase followers' support or loyalty

—104. More affection for the inclusive key-symbols (and objects to which they refer) in the name of which he operates

—105. Greater assumption of responsibility

—106. Better sense of humor

—107. Greater tact

—108. More sympathy for the underprivileged

—109. More idealizing of mother or surrogates

—110. More idealizing of father or surrogates

—111. Better health

—112. More pyknic or lateral in body structure

—113. More references to self in diaries and letters

—114. Greater self-congratulation

—115. More instrumental attitude toward party workers

—116. More attempts to justify instrumental attitude toward party workers

—117. Greater dependence of the granting of affection on receipt of indulgences from persons to whom it is granted

—118. More optimism

—119. More hours awake

—120. More guilt reactions

—121. Greater decline in nervous symptoms, and psychic "peculiarities"

—122. More self-recriminations upon the failure of demands for support and loyalty

—123. More doubts regarding decisions

—124. More sensitivity to "outside meddling in private affairs" (closed ego)

—125. Greater distrust toward declarations of loyalty by others

___126. More "fiery" type as contrasted with "colder" type

___127. More ruthless in employment of violence as means

___128. More aggression even if "irrational" toward those not meeting demands for affection

___129. More use of blame and criticism

___130. Stronger tendencies to inflict harsher deprivations on others in order to procure indulgences for self or allies

___131. More adjustive activity upon occurrence of deprivations

___132. More physical courage

h. PATTERN-CONFORMITY, THEORIST

___133. More emotionality in the use of symbols

___134. More success in writing or speaking on abstract aspects of politics

___135. Greater range of activities affected by anxieties

___136. More pessimism, brooding, etc., upon occurrence of deprivation

___137. A higher evaluation placed upon "inner life" than on life in the outer world as shown in diaries, etc.

i. AGITATOR

___138. More demand for support from large numbers of people

___139. More demands for immediate excited responses of support

___140. More insatiable demands for loyalty and support

___141. More indiscriminateness as to persons from whom loyalty or support is demanded

___142. More use of "all-or-none" reaction with reference to the support or loyalty granted by others

___143. More persistence despite failure of demands for support or loyalty

___144. Greater self-sacrifice in order to obtain grants of support or loyalty

j. ORGANIZER

___145. Greater social extraversion

___146. More unequal distribution of favors among those with equal claims

___147. More preoccupation with petty and routine details

___148. Greater routine imposed on others

___149. More reliance on inspiration as against premeditation in political and other activity

k. INSIGHT-FULL CHARACTER

___150. More deliberate inhibitions of rage

___151. More simulation of affection toward followers

___152. Greater disregard of promises

___153. Greater violation of conventional behavior, if necessary, in pursuit of political goals

___154. Greater recognition of political activity as means of heightening one's emotional level

___155. Greater recognition of political activity as means of alleviating anxiety

___156. Greater recognition of political activity as means toward acquisition of wealth and/or prestige

III. ATTRIBUTES AT TIME OF ELECTION

A. *Physical*

___157. Greater weight

___158. Greater height

___159. More evenly proportioned

___160. More blondness

___161. More regular features

___162. Greater voice volume

___163. More widely accepted accent

___164A. Better health

___164B. Eating

___164C. Drinking

___165. Greater physical and nervous energy

___166. Older

B. *Mental*

___167. Better oratorical ability (word fluency)

___168. Better memory

___169. Better visualizing ability

___170. Greater speed of decision

___171. Greater inventive ability

___172. Better judgment and foresight

___173. Greater capacity for details

C. *Prestige*

___174. Longer residence of paternal ancestors in the United States

___175. Longer residence of maternal ancestors in the United States

___176. Greater prestige value of occupation of father

___177. Greater prestige value of paternal grandfather's occupation

___178. Greater prestige value of occupation of maternal grandfather

___179. Greater wealth and income of parents (item 36)

___180. Greater prestige of parents (item 37)

___181. Wife's social prestige greater (item 45)

___182. Wife's wealth and income greater (item 46)

___183A. Subject's wealth and income greater

___183B. Subject's social prestige greater

___184. Greater prestige value of subject's prepolitical occupation

D. *Political renown*

___185. Longer tradition of public service in family

___186. Longer in United States politics

___187. Fewer rebuffs in political ascension

___188. Greater prestige of political position reached

___189. Longer experience as a public administrator

___190. Longer experience as a legislator

___191. Longer experience as a judicial officer

___192. Greater number of electoral successes

___193. More favorable publicity secured along the political career line

IV. TECHNIQUES EMPLOYED

A. *More successful use by candidate of given channels of communication*

___194. Personal letters (more stimulating)

___195. Political mass meetings (a better platform performer)

___196. Small informal party committee meetings (better with small groups)

___197. Public documents (more ringing pronouncements)

___198. Pamphlets and books on political theory (more prolific, more original, more widely read)

___199. Mass displays or demonstrations (better showmanship)

___200. The press (more cordial relations with)

___201. Other media

B. *More successful in creating impression of universality*

___202. Greater use of vague and general words as compared with precise and specific words

___203. More elaborate politico-social theories employed

Positive symbols of identification

___204. America

___205. Constitutionalism

___206. Equality

___207. Democracy

___208. The Union

C. *More successful in winning response from groups*

a. OCCUPATIONAL GROUPS

Agrarian

___209. Wheat

___210. Cotton

___211. Corn

___212. Other

Labor

___213A. Unionized labor

___213B. Nonorganized

Business

___214. Manufacture

___215. Finance

___216. Commerce

___217. Consumers

b. INCOME GROUPS

___218. High

___219. Middle

___220. Low

c. MINORITY GROUPS

___221A. Religious—general

___221B. Catholic

___221C. Protestant

___221D. Jewish

___221E. Nonchurch

___222A. Racial white

___222B. Negro

___223. Linguistic

___224. Veterans

___225A. Temperance reform

___225B. Young vs. old

___225C. City dwellers vs. rural inhabitants

D. *More successful in winning response toward symbols of policy*

___226A. Imperialism
___226B. National defense
___227. Internationalism
___228. Judicial supremacy
___229. Executive leadership
___230. Congressional leadership
___231. Expansion (economic)
___232A. Contraction (economic)
___232B. Economic autarchy

E. *More skillful in assuming role of hero*

___233. As a great public administrator
___234. As a leader in warfare
___235. As an agitator

V. SOCIAL SITUATION AND PARTY ORGANIZATION

A. *Social situation*

___236. International tension level more favorable to candidate
___237. Internal political tension level more favorable to candidate
___238. Economic conditions more favorable to candidate

B. *Party organization*

___239. More money spent by party
___240. Party successful in preceding presidential election

___241. A larger number of congressional seats held by party
___242. Larger number of counties controlled by party in preceding presidential election
___243. Greater unity within the party
___244. Party contained persons of greater prestige
___245. Party contained fewer persons of negative prestige value

C. *Propaganda techniques*
   a. MEDIA

___246. Greater press support
___247. More mass meetings
___248. Better precinct canvassers

   b. PROMOTION OF CANDIDATES

___249. More successful in establishing illusion of victory
___250. More skillful in building up myths regarding candidate (affection for candidate)
___251. More skillful in gauging tempo of campaign

   c. COUNTERPROMOTION (DIABOLISM)

___252. Depreciation of opponent's personality (weakness)
___253. Attribution of guilt to opponent
___254. Attribution of aggression to opponent

INDEX